The Three Apostles
of Russian Music

The Three Apostles of Russian Music

The Soviet Avant-Garde

Gregor Tassie

LEXINGTON BOOKS
Lanham • Boulder • New York • London

Published by Lexington Books
An imprint of The Rowman & Littlefield Publishing Group, Inc.
4501 Forbes Boulevard, Suite 200, Lanham, Maryland 20706
www.rowman.com

6 Tinworth Street, London SE11 5AL, United Kingdom

Copyright © 2022 The Rowman & Littlefield Publishing Group, Inc.

All rights reserved. No part of this book may be reproduced in any form or by any electronic or mechanical means, including information storage and retrieval systems, without written permission from the publisher, except by a reviewer who may quote passages in a review.

British Library Cataloguing in Publication Information Available

Library of Congress Cataloging-in-Publication Data

Names: Tassie, Gregor, 1953- author.
Title: The three apostles of Russian music : the Soviet avant-garde / Gregor Tassie.
Other titles: 3 apostles of Russian music
Description: Lanham : Lexington, 2021. | Includes bibliographical references and index. | Summary: "Gregor Tassie studies the lives, work, and legacy of three musicians who were trail-blazers in the Soviet avant-garde and led modernist music in the 1920s. Mosolov, Popov, and Roslavets were popular composers who have been unfortunately forgotten. This book is the first study in English of their legacy" —Provided by publisher.
Identifiers: LCCN 2021046968 (print) | LCCN 2021046969 (ebook) | ISBN 9781793644299 (cloth) | ISBN 9781793644312 (paperback) | ISBN 9781793644305 (epub)
Subjects: LCSH: Music—Soviet Union—History and criticism. | Mosolov, A. (Aleksandr), 1900–1973. | Popov, Gavriil, 1904–1972. | Roslavets, Nikolaĭ, 1881–1944. | Modernism (Music)—Soviet Union. | Avant-garde (Music)—Soviet Union.
Classification: LCC ML300.5 .T39 2021 (print) | LCC ML300.5 (ebook) | DDC 780.947/0904—dc23
LC record available at https://lccn.loc.gov/2021046968
LC ebook record available at https://lccn.loc.gov/2021046969

Contents

Abbreviations		vii
Acknowledgments		ix
List of Figures		xi
Introduction		1
1	The Young Paganini	17
2	The Revolutionary Messiah	55
3	The Prisoner of Tashkent	91
4	The First Symphony	119
5	Cinema and Theater	159
6	1948 and Decline	201
7	Man and Machines!	227
8	The Stage Works	257
9	Trial and Renewal	281
Conclusion		307
Bibliography		339
Catalog of Works		349
Discography		359
Index		367
About the Author		385

Abbreviations

ASM	Association of Contemporary Musicians
Glavlit	Chief administration for literature publishing
Glavrepertkom	Chief Committee for Repertoire Control
ISCM	International Society of Contemporary Music
Komsomol	All-Union Communist Youth League
Modpik	Moscow Society of Drama Writers and Composers
Muzo	Music department
Muzsektor	State Music Publishing Department
Narkompros	People's Commissariat of Enlightenment
NKVD	Narodny Kommissariat Vnutrenykh Del [Secret Services]
ORKiMD	Organization of Revolutionary Composers and Musical Workers
PROKOLL	Production collective of student composers of the Moscow Conservatoire
PROKULT	Proletarian Culture
RABIS	Trade Union of Art workers
RAPM	Russian Association of Proletarian Musicians
SOPHIL	Soviet Philharmonic Society
VKP (b)	All-Union Communist Party (Bolshevik)

Acknowledgments

In listing those who have made this book possible, I would like to thank Professor Inna Barsova of the Moscow Conservatoire who herself discovered Mosolov through Mahler, to Professor Inna Romaschuk from the Ippolitov-Ivanov Institute in Moscow who brought so much fresh information about Gavriil Popov, and to Professor Marina Lobanova who for decades has unearthed the forgotten manuscripts by Nikolay Roslavets, and restoring them for today's audiences. Without these three Russian musicologists, so much forgotten music would still be lying in archives gathering dust. In addition, I am grateful to Professor Igor Vorobyov of the St. Petersburg Conservatoire who has organized festivals of avant-garde music in St. Petersburg and written four key source materials on Russian avant-garde composers.

I am grateful to Iosif Raiskin and to Professor Andrey Zolotov for their friendship and valuable advice, and to Professor Ekaterina Vlasova at the Moscow Conservatoire, to Leon Hakobian of the Moscow Academy of Arts, and to Elena Lobanova at the Gnessin Institute for their welcome suggestions and advice. During the course of my research in the music of Mosolov, Popov, and Roslavets, I widened my scope by including Arthur Lourié, Mikhail Matyushin, and Joseph Schillinger whose contribution to avant-garde music is both unique and unknown, with the exception of Lourié whose work has been slowly recognized in recent years. For reading through the early drafts and making valuable comments and pointing to errors, I would like to thank Brian and Linda Climie, and to a fellow writer and critic R. James Tobin and to Jeffrey Davis. Many thanks to my old teacher (and a dedicated Scottish avant-gardist) John Maxwell Geddes, to the staff at RGALI in Moscow, and to the Russian State Music Museum, to the St. Petersburg RSGALI, to many others for their kind assistance. All the translations from Russian texts, archival sources, literature, and poetry are mine. Most of all, I thank Courtney

Walsh my editor at Lexington Books and her assistants Shelby Russell and Matthew Valades for their hard work, much valued advice, and kind assistance in bringing this project to a successful conclusion. Finally I must offer my thanks to Claudia Patsch at Universal Edition in Vienna, and to Bernhard Pfau, Dagmar Schütz-Meisel, Yvonne Stern-Campo, and Christopher Peter at Schott Music in Mainz for their invaluable assistance. At last, I thank my dear wife Elena for her perseverance and loving kindness through many years of research.

Gregor Tassie

List of Figures

Figure 1.1	A Sketch of the Composer Roslavets. Song of the Blue Clouds by Kazimir Malevich 1907	20
Figure 1.2	In the Hours of the New Moon (First Page)	30
Figure 1.3	Roslavets Portrait, 1918	34
Figure 1.4	Roslavets Setting of Gnedov's Poem Kuk (Final Page)	42
Figure 2.1	Roslavets Portrait, 1927	75
Figure 2.2	Roslavets—Violin Concerto No. 1 (First Page of Second Movement)	80
Figure 3.1	Nataliya Roslavets in the 1920s	105
Figure 4.1	Popov—Septet (First Page)	128
Figure 5.1	Popov—1944	184
Figure 7.1	Mosolov—1928	231
Figure 7.2	Mosolov—*The Foundry* (First Page)	240
Figure 7.3	Mosolov—Piano Concerto No. 1 (First Page)	243
Figure 7.4	Mosolov—1928	246
Figure 8.1	Mosolov—The Hero (First Page)	261

Introduction

Russian music has shared a central place in the repertoire with the Austro-German classics and Italian opera, and its significance in the arts has become increasingly prevalent in recent decades. For many years, Russian ballet music dominated the theater scene with piano concertos by Tchaikovsky and Rachmaninov making up the core of Slavonic music in concert programs. To a degree unimaginable fifty years ago, the music of Shostakovich flourishes with more of the symphonies, concertos, quartets, and film music performed and recorded, all adding to his worldwide recognition. Much of this popularity owes to the *"Testimony"* purported memoirs by the composer. Elsewhere, the publication in three weighty volumes of Prokofiev's diaries allows us access to the innermost thoughts of the musician, and the controversial book about Prokofiev's first wife, Lina, presents a quite different portrait of this celebrated composer. The history of the Bolshoi Theater that staged operas and ballets by Prokofiev, and the scandalous *Lady Macbeth of Mtsensk District* by Shostakovich, has been opened up by two recently published books by Simon Morrison and Solomon Volkov, respectively. All of these have been eclipsed by the popularity of a fictional book on Shostakovich by Julian Barnes—*The Noise of Time*.

In the slipstream of this wave of curiosity for Russian music, other twentieth-century composers—Gubaydullina, Pärt, Shchedrin, Schnittke, and Weinberg—have become the focus for music lovers. This attention extends from opera and ballet, to symphonies, art songs, and chamber music by composers from the former Soviet Union. The creativity of Kancheli, Silvestrov, Terteryan, Tischenko, Slonimsky, Sviridov, Denisov, Ustvolskaya, and others has become better known through CDs, streaming, and YouTube, but less so in the concert hall. The fact that listeners in the West are coming to terms of a huge musical diversity is perplexing because so little is known about the composers and their music. Almost all of these composers were influenced by Scriabin, Stravinsky, Prokofiev, and Shostakovich. However, there were other hugely important composers who lived in the period of the "Silver Age" that witnessed the loud arrival of modernism. Boris Kustodiev's painting of a giant Russian Bolshevik brandishing a red flag among rioting crowds in Moscow captures strikingly the moment of the revolution. There are two different images conjured up from the painting: firstly—the violent momentum of the uprising; secondly—a fresh page in history had been turned.

Of course, the revolution led to the emigration of several million Russians from the former ruling class and a large section of the intelligentsia. Among the émigrés were musicians and composers: Chaliapin, Cherepnin, Grechaninov, Koussevitzky, Heifetz, Medtner, Prokofiev, and Rachmaninov, and those writers, philosophers, and scientists who could find no place in the Soviet republic. The Civil War and War Communism brought poverty and despair to many who did not support the new Bolshevik regime. The revolution divided the old Russia for brothers and sisters, and fathers and sons who suddenly discovered themselves on different sides. Among those who welcomed the Revolution were the avant-garde futurists and symbolists who sought to replace the old regime with fresh and dynamic ideas.

One of the poets who was intoxicated by the events of 1917 was the symbolist Alexander Blok who wrote that, "I see the Russia dreamt of by our great writers in their frightening and prophetic dreams; I see the Petersburg envisioned by Dostoyevsky, the Russia that Gogol called a rushing troika. Russia is a storm."[1] Blok saw the revolution as inevitable, as a "cataclysmic, purgative, musical experience that would transform individuals, possibly the world." In a letter to the poetess Zinaida Gippius in 1918, he wrote, "Do you really not know that Russia will no longer exist? . . . That the world is clearly reconstituted? That the 'old world' is already dissolved?"[2] In the end, "Blok's greatest artistic response to the revolution was *The Twelve*, a poem that concludes, as does *The Book of Revelation*, with the appearance of Christ."[3]

Blok was just one of a richly talented group of men and women who saw the events of 1917—not as a cause for despair—but as a source for hope and confidence in the future. The "Silver Age" of Russian literature, music, theater, and art hugely influenced European culture before the Great War; however, the postrevolutionary period represents one of the most prodigious epochs that defined Russian culture for decades afterward. The symbolists and futurists through Proletkult formed an extensive arts movement at workplaces and schools in the new Soviet republic. Francis Maes—a music historian from the Netherlands—explains that

> the artistic vanguard, intent on playing the role of revolutionary pioneers, rallied under the banner of "left-wing culture." The journal *Lef* (Left) became the forum

of futurists and their heirs: the constructivists and adherents of the "Production Art" movement. The actor and director Vsevolod Meyerhold, for one, tried to attain "October in the Theater," as he called his project—an extended program that would allow the theater to participate in the social transformations wrought by the October Revolution. In his view, the theater had to become a model of the new life.[4]

His concept of biomechanics emphasized body language as a fresh means of expression, as Irina Gutkin explains, "His experiments were widely used outside the theater as well, for instance in the 'theatricalization' of military training, in experiments with the use of rhythmic movements in the factory, and above all in the sports parades that became a distinctive feature of Soviet culture in the 1930s."[5]

The mass festivals in Petrograd, Moscow, and other cities embraced hundreds of thousands of people—many of whom had never taken part in the arts. The new dynamic of free arts and theater schools, together with music clubs and creativity, imbued a common theme of festivities that celebrated a new age for the people. The Petersburg musicologist Igor Vorobyov reports that "many avant-gardists took part in the revolutionary and socio-political events (Mayakovsky, Lourié, Roslavets), and others took part in the Civil War (Mosolov), at the beginning of the 1920s they gave their energy to organizing clubs, studios, institutes, the purpose of which was organizing the education of a new generation on the base of contemporary, revolutionary art (Malevich, Tatlin, Rodchenko, Matyushin, Mayakovsky, Deshevov and others)."[6] The American musicologist Boris Schwartz wrote that Roslavets "is now recognized as one of the important pioneers in the evolution of non-tonal serial music."[7] His music was considered in symposia and concerts in the United States in 1967–1968 along with other composers Lourié and Hershkovitz.[8] Schwartz notes further that "Scriabin, and Roslavets, Lourié and Golyshev, among others, pursued their own theories in the field of non-tonal music and the use of the tonal row. Had it not been for the premature death of Scriabin in 1915, Moscow might have become a citadel of atonality, side by side with Vienna."[9] He was among those like Glière, Vasilenko, Vlasov, Fere, and Ippolitov-Ivanov who taught systematically in remote parts of the country.[10]

However, the narrative of the Soviet avant-garde musicians is largely unknown and remains an under-researched topic in music studies. This monograph will examine three of the most outstanding musicians in the fresh wave of composers that arose before and after the October Revolution. The impact of this new music had a great influence on their contemporaries—positively and adversely. Indeed, it was the explosive, astonishing musical works by Mosolov, Roslavets, and Popov that helped spark the music of Shostakovich, Prokofiev, Kabalevsky, and the second and third wave of avant-garde composers. In the final chapter, we will look at three other avant-gardists who made important contributions not only to Russian but significantly to twentieth-century American music—Matyushin, Lourié, and Schillinger. The influence that these new ideas played in Russian art is elucidated by Igor Vorobyov, who claims it was "the avant-garde who dominated contemporary life before and after the revolution through major works by Kamensky, Mayakovsky, Meyerhold *Mystery Buff*, the *Red Wind* ballet by Deshevov, *Ladomir* by Khlebnikov, *Ulyalayevschina* by Selvinsky, Shostakovich's Second and Third symphonies, *Le pas d'acier* by Prokofiev, Mosolov's *The Foundry*, and Tatlin's *Third International*."[11] All the composers that we will meet were influenced equally by the symbolist and futurist poets and painters in their music.

The ideas of the Russian futurists in the first decade of the twentieth century were similar to those of Filippo Tommaso Marinetti's "Il manifesto del Futurismo" (1909). The Italian poet rejected the quiet and passive laissez-faire of the Italian Ottocento society and called for the celebration of new technology, speed, and innovation.[12] In St. Petersburg, there appeared Elena Guro and Matyushin's manifesto "Trap for Judges" in 1910 which uniquely introduced "budetlyan" and Khlebnikov's unique "zaum" language. This group had already formulated its ideas between 1908 and 1910. The strictures of the Russian school were not as all-embracing as the Italian variant, and indeed when Marinetti visited Russia in 1914, he was ostracized by the Russian futurists, who detested his love of militarism, national-chauvinism, and antifeminism.[13] The distinguishing features of the Russian futurists were revolt against old values, anarchism, and mass actions, the rejection of traditional art, creation of new art forms, rejection of traditional forms of speech, and use of new speech forms, rhythms, poster art, slogans, and experimentation in new technology. Marinetti stipulated a series of eleven articles which call for "singing of the love for danger," that the "essential elements are courage, audacity and revolt," for "aggression, march, the leap, the slap and blow of the fist," for the "splendor of the world to be enriched by a new beauty through the speed of machines," and for "man at the wheel, and that beauty exists in struggle." These aspirations accorded with the Russian futurists, moreover Marinetti called for "poetry to be a violent assault on the forces of the unknown, to glorify war, and demolish museums and morality along with feminism, and for revolution."[14] Separating himself from Marinetti's creed, the St. Petersburg poet Igor Severyanin called himself an "Ego-Futurist" with his own "Prologue. Ego-Futurism" in 1911.

The Moscow-based poet David Burlyuk through his publishing house produced the Russian futurist manifesto in 1912 "*A Slap in the Face of Public Opinion*" which drew the Moscow, Kyiv, Kharkiv, Baku, Odesa and

Petersburg poets, painters, and musicians together in the "Hylaea" group. The Moscow group called themselves Cubo-Futurists picking up from the French Cubists whose art concentrated on the breakup of form, interplay of spatial planes, and the contrast of color and texture. The Cubo-Futurists adopted a new form of speech called "budetlyan" from the Russian words "budet—shall be, or I shall be." Their "new language" was based on neologisms and onomatopoeia, and Khlebnikov devised his "zaum" language based on anarchic and incoherent sounds. This scheme would be used in Matyushin's groundbreaking futurist opera *Victory over the Sun* in 1913.[15] There was another group called "Centrifuge" around Nikolay Aseyev, Boris Pasternak, and Sergey Bobrov who were associated with the *Lyrica* magazine and concentrated on rhythmic intonation and syntax and were more left-wing than the other futurists. In 1915, after exhibiting in several Cubo-futurist exhibitions, Kazimir Malevich launched his "Last Futurist Exhibition of Paintings 0.1" in Petrograd with thirty-six paintings by thirteen different painters in a similar style. Malevich was one of the most important figures and here explains his revolutionary concept,

> Under Suprematism I understand the primacy of pure feeling in creative art. To the Suprematist, the visual phenomena of the objective world are, in themselves, meaningless; the significant thing is feeling, as such, quite apart from the environment in which it is called forth.[16]

Suprematism expresses through a combination of limited colors in simple geometric lines squares, circles, and rectangles forming different dimensions and portray an inner movement of equal asymmetrical Suprematist works. Malevich demanded that suprematism must be the first step to "pure art," that is to bring closer the creativity of man and nature.[17] Futurism influenced the early Soviet cinema, notably Eisenstein's "The Strike" (1925) that was thought to be "the modern futurist art form par excellence" in that the movie events can be speeded or slowed down to create an impression different in time. Many of the futurists were actors, painters, musicians, and poets, and the leading actor and poet Vladimir Mayakovsky also painted and took an unambivalent involvement in politics; however, the futurists were regarded as idealists and lost their momentum in the 1920s, while many aspects of futurism became part of Soviet culture and ultimately their activities declined in the 1930s. Part of their contribution to Soviet art would be the adoption or assimilation of their symbolism and slogans as part of the huge demonstrations and festivities through until the end of the Soviet Union in 1992. Igor Vorobyov once more enlightens us that,

> In the first years of Soviet power, the festive events were scrupulously prepared. There was a remarkable social-political aspect involved in the organized mass

actions. Apart from the metaphors of past and present—the crowd scenes were based on historical events (in a huge production of "Seizing of the Winter Palace"—1920). These scenes essentially formed the methodology later extensively used by "left" artists of the 1920s and 30s. The aspiration to recreate the reality of historical events quickly led to "leftist" concepts of the "literary truth" (Mayakovsky) in film documentary (Vertov), photography, cinema (Eisenstein), and literary constructivism (Selvinsky). The artistic production attained a form of festive mythology by presenting the moral superiority of good over evil and transforming this positive foundation in the future.[18]

The introduction of the New Economic Policy (NEP) by Lenin's government in 1921 allowed for breathing space for the Bolshevik Party to gradually restore order not only in purely economic terms but also as a means of stabilizing social relationships in Soviet life. As Francis Maes tells us, "There was room for experiment again, and links with the outside world were renewed. Yet one could equally say that it was precisely during the time of the NEP that the characteristic Soviet culture emerged."[19] The social conditions of the day were reflected by the composers Roslavets, Lourié, Deshevov, and Mosolov in their music through "constructivism"—a theme shared with other poets, writers, painters, and architects. It was these composers—above all—who forged the new avant-garde. But what do we understand by the term avant-garde? The avant-garde is a description that advocates a change from the status quo—forward toward a bright new future. If this represents an ephemeral and overly generalized description, let us examine the exact meaning and its significance for the specific period under study.

David Nicholls of Cambridge University considers the avant-garde as follows: "in music can refer to any form of music working within traditional structures while seeking to breach boundaries in some manner."[20] However, Nicholls here is discussing the American variant. In the musical bible, Grove, the scholar Jim Samson states the term is used loosely to describe the work of any musicians who radically depart from tradition altogether.[21] In his study, the Russian émigré musician Larry Sitsky specifically names as avant-gardist composers: Arnold Schoenberg, Charles Ives, Igor Stravinsky, Anton Webern, George Antheil (in his earliest works only), Alban Berg, Henry Cowell (in his earliest works), Philip Glass, Harry Partch, John Cage, Morton Feldman, Richard Strauss (in his earliest work), Karl Heinz Stockhausen, Edgard Varèse, and Iannis Xenakis. Composers not in the category are Elliott Carter, Milton Babbitt, György Ligeti, Witold Lutoslawski, and Luciano Berio because—as Sitsky writes playfully—"their modernism was not conceived for the purpose of goading an audience."[22]

In his espousal of the extended avant-garde, the Italian essayist Renato Poggioli offers one of the earliest analyses of the phenomenon in his *Teoria dell'arte d'avanguardia*. Through his survey of the historical, social, psychological, and philosophical aspects of vanguardism, Poggioli reaches beyond individual instances of art, poetry, and music to show that vanguardists may share certain ideas or values which manifest themselves in the nonconformist lifestyles they adopt: He sees vanguard culture as a variety or subcategory of Bohemianism.[23] In an attempt to both clarify and advance Poggioli's study, is the German literary critic Peter Bürger's *Theory of the Avant-Garde*, which examines the establishment's grip upon socially critical works of art suggesting that in collusion with capitalism, "art as an institution neutralizes the political content of the individual work." Bürger's definition of avant-gardism distinguishes it from modernism, for example, avant-gardism rejects the "institution of art" and challenges social and artistic values and so necessarily involves political, social, and cultural factors.[24]

It may not seem so bizarre a consequence—in this study—that the association of leftism and the avant-garde is often credited to the influential thinker Henri de Saint-Simon, one of the forerunners of socialism. He believed in the social power of the arts and saw artists, alongside scientists and industrialists, as the leaders of a new society. Saint-Simon, in 1825, espoused, "We artists will serve you as an avant-garde, the power of the arts is most immediate: when we want to spread new ideas, we inscribe them on marble or canvas. What a magnificent destiny for the arts is that of exercising a positive power over society, a true priestly function and of marching in the van (i.e. vanguard) of all the intellectual faculties!"[25]

Almost two hundred years after Saint-Simon's writings, it seems the term of the avant-garde—in the twenty-first century—is again in vogue, as the Faroese-Danish fashionista Barbara í Gongini writes, "Rejecting the common mentality and nurturing originality has allowed those who are free in mind to shape the future. Innovation is the key to success."[26] The Oxford English Dictionary definition is wholly suitable to our purpose by associating the terminology with "works by artists of the Russian avant-garde."[27] Interestingly, the global character of the phenomenon places New York as a locus—"New York is the international capital of the musical avant-garde."[28] The dubbing of the terminology of the avant-garde for the arts has an extremely stylish context with the controversy of certain artworks attracting huge audiences; however for avant-garde music, often notoriety creates negativity in the eyes of the middle ground of society. In academia there has always existed a lively discourse on avant-gardism in music and this may refer for instance to Erik Satie's 1893 *Vexations*, which asks for the pianist to repeat a theme 840 times, or Pauline Oliveros's 1964 *Duo*, for accordion and bandoneon players riding a seesaw, with optional mynah bird obbligato. One of the most outrageous examples of avant-garde music is a composer who studied with one of the Russian avant-garde to be discussed in this book—John Cage, whose remarkable 4′33″ (1952) involves the soloist sitting quietly at the piano without touching the keyboard.

The utopia of the futurists and the other champions of revolutionary change found that War Communism, in particular, led to the throwing away of some elements of the avant-garde and other qualities that were embraced by Soviet art. In the opinion of Maes, "Although these men's work was revolutionary, it was not 'Soviet' in the strict sense of the word. The pre-revolutionary intelligentsia was simply co-opted by the regime as long as it provided useful propaganda tools."[29] After Cherepnin, Medtner, Prokofiev, and Rachmaninov left Russia, their place was taken by new composers Deshevov, Kabalevsky, Khachaturyan, Knipper, Mosolov, Polovinkin, Popov, Roslavets, Shebalin, and Shostakovich. Others, as we know left to further their careers, or some departed only to fall into ignominy. There were key educators such as Boris Asafyev, Vladimir Shcherbachev, and Ivan Sollertinsky in Leningrad, while, in Moscow, there was Nikolay Myaskovsky, Reinhold Glière, Nikolay Zhilyaev, and Boris Yavorsky unstintingly upholding innovative musical thought. They would ensure a continuation of the generations through concerts, publishing, and teaching.

In the 1920s, Soviet society threw up several associations founded to promote Marxist ideology through music and the arts. These were led by workers who participated in the Revolution and the Civil War—some had learned music in Red Army regimental bands and included young communists who wanted to destroy the old world by replacing it with something quite different. These groupings included supporters of different revolutionary leaders, particularly Bukharin and Trotsky. There were those such as Alexey Sergeyev who was in the outlawed Social-Revolutionary Party. Lev Shulgin, David Chernomordikov, and Lev Lebedinsky were the leaders of the Russian Association of Proletarian Music (RAPM) that attempted to destroy not only modernism but also traditional music. The RAPM was a political group formed of a few individuals who forced their way into musical life solely through their political allegiances and networking skills. They occupied influential positions at the Agitation Department of the State Music Publishing (Muzsektor), and the RAPM became an advisory body to the latter.[30] Only Alexander Kastalsky (1856–1926), a composer of liturgical music and the director of the Moscow Synod School, gave the group any musical credibility, while the other members possessed little compositional knowledge or skill. There were other groups like the Organization of Revolutionary Composers and Musical Workers (ORKiMD) that was set up as a breakaway group (led by Shulgin and Sergeyev) from the RAPM in 1925. At the same time, the emergence of the Production Collective of Student Composers (Prokoll) at the Moscow Conservatoire sidestepped both the Association of Contemporary Music (ASM) and RAPM by pursuing proletarian opera and choral works.

The Cultural Revolution launched by the Bolshevik Party in 1928 gave exclusivity of power to the RAPM over music publishing, education, radio, opera and ballet, and orchestras. This led to students at the Moscow Conservatoire Bely, Davidenko, Shekhter, and Koval joining its ranks. Not only was modernism attacked, but other targets included jazz, and "light music" for its "degenerate" and "pro-western" origins. The alternative was revolutionary songs and choral works based on patriotism and mass songs. Rabfaks or worker's schools were set up in the conservatoires to replace the traditional curriculum, with entrance permitted only for sons and daughters from working families without needing any examinations.[31] This failed to achieve any positive outcome, and, in 1932, in the Bolshevik Party's restructuring of culture, the RAPM was dissolved, and the Union of Composers was established with state support to unite all composers under one body, centralizing Soviet musical life, allowing the Union's members control of publishing and the commissioning of new music. Composers would discuss new music and agree on what was to be performed and published through their media outlets. In 1934, the concept of socialist realism was unveiled by the writer Maxim Gorky with backing by the Bolshevik Party and adopted as the new aesthetic covering all genres of Soviet culture. The Netherlands musicologist Francis Maes argues,

> Applied to art, Gorky's picture comprises two characteristics essential for socialist realism: first, the artist must see reality in its evolution toward the socialist ideal; second, individual creativity must make way for communal and comparable work. The first aspect reflects the difference between socialist realism and nineteenth-century realism: the critical view with which reality used to be observed has become outdated because reality has moved positively ahead. The second aspect means the rejection of the "l'art pour l'art" principle. Every manifestation of autonomous aestheticism would henceforth be labeled 'formalism. (. . .) Socialist realism was both the consequence and the negation of avant-garde trends. It held fast to the aesthetic utopia of Russian modernism, in which art played an active role in the creation of life; at the same time, it curbed the ambitions of art.[32]

However, some philosophers looked at the concept differently, for them, as Nikolay Chuzhak wrote, the working class was "the Pygmalion who brought to life the Galatea of Futurism and turned the evolutionary tasks of art into the task of creating the revolution."[33] The reality of the Soviet experiment was as Maes informs, "The vague symbolist idea of the future was now given a clear shape: that of communism."[34] In Russian music, constructivism superseded futurism in the 1920s by seeking the end of traditional sounds through using industrial and urban sound effects. The most characteristic of this was the Symphony of Foghorns by Avraamov in 1922, in which the "instruments" were foghorns, factory sirens, artillery, machine guns, and airplanes in a celebration of the revolution.

The new historical-sociological conditions caused the ostensible disappearance of the avant-garde in the 1930s; nevertheless, composers never ceased exploring new means of expression—their music was simply not performed anymore, or at least in public. Somewhat symptomatic of current musicology is the paucity of scholarly researched analysis and evaluation reflected by thinly documented concert programs and CD booklets. This dearth of information prevails in the recordings of Prokofiev and Shostakovich—naively marketed under the banner—"Under the Shadow of Stalin" or "Shostakovich against Stalin." The revival of cold war stereotypes lends a false narrative about these and other Soviet composers—and regrettably—the drive for sensationalism extends to speculation.

The disparity between academic research in Russian and German music of the twentieth century is revealing. The approach of musicologists toward German composers who were active during the Third Reich, such as Richard Strauss, Paul Hindemith, or Carl Orff, largely overlooks their relationship with the Nazis. The popularity of such works as *Carmina Burana* by Orff and Strauss's *Der Rosenkavalier* seemingly deter writers from criticism. Conversely, music writers are not immune to dealing with Soviet musicology. "In the case of Shostakovich, as of Richard Strauss," the Manchester musicologist David Fanning noted,

> the romantic ideology of doomed, suicidal genius is a potent but very partial myth. (. . .) This mythological dissident Shostakovich has enjoyed two decades of authority in music journalism, popular music writing, and on the internet; and it is an accident of the different methodologies and publishing practices of journalism and scholarship that musicologists were apparently slow to counter it.[35]

Regardless of the swelling interest in Soviet music, cold war mentalities predominate discussions and media coverage amid a hesitancy to examine original documents from the period. There is a misunderstanding that is echoed in Fanning's appraisal,

> There has also been a reluctance to evaluate Soviet music on the same technical and aesthetic levels as Western post-war art music, on the assumption that it must by its very nature be regressive and "unfree." More broadly still, the relatively slow pace at which musicology has followed Slavist literary and historical studies (. . .) has meant that Shostakovich has been viewed through a very crude

lens (in particular the Manichaean "for-or-against" syndrome noted above), and this has hardly encouraged a sophisticated understanding of the paradoxical nature of Soviet musical culture and its products.[36]

In the first decades of the twenty-first century, there has been a return to a "cold war" between the West and Russia—reviving old stereotypes—indeed "Russophobia" demonizes almost everything Russian.[37] This negativity is not shared by the Moscow-based musicologist Levon Hakobian, who explains,

> It seems that the dominant Western notion of the life under Hammer and Sickle, promoted by the Cold War propaganda and underlying numerous works of fiction, films and pieces of journalism (. . .), was reduced to a handful of definitely unpleasant constituents: GULAG, KGB, a militaristic euphoria, hard-drinking, a bureaucracy in splendour and working people in misery, empty shops and endless lines, dismal faces of passers-by in the streets and bombastic propaganda about the regime's successes. Accordingly, only two categories of humankind in Soviet society were worthy of attention: on the one hand, a cynical, cruel, corrupt communist elite, and, on the other, a courageous handful of dissidents. As for the rest of the population, it was considered an amorphous and sterile mass of silent conformists.[38]

Hakobian believes that the Soviet system was more benign than that commonly perceived by writing,

> It overlooks the existence of a highly specific and rich spiritual atmosphere elaborated by several generations of "conformists"—that is, properly speaking, by the common efforts of the country's intellectuals and creative people—that represents one of the most powerful realities of the Soviet epoch and, *sub specie aeternitatis*, may be regarded as an achievement of utmost importance (however unintentional!) by the communist regime.[39]

The contribution by Russian specialists can be strangely inconsistent and provide unfamiliar upshots, for instance, the renowned scholar Israel Nestyev authored highly respected works in the USSR. However, during "glasnost" in the 1980s, he switched from being an adamant scion of "formalism" to questioning the former tenets of Soviet musicology, including his writings. Of course, other musicologists in the former USSR—averse to Marxist ideology—celebrated the collapse of the system.

At the heart of the criticism of Soviet culture is not the state funding for theaters, and musical institutions, offering benefits for musicians largely unsurpassed elsewhere. Music education was free, concert tickets were affordable, and musical literature was widely available. The concept of realism in painting, architecture, literature, and cinema is accepted universally. Today, many years after the fall of the Soviet Union, there nevertheless appears to be a huge market for paintings by futurist, and avowedly "socialist realist" artists. Extraordinarily, at Sotheby's in London—as recently as 2017—works by Soviet modernist painters and artists (Kandinsky, Malevich, Rodchenko, and others) sold for unexpectedly high prices.

Soviet composers achieved both success and notoriety in the West long before the Nazis spread their malicious poison. Modernist music in Europe and America became restrained in its language; however, many Soviet musical works were stunningly successful under the batons of Leopold Stokowski, Eugene Ormandy, and Arturo Toscanini. Certainly, the orchestral works by Myaskovsky, Mosolov, Shostakovich, Kabalevsky, and Khachaturian were popular among new audiences.[40] Interestingly, Shostakovich's *Lady Macbeth of Mtsensk District* opera caused as much uproar not for its "formalism" but for its "vulgarity" in the *New York Times* as it did in *Pravda*.

Nevertheless, the first wave of the Soviet avant-garde embraced a diverse coterie of composers that advanced the boundaries of modernism on a worldwide scale. This book focuses on three composers whose affiliation was shared only in the ASM. The most prominent of the "apostles" was Nikolay Roslavets—who invented serial music before Arnold Schoenberg—with his "theory of the synthetic chord." However, in time, Roslavets, according to Boris Schwartz, was "completely expunged. If his name happens to be mentioned, it is either with rancor or ridicule for allegedly (. . .) being the 'Russian Schoenberg.'"[41]

Gavriil Popov influenced Shostakovich, and for the first time used electronic music in film with the groundbreaking Thereminvox. Popov's First Symphony was banned long before Shostakovich fell under a cloud, and his film scores used an experimental montage of music in the cinema of the 1930s. The third of the "apostles," and arguably the most exciting of all—Alexander Mosolov—was a leading constructivist and brilliantly gifted musician. Mosolov authored bitingly satirical songs, an antiromantic piano concerto, and four operas. The notoriously brief and explosive symphonic cameo *The Foundry: The Music of Machines* shares a common language with music by Varèse, Hindemith, Honegger, and Poulenc, yet Mosolov's piece is arguably more spectacular and individualist. Out-riders in the avant-garde circle are Vladimir Shcherbachov (1889–1952), the tutor of Popov and Shostakovich, and composer of five symphonies. More than twenty symphonies were written by the nephew of Anton Chekhov—Lev Knipper (1898–1974). His music adopted diverse styles while living conceivably the most astonishing life of all.[42] Somewhat by accident, the futurist Arthur Lourié was appointed "Minister for Music" in the Bolshevik government—yet, he changed his style after emigration. A protégé of Scriabin—Samuel Feinberg

(1890–1962) was a brilliant pianist and teacher who wrote stunningly esoteric sonatas and three celebrated piano concertos. Joseph Schillinger is famous for teaching George Gershwin, and both Schillinger and Nikolay Zhilyaev (1881–1938) left behind many musical pieces and treatises deserving of further archival research. The early death of Alexey Stanchinsky (1888–1914) robbed the world of a brilliantly gifted musician whose piano music foreshadowed Stravinsky and Bartók. The mysticism of Scriabin influenced Nikolay Obukhov (1892–1954) and Ivan Vyshnegradsky (1893–1979), who later experimented with micro-tonal music. The Ukrainian Yefim Golyshev (1897–1970) lays claim to have invented serialism; however, after emigrating to Paris earned his living as a bricklayer.

The invention of the Thereminvox offered a new potential instrument for the Russian avant-garde in their search for new means of expression. Of course, the Italian futurist artist and composer Luigi Russolo (1885–1947) experimented with new forms of musical instruments in the 1910s with his manifesto *L'Arte dei Rumori* (The Art of Noises) and his Intonarumori noise-creating devices. In 1920, a brilliant young engineer in Petrograd Lev Sergeyevich Theremin (1896–1993) designed a device that was based on radio waves transmitted over a short distance which responded to hand and arm movement creating sound. The Thereminvox was demonstrated to Lenin in 1922 who was able to perform Glinka's *The Lark*. Theremin also designed one of the first television devices in 1925, and during his career designed security systems for American prisons. Musicians in Frankfurt and Berlin heard the Thereminvox in 1924, and, in 1928, Theremin moved to the United States where a patent was taken out for his instrument establishing his own company which developed a range of electronic devices, cooperated with RCA, and was supported by the Rockefeller family, among other businessmen. In 1938, he returned to the USSR and continued his research work (although he was accused of being a spy and spent several years in a labor camp where he continued his experiments). The Thereminvox continues to be used in concerts both in Russia and in Europe to this day.

The phenomenon of the Soviet avant-garde was matched by innovative methods in musical performance. One of the most radical innovations was that by a professor of violin at the Moscow Conservatoire—Lev Tseitlin (1881–1952), who established an orchestra without a conductor. Persimfans (The First Symphony Ensemble) was based on professional musicians from the Conservatoire and the Bolshoi Theater Orchestra, whose Sunday subscription concerts at the Bolshoi, and at factories and other workplaces were extraordinarily successful. They also gave premieres of music by Prokofiev, Stravinsky, and Myaskovsky. The group performed a complete Beethoven symphonic cycle in Moscow—although their concert life lasted from 1922 to 1932, it became a paradigm for ensembles in Belgium and America.

Recently, in the twenty-first century Persimfans has been restored to concert life in Moscow.

This study of the Soviet musical avant-garde narrates the life and music of three leading avant-garde composers, or apostles of Soviet music, and of other neglected composers active between the First and theSecond World Wars. The contributions by Mikhail Matyushin, Arthur Lourié, and Joseph Schillinger will be discussed in the final chapter when we also reflect on the significance of the avant-garde in Russia and worldwide. As there are few if any recordings by either Matyushin or Schillinger, I have added to the discography the website addresses where some of their works may be found. As we will see, following the Silver Age in the first decades of the twentieth century there entered a brief period that brought a rich vein of musical discovery, and in today's more sophisticated world we are better able to appraise this fascinating chronicle of these immensely gifted trailblazing Russian musicians.

NOTES

1. Blok, Alexander, "The Intelligentsia and the Revolution," *Znamya Truda*, February 1, 1918.
2. Suss, P, "Na iskhode" (Nearing the End), *Rech*, October 15, 1917. Quoted in Hackel, Sergey, *The Poet and the Revolution*, Oxford University Press, 1975, 149.
3. Hackel painstakingly documents the apocalyptic sources and references in Blok's controversial masterpiece, pointing to Blok's annotated Bible and Bely's gloss on *The Book of Revelation* as being the most relevant. Klara Moricz, "Introduction," *Funeral Games in Honor of Arthur Vincent Lourie*, Oxford, Oxford University Press, 2014, 9.
4. Maes, Francis, *A History of Russian Music*, London: University of California Press, 2002, 240–241.
5. Gutkin, Irina, "Legacy of the Symbolist Aesthetic Utopia: From Futurism to Socialist Realism," 183–84, eds. Irina Paperno and Joan Delaney Grossman, *Creating Life: The Aesthetic Utopia of Russian Modernism*, 1677-06. Stanford, 1994.
6. Vorobyov, Igor, *Russkiye avangarda i tvorchestvo Aleksandra Mosolova 1920–1930 godakh*, Sankt Peterburg: Kompozitor, 2006, 28–29.
7. Schwartz, Boris, *Music and Musical Life in Soviet Russia 1917–1982*, Bloomington: Indiana University Press, 1983, 87.
8. Schwartz, Boris, *Music and Musical Life in Soviet Russia 1917–1982*, Bloomington: Indiana University Press, 1983, 454n.
9. Schwartz, Boris, *Music and Musical Life in Soviet Russia 1917–1982*, Bloomington: Indiana University Press, 1983, 426.
10. Schwartz, Boris, *Music and Musical Life in Soviet Russia 1917–1982*, Bloomington: Indiana University Press, 1983, 133.

11. Vorobyov, Igor, *Russkiye avangarda i tvorchestvo Aleksandra Mosolova 1920–1930 godakh*, Sankt Peterburg: Kompositor, 2006, 29.

12. Marinetti, Filippo Tommaso, "Manifesto del Futuristi," *Gazzetta dell' Emilia*, February 5, 1909.

13. Marinetti later became active in the Italian fascist movement—author.

14. Marinetti, Filippo Tommaso, "Manifesto del Futuristi," *Gazzetta dell' Emilia*, February 5, 1909.

15. The leading Cubo-futurists were Khlebnikov, Guro, the Burlyuk brothers, Kamensky, Mayakovsky, Kruchenykh, and Livschitz. The principal Ego-Futurists were Severyanin, Ivanov, Larionov, Shershenevich, and Gnedov—author.

16. Malevich, Kazimir, "Suprematism" Part II, *The Non-Objective World*, Munich: Bauhaus, 1927.

17. Malevich's group of Suprematist artists included Rozanova, Popova, Clyun, Udaltsova, Ekster, Suetin, Lissitzky, Khidekel, Puli, and Rodchenko—author.

18. Vorobyov, Igor, *Russkiye avangarda i tvorchestvo Aleksandra Mosolova 1920–1930 godakh*, Sankt Peterburg: Kompositor, 2006, 79.

19. Maes, Francis, *A History of Russian Music*, London: University of California Press, 2002, 243.

20. Nicholls, David (ed.), *The Cambridge Dictionary of American Music*. Cambridge and New York: CUP, 1998, 122–124.

21. Sampson, Jim, "Avant-Garde," eds. Stanley Sadie and John Tyrell, *The New Grove Dictionary of Music and Musicians*, second edition, London: Macmillan, 2001.

22. Sitsky, Larry, *Music of the Twentieth-Century Avant-Garde: A Biographical Sourcebook*, Westport, CT: Greenwood Press, 2002, xiv.

23. Poggioli, Renato, *The Theory of the Avant-Garde*, Belknap Press of Harvard University Press, 1968, 11, translated by Gerald Fitzgerald.

24. Burger, Peter, *Theory of the Avant-Garde*, English translation by Michael Shaw, forward by Jochen Schulte-Sasse, *Theory and History of Literature*, volume 4, Manchester University Press, University of Minnesota Press, 1984.

25. Beuys, Joseph, "Avant-Garde Art: What's Going Up in the 80's," Edinburgh International Festival, The Richard Demarco Gallery, 1980.

26. Gongini, Barbara í., "Avant-Garde Fashion" *A Modern Definition*, 2017. https://barbaraigongini.com/universe/blog/avant-garde-fashion-a-modern-definition/.

27. https://en.oxforddictionaries.com/definition/avant-garde.

28. https://dictionary.cambridge.org/dictionary/english/avant-garde.

29. Maes, Francis, *A History of Russian Music*, London: University of California Press, 2002, 243.

30. Maes, Francis, *A History of Russian Music*, London: University of California Press, 2002, 252.

31. Maes, Francis, *A History of Russian Music*, London: University of California Press, 2002, 253.

32. Maes, Francis, *A History of Russian Music*, London: University of California Press, 2002, 255–256.

33. Chuzhak, Nikolay, quoted in Gutkin, "Legacy of the Symbolist Aesthetic Utopia," 194.

34. Maes, Francis, *A History of Russian Music*, London: University of California Press, 2002, 256.

35. Fairclough and Fanning, *Cambridge Companion to Shostakovich*, CAM, 2008, 1.

36. Fairclough and Fanning, *Cambridge Companion to Shostakovich*, CAM, 2008, 2.

37. Russophobia has appeared in diverse areas of public life from alleged drug abuse in sports leading to bans on Russia's Olympic team, alleged interference in US and other country's elections, attempted assassinations of former spies living in the West, and spreading "fake news" in the West through their news agencies—author.

38. Hakobian, Leon, "Introduction," *Music of the Soviet Era: 1917–1991*, Second edition, London: Routledge, 2017, 1.

39. Hakobian, Leon, "Introduction," *Music of the Soviet Era: 1917–1991*, Second edition, London: Routledge, 2017, 2.

40. Myaskovsky's Tenth, Eleventh, Thirteenth symphonies, and Fourth String Quartet did experiment with serialism—author.

41. Schwartz, Boris, *Music and Musical life in Soviet Russia 1917–1981*, Bloomington: Indiana University Press, 1983, 86.

42. Following his death in 1974, it became known that Knipper had worked for the secret services and during the war was delegated to carry out an assassination on Hitler in the event of the Nazis capturing Moscow—author.

Chapter 1

The Young Paganini

The Roslavets family name originates from the river Rosl, which flows through the Chernigov district and the hamlet of Roslavka.[1] Interestingly, the register of nobility titles of the Russian empire denotes that the Roslavets was a noble peasant family.[2] This clarifies the mystery and falsehoods that shroud the early years of Nikolay Andreyevich Roslavets.[3] According to his autobiography, Nikolay's father was a serf who fought at the Shipka Pass during the Turkish campaign (1877–1878). On returning home, he was granted the right to buy property and, little by little, gained the freedom to become a civil servant. Nikolay Andreyevich was born in the town of Surazh in the Chernigov district on the border of Ukraine and Russia on December 23, 1880 (January 4, 1881).[4] As a child of seven or eight years, the local violinist Belodubrovsky writes "somewhere in these fields, a boy strolled, caught fish (a passion which proved short-lived), mastered how to make musical instruments from reeds, wood, and horns, tended after horses at night, then returned to a peasant hut, unsuspecting how fate would turn him into a musician of world fame."[5]

Far from civilization, Surazh was a god-forsaken hamlet where the peasants lived in deepest poverty, the nearest railway was sixty kilometers away, and the only way to make a decent living was to move to the nearest town. We know from a relative of the painter Malevich that "the Roslavets family were quite impoverished, the father Andrey Stepanovich was a writing clerk in the police department, and the mother was an alcoholic."[6] It is even more remarkable that Nikolay Roslavets found the means to become a celebrated musician; however, the attraction to music came from his uncle. At seven or eight, Nikolay learned to make and play the violin at his uncle's workshop later joining a band of two violinists, and a double-bass player. He recalled that "I can't disguise the fact that—apart from my uncle's 'compositions'— we played several of my own 'polkas or kozachoks'. During the gap between my studies, for two winters I attended the local primary Zemstvo school from which I graduated with an award and diploma."[7] At the age of twelve, Nikolay followed his father to work at a railway office in Konotop. There he mastered the violin with a Jewish musician and organized his band of two violins, flute, and drummer. One sign of the band's reputation was that they joined a circus on tour. After a few years, Nikolay moved with his father to the regional center of Kursk, working as a clerk on the Moscow-Kiev-Voronezh Railway.

ABASA AND MALEVICH

A major step came at sixteen, when Nikolay began studying music theory and harmony with Arkady Maximovich Abasa (1843–1915) at a private music school in Kursk. Abasa's teaching gave Roslavets his happiest memories, writing later that Abasa inspired in him the capacity "to work and study art unselfishly, not for other ill-advised aims, but for that ideal in life which was instilled in me and other pupils."[8] Roslavets dedicated his *Prélude pour Piano* (1915) to his memory.

Music was not the only attraction because Nikolay was also interested in painting. Kazimir Malevich tells us that he and Roslavets first became acquainted in Konotop when they were both members of an art club there. This lifelong friendship developed when they were both working on the railway in Kursk, as the painter recollects, "Nikolay Roslavets played the violin and was better at drawing than I was—and he painted too."[9] The growing enthusiasm for music led Roslavets to conduct in Polish church concerts, while working in the railway office, and studying music with Abasa, as he writes, "Directing both choir and orchestra, I managed to gain valuable musical preparation which helped me somewhat in future years."[10] Valentina Zaitseva—Malevich's sister—recalls that her mother gave him a violin "which he had dreamed of and helped to launch his musical career."[11] At the age of twenty-one, Roslavets's desire for a profession in music led him to move to Moscow (Malevich and his wife and two children did not make their move until 1904) as he writes, "I had managed to save 200 roubles from my earnings, and contrary to my family's wishes, in 1902, I moved to Moscow where after undertaking an examination, I was taken into the violin class at the Conservatoire."[12]

THE MOSCOW CONSERVATOIRE

Roslavets entered the class of one of the finest virtuosi in Europe. Jan Hřimalý (1844–1915) was born in the city of Plzen—the son of Vojtech, a distinguished organist, and composer—and he studied with his brother Vojtech Jr. before enrolling in Professor Moritz Mildner's class at the Prague Conservatoire. After six years as the concertmaster in Amsterdam, in 1869, Hřimalý arrived in Russia, and five years later replaced Ferdinand Laub as head of violin studies at the Moscow Conservatoire.[13]

With the bow of professor Hřimalý
All the fiddlers sang,
Striking their feet like a fist.[14]

Hřimalý's teaching at the Moscow Conservatoire spanned forty-six years (until his death), fashioning a distinguished lineage of master violinists second only to the St. Petersburg Professor Leopold Auer.[15] Among the winners of the illustrious gold medal were Iosif Kotek; Alexander Pechnikov; Georgy Konius; Mikhail Press; Alexander Mogilevsky; the violist, conductor, and composer Vladimir Bakaleinikov; Mikhail Erdenko; and Igor Guzikov.[16] The musicologist Leonid Raaben enlightens us on his teaching: "Actually, Hřimalý directed great attention to technique, and was a genuine pedagogue methodist: his essays 'Exercise in scales' and 'Exercises in double notes' were studied by generations of violinists."[17] It would appear that Roslavets's love for the chamber genre, if it wasn't born there, was secured in Hřimalý's class for string quartet.

At some point, possibly owing to the standard of his fellow violin students, Roslavets resolved to become a composer because he began studying counterpoint, fugue, and musical form with Mikhail Ippolitov-Ivanov and Alexander Ilyinsky, and orchestration and free composition with Sergey Vasilenko. Two years after Roslavets enlisted at the Moscow Conservatoire, Malevich followed him to study painting in Moscow. The two friends shared visits to the galleries, opera, ballet, and literary evenings. There remains little tangible suggestion of how they lived during these years—one auspicious example dates from 1907, when Malevich dedicated a painting to his friend entitled "A sketch of Nikolay Roslavets" (Song for a Light-Blue Cloud). The picture depicts a young naked man playing the violin.[18] Signs of his innovative and independent character can be observed in his developing friendships with the futurist poets Aristarkh Lentulov, Vasily Kamensky, and David Burlyuk—adherents of the literary avant-garde in Russia .

Following the 1905 Revolution, the Conservatoire was temporarily closed. It was at this time that Safonov resigned as Rector, and Ippolitov-Ivanov appointed as his replacement. There was a break in studies and in 1906, Roslavets returned home and met with his brother, who had been released from a Japanese prison camp after the Russo-Japanese war. The homecoming "was marked with song, music, and happiness. Many people sang, and played

Figure 1.1 A Sketch of the Composer Roslavets. Song of the Blue Clouds by Kazimir Malevich 1907. *Source*: Collection of Stedelijk Museum Amsterdam.

music."[19] According to his mother-in-law, Nikolay "was attentive to both family and friends, and was equally industrious and kind-hearted. Determined in both in his judgments and actions, he neither flattered nor patronized anyone. The easy life was not for him. He loved his work and gave himself completely to it."[20]

During his studies with Ippolitov-Ivanov and Ilyinsky, Roslavets composed more than 100 fugues, and his notebooks "Forms of Musical Composition" (1908–1910) contain examples of transitory two-part and three-part songs, sonatas, and rondos. In January 1910, he presented his teachers with a Sonatina for Violin and Piano.[21] These were in traditional style, however, with new ideas circulating among students, Roslavets was already seeking for new expressive forms, as he wrote years later, "I was extremely radical and owing to my point of view on numerous occasions suffered from occasionally a lack of sympathy."[22] Roslavets's reminisces how his increasingly rebellious views caused controversy among his professors; however, his distinctly youthful outlook enhanced the development of groundbreaking ideas.

> During my studies at the Conservatoire, regardless of all kinds of wickedness committed against me by the professors, I somehow completed the Conservatoire. At the time, I wanted to throw out everything that I learned there together with all its related baggage.[23]

If his professors got little recognition from Roslavets, at least he did have much respect for his violin professor, as his mother-in-law informs us.

As a student at the Conservatoire, in his routine work, he distinguished himself both through the independence of thought and originality in musical coherence and consequently clashed with his professors. (. . .) It was for this that his student pieces were rarely performed at the Conservatoire, and even less so in public. Of all his Conservatoire professors the only one for whom he had any warm feelings was the late J. V. Hřimalý.[24]

One of Roslavets's professors, Vasilenko commented disapprovingly about "his mediocre talents and lack of great musical knowledge—he possessed an enormous craving for innovation. At that time, he was corresponding with all sorts of young, Western composers whom I had never heard of, and the emerging Schoenberg had become his God. It was difficult to deal with him, and the music that he was writing was completely unacceptable."[25]

Sergei Nikiforovich Vlasenko (1872–1956) composed in almost every genre from opera and ballet to the early cinema while enjoying a second career as a conductor. His compositions have a mysticism, faithfulness to Russian folklore, and particularly Cossack song. That was most discernible in the stage works performed under his baton at the Mamontov Opera and later the Bolshoi Theater.[26] Vasilenko's interest in symbolism and exoticism from the Silver Age influenced Roslavets. Vasilenko was fascinated by Scriabin's mysticism, and his early works embrace modernist expressionist influences—it is curious that he was so dismissive of Roslavets. Indeed, the very title of Vasilenko's opera *Children of the Sun* produced at the Bolshoi Theater in 1929 invokes the symbolists.[27] Belodubrovsky writes that Roslavets imbibed the scents of the Silver Age in Russia in the years before the First World War together with the styles and fashions of the period. "He was attracted to the poetry of Blok and Bryusov, Severyanin, and Burlyuk, and Verlaine in their diverse and individual orientations."[28]

In time, Vasilenko would have cause to modify his opinion of Roslavets.

I was not looking forward to hearing his latest work. I thought it would be some kind of cacophony, and he declined to show it to us until it was complete. However, to my surprise, the cantata with its equally strident and succinct harmonies was suitable, and the culmination and brilliant orchestration proved wholly satisfactory. The examination board fretted over it, and the professors' present—Ippolitov-Ivanov, Kashkin, Kruglikov, and Grechaninov were all convinced that this was a young composer who expresses something new—so much so that they awarded him the Silver Medal.[29]

One other of Roslavets's teachers in composition at the Conservatoire was Mikhail Ippolitov-Ivanov (1859–1935). He belonged to the late nationalist school and embraced the rich harmonic orchestration of Rimsky-Korsakov—without necessarily the invention of his contemporaries—he never shied away from fresh ideas. Ippolitov-Ivanov wrote works on Catalan, Caucasian, and Central Asian harmonies, and like Vasilenko, later embraced socialist realism. As a conductor, Ippolitov-Ivanov undertook the world premieres of Rimsky-Korsakov's *The Tsar's Bride* and *Kashchey the Immortal* at the Mamontov and Zimin private companies and conducted at the Bolshoi Theater from 1925.

Ippolitov-Ivanov assumed the Rectorship when it reopened in 1906 through until 1922. However, his great contribution to Russian music was the completion and orchestration of Musorgsky's *The Marriage* in 1931. This underestimated musician instilled in Roslavets's orchestral technique the legacy of the folklore tradition. Among his other students were the pianists Goldenweiser and Igumnov, and Glière who tutored Prokofiev and Myaskovsky. Nonetheless, Roslavets was unimpressed. "They taught me at the Conservatoire as they were taught 100 years ago. Imagine that I completed the Conservatoire in 1913 and that I had to write as they did 100 years ago. They didn't even try to teach Scriabin that."[30]

Alexander Alexandrovich Ilyinsky (1859–1920) is the most underestimated of Roslavets's teachers; curiously, Ilyinsky's music was listened to by infinitely more people than any of his illustrious pupils. He was educated in the First Cadet Corps in St. Petersburg (his father was a physician in the Alexandrinsky Cadet Corps), and his musical gifts were so sophisticated that he gave recitals of his piano compositions.[31] Ilyinsky's most significant composition is the four-act opera based on Pushkin's *Bakhchisaray Fountain* (1915), as was the symphonic scherzo *Croatian Dances*, and his *Eros and Psyche* based on Sophocles. The music for the latter was used in the Hollywood film *East of Java* (1935), the adventure serial *Flash Gordon's Trip to Mars*, and the Universal Pictures adventure series *Tim Tyler's Luck* (1938). Ilyinsky's *A Practical Guide to the Teaching of Orchestration* (1917) remains a study-work in Russia's music education.

Roslavets found shortcomings in his methodology: "The professor approached the piano and stated, 'this is the music of Scriabin.' (. . .) I began to explore as my inner being couldn't tolerate such anarchy."[32] Roslavets's fellow students included the Kalinnikov brothers Vasily and Viktor, Anatoly Alexandrov, and Nikolay Golovanov.[33] The Kalinnikov brothers were good composers in the traditional style, as was Golovanov, who was more infected by the mysticism of Scriabin. Golovanov became a celebrated conductor—one of Russia's greatest interpreters of the Russian nationalist school at the Bolshoi Theater. Alexandrov fell under the spell of Scriabin and wrote a rich number of works continuing his legacy, and was a talented teacher. Roslavets was called up for military service in 1902, however was allowed to continue his studies until 1911, when he shared his final year in the army.

The marriage to a fellow student Natalya Alekseyevna Langovaya (1888–1957) allowed Roslavets' support because he joined one of the wealthy Moscow families, allowing him the freedom to develop his musical career. He and his new wife lived at his mother-in-law's home at 38 Myasnitsky Street in downtown Moscow.[34] In Roslavets's final year of study, he took a crucial step in formulating his innovative system of composition. Written at a time of sweeping changes in Europe, the graduation work of Byron's mystery *Heaven and the Earth* impresses with its foreboding, expectation, and prophetic language. The symbolism apparent in the poet's work is appropriate to both time and place, evident in Andrey Bely's novel *Peterburg* with the catastrophic picture of the Romanov citadel, and contemporary with Georgy Chulkov's *Snowstorm* that illustrates a satanic masquerade. The foreboding of a great catastrophe amid groundbreaking societal changes inhabited much of Russian thinking and culture during this period. Typical of this was Anna Akhmatova's *Poem Without a Hero* (1913) that recreates the imagery of a devilish harlequin in St. Petersburg.

Early Compositions

Before the groundbreaking Violin Sonata, there were several vital student pieces, notably for violin and orchestra—*Rêvérie* (1907), the First Symphony (1910), and his symphonic poem *In the Hours of the New Moon* (1913). Also, there were miniatures for violin and piano, and romances set to poems by Konstantin Balmont, Vyacheslav Ivanov, Alexander Blok, Maximilian Voloshin, and Nikolay Gumilyov. Roslavets's piece for violin and orchestra *Rêvérie*—despite the heavy orchestration, reflects a stab at several forms that would evolve into his distinctive technique. The scoring comprises solo violin and harp with timpani and chamber orchestra. The mood is dreamy-reflective in the invocation of a romantic poem and with a lure to symbolism. The symphonic poem is a notion that he would continue, yet the *Rêvérie* is based on the traditional Moscow school. For Roslavets, this was but a stepping-stone. Lobanova considers that during studies with Ilyinsky, Roslavets was still 'paying a debt to the school by trying out different ensembles, forms, and formulas.'[35] Other student pieces included the first movement for a String Quartet in F,[36] a *Minuet* in G for String Quartet (1907), *Serenada* in D for two violins (1909), the *Poème Lyrique* in F for violin and piano, and *Dances of the White Maidens* for cello and piano (1912).[37] A common feature is Roslavets's experimentation with major-minor tonality.

The *Trois poèmes* for violin and piano, the first—*Poème douloureux* (1909–1910), compromises the intensity in chromatic tone with a measured academicism.[38] Roslavets adopts a graceful measure by eliminating the sense of power, while the shifting measure, the decorative development, and bleakness reveal the struggle for a new style. In the other miniatures of *Poème Lyrique* and *Poème*, Roslavets presents Scriabinesque motifs of exhaustion, passion, and flight. The violin and piano arrangements, the *Romance* (1908), and *Arabesques* (1909/1910), are more simple in their structure, and Roslavets's use of symbolism pre-echo the synthetic chord.[39] Three of Roslavets's pieces for violin and piano are *Morgenstimmung* in B (1907), dedicated to his wife, Natalya Alekseyevna Langovaya (with hints of his interest in German themes), and the *Elegy* in G, and *Serenada* in G (1908).[40]

Vocal Works

Roslavets wrote several settings for voice and piano to Balmont's *Summer Lightning* and *The Flower* (1909), as part of a traditional cycle and are reserved in their recitative style. More individualistic is another Balmont symbolist romance, *Moran*, or *The Evening Field* that departs from tradition by using an ingenious augmented mode.[41] This device became Roslavets's "visiting card" by using the augmented triad rather than Schoenberg's diminished triad.

Roslavets set the miniature *Swans* by the symbolist Vyacheslav Ivanov, in which there is a dominating recitative composed with elegance and assurance. Roslavets's experimental vocal cycles used triads with synthetic chord technique and involving consonance. The early form of the synthetic chord is evident in both the vertical and horizontal musical lines in his setting of Alexander Blok's *I Don't Remember Yesterday*. There is a kinship in later settings of *The Wolfs' Graveyard* and *Kuk* from his *Four Compositions for Voice and Piano* (1915). These all reject tradition by Roslavets's introduction of a concept of "compositions" in diverse arrangements. The Ivanov and Blok vocal miniatures are similar to Gumilyov's *Beatrice* and the cycles from Bely, Voloshin, and again, Blok (1910–1911), are more radical in their harmonics. Now, only a short step remained before the conclusive realization of the "synthetic chord."

If Roslavets was still experimenting with different styles and influences, a step forward was in the Symphony in C Major, in which he demonstrates an assurance both as composer and orchestrator. The symphony assumes a sonata-cyclic one-movement conception with the transition of leitmotifs and ideas bearing an affinity with Scriabin's *Poem of Ecstasy*. Roslavets's tempos are similar to those of Scriabin with a measured opening contrasting the main section underlined by the transformation of the *Andante* theme in the exposition. The mood of late romanticism abounds with drawn-out melodic lines. After the opening bars, the development is based on motifs of reflection and cries. The ostensible development of leitmotifs dominates the exposition in the three central segments.

Another hint of Scriabinism is the use of indications in his idiosyncratic idiom: *Intimo, Pienamento,* and *Solennemento*. The polyphonic style is expressed through leitmotifs of fatigue, crying, reflection, dreaming, and anxiety evocative of Scriabin, yet at quite distinctive tempos. The pulsating section marked *Intimo* in the exposition eases off and is followed by piercing motifs, flowing lines, and arabesques. It is here that Roslavets takes a different path, introducing a more individualist harmonic structure away from the classical-romantic tradition. The Symphony in C Major is one of the first steps to this technique and acts as a bridge to his symphonic poem *In the Hours of the New Moon*, which introduces his pan melodic and pan thematic notion.

Heaven and Earth

Roslavets's graduation work *Heaven and Earth* remains extant only in the piano score. Through shifting Byron's romanticism to symbolism, Roslavets bolsters up a sense of fear and expectation. In the first scene, the imagery of cries, incantation, and imploring switch against slow tempos, movement, and tranquillity dominates. The vocal writing adopts a declamatory form in the second and third scenes, with an idiom of monotony complementing the austere dramaturgy. The mood of expectation is stressed by sharp dissonance on the vertical line while colors dominate through forceful triads and sharpened intervals. There emerge episodes of Scriabinesque flight in which the leitmotifs of the heroes Asa and Agolibam rouse themes of tragedy and sadness, while the imagery of Irada and Japheth is expressed in a fugal passage. In the second scene, Roslavets employs richly gorgeous orchestration with solo parts for cello, brass, and the viola. Roslavets uses diminished seventh chords and declamation in the fantasy of the Spirits of the Earth that is more typical of romantic opera, while in the beautiful writing for woodwind, horns, timpani, and strings from the third scene, there are pre-echoes of *In the Hours of the New Moon*. In the final scene of the Flood, Roslavets's chorus sings: "The earth and heaven have come together, Jehovah have mercy, Jehovah!" Finally, the work closes on a gratuitous C major chord.[42] *Heaven and Earth* borders on symbolism and post-symbolism by Roslavets's embracing two contrary styles. The Biblical subject matter owes much to the symbolists' need to show a new form of life while contemplating at the same time the end.[43] It is easy to see how the juxtaposing of tradition with modernism may have been unwarranted for the examiners. As Vasilenko suggests in his memoirs, his professors saw signs of promise but not necessarily in styles they would have liked. Following a decade of studies at the Conservatoire, in 1912, Nikolay Roslavets graduated as a free artist, and awarded the Great Silver Medal (at the age of thirty-one) for his mystery cantata *Heaven and Earth*.

Roslavets consciously worked on ideas unfamiliar to the mainstream—revealing himself as a trendsetter—but his radicalism wasn't owing to an aspiration to originality. He started to "swim in the chaos of sound" at first instinctively, creating eloquently the sound which interested him—and in the process discovering several harmonic complexes which became an inseparable part of his style, as he shares here, "In the spring of 1913, a curtain opened before me, and after six years of single-minded creativeness (about 1919), I finally found the individual technique that allowed me the space in which I could express my artistic personality."[44] By the close of the fêted Silver Age, Russia was producing outstanding talents in the most diverse art forms; architects, painters, poets, actors, dancers, and composers represented distinct modernity—a trend to which Roslavets totally subscribed. Roslavets's drive to innovation was matched by a passion for politics because radicalism became deeply embedded in his consciousness during the bloodbath of the Great War, writing that, "The greatest inner concern pushed me upon the path of focused searching."[45] Roslavets described his musical obsession with no little candor. "All the knowledge and the technical tradition acquired by me at the Conservatoire seemed superfluous in my practical work, and considered outdated, trite and of little use in expressing my inner 'self,' and consequently, I dreamed of new, unheard of sound worlds."[46]

The Early Works

The years following graduation from the Moscow Conservatoire were most probably Roslavets's most fruitful and happiest period. It was a time when he discovered the great French poets and writers. However it was inspiration from his compatriots, notably the symbolists, that helped create his finest works—Balmont, Ivanov, Sologub, Gippius, Blok, Bely, and Bryusov—the acmeist Gumilyov and the futurists Severyanin, Burlyuk, Guro, and Kamensky. It was the vocal settings that gained him the first recognition. Derzhanovsky's journal *Muzika* was first to draw attention to his settings of Gippius's *Incantation*,[47] *I Don't Remember What Happened Yesterday* by Blok,[48] *The Swans* by Ivanov,[49] and *The Quiet Sunset* by Bryusov.[50] The songs embrace symbolism typical of his opera mystery *Heaven and Earth* and the symphonic poem *In the Hours of the New Moon*. The vocal miniatures are subject to illustrative settings and emotions through picturesque aspects of the texts and lack any disguised motifs or subtext. Lobanova considers that Roslavets's use of these poets is not because of their purely textual language, but in "the musical logic of the words and their catch phrases."[51]

The Russian Modernists

The search for "unheard of soundworlds" was not exclusive to Roslavets—he was but one among other musical explorers. The ground-shaking events in Russia influenced the arts through new-fangled ideas and conceptual schemes challenging the status quo. During the years of 1917 and 1918, Ivan Vyshnegradsky (1893–1979) developed a "musical continuum" birthing his organization of "micro-intervals." Two years before, Arthur Lourié (1892–1966) fashioned the notion in a musical form of "futurism," while the modernist and mystic Nikolay Obukhov (1892–1954) experimented in twelve-tone systems and electronic music. Contemporaneously, the Ukrainian painter and composer Yefim Golyshev (1897–1970), with his Piano Trio, hit upon a theory with some affinity to Roslavets's synthetic chord called the *Zwölftondauer-Komplexe*. One of the most exciting and brilliant prospects was Alexey Stanchinsky (1888–1914), whose exploration of asymmetrical time signatures ended only through his premature, tragic death. These composers endured success, but mostly failure—only Roslavets did not go into exile following the October Revolution. Roslavets's discovery of the synthetic chord and its practical implementation allows him to be considered the leading and most insightful master.[52] Here Roslavets shares his methodology with a fellow avant-gardist Avraamov,

> When I reflected upon the consequences of my work in 1913, I saw that this sound was more than proselytization. A composer inevitably arrives at a preferred sound and I started to write in this way. How does this happen? I examined the number of sounds in any composition, with 1-2-3-4 dominating the number of sounds that are adopted by one composer and adopted by others. This has its own logic. If we base ourselves on consciousness, then we have logic. Later, I began to explore the very form of these sounds and attempted to write thought-provoking sounds that I harmonized differently. I discovered an innovative concept. Thus, after ten years, I put together these thought-provoking sounds and harmonized them in a new manner.[53]

The first public performance of early works by Roslavets created something of a furor, as the critic Yevgeny Braudo reflects: "Those among us still recall the sensation that his first pieces caused."[54] Schoenberg was the composer with whom Roslavets was most often associated in his earliest compositions. The first hearing of Schoenberg's music in Russia was in 1909 when Sergey Prokofiev played the Austrian's *Drei Klavierstücke* Op. 11 causing great interest among young music lovers in St. Petersburg. Roslavets likely heard this concert as he refers to the music later in discussing Schoenberg's music. The performance of the F sharp Minor Quartet by Schoenberg in St. Petersburg caused him to go there again in February 1912.[55]

However, later in December that year, at the invitation of the conductor and promoter Alexander Ziloti, Schoenberg arrived to conduct his *Pelleas and Melisande* symphonic poem (1903).[56] Karatygin wrote in the local *Rech* newspaper,

> This was a remarkable event on the podium; there appeared a little man with a bald head and a burning, restless look, nervous gestures, and even in the quieter moments, a demonic passion. He is as lively as quicksilver, a small man who reminds one of a little Chinese Buddha. One thinks of figures from Hoffmann's fairy tales or the sinister stories of Edgar Allan Poe. However, the program, which I have before me, says nothing about Poe's dreams. The piece performed was the symphonic poem *Pelleas and Melisande* by the very paradoxical, daring, and perhaps, the most important of the German modernists—Arnold Schoenberg.[57]

There is no record of Roslavets meeting with the Austrian composer, and Schoenberg left Russia on the following day, and it is unlikely they ever met or exchanged addresses.

In general, the years between 1911 and 1917 are difficult to monitor; however, we know that Roslavets was called up in 1911, when he was completing his final year, and served in the Preobrazhensky Guards Regiment. Roslavets continued to compose and meet with members of the Russian futurist circle in Moscow and St. Petersburg. In March 1914, he suffered from tuberculosis and was released from active service. That proved a mark of providence as the Great War broke out just five months later, although he remained nominally in the reserves. Roslavets recuperated in Yalta, a popular health resort for the wealthy and aristocracy from the empire's major cities, and a warm climate to recover from illness. At this time, the town attracted Russia's celebrated and most aspiring artists of the futurists and many of his new friends in the arts.

In the Hours of the New Moon

Roslavets's *In the Hours of the New Moon* is influenced by Jules Laforgue (1860–1887). Marina Lobanova explains here that "the theme of the moon prevails in much of the poet's writing notably in the collection—*L'imitation de Notre-Dame la Lune* (1885) which appeared in Russia in the first decades of the 20th century."[58] The album is dominated by several poems *Clair de Lune, Litanies des premiers quartiers de la lune, Climat faune et flore de la lune, Dialogue avant le lever de la lune, Lunes en détresse, La lune est stérile*. We know that Laforgue's poetry influenced the missing Roslavets symphonic poem *The Death of the Earth*. It may be that this work foresaw aspects of Roslavets's masterly *In the Hours of the New Moon*. The piece starts quietly on harp, flute, horn, and strings—as if in a dream world, with shifting ideas, hinted at by a rising flute. The floating melodies create a mood with little dancing themes on the strings and woodwind. The whole orchestra presents a mesmerizing picture of calls on the brass, silky strings, while the harp, flute, and clarinet evoke a balmy summer night, summoning up kinship with Debussy and Scriabin. The languorous melodies are impressionist with a rising tempo on the woodwind, introducing a tantalizing idea in exquisite harmony until the horns threaten the idyll, and the dream ends suddenly. This composition reveals Roslavets's aspiration to concentrate his expression in the timbre and color mixed with feeling for time and musical form, as Lobanova explains, "the principle and stylization of emotions are apparent in the chamber and instrumental music by Roslavets during the 1910s."[59] Here, as Hakobian notes, the music "gravitates rather towards Skryabin: some of its pages create the impression of daintily orchestrated passages from Skryabin's late piano music ."[60]

Nocturne

The *Nocturne* for harp, oboe, two violas, and cello (1913) is important because Roslavets uses the synthetic chord with elements that are decoratively written in clearly thematic roles. "The prevalently diatonic modal harmonies (. . .) are reminiscent of Debussy."[61] The modulations in timbre are at the edge of musical form and strengthen both the dynamism and extension of the piece.[62] The *Nocturne* has a symmetrical framework with a reprise-coda, at the beginning of which, there is a synthetic chord in transposition with a quasi-tonal reprise. Additionally, a rondo and variations recur in an abridged form and eventually close in a reprise-coda. In the harp's first four notes of the *Nocturne*, there is—as its basis—a heptasonorous synthetic chord *d-e-fis-g-a-h-c*. The opening phrase has a muted transposition that is followed by rising quarter notes with three transpositions of the synthetic chord from *g*, *c*, and *f* and the final transposition assumes two forms of a vertical chord on the harp and a horizontal melodic chord on the cello.

Roslavets's decoration and color are quite different in the String Quartet No. 1 written in the same year, as Lobanova describes, "Here, the microthematics, dynamics, and motivic rhythm of the articulated kaleidoscope are what appears to interest the composer most of all."[63] Roslavets explores the potential of his expression innovatively both in the timbre and sound but differently with a controlled fluid potency. Roslavets's experimentation in the

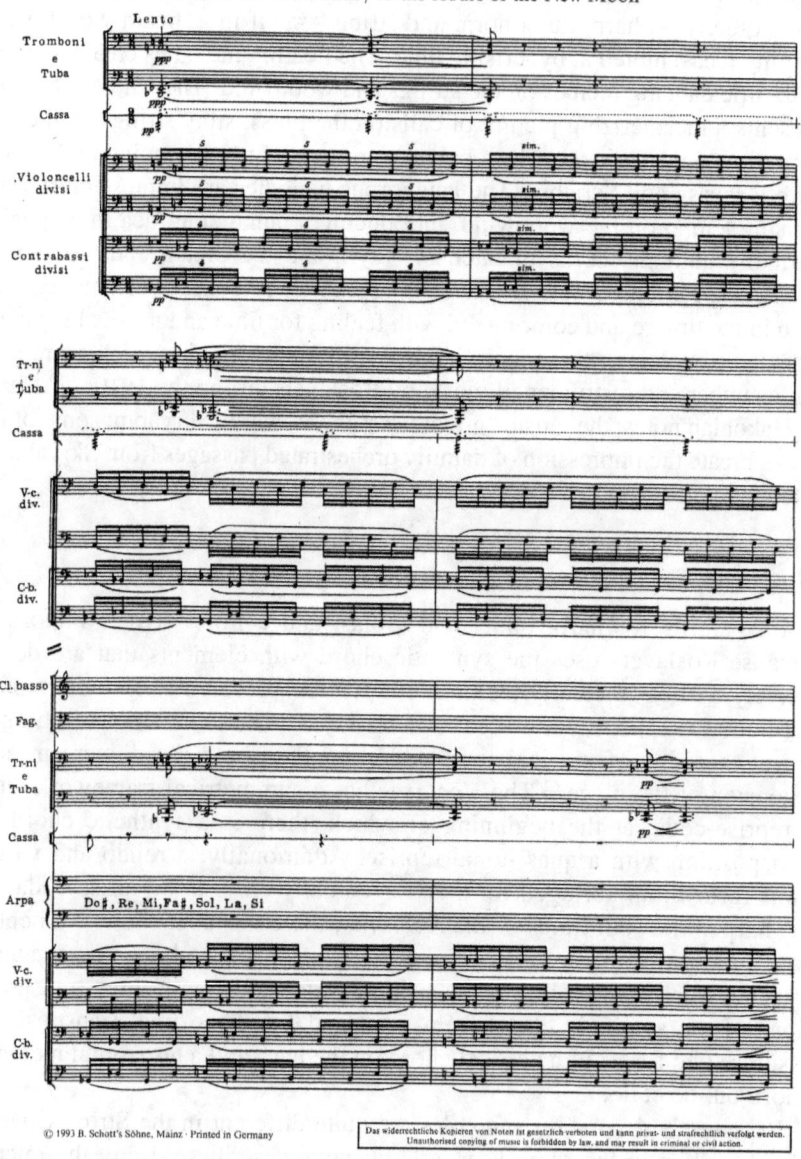

Figure 1.2 In the Hours of the New Moon (First Page). *Source*: Courtesy of Schotts Music.

quartet genre touches all expressive means and is of particular fascination in how he deals with rhythm and motif counterpoint.

Violin Sonata No. 1

Roslavets's first two violin sonatas explore the style and systems of sound, and significantly, the writing is for two virtuosi with an equal opportunity for expression. Experimentalism is most noticeable in the Violin Sonata No. 1 (1913), as the composer informs us that,

> During my early exploration in the spring of 1913, there emerged my first opuses—the Violin Sonata No 1, and romances (which were) published in the same year. (. . .) I expect, of course, an inescapable connotation of my principles and methods with those of Scriabin (late Prometheus period), and with Schoenberg; almost certainly, they will try to align my principles with these two innovative composers.[64]

Myaskovsky was the first to pronounce the magnitude of Roslavets's latest piece.

> One feels the association with an outstandingly original composition that somehow emerges from another world. In this sonata, one is convinced of the manifestation of surprisingly asymmetrical, and hitherto, stimulatingly memorable themes, of a wonderfully and deeply profound thematic work, with fashioned expression, richly stimulating designs, in absolutely perfect form (the sonata is in one-movement), the presence of dazzling harmonies and interesting episodes in the development (for example, the magnificent build-up to the reprise with the motif of the main idea in the form of *basso ostinato*), and a well-handled temperament, with power, and ferocity in discourse. In one word, the combination of these qualities strongly shows that in Roslavets' persona, we have someone who is a leading authority in composition. One cannot avoid mentioning that the themes of the sonata are so obvious and so systematic that they penetrate the whole work and are shared with multifaceted, distinctive harmonies giving it a very individual, and unique character.[65]

This could hardly have been a more welcoming appraisal of Roslavets as a composer and a promise of better things to come. Myaskovsky could find fault only with the technical difficulty which might hinder its popularity. It appears that Roslavets took this advice, for the Violin Sonata No. 2 (1917) has a greater simplicity and transparency. Written in July 1917 in a traditional three-movement form, it has an intensity, solidity of musical expression, and an unhurriedly meditative mood. Perhaps because of when it was written the manuscript was lost and has only been reconstructed from his notebooks.⁶⁶ Roslavets's *Poem for Violin and Piano* (1915) is fascinating for its breathtaking central passage and the culmination in which there permeates an inflexible strength, together with an asymmetry and tendency to free musical form. The transformation of the main idea occurs as if a sudden outburst which then terminates in blissful calm. The explosive force of the almost orchestral power of the piano surpasses that of the later Violin Sonata No. 4, the Piano Trio, and other pieces of the 1920s.⁶⁷

Roslavets's new organization of sound is presented painstakingly in his early piano pieces. The Piano Sonata No. 1 (1914) embraces a closed abstract program, reflecting upon Scriabin's late sonata-poems using a static, dynamic dramaturgy. Roslavets indicates what are surprising (for him) tempo indications: *Allegro con impeto (risoluto), Scherzando; con leggerezza, Moderato (Pieghevolmento), Moderato (con dolcezza), Moderato non troppo, Assoluto, Commodito; con delicatezza; narrante, Vivo (con sveltezza)*. At variance with Scriabin—these are inconsistent—the process from mystery and chaos to ecstasy is impressive, and the colors are distinct from both the context and period.

In 1914, now released from mundane barracks life, Roslavets sought to explore his theory of the synthetic chord, termed—the 'new organization of sound' by experimenting in diverse styles. In the Crimea, he composed his String Quartet No. 1, the *Nocturne* Quintet, and the remarkable art song *Daisies* (to Severyanin's verse) in 1913. Conceived in St. Petersburg and completed in Yalta, the setting of Gnedov's *Kuk* (1914) is surprisingly evocative and impressionist. The climate on the Black Sea coast inculcated a favorable effect on Roslavets composing the groundbreaking Violin Sonata, and his song cycle based on Verlaine—*Sad Landscapes*, and *Three Compositions for Voice and Piano*. If the setting for *Daisies* bows to impressionism—Roslavets had no trouble mixing with the futurist expressionism of *The Wolfs' Cemetery* set to David Burlyuk (1913)—and *Trois Compositions pour Piano* (1914). Roslavets set texts by Guro in his *Song for Harlequin* (1915) in a decorative theatrical fashion reflecting upon the World of Art.

The Piano Sonata No. 2 (1916) explores the possibilities of the instrument by trying new rhythmic formulas and developing unusual metric scales. Roslavets's fresh rhythmic ideas continue in his piano pieces—*Trois compositions* (1914), *Trois études* (1914), *Deux compositions* (1915), and *Prélude* (1915). Roslavets's *Trois études* have an engaging tranquillity; however, the *Quasi prélude* and the *Quasi poème* from his *Deux compositions* epitomize the exciting life force of modernism. The exploration of the gradations between sound and silence is noticeable in other piano pieces. The *Prélude* and the *Trois compositions* indulge in transparency and lightness without abandoning his proclivity for mysterious ornamentation.

Vocal Works

The cycle of Verlaine settings—*Sad Landscapes*—*Autumn Song*, and *Twilight* (1913)—reflects upon decorative modernism with arabesques and patterns. There are unadorned sounds in the harmonic development that enhance the beauty and dissonances through synthetic chord structures. In the *Autumn Song* and *Twilight*, there is a noticeable mirror-symmetry separate from its strophic structure. The exploration continued in *Three Compositions for Voice and Piano*, in Roslavets's setting of texts by Bryusov's *Quiet Twilight*, and two verses from Blok, *You Haven't Left*, and *The Wind Blows* (1913). On March 14, 1914, the symbolist poet Alexander Blok acknowledged receiving "Another two romances from Roslavets in Moscow." We do not know what his opinion was or indeed of Roslavets's relationship with the poet.[68] The timescale saw Roslavets developing friendships with many of the futurists both on the Black Sea and back home in Moscow. As we know, Roslavets had enjoyed friendships since his student period with several futurist poets. This period of Russian art had a transformative effect on many people as is most manifestly articulated by the artist Alexander Benois, who spoke of an age of expectation,

> Beauty is the last guiding star in the twilight sky where the spirit of the man of today dwells. Shaken loose of religion, the systems of philosophy conflict with each other, and in this monstrous concoction, we have one remaining absolute, one absolutely heavenly discovery—which is beauty. This must bring civilization to enlightenment, and it cannot allow itself to die amongst despair. Beauty hints at some custom of an association with everything.[69]

Futurism

Roslavets's aspiration to fresh, undetermined sound worlds was spontaneous in a historical and cultural context among many artists, painters, and writers of his generation. The feeling of "something is happening" was sensed among many in the first decades of the twentieth century. All of humanity seemed at the crossroads between dramatically sharp distinctions of old and new. Many were discussing the societal crisis in culture; *Der Blaue Reiter* association spoke of a "mighty shock to all our culture" that would be shared through expressionism in the arts. In the words of Stefan George, "I feel the breath of different planets." In the manner of novelty, there emerged fresh representatives of the most diverse movements—the artist Vasily Kandinsky spoke of a "new beauty" and new music over the "new word," and a "new structure of the word" among the futurists. As we know, Roslavets and Malevich were friends from their youth, both drawn to the painting and the arts and to radical thought. Interestingly, Kandinsky and Schoenberg corresponded for many years sharing their ideas on art and musical expression .

The Petersburg poet Igor Severyanin was among those who picked up the banner of futurism in Russia from the diminished Italian movement. The crusade embraced almost all the progressive poets and painters of the 1910s carrying through into the Soviet period. The Moscow-based group around David and Nikolay Burlyuk called themselves "Hylaea" and brought together Vasily Kamensky, Velimir Khlebnikov, Alexey Kruchenykh, and Vladimir Mayakovsky.[70] This grouping proved themselves the most tightly knit through the launch of the manifesto "*A Slap in the Face of Public Taste*" in 1912. David Burlyuk published the works of several poets, proselytizing futurism not only in Russia but in Europe and the United States. The aims were for experimentation of new ideas in the arts and rejection of everything that was tradition. Great writers of the past such as Pushkin and Dostoyevsky were to be "heaved overboard from the steamship of modernity."[71] This fully subscribed with Roslavets, who was a close collaborator with the futurists, and proselytized many of their ideals into the Soviet period. The fundamental tenets of the group were pronounced in their declaration,

Figure 1.3   Roslavets Portrait, 1918. *Source*: Courtesy of Marina Lobanova.

Only we—are the face of our Time. The horn of the time will cut us from literary art.

The past is dark. The Academy and Pushkin are unknowable to the hieroglyphs

Throw away Pushkin, Dostoyevsky, Tolstoy and all the rest from the Ship of modernity.

All these Maxim Gorki's, Kuprins, Blok's, Sologubs, Remizovs, Averchenkos, Chernys, Kuzmins, Bunins and all the rest need only a dacha on the river . . .

We order to read the laws of the poets:

1) To increase the dictionary and in its mass free and free words (Word-novelty).
2) For excessive hatred to existing language before us.[72]

The text of this manifesto is redolent in the social-cultural theater and provocative style of the futurists. The essence of the movement was a utopia. As Mayakovsky is claimed to have said in 1920 in addressing Einstein's discovery of relativity—"greetings to the science of the future from the art of today."[73] The movement embraced all the art forms in 1913, painting, architecture, theater, poetry, philosophy, and music. The theater director and actor Vsevolod Meyerhold formulated a revolutionary rejection of classical scenic models. "Turning in our hands a model, we have turned the revolutionary theater in our hands. We wanted to burn and crush the models; we have already approached this in that we can crush and burn the old methods of natural theater."[74] There was not always harmony among friends and associates—Kazimir Malevich wrote to Matyushin in 1914.

> Roslavets understands a bit more but, he, as an enthusiast, will see a little piece of imported cloth instead of a tie as something special—he isn't a futurist at all. He publishes much of his music to poems by Igor Sever(yanin) and Gnedov. The devil take it! I get so angry that he writes this, that, and the other, it seems I will soon give concerts myself just to show that all this is wrong. I keep on seeing these musical masses, blocks, layers of some 20 chords hurled into space, and the frozen mass of the musical cube. I genuinely hear how these 20 pood layers of sound float. And there is also the alogy of musical instruments.[75]

The motifs and symbolism of early Roslavets were of languor and flight, analogous with the mystic chord of the late Scriabin. However, with the synthetic chord, Roslavets was able to leave behind the influence of his compatriot. His letters inform of a reluctance to descend into dryness and aridity, more so Roslavets tried to grasp the era in which he was living through his music. The laconicism and aphorism coincide with greater attention to development and variations, and enabled in beautifying his austerely defined structures. As Myaskovsky noted, there is something in Roslavets's sphere of imagery and expressionism which reminds one of Schoenberg. However, in distinguishing between the expressionism of Schoenberg and Roslavets, there are divergent gloomy and logical moods—the presence of traumata is enlightened.

There is a clear example of Roslavets's emotional expression in his setting of *The Wolves' Cemetery*. There is an isolation—and in its' rhythm and colors, the harmonies are extraordinarily intense. In Gnedov's *Kuk*, all attention is to the text—its hidden expressive syntax and sound help beautify the music. As Malevich indicates, Roslavets was enticed by futurism, but critically was also drawn to other ideas—he simply took from futurism what he needed for his own expression. Of course, we know that during this period, Malevich formed his own group of Supremacists in a new revolutionary art form in Russia.

The year 1915 proved crucial in meeting with leading artists and writers—somewhat anecdotally, Mayakovsky said of him: "What silly sheep hasn't heard of Roslavets!"[76] The futurist collection—*Spring Counter Agency of the Muses*—comprised of poetry by Aseyev, Belenson, David and Nikolay Burlyuk, Bolshakov, Varavin, Vermel, Kamensky, Kanev, Mayakovsky, and Boris Pasternak was published in April 1915, with artwork by the Burlyuk brothers and Lentulov and a play by Khlebnikov. Roslavets was the only composer involved at this time. The cover significantly marked the passing in April 1915 of Scriabin. In a letter to Matyushin, on October 19, 1915, Malevich wrote.

> We have in Moscow something new, quite unexpectedly, I received an invitation as a professor of new painting to a just-opened studio-theater in Moscow. I go there, and there I find the whole company of "Bubnovo valet" and Roslavets was acquainting his listeners with *solfeggio*. (. . .)[77] I was daft enough to tell Roslavets that contemporary music must express plastic music and have length and width to move musical masses through time, with which dynamism of musical masses must change in state, which is holding to the sound mass in time.[78]

Malevich found more to appreciate in his old friend's music again when he wrote to Matyushin on February 14, 1916.

> If we look at a mass of scattered flower petals. And suddenly over these petals there walks a cladded horse, stamping and crushing everything, you see how the stiff hoof flattens and destroys the pallid forget-me-nots, carnations, violets, and besmirched chrysanthemums. Roslavets has not taken the path of graphic realism with the jangle of futurism and musical Impressionism. But he has approached

musical forms without expressing anything apart from the sound. A small piece says a lot because of its directness, and the tension is concentrated through the forceful energy in sound, obvious for its great boldness, by the terrible crashing chords, daring treatment, and steadfastness. But suddenly this steel-clad horse, stamping with a firm iron leg, stops and collapses into some familiar and well-known mood, as if it's necessary to expect a snore, or a whimper from it—as if he's fascinated by the fading evening twilight. And if he manages to break away from the vestiges of musical "nocturnes," then his power will become even more terrible and merciless in tone.[79]

Lobanova notes here that Malevich pinpoints one of Roslavets's crucial elements in 'his aspiring to objective creativity, an artistic message, without any subjectivity, as Roslavets would have said, "chaos."'[80] In time, Malevich would be increasingly appreciative of Roslavets by calling him a "colossal Russian composer."[81] Roslavets responded in kind, albeit through Natalya, regarding Malevich's programmatic pamphlet *From Cubism to Suprematism*.[82] "My little booklet has affected Roslavets, his wife wrote to me, that he is fired up and he wants to write his declaration, he wants to preach to the people."[83] This was the inspiration for Roslavets's essay *Art and the Psyche of the Masses*.[84]

Malevich responded to Roslavets.

Oh, how much I wish that the three of us could expose the challenge of the new day. He has invigorated me—my brain is on fire: You burn with truth and we are assured in our trio as the true believers. And our skeletons will ascend the exalted space before there has come—the wonder of wonders.[85]

Roslavets was not attracted however to "futurist instrumentation" or by "the music of noises." Other composers found different expressive techniques, as Lobanova informs us, "Finally, it became clear that the Russian futurists linked the 'music of the future' with the uniform twelve-note temper—in the famous 'opera in two deimakh and six scenes,' *Victory over the Sun* to texts by Alexei Kruchenykh, and music by Mikhail Matyushin and decorations by Malevich (. . .) using a quarter-tone system."[86] In presenting the futurist "Budetlyan" theater, the opera was staged on December 3 and 5, 1913, in the Luna Park on Ofitsersky Street, St. Petersburg. The opera is about throwing away old art forms and creating new unknown art forms, in a synthesis of poets, artists, and the composer—it was a radical conception of futurism. The music was sharp and dissonant, with the characters being parodies of the personages depicted. This opera will be discussed in more detail when we examine Matyushin in the final chapter.

From the beginning, Roslavets was involved in the St. Petersburg "Union of Youth" started in 1910 by Elena Guro (1877–1913) and her husband, Mikhail

Matyushin (1861–1934) and Pavel Filonov (1883–1941). Three years later, the "Hylaea" futurists joined with the "Union of Youth" in collaborating on theater productions by Mayakovsky. During this period, Roslavets lived just yards away from the School of Art and Architecture where Mayakovsky was teaching, along with David Burlyuk and the other futurists. According to Lentulov's daughter, Roslavets regularly performed his music at the futurist gatherings in Aristarkh Lentulov's home.[87] The ideology of futurism features in several of Roslavets's writings. This statement dates from the mid-1920s and reveals the often contradictory views of Roslavets in his association with futurism.

> Opera, as a musical form, is dead. In the next 20 years—no one will write opera—they will work on symphonies or chamber music. There are no librettos that are satisfactory, and dramatists avoid writing librettos. More so, after Wagner, people have stopped writing operas; what is called opera has become, in actuality, a special form of symphonic music. The Wagnerian music dramas were the moment of the death of opera. The desire for revolutionary opera—is a question of Soviet self-esteem. Do we need such a realization? "To freshen up" the Bolshoi Theater is not for this—it is opera that is dying; here is the road. It is not possible to shield the proletariat from major operatic triumphs, but it is needed to demonstrate these as a cultural-educational exercise—that is transforming the Bolshoi Theater into a kind of museum.[88]

We know that Roslavets was attracted to opera with his *Heaven and Earth*, and he wrote a "heroic opera in five acts and eight scenes"—*"The City of a Great Planet,"* which we know of only because of the libretto *"To the Sun!"* from texts by Bryusov that was published in 1911. Roslavets preferred writing for chamber genres; however, writing symphonies—despite as many as seven attempts—proved beyond him. As the futurists believed in and proselytized abstruse language, the hope was that Roslavets's synthetic chord would become the musical language in Russia, just as Esperanto would be an international medium of discourse, here utopian theories had reached their apogee.[89] As one of the futurists Velimir Khlebnikov declared: "Abstruse language is the leading world language in its womb. Only it can unite people."[90]

In Roslavets's vocal works, there is an extraordinary feeling for poetry, and the meaning or sense of the written word. Roslavets based himself on the phonetics, rhythm, the sound of syntax, words, and the syllable of his chosen text. There was always a distancing in Roslavets from the emotionality of his text, perhaps owing to the time of the composition.[91]

First Publications and Recognition

Aristarkh Lentulov's futurist artwork adorns the first edition cover of Roslavets's Violin Sonata No. 1, while David Burlyuk provided the frontispiece of the *Deux compositions* (1915) with the epitaph "Together to the new, unknown world!"[92] The evident mutual respect for another futurist poet is in the dedication, "To our genius of a singer, to our dear Vasya Kamensky. Moscow, 4 January 1916, from the author Nik. Roslavets."[93] Another dedication to his wife, Natalya—and one of his most superb pieces is the setting of *Flight* (1915). Roslavets taught Natalya Langovaya music theory when she was studying at the Conservatoire.[94] Furthermore, Roslavets helped his wife write about music, for it is her pen that authored an article on French modernist music in *Musical Culture* in 1924.[95] Roslavets's *Three Compositions for Singing and Piano*, in both their style and thematic structure, employs the synthetic chord. There is a thematic affinity between *The Wind Blows* and his later *Flight*. Myaskovsky identified the divergence in original technique between Roslavets and Scriabin in his review of the *Three Compositions for Singing and Piano* and the vocal cycle *Sad Landscapes* from Verlaine.

> Here are works that will hardly be recognized soon—even at the speed by which musical consciousness grows at present. The harmonic language of the composer, the wonderful turns of his themes, the reflective contours of his writing—all of which are so unusual and foreign to us—even Scriabin's latest adroit inventiveness—are undoubtedly due for prolonged neglect, and perhaps even anger. Yet, there is so much in Roslavets' harmonies. These are the relentless six-seven-eight sonority chords, with their inimitable introduction, almost extraneous repetition, quite often echoing recent Scriabin compositions—that they sound deafening to the contemporary listener, harsh in the lower registers and silvery sounding on the high notes, and also (. . .) lend the impression of some kind of metier, dreariness, yet all the same, one gets the same feeling because Roslavets doesn't share the same harmonies as Scriabin, as if there is the basic principle in which there is missing a steadfast, steely logic, that undoubtedly is still so organic, integral and individual as in Roslavets' composition.[96]

Uniquely, Roslavets shared with Scriabin the aspiration to create a new system of musical technique, and they have many things in common, notably the perfection in creativity, the accuracy in composition, and denial of free improvisation.[97] Sabaneyev also affirmed the independence of musical thought when comparing the two composers.[98]

> Roslavets takes several defined sounds which he considers synthesizes the quality of all former basic sounds in musical theory. Old music is based on three sounds: major, minor, diminished, augmented on septachords of different types. Roslavets pursues his task with almost mathematical clarity: to create a sound which would in the least number of sounds end in itself as parts of all these

former sounds. And he finds his "leading sixth sonority." (. . .) Both the melody and harmony of Roslavets' music and its rhythm seem to be the main starting point of his criteria.[99]

Here, Roslavets specifies the essence of his new system of tonality. "All the harmonic formulas of the classical system (major, minor, augmented and diminished triads, dominant ninth chord, ninth chord, diminished seventh chord, various secondary seventh chords and derivative chords with chromaticisms, etc.)."[100] This all relates to his piano and chamber music and the song cycles from the 1920s through until the 1930s. In one of the settings of his *Four Compositions for Singing and Piano*, Roslavets illustrates the potential of his technique to the avant-gardist composer Arseny Avraamov. "Generally, in the harmonic construction of *Kuk* lies the 'gamma' of the scale comprising eight sounds: (*c*), *d, es, f, fis, as b, h.*"[101] What is curious is that Roslavets doesn't allude to the synthetic chord here. "The harmony in *Kuk,* albeit, in the seventh-sonority, its development, so to speak, inclines towards the 'eighth-sonority'—an inclination which is more observant in the harmonic analysis of the composition and is very obvious."[102] Each of the settings by four different poets embraces fundamentally different themes of the grotesque, of love, grief, and joy, sadness, and exhilaration all in vibrant colors. In each setting, Roslavets chooses appropriately selected music in different harmonies and structures, as explained here by Leon Hakobian.

> The synthetic chord technique remained Roslavets's exclusive property, but the kind of musical utterance associated with it—restricted to a narrow scope of refined and rich, but ultimately monotonous harmonies, impulsively variable in rhythm and tempo, gravitate towards the mystic and sensual and avoiding references to "democratic" genres—is characteristic of a number of noted composers who were active in the early post-revolutionary years and became prominent members of the ASM.[103]

Initially, as an experiment, Roslavets decided to use a text—*Kuk* by the ego-futurist poet Vasilisk Ivanovich Gnedov (1898–1978). Founded by Severyanin, ego-futurism was a trend within futurism which attacked contemporary verse by diminishing the number of letters and words used. Vasilisk Gnedov was a close friend and fellow-thinker of Roslavets at this period before the October Revolution. Gnedov was born to a merchant's family in the Don area and was educated at the Rostov on Don technical school (from which he was expelled). In 1912, he moved to St. Petersburg where he was inspired by Igor Severyanin's ego-futurists. In 1913, his poems were published under the titles "*Host to Sentiment*" and "*Death to Art.*" In the following year, together with Pavel Shirokov, he published another collection,

"*Book of the Great.*" His readings consisted solely of gesticulating his hands and crying out words while crouching down sideways, and uttering words of his "poem." Following the collaboration with Roslavets, Gnedov enlisted in the army and fought in the October Revolution. In 1921, he gave up his literary activities, but continued to write poetry working as an engineer, in 1925, he joined the Communist Party, and was arrested in 1936, and spent twenty years in the labor camps. After rehabilitation, he continued to write, and many of his early futurist works appeared again. He was called the "Generalissimo" of the futurists. As the poet was exploring a new expressive language, the composer sought for "new harmonic forms."

Kuk! I am. Where's the vulture? The nests of the chicks have swelled,

The chicks have yellow-mouthed the forest . . . Kuk! I am. The vultures were gloomy.

The forest is yellow-white colored, Kuk, Kuk: Kuk![104]

Here after creating a relaxed world of "theatrical" poetry, Roslavets strengthens the central idea, so that in the opening synthetic chord, the linked notes act as a "bridge," like a leit interval of a triton. In the spring of 1914, after Roslavets and Gnedov had both recovered from tuberculosis, they collaborated on an opera *The Seven-Humped Camel* for the futurist theater "Budetlyan" of Velimir Khlebnikov. One other project—inspired by Malevich—was producing a magazine *Supremus* that also involved Roslavets—however like the opera—never left the drawing board despite a libretto by the futurist poet and painter.[105]

Roslavets's setting for *The Wolves' Graveyard* is from Burlyuk's futurist poem about the final resting place for Russian poets and writers.[106] David Burlyuk (1882–1967) and his brother Nikolay inspired several of Roslavets's vocal works before 1917. The two brothers were born the sons of an agronomist in the Kharkiv region of what is now Ukraine. Attracted to painting, Burlyuk studied with Willi Dietz, and the Slovenian Anton Ažbe in Munich, and with Fernand Cormon at Montmartre in Paris. Returning to Russia, he became one of the most radical artists, working with Mayakovsky between 1911 and 1914 on the futurist "*The Trap of Judges*" and "*A Slap in the Face of Public Taste*" manifestos. Owing to his glass eye (following an accident), Burlyuk was given exemption from the Great War. He narrowly survived pogroms in 1918 and left for Ufa, where he organized exhibitions, and together with Mayakovsky, and Kamensky toured the Urals and Siberia. In 1920, he emigrated with his family to the United States where he continued to organize art exhibitions. Mayakovsky said of Burlyuk, "My genuine teacher,

Figure 1.4 Roslavets Setting of Gnedov's Poem Kuk (Final Page). *Source:* Courtesy of Schotts Music.

he showed me how to write. Every day he gave me fifty kopecks so I wouldn't starve." Burlyuk sought new ways of expression through painting and writing poetry in radical ideology—he was the first to use collage in art. Roslavets recreates the dark mood of Burlyuk's poem with a drone-like tonality, in a quietly mysterious mood. The hazily sketched colors dominate the funereal semantics by an innovative evocation of the St. Petersburg cemetery.

> All the cemetery is dimly lit up. As if a low closed. The life's of the past wicked.
>
> In shadowy ice. Over the cemetery unsteadily hang. In the unsteadying sparks hover.
>
> As every inch of clay is pushed aside. The wise hand's grasp.[107]

Burlyuk's poem is the third in his collection of *Four Compositions for Singing and Piano*, together with Severyanin's *Daisies*, Konstantin Bolshakov's *You Carry Love In The Sought-After Flacon*, and Gnedov's *Kuk*. Roslavets's settings, unsurprisingly, did not meet with understanding from progressive musicians of the day. It is not surprising that Roslavets's work was misjudged by Avraamov, who was also exploring innovative musical expression at the time.[108] The distinguished composer and musicologist Boleslav Yavorsky disparaged the song cycles: "we are attempting now to read poetry as if it were prose, yet before which, we probably read prose like motoric poetry."[109]

Vasily Kamensky (1884–1961) was born a serf's son on a riverboat on the Kama, near Perm in the Urals. He lost both parents at a young age and was brought up by his aunt, spending much of his childhood helping his uncle on the boats. Kamensky worked at a newspaper in Perm where he authored short articles and poetry, becoming close to Marxism and joined a theater company touring all over Russia. On his return, he led a strike and was imprisoned, after which he traveled to Istanbul and Teheran. He studied in Moscow as an agronomist and reprised his journalist career through which he met Burlyuk and Khlebnikov, and began studying painting, and organized exhibitions in St. Petersburg, Moscow, and Perm. Kamensky pioneered air flight in Russia, traveling to Paris and after buying a Bleriot aircraft, crashed it, and took the parts back to Perm for repair. The dream of flying occupies many of his poems. After the October Revolution, he worked with the "Lef" arts organization, collaborating with Meyerhold, and writing futurist poetry. One of his books, *Emelyan Pugachev*, was used as the libretto for Koval's opera at the Kirov Opera in 1942, for which he received the Stalin Prize. He lost both legs and was paralyzed from 1948 until his death.

Based on Kamensky's poem, Roslavets's *Flight* (1915) abandons the ornamental figurations of arabesques, and indeed of symbolism. Instead, Roslavets chooses semantics in individual fragments, by using ostinato to imply movement, as Lobanova delineates, "In the sphere of 'musical theater,' the symbolic masks take on new images."[110] Kamensky was one of the outstanding futurists, and this setting by Roslavets illustrates one of his strikingly fresh compositions in the genre. Lobanova again tells us that "the original rhythmic arrangement by which the composer abandons traditional writing in 2/4 time has a conventional character: Roslavets works with a rhythmic formula, from the first measure and in variations throughout the entire piece."[111]

> Little turquoises, uoises. Flying and ing. In the rays of the valley. While earth is silent.

> The wings unfolding. Flapping speed. The plains are alight. Birds are kings. In the air, air, Spirits are afresh. Somehow reluctant. To know of the earth. The wings of the will.[112]

The setting for the symbolist Blok's *My Prophecy Is Fulfilled* (1919) explores methodology and rhythm. Roslavets's conception of "secret theater" in Yelena Guro's *Song of the Harlequin* (1915) reflects the prerevolutionary period. The illusion of life as a theater, with a tear, shed for the beautiful life and regeneration through the dreaming of new, unknown sound worlds. There is an extraordinary elegance, beauty, and enlightenment permeating Roslavets's setting of Voloshin's eponymous poem *Through the Almaz Curtain* (1918). This vocal piece reveals a major composer and heralds his finest work. A new source for inspiration was the symbolist Zinaida Gippius. Roslavets's setting departs from the formality of the "art song" or "romance." Again, the motif of cries from his *Incantation* is reprised. The third setting *Suddenly* is unfortunately lost to us.[113]

The great imposing building where Nikolay and Nataliya Roslavets lived in Moscow belonged to Professor Alexey Petrovich Langovoi (1867–1939), a specialist in therapeutic medicine who lectured at the University. Langovoi was a member of the Moscow State Duma, and a leading art collector and au fait with many artists of the day and notably with the portraitists Serov, Grabar, and Milyutin. Several portraits were painted of this distinguished surgeon and benefactor of the arts. Langovoi enjoyed a rapport with his son-in-law, for they shared a lure to contemporary art, and both may have influenced each other through the daring new art forms emerging in the first decades of the twentieth century.

Roslavets's own paintings were exhibited at Langovoi's showings—the surviving canvasses reveal a style unpretentiously close to impressionism. Langovoi arranged soirees at home, where Roslavets's music was heard long before they were in public.[114] The portraitist Grabar characterizes Langovoi with this unflattering anecdote: "Would it not have been appropriate if Serov portrayed A. M. Langovoi—a member of the Moscow Duma and art collector—in such a flattering pose—someone more and more inclined to the latest modernism, yet happens to be more and more repulsive?"[115]

Roslavets's compositions during the Great War won important recognition from leading musicians of the day. Roslavets had an influential supporter in Moscow, since 1909, in the music publisher and composer Vladimir Derzhanovsky, and the very first issue of Derzhanovsky's journal *Muzika* in 1910 favorably reviewed Roslavets's early works. Derzhanovsky was a promoter and arranged concerts where Roslavets's romances were sung by his wife—the mezzo-soprano Yelena Koposova to whom Roslavets dedicated the Guro setting—*Song of the Harlequin* in 1915. At the beginning of the same year, Roslavets sent Derzhanovsky his *Nocturne*.[116] As we know, the Violin Sonata had been praised by Myaskovsky, and in the years to come, the two composers would develop a close friendship. Myaskovsky noted in a letter,

> Roslavets has sent me his Quartet and *Nocturne*. I have only glanced at them briefly and have yet to look at them at length (I received them on 7 March and, as yet, haven't written to thank him for them, although I do have his address). Please express my sincere gratitude to him, and send my apologies for not responding because everything is so frantic down here. When things have calmed down, and I have collected my thoughts, I will write.[117]

At this time, Myaskovsky was stationed near the front line at Peremysl, and his letter indicates how highly he regarded Roslavets's music. One other influential friend of Roslavets was the St. Petersburg composer, music critic, teacher, and physician Vasily Karatygin, who officiated at contemporary music evenings in the capital. In this essay "The latest tendencies in Russian music" Karatygin allow us an early appreciation of Roslavets,

> The Muscovite [sic] Roslavets has only begun to make his mark on the composing path. The opuses published to date (a string quartet, a quintet for oboe, two violas, cello and harp, a violin sonata, and romances) bear witness that this composer promises to be the most radical of all our contemporary composers. The influence of Schoenberg and the modern French (composers) continue to prevail in Roslavets' works. It seems that this person is talented, but what flawless instances of his talents may emerge in the development of his personality—are matters for the future, but, at present, it is difficult to make a sure guess.[118]

This rather cautious assessment contrasts with those by his contemporaries, the Petersburg critic Yevgeny Braudo reflected on the first pieces by Roslavets. "In this young composer, one would like to see a fellow-traveler of the latest West-European musical style. But Roslavets is so unique that he cannot be defined as the 'Russian Schoenberg,' no more than the latter could be called the 'German [sic] Debussy."[119] Throughout his career, of all his colleagues Myaskovsky seemed to grasp the essence of Roslavets as a musician and composer, here he appraises the affinity between the Russian and the Austrian composer in their stylistic kinship.

> There is one artist whose harmonic style appears to be shared by Roslavets, and this is Arnold Schoenberg. But in the personality of Roslavets, we see a selfless and greatly significant composer—all the clear-cut similarities are no more than that—similarities: in the romances before us (*Three Compositions for Singing and Piano* and *Sad Landscapes*), there appears to be a distinctive, and shared tonality, which reveals a self-assured creative personality, but the tone, though presently difficult to grasp, shows unambiguous evidence of the composer's inimitably divine expression, and the original and distinctive vigor of his musical thought.[120]

Certainly, both Myaskovsky and Braudo considered that with his growing catalog of music, "Roslavets is revealed as a master and trailblazer among dozens of trend-setters."[121] The prerevolutionary years were a richly inventive period in exploring the new tonal system of music. However, there would emerge great opportunities both as a composer and in public life—and so turn an exciting new page for music in Russia and beyond.

NOTES

1. *Chernigov district list of village and towns*, 1859 census, St. Petersburg, 1866, 185, 187, 189.

2. Lukomsky, Troinitsky, *General List of Russian Nobility*, State Russian Government, St. Petersburg, 2004, 145.

3. There are three different biographies with conflicting dates and places of birth, and finding the truth behind the legend has been a matter for astute research something made even more difficult a century afterward and after changes in the different regimes in Russia and the Ukraine during the last hundred and thirty years. Surazh was a small district town, where Roslavets was accredited as 'a peasant from the Gordeyev hamlet of the Surazh district' in his military pass. Other pieces of his early biography indicate that rather than coming from a poor peasant family, Roslavets's father was actually a skilled worker and frequently traveled around the local district working for the railway company; indeed it is highly unlikely that a family of 'poor peasants' could afford to send their son to a school at a Zemstvo and receive a musical education there. The 'autobiography' written by Roslavets, and published in 1924, was aimed at forestalling attacks on his background and ostensibly designed to present himself as being from a poor impoverished background. The third biography that exists, and which contradicts some of the formerly stated information, is by the composer's mother-in-law. There are some inaccuracies regarding the birth date given by Olga Langovaya; the most accurate date is from Roslavets's military

service documents where the birthdate of December 23 (old style) is confirmed by his diploma on graduation from the Moscow Conservatoire. The recollections of Malevich's sister, Victoria Stepanovna Zaitseva have been scrutinized, and certainly the minutiae that Andrey Roslavets cooperated for the Tsarist police would have been information that the composer wanted suppressed—author.

4. Roslavets, Nikolay, "O sebye i svoim tvorchestva," *Sovremennaya Muzyka*, V. 1924, 134–135.

5. Belodubrovsky, Mark, "Nash zemlyak," *Sovetskaya Muzika*, No. 5 1989, 105.

6. Zaitseva, Viktoria Severinova, "Vospominaniya o brate," *Malevich o sebye, Sovremmeniki o Maleviche. Pisma. Dokumenty, Vospominaniya. Kritika.* V 2 tom/ I. A. Vakar, T.I. Mikhenko, Moscow, 2004, t.2., 6.

7. 6 Roslavets, Nikolay, "O sebye i svoim tvorchestva," *Sovremennaya Muzyka*, V. 1924, 134–135.

8. Roslavets, N.A., "Abaza A.M.," *Muzyka*, 1915, No. 208, 71.

9. Malevich, Kazimir, "Detsvo i yunost Casimira Malevicha," *Avtobiografii khudozhnika*, Stockholm, 1976, 126.

10. Roslavets, Nikolay, "O sebye i svoim tvorchestva," *Sovremennaya Muzyka*, V. 1924, 134–135.

11. Zaitseva, Viktoria Severinova, "Vospominaniya o brate," *Malevich o sebye, Sovremmeniki o Maleviche. Pisma. Dokumenty, Vospominaniya. Kritika.* v 2 tom/ I. A. Vakar, T.I. Mikhenko, Moscow, 2004, t.2., 6.

12. Roslavets, Nikolay, "O sebye i svoim tvorchestva," *Sovremennaya Muzyka*, V. 1924, 134–135.

13. In Russia, he was called Ivan Voysekovich and it is of note that Tchaikovsky in his reviews several times mentioned the Czech violinist and followed his rise as a virtuoso in Russia. Tchaikovsky's first mention is of his playing in a String Quartet in 1872, and described his performances of the Viotti Concerto No. 22 three years later. 'The violinist Mr. Hřimalý magnificently played the Vientan Concerto, and was worthy of a noisy approval by the public. The quality of this virtuoso pales before the colossally talented Mr. Laub of which our public is spoilt. Nevertheless one cannot deny the great achievement of Mr. Hřimalý, and particularly for his great technique and wonderful clarity and thoughtful performance. His tone is quite strong but is not the most agreeable. In any case, if he is not first-class, then all the same he is wholly remarkable virtuoso that we have in Moscow, after Laub, he is perhaps the first.' As noted, Hřimalý was active in chamber music and was the leader of the Quartet of the Moscow branch of the Russian Music Society whose members were at this time, Brodsky, Gerber, and Fitzenhagen. Tchaikovsky wrote: 'If the Moscow Quartet have experienced the regrettable loss in the person of Mr. Laube, then perhaps now it has achieved a relatively equal strength of all its four performers.' This was in response to a performance of the Beethoven Quartet in B flat. In Moscow, the Czech was leader of the symphony orchestra of the Russian Music Society. Tchaikovsky added in another critique of the day, 'Hřimalý has given one the sense that his [. . .] strong point is quite enough as to occupy a prominent place among the most celebrated virtuosi of our time.' The Russian musicologist Vladimir Rabey writes that: 'It would appear that Tchaikovsky was impressed by the Czech musician's paradigm as a master musician

who constantly works on improving his mastery. Nevertheless, the opinion of such an authoritative critic impels us to pay attention to consider him as personality, both as an artist and teacher.' As leader of the Moscow String Quartet, Jan Hřimalý co-premiered the string quartets No. 2 and No. 3 by Tchaikovsky in 1874 and 1876, respectively. He also took part in the first private hearing of the Piano Trio in 1882 and may well have given the premiere—author.

14. Raaben, L., *Istoriya Russkovo i sovetskovo skripachnovo iskusstsvo*, Leningrad, 1978, 81. Translated by the author.

15. His pupils which included Elman, Heifetz, Tsimbalist, and Polyakin—author.

16. It is supposed Hřimalý taught Mitrofan Vassilyev the first violin teacher of Sibelius. His students continued the Moscow violin tradition in China and America in the twentieth century. Notably, Stolyarov became the teacher of David Oistrakh, and Nathan Milstein. The distinguished composer Reinhold Glière and the conductor Konstantin Saradzhev were among his pupils.

17. Raaben, L., *Istoriya Russkovo i sovetskovo skripachnovo iskusstsvo*, Leningrad, 1978, 80–81.

18. *Detsvo i yunost Kasimir Malevich*, Harsevitch, Stockholm, 1976, 127.

19. Roslavets, E.F., *Sovetskaya Muzyka*, No. 5, 1989, 105–106.

20. Roslavets, E.F. *Sovetskaya Muzyka*, No. 5, 1989, 105–106.

21. RGALI, f.2659, op. 1, ed. kh. 68.

22. Roslavets, "O sebye i svoim tvorchestva," *Sovremennaya Muzyka*, V. 1924, 133.

23. RGALI f.2659, op. 1, ed.khr. 72, l. 20.

24. Langovaya, Olga, "Nikolaj Andreevic Roslawetz," manuscript, Lobanova, Marina, *Nikolay Roslavets i kultura i evo vremeni*, Moscow: Petroglif, 2011.

25. Vasilenko, S.A., *Vospominaniya*, Moscow, 1979, 169.

26. Vasilenko was from an aristocratic family, and regardless of his interest in the arts, his father required that he study law at Moscow University. Through the composer Sergey Taneyev he met Tchaikovsky which decided his future in music. He studied privately with Grechaninov, Protopopov, and Conius before he enlisted at the Conservatoire in 1896 where he studied composition with Taneyev, Mikhail Ippolitov-Ivanov, and conducting with Vasily Safonov. He was awarded the Gold Medal in 1901, after which he began teaching at the Conservatoire himself five years later. During this interlude, Vlasenko traveled widely all over Europe, Austria, Norway, Germany, Italy, Switzerland, and Turkey. His status in Moscow's musical life was enhanced when he became organizer and conductor of the historic concerts of the Russian Music Society for ten seasons until 1917. During the Soviet epoch, Vasilenko did not find it difficult to adapt his creativity to socialist realist themes as his opera of 1939 *"The Great Canal"* discloses, and he wrote arrangements from Turkmen folk music, and during a busy career composed seven operas and ballets, and five symphonies, the first of which dates from 1906. One of his symphonies is based on Italian folk themes and is orchestrated for domra and Russian folk orchestra. Vasilenko's compositions are finely orchestrated reflecting the influence of the nationalist school, perhaps the most notable works are those influenced by the symbolist poets of the fin de siècle; the song cycles on texts by Blok, Ivanov, Bryusov,

and Balmont date between 1906 and 1913. Orchestral pieces of the period reveal his interest in exotic themes: "The Garden of Death" and "The Flight of the Witches." In 1929, he wrote an opera based on Maxim Gorky's *"Children of the Sun"* which was staged at the Bolshoi Theater, as was his *"Christopher Columbus"* four years later. If Vasilenko was enormously productive in composing many works in diverse genre, few are distinguished by innovative ideas or any exceptional individualism—author.

27. Another factor where Vasilenko may have found affinity with Roslavets was in the sonatas written for violin and viola greatly influencing his pupil through his composing career. Why then was Vasilenko critical about his pupil? Roslavets was already deceased and forgotten, and following the 1948 affair, Vasilenko was audacious enough to mention his student, for everyone had closed their memory to Roslavets—author.

28. Belodubrovsky, Mark, *Sovetskaya Muzyka*, No. 5, 1989, 106.
29. Vasilenko, S.A., *Vospominaniya*, Moscow: Kompositor, 1979, 169.
30. RGALI f.2659, op. 1, ed. khr. 72, l. 20.
31. Between 1875 and 1879 he served in the artillery, and as from 1881 until 1885, he studied at the Prussian Royal Academy of Arts with Woldemar Bargiel, Theodore Kullak, and Nathaniel Betcher in counterpoint, fugue, orchestration, and composition. Ilyinsky furthered his schooling by attending lectures at the Faculty of Philosophy at the University of Berlin. He graduated as a correspondence student from the St. Petersburg Conservatoire as a free artist and lectured in piano, musical theory, and composition at the Moscow Philharmonic Society until 1905, after which he was employed at the Faculty of Composition at the Moscow Conservatoire. Described as "the most endearing man, unusually simple and kind, he is an excellent musician, of no great creative gift, but an excellent technician and is a German through and through." Thus was Ilyinsky described by Stepan Smolensky the leading choral musician of the day, and we have no better reminiscence of the man as a musician and human being. He wrote monographs on Beethoven, Wagner, and Glinka; a collection on composers between the ninth and the twentieth century; and several books on musical theory—author.
32. RGALI f.1., ed. khr. 72, l. 20.
33. In 1915, the distinguished soprano Nina Koschitz sang several Ilyinsky romances under Ilyinsky in a popular symphony concert at the Bolshoi Theater and his music was shared with pieces by Tchaikovsky—author.
34. Lobanova, Marina, *Nikolay Roslavets i kultura evo vremeni*, Moscow: Petroglif, 2011, 37.
35. Lobanova, Marina, *Nikolay Roslavets i kultura evo vremeni*, Moscow: Petroglif, 2011, 212.
36. G.Ts.M.M.K. f.373. ed. chr. 2.
37. RGALI, f. 2659, op. 1. ed. khr. 17, 19, 26, 21.
38. RGALI, f. 2659, op. 1. ed. khr. 20.
39. RGALI, f. 2659, op. 1. ed. khr. 20.
40. RGALI, f. 2659, op. 1. ed. khr. 18.
41. RGALI, f. 2659, op. 1. ed. khr. 47.
42. RGALI, f. 2659, op. 1. ed. khr. 49 and G.Ts.M.M.K. f. 373, ed. chr. 14.

43. Bryusov, Valery, *Dnevniki*, Moscow, 1927, 13.
44. Roslavets, "O sebye i svoim tvorchestve," *Sovremennaya Muzyka*, V. 1924, 134.
45. Roslavets, "O sebye i svoim tvorchestva," *Sovremennaya Muzyka*, V. 1924, 133.
46. Roslavets, "O sebye i svoim tvorchestva," *Sovremennaya Muzyka*, V. 1924, 133.
47. *Muzika*, 1911, No. 10, 238.
48. *Muzika*, 1911, No. 53, 1201.
49. *Muzika*, 1911, No. 54, 1230.
50. *Muzika*, 1913, No. 114, 79.
51. Lobanova, Marina, *Nikolay Roslavets i kultura evo vremeni*, Moscow: Petroglif, 2011, 231.
52. Serebryakova, L.A., "Roslavets," *Russkiye kompositori*, Yekaterinburg: Ural LTD, 2001, 273–274.
53. RGALI, f.2659, op. 1, ed. khr. 72, l. 21.
54. RGALI, f. 2659, op, 1, ed. kh. 99, l. 28, Braudo, E.
55. Roslavets, "O sebye i svoim tvorchestva," *Sovremennaya Muzyka*, V. 1924, 136.
56. The concert took place at the Philharmonic Hall on Mikhaylovsky Street with the Ziloti Orchestra on December 21. There were three rehearsals arranged for Schoenberg who found the ensemble excellent, drawn from members of the Imperial Court Capella Orchestra.
57. Stuckenschmidt, *Schoenberg*, London: John Calder, 1977, 181.
58. Lobanova, Marina, *Nikolay Roslavets i kultura evo vremeni*, Moscow: Petroglif, 2011, 222.
59. Lobanova, Marina, *Nikolay Roslavets i kultura evo vremeni*, Moscow: Petroglif, 2011, 244.
60. Hakobian, Leon, *Music of the Soviet Era 1917–1991*, London: Routledge, 2017, 28–29.
61. Hakobian, Leon, *Music of the Soviet Era 1917–1991*, London: Routledge, 2017, 28.
62. Lobanova, Marina, *Nikolay Roslavets i kultura evo vremeni*, Moscow: Petroglif, 2011, 241.
63. Lobanova, Marina, *Nikolay Roslavets i kultura evo vremeni*, Moscow: Petroglif, 2011, 244.
64. RGALI 2659, op. 1, ed. khr. 76a., l. 003. Ob. 4.
65. Myaskovsky, Nikolay, *Muzika*, No. 197, 1914, 544.
66. Lobanova, Marina, *Nikolay Roslavets i kultura evo vremeni*, Moscow: Petroglif, 2011, 245.
67. Lobanova, Marina, *Nikolay Roslavets i kultura evo vremeni*, Moscow: Petroglif, 2011, 246.
68. Blok, Alexander, "*Zapisniye knizhki*," 1901–1920. Moscow, 1915, 216.
69. Benois, Alexander, "Khudozhestvennoye heresy," *Zolotoye Runo*, No. 2, 1906, 86.

70. Terras, Victor, *Handbook of Russian Literature*, Yale University Press, 1990, 197.
71. Lawton, Anna and Eagle, Herbet, *Russian Futurism through its Manifestos 1912-1928*, Cornell University Press, 1998, 1-3.
72. Katanyan, V., "Mayakovsky," *Khronika zhizni i deyatelnosti*, fifth edition, Moscow, 1985, 62-63.
73. Jacobson, Roman, *Rabotu po poetiki*, Moscow, 1987, 420.
74. Meyerhold, *O Teatre*, St. Petersburg, 1913, 7.
75. Letter Malevich to M.V. Matyushin, May 1914(?), *The Artist, Infinity, Supremacism* unpublished writings 1913-1933, vol. IV, Borgen Copenhagen, 1978, 208-209.
76. From reminiscences of Roslavets's second wife, M. B. Babenko, RSGALI, f.2659, op. 1, ed.khr. 99a.
77. The "Bubnovy valet" also known as the "Jack of Diamonds" was an arts circle influenced by French art and included Kandinsky, Larionov, Lentulov, Goncharova, Kuprin, Konchalovsky, and others. It broke up gradually from 1916 and was revived in 1927—author.
78. Malevich to M.V. Matyushin, publication by E.F. Kovtun, *Ezhegodnik rukopisnovo otdela Pushkinsovo doma na 1974*, Leningrad, 1976, 188.
79. Malevich, Kazimir, "Malevich o sebye." *Sovremmeniki o Maleviche. Pisma. Dokumenty. Vospominaniya.* Tom 1. Moscow, 76-77.
80. Lobanova, Marina, *Nikolay Roslavets i kultura evo vremeni*, Moscow: Petroglif, 2011, 187.
81. Malevich, Kazimir, "Malevich o sebye." *Sovremmeniki o Maleviche. Pisma. Dokumenty. Vospominaniya.* Tom 1. I. A. Vakar, T.I. Mikhenko, Moscow, 2004, 81.
82. Published in Moscow in 1916.
83. Malevich, Kazimir, "Malevich o sebye." *Sovremmeniki o Maleviche. Pisma. Dokumenty. Vospominaniya.* Tom 1. I. A. Vakar, T.I. Mikhenko, Moscow, 2004, 99.
84. RGALI. f.2432. op. 1. ed.khr. 266. l..69.
85. Malevich, Kazimir, "Malevich o sebye." *Sovremmeniki o Maleviche. Pisma. Dokumenty. Vospominaniya.* Tom 1. I. A. Vakar, T.I. Mikhenko, Moscow, 2004, 99-100.
86. Lobanova, Marina, *Nikolay Roslavets i kultura evo vremeni*, Moscow: Petroglif, 2011, 188.
87. Lentulova, M., "Khudozhnik Aristarch Lentulov," *Vospominaniya*, Moscow, 1969, 19-20.
88. Roslavets, N., "Omolozheniye operi i baleta," *Zhisn iskusstva*, No. 6, 1926, 9-10.
89. Lobanova, Marina, *Nikolay Roslavets i kultura evo vremeni*, Moscow: Petroglif, 2011, 191.
90. Khlebnikov, V. *Sobraniye proizvedeniye.* Tom 5. 236.
91. Lobanova, Marina, *Nikolay Roslavets i kultura evo vremeni*, Moscow: Petroglif, 2011, 228.
92. Belodubrovsky, Mark, *Sovetskaya Muzyka*, No. 5, 1989, 106.
93. RSGALI, f.1497, op. 1.ed.khr. 57.

94. RGALI, f. 2659, op, 1, ed. kh. 18.
95. Roslavets, Natalya N.R., "Music in Post-war France," *Muzykalnaya Kultura*, 1924, No. 3, 201–209.
96. N.M., *Muzyka*, No. 197, 2014, 542–544.
97. Lobanova, Marina, *Nikolay Roslavets i kultura evo vremeni*, Moscow: Petroglif, 2011, 165–166.
98. Sabaneyev, Leonid, "Russkiye kompositori, II Nikolay Roslavets," *Parizhkii Vestnik*, 1926, III. 31.
99. Sabaneyev, Leonid, "Russkiye kompositori, II Nikolay Roslavets," *Parizhkii Vestnik*, 1926, III. 31.
100. Roslavets, Nikolay, RGALI, F. 2659, op. 1, ed. chr. 72. l.7.
101. Roslavets, Nikolay, "Druzhestvenny otvet Ars. Avraamovu," *Muzyka*, 256.
102. Roslavets, Nikolay, "Druzhestvenny otvet Ars. Avraamovu," Muzyka, 256.
103. Hakobian, Leon, *Music of the Soviet Era 1917–1991*, London: Routledge, 2017, 33.
104. Gnedov, Vasilisk, "Kuk," Moscow: V. Grosse, 1913—translated by the author.
105. Lobanova, Marina, *Nikolay Roslavets i kultura evo vremeni*, Moscow: Petroglif, 2011, 44.
106. The Volkhov graveyard in St. Petersburg which was founded in 1756 also contains the remains of many distinguished Russian scientists, revolutionaries, and explorers—author.
107. Burlyuk, David, "Volkhovo kladbische," Moscow: V. Grosse, 1914—translation by the author.
108. Roslavets, Nikolay, "Druzhestvenny otvet Ars. Avraamovu," *Muzika*, No. 215, 1915, 193.
109. Yavorsky, B. L., *Statii, Vospominanyii, Pisma*, Moscow: Muzyka, 1972, vol. 1, 497.
110. Lobanova, Marina, *Nikolay Roslavets i kultura evo vremeni*, Moscow: Petroglif, 2011, 239.
111. Lobanova, Marina, *Nikolay Roslavets i kultura evo vremeni*, Moscow: Petroglif, 2011, 239.
112. Kamensky, Vasily, "Flight," *Spring Counter agency of the Muses*, Moscow: V. Grosse, 1914,—translation by the author.
113. The settings to Gippius would suffer for the poetess would prove a scandalous figure in the early days of Soviet power because of her religious views and indeed she emigrated shortly afterward—author.
114. Lobanova, Marina, *Nikolay Roslavets i kultura evo vremeni*, Moscow: Petroglif, 2011, 40.
115. Grabar, *Valentin Serov v vospominaniyakh, perepiska i dnevnikakh*, tom. 2, Moscow, 321.
116. The weekly journal *Muzika* published between 1908 and 1917 by Vladimir Derzhanovsky in Moscow is most amenable to new music—author.
117. Myaskovsky, N. Ya., *N. Ya. Myaskovsky*, tom 2, Moscow: Muzyka, 1964, 393.

118. Karatygin V. "Noveishiye techeniya v russkoy muziki," 109.
119. Braudo, Y., "Na konzertakh (O Roslavets i Gr. Krein)," *Novy zritel*, No. 13, 1924.
120. N.M., *Muzyka*, No. 197, 2014, 543.
121. Braudo, Y., "Na konzertakh (O Roslavets i Gr. Krein)," *Novy zritel*, No. 13, 1924.

Chapter 2

The Revolutionary Messiah

After the catastrophe of the Russian military defeat in 1916, the Cossack troop rebellions and the workers' strikes forced the overthrow of the Romanovs by the following spring. The futurists welcomed the Russian Revolution, for they had long aspired to usurp the old traditions and called for "Let the streets be a place for everyone to celebrate art." Roslavets reflects that he was at the heart of events, "My revolutionary, Soviet, and public activities are there for anyone to see, and hence there was no need to declare a 'political platform.'"[1] The futurists could visualize their utopian dreams coming to life; however, their movement had already attained its hiatus two years before, but they would play a decisive role for the culture of the revolution. Together with his compatriots, Roslavets found himself in a quite new world because there now came an outlet for his radicalism in music, as his biographer Marina Lobanova tells us, "at once, following the February 1917 Revolution, the composer became one of the leaders of cultural life."[2]

This acknowledgment overlooks the bitter controversy and incongruities which plagued many artists during the first years of the revolution. In this period of swiftly moving changes, the career of Roslavets can best be followed through the concert programs, reviews, posters, and handbills of the time. On the other hand, his political affairs can be witnessed in the transcripts and letters of the cultural administration of the young Soviet republic. As we shall discover, few figures in the arts played such an intense degree of involvement in constructing a radically new society—with music at its core. These papers inopportunely and uniquely offer a hint as to the origins of Roslavets's subsequent and tragic fall from grace.

FUTURISM AND THE REVOLUTION

The aesthetic utilitarianism and imbibing of mass genres of futurism were wholeheartedly embraced by Nikolay and Natalya Roslavets. On March 26, 1917, at a meeting at the Hermitage Theater in Moscow under the heading "The First Republican Evening of Art," leading futurists including Mayakovsky, Kamensky, Burlyuk, Gnedov, Lentulov, Yakulov, Tatlin, Malevich, and Roslavets addressed an audience of art workers. As Vasily Katanyan, Mayakovsky's biographer, informs us, "Everyone spoke about the need to bring talent onto the street and give art to the masses of workers—so these democratic tasks always entered into the program of futurism."[3]

This refers to the February/March 1917 Revolution during which different groups of artists came together—Blok and Mayakovsky, Khlebnikov, and Bryusov accepted the revolution as some form of religious event transforming the reality of the mystery. As Lobanova writes, the slogan was "bring the theater into public life." That is on to the streets, and theatrical motifs dominated poetry, literature, and painting. The creation of "mass events" was influenced by the symbolist conceptions of "temples of events," of "theater," expressing the "cathedralism" proselytized by Vyacheslav Ivanov, Fyodor Sologub, Dmitry Filosofov, and the idea of "theatricalizing the theater" of Nikolay Yevreinov, the "tragic farces" of Vsevolod Meyerhold and Alexander Tairov, the theory of the futurists, and boundless art. These were brought together from diverse theatrical concepts in a special quality of life.[4]

The Proletkult concept originated from the ideas of Bogdanov, Gorky, and Lunacharsky after the 1905 Russian Revolution by advancing an intellectual-based theory of using art to advance socialism. Bogdanov was opposed by Lenin, who believed that this was just idealism and not Marxist. These ideological differences would develop in years to come by the Proletkult becoming separated from the Soviet state institutions. At first, the Bolshevik Government supported the Proletkult in facilitating the revolutionary dramas played out on huge squares presenting historical symbolist spectacles. In central Moscow, celebrations of the revolution staged farces portraying Russian lubok, colorful posters, flowers in the style of the "Bubnov valet," by the supremacists Malevich, Konchalovsky, and Lentulov on November 7, 1918. At an event on July 19, 1920, in Petrograd "To the World Commune" organized by the Petrograd theater societies, some four thousand Red Army troops were mobilized, and thousands of actors and workers, totaling forty-five thousand participants. There was an allegoric nature to the events depicting the storming of the Bastille and portraying historical figures. The atmosphere can be sensed in this memoir by the young artist Alexander Labas, "It seemed as if we were living on an active volcano, but we felt ourselves great—this is us;

the youth of the revolutionary period could never be better. . . . We wanted to feel and understand everything and express it through our art."⁵

The divergence in the ideology of Proletkult and the Soviet Government's later arts policy are the key to understanding the fall from grace by Roslavets in the 1930s. This ideological struggle was not grasped during the heady moments of the taking of power by the Bolsheviks in 1917 and would only come into play in the bitter debates in the 1920s and 1930s. In the revolutionary months of 1917, activists went out to organize the workers and peasants around the country. Nikolay and Natalya Roslavets were sent to the town of Elets in central Russia, where they organized open-air concerts, talks, and other cultural events.⁶ We know from Malevich that Roslavets opened a music school where he taught composition and the violin to children of the poor.⁷ A theater workshop was established to boost popular support for the revolution, and Natalya Roslavets edited the new local paper *Sovetskaya Gazeta*. Most significant was the opening of the Peoples University, making available free education to help overcome illiteracy.⁸

The degree of Roslavets's involvement during this period is reflected in his election as chairman of the Elets Soviet of Deputies in December 1917. The ensuing months were among the stormiest periods of the Civil War that witnessed atrocities on both sides, by former allies and colleagues.⁹ None of which is accounted for in his autobiography; however, he did later give a fleetingly muted account. That this document remained unpublished for many years underlines the fact that Roslavets's association with the SRs (albeit briefly) would have been compromising.¹⁰

> In Elets, as a delegate from the "Union of Workers Intelligentsia," I was elected to the Soviet of Working People's Deputies. I joined the local Social-Revolutionary Party, and during the October Revolution—against the policy of the party—fought the Menshevik SRs who controlled the Soviet. Together with revolutionary workers, we organized the Red Guard, and in December, threw out the Mensheviks, and assumed "Bolshevik" power of the Soviet, and I was elected as its Chairman. However, the SRs discussed my actions and expelled me, so I joined the "left" SRs and became their Chairman. After the "left" SR revolt (in July 1918), I left the party, and together with Comrade Zaks, formed a group of Narodnik-Communists, and shortly afterward joined the Russian Communist Party (Bolshevik).¹¹

Following the October Revolution—when performances at theaters and concerts largely continued without interruption—cultural life underwent a significantly radical transformation. The futurists arranged street theater and demonstrations with music playing a powerful part in winning over people to the revolution. Belodubrovsky argues that the postrevolutionary period was dominated by romantic terminology with a characteristic slogan *Give us!*[12] Characteristically, Roslavets wrote the music for Mayakovsky's celebrated poem *Give us, Give us!* "Roslavets' activities were forever linked with Proletkult and the 'musical Left.' The polyphony and multiple layers of his prerevolutionary music that polarized between the 'old' and the 'new,' in the postrevolutionary years, (was) expressed in an extraordinarily sophisticated manner."[13] Roslavets's activities in Proletkult saw him collaborating with the leading figures in the organization, and his music became transformed through agitational songs, choruses, and hymns celebrating festivities and meetings, demonstrations, and street theater. Here Lobanova elucidates,

> The first effect was a simplification in his language and withdrawal from the synthetic chord by turning to traditional harmony or "developed technique," in which the principles of the "new system of organizing sound" were combined with traditional tonal structure. The most prevalent and fruitful means of this "developed technique" are in Roslavets' instrumental pieces.[14]

The scholar Ekaterina Vlasova comments that Roslavets's political consciousness was unique among Russian composers and reflected in the appointment to responsible roles. He was a member of the Executive and Head of the Cultural Affairs department of the Bolshevik Government, and, in 1918, Roslavets was elected as a member of the Moscow Soviet of Workers and Peasants Deputies.[15] The only other musician of the day to take such an active part was the futurist composer Arthur Lourié's appointment as "Minister for Music" in the Bolshevik Government in 1917.

Agitprop

Roslavets's music during the Revolution and Civil War generally reflects upon the transformations in Russian society. Futurists and writers organized street art, and agitprop trains transported the ideas of the revolution all over the country. Roslavets's most popular agitational songs include *On the First of May* (from the cycle *Revolutionary Songs*), highly regarded was *The Textile Worker* (from the series *Poems of the Working Profession*), *The Last Wonder*, and *The Shots Ended* (from the sequence *Songs of 1905*). Roslavets's songs—*The Textile Worker, On the First of May, The Foundry Worker*, and *In the Fields*—are extraordinary for their exhilarating freshness and simplicity and pre-echo the choruses by Georgy Sviridov—the trailblazer of the New Russian school in the 1950s.[16] The texts were by Proletkult poets and writers and the amateur musicians who later formed the RAPM and ORKiMD. Roslavets's finely crafted solemnly militant compositions were called "models of revolutionary creativity."[17]

In January 1919, Roslavets was elected chairman of the Board of the Moscow District Art Workers Union—RABIS, with the responsibility for organization and administration. The Proletkult activities were significant judging from Roslavets's reporting in July 1920, that as many as forty-two composers were working on one hundred different projects for choirs, folk instruments, and wind bands.[18] The abstract painter Vasily Kandinsky was influential in the Arts Section of the Commissariat of Enlightenment, when Roslavets was in the Music Section. Kandinsky was the vice president of the Russian Academy of Art, where the modernist musician Leonid Sabaneyev worked and who simultaneously was building contacts with arts groups in Europe, corresponding with the ASM reaching out to the West. Roslavets was active in the Russian Academy of Arts, where the ASM concerts were regularly held.

Roslavets was one of the crusaders in establishing a Union of Composers and Musicians in 1919, long before its formal foundation by the RCP(b) in 1932. Roslavets helped establish the ASM, which operated under the Music Department of the Commissariat of Peoples Enlightenment—effectively state funded. On October 17, 1919, under the signature of Arthur Lourié—the head of the Music Department, Roslavets's membership card states: "Formed by MUZO, under NARKOMPROS for a) the study of contemporary music b) the propaganda of contemporary music c) the publication of the member's works, etc."[19] Roslavets became the chairman of the Composer's Section of RABIS in 1920 and reported back regularly on its activities, for which he became known wittily as the "organizer of sound" among his colleagues.[20]

In 1921, Roslavets wrote to the party branch at RABIS, resigned as chairman of the RABIS Board, and from the Moscow District Soviet of Workers and Peasants Deputies. Here is Roslavets's letter explaining that he had not written anything since the February Revolution and that it was impossible to play a role in the party while trying to pursue an active music career.

> In consideration of the end of the Civil War and the Party's transfer towards peaceful construction. (. . .) Unfortunately, as has become clear, it is not realistic to combine my creative cultural work with the Party's organizational work. This need for freedom to create works of art and balance one's time with my place of work cannot be tolerated in the Party organizations. (. . .) I announce my resignation from the ranks of the Party—believing that this loss will be compensated for by strengthening my musical contribution, and my contribution to the proletariat will continue as strong as before—irrespective of being out with the Party ranks.[21]

Unwittingly, this ostentatious withdrawal from politics resulted in misfortune as Roslavets squandered the influence that he enjoyed in the party and state apparatus. Roslavets's political commitment is questioned by Vlasova, who writes that Roslavets left the Bolshevik Party because he was afraid of losing his positions owing to the purge against the SR Party.[22] After the conquest by the Bolshevik Party over their opponents in the bitterly fought Civil War, it was a time when careerists were joining the party and becoming part of the state network. In the 1920s, the positions of power and authority once occupied by Roslavets were engaged by people from the other end of the political spectrum, and who happened, in time, would prove to be his most bitter enemies.

Postrevolutionary Compositions

When Roslavets wrote that he had composed little since the February Revolution, in actuality, he had never stopped writing music. Between 1917 and 1922, the composer wrote three sonatas for violin and piano; the only piece which remains complete is the Violin Sonata No. 4; the Third and Fifth Sonatas are both lost. The Fourth Violin Sonata was written in Moscow in August 1920. The kinship with his past works is noted here by Lobanova, "The language is like that of his earlier violin sonatas, with extraordinary means of expression and a penchant for monumentalism, simplicity, and laconicism."[23] Myaskovsky was impressed: "there is the sense of a genuine inner framework, (. . .), he has shaped sharp and unequivocally extraordinary pages."[24]

The String Quartet No. 3 (1920) is among the composer's finest chamber works. Here, in exploring the synthetic chord, Roslavets uses a vertical chromatic line with micro-thematics and unclassical rhythmic formulas, and intensely driven polychromic processes. The one-movement structure is based on time measures with hesitant agogics and partial switches in tempo creating an extraordinary rhythmic pulse. Roslavets forms a pattern that realizes its theoretical locus through a "new rhythmic form."[25] In the Third String Quartet, the theme of the crucifix is characterized by the markings "misterioso." Roslavets used montage imagery—albeit in a simplified form—in his agitational songs. However, the montage in the Third Quartet is based on micro-thematics, using small units of no more than a motif or phrase, while more developed ideas are introduced. Another crucial element is the use of intensely developed polyphony. It is the polyphony that secures the rhythmic and time variance in the score. The innovative polyphony, the rhythmic, thematic, harmonic organization of the quartet conflicts with form. Roslavets experimented with the limitations of sonata form where classic interval norms transpose the main and closing parts in the reprise. The stylistic dissonance in the Third Quartet is not a compromise or a synthesis of "innovation" and "academism" and this was continued by Roslavets during the 1920s.[26]

The trend recurs in Roslavets's piano trios. The Piano Trio No. 2 (August 23–October 13, 1920) synthesizes the conventional scheme with groundbreaking harmonies and rhythm. There is a link between traditional harmony and cyclical structures in this one-movement piece. The harmonic colors are typical for Roslavets's "synthetic chord" in the augmented mode. This work was restored for performance only in 1989.

Roslavets further explored the synthetic chord in vocal compositions based on the symbolist poets—Bryusov, Sologub, and Pavlovich. The setting of Bryusov's *On the Saim* (1920) was to be the first in a cycle, the second was *In the Glittering Prosperous Distance*, the third setting of *Two in the Boat* (1920), are lost. Lobanova suggests that the texts of *On the Saim* were perhaps "mystical-symbolist" and would have been proscribed.[27] The use of the synthetic chord in the Bryusov settings takes the keyboard writing to the heights of expression. The ornamentation reveals modernism, and the romance is both intensive and laconic in the narrative—more than the neoclassicism that later fascinated Roslavets. They were premiered by K. G. Arle-Tich and B. B. Tich on November 27, 1924, at the Chamber Hall of the Moscow Conservatoire. On the same evening, several of Roslavets's song cycles were performed: *I Was Awoken Early*, *Sinless Dream* (from *Songs from the Past*), with the earlier songs *Autumn Song*, and *Quiet Twilight*. Roslavets here informs of his writing as if in a style ideologically foreign to him.

> The works date between March and May 1920. Owing to circumstances beyond the control of the composer—only now have they come to light—almost a decade after their composition. It is for this reason that they are presently ideologically out of date written in a tone long since alien to the composer. The composer has re-evaluated these works only to experience the resolution of formal problems toward developing his principles and methods in organizing sound material.[28]

The vocal cycles were published neither in 1920, nor in 1929, for reasons that we will discover. There is a kinship of the Sologub settings with the four miniatures—*I Was Awakened Early*, *My Steppe*, *Quiet Lullaby*, and *Sinless Dream*. These vocal pieces share meditative lyricism, dreamy moods, and embraced late romanticism. In January 1919, Roslavets completed his vocal cycle with four poems by Zinaida Gippius—some of his finest works in this genre. Lobanova believes 'the motif—of the calling, or a summons prevailed in many of Roslavets settings,' notably in *Incantation*, while *The Spring Wind* reprises much of his writing for Kamensky's *Flight*, and the third, *Cocks*, is beautifully expressive and vibrant. Roslavets uses the synthetic chord technique in all these songs. Regrettably, the third setting *Suddenly* is lost. Owing to the religious content, the pieces were not published in the lifetime of the composer.

In his response to the sudden death of the symbolist Alexander Blok in 1921, Roslavets used texts by the poetess Nadezhda Pavlovich for the cycle—*In Memory of A. Blok* (1922). The songs are remarkable for their enlightened intensity, modernism, and humility in a form more familiar in his agitprop work. The cycle assumes a ceremonial funereal mood, evocative of demonstrations and marching songs. The song *He Is in the Coffin* is theatrically dramatic, and the mood continues with a bell-like incantation in *Look, at the Wide Open Sky*. The final *Holy Mother! His Autumn* is an epilogue to a great happening or event.

Roslavets in Kharkiv

Following four years of intensive activities in Elets and Moscow, Roslavets moved to Ukraine, where Natalya was employed on a project in Kharkiv (then the capital of Soviet Ukraine). In May 1921, Roslavets returned to teaching as a professor at the Music Academy and appointed head of Artistic Education at the Commissariat of Enlightenment of Ukraine.

His letter of reference is laudatory, "Comrade Roslavets is one of the leading workers in musical education in Moscow, he is energetic and talented, a magnificent organizer, and immeasurably well-educated. Comrade Roslavets is one of the most brilliant composers of our time and has stipulated that his composing is not to be disturbed."[29]

The city boasts an enlightened history for distinguished writers such as Adam Mickiewicz, Goethe, and Ivan Franko who were associated with Kharkiv University, and possesses a fine Opera and Ballet Theater. Following the liberation from German troops in 1919, the new Soviet powers decreed Kharkiv as the new capital of Ukraine. However, the city suffered from chronic food and fuel shortages. In his first weeks, the traumas of war and revolution seem to catch up with Roslavets as he was diagnosed with pneumonia and underwent what appears to have been a nervous breakdown. Natalya and Nikolay Roslavets occupied a small flat with an Shrëder piano in a quiet locality on 5 Eparkhalnaya Street allowing him necessary conditions for composition. Owing to his state responsibilities, Roslavets sat on numerous committees and became entangled in proscribing operettas at the Kharkiv State Opera Theater.[30] Roslavets met with the young modernist composer Iosif Schillinger, who was energetically involved in the city's musical life. (We shall assess Schillinger's music in the conclusion.) At a concert in January 1922, both Roslavets's and Schillinger's music was performed at a concert of contemporary Russian romances by Catoire, Medtner, Gnessin, Prokofiev, and Stravinsky. According to the concert bill, most of the pieces were local premieres, although we don't know which songs were programed.[31] On February 13, 1922, Roslavets gave a talk at the "Young Peoples Philharmonic."[32] There was a thriving appetite for modernism in the city for in the spring of 1922, Roslavets helped establish the "Society of New Art," including Schillinger, the futurist poets Petnikov, Akimov, and others.[33]

It was in Ukraine that Roslavets wrote the second of seven unfinished symphonies (which is still unaccounted for). If he was enthusiastic in exploring the potential for his synthetic chord in chamber ensembles, the ambition to write for larger ensembles was a constant allure. Sabaneyev considers that Roslavets started a four-movement symphony in 1919 before he traveled to Kharkiv, yet considering Sabaneyev's fallibility, and his subsequent antipathy, there might not be much veracity in this story. It is likely that the themes of this projected symphony appear in other compositions written in Ukraine. Roslavets did sketch three movements of another symphony in Kharkiv, as the remaining sketches show passages for a solo violin, and two solo cellos in energetic passages until the entry of the woodwind. The archives contain what is a *Lento* movement scored for a three-part orchestra which has a date November 24, 1922. There is no record of any performances, although professional orchestras were available. Perhaps, it was illness and the teaching burden that hindered him from completion. Roslavets's Second Symphony dates from Kharkiv in 1923, and the thematic material is quite dissimilar in style and content from his previous drafts. Roslavets was so confident in this new symphony that he shared the details with his colleagues back in Moscow.

> N. A. Roslavets (. . .) proposes to present a Septet of voices with an orchestra in his newly written symphony. By no means will this be for a choir, but an ensemble of seven individual timbres across seven ranges: soprano, mezzo-soprano, contralto, tenor, baritone, bass, and low bass (contra-octave). Certainly, the problem of using this extraordinary "vocal orchestral group" wholly depends on the composer's talent and ability. Roslavets himself anticipates a whole number of refreshing opportunities that will surely lead to a refined orchestral sound. He has recently written a Sonata for Cello and Piano (his second), a Piano Trio (in one-movement, his Second), a Fifth Sonata for Violin and Piano (1922–23), several romances to text by the symbolist Fyodor Sologub and Nadezhda Pavlovich, a Symphony in four-movements and a Symphonic Poem from Baudelaire *Man and the Sea* (1921, the first in a large symphonic triptych). Presently he is writing a String Quartet.[34]

Alas, nothing remains of this symphony with a septet of voices, or of the symphonic poem *Man and the Sea* by Baudelaire.

Chamber Music

Of the two Cello Sonatas composed in Kharkiv, the First Cello Sonata (1921) experiments in fusing the synthetic chord with free tonality. "The impulsively vigorous main idea is written in sonata form, outlining the positive interval of a synthetic chord—a triton, with a high *e* note."[35] The Second Cello Sonata (1922) was premiered in Moscow by Maria Mirzoyeva and Sergey Shirinsky in 1926.[36] The Piano Trio No. 3 dates from April 1921. So pleased was he with this outstanding piece that Roslavets dedicated it to the virtuosos of the Moscow Piano Trio: V. I. Dillon (piano), U. M. Goldstein (violin), and Semyon M. Shpilman (cello). The Third Piano Trio was premiered by their dedicatees on November 27, 1924, at the Chamber Hall of the Moscow Conservatoire. Myaskovsky was suitably impressed that

> this vision, unfalteringly, and somewhat insatiably, transports one into the discordant future, yet, this is entirely a foretaste and hint of the future, and most likely of the far off (future); there is a shudder of life in the whole thing, albeit this is not always clearly felt, but it is even more advanced when realized, in just one detail, or as an abstraction of an idea or the creation (. . .) in a moment of utmost elevation (the culmination of the exposition and the repeats) is all lavishly fluent, yet somewhat passive in their bleakness.[37]

The themes of the Third Piano Trio share a kinship with early symbolism and may perhaps be judged as small branches growing ever higher upward. The sense of harmonious breathing introduces a coldness, whereas conventional themes have a mirror-like symmetry, with "waves" of melody palpable in the *accelerandi* and *diminuendos*. From the opening bars, the melodic-dynamic contours give steadfastness and vigor to the unwinding themes. The piano scoring is rich and "orchestral" using all the facets of the modern concert piano, Lobanova notes that Roslavets embraced a "paradoxical synthesis of invention and traditionalism, aspiring to breaking with norms, and simultaneously—to a new rigorous law defining the creative individuality of Roslavets, particularly with a style orientated on futurism and new academicism."[38] The composer and critic Leonid Sabaneyev evinced the difficulties of his music in a concert review on March 18, 1924:

> Roslavets—is a forceful representative of musical modernism through his use of the most intricate harmonic complexes. But his creativity lacks that "common fascination," that label from which the "modernists" suffer, and this— undoubted individuality, is somewhat ferocious and secure in relating to the sound. His music is a world of organized sounds, in which there is huge integrity and logic, but is abstract, and, it seems, emotionalism does not enter into the composer's responsibilities. Roslavets has a skilled individual and profound

mastery, but the extraordinary sound of his compositions will hardly make them soon accessible to the public.[39]

If Sabaneyev had already pointed to his negativities, another writer more favorable to Roslavets pointed to other characteristics in his music.

The systematic, logical reserve, and dogged pursuit of relentlessly stated artistic aims—such are the strongest qualities in the musical profile of N. A. Roslavets. The rigorous reserve of musical constructivism allows Roslavets' music that special charm, making it not only accessible but wholly convincing for broad groups of listeners, especially those uninvolved in matters of musical creative methodology, upon which his composing is based.[40]

This appraisal reveals how diverse were the judgments on Roslavets's music, and this was from two writers who were on the side of modernism and new ideas. Following his emigration, Sabaneyev wrote more broadly about his old friend,

Nikolay Roslavets as a composer is a phenomenon of unusual originality. There are in him, (qualities of his being) both a thinker and an artist. Russian musical creativity, which normally is flowing in pure emotionality, is least interested in music as structure, and music as organized sound. Music for Russian composers is usually about the "language of feelings," and the discourse of emotion and moods. Roslavets has a quite different approach to music: for him, music is a structure of organized sound material built from scientific, and almost rational principles, with a completely controlled consciousness at each moment of creativity. This is what Taneyev dreamed about—another type of architect in music, who foresaw an intuitively profound organic family of musical laws with the mathematical, inner logic of musical structure. But Taneyev was also associated with musical tradition: believing that this logic can be researched in examples of classical works. Roslavets has progressed further: he builds upon the laws of musical structures quite independently from past experience and opens the path to innovative horizons, but in the frame of strict musical logic. We can see the creativity of Scriabin, who was less firm and precise. Scriabin was thus intuitive and not an architect. . . . Roslavets has a tectonism, and his mathematics in musical creativity matches academicism. This is an original and exceptional type of innovator and academician. He is not interested in emotion as such. For him, music is not about the language of feelings, but expression of an organized psychic world. He is interested not in emotion in itself, but placing it on a musical canvass with other "organized emotions," irrevocably leading to the organization of sound. Roslavets is a genuine master of sound, loving his mastery as a working specialist loves his sounds as his trade. He writes neither one note, nor one phrase. Everything is prepared and thought through to the last step. . . .

But it would be a mistake to think that he writes dry and unengaging music. It appears despite the mathematical sources of his structures; his music seems expressive and full-blooded and produces the impression of something quite new. . . . The mastery, technical perfection in performance, and the unusual conviction of the composer's principles—place him in the front rank of composers in the USSR, where he is placed on the left wing of the composers camp.[41]

Lobanova writes that the "logical conclusion of Roslavets" searching was the creation of his own pedagogical systems, in which he fanatically believed declaring: "This system will last two hundred years."[42] The tragic transformation in history did not allow the possibility of either the accuracy or fallacy of Roslavets's prophesy. Regardless of which, the "new system of organizing sound was and remains one of the most interesting experiments in contemporary music."[43]

Roslavets as Head of Repertkom

Nikolay Roslavets's return to Moscow coincided with his appointment to a leading role in education, music policy, and publishing. This proved to be the most eventful period of his career, if it had a detrimental effect on his composing; nevertheless, he proved himself courageous and principled in defending his musical ideas against his opponents. Roslavets was appointed head of Policy for Music (Glavrepertkom) at the State Publishing House (Muzsektor) in October 1924, a role he held until January 1930. In the capital, Roslavets found himself among rancorous debates about the arts in society. His opponents came from the RAPM and ORKiMD who wanted to exclude almost all traditional classical and modernist music. The phenomenon was familiar to many artists, and writers whose past caused concern if not disguised under more common garb. In parallel with the writers Yesenin, Zamyatin, Pilnyak, and Bulgakov, Roslavets had to veneer over several undertakings and interactions by him between 1910 and 1921.[44]

Under Roslavets, Glavrepertkom (the chief editor of music repertoire) criticized the Bolshoi Theater by denouncing the appearance of the Tsarina Catherine the Great in scenes from Tchaikovsky's *Queen of Spades* and Rimsky-Korsakov's *Christmas Eve* as "monarchist propaganda." Whereas the proponents of the soft line at Narkompros may have been ambivalent, the editing bodies championed regulation and control of literature, and artistic productions, maintaining that artistic merit never mitigated problematic content.[45] Roslavets was no exception to the rule, but his orientation made him the champion rather than the denigrator of music that the radicals on the musical ultra-left rejected. As Neil Edmunds points out, there were those ASM musicians who didn't hold back from criticizing the ultra-leftist musicians. "Two individuals who fell into this category were the composer, Nikolay Roslavets, and the critic Leonid Sabaneyev. (. . .) Roslavets, for instance, in a clear reference to the ultra-leftist RAPM, and ORKiMD claimed that "Russian composers have fallen silent while the organization of Russian musical life stagnated, and complete anarchy (. . .) caused by a peculiar form of the celebrated 'hack' has set in."[46] The fact that Roslavets used terms, such as "khaltura" (a potboiler or hack), favored by the proletarian music movement's ideologists to describe the composers of light music, added to the power of his criticism.'[47]

Both Roslavets and Sabaneyev—according to Edmunds—were against viewing early Soviet musical life as a battle between antagonistic factions. Roslavets, for instance, had been head of the repertoire section of Moscow Proletkult's music department and remained an enthusiastic supporter after it lost its autonomy.[48] The American musicologist Anna Ferenc points out that Roslavets had written several pieces for workers, notably *Pryzyv* (*The Call*) and *Fonar* (*The Torch*) at the Proletkult studios, and he considered that these songs "could help with the ideological organization of the masses."[49] Additionally, Roslavets lectured at the Proletkult club's music department, among which were subjects such as *Music and the Machine*, *The Origins of Music*, *The Choir Past and Present*, and *Classical Music*, the two latter courses being of a practical nature while the first two were purely theoretical.[50]

The Proletarians versus the Modernists

The 1920s were a period of bitter fighting between the composers of the ASM and the proletarian musicians of RAPM, the root of which is unveiled by one of the ultra-left musicians Yuri Keldysh. "This organization (ASM) did not become popular among composers and didn't win enough authority. This was linked mainly with the general personality of the main leader of MUZO A. Lourié—a real decadent, eclectic, but with a pretension for innovation and originality. In his duties, Lourié used self-promotion and supported such musical adventurers, while hiding behind noisy, apparently revolutionary declarations about the basic renewal of language and form of contemporary music."[51] Not only being a firm critic of the modernist composers, Keldysh would be a staunch adversary of Roslavets in the coming months and years.

In 1923, several maneuvers were launched to impose control of the conservatoires and music schools by the newly formed RAPM against what they considered "decadent," "Western-orientated," and "bourgeois" musicians.

Workers' faculties or Rabfaks were to control the entry of students from poor backgrounds and expel those students from the intelligentsia and former ruling class. A third of students were expelled under dubious accusations and replaced by young people without any music background. The "Red Professors" was established to oversee this process and ensure the teaching methodology would switch from what they called "harmful bourgeois" ideology. In essence, the conservatoires were to become "factories of music" and academic study was to be limited. The RAPM members were mostly young people with little musical education: former members of military bands of the Red Army. Sergeyev, Shulgin, Lebedinsky, Keldysh, Korev, and Bryusova were among the prominent activists. The type of ideology behind this major restructuring of musical education may be observed by this editorial in the ultra-left newssheet.

> In a society based on private property, the artist produces goods for the market, he needs buyers. Should we bring pleasant, sweet biscuits to this small minority when the workers and peasant masses need black bread? (. . .) Art serves the people. It must go to the deepest roots in the very center of the broad working masses. It must unite feelings, thoughts and wills of these masses, and raise them higher.[52]

The RAPM and ORKiMD launched a wave of actions against those whom they considered were harmful to socialist culture. In late 1923, several devastating blows fell upon the ASM—allegedly due to low sales—the State Publishing House closed *To New Shores* (*K Novym Beregam*). The GPU arrested Professors Lamm and Gĕdike in the spring of 1924, Lamm was held in Butyrskaya Prison for three months, and the homes searched of distinguished musicians causing the psychic illness of Professor Gĕdike.[53] All of which helped to drive away the musicians who had been working with the publisher since the Civil War. The editorial board of *Musical Novelty* (*Muzikalnaya Nov*)—which replaced *K Novym Beregam*—was led by ultra-left party members whose criticism of the Conservatoires and concert life further alienated the musical community.

Editor of Musical Culture

The newly appointed head of the State Publishing House, Otto Schmidt asked Roslavets to win back members of the ASM through a new journal that would be Marxist in orientation and address the implications of the revolution for music. This mission corresponded with that of Alexander Voronsky, who, as the editor of *The New Red* (*Krasnaya Nov*), tried to cultivate the support of "fellow traveler writers." The general tone of this "soft line" demanded efforts to win over musicians, not terrorize them into silence. The new Soviet republic had already lost outstanding musicians and composers with the departures of Cherepnin, Koussevitzky, Chaliapin, Lourié, Rachmaninov, Prokofiev, Medtner, and Grechaninov to the West. The government did not want to lose more composers and musicologists; however, through the continuing attacks by RAPM, the "brain drain" would resume.

It was not until July 1924 that *Musical Culture* (*Muzykalnaya Kultura*) appeared under Roslavets's editorship, and he quickly proceeded to hire the ASM members Asafyev, Belyaev, Derzhanovsky, Myaskovsky, Sabaneyev, and Yavorsky. Like other periodicals *Contemporary Music* and *To New Shores* (both produced by the ASM), the new journal combined sound scholarship and focused on contemporary music. Quarter-tonal, atonal, and machine music received extensive coverage, as did Georgy Konius's "metro tectonic" method of formal analysis. What distinguished *Musical Culture* was its explicit concern with the relationship between radical art and politics—in other terms, the attitude of the avant-garde to Soviet society.

Nikolay Roslavets's stature as a composer and political front-runner was now at its zenith. His editorship led to vitriolic debates with the ultra-left over the future of music in the country, and no one more than Roslavets took the battle to the RAPM than he did—a factor which ultimately led to his demise. Roslavets sneered at his critics—often in mockery—dismissing his enemies through the sheer force of argument. Roslavets appeared to delight in making fun of his detractors. "If we cross out the title *Hymn of Thanksgiving* in Beethoven's Quartet op. 132, and substitute *Festive Victory Celebration of the Red Army*, or *Opening of the Baku Tram Line*—does this in any way change the content of the quartet?" Roslavets's leader "Music is music, not ideology" was directly targeted at the RAPM.[54]

In the first issue of *Musical Culture*, Roslavets argued that the Russian proletariat, through sheer necessity, had to focus on economic and political concerns, and, because it was now the ruling class, the workers had to destroy the culture of its former oppressors and only then build a socialist culture. But to do so, the young culture of the Russian bourgeoisie must be first understood and mastered. This project could not be achieved in Roslavets's opinion by "simplifying" music to correspond to the current level of the masses' cultural development. The aesthetic preferences of workers and peasants in this transitional era reflected a "non-culture" from social, economic, and political oppression rather than the offspring of a new artistic awareness. The building blocks of genuinely revolutionary music would be the new tone systems developed by composers like Roslavets, not folk song, and traditional forms (particularly in *sonata-allegro* form) that were idealized by the RAPM.[55] Roslavets staunchly defended avant-garde music, which still remained so inaccessible to many audiences. Trotsky alluded to these ideas in his pamphlet *Literature and Revolution* (1924) that specifically proletarian culture would never exist because the proletarian dictatorship was transient.[56] Roslavets was forthright and somewhat mischievous in saying that he was no "proletarian" composer,

> I am so "bourgeois" that I consider the Russian proletariat—the legitimate inheritors of all culture—worthy of that culture and its finest music. And therefore, it is explicitly for (the Russian proletariat) I am writing my symphonies, quartets, trios, songs, and other "head crunching" works. . . . I am convinced that I will live to see the day when the proletariat will finally understand my music.[57]

The scholar Marina Frolova-Walker associates the antipathy of the RAPM to Roslavets was because his views on music were similar to those of Trotsky, but Roslavets's views on the arts in Soviet society predate Trotsky's pamphlet. As Trotsky's biographer, the Russian historian Dmitry Volkogonov, explains, "his interest in art, (was) visiting museums and galleries, and writing articles of a professional standard on artistic topics for the Kyiv newspaper. He took (his wife) Natalya to the Vienna opera but confessed that his appreciation of music was no better than primitive."[58] Considering Trotsky's ostensible musical ignorance, it would rather appear it was the politician who was espousing Roslavets's doctrine in his thesis. Frolova-Walker tries to explain that Roslavets saw the arts in socialist society as if "through the lens of Trotsky's view of Marxism," but it was Trotsky who was adopting the composer's standpoint and of the Italian philosopher Antonio Labriola (1843–1904). It is well known that Trotsky plagiarized other people's ideas by proselytizing them as his own. Even the famous Trotskyite notion of "permanent revolution" was taken from none other than Karl Marx.[59] Lobanova notes that in 1929, following Trotsky's exile, it is surprising that those RAPM members who condemned Roslavets "were not embarrassed that just recently they had enthusiastically quoted both Trotsky and Voronsky in their speeches."[60]

We have a vignette of Nikolay Roslavets during this enormously focused and intensive period. A student of Roslavets—Pyotr Vasilyevich Teplov (1889–1992)—wrote of him being in a happy, upbeat mood,

> Nikolay Andreyevich was dusky, with a beard and mustache and loved to laugh. . . . The mid-1920s was a enjoyable moment in time. N. Roslavets . . . appeared full of energy and hope, (at this time) the RAPM members were not expected by any of us (later they prospered in beating us). The publishers were situated "behind" the former Jurgensons music shop on Neglinnaya Street, and entry was through the shop. Along one side of a long corridor, music scores were displayed behind the counters, leading to (rooms containing) the

main storeroom. In one of these rooms, Roslavets signed off a new publication. Ceaselessly, colleagues arrived to see him . . . composers, and musicologists. . . . On my arrival, Leonid Sabaneyev was already there . . . one had to wait for a little. . . . We then entered another room with a grand piano. Some of the other editors (including Myaskovsky) were there. "Well, we are in the middle of an audition!" I played through some piano miniatures. . . . This was Moscow in 1924.[61]

It was at this time that the proletarian musicians attempted to seize control of theater and concert programming. The repertoire had to be changed as they called for, "Any devilish stuff like *Faust* or *The Demon* has to be thrown out. And to take its place—anything connected with the mass movement, (. . .) and with social content."[62] Such works as *The Tsar's Bride*, *The Force of Evil*, *Boris Godunov*, and *Askold's Grave* were suitable; however, operas like *Tosca* became *Life for the Commune*, or *Struggle for the Commune*, Glinka's *A Life for the Tsar* was renamed *For Hammer and Sickle*, while Meyerbeer's *The Huguenots* became *The Decembrists*. Not only were operas rechristened, but the librettos were updated with revolutionary content. The ultimate failure of these productions led to their withdrawal by the end of the 1920s.

Owing to the unforeseen cancellation of the ASM concerts, Derzhanovsky solicited the facilities of the State Academy for Scholarship in the Arts (GAKhN), where recitals proceeded without having to wait for cancellations by Muzsektor.[63] The opening recital was devoted to Hindemith, the follow-up concert featured music by Roslavets, Melkikh, Vasilenko, and Dzegelyonok, and at the third evening music by *Les Six*.[64] The latest Soviet music was now being published by Universal Edition in Vienna and distributed worldwide. Notably, the March 1924 edition of their trade journal *Musikblätter des Anbruch* was wholly devoted to Soviet music. This Western outlet led to criticism from the RAPM—as Veprik informed Bryusova—a leading member of the "Red Professors" at the Moscow Conservatoire. "The journal is quite scandalous. If you were to believe it—we have four geniuses: Myaskovsky, Alexandrov, Feinberg, and Roslavets—all the rest are rubbish."[65] Despite the hostility, the ASM concerts continued successfully with music by Bartók, Casella, Kodaly, Honegger, Krenek, Schoenberg, Webern, and Cyril Scott.

Roslavets fell in the firing line from the extremists for leading the ideological attacks in the media on their activities. An added source for malevolence was Roslavets's role as a censor at the State Publishing House and his choosing what was to be published or not. This position of influence allowed him control over the content of the ultra-leftist RAPM journals *Musical Novelty*, *Music and October*, and the first issues of *Proletarian Musician*. Hence, it is perhaps not surprising why there was so much hostility aimed specifically at Roslavets until the 1932 debacle.[66]

Only three issues of Roslavets's *Musical Culture* appeared—for according to a letter from Derzhanovsky to Asafyev—there were differences on the whole project. The new head of Muzsektor (Music Publishing)

> Yurovsky informed Roslavets officially that the journal would be closed because it's a loss-maker and a source of trouble. Roslavets was given to understand that he had no future at Muzsektor. They argued, and Roslavets left as if to resign. But he changed his mind on the way thinking that his resignation would mean the triumph of the events around Sergeyev, and Chernomordikov. So instead of giving his resignation, he went to brew up some trouble at the Rabis CC (the Art Worker's Union), where he spoke to Slavinsky (the chair). As a result, if he's right, we can soon expect an audit of Muzsektor, etc. etc. etc., and there'll be a war against Yurovsky, with Roslavets as its instigator, and all the forces of RABIS as his army.[67]

As we will discover, this episode proved just the beginning of a struggle between Roslavets and the proletarian musicians.

Lev Lebedinsky—a prominent member of the RAPM—dismissed Roslavets's critiques as "lightweight and gibberish."[68] Roslavets was accused of "drawing a terrifying picture of musical culture destroyed by the working class."[69] Roslavets's music was criticized for "lacking artistic sensibility and feeling for artistic truth, without creativity (. . .), and for long disguising this creative void with supposedly original, constructivist fabrications."[70] Condemnation was targeted at his revolutionary songs and other poster art, and Lebedinsky added that Roslavets was cynical and wanted to "cultivate bourgeois music, while at the same time claiming that he takes no part in promoting it."[71] Lebedinsky criticized Roslavets's mass-produced pamphlets *Music for Everyone* (*Muzyka dlya Vsekh*), believing that their allegedly harmful political line was inappropriate for a working-class readership.[72]

As we know, in 1919, Roslavets was a founding member of the ASM with Myaskovsky, Sabaneyev, Belyaev, Shebalin, and others. Frolova-Walker writes that the Myaskovsky-Lamm circle considered Roslavets as an adverse presence in the ASM. "Roslavets was no less alien, and often problematic, but potentially too useful to be rejected, thanks to his party connections and his post in the newly established censorship organization, Glavrepertkom."[73] The ASM journal did not suit those who disapproved of its alleged cosmopolitanism and failure to adhere to dogma.[74] *Music and the Revolution* was the house journal of the ORKiMD, a leftist music group that gave space to Asafyev, Belyaev, and Sabaneyev in its columns, yet, excluded Roslavets owing to his editorial activities in banning the proletarian musicians. According to the American scholar Amy Nelson,

Roslavets was a composer first and a music critic second. He was a member and supporter of the ASM but did not belong to its social circles, nor was he on the faculty at the Conservatoire. A unique and compelling figure, Roslavets was one of few musicians who worked for a politically creative policy and the only professed Marxist in the modernist camp. While many in the intelligentsia petitioned the state for support and preference in this period, Roslavets was in a unique position to shape policy toward music in general. An influential and outspoken proponent of his vision of cultural transformation, Roslavets both influenced and responded to the ambiguous and often treacherous political dynamics of the NEP order.[75]

The musicologist Kirill Tomoff identifies Roslavets as

> a fiery polemicist in the 1920s who thought that political and social revolution called for new, revolutionary innovations in composition. Roslavets and those who shared similar visions fancied themselves the musical avant-garde, but most members were considerably more conservative and included conservatory professors and young talents like Dmitry Shostakovich.[76]

The early work of Shostakovich has many examples however of avant-garde tendencies, particularly in his opera *The Nose*, several chamber pieces, and the Second and Third symphonies.

In 1924, the ASM began producing *Contemporary Music* under Vladimir Derzhanovsky (formerly editor and publisher of the pre-1917 *Muzika*). The assistant editors were Leonid Sabaneyev and Viktor Belyaev and featured enthusiastic articles and reviews of both new domestic and Western music, notably from Prokofiev, Stravinsky, Bartók, and Hindemith, as well as Myaskovsky, Roslavets, Feinberg, and Alexandrov. The journal published the thesis of Arseny Avraamov—the composer of *Symphony of Foghorns* (1922), and his theory of metrotechtonics became a topic for fierce debates between Georgy Konius, Sabaneyev, and Roslavets. Viktor Belyaev discussed the latter's "new system of sound,"

> in the person of Roslavets, contemporary music possesses an absolutely foremost and quite idiosyncratic composing figure—a master who has attained absolute freedom in applying the sound material expressed by him, (this is) a musician who is creating in a new sound world discovered by him and which so far, apart from him, no one else has used.[77]

The essay *Where Are the Russian Composers?* by Roslavets became a noteworthy contribution to the debate,

> For anyone interested in Russian contemporary musical culture and who follow its affairs in the papers and journals, it must appear as if only three or four composer's names are comfortable within the tight circle monopolized by the press. That is not the case: there are more than a few vigorous workers in the field of Russian music. Those "titans" about whom so much is written and heard—in essence—the yardsticks—point the way forward in contemporary music. However, those "minnows" or mass song composers about whom the press do not want to know, are not so few but perhaps are too many in such an enormous union like the USSR.[78]

This was another example of the hostile attacks by Roslavets against the proletarian musicians of RAPM. The campaign came into the open at a meeting of the "Red Professors" at the Moscow Conservatoire on May 26, 1924. As a keynote speaker, in his statement: *On New Methods in Forming a Professional Composer*, Roslavets empathized with the "Red Professors" and their leader Nadezhda Bryusova that "knowledge of the disciplines was essential." One of the RAPM members, Vinogradov, was more sweeping in his response. "The Conservatoire must prepare the composer who responds to the needs of the masses, and not be misunderstood by them, (however) the compositions of a 'contemporary' composer doesn't meet their demands." Rabinovich, another RAPM acolyte, commented: "It appears that in most points, Comrade Roslavets' disposition coincides with that of the Red Professors. But he doesn't deal with the main shortcoming of the 'contemporary' school—taking the composer away from the masses."[79] Mikhail Gnessin shared Roslavets's view, but the decline in relations was now so bad that the RAPM chairman Lev Lebedinsky broke off all relations with Roslavets.[80]

The revolutionary song movement was not always successful in finding their audiences among the Soviet intelligentsia. Sabaneyev characterized mass songs by "proletarian" composers in the following terms: "In almost all of them, the idea of good spirits is realized in a primitive march rhythm, while their tunes echo the old-fashioned tsarist military music, which in its turn, had its roots—alas—in operetta."[81] Roslavets made a similar criticism of the efforts of the RAPM composers and for which he suffered ignominy; however in 1926, Sabaneyev emigrated to the West and avoided any possible consequences of his criticism.

Like a rolling stone gathering moss, Roslavets collected more and more enemies; some endlessly counseled against him, a little-known composer Kovalev complained that "Roslavets was behaving as if he was sacrificing himself for the common good." Following the scandalous reigns of Lourié, Lamm, and Chernomordikov, he couldn't publish his music. Roslavets had to stop publishing his work for six months at least and is accused of delaying

Figure 2.1 **Roslavets Portrait, 1927.** *Source:* Courtesy of Marina Lobanova.

publishing while his compositions were piled up high at the printers.[82] Only seven pieces by Roslavets were published by Muzsektor between 1923 and 1924, whereas fourteen of his agitprop songs were published between 1925 and 1927, and four were published at his own cost between 1926 and 1929.[83]

New System of Tone Organization

The new system of sound was developed from approximately 1909 through to 1919, a ten-year process, yet as we know, he continued to experiment by sometimes blending tonality with his synthetic chord technique. Roslavets used the six to nine pitches of the synthetic chord—horizontally to construct the melody and vertically, to create harmony. The opening synthetic chord assumes several functions of the tonic, reappearing often at the culmination. The range and technical capabilities of the modern piano were particularly attractive for Roslavets.

The piano sonatas and vocal and chamber pieces of the 1920s share a harmony with the mystically inspired work of Scriabin. Refuting the charges that the modernists "fetishized the creative process," Roslavets denied the presence of any outside "inspiration" in his music. "I know that the creative act is not some 'mystic trance' or 'divine discovery,' but rather a moment in the highest exertion of the human intellect for its attempt to transform the unconscious (subconscious)."[84]

Picking up the ideas of the futurists, Roslavets considered Russian classical music an "outgrowth of a feudal culture" that deserved to be swept aside by the Revolution, "Russian musical culture—still unsteady, still without strong roots-was completely routed by October."[85] Roslavets felt that his music belonged to the future however was dedicated to developing the musical sensibilities of the masses without patronizing them. We know that he made numerous contributions to revolutionary-agitational literature for worker's clubs. These agitprop songs, many of which employed a modified version of the New System of Tone Organization, aroused scorn from the RAPM and misunderstanding from his associates in the ASM who considered them a source of embarrassment and those who were eager to revive interest in his "serious" music.[86] Amy Nelson portrays here the significance of Roslavets and the "modernists" during the 1920s,

> It is alleged that Roslavets exhibited some of the aesthetics of negation and much of the avant-garde, interventionist political rhetoric that characterized the phenomenon in other artistic fields. He was, however, rather atypical of the Soviet modernist community as a whole, in which the eclectic flirtation with atonality, and his perceived interest in neoclassicism, and the rather self-conscious appropriation of urban popular music that typified musical modernism elsewhere in this period was also found in his work of this period. The referential framework for the ASM and the Leningrad modernists was not the artistic avant-garde whose tragically successful quest to establish a truly revolutionary culture has been delineated by Groys and Clark. Instead, musically as well as ideologically, the musical modernists were fairly well-integrated members of the musical establishment, and official policy supported and was defined by these groups rather than the militants on the musical left.[87]

Here the English musicologist Neil Edmunds explains the essential cause of friction between the diverse musical groups in the 1920s,

> ASM claimed that music and ideology should be separate, and advocated contemporary Western music and compositional techniques, such as serialism. That resulted in an emphasis on form rather than content, and music composed in an idiom that the masses would find difficult to comprehend. There were in practice, however, supporters of ASM like Roslavets whose work had a clear ideological content, and compositions by composers on both sides that imitated the machines with which the proletariat was familiar.[88]

This accusation of being concerned with musical form, rather than content, would become the core of the attacks against so-called formalist contemporary composers for many decades in Soviet music, particularly after the line of "socialist realism" was introduced in 1934. In the 1920s, Narkomprom mostly unheeded rather than opposed the RAPM, although the latter encountered genuine enmity at the State Publishing House from Roslavets, who used his *Musical Culture* to promote his conception at odds with the "back to Beethoven" program of RAPM. As a political editor, Roslavets had censorial control over *Musical Novelty* that could be mitigated only partly by the RAPM supporters in Narkomprom, such as Chernomordikov, Sergeyev, and Shulgin. When the RAPM launched a direct attack on "his" journal, Roslavets exercised this authority freely, prompting the proletarian musicians to appeal to "higher authorities."[89] Ultimately, both sides lost because the party organization at Muzsektor decided to close both journals down at the end of 1924—here was the consequence of Roslavets's loss of influence through being out of the ruling party's trusted membership.[90]

Anna Ferenc argues that, "After the Revolution, Roslavets naively defended his pre-Revolutionary compositional creed by drawing an analogy between his emancipation of music from outdated conventions and the new socialist structuring of society."[91] It can be contended, however, that Roslavets developed his ideas thoroughly and consistently over many years when he was collaborating with the Futurists. His ideology almost fully identified with the casting out of the old structures in art and society, abandoning of old tradition, his castigation of opera for a new form of music in which his own sound structures would play a firm part in future society. Rather than being a futurist, as we have seen Roslavets was more of a collaborator with some of their ideas, for utopia was not part of his artistic credo. It was clear the composer believed that the synthetic chord offered a new system of sound that could play a key part in Soviet music and unequivocally attacked those who disagreed. In the critical year of 1924, Roslavets voiced his philosophy:

> To leave behind the contemporary impressionist and expressionist anarchy, which is leading musical art into a cul-de-sac, one must advance in the direction of (. . .) realizing new laws of musical thinking, a new logic of sound, and a new vibrant, and rigorous system of sound organization. We need neither the unbalanced neoclassicism, quietly suckling from two mothers, from "yesterday" and "today" nor the barbarism of European music that makes a toxic swing from Debussy to Negro (jazz). What we need is a strong balanced system with fresh thoughts and fresh perceptions of sound—based on new views and a new view of the world. (. . .) A real, well-founded, harmonious art can be developed only upon the groundwork of a certain agreed structure, a model, and theory.[92]

If Roslavets's ideas here relate with those of Hauer and Schoenberg, the Russian came to his ideas separately. In his mammoth pioneering study of Soviet music, the American musicologist Boris Schwartz tried to dismiss Roslavets owing to the apparent force and influence of Scriabin, who "overshadowed such minor experimentations as Vladimir Rebikov and Nikolai Roslavets."[93] Nonetheless, Richard Stites considers Roslavets was more illustrious than Schwartz made out for he had already abandoned classical music and was matching Western modernists such as Bartók, Honegger, Ravel, and Hindemith in comparison "with some daring Russian practitioners such as Nikolay Roslavets; proletarian choral music exalting revolution; and machine music."[94]

In 1925, at a gathering of arts workers, the Commissar for Enlightenment Lunacharsky attempted rather patronizingly to portray the problems for the workers' appreciation of the arts, "it is impossible to say, that Repin's paintings are so difficult to understand. Understanding here is not quite what is wanted by the proletariat. But paintings by some futurists are not clear to the proletariat because the worker says: 'maybe it is revolutionary, but the devil knows, you can't make it out.'"[95] At this meeting, the RAPM and ORKIMD launched an intense campaign on eradicating "bourgeois culture" as they perceived was epitomized by the ASM, and especially by Roslavets and to grasp a monopoly in Soviet music. Roslavets was identified as the principal enemy. The proletarian musicians Shulgin and Lebedinsky called for destroying their opponents, using ideological labels. Unfortunately, more cruder instruments would come into play in the RAPM warfare against Roslavets and his colleagues in the ASM.

Piano Music

Regardless of Roslavets's work as an editor and campaigner against his ideological enemies, outstanding music continued to pour from his pen. In the growing catalog, the Piano Sonata No. 4 (1923) was premiered by Pavel Kovalev on April 12, 1924, in Moscow (unfortunately the Piano Sonata No. 3 is deemed lost). The Piano Sonata No. 5 (May/June 1923) refashions orchestral effects in virtuoso style, as Roslavets's biographer notes, "There is a measured laconicism bordering on pretentiousness mixed with decorative outlines, and is detailed in the style of a musical painting with the contrasting hues laid out broadly, in powerfully detailed sounds."[96] Roslavets did not return to the genre until 1928, with the Sixth Piano Sonata, of which only fragments remain. Roslavets may have lost all interest in this latter piece because he omitted it from his catalog.[97] The musical press announced the composition of a four-movement Piano Quartet in 1924.[98] Only one movement remains of a Piano Quintet dating from the same year.[99]

Through the agreement between Muzsektor and Universal Edition, Roslavets's scores were published simultaneously in Moscow and Vienna. The Cello Sonata No. 1 (1921) was premiered on November 6, 1924, in Vienna, and in the following year, New Yorkers heard several works by Roslavets in a recital shared with music by Feinberg and Myaskovsky.[100] Roslavets's music was praised by Darius Milhaud when he conducted both his and other music by *Les Six* in the USSR in 1926. Sabaneyev's letter to Roslavets mentions that the French composer "welcomed (hearing) your works, and it seems that he met with you in Moscow." Regardless of Sabaneyev's criticism, it would appear that he actively promoted the early Roslavets's chamber pieces in Western Europe.[101] Sabaneyev took Roslavets's scores with him to America, and the Russian émigré pianist Pavel Kovalev (the dedicatee of the Fifth Piano Sonata) championed his works there.

Violin Concerto No. 1

It is quite remarkable that this intense period led to some of Roslavets's best work—bizarrely, mostly unperformed and unpublished. A common feature seemed to be that when he started a composition, he didn't always find the time to finish it. The most significant orchestral piece is the Violin Concerto No. 1—started on July 3, 1925, at his dacha in the village of Dubka, and completed at the Roslavets's home at 22/3 Leontyevsky Street in Moscow that autumn. The Violin Concerto was first heard (the first and second movements from the three-movement piece) at the State Academy of Arts in Moscow on May 29, 1929. The ASM concert featured the performers P. Ilchenko and P. Nikitin in the arrangement for violin and piano. According to the contract initialed by the composer and Alexander Yurovsky, the full score was to be published two years later, but this never happened.[102] There were more performances in the Soviet Union, but it was only heard in the West at IRCAM in Paris on October 7, 1979. The full orchestral version was premiered at the Moscow Autumn Festival on November 18/19, 1979, with Tatyana Grindenko and the Moscow Philharmonic Orchestra under Fyodor Glushenko—fifty-four years after its composition. The original manuscript was discovered only in 1989 by Marina Lobanova at the RGALI archives.[103]

The opening idea takes the form of a synthetic mode that develops a twelve-note sequence that is reprised in the finale. There is a similarity of Roslavets's treatment of the synthetic chord and synthetic mode with his setting to Voloshin's *Through the Almaz Curtain* (1918). Neoclassicism appears in the traditional three-movement arrangement—unlike the early single-movement *Rêverie* for violin and orchestra. The writing for violin is technically challenging—with a "dialogue" of voices—however the residing force of ensemble performance dominates throughout. The *Allegretto grazioso*, in

Figure 2.2 Roslavets—Violin Concerto No. 1 (First Page of Second Movement). *Source*: Courtesy of Schotts Music.

sonata form, is rather mysterious and gray, yet, the original dramatic image leads with dynamic roles for the harp, piano, strings, and woodwind, and a dramatic burst of tension following the extended solo entry by the violin. There is an unwavering meditative atmosphere in the *Adagio sostenuto*, and the woodwind, brass, and percussion become interlocutors with the soloist. In the finale, *Allegro moderato risoluto*, the timpani brings tension and power, and passages of quiet reflection emerge from the use of intense polyphony which provides a structural balance. Roslavets finds an equilibrium between the static and dynamic forces, presenting a feeling of expectation, concentration, and ultimately of silence. This is among Roslavets's surviving masterpieces and the most ambitious completed composition from this period. When he heard it, the modernist Soviet composer Edison Denisov declared that "this is one of the finest concertos of the 20th century, in any case, in my opinion, the second in significance after Berg's concerto."[104]

Professor Elena Dolinskaya considers that Roslavets's concerto was a notable event in symphonism,

> The monumental three-movement cycle of the Violin Concerto is notable for the dominant role of analytics. A free world of imagery flows from a mono-thematic conception. Here the chamber environment is unified with a colossal sound, but is meditative in the vitality of ostinato complexes.[105]

Roslavets's exploration of chamber music now extended to one of the neglected string instruments—the Viola Sonata No. 1. Dedicated to Vadim Borisovsky—the violist of the Beethoven Quartet, the sonata was completed on August 6, 1926. There is here a kinship with the First Cello Sonata—the work demonstrates a technique reminiscent of modernism based on the chromatics of the synthetic chord. That was not his first attempt—as there are sketches for another Viola Sonata from 1925—regrettably, it is virtually impossible to reconstruct the music from the rough draft.

A New Sound System

At the First All-Union Conference on "Musical Enlightenment" on March 13, 1926, Roslavets shared the platform with Lebedinsky of RAPM. Roslavets said he was appalled by the products of the "Five Years after October" record factory, whose output consisted primarily of gypsy music and other "vulgarity."[106] Yet he recognized that strict regulation might lose the company its commercial value and put the factory out of business. Furthering the futurist ideology of throwing out the old and bringing in the new, Roslavets proposed getting rid of the Rimsky-Korsakov system in favor of giving preference to "practice over theory" to help cultivate originality. The opposition came from a formidable alliance of nonparty specialists (Konius and Yavorsky) and party members (Vinogradov and Lebedinsky).[107] With this newly founded temporary "coalition" of ASM with RAPM, Roslavets's hopes of a professorship at the Conservatoire proved dead in the water. As a preamble to a possible appointment, Roslavets's candidature was discussed at the Red Professors' factional meeting ensuring that he was never appointed.[108] A vitriolic piece aimed at the composer by Lev Kaltat wrote, "Our task remains that Roslavets should recognize (. . .) the progress of new proletarian music—however, this is hopeless and useless—we have to expose the bourgeois essence of Roslavets and others like him, and isolate them ideologically from Soviet music and limit society from any influence by such 'theoreticians.'"[109] Lunacharsky criticized the ASM composers, "Bourgeois individualism leads to division among creators and to aristocratically distant creativity understood only by particular groups of intellectuals. (. . .) Contemporary music in almost all of Europe has fallen into a collective sin of formalism."[110] Here was the mention of the dreaded sin of "formalism," the name-calling and verbal abuse of which would blight Soviet music for decades.

In 1927, both the RAPM and ORKMID intensified their campaigning against the "contemporary" musicians, who were now accused of formalism. Here the musicologist Marina Lobanova clarifies,

> The futurist poets came under attack for "subjectivism," "intellectualism," "abstruseness" condemning Kruchenykh, Khlebnikov, Mayakovsky, Kamensky, Guro, Chagall, Meyerhold, and in music, Stravinsky, Schoenberg, and Roslavets. Under one headline, the names verify that this was purely about ideological guilt—in one basket, there were representatives of diverse artistic tendencies including those unconnected with constructivism. As proof of which is the apparent heresy of Roslavets in his famous expression about "expressing my own self 'I am' dreaming about new, "unheard of worlds of sound."[111]

Finally, there came a warning from the proletarian musicians: "Constructivism (. . .) in its extreme appearances (intellectualism, formalism, and the fetishism of creativity), is the latest creation of a bygone culture and an appropriate screen for those who oppose the building of a new life."[112]

The campaign continued in the musical press through 1928. In a vitriolic article against several leading modernists, firstly aimed at Mosolov, and Roslavets, Viktor Bely tore into Roslavets because he defended Stravinsky and Schoenberg and hence supported "bourgeois decadence, and cultivated deep ideological roots with decadent Western culture," and for his allegedly belonging to a "left front," and of "contemporary music." Roslavets's prerevolutionary compositions were denounced for their "gaudy futuristic covers," for expressing "a petty-bourgeois reactionary tendency in music, and in his agitational works."[113] All the more forces were thrown against the contemporary musicians, RAPM, Prokoll, and the Academic Commission of the art workers union RABIS denounced the ASM for "producing profoundly decadent works by their members for new revolutionary Russian music and for spreading false information to the West about the ideological face of our Union."[114] Against the volume of such attacks, and when his colleagues were hiding for cover, Roslavets remained unbowed and continued to proselytize his ideas. Roslavets exposed the music of his opponents, pointing out that "the work of the leading Proletkult composers—Dmitry Vasilyev-Buglay, Boris Krassin, Grigory Lobachev, Lev Shulgin—was based on three sources: 'military march-like primitivism,' the elements of *style russe* and—as a somewhat loftier element—the elements of impressionistic harmony."[115]

In his thesis *The New System of the Organization of Sound and New Methods in Teaching Composition* (1926–1927), Roslavets introduces a new definition in the concept of harmony. "There is no definitive, absolute, unified system of music." writing that, "the classical system is but a stage in the process of achieving unorganized musical material in sound. The education of sound extends to more complexity from nonchordal sounds (shrieking complex seventh chords, then nine) to altered chords. As a result of which the movement by Liszt, Wagner, Reger, Richard Strauss, and Scriabin led to breaking classical tonality—it became transformed through its chromatic system and is relative only to tonality. Here is the basic withdrawal to atonality or omnitonality. Debussy broke away from the classical system by departing from the tonal principle."[116]

Here Roslavets's views and approach generally coincide with the Schoenberg school: the dominant historical character of classical tonality, the gradual tonal attainment of the musical scale and withdrawal to a chromatic system. Roslavets reflected that Schoenberg's departure from "nonchordal thinking" started with his *Drei Klavierstücke* (1909), while in Russia, the trend started with Scriabin's *Prometheus* (1910), and in Roslavets's works. Roslavets here categorizes the system of harmony: "The synthetic chord is the principal harmonic six-note new system, including in itself, the main harmonic formula of the classical system (major and minor, augmented and diminished, dominant ninth chord, ninth-chord, diminished seventh chord, different views of 'leading' seventh chords and chords of 'fluctuation,' produced from the main, etc."[117] This seventh chord is required to transform by itself the principle of classicism.

Return to Agitprop

We know that during the Revolution and the Civil War, Roslavets was passionately involved in writing agitational pieces for meetings, events, and demonstrations, and this continued through the 1920s with Roslavets's songs, hymns, and marches. Among the most popular were his *Hymn to the Soviet workers-peasant militia* to words by Vyatich-Berezhnykh (1926), *The Communist International*, and his *Communist Funeral March* (1923).[118] Roslavets's most significant works in this form are the cantata *October* (1927), and the symphonic poem *Komsomoliya* (1928), *The Song about 1905, Songs of the Working Women and Peasant Women, Songs of Revolution*, and *Poems of the Workers*. The cantata *October* marked the tenth anniversary of the October Revolution. The composer shared his thoughts with the media:

> The cantata is for two singers, choir and orchestra and is based on poetry by Vasily Alexandrovsky, Vladimir Kirillov, and Sergey Obradovich. It begins with a four-measure "epigraph" in which three trumpets, in unison, introduce the main triumphant theme bonding together the cantata. There are five movements:
>
> 1) "Uprising" (Alexandrovsky)—orchestral and choral symphonic picture describes the moment of the October uprising, struggle, and victory.
> 2) "25 October" (Kirillov)—solo baritone with orchestra—glorifying the great day of the working-class victory.
> 3) "The spirit sings louder" (Alexandrovsky)—orchestral/choral section reflecting the mood of the victorious masses and the call to all "slumbering" masses, demanding they awake, arise, and "burn the rotten past."
> 4) "Express" (Obradovich)—solo soprano with orchestra,—portraying the express train traveling across the fields, and Komsomol members at the windows espy an old man with a pipe who reflects about the revolution and is called to cast aside his years and march to the sun in your native country, for the world will be built differently.
> 5) Finale—"Greetings to the Comintern" performed by both soloists, choir, and orchestra. The call of the Russian proletariat to everyone, "the young in heart," glorifies the "Hammer and World Sovnarkom" [Soviet government] and struggle on earth for the "sun of universal love."
>
> The culmination in the finale is embodied by an exhilarating degree of tension and bombast. In the cantata, the composer departs from his customary "orchestration" as he says the writing attempts to create monumentalism in the "decorative" style intended to achieve maximum emotional force.[119]

The opening movement takes the form of a *sonata-allegro*, while the third movement is a funereal march, and the second and fourth movements are a *march* and a *scherzo*. The work is in the style of agitprop, with little lyricism or romanticism; the introduction of soloists is a kind of oratorical declamation in an exhortative manner. The fresco style lacks detail and objectivity in structure, yet harmonizes with the spirit of the agitational art of the postrevolutionary period which sought a rhetorical and allegorical nature clear in presenting both ideology and symbolism. The first movement *Uprising*, follows the poster art form which is underscored by developing to a rhetorical argument, using the keynote phrase—"We raze the old, and destroy it." A fanfare accompanies this leitmotif phrase—and acts as a call sign throughout—of the cantata. The choral recitative gradually becomes a driven ostinato supporting the tension for the culmination in the celebratory, victorious C major. In the second movement, *25 October* there is an allegorical choral imagery, and a march-recitative develops its theme in a generally symbolic spirit. In the third section, *The spirit singing louder* is in the form of a montage with a revolutionary narrative unified by the leitmotif and reprise. The fourth movement fulfills the role of a dramatic pause in ostinato form portraying movement. The contrast between the other sections creates a chamber-like ensemble (without contra-bassoon, trombones, and trumpet), with the enlightened voice of the mezzo-soprano. The hint of the leitmotif presages the denouement of the finale and psychologically prepares the listeners. In the finale, following the proclamation of the main idea, there begins a lapidary march with a clear tonality in C major (a kinship with his graduation piece *Heaven and Earth*), and introducing a double fugue into the exposition. The cantata *October* was written in May–August 1927, and premiered at the Hall of Columns in Moscow on December 4. The concert also billed Shostakovich's Second Symphony *To October*, Mosolov's *The Foundry*, and Polovinkin's *Prologue*.[120]

In 1927, Roslavets's position in Soviet music was positively evaluated by *Pravda*, "His music . . . is a call to the creative recognition of new laws in musical thought, original, clear and exact systems of musical organization (. . .) of vitally inspired success supplemented by precious innovations."[121] This compelling appraisal was not shared by the RAPM press, where Roslavets was dismissed as "decadent," and a "genuinely bourgeois ideologist."[122] These two contradictory opinions reveal how differently his music was judged and divided opinion. The RAPM critic Semyon Korev found the stylistic change of the cantata largely welcome, yet expressed reservations,

> The *October* cantata signals a positive and happy stage of Roslavets' career, and to some extent, a watershed. The composer approached the cantata with the accrued achievements of his creativity and with all his bourgeois philistinism. He expressed all the positive traits and the revolutionary artistic capability in his creativity. But at the same time, Roslavets discards his past by embarking along

the path of the mass composer. This work does not suffer from the main shortcomings of the composer's earlier music, which is an unforgivable barrier (in performance). The *October* cantata is quite immediate and populist. There is no trace of contrivance in the cantata's character but Roslavets perhaps went too far in the other path—of emotionalism. But the consequence of this hyperbole is in the cantata's great impact, freshness, and popular appeal. Above and beyond, of all the October musical works, this cantata is most appropriate for a jubilee: it is solemn without pomposity and colorfully uplifting, without being pretentious.[123]

Other critics applauded Roslavets for abandoning his customary "constructivist principles" in favor of a more accessible style.[124] This was the highest-profile event of the tenth anniversary happenings, and the apogee of the ASM's promotion of over one hundred concerts in the Soviet capital. This ostensible success was quickly met with a terrible reversal.

NOTES

1. Roslavets, "O sebye i svoim tvorchestva," *Sovremennaya Muzyka*, V. 1924, 137.
2. Lobanova, Marina, *Nikolay Roslavets i kultura evo vremeni*, Moscow: Petroglif, 2011, 46.
3. Katanyan, *V. Mayakovsky—Khronika zhizni i deyatelnosti*, Moscow, 1985, 127.
4. Lobanova, *Nikolay Roslavets i kultura evo vremeni*, Moscow: Petroglif, 2011, 279–280.
5. Labas, A., "Vospominaniya," Rukopis. Arkhiv A.A. Labas.
6. RGALI, f. 2659, op, 1, ed. kh. 91, 1–2.
7. GTG, f. 25, ed. kh. 9, l. 22.
8. Podmarkova, L. A., *N. A. Roslavets—kompositor, pedagog, obshestvenniy deyatel*, Elets, 2003.
9. RGALI, f. 2659, op, 1, ed. kh. 89, l. 28–29; ed. kh. 95, l. 4 ob.
10. *Razgon*, Ovrutsky L. *Terror ugnettennikh i terror pobeditelei*, Rodina, No. 5, 1990, 37.
11. Roslavets (manuscript), Frankfurt-am-Main, 1997, *Roslawetz und Kultur und seiner zeit*, 40.
12. Belodubrovsky, "Nash zemlyak," *Sovetskaya Muzika*, No. 5, 1989, 105.
13. Lobanova, Marina, *Nikolay Roslavets i kultura evo vremeni*, Moscow: Petroglif, 2011, 279.
14. Lobanova, Marina, *Nikolay Roslavets i kultura evo vremeni*, Moscow: Petroglif, 2011, 286.
15. Vlasova, E.S., *1948 god v sovetskoy muzyki*, Moscow: 21 Classika, 2010, 29.

16. Severina, I., "Novaya simfoniya Nikolaya Roslavetsa," *Rossiskaya Muzykalnaya Gazeta*, 2002, Nr. 2, 8.
17. RGALI, f. 2009, op. 1, ed. kh. 122, l. 27.
18. Roslavets, "Otchet o rabote Lekstionno-repertuarno-izdatelskoy sektsii I konzertnovo podotdela muzykanovo otdela Moskovskoy proletkulta," ed. S.R. Stepanova, *Muzykalnaya zhizni Moskvy v pervye gody posle Oktyabya 1917–1920. Khronika, dokumenty, materialy*, Moscow: Muzyka, 1972, 290.
19. RGALI, f. 2659, op, 1, ed. kh. 92, l.1.
20. Braudo, Yevgeny, "Organizator zvuk," *Vestnik rabotnikov iskusstsv*, 1925, No. 2, 14.
21. RGALI, f. 2659, op. 1, ed. kh. 96, l.1.
22. Vlasova, E.S., *1948 god v sovetskoy muziki*, Moscow: 21 Classika, 2010, 29.
23. Lobanova, Marina, *Nikolay Roslavets i kultura evo vremeni*, Moscow: Petroglif, 2011, 330.
24. Myaskovsky, Nikolay, "Na konzertakh sovremennoy muziki," *Muzyka*, 230.
25. Lobanova, Marina, *Nikolay Roslavets i kultura evo vremeni*, Moscow: Petroglif, 2011, 320.
26. Lobanova, Marina, *Nikolay Roslavets i kultura evo vremeni*, Moscow: Petroglif, 2011, 322.
27. RGALI. f.2659. op. 1. Ed. chr. 53. L. 4.
28. G.Ts.M.M.K. F. 373. Ed. chr. 11. L.13.
29. Letter of reference from Professor Levenstein, RGALI, f. 2659, op. 1, ed. kh. 98, l.1.
30. "Sud and operetkoy," *Teatralny Izvestiya*. No. 2, 1921, October 13, 1921, 3.
31. Schillinger, I.M., "Zapiski kompozitora, Novaya era muziki," *Teatralny Izvestiya*. No. 4, 1922, 23-24/1/1922, 3–4.
32. *Khudozhestvennii Mysl*, No. 1, 1922, February 18–25, 1922, 11–12.
33. *Khudozhestvennii Mysl*, No. 5, 1922, March 18–25, 1922, 21.
34. "Personalia," *K Novym Beregam*, No. 1, April 1923, 55–56.
35. Lobanova, Marina, *Nikolay Roslavets i kultura evo vremeni*, Moscow: Petroglif, 2011, 326.
36. RGALI, f.2659. op. 1. Chr. 28. l, 20 ob.
37. Myaskovsky, "Na konzertakh sovremennoy muziki," *Muzykalnya kultura*, No. 1, 1924, 66–67.
38. Lobanova, Marina, *Nikolay Roslavets i kultura evo vremeni*, Moscow: Petroglif, 2011, 254.
39. RGALI. f.2759. op. 1. Ed. khr. 99. L. 27.
40. Braudo, Yevgeny, "Avtorskii vecher N. Roslavetsa," *Izvestiya*, February 17, 1926.
41. Sabaneyev, Leonid, "Russkiye kompozitori, II, Nikolay Roslavets," *Parizhkii Vestnik*, 1926, III, 31.
42. RGALI, f.2659. op. 1. Ed. khr. 72. l. 7.
43. Lobanova, Marina, *Nikolay Roslavets i kultura evo vremeni*, Moscow: Petroglif, 2011, 278.

44. Lobanova, Marina, *Nikolay Roslavets i kultura evo vremeni*, Moscow: Petroglif, 2011, 44–45.
45. Glavlit, RGALI, f. 2030, 1060.
46. Roslavets, "Sem let Oktyabrya v muzyke," *Muzykalnaya Kultura*, No. 3, 1924, 182.
47. Edmunds, Neil, *The Soviet Proletarian Music Movement*, Oxford: Lang, 2000, 27–28.
48. Roslavets, "Sem let Oktyabrya v muzyke," *Muzykalnaya Kultura*, No. 3, 1924, 184–186.
49. Ferenc, Anna, "Reclaiming Roslavets: the troubled life of a Russian Pioneer," *Tempo*, No. 182, 1992, 8.
50. Schwartz, Boris, *Music and Musical Life in Soviet Russia 1917–1982*, Indiana UP, 1983, 96.
51. Keldysh, Yuri, Sovetskoye Muzykalnoye stroitelstvo v pervye gody posle Oktyabrya, *Istorii muzyki narodov SSSR.*, 1970. T. 1, 57.
52. *Muzykalnaya Nov*, No. 10, 1924, 5.
53. Roslavets to Slavinsky, RGALI. f. 2659. Op. 1. Ed.khr. 80. L. 1–6.
54. Roslavets, *Muzikalnaya Kultura*, No. 1, 1924, 50.
55. Roslavets, "Dialektikus, O Reaktionnom i Progressivnom v Muzyka," *Muzykalnaya Kultura*, No. 1, 1924, 48–49.
56. "Nashi zadachi," *Muzykalnaya Kultura*, 1(1924), 3–4.
57. Roslavets, "O sebye i svoim tvorchestve," *Sovremennaya Muzyka*, V. 1924, 138.
58. Volkogonov, Dmitry, *Trotsky: the eternal revolutionary*, London: HarperCollins, 1997, 52.
59. Marx, Karl, *The Holy Family*, Moscow: International Publishers, 1956.
60. Lobanova, Marina, *Nikolay Roslavets i kultura evo vremeni*, Petroglif, Moscow, 2011, 111.
61. Teplov, Pyotr. "Nash Zemlyak," Mark Belodubrovsky, *Sovetskaya Muzyka*, No. 5, 105.
62. Tsenovsky, A. "Operny teatr," *Muzykalnaya Nov*, No. 9, 1924, 23.
63. Walker, *Music and Soviet Power 1917–1932*, London: Boydell, 2017, 107.
64. Walker, *Music and Soviet Power 1917–1932*, London: Boydell, 2017, 107.
65. Veprik to Bryusova, RGALI, f.2444, op. 2, e.kh. 67, ll, 4–5.
66. Edmunds, Neil, *The Soviet Proletarian Music Movement*, Oxford: Peter Lang, 2000, 30.
67. Derzhanovsky to Asafyev, December 16–17, 1924, RGALI, F. 2658, OP. 1, E.KH. 542, L.8.
68. Lebedinsky, "Otchet o deyatelnosti soveta Associatsii proletarskikh muzykantov, borbe za proletarskoy muzyki i dalneishikh zadacha RAPMa," pt. 1, *Proletarsky Muzykant*, No. 3–4, 10.
69. Lebedinsky, "Otchet o deyatelnosti soveta Associatsii proletarskikh muzykantov, borbe za proletarskoy muzyki i dalneishikh zadacha RAPMa," pt. 1, *Proletarsky Muzykant*, No. 3–4, 10.
70. Ferenc, Anna, "Reclaiming Roslavets: the troubled life of a Russian Pioneer," *Tempo*, No. 182, 1992, 9.

71. Lebedinsky, Lev, "Otchet o deyatelnosti soveta Associatsii proletarskikh muzykantov, borbe za proletarskoy muzyki i dalneishikh zadacha RAPMa," pt. 1, *Proletarsky Muzykant*, No. 3–4, 10.

72. Sabaneyev, *Muzyka v Klube*, (Moscow), 1926, 9.

73. Walker, *Music and Soviet Power 1917–1932*, London: Boydell, 2017, 86.

74. Hakobian, Leon, *Music in the Soviet Era 1917–1991*, London: Routledge, 2017, 28.

75. Nelson, Amy, *Music for the Revolution: Musicians and Power in Early Soviet Russia*, Pennsylvania UP, 2004, 93.

76. Tomoff, Kirill, *Creative Union: The Professional Organization of Soviet Composers 1939–1953*, Ithaca, NY: Cornell UP, 2006, 17.

77. Belyaev, V., 'Muzykalnoye vystavki,' *Muzykalnya kultura*, No. 1, 1924, 68.

78. Roslavets, Nikolay, *Sovremennaya Muzika*, 1924.

79. RGALI, f. 2009, op. 1, ed.khr.27, l. 29.

80. Vlasova, E.S., *1948 god v sovetskoi muzike*. Moscow: Klassika, 2010, 34.

81. Sabaneyev, "Muzika posle Oktyabya," *Rabotnik prosveshcheniya*, 1926, 29.

82. Kovalev letter to Tyuneyev, July 31, 1924, Svetlana Martynova, "Pavel Lamm v tyurmakh I sslykhakh: Po stranitsam Vospominanii O. P. Lamm," *Trudy Muzeya Muzykalnoye Kulturi: Almanakh*, vol. 2, Moscow, GTSMMK, 2003, 112–115.

83. RGALI, f.2659, op. 1, ed. khr. 100.

84. Roslavets, "O sebye i svoim tvorchestve," *Sovremennaya Muzyka*, V. 1924, 136.

85. Roslavets, *Muzykalnaya Kultura*, 1924, 3.

86. "Khorovaya rabota v Soyuz tekstilshikov," *Muzyka i Revolution*, 1, 1926, 37.

87. Nelson, Amy, *Music for the Revolution: Musicians and Power in Early Soviet Russia*, Pennsylvania UP, 2004, 63–65.

88. Edmunds, Neil, *The Soviet Proletarian Music Movement*, Oxford: Lang, 2000, 306.

89. Roslavets, "Beglym ognem," *Muzykalnaya Kultura*, 1924, 8, 13–17.

90. Nelson, Amy, *Music for the Revolution: Musicians and Power in Early Soviet Russia*, Pennsylvania UP, 2004, 91.

91. Ferenc, Anna, "Music in the Socialist State," ed. Neil Edmunds, *Soviet Music and Society*, London: Routledge, 2009, 11.

92. Roslavets, Nikolay, "Nikolay Roslavets," *Sovremennaya Muzyka*, 2, 1924, 35.

93. Schwartz, Boris, *Music and Musical Life in Soviet Russia 1917–1982*, Bloomington: Indiana UP, 1983, 9.

94. Stites, Richard, "Russian Popular Music to 1953," ed. Neil Edmunds, *Soviet Music and Society under Lenin and Stalin*, London: Routledge, 2009, 21.

95. Osnovy Khudozhestvennii Obrazovaniya (speech by Lunacharsky at the opening of a methodical meeting on art education April 6, 1925/*Muzykalnoye obrazovaniye*, No. 1–2, 1926, 14.

96. Lobanova, Marina, *Nikolay Roslavets i kultura evo vremeni*, Moscow: Petroglif, 2011, 333.

97. RGALI. f. 2659. op. 1. Ed. chr. 45.

98. *Sovremmennaya Muzika*, vypusk 5., M. 1924, 139.
99. RGALI, f.2659. op. 1. ed. chr.29.
100. *Sovremennaya Muzika*, No. 7, 44.
101. RGALI, f. 2659, op. 1, ed. kh. 86.
102. Lobanova, "Nakhodki," *Sovetskaya Muzika*, No. 10, 1989, 32.
103. RGALI, f.653, op. 14, ed.khr. 14.
104. Denisov, Edison, "Ne lyublyu formalnoye iskusstsvo," *Sovetskaya Muzika*, No. 12, 1989, 18.
105. Dolinskaya, Elena, Ed. Tarakanov, *Istoriya Sovremennoy Otechestvennoy Muzyki*, vypusk 1, 1917–1941, Moscow, 1993, 175–176.
106. GARF f.298, op. 1, d.127, ll.114–114ob.
107. RGALI, f.658, op. 6, d.55, ll.1–8.
108. RGALI, f.2009, op. 1, ed. Kh. 27, 1.15.
109. Kaltat, Lev., *O podlinno-burzhasnoi ideologii gr. Roslavetsa*, 1926, 34, 42, 37.
110. "Nash Muzykalnyy front," *Materialy Vserossiskaya muzykalnoy konferentsii*, 19, 24.
111. Lobanova, Marina, *Nikolay Roslavets i kultura evo vremeni*, Moscow: Petroglif, 2011, 100.
112. E.M., "Poslednee slovo otzhivayuschey kultury," *Muzyka i revolutsiya*, No. 9, 1927, 4–6.
113. Bely, Viktor, "Levaya fraza o muzykalnoy reaktsii," *Muzykalnaya obrazovaniye*, No. 1, 1928, 43–47.
114. "Pisma v redaktsiyu," *Muzykalnaya obrazovaniye*, No. 2, 1928, 38–39.
115. Roslavets, Nikolay, "O pseudo-proletarskoy muzike," *Na putyakh iskusstva*, Moscow, Proletkult, 1926, 187.
116. RSGALI, f. 2659, op. 1, ed.khr. 72, l. 6.
117. RSGALI, f. 2659, op. 1, ed.khr. 72, l. 6.
118. RGALI, f.2659, op. 1, ed.khr. 55, l. 1–4.
119. N. "Kantata Oktyabr," *Rabis*, November 22, 1927, No. 45 (45). 11.
120. Drozdov, A., "Simfonicheskoye konzert GAKhN," *Muzika i Revolutsiya*, No. 12, 1927, 29.
121. *Pravda*, November 8, 1927.
122. Kaltat, Lev, "O podlinno-burzhasnoi ideologii gr. Roslavetsa," *Muzykalnaya Obrazovaniye*, 1927, 3–4.
123. Korev, Semyon, "Sovetskaya simfonicheskaya muzyka: jubilniye Oktyabrsiye kontserti," *Sovetskoye Iskusstvo*, No. 7, 1927, 51–52.
124. A.B., "Cantata N. Roslavetsa Oktyabr," *Sovetskaya Muzyka*, 24, 1927, 39, 40–43.

Chapter 3

The Prisoner of Tashkent

In March 1927, Roslavets made his only known trip outside the USSR when he embarked on a Black Sea cruise from Odesa to Constantinople and Athens.[1] Curiously, the composer's foreign travel was limited because his works were now successfully published and performed in Europe, America, and elsewhere. The voyage was not an idle one for he worked on a new chamber piece. The Piano Trio No. 4 is framed in four movements—the accents of the first theme from the first movement are strongly rhythmic by continuing exploration of the synthetic chord.[2] Lobanova discovered the mistakenly attributed score for a Violin Concerto as parts for the Fourth Piano Trio, while the first movement was discovered elsewhere.[3] Roslavets adopts a four-movement structure with the opening movement shifting to a second *attaca*. The Fourth Piano Trio employs an expanded harmonic technique founded on synthetic chord chromatics in traditional structures of triads and absolute tonality. The Fifth Piano Trio is mentioned in Roslavets's catalog; however, it appears that this piece shares a fate with other abandoned pieces.[4]

Sabaneyev wrote that Roslavets's early compositions "were colored in ultra-modernistic hues, with bold, complex harmonies in which musicians could discover nothing at first but wild cacophony. At that time, his work met with little sympathy, and somehow he wasn't part of any composers group of the musical world of the time."[5] This rather disingenuous statement contradicts his previous opinions and tells us more perhaps about Sabaneyev. We already know of Roslavets's friendship with Myaskovsky and Derzhanovsky and other Moscow contemporary composers from the 1910s and 1920s, and of course with the futurists. However, Sabaneyev here is correct in that "Roslavets finally had to make some concessions, and his revolutionary compositions, written for workmen's clubs, differ strongly from his serious compositions." Sabaneyev called him "a miniaturist in tonal matter; like both Scriabin, and Schoenberg, he lovingly writes out the minutest details, the only thing where his later compositions differ from his earlier ones is a greater perfection of elaboration, an ever-growing academic formalism and a striving for precision, harmoniousness and abstract perfection."[6]

As arguably the most flamboyant and controversial of the modernists, and the only one who dared oppose the proletarian musicians, few were surprised that Roslavets's *October* was criticized by the RAPM hacks.[7] Similarly, the ORKiMD expected that revolutionary music should be "strong-willed, dynamic, and easily understood."[8] Certainly, in 1927, the pressure on Roslavets and other modernists to reform was intensified by an editorial in *Music and Revolution.* "There is perceived in our musical life a treacherous leaning to evaluate works of art exclusively based on their talent, originality, and vibrant individuality."[9]

On March 8, 1928, the stark differences within Soviet music emerged at the Glaviskustsvo Conference at which Roslavets expressed his views on the current state of the musical theater. His speech reprised his ideas of the futurists before the revolution by throwing away old traditions and starting everything anew,

> The arts of today are already beginning to resemble something like a retirement home in its "dead" hours. To be at the opera for a couple of hours or somewhere like this—is a "dead" hour, just like retirement homes. There have appeared religious tendencies that didn't exist three years ago. You, yourselves, are aware of the colossal success of *Kitezh* by Rimsky-Korsakov. What has not been said about this brilliant music, that this is "wonderful," and everything representative of that "brilliant music" . . . this opera has appeared now, not three years ago, but today, and bears witness to the mysticism, and diverse religious leanings that are reappearing in our everyday life. . . .
>
> To strengthen our theatrical-musical front and the so-called genuine Soviet play with "ideology," must reflect the ideology of today. There must be a bitter struggle against the reaction that I have described, and should strike audaciously to (. . .) struggle against today's reactionaries. And by what means? There must be a revolution from above—you can't do just anything—a revolution from below is inconceivable. . . . Do the state and party have the methods and power to embark on this struggle? I think that after ten years of experience, it has. (. . .) By unleashing the struggle, do we need to keep the old opera? I would say not. I think that the operatic form is more uncertain . . . and it isn't indispensable. What form will be positive here? I believe that in this searching—a new creative format will come."[10]

Roslavets's readiness to express his views distanced himself from the ASM members, most of whom were unwilling to engage in debate with the proletarian musicians. Despite raising the issue of closing opera theaters and banishing the so-called reactionary repertoire, nothing Roslavets said made any difference. Roslavets's espousing of the futurist project of overthrowing old traditions was not shared by his colleagues in the ASM, and neither were they by the RAPM or ORKiMD. The attacks in the 1920s, by RAPM, were intended to grasp total control of the concert halls and theaters, and of repertoire, and ultimately were a rehearsal for the Zhdanov affair in 1948, in which the terminology of "cosmopolitanism" and accusations of "profound, ideological affinity with decadent, Western culture" were reprised.[11] The RAPM and ORKiMD wanted an exclusivity of power in Soviet culture, and for a simplified musical language easily accessible to the masses. The scholar Ekaterina Vlasova considers that neither his unimpeachable class origins, nor his "revolutionary public statements, and his forced assimilation of the mass song could save him from the worst and harshest criticism."[12]

AGITPROP MUSIC

Roslavets's most ambitious piece after his cantata *October* was the symphonic poem *Komsomoliya* (1928) marking the tenth anniversary of the Young Communist League (Komsomol). The work has a harmonic structure based on the "synthetic chord," serving to neutralize post-romanticism. *Komsomoliya* is extraordinary not only for its "experimentalism" but also for the unusually large orchestra.[13] "The leitmotif appears as a fervent signal on the trumpet, in the cornet trumpets' bright timbre, and the ringing colors of the whole orchestra."[14] In the dominant is the almost kaleidoscopic microthematic movement of its energetic marches, presenting diverse blocks of colors in sound patterns, and clusters.

Komsomoliya seeks to invoke both the imagery and spirit of the mass demonstrations in the first decades of Soviet power. It seemed as if the perfection, finality, and inner organism, and the montage of autonomous, selflessly rich sound clusters evoked Pavel Filonov's creations. Roslavets's opponents were not impressed however, and responded by sarcastically suggesting an association with Nietzsche in that Roslavets is trying to be a "superman, interested in nobody and uninteresting to anybody."[15] No longer was Roslavets referred to as "Comrade" but addressed "Mister" or simply "Citizen." This was an extraordinary nuance as if placing Roslavets outside Soviet life and of public discourse. This was only the beginning of a sharply renewed campaign that would culminate in a tragedy that few could have prophesied.

Many agitprop compositions by Roslavets celebrate the festivals of the Soviet calendar; the workers' songs—*Poems of the Working Profession*

(1924–1928)—were performed widely. The cycle includes *The Weaver* for female voice and piano, based on a text by S. Litkovsky, in a similar vein is *The Seamstress* to words by G. Korenev, while *The Miller* is based on the poem by A. Shatalov for choir with piano accompaniment, as is *The Turner* from a text by Y. Tverdov.[16] As Lobanova cites, these all "resemble allegorical social masks akin to the personages depicted in the 'mass actions' and the 'Window of ROSTA' in which amateur theater is created, characterizing the new world of revolutionary imagery."[17] In a similar mood and style is Roslavets's chorus—*The Workers Fortress* (1926), based on a text by A. Pomorsky.

The events of 1905 were the subject of a state commission to theaters in Moscow and Leningrad to mark the twentieth anniversary of the first Russian revolution, which motivated the compositions by Korchmarev, Krasev, Myaskovsky, and Roslavets.[18] *Bloody Sunday*, marking the 1905 slaughter of St. Petersburg demonstrators, was realized in Roslavets's highly praised *Songs of the Year 1905* (1925). From a text by A. Andreyev—the rhetoric of revolution permeates *The Last Wonder*, by invoking marching songs, funereal imagery, and oratorical pathos. *The Guns Have Fallen Silent* from Tarasov's poem, together with *Mother and Son* from G. Galin, shares a clear tonality in rhythm and declamation.

Regardless of Roslavets's socialist realist music, the RAPM journal *Musical Education* was not in any way convinced but wanted still more of it,

> Roslavets' compositions (*The Last Wonder* and *The Guns have Fallen Silent*) (. . .) prove that simplicity doesn't signify a decline in standards and that the best results are achieved by the most modest means. We need great symphonies, musical dramas, and perhaps new forms of music which can be both modern in form, and content, and take music forward, we can't forget that most of our auditoriums are full of workers and peasants unprepared for complex forms but want genuine art. (. . .) Roslavets' two vocal compositions approach this idiom by creating music for the masses and this must greatly hearten the consciousness of any contemporary musician. (. . .) Should the artistry be transformed and accustomed to the social demands of the present-day?[19]

A popular theme was the Decembrist revolt suppressed by Tsar Nikolay I in 1825 which involved writers and members of the aristocracy. Roslavets's *The Decembrists* use settings from Pushkin's *Epistle to Siberia* and the Decembrist poet Odoyevsky's *Reply to the Epistle to Siberia* in a diptych with a distinctly laconic bravura.[20] Roslavets assumes a romantic ballade manner and a hymnic tone. The emotional intensity and powerful sequence of keywords are subject to a reserved conveying of the logic and semantics of the poems.

Roslavets's *Songs of the Working and Peasant Girls* (1925–1926) for amateur or semiprofessional workplace choirs was widely popular. Interestingly, this theme was contemporaneously advanced in Germany by Schoenberg's pupil Hanns Eisler and by Paul Hindemith writing for workers' choruses. Roslavets's other works include Dorogoichenko's *Lullaby Song* for voice and piano and *The Miller* for mixed choir from S. Dolnykova, and the *Song about the Red Banner* for a female chorus from A. Bogdanov's poem.[21] The Soviet hero is represented in his *Songs of the Revolution* cycle (1921–1926), *Flowers of Metal* based on M. Gerasimov is unfinished, however. Roslavets' setting of *In the Fields* by P. Oreshin, *October* to S. Rodov, the refrain *The Smith* from a poem by S. Obradovich, *On the First of May* again has Oreshin's poetry while Bryusov's translation of the Flemish writer Emil Verhaeren's poem *Uprising* are all in the spirit of poster art.[22] These songs fluctuated between tonality and synthetic chord technique, indeed Roslavets's modernism didn't hinder him in reaching a wider audience at all, for the synthetic chord technique proved popular among workers. There were other songs akin to light stage songs using words by P. Druzhinin *The Wife's Share*, and *Skates* from lyrics by A. Shiryavets (1929).

Several of Roslavets's revolutionary songs managed to outlive their author through to the final years of Soviet power. Roslavets's commission in honor of the Civil War hero Kliment Voroshilov (1930) is a celebratory march for military band,[23] and the arrangement for Mayakovsky's *Give Us!* (1930) is perhaps the most popular of all his works.[24] Of great popularity among workers' clubs was the Komsomol march *Knock the Door* in an arrangement for the poem by I. Utkin and the two-part chorus *The Drum* with balalaikas and piano (1930).

Roslavets's Modernism

The concept of "constructivism" influenced many artists, musicians, and writers of this period. The artist Pavel Favorsky touched on the concept of space and time, construction, and composition. As we know, from his setting for Kamensky's futurist *Flight* composed before the revolution, Roslavets was fascinated by the "urban song" and the propelling movement of engines; notably, the fourth section of his cantata *October* characterizes locomotion. This theme was similarly invoked in *Pacific 231* by Honegger and Mosolov's *The Foundry*, and the more ambiguous Arseny Avraamov's *Symphony of Horns* (1922). Another work in this idiom of machines and motion is the symphonic poem by Roslavets based on a text by Zharov—*The Black City* (1929). Roslavets gives its premiere as taking place in Leningrad in the spring of 1930; however, the score has completely disappeared.[25]

The style of Prokofiev and Stravinsky was alien to Roslavets, as he writes that, "There is no break in the line of musical development in my work, in the synthetic system there is—classicism, romanticism, impressionism, and the polytonalism systems."[26] For Roslavets - the models were Beethoven- as discussed in his thesis- "Back to Beethoven." Roslavets also was skeptical to Debussy believing that he lacked substance and that his music only gives the impression of timbre and beauty.[27]

Nevertheless, despite disagreements with some of his colleagues in the ASM, Viktor Belyaev continued writing that Roslavets was "resolute and at the highest level in the rich and cherished creative work" through "organizing tonal methodology and creatively founding elements of sound."[28] If he had criticism for some of the European modernists, in his important review of Schoenberg's *Pierrot Lunaire*, Roslavets believed that the Austrian was "under the banner of constructivism," a "revolutionary," and "instead of a merging together, a conflict has developed in which the collision of two dissimilar creative individualities struggle for the image of art."[29] Here Roslavets develops upon his argument,

> The image of Pierrot portrayed in Schoenberg's music is no longer the translucent Pierrot with his tender sighs in which one wonders at an affinity with the fragile harmonies of Debussy, but, this is the Pierrot of "metal and concrete," the child of the modern industrial giant city—unrecognized by mankind—for this is a new Pierrot, in whose sighs, the rasp of metal is heard, along with the roar of propellers, and the noise of automobile sirens. The Pierrot of Schoenberg is indeed breaking toward a positive result, but the source of positive energy seems here not to be the moon, but an enormous electric propeller.

In exploring the contradictions in Schoenberg's *Pierrot Lunaire* and the divisions between old and new, Roslavets found an incongruity in his writing between the old impressionism and new-fangled industrial rhythms. "The 'innovator-traditionalist' of Schoenberg found a true ally in the 'decadent-futurist' Roslavets."[30] In another essay, Roslavets was categorical in writing about new trends in Soviet music,

> We are the smiths of new living forms, and realists, we are the people of the earth standing firm and looking keenly at the future through the prism of the will, of reason and science. According to our outlook and our psychology, we are molding our culture. We know that it is still young and imperfect, as are we ourselves. Let this be! Maturity and perfection will certainly come in its own time—the future is ours![31]

Political Disputes

In his role as the political editor of Glavrepertkom, Roslavets attended a meeting in June 1929 on the future of music that was arranged by the Agitprop

Department at the CC VKP. The chair of the discussion was the former journalist, diplomat, and Prokoll activist, Platon Kerzhentsev (1881–1940).[32] This conference embraced all factions in Soviet culture. Vlasova here discusses Roslavets's political position at this time,

> (his) social and aesthetic views were distinguished by extreme radicalism. In the documents of Glavrepertkom of the 1920s, the eminent signature of Roslavets (the initial and first letters of his surname) as political editor featured on many orders, letters, and statements, none of which add anything to the starry-eyed niceties of the composer's biography. At the above-mentioned meeting, he along with E. Braudo, S. Korev, and I. Novikov—as members of the working presidium—each spoke from the main report ("On the tasks and forms of the stage") and were categorical in their views and lively in the debate.[33]

Regardless of the disparagement of contemporary musicians, it is worth mentioning that the Commissar for Enlightenment Lunacharsky flagged up that some sort of compromise might be in the air. "There continues to be an accepted fraternal exchange of opinions, and a common position is progressively evolving."[34] However, Lunacharsky willfully ignored the intensity of the debates and attacks on the ASM composers. Among others present were activists from the RAPM—Gorodinsky, Vinogradov, Rabinovich, Lebedinsky, and Chelyapov from the ASM. Speaking on the most disturbing factors in Soviet music, Roslavets stated: "There is in the short term a deficit in musical cadres, and we cannot move forward without resolving this problem."[35] Among the items discussed were repertoire policy and many of the agreed positions were shared by Roslavets. However, a more reflective opinion comes from Vlasova: "It would be more accurate to state that Roslavets expressed not his radical judgment about the correct existence of traditional genres of opera and ballet, but simply declared the position at the time of his leadership."[36]

Following the launch of the Cultural Revolution in 1928 by the VKP(b), many productions of Soviet and Western music were postponed or canceled, including at the Bolshoi Theater of Prokofiev's ballet *L' pac d'acier*, the opera *The Nose* by Shostakovich, and the ballet *The Four Ages of Moscow* by Polovinkin, Mosolov, Shostakovich, and Alexandrov, and Hindemith's chamber opera *Neues vom Tage*. These revocations were engineered by the RAPM members who dominated the arts councils of the leading Soviet theaters. Lebedinsky proudly documented his contribution,

> We attempted to influence, one way or another, the work of the various commissions which served the Bolshoi Theater linked with the reactionary group of artists, musicians, and directors, and most recently we responded to events at

the Bolshoi Theater (a press campaign) through *Soviet Art*. . . . In regard to the contemporary crowd, again in the arguments expressed through *On the Literary Post* we gave our view on a whole number of musically decadent contemporary composers.[37]

One other RAPM front-runner, the musicologist Yuri Keldysh espoused. "Prokofiev's ballet (*L'pac d'acier*) certainly has nothing in common with our revolution, and if it somehow reflects upon it, shows hostility in a somewhat outrageous manner, it's cheap, and conspires against the revolution."[38] During the meeting, the works of modernists such as Prokofiev, Krenek, Schillinger, Shreker, and Roslavets were denounced as being "ideologically alien" from "class enemies."[39] The real models of proletarian music, in Marian Koval's opinion, were Viktor Bely, Alexander Davidenko, and Boris Shekhter (the RAPM composers). Unhappily, for Roslavets and the ASM, the Commissar of Enlightenment Anatoly Lunacharsky shared this view. "Bourgeois individualism leads to a rift between the creator and aristocratically secure creativity, which is understood only by different groups of the intelligentsia."[40] The solitary voice in opposition at the conference was that of Nikolay Roslavets.[41] Of course, we know that Lunacharsky was one of the founders of Proletkult, which promoted proletarian art and culture; hence, it is clear he would have little sympathy for the modernists.

The RAPM lexicon was malicious in hugely exaggerating their opponents' perceived threat—"reactionary priest-black-hundreds," "Menshevik-saboteurs," and using terms like "fascists" and "priest's groupings" were typical in attacking the Moscow Conservatoire and the Soviet Philharmonic Society (SOPHIL).[42] A performance of Respighi's *The Pines of Rome* upset Lebedinsky so much that he complained that "this march seems like the finale of the whole work, and an apotheosis of Fascism."[43] Those deemed as "fascists" included all émigrés and white guards, and "the creativity of Prokofiev, one must consider his works then, as the works of a fascist." Stravinsky was denounced as "a mystic" bearing "an affinity with the fascists."[44]

In a leader of the RAPM paper *Music and the Revolution*, the ultra-left musicians attempted to link musical constructivism and abstruse futurists with foxtrot music. "Any sort of abstruse futurism doesn't express anything; it represents its open declaration that we shall take some mixture of strange sounds without any inner order. This is undoubtedly the most absurd position which has been taken by this new art." Mayakovsky was sharply criticized for his satires *The Bedbug* and *The Bathhouse* staged at Meyerhold's theater. In 1928, he was rejected by the proletarian writers as a "fellow-traveler," rather than a great working-class writer. Ultimately, Mayakovsky relented and joined the proletarian RAPP; however perhaps in shame, he resigned before his tragic suicide in 1930. The futurists had lost traction because many of their ideas and slogans had been embraced by the Soviet cultural apparatus. Its constructivist projects were assumed by the Union of Real Art (OBERIU) in 1928 by Daniil Kharms and Alexander Vvedensky who tried to revive futurism by presentations at universities and theaters. Kharm's satirical play *Elizabeth Bam* proved a forerunner (albeit picking up from Matyushin's *Victory over the Sun*) of the "Theater of the Absurd." Shostakovich dedicated his First Symphony to Kharms. The unrepentant Suprematist Malevich encouraged them to "Go and stop progress!" by allowing performances at his studio in Leningrad. OBERIU was closed down around 1931, when socialist realism was becoming the new artistic trend (it was revived and became hugely popular from the 1980s in Russia, forming the missing link between the early futurists and today).

Not satisfied with blocking productions, in 1930, the RAPM attempted to take complete control of the Soviet theater and monopolize Soviet music. The chief conductor of the Bolshoi Theater, Nikolay Golovanov, was declared a "reactionary" and one of the "black hundreds" (a racist extremist group in Tsarist Russia), leading to his sacking from both the Bolshoi Theater and SOPHIL. Similarly, many of the staff of SOPHIL were dismissed.[45] Foreseeing the turn of events change irrevocably, in 1929, the ASM was dissolved by its members, and in its place, the All-Union Society of Contemporary Musicians was established to promote modern music inside the USSR and abroad. Nevertheless, links with the International Society of Contemporary Musicians were curtailed.[46]

When Nikolay Roslavets left the organization, he remained nevertheless a trusted servant of the Bolshevik Party. In 1929, Roslavets remained one of three political editors (theater, cinema, and music) at Glavrepertkom. Now, he attempted to widen his scope of work and his influence, and, in 1928, started lecturing at the Stravinsky School of Vocal Art, and the First Moscow Music Technical School, Additionally, from January 15, 1930 to September 31, 1931, he was a music consultant at the Moscow Region Department of Publishing and Literature. The work that gave cause for controversy however was being head of Music at the Tea-Kino-Pechat publishers—a post he held until May 1930 when he was dismissed for allegedly committing "political errors."[47]

The Purging of Roslavets

As a consequence of the party's Cultural Revolution, the shake-up at Glaviskustsvo in February 1930 set the agency upon a radical course. Roslavets lost his job to Sergeyev of the RAPM—who was replaced later by Semyon Korev—another cohort from the RAPM.[48] The back history to these developments was that Roslavets was falsely accused of publishing his own compositions and ritually drummed out of both Glavrepertkom and Glaviskustsvo.[49] The methods could best be termed as "fake news" under the slogan of "the struggle with eclecticism and formalism in musicology." Lebedinsky purportedly "unmasked" a group propagating formalist [musical] literature in the publishing house Triton, Academia, and the Music Publishing State Publishers and acted to shut the private publishers down.

The Association of Moscow Authors (AMA) was attacked for proselytizing "gypsy music" and "foxtrots," and ignoring the RAPM composers and corruption. Roslavets was accused of being culpable through the private cooperative Tea-Kino-Pechat.[50] The campaign against AMA was linked with the campaign against Roslavets which was fabricated by Alexey Sergeyev, Yuri Keldysh, and Semyon Korev. Roslavets was specifically accused of "a) conniving the composers of 'foxtrot' and 'gypsy music'; b) carrying through his policy of obstructing the works of proletarian composers; c) patronizing the Association of Moscow Authors ('AMA'), as a 'fake-cooperative,' a 'private market' Mr. Pereselentsev (presently imprisoned for his 'dealings' for four years); d) working in the Tea-Kino-Pechat, helping 'AMA,' that is to 'merge' into a private company with the Tea-Kino-Pechat; e) and published his own musical works."[51] These indictments, including taking bribes, effectively finished Roslavets's career in Soviet public life, or were intended to, but as we will see, they were only incriminating and failed to achieve the results intended. Going on the counterattack, Roslavets argued at the Central Commission to cleanse the Soviet apparatus from the RAPM who were flooding society with their music of "hoorah agitational," "cheap chanson," "vacuous," and other "unacceptable musical forms."[52]

However, in his response, Sergeyev incriminated Roslavets for "departing from the class line," patronizing gypsy music and foxtrots, and taking bribes. All these accusations were aimed at sacking Roslavets and further blacklisting him.[53] Roslavets adopted several tactics to win his case- appealing to the Drama and Modpik Composers Section - he accused his opponents of not "even being musicians" yet thought themselves good enough to judge him. He also said that the cooperative was the only publisher for his work now because the RAPM had control of the State Publishing House and were snubbing his music.[54] Roslavets claimed that the "RAPM was trying to discredit him (. . .) and banish him—as a proven class enemy—from Soviet employment."[55] There was some back history with Sergeyev in particular because Roslavets had exposed Sergeyev's infamous past when "Sergeyev was a counter-revolutionary in 1918."[56] Sergeyev was a former member of the S-Rs of which Roslavets had been a member; however, Roslavets was in the "left" group whereas Sergeyev was in the "right" faction.

At the plenary meeting—seeing Roslavets had won over his audience—the RAPM members stormed out of the courtroom. The court decided in

Roslavets's favor, and Bely, Davidenko, Shekhter, and Koval (all members of RAPM) were publicly rebuked.[57] This episode proved no more than a temporary rehabilitation. Intending to maximize the campaign against Roslavets and petitioning for public condemnation, the first shot in a revived campaign became the pamphlet "A Shameful Document" in which the RAPM condemned the judgment and managed to entice support in *Proletarian Musician* from Konstantin Igumnov, Heinrich Neuhaus, Reinhold Glière, and Dmitry Shostakovich. The distinguished piano teacher Igumnov wrote that the proselytizing of gypsy-foxtrot and so-called light music is essentially cabaret and upsets the listener.[58] Shostakovich wrote a detailed letter identifying four measures required to eradicate the "harmful light music" censuring the control bodies for allowing this genre to be broadcast and recorded, and workers clubs for popularizing this music and expel the composers who were responsible.[59] The musicologist Hakobian writes that Shostakovich's statement must be assessed "as blameworthy, bordering on political denunciation. This is perhaps, the most discreditable document that has ever appeared under Shostakovich's name. But it confirmed Shostakovich's loyalty towards the RAPM and showed once more that in the person of Shostakovich they had a valuable potential ally."[60]

Just a short while before, Shostakovich had orchestrated the hugely popular Vincent Youmans's song *Tea for Two*, or *Tahiti Trot*, even using it in his ballet *The Golden Age*. The piece was now condemned as being decadent by Zhitomirsky. "I consider as a political mistake, the permission by me to the conductor Malko to arrange my orchestration of '*Tahiti Trot*,' from my ballet '*The Golden Age*.'"[61] Shostakovich was trying his best to avoid any trouble but was apparently quite ready to implicate others. Interestingly, the *Proletarian Musician* wrote that Shostakovich was a progressive and active fellow-traveler. This was mostly owing to his work at the Leningrad Theater of Working Youth (TRAM) of which he was as good as music director. Hakobian mentions that "the proletarians had every reason to sympathize with Shostakovich due to his sharp attacks upon light music."[62] The crusade against Roslavets now gained the backing of the proletarian writers' body RAPP who condemned the "clearly expressed right opportunism construed by the hostility of a known number of specialists working in musical establishments, trading in ideology."[63] The authority of the influential proletarian writers' body was decisive in the palpable demonization of Roslavets.

There were voices of reason—however—but they were only expressed in private. The campaign of public deification aroused the puzzlement of the leading Leningrad musician Boris Asafyev writing to his Moscow friend Derzhanovsky: "What has happened to Roslavets? I can't make head or tail of it. At the Conservatoire, I had to sign some piece of paper against all manner of musical nonsense, and for some reason, Roslavets' name was mentioned as being a 'supporter,' or something like that. We do need to combat vulgarity, but I can't understand what Roslavets has to do with it—he's always been such a serious man."[64] Roslavets's dismissal notice was unrefined and straightforward,

> For the deficiency of a strong class line in his work, expressed in an unacceptable struggle against elements of musical deceitfulness on stage, for masquerading as a writer and a performer of light, foxtrot, and gypsy music and publishing at "AMA"—a private publishing house in an explicit musical sham, Citizen Roslavets is removed from work in the 3rd category and banned from working as a political editor in state organizations for two years.[65]

The description of Roslavets as a composer of light music was no less than an attempt to destroy his credibility as a composer, musician, and teacher. The saga of incrimination through Roslavets's renunciation of the accusations— Roslavets as a former party member—now had to demonstrate his loyalty to the party.[66] This "atonement" was undertaken through Roslavets coediting (with Mikhail Krasev) an atheist booklet *Godless Songs*, which could hardly have proved disagreeable to the Marxist composer.

Roslavets was not alone for—in the same year, 1930, his friend from childhood, Kazimir Malevich was cross-examined and briefly imprisoned upon returning from his exhibition in Paris,[67] and his work impeded until his death from cancer five years later.[68] During a decade of editorial work, Roslavets had incurred the wrath of many fellow composers (both modernists and proletarians) for banning their works from publication and performance. The RAPM petition against Roslavets proved a popular option for many in getting their own back against him. Indeed, when the Union of Composers was established a year later, Roslavets was not even invited to be a member, a factor which considerably restricted the publication and public performance of his music.[69]

The Exile to Tashkent

Roslavets was one of the few who didn't choose foreign exile following venomous attacks from the ultra-left extremists of the RAPM and ORKiMD. Leonid Sabaneyev had emigrated in 1926, and another avant-garde composer Joseph Schillinger decided not to return from the United States in 1929. Perhaps, like Myaskovsky, Shebalin, Asafyev, and other colleagues, Roslavets felt he owed a duty best served in the Soviet Union. In the opinion of his family, Roslavets's best option was to disappear before matters deteriorated further. There was a program of sending engineers, scientists, and musicians to Central Asia to develop life there. Likewise, students who had graduated from university and colleges were sent out to the far-flung regions to develop the economy. Several composers including Davidenko, Shebalin, and Mosolov went to study folklore, and as a result, wrote music based on local cultural traditions. The country chosen for Roslavets was the huge territory of Uzbekistan. Unlike Ukraine, there was little tradition of Western classical music there, and the capital of Tashkent proved a new experience—infinitely more challenging than that in Kharkiv. It also came following the breakup of his long-standing marriage to Natalya Alekseyevna Langovaya, with whom he shared twenty years of life and work since meeting as students at the Moscow Conservatoire.

For Roslavets, the position of considerable responsibility in the burgeoning music life of the republic was a sign that his expertise, understanding, and authority in music were valued and necessary. There is no evidence as to how this appointment came about; however, it proved timely. The Soviet Government was intent on developing the cultural life of the Central Asian republics by drawing experienced musicians from the European USSR to explore indigenous culture and teach a new generation of musicians. This was not Roslavets's first acquaintance with Central Asian culture for he made arrangements of Turkmenian folk music in classical traditional form. Taken by the strikingly colorful Turkmen folk ideas, he wrote a String Quartet entitled *Turkestan* (1930) for a competition arranged by the Soviet Turkmenian Government.[70] Roslavets claimed there was a considerable success from the public performances, but this piece is now missing.

Roslavets traveled to Tashkent in the summer of 1931, on a date verified by his second wife Maria Vasilyevna Fillipova.[71] His period of employment at the Tashkent Music Theater (named after Sverdlov) began on September 1, 1931.[72] There is no little irony that this new responsibility was welcomed by his former intimate and spouse of many years, Natalya wrote from the Crimea. "Greetings from Novy Afon and congratulations on the Uzbek proposal of which I wholeheartedly approve."[73] Roslavets's two-year contract as the Music Director and Conductor at the Sverdlov Music Theater was concurrent with Director of Music at the Uzbek Radio Center. These positions would prove a great influence on the development of classical music in the emergent country, offering huge potential. Roslavets's contract dates from 1930, but, as we know he only started in September 1931.[74] This delay in taking up the position was caused through awaiting the completion of the legal processes in his favor.

Uzbeki Music

Roslavets was well set to make a pioneering path for music in the Soviet republic. During his tenure, he wrote the premiere stage works and symphonies on

Uzbeki themes, led the way for the nationalist school, and trained the radio and theater orchestras there. Roslavets's move to Central Asia caused a transformation in living conditions; during the summer, it can reach 50 degrees centigrade, and in winter months drop to minus 20. Traditional Uzbeki music is conveyed through the sixteenth-century Shashmagomi—the Central Asian classical style from Fergana and Samarkand. This style comprises six magomi or mugamis written as a structure in six modes similar to traditional Persian music. Shashmagomi begins on a *pianissimo*, with interludes of Sufi poetry, and gradually climbs to a culmination before returning to the opening tone. Magomi are expressed either orally, or through folk instruments such as the Tanbur, an extended long-necked fretted lute; the Dutor, a long-necked fretted lute used widely in Central Asia, or the Chang-an instrument like the zither; and the Qu'oshnay, a clarinet-like instrument made from reeds. Writing for these instruments and understanding the semantics was challenging. The musical notation was initially recorded by Russian musicologists who traveled there following the Romanov conquest of what was then called Turkestan.

Nevertheless, Roslavets could not forget the circumstances of his position—in a photograph sent home—he makes an ambiguous, albeit gallant nod to Lermontov's famous novel, writing. "To dear Mukhonke, from the prisoner of Tashkent."[75] The absence of debates and attacks allowed a sanctuary of quiet seclusion for Roslavets, and we do not know of his associations with the artistic community in the city, or even if he traveled to other towns in the republic. His demanding lifestyle could well have precluded him from doing so, but interest in folk culture may have encouraged his traveling beyond Tashkent.

In Uzbekistan, the living conditions and climatic severity imposed an oppressive idiom in which he found returning to composition difficult and indeed traumatic. Writing to his wife, he seemed despondent. "In the courtyard, there is a well from which I can draw water. The water is fine, but even carrying the bucket is challenging."[76] With the hard lifestyle, Tashkent's music director discovered that his musical duties were equally complicated: "Tomorrow morning at 11, there will be a general rehearsal, and an evening performance (premiere). I write music day and night, and the copyist barely keeps up with me."[77]

Roslavets's Uzbeki Compositions

The initial fruits from Roslavets's new environment were a ballet on Uzbeki themes *Pakhta* (*Cotton*). The libretto of the three-act children's pantomime ballet by L. Voschene portrays the struggle of cotton farmers under Tsarist

Figure 3.1 Nataliya Roslavets in the 1920s. *Source*: Courtesy of Marina Lobanova.

rule. The musical language is of a different style from a decade before. Here, he portrays eastern idiom by introducing Shashmagomi—Roslavets extensively employs ostinato and recreating solo instrumental parts with frequent use of divertimenti. The score benefits from the richly uninhibited orchestration typical of Roslavets's most successful works. The stage premiere in Tashkent of *Pakhta* was on April 21, 1933, was repeated the following evening. The wealth of rich local folklore attracted the composer, and suitably pleased, Roslavets decided to take several subjects in composing a large-scale orchestral work on Uzbeki themes for a symphony based on Shashmagomi motifs. The potential of a symphonic piece would be perhaps more stimulating than an ostensibly unpretentious ballet for young people and children. Here, Roslavets outlines his thoughts on his latest music,

> During my work on the ballet *Pakhta*, I was inspired by the idea of a great symphonic work to commemorate the 15th anniversary of October (. . .) which would invoke the heroic labor, struggle, and victory of the proletariat. This work will have a far-reaching form in symphonic music and be fashioned entirely on themes and motifs from Uzbeki folk music (with the extensive usage of folksongs from the post-October period). The symphony will be for a large European orchestra combined with an ensemble of Uzbek national instruments, with these two groups forming one integral group. The proposed name of this work will be "Soviet Uzbekistan—a symphony of labor, struggle, and victory."[78]

We know Roslavets composed the symphony during the blisteringly hot summer between June 1 and September 1, 1932, and the writing resonates with the ballet's idiom. It would appear that the symphony was experimental by using folklore motifs in a large orchestral score and strange that he didn't attempt to get many performances—perhaps for fear of criticism and for being out of character from his previously more illustrious and daring scores. The Uzbeki symphony was successfully performed under his direction by one of the symphony orchestras at his disposal. With a rather customary lack of ambition, perhaps through dissatisfaction, or the reluctance to pursue such a large-scale opus, following completion—no more performances were given.[79]

Roslavets was motivated to write a traditional symphonic work based on Uzbeki motifs, stimulated by the richly vibrant folk culture. In a relatively short spell between December 1932 and the following January, he wrote a symphonic poem *Girya* for the national instrument—the Dutar and solo voice and symphony orchestra. The work was written for the celebrated Uzbeki singer and virtuoso folk musician, Yunus Radzhabov, who played the Dutar. Roslavets didn't give his enemies subject for criticism and employed the traditions of the nationalist school in the form of variations on Uzbeki themes. Curiously, Roslavets uses an accordion in addition to the Dutar (which is akin to a long-necked fretted lute) and approaches the theme more freely than in any previous compositions. There is a clear aspiration to capture the spirit of the Orient, revealing manifest inventive devices in his orchestration, but, no less one feels the notion is somehow alien to him, and no more than an experimental side note. One other composition where Roslavets uses Central Asian harmonies is in the *Four Uzbek Songs* for Piano Trio, which was—in the words of the composer—"written for the Radio" and "performed frequently" in Tashkent.[80]

Turkmenia and Uzbekistan were not the only beneficiaries of his pioneering writing, for the opulently vivid music of the Caucasus became another subject for attention. Chechnya has a remarkably rich musical heritage, and its folksongs were discovered by one of the Decembrists exiled there in the first decades of the nineteenth century, and more recently in the 1920s by the proletarian musician Alexander Davidenko who collected historical, romances, dance, and ceremonial songs there. Davidenko's collection of thirty Chechnyan folksong arrangements was published in Moscow in 1926. The musical language has a kinship with Central Asian mugamis, including the colorful lesghinga, and many instruments have associations with Russia and Central Asia. Roslavets made arrangements of Chechen folk music for a four-stringed Chechen national instrument, similar to the domra (1934–1935).

Return to Moscow

Roslavets's spell in Tashkent did not witness any deflection from exploring innovative musical ideas and refining the "synthetic chord." He continued to research musical theory, and his compositions espouse his groundbreaking method of composition, even if they were now largely confined to the bottom drawer. With the conclusion in 1933 of his contract at the Sverdlov Music Theater and Radio Center, Roslavets's seclusion in Tashkent was effectively over when he received an honorary diploma from the Uzbek Government. Upon returning in November 1933, he was appointed to a lectureship at the State Music Polytechnic Institute in Moscow. He was also contracted as a producer at the All-Union Radio Committee (until 1935), sharing this with the directorship of the All-Russian Concert Association until 1939. Another important administrative duty was as the head of the section of scientific associates at RABIS.[81]

The lectureship was a fruitful period in his career, and he took students in conducting from military bands. One of the advantages of such a commendable position was that he was allowed an officer's uniform. There were other demands for his services, augmenting his salary from teaching, over two months, Roslavets worked as the senior music editor for control of entertainment and repertoire policy at the Moscow City Soviet.[82] To occupy such an ostensibly important editorial position implies that Roslavets still had friends who supported him, and most importantly his experience and knowledge were welcomed. In the years to come, he could reflect on the administrative activities he shouldered in the Soviet music world,

> I am an old activist in public affairs—a composer and teacher (a peasant by background), and from the first days of the revolution—I went over unreservedly to the proletariat and all my strength and knowledge has been given to serving them. From 15 May 1923 until 15 January 1930—that is almost seven years—I worked unceasingly in the Chief Repertoire Committee as the Political Editor of the Theater and Music Section, and not for a minute have I broken from my civic duties, music teaching, and public activities, as a member of the Executive of the Association of Contemporary Music, the Chair of the Bureau of the Composer's Section of Modpik, and a staff member on almost all Soviet arts journals. Comrades, I am no appeased intellectual, nor am I without sentiment, when necessary I have laid down my pen and taken up arms in defense of the proletarian revolution (the defense of the uprising by counter-revolutionaries in Elets in 1919, and the Chairmanship of the Elets Council of Workers and Peasants Deputies), and with the same hands which have written symphonies, I have signed the death warrants for White Guards and Counter-revolutionaries.[83]

We know that Nikolay Roslavets was no shrinking violet, but neither was he a Robespierre, and after the Civil War, he exchanged the gun for the pen and no less forcefully attacked his enemies—and for that he ultimately paid a heavy price. There are in Roslavets's words more than a little irony because he never completed any symphonies, except one for chamber orchestra. Certainly, throughout his career, Roslavets enjoyed influential associates in Myaskovsky and Derzhanovsky who could provide necessary references to government institutions. If both the ultra-leftist RAPM and VAPM were now dissolved, their former members remained just as active. Roslavets's enemies remained influential enough to close Moscow's concert halls to him. The theory of the synthetic chord was expounded by Roslavets in several treatises during the last decade of his life, including works on counterpoint and the fugue.[84] Gathering dust in archives are his notebooks of musical notations from Central Asia (1937).[85] Roslavets's essays also reflect on his continuing faith in Marxism and embody an enormous study of aesthetic and musicological literature. To date, all of these valuable theoretical studies on music education and music theory remain unpublished.[86]

Chamber Symphony No. 2

We know that since his student years the symphonic genre allured Roslavets, yet no completed composition ever emerged, and this craving continued to ferment within him. There remain in the archives, two drafts of incomplete symphonies by Roslavets for a Symphony in G major written during the 1930s.[87] The forceful symphonic nature of the *Allegro giocoso*, in a poignant scherzo style, attains all the prerequisites in the classical sonata-symphonic cycle. There are sketches for "A work for symphony orchestra" written in the rondo form with a scherzo and finale. Roslavets's conventional three-part orchestra employs an extra cornet and harp, in a befittingly elegant style, additionally shifting the themes in numerous string solos. Without contravening the restrictions of the traditional major-minor system, the piece is appropriately tranquil and meditative. The masterly *Allegro giocoso* is written with the free use of both form and standard ranges. There exist fragments of another symphony dated September 29, 1942, written when he was seriously ill—regrettably, the composer never left his final thoughts in this genre.

If Roslavets failed to complete a major symphony—not unlike Schoenberg—the Russian modernist was only able to realize his dream in the more intimate chamber idiom. There were two attempts to write a Chamber Symphony over ten years. There are sketches in the archive for a Chamber Symphony which Roslavets started on November 11, 1926. In the remaining drafts, there is a framework for two movements, proving unambiguously, that it isn't linked with the 1934 piece. Roslavets gave importance to this later Chamber Symphony, documenting it in his catalog of works—without any acknowledgment of the sketches from 1926. This substantiates the fact that the composer (as was his habit) had lost interest and started a quite new work. We can see an example of this from the student years at the Moscow Conservatoire when Roslavets destroyed his "old" manuscripts. Roslavets's student piece *Finnish Fantasy* was praised by Vasilenko for being "well written, with an excellent theme, and agreeable harmonization," and well orchestrated, so when Vasilenko wanted to conduct it with the students' orchestra, Roslavets told him the score was destroyed. Roslavets explained that "the Fantasy was old," and "I had found something new." Such a manner of working characterizes both the limits and demands that this obsessively exacting musician placed upon himself.[88]

The contemporary Russian composer Alexander Raskatov (1953–) nevertheless "reconstructed" the material of the 1926 Chamber Symphony, with the minimum use of archive documents.[89] The 1926 sketches represent a purely academic interest in Roslavets's compositional technique, and his "new system of organization of sound" with a specific harmonic design, and, as in many other cases, Roslavets schematically noted the harmonic center in several of the fragments. Nevertheless, Raskatov's reconstruction of the First Chamber Symphony remains important to understanding Roslavets's creativity.[90] Nevertheless as we know, he may not have wanted to pursue the themes of this particular piece.

However, as we will see, the Chamber Symphony No. 2 represents some of Roslavets's finest work before the fatal illness that broke his health and well-being and is one of the pinnacles of his "academic innovations" written in the USSR. It would appear that Roslavets had a particular ambition for his new piece even before he finished the orchestration and sought approval from the most authoritative composer of the day,

> Dear Nikolay Yakovlevich, I present you with the score of the first movement from my Chamber Symphony and ask you either to love it or just pity it. It's a misfortune that I didn't manage to complete the orchestration, for only three pages remain (to be completed). I ask you not to hold anything back please (in criticism). I am awfully sorry for this embarrassment (not really my fault!). Yours respectively, Nik. Roslavets.[91]

As we know, Myaskovsky was a long-term advocate of Roslavets's music, and at this time Myaskovsky was a consultant both at the Composers Union and the Moscow Philharmonic,

> The Chamber Symphony realized by Comrade Roslavets' arrangement assumes a conventional harmonic and melodic style (approaching late Scriabin, and to a

degree, Schoenberg), but is to a certain degree, distinguished from those (of his) recent works familiar to me by this composer, which has a more transparent quality and greater clarity and expression in their thematic material. In particular, I have to point to the energetic, translucent leading and closing themes in the first movement, and the colorful scherzo (third movement) with its fantastic main theme, the animated second (movement), and the poignant song-like third (movement); the dynamic finale is excellent (as is the third movement), with a lively first theme and a passionately lyrical central passage. The technical subtext in Comrade Roslavets' symphony has been superbly fashioned, and in it's form (the subtext, to be truthful, seems a little academic, particularly, owing to the nature of its thematic and polyphonic material). Considering the harmonic and intonational language, the performance of Comrade Roslavets' symphony will be a challenge; however, its extraordinary elements in composition demand public performance.[92]

As we see, Myaskovsky was well impressed; however, it was never performed in the composer's lifetime. The Chamber Symphony No. 2 was written between May 1934 and February 1935, and Roslavets avoided any simple harmonic choices that distinguished his other works from this period. The piece demonstrates enormous potential in the "new system of organization of sounds" and Roslavets openly "mixes the harmonic technique" that was so successfully formed and implemented in the 1920s.

The groundbreaking tonality, fashioned on a chromatic base, is merged with an expansive tonality associated with late classical major-minor arrangements. The harmony of this innovative and astonishingly advanced composition, employs rich polyphony, and a never-ending use of semantics. That corresponds with the "new counter-point" accentuating Roslavets's pan-melodic and pan-thematic designs. The comprehensive expressive means and compositional-dramatic resources used in this piece represent the highest moments of creativity.[93] There is a parallel with Schoenberg's Chamber Symphony, in the "sequence of fourths" played on the bass-clarinet which echoes the leitmotif horn call in the Viennese composer's masterwork. It is almost as if he is paying masked reverence to Schoenberg from afar. Roslavets uses folksong and introduces colorful jazz stylizations (invoking comparisons with Weill, Eisler, and Wellesz). Throughout, his orchestration is masterly, and, in the slow movement introduces a blend of atmospheric moods, all of which create great expression and transparency—like Shostakovich—he uses the piano as a solo instrument. The scherzo emerges as a fantastic fairy tale sketched in brilliant colors, and at its heart is an Uzbeki folk theme on the woodwind, which is countered by *tremolando* strings. The finale embraces a dynamic idea that leads to a march and ultimately, following a dreamy passage, to an exhilarating and satisfying culmination.[94] In the context of symphonic works written during the 1930s, Roslavets's symphony justifiably stands with Popov's First (1934), Shostakovich's Fourth (1936), and Myaskovsky's Tenth and Seventeenth (1930).

Violin Concerto No. 2

Another important work of this period is the Violin Concerto No. 2 in D (1936). Roslavets introduces a switch from his First Violin Concerto, for here he adopts the customs and traditions of the Russian academic school. Nevertheless, both of the Roslavets's concertos observe all tenets of the concerto genre in the three-movement cycle: employing sonata form in the first movement, while in the second, there is an intricate three-part scheme with a cadenza, and in the finale—a rondo with all the conventional bravura. The concerto embraces the orchestral scoring of the nineteenth-century Russian classics. Roslavets's cadenza demands crucial melodic-thematic attention in the lyrical episodes and a virtuosic figuration of counterpoint in the development sections. The themes and tone colors are conventional with its chant-like themes alternating with diminutive accents through the major-minor system blending with pentatonic qualities.

The first movement, *Allegro moderato*, is distinguished by numerous repeats, and a variational form which the intonational formula creates an ostinato effect. The orchestra is for a chamber-sized ensemble with numerous solos. Roslavets adopted a tempo with expression at the brink of musical form. The harmonic resolution remains academic—the tonal plan is determined by the relationships corresponding to conventional form and harmony. Roslavets reprises his favored adoption of mono-thematics: both the main theme from the *Adagio* and the *Rondo finale* are related to the harmonic pattern of the first movement. This concerto was destined for Roslavets's already bulging bottom drawer, and like his Chamber Symphony, was never performed in his lifetime. This was disappointing particularly for the new generation of Soviet violinists: David Oistrakh, Boris Goldstein, Leonid Kogan, and Elizaveta Gilels. It is not known even if Roslavets showed his manuscript to his colleagues, or if it was shared with the coterie of Pavel Lamm's friends at the Conservatoire.[95]

This was the last orchestral work by Roslavets that he completed, the remainder of his pieces were for his favorite instrument—the violin. The Five Pieces for Violin and Piano include *Gavotte*,[96] *Scherzo*, *Waltz*, *Lullaby*, and a *Dance*.[97] Another series for violin and piano were for students—the *Seven Pieces in the First Position* represent a considerable addition to schools and college courses.[98] This dates from the 1930s, and the *Invention* is exactly that—a brilliant virtuosic polyphonic piece. The meditative *Nocturne* (1935) has a singing melody which invokes popular revolutionary songs of the 1920s and 1930s.

A sense of anxiety is evident from Roslavets's pleading for the fees from a *Potpourri-Fantasy on Themes from Popular Soviet Songs* for xylophone and piano commissioned by the Moscow Variety (Theater). "All these pieces have become popular and have been often performed in concerts by the Moscow Variety."[99] In 1938, Roslavets was pensioned from his state duties and suffered his first heart attack which resulted in temporary paralysis of his arms and legs, and partial loss of speech. This was the first in a prolonged decline foreshadowing his death just five years later. In 1939, he was appointed Artistic Director of the State Ensemble of Gypsy Song and Dance. Roslavets wrote music for sports parades and continued to search for innovative means of expression. His tenaciousness may be witnessed in these words. "Genius is but a matter of patience. Those who wish to rise above people must prepare for struggle and not retreat before whatever difficulties may arise. Sluggishness in creating great works demands whatever significant conditions or they may be augmented through a cynical preparation to live in poverty."[100]

Here the authentic Roslavets is speaking rather than the humble creature who appeared to have succumbed to his fate. Among his final works, there is evidence that Roslavets had not compromised his values by continuing to employ his new system of musical tonality. In 1940, owing to Myaskovsky and others, Roslavets was given membership of the Union of Composers Music Fund. This prevented him from being called up for military service during the war.

Retirement and the Last Works

The Quartet No. 5 in E major (February 1941) was composed following his second serious illness and reveals Roslavets's capacity to write extraordinary music.[101] Here Roslavets writes in the academic, classical structure and the piece abounds with crisp, audacious harmonies. There are hints of some of his finest compositions notably in the third movement with the elusive pan-thematic structure, as Belodubrovsky writes, "But the Fifth (String) Quartet stylistically represents a great work in synthesizing the naturalism of the Russian urban romance with its openly democratic intonation in a polyphonic chromatic style."[102] Roslavets's unraveling of the traditional arrangement is dominated by a harshly dissonant consonance in a chromatic vertical line reminding us of the synthetic chord. The violinist and music teacher Belodubrovsky expands on the composer's methodology,

> Roslavets wrote music in different styles, in a range of artistic and theoretical styles. These included his freely advanced serialist scheme, and predicting the

development of sonority (with the synthetic chord as an individual harmonic cluster), and a new Russian style, with innovative neorealism in his later works. (. . .) In the center of his imagery is man in a milieu with nature and in a wider perception of the cosmos.[103]

The leading composer of the "new" Soviet avant-garde in the 1980s, Edison Denisov, wrote about the influence of Roslavets, "It's not right that there have been expunged from the history of Soviet music such wonderful composers as Roslavets, Mosolov, Lourié, without mentioning any others. More than half of Roslavets music is lost."[104] The Violin Sonata No. 6 in C minor (1941)[105] was mislaid and languished in the archives for many years under the manuscript of the *Legenda* that was composed in the same year.[106] The valedictory violin sonata is in three movements and embraces his later works by absorbing the whole chromatic palate and is meditative throughout with the same material reprocessed with the synthetic chord repeated. The short piece for violin and piano *Legenda* (1941) is beautifully written in a late romantic style. Belodubrovsky was disappointed initially by Roslavets's *Twenty-Four Preludes for Violin and Piano* (1941–1942) and shares here his impressions of Roslavets's violin pieces—*Legenda* and the cycle of *Twenty-Four Preludes for Violin and Piano*,

> I was troubled at first by such trite material being taken seriously (Shostakovich). It was extraordinarily unstructured. I was disappointed by the apparent inorganic unity of emotion, the familiar intonation, and rationality. There came the thought: "What is this?" Was this a reaction to the psychological trauma of the 1930s? Was this weak creativity? Or was this just "violin music" in its most archetypal manifestation, with "thoughts" and "timeless movements?"

Belodubrovsky performed *Legenda* in a radio broadcast and received a poem from a listener which seemed to portray the essence of Roslavets's music in a poem by Anna Akhmatova,[107] "All that once. Happened to me. . . . With fresh loss, I return home."[108]

Mark Belodubrovsky who studied and researched Roslavets's violin scores and who has helped organize festivals of his music in recent years finds unique aspects in his creativity which has yet to be fully appreciated by the music world; here he describes some of his late works written when Roslavets was gravely ill.

> The music is from a quite different world. The unimpeachable and contemplative invocation of Tchaikovsky and Taneyev, however this piece belongs to the 20th century. There is a nostalgia like a lacrimosa—almost an epitaph to life. (. . .) The music is lyrical and needs to be played as it is both open and modern.

Its character in many ways is defined by the popular romance—the *Legenda* is predictable, although masterly written (there is a citation from the old romance *Don't Leave, but Stay with Me*). There is a feeling of great organic fusion in the cycle of the *Twenty-Four Preludes*.[109]

At the outbreak of war, Roslavets stayed in Moscow despite many state institutions being evacuated. Roslavets's visitors were restricted to his loyal devoted students and old friends like Myaskovsky. He was diagnosed with cancer in his left kidney, but it was a second heart attack that took the life of Nikolay Andreyevich Roslavets on August 23, 1944.[110] At his funeral at the Vagankov Cemetery, students, friends, and composers paid their final respects to a colleague and friend who was never fully celebrated in his lifetime.

NOTES

1. He arrived in Athens on March 27—author.
2. The origin for the Piano Trio No. 4 was noted on a photograph taken in Athens—author.
3. Lobanova, Marina, "Naidenniye rukopisi N.A. Roslavetsa," *Sovetskaya Muzyka*, No. 10, 1989, 32.
4. RGALI, f.2659, op. 1, ed. khr. 100.
5. Sabaneyev, Leonid, "Russkiye kompositori, II. N. Roslavets," *Parizhkii Vestnik*, March 31, 1926.
6. Sabaneyev, Leonid, "Russkiye kompositori, II. N. Roslavets," *Parizhkii Vestnik*, March 31, 1926.
7. Bely, Viktor, "Levaya fraza muzykalnaya reaktsii," *Muzykalnaya Obrazovaniya*, No. 1, 1928, 43–47.
8. "Velikii Octobrya," *Muzyka i Revolutsii*, 11, 1927, 5–6.
9. Bely, Viktor, "Levaya fraza muzykalnaya reaktsii," *Muzykalnaya Obrazovaniya*, 1928, 1, 43–47.
10. RGALI. f. 645, op. 1, ed.khr. 147, l. 159–163.
11. Lobanova, Marina, *Nikolay Roslavets i Kulturi i evo vremeni*, Moscow: Petroglif, 2011, 98.
12. Vlasova, Ekaterina, "Venera milosskaya i printsipi 1789 goda," statii pervaya, *Muzykalnaya Academia*, 1993, 2.
13. "*Komsomoliya*" was premiered by the Symphony Orchestra and Choir of the Moscow Capella and broadcast live on Comintern radio from the Kuchmeister club in Moscow on September 30, 1928. The composer passed the score to the State Music Publishers; however, it was not published until 1990 and only performed again on October 6 that year by the New Moscow Symphony Orchestra under Konstantin Krimets through the auspices of the "Heritage" Festival—author.
14. Lobanova, Marina, *Nikolay Roslavets i Kulturi i evo vremeni*, Moscow: Petroglif, 2011, 317.

15. Alekseev, *Muzykalnaya obrazovaniye*, 1924.
16. RGALI, f. 2659. op. 1. ed. chr. 56. l. 1–3.
17. Lobanova, Marina, *Nikolay Roslavets i Kulturi i evo vremeni*, Moscow: Petroglif, 2011, 289.
18. Kleiman, Levina, Bronenosets "Potemkin," Moscow, 1969, 24.
19. Vygodsky, "1905 god v muziki," *Muzykalnaya obrazovaniye*, No. 1–2, 1926, 63.
20. Odoyevsky, Alexander Ivanovich (1802–1839).
21. G.Ts.M.M.K. K, f.373, ed.khr. 13.
22. RGALI, f.2659, op. 1, ed.khr. 58. l. 1–4; ed. chr. 53. l. 6–11; ed. chr. 56. l. 4–8.
23. RGALI, f.2659, op. 1, ed.khr. 92, l. 15.
24. RGALI, f.336, op. 5, ed.khr. 38, l. 21–24.
25. Further evidence comes from a postcard of February 9, 1929, sent to his student Pyotr V. Teplov in which he mentions the score of the new composition. Lobanova, 308.
26. RSGALI, f. 2659, op. 1, ed.khr. 72, l.22–23.
27. RSGALI, f. 2659, op. 1, ed.khr. 72, l.6.
28. Belyaev, Viktor, "Muzykalnoye vystavki," *Muzykalnya kultura*, No. 1, 1924, 68.
29. Roslavets, Nikolay, "Lunaire Pierrot," Arnold Schoenberg, *K Novym beregam*, No. 3, 1923, 32.
30. Lobanova, Marina, *Nikolay Roslavets i Kulturi i evo vremeni*, Moscow: Petroglif, 2011, 301.
31. Roslavets, Nikolay, "Sovetskaya Muzika," *Rabis*, No. 43(85), November 8, 1927, 8.
32. He was appointed head of the Committee for Arts in 1936—author.
33. Vlasova, Ekaterina, *1948 god v sovetskoi muziki*, Moscow: 21 Classika, 2010, 45–46.
34. Lunacharsky, Anatoly, "Teatr sevodnya," 55.
35. Kerzhentsev, Platon M., "Puti razvitiya muziki," Stenograficheshy Otchet Soveschaniye po voprosam muziki pri APPO TsK VKP(B). Moscow, 5–8.
36. Vlasova, Ekaterina, *1948, god v sovetskoi muziki*, Moscow: Classika, 2010, 86.
37. Lebedinsky, Lev, *8 let Borby za proletarskoy musiku*, Moscow, 1931, 50.
38. Keldysh, Y., "Stalnoy skok Prokofieva," *Muzykalnoy obrazovaniye*, No. 3, 1928, 44.
39. "Puti razvitiya muziki," *Stenograficheshy Otchet Soveschaniye po voprosam muziki*, 1930, 27–28.
40. Lunacharsky, Anatoly, "Nash muzykalnyy front," 19, 24.
41. Lunacharsky, Anatoly, "Nash muzykalnyy front," 174–175.
42. Sophil was the leading promoter of symphonic concerts in the capital—author.
43. Lebedinsky, Lev, "O muzykalnoy praktike, obshestvennikh gruppirovkakh muzykantov k nashey politike po otnosheniyu k nim," *Proletarsky muzikant*, No. 2, 1930, 5.

44. Lebedinsky, Lev, *8 let Borby za proletarskoy musiku*, Moscow, 1931, 41–42.
45. "Prigovor suda po delu SOPHILa," *Vechernaya Moskva*, March 24, 1931, 1–2.
46. "Novy ustav associatsiya sovremennoy muziki," *Sovremennaya Muzika*, No. 32, 1929, 5–7.
47. RGALI, f. 2659, op. 1, ed. kh. 95, l. 4. ob. 6–9.
48. Vlasova, E.S., *1948 god v sovetskoy muziki*, Moscow: 21 Classika, 2010, 29–30.
49. Korev, Semyon, "Glaviskustsvo," *Proletarskaya Muzyka*, No. 3, 1930, 29–30.
50. "Dovesti do kontsa borbu s nepmanskoy muzikoy," Moscow, 1931, 93.
51. "Dovesti do kontsa borbu s nepmanskoy muzikoy," Moscow, 1931, 93.
52. RGALI. f. 2659. op. 1. ed. khr. 94. L. 4–5.
53. RGALI. f. 2659. op. 1. ed. khr. 94. L. 6.
54. RGALI. f. 2659. op. 1. ed. khr. 94. L. 7–8.
55. "Dovesti do kontsa borbu s nepmanskoy muzikoy," Moscow, 1931, 94.
56. Mende, Wolfgang, "Music censorship in the era of NEP and Cultural Revolution: The case of Nikolay Roslavets," *1948 and All That: Soviet Music, Ideology and Power*, 27-8/11, Cambridge, UK, 2009.
57. RGALI. f. 2659. op. 1. ed. khr. 94. L. 9–15.
58. Igumnov, Konstantin, Anketa, "Proletarsky muzykant o legkom zhanre," *Proletarsky muzykant*, No. 2, 1930, 22–25.
59. Shostakovich, D.D., Anketa, Proletarsky muzykant o legkom zhanre, *Proletarsky muzykant*, No. 2, 1930, 22–25.
60. Hakobian, Leon, "Shostakovich, Proletkult and RAPM," *Shostakovich Studies 2*, CUP, 2016, 267.
61. Shostakovich, Dmitry, *Proletarsky muzykant*, No. 66, 1930, 25.
62. Hakobian, Leon, "Shostakovich, Proletkult and RAPM," *Shostakovich Studies 2*, Cambridge UP, 2016, 266–267.
63. "Dovesti do kontsa borbu s nepmanskoy muzikoy," Moscow, 1931, 91–92, 96–98.
64. Asafyev to Derzhanovsky, 7/4/130, G.Ts.M.M.K., f. 3, e.kh. 2, No. 855.
65. Roslavets E. F., archive, Lobanova, Marina, *Nikolay Roslavets i Kulturi i evo vremeni*, Moscow: Petroglif, 2011, 99.
66. Vaxberg, Arkady, *Tsaritsa dokazeltelstv: Vyshinsky in evo zhertv*, Moscow, 1992.
67. Malevich in 1934 was diagnosed with cancer and died in Leningrad on May 15, 1935.
68. Vakar, Mikenko, *Malevich o sebye, sovremmeniki o Malevichi, Pisma, dokumenty, kritiki*, tom 1., Moscow, 2006, 542–558.
69. Interview with Inna Barsova February 2018.
70. RGALI. f. 2659. op. 1. ed. kh. 100.
71. RGALI. f. 2659. op. 1. ed. kh. 95. l. 5ob.
72. RGALI. f. 2659. op. 1. ed. kh. 95. l. 5ob.
73. RGALI. f. 2659. op. 1. ed. kh. 85.
74. RGALI. f. 2659. op. 1. ed. kh. 95. l. 5 ob.

75. RGALI. f. 2659. op. 1. ed. kh. 81. l. 2.
76. RGALI. f. 2659. op. 1. ed. kh. 81. l. 3.
77. RGALI. f. 2659. op. 1. ed. kh. 81. l. 4.
78. RGALI. f. 2659. op. 1. ed. kh. 93. l. 7.
79. RGALI. f. 2659. op. 1. ed. kh. 92. l. 17.
80. RGALI. f. 2659. op. 1. ed. kh. 100.
81. *V mire muzyki*, Moscow: BSE, 1981, 5.
82. RGALI. f. 2659. op. 1. ed. kh. 95. l. 9 ob.
83. RGALI, f. 2659, op. 1, ed. kh. 94, l. 4, 6 oborot.
84. *V mire muzyki*, Moscow: BSE, 1981, 5.
85. RGALI. f. 2659. op. 1. ed. kh. 69. l. 21–30.
86. "Working Book on the Technique of Musical Composition. Parts of Theory and Practice. Research" (1931). Another study "Research on musical sound and tonality" probably was written in Tashkent (1933). A major paper of eighty pages "Pedagogical Principles of the New System of Musical-Creative Education" (1930) and there is a disposition for a book called "The New System of Composer's Education. Course of the Norms for Theoretical and Practical Attainment of Methods and Means of Musical Composition" (1935).
87. RGALI, F.2659. op. 1. ed. kh. 16.
88. Vasilenko, S., *Vospominanii*, Moscow: Kompositor, 1964, 169.
89. Lobanova, Marina, "Strasti po Nikolaye Roslavetsu," *Rossiskaya Muzikalnaya Gazeta*, No. 10, 2002, 7.
90. In preparing Roslavets's works for publication in the 1980s, Lobanova attempted to clarify the fate of the Second Chamber Symphony, in fulfilling the requests from Festival organizers in *Naslediye* and *Moscow Autumn*, and the German music publishers B. Schott und Sohne. At that time, the traces of the Chamber Symphony hadn't been found in the personal archives of Roslavets or of Myaskovsky in TSGALI and G.Ts.M.M.K., nor in the archives of the Composers Union or Muzfond, in which there could have been the Chamber Symphony written under contract from the Composers Union. Lobanova elucidated that all the manuscripts of works by Soviet composers preserved earlier in archives and libraries of the Composers Union and Muzfond were in their time transferred to the G.Ts.M.M.K. All these circumstances held back publication of the Chamber Symphony No. 2. The score of the Chamber Symphony allows one to clear up the period and place of composition—author.
91. RGALI. f. 2659, op. 1. ed. kh. 147. L. 2. First published "Nikolaj Andreevic Roslawetz," Frankfurt-Am-Main, 1997, *Roslawetz und Kultur und seiner zeit*, 213.
92. RGALI. f. 2659, op. 1. ed. kh. 98. l. 3. First published "Nikolaj Andreevic Roslawetz," Frankfurt-Am-Main, 1997, *Roslawetz und Kultur und seiner zeit*, 212–213.
93. Lobanova, Marina, *Nikolay Roslavets i Kulturi i evo vremeni*, Moscow: Petroglif, 2011, 344–345.
94. Roslavets's Chamber Symphony was first published and recorded in 2005 by the BBC Scottish Symphony Orchestra under Ilan Volkhov in Glasgow—author.
95. The concerto was premiered by Alina Ibragimova and the BBC Scottish Symphony Orchestra under Ilan Volkhov in 2008 in Glasgow—author.

96. RGALI. f. 2659. op. 1. ed. chr. 33. l. 18. Probably dates from 1935. The archive date of 1908 is wrong—author.

97. G.Ts.M.M.K. f. 373. Ed. chr. 9,4,6,10.

98. RGALI. f. 2659. op. 1. ed. chr. 33. l. 34.

99. RGALI. f. 2659. op. 1. ed. kh. 93. l. 10.

100. RGALI. f. 2659. op. 1. ed. kh. 62. L. 11–12.

101. G.Ts.M.M.K. f. 373. ed. chr. 1.

102. Belodubrovsky, Mark, *Sovetskaya Muzyka*, No. 5, 1989, 108.

103. Belodubrovsky, Mark, *Sovetskaya Muzyka*, No. 5, 1989, 108.

104. Denisov, Edison, "Ne lyublyu formalnoye iskusstsvo," *Sovetskaya Muzika*, No. 12, 1989, 18.

105. Written for violin and piano, because of its late romanticism, Lobanova thought its origin in the 1930s; however, Pyotr V. Teplov (Roslavets's pupil) who presented the score to the Glinka State Music Archive. In three movements, the reconstructed sonata was published by Schott Musik International.

106. G.Ts.M.M.K. f. 373. Ed. chr. 7.

107. Belodubrovsky, Mark, *Sovetskaya Muzyka*, No. 5, 1989, 108.

108. Akhmatova, Anna, "Putem vseya zemli."

109. Belodubrovsky, Mark, *Sovetskaya Muzyka*, No. 5, 1989, 108.

110. Many of his papers and scores were lost owing to the speedy remarriage of Roslavets's widow shortly after the funeral. She quickly sold his piano and violin and apparently took little care of his archive which led to the loss of many scores, newspaper articles, photographs, and personal documents relating to his life and career. Kholopov, Volnyuschaya Stranitsa Russkoi Muziki, www.composer.ru/xxmidi/st/Rosl_Holop01.html.

Chapter 4

The First Symphony

The author of one of the finest symphonies of his day—Gavriil Nikolayevich Popov today is best known for writing some of the most successful film scores in Soviet Russia. A sign of his immense musical gifts is that Popov wrote in almost every genre—pioneering electronic music—and the first to use it in the cinema. The source of his originality, extraordinary gifts, and humanity lies in the Cossack traditions of the River Don. The Don Cossacks were descendants of Slavs from the Dnieper in Southern Russia, and Goths from Caucasia. Known as the "Wild Fields," the lands once ruled by the Golden Horde were settled by Cossack tribes in 1444.

Lying in the foothills of the Caucasus, the Don region shares cultural traditions with the peoples of Chechnya, Kabardian-Balkar, Ossetia, Armenia, Georgia, and Azerbaijan. The Cossacks defended their beliefs fiercely and made a decisive contribution to the Romanov empire providing the most steadfast warriors in the campaigns of conquest. They also staunchly defended their rights of independence and often rebelled against Tsarist rule. Illustrious Cossacks in history—Emelyan Pugachev and Stepan Razin—led uprisings against Catherine II. Dmitry Turchaninov served as a General in the Union Army during the American Civil War. During the Great War of 1914–1918, fifty-eight regiments from the Cossack Host fought for Nikolay II's army. Their rebellious character was underscored when three Cossack regiments in Petrograd led the second Russian Revolution in March 1917—overthrowing the Romanov dynasty of over three hundred years. The Nobel prizewinner Mikhail Sholokhov's novels evoke the Cossack rebellions—portraying the passions of patriotism, of broken families, all of which reflect their breezy independence, chirpiness, and bountifully vibrant romanticism.

The Cossacks are universally renowned for their singing, and many songs have become widespread in Russian folklore, notably the *Black Raven*

(*Chorny Voron*), and *It's Good, Brothers' Good!* (*Lyubo, Bratsi, Lyubo!*). The notion of freedom and independence derives from an old term that distinguishes the Cossack peoples—detached from serfs, nobility, tradespeople, and the church—as the *Free People*.

EARLY YEARS

All the virtues of openness, the individuality of beliefs—combined with a passionate love of nature and art—were to be observed in Gavriil Nikolayevich Popov. He was born in the Don Cossack capital—Novocherkassk on September 12, 1904 (new style) the son of Nikolay Dmitrevich Popov—a teacher of Russian, logic, and psychology, and the director of the Stepanov Gymnasium.[1] According to his diary, Nikolay Popov taught his son "the violin, choral conducting, composing music, and the inculcation of his world outlook, acquiring of diverse knowledge, and the opening of his artistic potential."[2] He encouraged Gavriil to study Chekhov, Turgenev, Goncharov, and Tolstoy.[3] Lyubov Fyodorovna—his mother played the piano and began teaching her son when he was six. Gavriil noted in his daily journal, "From my early years she gave me a love for music: apart from my parents' musicality, we heard vocal and quartet music at home when my father's colleagues visited."[4] The young boy's love for music soon became a driving force, and at the age of seven, Gavriil began studying privately with David Grigorovich Marshad, noting in his diary that, "In 1915, at the age of 11, I gave my first public concert with students of Presman at the Rostov Conservatoire (in aid of wounded and sick soldiers of the Russian army)." He began studying with Professor Matvei Leontovich Presman (1870–1941) at the Rostov on Don Conservatoire in piano and music theory. Writing in his diary, he noted that, "It was in 1919, at the age of 14 ½ years, that I began composing. At that time, there appeared in the press a (positive) review of my first performance."[5] It was Presman who transformed Popov's youthful gifts into becoming a professional musician. In Moscow, Pressman shared piano studies with Rachmaninov and Scriabin under Nikolay Zverev and Vasily Safonov.[6]

The bitterly fought Civil War saw the city of Rostov switch sides several times, inflicting civilian casualties. The events were recorded by Gavriil, "The whole day there was artillery shelling and machine gunfire; near us (at the corner of Bratsky and Sennaya), two machine guns were constantly in action. Papa wouldn't let me go to my music lessons."[7] A week later, he wrote that the Whites left the city after just two days, and "a shell fell on our home."[8] Popov's mother died from cholera in July 1919, after evacuating to Yekaterinodar (now called Krasnodar). All of these events imbued in Gavriil a mental toughness that would shape his future career.

On July 12, 1921, Nikolay Popov was arrested owing to false accusations by his neighbors.[9] Gavriil's diary became a sanctuary of his deepest thoughts, writing "1) release of my father. 2) enter the polytechnic institute, 3) enter the conservatoire, 4) relationship with Zina, 5) relations with Tanya."[10] Following an investigation, his father was released after six weeks' imprisonment. To make ends meet, Popov started teaching while studying at the Faculty of Architecture at the Don Polytechnic Institute, and the Faculty of Mathematics of Rostov State University in 1921–1922. Recording in his diary, Popov noted that, "In the spring of 1922, I passed all the examinations for the Department of History of Arts at the Don Archaeology Institute in Rostov. I studied draftsmanship at the Rostov Design School."[11] Gavriil's diverse interests had framed his future to make his way in life, and in actuality, he was a jack-of-all-trades.[12] One wonders here if Gavriil had reconsidered music as a career, or was this simply a means of broadening his knowledge of life? Soon he would be impelled to make a choice as two different paths opened up for him as he confides that, "Today, I wanted to join the Vladikavkaz Railway as a draftsman, but Presman offered me a place in the Opera Theatre."[13] Presman, as director of the Opera Company, helped Gavriil to make his mind up. The choice for Popov was more beneficial as he noted in his journal, "I shall work five hours every day. The salary shall be perhaps 100–150,000. . . . This work is certainly more interesting than draftsmanship and more valuable by getting to know opera."[14] Gavriil was now the breadwinner for his large family. His stepmother—as he noted in his diary—"Adele Vasilyevna cannot presently alone feed all our family. . . . There is nothing left to sell. . . . Yet, three hungry stomachs cannot help themselves."[15]

First Compositions

Gavriil Popov's early piano pieces of 1920 reveal both influences of impressionism and the national school—*In the Style of Lyadov*, *Etudes in the Spirit of Rachmaninov*, and *Idyll in the Style of Rimsky Korsakov*, *Thoughts about the Sea*, *Joy*, *Sadness*, and *Musical Burst*. Another fourteen piano pieces date from 1921, and he began giving opus numbers to his piano works. The desire to study music in Petrograd came through the lectures given by Mikhail Gnessin (1883–1957) in August 1921, and as he informs us through his diary, became, "One of my first musical mentors was the composer Mikhail Gnessin."[16] Popov's *Musical Burst* and *Caprice* were praised for their monothematic and harmonically fragile nature. The consequence of Gnessin's guidance was that Popov started studying harmony and modern European composers.

Popov now entered the class of the pianist, composer, and teacher Vasily Vasilyevich Shaub (1890–1941). Shaub opened Scriabin's mysticism, exoticism, and eroticism up to Popov, which influenced the programs for his recitals as he noted,

> The mysticism of Wagner is intelligent, and clear (in that it is towards mysticism), as well as formulated in leitmotifs (the intervention of rationalism to leitmotifs becomes an allegory). Scriabin is inclined to fiery spiritualism and real spiritual existence—not through impassioned passions and feelings—but genuine passions and not isolated conflicts of good and evil, but the eternal struggle.[17]

Another corollary was Shaub's lectures on orchestration and the Beethoven symphonies. A fresh discovery was hearing his teacher's piano music, as his diary tells us, "I was taken by his creativity."[18] New horizons opened up for him, as he relates, "I am already close (Shaub) to the enigma of modernism. The foundation of these depths and outstanding achievements in this area are in the creativity of A. N. Scriabin."[19] Shaub had now become his spiritual father. There was early evidence of the lethargy that would prove a thorn in his personality when Shaub reproached Popov that he would make a composer out of him, but he needed to work more.[20]

Petrograd-Leningrad

In August 1922, Gavriil Popov's journey to Petrograd for the entry examinations to the Institute of Engineering and the Conservatoire was enabled by a loan from his father.[21] His biographer Inna Romaschuk notes his diversity of interests: "Popov sensed the appeal of composing music. However, the interests to literature, mathematics, and architecture never faded away."[22] He was full of creative ideas and hopes. Nevertheless, an unknown prospect awaited him in the Northern capital that would become his home for the next twenty years.

Popov entered the composition class of Maximilian Shteinberg and the piano class of Maria Barinova. Barinova (1878–1956) had studied with Rimsky-Korsakov, Josef Hoffmann, and Ferruccio Busoni and was one of the finest pedagogues in Russia (who openly held anti-Soviet views). Shteinberg (1883–1946) was also a pupil of Rimsky-Korsakov and had married his daughter Julia (who was herself a composer). The city boasted a wealth in the arts and some of the finest museums and galleries in Europe with stages on which celebrated singers and dancers regularly performed, and the French and Italian renaissance architecture allowed the city to be known as *Venice of the North*.

Concurrently, Popov attended lectures at the Institute of Art History and the Faculty of Architecture of the Polytechnic Institute (1922–1923).

As Romaschuk informs us, "He was, in a word, interested in everything: from intense contemporary innovations to the predominately European music at the Philharmonic."[23] Popov joined the Leningrad branch of the ASM through whose concerts, he became increasingly attracted to modernism. Popov identified Schoenberg as "my new, wonderful composer," yet shared with Shostakovich a disfavor for dodecaphony. "Schoenberg's influence is in its laconism, contrasts (dynamic determination and penetrating sound, unity of common severe colors)."[24] The music of Paul Hindemith liberated a dynamic-linear aspiration for instrumentation expressing the character of dynamics, rhythm, and movement. Popov was overwhelmed by Stravinsky's "*Petrushka* is such a delight, such joyousness, and light! But Hindemith? This is red-hot 'urbanism' which ruptures the blood cells and cultivates one's thoughts, Stravinsky, Schoenberg, Hindemith, and Prokofiev are my stars."[25] In his second year, Popov moved to the classes of Leonid Nikolayev and Vladimir Shcherbachov. Nikolayev (1878–1942) was a student of Safonov in piano (as was Shaub), and Taneyev, and Ippolitov-Ivanov in composition at the Moscow Conservatoire. Shcherbachov (1887–1952) was the "modernist" at the Conservatoire.[26] Nikolayev's class included the future of Russian pianism: Maria Yudina, Vladimir Sofronitsky, and Dmitry Shostakovich. Popov studied counterpoint, orchestration, form, and free composition with Shcherbachov, who it is claimed "united Russian song with the fugue" through developing this methodology from Glinka and Taneyev. He inculcated the concept of melodically conceived images mixing folklore with polyphony. One of the important features of Shcherbachov's teaching was using a melodic "cell" in the orchestral lyric range (Aria, Melody). Popov's first piano pieces in Petrograd were a cycle called *Images*, with another two pieces *Le Fond*, completed on August 19, 1923, and *Retentissement* between October 25 and November 7, 1923. It appears these two earlier pieces were experimentally tentative and shelved.

Purge at the Conservatoire

In May 1924, as part of a nationwide process led by the RAPM and ORKiMD, Popov was "purged" from the Conservatoire. This was through the campaign by the proletarian musicians to set up Rabfaks and exclude students whose backgrounds may be judged as politically suspicious. Popov's anger was restricted to his diary, "I have been expelled from the Conservatoire: private fury. It will be more difficult, but the devil with it."[27] Popov, his friend Boris Arapov, and another ten students were let go. The reason ostensibly given for his removal was "academically of average ability, without any potential."[28] Ekaterina Vlasova has written that such expulsions served to ostracize young people and often led to suicides, although she fails to provide examples of this.[29]

Responding to this thinly disguised maneuver by the Leningrad faction of the RAPM, the Conservatoire Rector Glazounov appealed for reinstatement by sending a glowing character reference to the deputy head of the Commissariat of Enlightenment Pokrovsky.[30] Additionally, Professor Nikolayev appealed to the distinguished musicologist Boleslav Yavorsky in Moscow. Throughout this appeal process, Nikolayev and Shcherbachov continued teaching Popov—pro bono—so highly did they judge his talent.[31] Popov was then considered a great piano soloist of the future, rather than as a composer, and to emphasize his potential and make a living, he began giving recitals at Leningrad concerts of new music. Popov, the young virtuoso made a reputation for his prodigious expression, exhibiting the vibrancy associated with an extraordinary technique and sound quality.

During this imposed "gap year"—and to mark his twentieth birthday—Popov gave a recital of Bach-Busoni, and Liszt in Rostov on September 12, 1924. There followed similar solo concerts in Moscow and Leningrad.[32] Popov took in private students and worked as a repetiteur at the Verbova Dance Studio, and the No. 40 labor school. He continued attending his art lectures and became increasingly active in the ASM Leningrad branch.[33] Following this year of "penitence," Popov was readmitted to the Conservatoire in 1925. The readmittance owed greatly to the efforts of Yavorsky, and in gratitude, Popov presented his freshly composed *Expressia* to the venerated musicologist/composer elucidating his thoughts in writing it on the score. Indeed, Popov's explanation of the arguments for his composition became a force of habit.

First Mature Compositions

In February 1925, Popov composed his piano prelude *Expressia* giving it Op. 1—the first of two pieces. Writing to Yavorsky, Popov explained: "This is an attempt in a possibly laconic form to realize the highest [degree of] expression by using conflicting elements, for example, 1) serene songlike melodic sketches, 2) important fluctuating lines, [*Melodie*] 1) a 'bare' melody, 2) harmonically intense poignant voices" through emphasizing "the play of colors."[34] In confiding to his diary, "*Expressia*—is my favorite, precious, profound and aspiring, tender and simple, stern and caressing work. Shall I be able to compose something better than *Expressia*?"[35]

The second prelude *Melodie* was finished on December 25, 1925—here Popov uses Shcherbachov's notion through mixing his own thoughts in a polyphonic development of melodic forms.[36] As he explains in his journal,

"In this *Melodie,* there is something simple, of deep sadness, and which is simultaneously joyous."[37] The composition of *Melodie* dates from the blissful summer weeks following his marriage to Olga Palui—a fellow student—to whom the prelude is dedicated. These compositions reveal an advance in engaging with folklore and a trend toward constructivism and expressionism. He realized that now he was a different, more mature composer, and consigned his youthful pieces to the bottom drawer.

Popov dedicated his *Expressia* to Schoenberg as an evocation of the Viennese master in Slavic colors. All four pieces (including the earliest *Images* cycle—*Le Fond* and *Retentissement*) were promoted by the Circle of New Music at a concert on April 6, 1926. The press response was encouraging in calling "Popov, talented, and sounding remarkable, but acerbic (Scriabinesque)."[38] Another media notice was more supportive: "The young, clearly gifted G. Popov—who played his piano pieces—has become prominent among Leningrad composers. His *Expressia* and *Melodie* are perhaps not entirely individual, but all the same are highly promising dynamic compositions."[39] The two preludes served as a propitious prequel for the *Septet*—the most significant of Popov's early compositions—and which revealed his enormous potential. When Darius Milhaud visited Leningrad in 1926, Popov was invited to play his own compositions privately at an event facilitated by Asafyev.[40]

Popov's *Vocalise* in A major (dedicated to T. P. Todorovaya) dates from June 1926 and was published by the private Triton publishers in the following year (this earned him 40 roubles). It was premiered at a concert of friends of chamber music on October 25, 1926, in Leningrad. The review praised it as "pleasant and profound."[41] The modernist musicologist and gifted wordsmith Boris Asafyev noted that "the path of lyricism by Leningrad composers is essentially identified by two dates: in July 1926 there appeared in the *Vocalise* by Gavriil Popov musical content of an equal richness in melody and symphonic intensity."[42] Popov's second *Vocalise* was composed in April 1927 and performed on June 18, 1929, by Natalia Rozhdestvenskaya in a radio broadcast concert. It has not been published. The third *Vocalise* written on May 3–4, 1929, remains only in sketch form.[43] Other incomplete works include the *Concertino* for Violin and Piano, Op. 4 (1926) which has only six pages comprising 130 bars, and the *Dance Suite*, Op. 5 for piano in drafts for two numbers. The Leningrad ASM branch programed Popov's *Melodie*, Ryazanov's *Chant*, Tyulin's *From the Depths*, and Shcherbachov's *Invention* in a piano recital on April 12, 1927.[44] On December 14, 1927, Popov played his *Melodie* and *Expression*, and accompanied E. N. Goldenberg in the *Vocalise* No. 1, Op. 3 at the State Academy of Arts and Sciences.

The Septet

The year 1926 was auspicious for modernism in the USSR with Mosolov's First String Quartet, First Piano Concerto, *The Foundry*, Vladimir Deshevov's *The Rails*, Shostakovich's First Symphony, and Leonid Polovinkin's *The Telescope* all being heard in concert. This was as if a new page was turned in Russian music—a fascinating occurrence in avant-garde music. The graduation work that opened up Popov's career and won him speedy recognition in the USSR, Europe, and the United States was the *Septet*, Op 2. At the start of the momentous year of 1926, Popov's chamber piece started off as a *Sextet*, and it was only after rehearsals in late January that he decided to introduce a double bass to strengthen the sound picture. Four months later, this masterly composition became the *Septet*. The scoring is for flute, clarinet, bassoon, trumpet, violin, cello, and double bass. Initially, only the opening two movements (*Andante con moto* and *Allegro energico*) were heard on May 31, 1926, at the Leningrad Circle of New Music concert conducted by Shcherbachov (to whom it is dedicated) at the Fourth Music Technikum. The program included Berg's Piano Sonata, Shostakovich's *Aphorisms*, and Zhivotov's *Nonet*. Popov's *Septet* was published by Muzsektor in Moscow, by Universal Edition Vienna, and in Leipzig in 1928. In its original variant, Popov's *Septet* bore the subheading "Chamber music for seven instruments." There were many who were in awe of Popov's brilliantly written chamber piece, for in an unpublished essay, "The Leningrad Lyricists," the Leningrad wordsmith Asafyev succinctly categorized the *Septet* as "an ensemble of a new type."[45]

The complete premiere of the *Septet* on December 13, 1927, at the Maly Hall of the Moscow Conservatoire was remarkably successful (the *Largo* and *Allegro energico*, date from November 1926). As Popov enthused to Asafyev, "Everything sounded really fantastic—the third movement sounded absolutely amazing. What good luck to have heard my score, the first one performed from the very start by first-class (musically and technically), astonishing Moscow musicians (the ensemble was led by the cellist V. L. Kubatsky)."[46] Popov continued "I can enlighten you that the *Septet* 'was approved'! The *Septet* reassured me of my immaculate managing of the score. I will tell you everything later. Both your essay and analysis of the *Septet* are available. My trip has been generally satisfactory."[47] According to one review, the *Septet* "expressed highly individual creative ideas, while being naturally deeply national. . . . Popov's potency is in a wonderfully melodic and thematic inventiveness, and an ability to develop musical ideas organically."[48] Belyaev noted specifically Popov's "*inclination* to the West."[49]

In the *Septet*, one can hear Russian song melody (in the pastoral solo flute at the opening theme of the first movement (*Moderato cantabile*), and the (*Largo*) and a Tango rhythm in a passage of the second movement (*Allegro*), and foxtrot rhythm in the central part of the third movement). The theme of the Trio scherzo and an idea from the *Largo* lend a hint of parody. Hakobian wrote: "Though not free from some stylistic dependence on Prokofiev and Hindemith, possibly also Stravinsky, the work—especially its middle movements, *Scherzo (Allegro)* and *Largo*—is full of attractive details and was justly appreciated as a brilliant achievement."[50]

There is a parallel with Shcherbachov's *Nonet* written for voice, flutes, harps, string quartet, and dancer. There is a clear association in Popov's dedication.

> Almost as if a model—Popov recreates the resonance and atmosphere of the opening bars of the *Nonet*, with similar reticent motifs of the harp, created by the *flageolets* and muted strings. However, contrary to giving the *accent* to the voice, Popov strengthened the melodic instrumentation by creating a distinct singing melodic texture, while backing away from vocalization (at the beginning of the first movement). Shcherbachov's *Nonet* is full of colors and dynamics, as if synthesizing different art forms—more like a *chamber* structure. Popov's more logical scheme in the *Septet* is in recreating a symphonic model (in four movements) in the chamber genre.[51]

The Moscow scholar Lyudmila Nikitina notes an affinity with Stravinsky in the song which opens the *Septet* and also in the harmonies and intonation. "In the *Septet* there is something different: the feeling of several processes—as if all the conceivable emotional and expressive elements were coming together in a single space."[52] Romaschuk considers the *Septet* appeared at the crossroads of those emotional constants which revealed the joyous feelings of sharing in the creation of a new world. "It is no accident that the *Septet* became virtually the first work in our country to be a model for symphonism in the chamber genre."[53] In 1971, after many years, Popov decided to rechristen it as his Chamber Symphony when it was reprinted by Sovetsky Kompositor.[54]

Grosse Klaviersuite

Enthused by the success of the *Septet*, Popov's next major piece was the *Grosse Klaviersuite*, written between April and November 1927; it is dedicated to his fellow student and pianist Maria Yudina. The opening *Invention* was premiered separately by Popov in the Glazounov Hall of the Conservatoire, and the whole suite was heard in an ASM concert on November 25, 1927, in Leningrad. The piece was published both in Moscow and by Universal Edition in 1931. Once again, the response was positive: "this notable stamp of maturity shows remarkable progress in mastery."[55] The

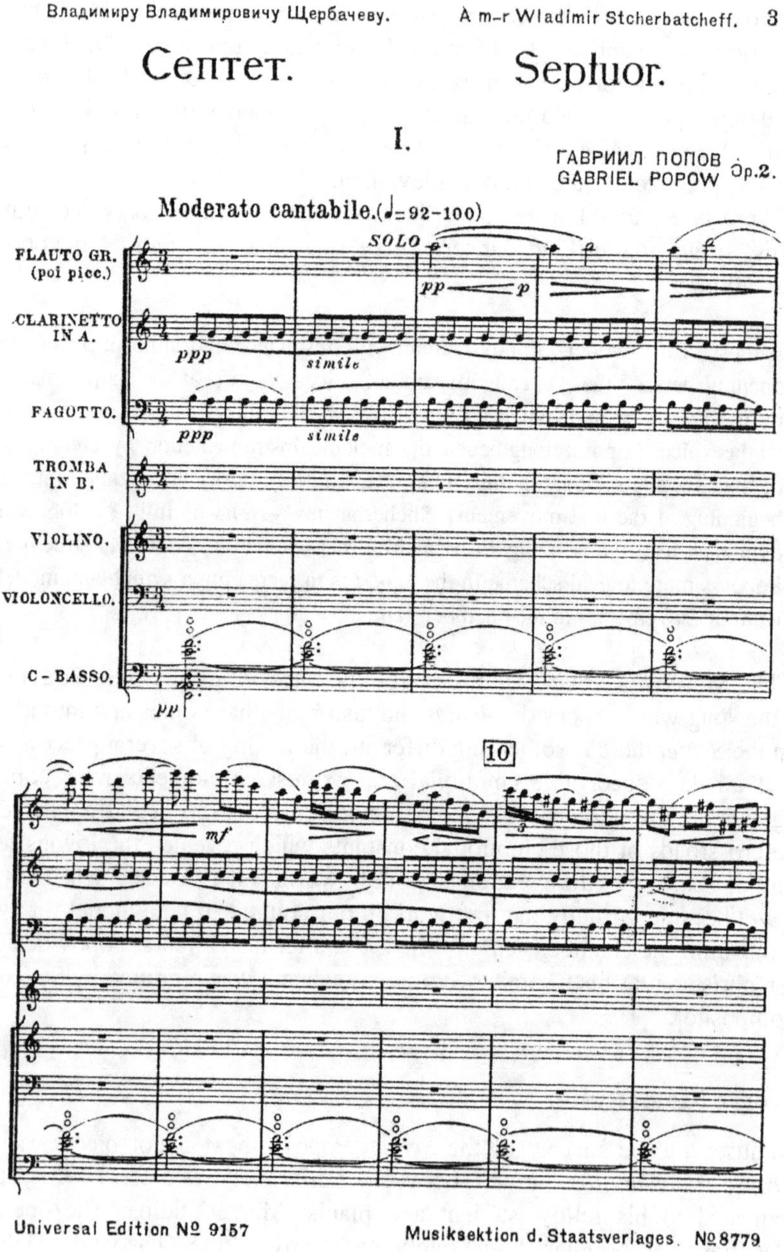

Figure 4.1 Popov—Septet (First Page). *Source*: © Copyright by Universal Edition A.G., Wien.

Leningrad composer Bogdanov-Berezovsky enthused about "the assured, undoubtedly expressive and original piano writing."[56]

With its icy neoclassicism, the *Grosse Klaviersuite* lacks any hint of romanticism, mysticism, or impressionism, and was unlike anything in Russian music at the time. In the opening *Invention*, there is a ferocious bellicosity with a sweeping passion in the harsh leaps and flashes of dissonance. The second movement *Choral* uses block chords with its subtly pulsating rhythms, and there is an unpretentious bi-tonality in the third movement *Lied*. Here there is a nod to Popov's childhood hero Chopin; however, this is but the calm before the storm. In the *Fugue*, the counterpoint is wild and harsh with the quasi-Bachian sequences. The music is anti-tonal and unrelentingly brusque. Interestingly, the opening idea appears in the primary theme of Shostakovich's Tenth Symphony (1953), something Popov alluded to when he first heard it. The connotation is hardly surprising as both works share energy and dynamism, mixed with the grotesque, irony, and brilliance.

Asafyev's Mentoring of Popov

The composer and musicologist Boris Asafyev (1884–1949) was the most distinguished wordsmith of the Leningrad music school. Here he appraises Popov's youthful promise as a potential modernist among other Leningrad musicians,

> Beginning roughly from the mid-twenties—among a group of young Leningrad composers—there began an aspiration to struggle for the Melos (the melodic principle in its immeasurable shades and possibilities, where it is in organic unity with rhythm, like breathing), and for expressing living intonation in each of the musical elements, and in the *voices*—in the broadest sense—and bring it to the listener.[57]

Before the cataclysms ahead in his career, it is worthwhile to consider this accurate judgment by Asafyev of this modernist.

> Popov has an intense and sharp feeling for line, with a powerful sense for form—all heard in his orchestration, and the ability to project the musical flow intensively, submitting it to his structured development. Every part of the cyclical chamber works by Popov is recognized as a new achievement to a final goal, he is driving himself more. (. . .) Popov shares an affinity with several works by Hindemith. (. . .) The *Septet*, and the *Grosse Klaviersuite*, appear to be Popov's most dominant and individual works at present. (. . .) He delights in persuasively flexible melodies. In the *Septet*, there unravel a number of expressive measures which share a penchant for apathy, passion, and seminal energy, and to spirit

and joy. The development is through the dialectic of form, and through form, not as self-governing *literary* (programmatic) ideas.⁵⁸

Popov met Paul Hindemith after hearing the Second Quartet when the German composer and violist toured with the Amar Quartet to the USSR in 1927.⁵⁹ As he tells us through his journal, "The latest form, material, polyphony, clarity, and life are brilliant, and Hindemith's (own) sound and ability to play the viola is captivating, creating joy and happiness in life. Now, I want to write a quartet. It's a long time since I experienced such happiness from music as today."⁶⁰

Popov continued to perform on the concert stages of Leningrad; the Russian premiere of Stravinsky's *Les Noces* involved Popov (deputizing for Shostakovich) with the other piano parts taken by Maria Yudina, Issay Renzin, and Alla Maslakovetz, with the Glinka State Choir, under the direction of Mikhail Klimov on February 9, 1927. Popov shared performances with his fellow student Shostakovich in piano arrangements of Stravinsky's *Apollon musagets*, and *The Rite of Spring*. Shostakovich was again his partner in a performance of the Mozart Concerto for Two Pianos K.365 under Fritz Steidry and the Leningrad Philharmonic Orchestra on November 23, 1927. Popov recalled that he "played the second piano. It was a fine success."⁶¹ However the local critic was not so enthusiastic unfortunately—"there was a complete lack of understanding. Too 'weighty' a piano sound, and not in the manner of the 'youthful' Mozart, which completely ruined the piece."⁶²

Popov's diary reveals his feelings and the reflection of his country in his music: "John Reed's book arouses in me great joy for everything that happened in 1917, for the Bolshevik Revolution of 25 October.⁶³ This joy is expressed in my enhanced musical creative energy. The description of the workers' funerals who fell in Moscow during the Civil War with the Junkers motivated me to write a 'funeral march.' I wrote a line of uninterrupted steps: of a slow, heaviness turning into a cry. It is uniformly severe and staunch. I don't know if I will continue this idea. I imagined this as a march in orchestral sound: strings and timpani."⁶⁴ In his still-to-be written First Symphony, Popov would express more fully his thoughts about the Revolution. In 1927, an anthology of new music by Leningrad composers entitled *Northern Almanac* was published by the private publisher Triton. The collection—in homage to the *Album* produced by *Les Six* who had taken the example of the Russian *Mighty Handful*—featured the work of Ryazanov, Shcherbachov, Tyulin, Popov (*Vocalise*, Op. 3), and Deshevov.⁶⁵ The print run was thousand copies.⁶⁶

Three more works by Popov were published between 1928 and 1932 by Universal Edition in Vienna: the *Expressia* and *Melodie*, Op. 1; the score and parts of the *Septet*, Op. 2; and the *Grosse Klaviersuite*, Op. 6. Typically, the

UE print run was between two hundred and five hundred copies (the largest print run was for the *Grosse Klaviersuite*).[67] The choice of the composers published by UE belonged to Muzsektor. In all, 110 Soviet composers were published and distributed through the Vienna publishers. The author Olesya Brik commented that "practically all significant composers of Moscow and Leningrad, both recognized, and young were published."[68] It is notable that of the works sent to Vienna, nothing was dismissed because of the trust given to the Soviet agency. "The agreement excluded only politically tendentious musical works."[69] The sole exception was Fere's children's songs—*On the May Holidays*.[70]

The First Symphony

It was clear that with the *Septet*, and *Grosse Klaviersuite*, Popov was drawn to the symphonic genre, and it seemed just a matter of time before he would start on his first symphony. From his diary entries during in the last weeks of 1927, Popov disclosed that, "I have sketched several bars of my symphony (1st movement)."[71] As we know, Leningrad's vibrant concert life allowed Popov many sources of influence and inspiration for his compositions. Hindemith remained an influential figure for Popov, now he heard the German composer's freshly conceived *Kammermusik* No. 5 for viola and chamber orchestra, as he wrote to his wife,

> it sounds wonderful in all parts. There is not the radiance of the sun, but I like the full "sense" of colors—full of indomitable energy and force. The second, slow movement with its unadorned and diffident lyricism (with human breathing). The first movement with a pouring of energy (viola solo), is close to the Bach violin sonatas, with modern metric measures intense against the sound of the mechanically-calculated sound of the orchestra. The third movement—elegant and modest *Mässig schnell*. Normally, such movements are characterized as a *Scherzo*. I want to use this vocabulary. The finale—rich, joyous music on the theme of the noblest B-major from a German military march. So uncomplicated, raucous, and jubilant.[72]

During the 1920s, Mahler's symphonies were frequently performed by the Leningrad Philharmonic Orchestra under guest conductors, and it is clear that although Popov does not here mention him—like his friend Shostakovich—Popov was strongly influenced by Mahler.

Popov was impressed by Otto Klemperer conducting the Leningrad Philharmonic, mentioning in his diary that "Beethoven's Third Symphony sounded profound and great. The energy of the strings in Beethoven represents for me—happiness and creative will power."[73] Tchaikovsky remained a strong influence, as he mentioned, "for his humanity and the enormously dynamic music."[74] In the first months of 1928, it appears that progress had been made and the symphony was already attracting interest. The Artistic Directorate of the Leningrad Philharmonic Orchestra was scheduling a premiere in the city's subscription series, as he described, "Today, I noticed that posters have gone up with the prospectus of the Philharmonic matinee concerts, and my symphony is planned there for 14 April (1929)."[75] However, this date passed because only the lengthy first movement was finished in 1928. As his teacher Shaub had foreseen, the lack of industry by Popov was becoming a flaw and a hindrance.

In May 1929, Popov played through Stravinsky's Piano Concerto with the conductor and composer Ernst Ansermet. Afterward, the Swiss maestro asked for the *Septet* score and expressed interest in the symphony. True to his promise, the following year Ansermet performed the *Septet* at a BBC radio concert in London. There was more interest from the visiting conductor Nikolay Malko who requested the symphony for a tour of Argentina. However, Popov refused to give him an incomplete score, complaining to his journal, "What a crank, how can I give him just *a piece* of it?"[76] Popov was encouraged by Stravinsky's ballet *Apollon musagets*, enthusing in his dairy, "In every bar there is an intensity, profusion of melody, energy of thought, and a great mastery of form. I could not tear myself (away) from three or four pages until 9 o'clock."[77] The rest of his evening was spent on his symphony. Asafyev appealed in the media for "the creation of symphonies which avoid personal feelings, in their subjective-psychic consistencies, and which 'tell the drama of life.'"[78] The writing of his huge symphonic work was proving a major task which he found difficulty in mastering, as he explained confiding in his journal, "I am increasingly searching for a dramatic (symphonic) musical structure. I am exploring for a scheme and a method." In May 1929, almost two years since beginning the symphony, he was still nowhere near finishing it. On June 23, once more he played through the symphony, noting in a jot, "I like the Coda more now. Alongside the murmuring violas (a prolonged *pianissimo* in the *Corno* and *Trombe sord. Con Sord* (harmony) the melody sings (from the second idea) on the first and second violins (*sordini*). It should sound fragile and deeply passionate."[79] Once more, as his diary intimated, Shcherbachov discovered "a common orchestral *inelegance* and (he) recommended spending more time on the second movement, and not wasting time on details in the first movement. (. . .) He praised it in general terms. He is concerned mostly with my orchestration. On this I differ with him; although I am aware of possible errors in orchestration, I can really hear and feel the *spirit* of the orchestra."[80] After playing through the first two movements to Prokofiev, he thought that he didn't like it, noting in his journal, "It was interesting to hear about Prokofiev's orchestration studies in Rimsky

Korsakov's class (he received a mark of 3 in the examination)."[81] However, Prokofiev only masked his admiration for the symphony. Somewhat later, in a letter the theater director Meyerhold told Popov "Prokofiev likes you very much. He sparked in me the fire of sympathy for you."[82]

In October 1929, Sollertinsky—the artistic head of the Leningrad Philharmonic—asked when the symphony would be ready, Popov promised "to finish it in three months."[83] Popov's neighbors in his communal flat were just as interested and disturbed by the symphony's progress, or lack of it, when they heard Popov's singing and repetition of themes on his battered upright piano. The disturbances caused Popov to complain that, "This is oppressive beyond words!"[84] This rather seemed an ironic augury of the impending public disapproval of the Popov symphony.

Two years after starting his magnum opus, in November 1929, as his diary informs us, "I am still working lethargically on the second movement. The muted trumpets are singing, the cellos play *pizzicato*, and the oboe plays an *espressivo* note. . . . I can't wait to hear all of this in the orchestra."[85] Unfortunately, Popov's prolonged nurturing of ideas, and distractions from theater and cinema work inexorably obstructed the completion of the symphony. Another interruption was his teaching about which he grumbled, "If one could give up lecturing at the technical college and my private lessons—I might be able to manage it. . . . In the middle of the second movement, I have found a quite classic Scriabinesque harmony (thanks to several interruptions) in a cadenza. And later there is a Wagnerian sound on the cornet solo. What is going on?"[86] Popov was impressed by Shostakovich's industry, envying, "If I could reach just half his rhythm!"[87] Adding again in his diary, in admiration. "He infects me with his lively creative energy. Only Shcherbachov had this effect on me before."[88] Regrettably the "infection" was minimal, and the symphony dragged on at the same pace as before.

Shostakovich told Popov that 'the second movement was (in the strings before the *Wagnerian* theme) "wonderful" in one passage.'[89] Apart from teaching, an unexpected networking opportunity came from a Moscow conference to discuss opera, and an invitation from Abram Room to write a film score in Kyiv. The latter project would take up two valuable months. In the meantime, a positive relationship developed at the conference with the theater director Meyerhold. Popov boasted in pride in his diary that "Meyerhold, Guzman, and I have formed a united front in fighting for real Soviet music."[90] The head of repertoire at the Bolshoi Theater Guzman stated that "opera must be understandable to the worker."[91] At first, in a letter home, Popov was enthralled by Meyerhold, "by his setting out the problems clearly and profoundly, *great* questions in art, about the epoch, of *core* slogans, and the present-day ideas of vast construction, is all inescapably tearing away from the petty-minded, red-hot everyday form of life."[92] During a conference break, in a letter Popov wrote that he agreed with Meyerhold, "that we musicians are shambolic: certainly, we didn't know what pieces were banned by Muzsektor, and we didn't send this list to you for the discussion with Bubnov. I would like to blame the lack of organization on other Leningrad composers, but I am also to blame."[93]

The longer he toiled over the symphony the more that Popov became depressed, whining in his diary that, "I am essentially inept, I look at Krenek and Shostakovich, and see how innovative, and resourceful they are, and what am I?"[94] Shostakovich's new opera *The Nose* at the Mikhaylovsky Theater on January 27, 1930, impressed him, writing in his diary, "Shostakovich's orchestration is brilliant. (. . .) It is fascinating: how can I even attain half of his orchestral and melodic brilliance?"[95] The second movement *Largo* of the symphony was completed at the beginning of February 1930, and again shared his work with Shcherbachov, noting, "There is no discord regarding the music and form (construction)! He made some comments on the orchestration. Trivial issues. I have now started on the third movement."[96] In May 1930, for the first time, Popov heard his orchestral music in the theater production of *Oil*, recording in his diary that, "It was a huge achievement. It sounded forceful, expressive, and dynamic."[97] The opening review praised its "dynamic intensity."[98] Apart from lethargy, it seemed from his journal that instrumentation was a problem for Popov buried himself in a study of orchestration. "Composing technique is the *foundation for expression in the artistic* form of ideas, and consequently, of my own consciousness."[99] Returning from a holiday cruise on the Volga, there was news from Malko in Prague, and Berlin. Mikhail Druskin in Germany asked about the symphony. Malko wanted to conduct it, whereas Druskin wanted to give the score to Klemperer, Kleiber, or Scherchen who all expressed interest. These caused Popov no little angst as he recorded, "A groundswell of shame overwhelmed me reading these postcards."[100] The symphony's completion continued to elude him, as he confided in his journal, "After eleven pages, I cannot wrap up the finale. True, it's a long time since I worked properly—for eight, or ten, or twelve hours a day. (. . .) There is so much tension, melodic movement, and passion. This is like cement solidifying into concrete—exhausting all my thoughts and ideas."[101] Popov looked over Stravinsky's *Rite of Spring*, relishing not only the technique but also the mastery and brilliant musicianship. As always, Shostakovich remained a source of admiration for Popov, writing that, "His musical and orchestral gifts are inspiring and heart-warming."[102] More interest in the symphony came from another source in Germany from the young Soviet conductor Lev Ginzburg, who informed Popov that, "I am very interested in Shcherbachov's *Symphonietta*, and your symphony. (. . .) I do not know if the Radio (in Berlin) will allow me a four-part orchestra. I impatiently await the score, to judge it better. In any case, the performance is guaranteed following the wonderful success of your *Septet* in Stuttgart."[103]

Another diversion was writing music for the Leningrad TRAM theater *Vstrechny*. Popov was distraught from more domestic problems noting in his diary, "I have been beaten (. . .) because from morning till night—(until 1, 1.30 am) (my flat) is full of noise—often loud—from radio broadcasts, and K.M. Morozova's singing, either her piano playing or that of her daughter."[104] Living in a communal flat led to him searching for accommodation during his film work on one of the first Soviet sound movies *Song*. Shostakovich praised his incidental music for *Vstrechny*, telling him that hearing his orchestral music would give him confidence. The press reported that Popov's score "was unusually clear, and theatrical."[105] On December 12, 1930, we know from his diary, Popov met with Meyerhold and the conductor Samosud. "In principle, Meyerhold agreed to work with me, and soon we will start looking at themes and librettists who can match both Meyerhold's and my creative principles."[106]

The project was Meyerhold's production of *A List of Benefits*, which played an important element on Popov's career and Soviet theater in the 1930s. The celebrated actor/director had collaborated with Shostakovich on Mayakovsky's satire *Bedbug* developing a valuable partnership, now Meyerhold invited Popov to stay at his flat just off Gorky Street. However, the frequent distractions in the Meyerhold apartment led him to write his score at the theater. A new element was using jazz syncopation, an idea given to Popov from hearing a soprano saxophone in a piece by Shebalin.[107] After five or six days of frenetic activity, on May 12, the last twelve musical numbers were complete, Popov was enthused noting that, "Meyerhold was delighted, and Raikh (Meyerhold's wife, Zinaida) smiled contentedly. The musicians congratulated me enthusiastically."[108] Popov recycled his *Largo* from the *Septet*, and as he mentioned to his wife, "Meyerhold said this theme (the second in E minor) is brilliant. He is terribly passionate about it. . . . But Raikh (. . .) doesn't hear anything. She seems indifferent to music."[109] Moscow life disappointed Popov, making him homesick writing to his wife, "It's frustrating and congested. I miss Leningrad."[110] One more commission from the Red Theater production of *Class* engaged Popov until July, after which he and his wife took a holiday at Solntsy, in the Gulf of Finland. The symphony's completion was prioritized for the summer weeks.

Popov's resumption of work on the symphony quickly uncovered fresh glitches in the finale complaining that "I still don't have any discernible themes relating to the 'finale'—in closing the preceding symphonic development."[111] Progress was made by October, and he was confident enough to show his symphony to Asafyev. "I experienced a tangible happiness and satisfaction from such appreciation for my most compelling work."[112] At the end of November 1931, the Popov's moved to their new home in Detskoye Selo in Leningrad's green belt. This was a spacious flat in the semicircle housing quarter of the Catherine Palace given to arts workers. The fresh air and greenery of the environment helped finally the completion of the symphony's first version on January 17, 1932. At last Popov could confide in his diary that "the symphony has emerged with musical substance, passionate emotions, and a very clear intensity in the ideas. My opinion is shared by Asafyev, Arapov, Meyerhold, Tolstoy, Bogdanov-Berezovsky, Kochurov, and many others. Shcherbachov also played it through and responded positively (. . .), only expressing concern over the first movement orchestration."[113]

Popov believed that his newest work would prove an important contribution to contemporary repertoire, and regardless of Myaskovsky's symphonies and those by Shostakovich, he complained about the lack of new works, writing to Malko that, "Here at the Philharmonic, there is absolute poverty in the Soviet symphony. There is nothing to play, composers aren't writing symphonies. There are hopes for two new symphonies: my own and that by Shaporin." Further, Popov enlightened the conductor Nikolay Malko about a project (with Meyerhold) to write a Soviet opera based on texts by Alexey Tolstoy. He added about his fascination with Hindemith, Stravinsky, Berg, Krenek, Schoenberg, Prokofiev, and Richard Strauss. In addition to asking Malko for new scores from Europe, he also asked him to bring a Parker pen.[114]

It now seemed problematical to get his new symphony published. On October 2, 1931, at a meeting of the Association of Theater and Concert Composers (Vseroskomdram), Shebalin severely criticized the RAPM for taking over control of publishing saying that, "Such comrades: Feinberg, Shcherbachov, Polovinkin, Shenshin, Kryukov, Mosolov, Gavriil Popov, and a whole number of others that one could name. (. . .) Nothing is being published (. . .) apart from that of the proletarian musicians, and all other composers are being slowly, but surely chased away. Why is it so impossible to write orchestral music? There is already a very real need for it."[115]

Opera

The project for an opera based on a libretto by Tolstoy was announced in the media in the spring of 1931. "In the forthcoming season of the Theater of Opera and Ballet there will be a new opera, on which V. E. Meyerhold and the composer G. Popov have started to collaborate."[116] However, the libretto of this unrealized project was ultimately written by Dmitriev, not Tolstoy, and crucially, the music did not involve Popov. The plan was for an opera about Civil Rights in the United States, yet the problem was accessing archival material. Popov suggested to Meyerhold in an epistle that they should go to the United States to feel the "actual atmosphere and get familiarity with the lifestyle and pulse of the American negro."[117] The apparent betrayal of Popov's friend Alexey Tolstoy to write the libretto—not for his planned opera—but for Shostakovich greatly upset him. Furthermore, Popov was the last person to hear about the aborted project. In a letter to his wife, Popov intimated that he was now disheartened by Meyerhold, who appeared to be "superficial," and seemingly had little respect for Popov. "I refuse to write this opera. He doesn't allow me two words of my own."[118]

The suicide of the writer and actor Mayakovsky came as a shock to many of his friends, including Popov. His initial response was a *Symphonic Requiem in Memory of Vladimir Mayakovsky*.[119] However, there emerged sinister gossip about his new symphony. Now that his symphony was largely completed, a threat emerged from the RAPM against the Leningrad modernists specifically concerning Popov's symphony. The RAPM newssheet *Proletarian Musician* published a report from the Leningrad branch in which the secretary Vladimir Jokhelson wrote that "regardless of the shift by Shostakovich, he remains far from being a fellow-traveler. On the other hand, there is pressure from the right elements, for example, from Popov, whose speech at the composers' conference was extremely typical (of him). There are already emerging reactionary politics in his words."[120]

Composers Union

After the Cultural Revolution of 1928, following the disbandment of the ASM, and the shutting down of the RAPM, the transformation in the arts was unfolding rapidly with the foundation of the Union of Composers. The inaugural meeting on April 23, 1932, was chaired by the new Narkompros commissar Nikolay Bubnov. Leningrad composers were represented by Popov, Shostakovich, and Shteinberg. Notably, the Moscow composing contingent was represented by Mosolov, Gnessin, and Shebalin. This was on the eve of the publication of the party resolution "On the Restructure of Literary and Arts Organizations" formally disbanding the left arts organizations and founding of the Union of Composers. The speeches mainly touched on the harmful activities of the RAPM, and the abnormal relations which had resulted from their misrepresentation of the party's arts policies. The speeches (Shebalin, Shostakovich, Gnessin, Mosolov, Popov, and others) offered a long list of examples showing the complete ignorance by the RAPM leadership to fellow-travelers in music. However, those present agreed that "RAPM had taken an incorrect line" (as stated by Arkadyev) while the RAPM leadership had lost their trust (verified by Shebalin, Shostakovich, Mosolov, and others). The leadership of RAPM was given the opportunity of acknowledging their ill-conceived ways; however, they declined to do so, unaware that a decision had already been taken to disband them. Popov recorded in his diary:

I was the third person to speak following Shebalin and Shostakovich. I spoke for thirty minutes on two issues, (1) the background to the development of the RAPM movement in Leningrad and their relationship with fellow-traveler composers and (2) the development of symphonic music in the USSR. I voiced both the positive and negative aspects of Leningrad music in the last three years and on the series of facts relating to the shameless slandering of different fellow-travelers, and inability to find a working relationship with fellow-travelers, and creating an atmosphere of hostility, slandering of fellow-travelers on the pages of the RAPM press without justification; conveying examples of slander against me, placing insulting letters to the editors, without any verification and grounded truths the most serious accusations of composers of "reactionary politics," "underground" struggle against the RAPM and other delights. I mentioned the shameless fact of the RAPM excluding me from the teaching post at the Central Music Technical College, part of a strategy of blaming me for reactionary methodology (without any previous contact, report, or discussion), and against the protests of my students, under the pretext of "rationalizing cutbacks."[121]

In May 1932, Popov played his symphony to fellow professionals at the Bolshoi Theater, as he wrote to his wife,

Most of those who listened were unknown to me. (1) conductors of GABT [Bolshoi Theater] (2) soloists from the orchestra, (3) theater directors. The director [Malinovskaya] is not in the city. In charge was Arkanov [her depute]—the very one who approached both me and Tolstoy. Following the performance, they shared their impressions [in groups]. My friend, the German bassoonist—Binner is a student of Hindemith, and who played my *Septet* strongly endorsed the symphony. The piano was in poor condition. [The staff conductor] Melik-Pashayev told me how much clearer the symphony was in the second audition—and his enjoying it.

Arkanov also approved Popov's projected opera about black history in the United States.[122] Although this may have been a red herring because Popov already thought the opera wouldn't happen. Later in 1932, the Bolshoi Theater and *Komsomolskaya Pravda* organized the All-Union Competition in commemoration of the 1917 revolution. This event presented an opportunity for Popov. On October 10, he played his symphony to the Bolshoi Theater directors, plus Golovanov, Gnessin, Goldenweiser, and Myaskovsky—several of whom had heard it in the spring. Two weeks later, Popov was informed that he shared second prize with Shebalin's *Lenin* Symphony, Op. 16, and Shaporin's Symphony in D minor, Op. 11 with no first prize awarded. There was still no date for the symphony's premiere in Leningrad.

In August 1932, the idea of a chamber opera surfaced when Popov met the librettist, Eduard Krimmer. The subject was Yevgeny from Pushkin's *The Bronze Horseman*. Several composers were drawn to this subject including Glière and Myaskovsky. Popov acknowledged the problems in his diary, "The difficulty in setting Pushkin's poems and perhaps, the composition—from Pushkin's period—requires modification by Pasternak, but I don't know him personally."[123] Without waiting for a libretto, Popov immediately started on the stage work, so much so that he was confident to play the music to friends. Out at Detskoye Selo—at their new home—after a supper with Tolstoy, Meyerhold, and Raich, Popov played through Yevgeny's aria. Apparently reconciled, Popov noted that "Meyerhold kissed me. I told him of my work on the *Bronze Horseman* during the summer. . . . 'Pushkin with jazz!' speaking of the Aria-Tango." So taken was Meyerhold with the idea and Popov's music, he promised to stage the opera in Moscow.[124] There was interest too from Arkanov at the Bolshoi Theater who suggested a commission for the stage work.[125] In March 1933, and without any confirmation, Popov approached Samosud, the music director at the Mikhaylovsky Theater. Instead of Tolstoy, Spassky was now writing the libretto for *Poor Yevgeny* and asked for an advance of 5,000 roubles.[126] However without any contracts and no libretto, three years later, trying to revive the idea, Popov asked the writer Osip Brik to write one, yet again no progress was made, and this became another lost project for Popov, although he recycled the music later.[127]

Debates about the First Symphony

In the spring of 1933, Popov's symphony was considered important enough for a two-day discussion at the Leningrad branch of the Composers' Union. The event started positively for it was his friend Boris Arapov who introduced the debate.

> Popov is primarily exploring for a modern language, and for fresh content which is both innovative in form and technique. We have often what (are termed) ground-breaking works in both program and name, (but) not revolutionary in language, in mostly archaic means. Many find analogies in Popov's vision with Mayakovsky's stimulating originality. Mayakovsky also followed a path of revolutionary innovation. In Popov's case, all this audacious novelty is not experimentation for the sake of it, but clutching at new ground-breaking sounds. Popov's symphony through its' conceptual plan and masterful quality is wholly original, and its revolutionary content is unquestionably ours (Soviet).

In following up, Shostakovich commented that he "is a great and enthusiastic admirer of this symphony, but I am concerned (as to) when will this symphony be finished, and when will it be possible to hear it?" The first note of dissent came from Arseny Gladkovsky, who said he was attracted to the energetic pulse, and the effort yet the main flaw is in its great intensity which overwhelms the listener. Pyotr Ryazanov reflected on the subject matter. "The symphony is a document of time, and essentially of the revolutionary period, and most of all realizes a man's consciousness during this definite period. This symphony is typically characteristic of the literature of the mid-twenties when Pilnyak, Zamyatin, Alexey Tolstoy were dealing with this issue. Typically, Popov's s work coincides with Meyerhold's *A List of Benefits*. The path of Meyerhold is akin to that taken by Popov." Benedict Pushkov saw both positives and negatives:

> I don't think that in its first hearing the symphony will be understood by the audience, nor do I think it will be welcomed, appreciated and in any way be inspiring. I endorse the momentous candor and nobility of the symphony. The subject of this symphony is not stationary, it builds onwards. The symphony begins on a profoundly individual question—as a sort of psychological plan—ending with a societal generalization, and looks to the future, historically and objectively. The symphony is positively structured as a Soviet symphony should be, however at the same time I sense something that I cannot quite agree with.

The final speaker in the two-day debate was Mikhail Glukh:

> I only heard the symphony today and my first impression was extraordinarily compelling, and undoubtedly we have a very powerful work, a great one which speaks of a composer who follows a unique path. The problem arises from the subject matter of the symphony which is the composer and the revolution, and the intelligentsia and the revolution. What belief do the intelligentsia have in the revolution, and what is the view presented here by Popov? The feeling of the revolution as a great moving force, which appears in the prologue to the work, is what Popov gives us without doubt. The profundity of the work is enormous, but it is adversely obscured, and I consider that this comes from something that is not quite palpable.[128]

In response to the criticisms raised, Popov agreed to rewrite some parts of the symphony before the Leningrad Philharmonic premiere.

Invitation to London and Paris

In the autumn of 1933, the visit by Prokofiev to Russia opened up dramatically new possibilities for Popov. Prokofiev told him that the *Septet* was very well received at the Paris premiere.[129] But he was soon brought down to earth when he played chess with Prokofiev, as he confided to his journal, "I was absolutely thrashed."[130] Popov expressed a desire to perform in the West, and suitably impressed, on returning home, Prokofiev invited him to Paris for concerts of his music, and a BBC broadcast in London. Prokofiev mentioned the financial arrangements, writing to Popov from Paris.

> To arrange a concert exclusively of your works is hardly feasible, but I have two firm proposals for you, 1) the Paris contemporary music society Triton invites you to play your Trio (song and sonatina) (Two Vocalises, Op. 3, and several piano pieces) on 13 April, for a fee of 500 francs, 2) London radio (British Broadcasting Corporation) proposes you play for them on 15 April, the Trio, and a group of solo items, for a fee of fifteen guineas, which is 1200 francs. They are both confirmed. (. . .) Finally, if the symphony is performed, then you will receive 300 francs for the score, and perhaps another 100 francs as the author's fee.[131]

Prokofiev asked him to make haste and arrange his train tickets and foreign passport, emphasizing the significance of the London engagement, both financially and musically. Popov was advised to send word of his intentions and the symphony to Paris. Popov noted that "The symphony is programmed for a Paris performance at the end of April under Desormiere ('similar in character to Ansermet, but younger')."[132] This proposed concert was based on the promise by Popov to send the score in mid-February. However, the orchestration was not completed until March 31, 1934, and the Paris concert never took place. In a third letter, Prokofiev said the Paris premiere of the symphony could be postponed until May or even October.[133] Prokofiev sent the contact details of Edward Clark at the BBC in London who would arrange a work permit for him, but again nothing happened. Whether it be through lethargy or lack of a business-like approach, Popov never did send the score or travel to London (at least for another thirty years). Certainly, the extraordinary efforts taken by Prokofiev to get Popov's music heard in Europe were salutary, and, if they had succeeded, perhaps Popov's career would have taken a quite different course.[134]

The first orchestral piece by Popov to be heard at the Leningrad Philharmonic was not the First Symphony, but the colorful Symphonic Suite No. 1, Op. 12 on April 6, 1934. Based on a popular film score, the conductor was the Englishman Albert Coates. The acquaintance with Popov's music led to Coates suggesting that he write a violin concerto, as he mentioned in his diary, "He spoke about my 'melodicism,' and of my affinity with Tchaikovsky."[135] The idea of a violin concerto motivated Popov, and by the end of the year, he had written seventeen pages of the opening movement. As always, Popov showed his score to his teacher who spoke about the unnecessary length of the exposition of the main theme (repetition, and in the same tonality), and to Shostakovich who commented on "the premature appearance of the tonality (E major) of the secondary idea at the end of the exposition of the main theme."[136] The Popov Violin Concerto would be subject to numerous revisions in the coming years.

On December 28, 1934, Vladimir Dranishnikov conducted the Symphonic Suite No. 1 with the Moscow Radio Orchestra. The work was praised by Myaskovsky, Shebalin, Kabalevsky, Knipper, and Alexandrov. Popov was given a reception at the National Hotel nearby, and later at the House of Unions hosted by Moscow Radio and the Komsomol. Back home in Leningrad, he took in performances of Stravinsky's *Le roi des étoiles* and *Les noces* at the Capella. Popov informed that, "The music is brilliant; (but) the performance was disappointing."[137]

Shostakovich's opera *Lady Macbeth of Mtsensk District* impressed Popov enormously. "I am convinced again that the second act (two murders and one vision) is brilliant for its dramatic force, clear expression (all elements of the writing), and the wonderful lyricism."[138] Popov ranked the opera with Berg's *Wozzeck*, *Oedipex Rex* by Stravinsky, and Shostakovich's *The Nose* as the finest of the twentieth century. In another diary entry, Popov regretted that the ever increasing volume of cinema work was breaking his willpower and daily systematic work.[139] Malko asked the score of the Symphonic Suite No. 1 for his Danish Radio Symphony Orchestra, suggesting that the broadcasts could be picked up in Leningrad.[140] In the first week of January 1935, Popov got a letter from Artur Rodzinski—the music director of the Cleveland Orchestra—complaining that he could not make out details in his score of the symphony. Rather than dispatch a fresh copy, Popov asked him to return the score with his questions—this unfortunately never happened, and another possibility was lost. Rodzinski had premiered Shostakovich's *Lady Macbeth* in New York and was actively promoting new Russian music in the United States.[141] A performance of Schoenberg's Variations for Orchestra by the Leningrad Philharmonic under Steidry disheartened Popov noting that, "Schoenberg's principle (absence of modality, 12 tone key etc.,) does not satisfy me."[142]

Completion of the First Symphony

We know that the first version of Popov's Symphony was completed in January 1932.[143] The work is scored in three movements for a huge orchestra and demonstrates the characteristics which became Popov's hallmark: the employment of rich textures combined with weirdly fluctuating syncopations, mingled with irony, grotesque, and pathos. Popov introduced the dedications from the intended Mayakovsky Requiem: "To my dear father. The working man and champion of the Proletarian Cultural Front (Education of Young

Workers). I dedicate this symphony, (1) the first movement *Struggle and Defeats*, (2) the second movement *Humanity* and, (3) the third movement *Energy, Will, and Joy of Labor of the Conqueror.*"[144] On the title page of the manuscript, Popov wrote "*Sturm und Drang.*"[145]

Before the orchestral premiere, the symphony was heard in both Moscow and Leningrad in the piano score to musicians, composers, and friends. In these private hearings, many were struck by the brilliance and freshness of the writing. The symphony was thought by the Secretary of the Composers' Union in Leningrad to be "a considerable success for Soviet symphonic music."[146] Popov enlightened readers in the Composers Union journal that, "Soviet symphonism is a new type of musical composition which ought to permeate the creative practice of the composer. . . . Soviet symphonism must spread its influence into the forgotten, backward areas of instrumental and vocal music . . . through sincere revelatory emotion, and intensifying the socio-political ideas in the literary texts for vocal compositions."[147]

Shostakovich and Popov continued to share their latest music by playing through themes and ideas as they wrote them, mentioning in his diary that, "Yesterday Mitya Shostakovich was here. I played my symphony to him. He likes the finale. He is reticent regarding the remainder, which probably means that he didn't like it."[148] Popov was being overly modest, or disingenuous, because Shostakovich praised the strings in the second movement, as "wonderful." Many years later, Shostakovich reflected: "In my view, this is one of the most outstanding symphonic works, and influenced, not only my creativity, but that of other Leningrad composers during the 1930s."[149] Romaschuk considers that "a great deal of what was perceptible in (Shostakovich's) Fourth Symphony was already revealed in Popov's First."[150] This influence from Popov's symphony is manifest in the enormous inner propulsion of ideas, the content of which demands fluctuating diverse passages, the intensity of flowing, and substantially distinct images. The English musicologist David Fanning wrote of the finale's perpetual motion where all sorts of ideas fly about notably on piccolo and xylophone which "Shostakovich would remember in the finale of his Fifth Symphony and the second movement of his Seventh (. . .) he would draw on its hyperbolic C-major conclusion-albeit in heavily ironized form-for the corresponding pages of his equally ill-starred Fourth Symphony."[151] Shostakovich's biographer Marina Sabinina noted that in both symphonies there reoccur the similar "intensifications, multi-textured composition, thematic indulgence, and congestion."[152]

European modernism was relevant as the scholar Elena Dolinskaya writes, "a special role was played by (the use of) experimental methodology that reflected the latest tendencies of modern European orchestration."[153] In the 1930s, Popov's symphony was highly commended by a wide-ranging number of musicians and others in the arts: Prokofiev, Asafyev, Meyerhold, the novelist Alexey Tolstoy, and the conductor Ernst Ansermet. Shostakovich stated that it was a remarkable phenomenon in Soviet music.[154] Dolinskaya gives her insightful appraisal that

> the symphony represents the psychological restoration of a personality during revolutionary events—in a massive three-movement cycle. The organic unity of the movements takes an integrated line of development and continual resolution of lyric imagery of the main theme of the first movement: such as the intonation in the complexity of the main idea, as an integral image in the *Largo*'s secondary idea. The metamorphosis of the main theme of the first movement (*Allegro energico*) is linked to the beginning of the (*Finale*) *Scherzo*. Here the composer is trying to build up with jazz-like means (syncopated rhythms with changing accents, half-tone changes of pronounced non-accords). Here there arises contrasting, and for Popov, characteristically stylistic declinations, necessary for determined concretized images in opening up his musical ideas.[155]

In distinguishing between a *pure* symphony where there is no literary, or visible *concept*, unlike for the cinema or theater, in a letter to Malko, Popov believed the listener has to "enter into the process of the symphonic flow by grasping the nature of shifting ideas, emotional tensions, (. . .) of repose, again movement, collisions of dreams, their struggle and divergent inward symphonic forms."[156]

The massive opening movement of twenty-two minutes—*Allegro energico*—is based on a richly polyphonic sonata form. The orchestral canvass embraces different ideas—as if independent of each other—hinting at Varèse's essays on "spatial" music. It is unlikely, however, that Popov was aware at the time of *Amériques* or *Arcana*. The second movement, *Largo con moto e molto cantabile*, is founded on a seemingly everlasting richly emotional theme on the oboe. The third movement, *Presto*, combines a brilliant *Scherzo* with a buoyant closing coda that mesmerizes with its percussive astounding finale. That Popov's First shares ideas in several of Shostakovich's symphonies are perhaps as much a reflection of deference by Shostakovich to Popov's prodigious talent. Hakobian considers that the first movement "could serve as an immediate model for the first movement of the work by Shostakovich, (. . .) with enormously enlarged sonata forms with numerous and variegated 'extra' insertions."[157] Popov's friend and colleague, Boris Arapov, wrote that he interpreted the narrative of the symphony as the "fall, struggle, fall, a further struggle; finally, victory and the confirmation of a new beginning in life."[158]

The First Symphony was premiered on March 22, 1935, by the Leningrad Philharmonic Orchestra under Fritz Steidry to a mostly hostile audience. The performance disappointed Popov writing in his journal that "the symphony was under-rehearsed—slow tempi, unsatisfactory nuances of separate groups in tutti. This is the result of a lack of rehearsal: four general and four group (rehearsals). If there were another two general (rehearsals), then everything would have been much clearer and emotionally suitable."[159] Characteristically, Popov took some of the blame on himself. One of the problems was the failure by the musicians to understand it, and they mounted a fierce resistance to giving a successful debut, as was to be repeated with Shostakovich's Fourth Symphony a year later. The part played by Steidry is difficult to comprehend as the conductor was highly regarded for his advocacy of Schoenberg and the New Vienna School. On the following day, with remarkable speed the Leningrad Regional Repertkom banned the symphony.[160] Popov's immediate thoughts were shared in his diary,

> The upshot is that it is necessary to spend a month cleaning up the score in the tutti and some minutiae. Pushkov told me yesterday that the Oblast Repertkom has banned my symphony. . . . This was verified by Jokhelson in a phone call to Pushkov. Repertkom is Obnorsky. He didn't like it, so he banned the symphony. (. . .) It's an astonishing moment. Repertkom didn't wait for any discussion or any reviews. They simply banned it. If this is confirmed, then I will have to spend time in Moscow to clarify matters. But I have to write (a film score) for Room. How will I manage this and be able to concentrate on *The Severe Youth* commission?[161]

The following day, Popov managed to see the transcript banning his symphony.[162] "Impermissible performance of his (work), because it reflects an unfavorable ideology to our class."[163] Prokofiev, Asafyev, Shebalin, and Shaporin all petitioned for a lifting of the ban.[164] The composer Mikhail Yudin expressed an opinion thought to be widely shared by those who heard the symphony. "Often, when listening to Popov's symphony, there arises an association with Filonov's paintings—the canvasses of which are all masterly detailed, and in sum, give the notion of a nightmare. The finale is the most poster-like in its irony"[165]

The premiere of Popov's symphony took place during a disturbingly transformative period in the country, and more importantly in Leningrad. It was on December 1, 1934, that Kirov, the leader of the city's party, was assassinated at the Smolny headquarters which led to the arrests of thousands of people in the city. Between February 29 and March 27, 1935, some 35,000 people were arrested on suspicion of being enemies of the state. The Politburo stated in a resolution on January 26 that the perpetrators were arising from "the terrorist activities of the Trotskyist-Zinoviev counter-revolutionary block" adding that "Leningrad is the only city where there remain so many former Tsarist officials and their lackeys, former gendarmes and policemen . . . and they are continuing to hinder our administrative work everywhere."[166] Some 4,393 former officials were shot and hundreds more were sent to labor camps. One of the significant factors in the overnight banning of Popov's symphony was that the head of Leningrad's Glavrepertkom Boris Obnorsky was formerly the head of the Zinoviev Communist University in Leningrad between 1922 and 1929. With this colorful back history, Obnorsky may well have been fearful of repercussions against him if he was not seen to take strong action against works which might have been considered controversial. The fact that the symphony's premiere was not a success with either musicians or the audience will have been the determining element in banning it.

Lifting of the Ban

Popov's ministrations in Moscow were successful, for, at the end of April, the ban was lifted by the head of Moscow Repertkom—Osaf Litovsky. Nevertheless, unsatisfied with this decision, the former RAPM member—Jokhelson set up a debate at the Leningrad Composers' Union to build the campaign against the symphony.[167] Here it is important to note that two years before Jokhelson had widely praised Popov's symphony in the media, so perhaps he was just trying to act safe. During the two-day debate (Popov could not attend as he was working on the film score in Kyiv, and in any case was not invited), the symphony was torn to shreds, despite support from a subdued minority. Popov was attacked for being allegedly "influenced by western bourgeois ideology," for individualism, and the failure to uphold socialist realism. This was from the head of the orchestra who acknowledged that he didn't know much about music. There was hope for a positive appraisal when Popov's friend Boris Arapov gave the opening statement by lending significant backing. "I wanted to say that the acquaintance of Popov with [the music of] Schoenberg, Stravinsky, Krenek, Bach, and Beethoven has all led to positive results."[168] This was nullified by the secretary Vladimir Jokhelson who said that he believed the press statement was verbatim, and that Glavrepertkom should enforce the ban. There was criticism from an unexpected source, Bogdanov-Berezovsky who may well have been terrorized by recent events in the city. "The score is dreadful because it doesn't fully realize the composer's conception. The musical-thematic text of this composition is more effective, and important than its orchestration. This work is essentially foreign to Soviet reality." The one-time ally of Popov concluded by saying that "Popov's symphony represented a forgotten phase. It seems to me that this is not the required path for Popov."[169] These words were disappointing because this friend (like Jokhelson) had previously favored the symphony in the media.[170]

Crucially, the backers of Popov's symphony were not present at this meeting; absent were Asafyev, Shostakovich, Scherbachov, and Shaporin, and there was no quorum of the "secretariat" of the Composers' Union (which included Popov). Jokhelson himself was dismissed for being "provincial and lacking in argument," and without the authority to ban the symphony.[171]

Popov was upbeat after meeting with satirist writers in Moscow en route to Leningrad from Kyiv, noting in his diary that "The brothers' Tur published a feuilleton in *Izvestiya* defending my symphony under the ironic heading *Extraordinary Love*."[172] The Moscow broadsheet called the banning "a clear example of the unnecessary and harmful exercise of administrative power. (. . .) In this entire atrocious affair, one cannot be happy just by the miserable revocation of the ban. In our country, there are too few composers, and fewer still of significance."[173] This came three months after its albeit formal renovation. In a further attempt to reinstate the symphony, in October 1936, Popov met Rafail—the head of the Leningrad Committee for Arts, outlining the history of Jokhelson's vendetta. Jokhelson now shared the Directorship of the Mikhaylovsky Theater with the Secretaryship of the Composers' Union—two highly important roles in the city. Rafail promised that he could only try to clarify matters.[174] The scandal over the banning, and the hostility which developed led to Shcherbachov, Arapov, and Tyulin attempting to restore a better atmosphere in the Composers' Union. This was extenuated after the scandal of "formalism" surrounding Shostakovich's *Lady Macbeth* and *Bright Stream*, and now there was little chance of ever resurrecting the symphony.

We know that Popov's symphony was familiar to leading conductors in Europe and America; candidates were literally queuing up to give the Western premier including Klemperer, Kleiber, and Scherchen, yet nothing came of it. The symphony's score and parts only resurfaced a decade after Popov's death in 1972. In a letter to Izaak Glikman many years later, Shostakovich recalled that Popov "was really a very talented person. His First Symphony (was) ruined by fighters against formalism, and it overflowed with some very good things."[175] Shostakovich later attempted to resurrect the symphony for performance. The musicologist Inna Barsova expressed an initial lack of interest in Popov when so few of his works were performed. "When we saw that he was awarded the Stalin Prize, we didn't think so much about him, no one thought his music was of interest, and when we discovered the First Symphony in Germany at a seminar, we were astonished. His widow, Zara Apetyan kept the score, and it was passed to the Glinka Museum; the radio made recordings of symphonies which were then unknown."[176]

A year after the fiasco of his own symphony, in 1936, Popov heard the first movement of Shostakovich's Fourth Symphony. After hearing the whole work played by the composer, he exclaimed—"brilliant. It's undoubtedly his finest creation."[177] Popov thought the finale was "wonderful music. Very profound. It ends very well. On a dominant lamenting on a low register with divided Celli and Bassi and (in) a broad usage of violas, violins I and II to sol, solo, dying, celesta."[178] The extraordinary nature of the construction of Popov's First Symphony is explored by Igor Vorobyov. "The form of the avant-garde utopia in symphonic music, like Scriabin, was stretched out in a spherical form. This spiral form was based on the variable opening thematic complex which was a characteristic in Shostakovich (2nd and 3rd symphonies), *Komsomoliya* by N. Roslavets, *October* by I. Schillinger (this idea will be taken in the 1st and 3rd movements of G. Popov's First Symphony)." Vorobyov states that in the 1920s and early 1930s, Soviet composers continued to use Scriabin's model of the culminatory finale in attempting to replicate the festive coda of the Symphony No. 5 *Prometheus* and especially in the Symphony No. 4 *The Poem of Ecstasy* in aspiring for "forward and upwards."[179]

The disappointment at the failure of his symphony led Popov to start writing a quite new work in the summer of 1935, enthusing in his diary that,

> In my Second Symphony, I want to tear apart the banality of public taste, roaring with desperate power and passion. . . . I want to portray the immense roar of stimulating dynamic thinking, and the utmost, and most subtle, sincere sensitivity. . . . They will say it's unfathomable! Yes, it may be unfathomable today. But tomorrow, it will be so clear and vital—they'll say it could never be otherwise.[180]

It appears that his new symphony was slowly taking shape for a year later, again confiding to his journal,

> Right now, my Second Symphony has started to sound very clearly inside my head, in detail, with impassioned sharpness, and its form is absolutely unusual. The first theme is extraordinarily boisterous, and there is a massive blow with a tutti chord and a powerful *fortissimo* (unison) on strings of the opening idea, without harmony, without any accompaniment.[181]

The Petersburg music writer Iosif Raiskin considers the "unwritten symphony by Popov shares the fate of Berlioz's Symphony in A minor, of which the composer dreamt and which we know was never written due to a misfortune in his private life."[182] Popov gave the Opus 23 to the incomplete Second Symphony, but only seven pages remain in the archives, dated March 12, 1937. Many years later, this has been scored out and written in the score "for the 6th symphony," again erased out, "for the 7th symphony." The projected Seventh Symphony was never finished. The wartime Second Symphony Op. 39 is quite unrelated to these sketches.[183]

While it was the symphony that was Popov's idée fixe, writing for the theater and cinema helped earn a living—and some passing glory—Popov felt that this secondary career, albeit financially lucrative, was holding him back—certainly, he would have written more symphonies if he enjoyed financial support. If anything, the work for theater and film helped experimentation to enhance his expression (he was first to use electronic instruments in the cinema), and additionally, impose a discipline in keeping to deadlines.

Regardless of lifting the ban, the scandal remained, and Popov's name and reputation were worth little for the assignment to write a film score for *Land of the Soviets* ended in disaster. As the film moved to completion, Esfir Shub (who had worked with Popov for her *KShE* documentary) whinged in a letter to the composer, "I so much wanted my picture to include your classical music. The conductor Shteinberg and Kryukov are now going to realize this. These are challenging times. Your name is banned here. I don't expect anything good from Kryukov. I cannot imagine my work without your music."[184] In August 1935, Eisenstein hired Popov for his *Bezhin Meadow* film about collectivization in Ukraine. Popov was enthused by the initial film rushes in October, considering it brilliant in its content, depth, and masterly in form.[185] However, the film was canceled owing to its controversial coverage of collectivization, and, even in the revival, it was Prokofiev's music that was used for the film score.

NOTES

1. In 1920, he became the director of a labor school of the first and second level, and at Rabfak, and lectured at Rostov University and at the Pedagogical Institute. He was head of the faculty of "methodology of teaching of Russian language and literature," Romaschuk, *Gavriil Nikolayevich Popov. Tvorchestvo. Vremya. Sudba*. Moscow: Institute Ippolotit-Ivanov Publishers, 2000, 321.

2. Apetyan Z.A., ed. *G. N. Popov 1904–1972—Iz literaturnovo naslediye. Stranitsi biografii*, Moscow: Sovetsky Kompositor, 1986, 344.

3. Nikolay Dmitrevich Popov (1883–1945) played violin and composed for the church choir that he directed. Following his graduation from the history and philology faculty of Kharkiv University in 1910 and worked as a teacher at Rostov University, *Gavriil Nikolayevich Popov. Tvorchestvo. Vremya. Sudba*, Moscow, 2000, 3 43.

4. Popov, Gavriil, "Autobiography, Romaschuk, Inna," *Gavriil Nikolayevich Popov. Tvorchestvo. Vremya. Sudba*, Moscow, 2000, 321.

5. Autobiography, Romaschuk, *Gavriil Nikolayevich Popov. Tvorchestvo. Vremya. Sudba*, Moscow, 2000, 321.

6. It was to Presman that Rachmaninov dedicated his Second Piano Sonata, opus 36 in 1913. When dismissed by the Russian Music Society in 1912, Rachmaninov wrote in defense of his colleague: "I personally consider Presman a most honourable

man and a highly talented pedagogue who loves his calling passionately." Presman conducted Rachmaninov's early opera *Aleko* in Rostov in 1902, and later premiered the Cello Sonata and the Second Sonata there. However, following the October revolution, in 1918 Presman returned to establish a private music school on the base of the previous RMO school in Rostov on Don which had been requisitioned as a hospital during the war—author.

7. Apetyan, Z.A. (ed.), *G. N. Popov 1904–1972—Iz literaturnovo naslediye. Stranitsi biografii*, Moscow: Sovetsky Kompositor, 1986, 194.

8. Apetyan, Z.A. (ed.), *G. N. Popov 1904–1972—Iz literaturnovo naslediye. Stranitsi biografii*, Moscow: Sovetsky Kompositor, 1986, 194.

9. Apetyan, Z.A. (ed.) *G. N. Popov 1904–1972—Iz literaturnovo naslediye. Stranitsi biografii*, Moscow: Sovetsky Kompositor, 1986, 206.

10. Popov, Gavriil, Diary August 22, 1921, *Gavriil Nikolayevich Popov. Tvorchestvo. Vremya. Sudba*, Moscow, 2000, 327.

11. Diary August 22, 1921, *Gavriil Nikolayevich Popov. Tvorchestvo. Vremya. Sudba*. Moscow, 2000, 327.

12. "I had learned the means of existence and began working at the age of 15 years by teaching piano and elementary maths. Between 1920 and 1921, under N. P. Speransky I assisted as a repititeur in the opera studio at the Rostov State Conservatoire, and from 1921 to 1922, I worked as a draftsman at the Rostov railway workshops." Diary, April 26, 1922, *Gavriil Nikolayevich Popov. Tvorchestvo. Vremya. Sudba*. Moscow, 2000, 328.

13. Apetyan, Z.A. (ed.) *G. N. Popov 1904–1972—Iz literaturnovo naslediye. Stranitsi biografii*, Moscow: Sovetsky Kompositor, 1986, 204.

14. Diary, May 26, 1921, *Gavriil Nikolayevich Popov. Tvorchestvo. Vremya. Sudba*. Moscow, 2000, 204–205.

15. Diary, August 11, 1921, *Gavriil Nikolayevich Popov. Tvorchestvo. Vremya. Sudba*. Moscow, 2000, 207.

16. Popov, "Autobiography," *Gavriil Nikolayevich Popov. Tvorchestvo. Vremya. Sudba*, Moscow, 2000, 321.

17. Diary, September 4, 1921, *Gavriil Nikolayevich Popov. Tvorchestvo. Vremya. Sudba*, Moscow, 2000, 210.

18. Diary, December 1, 1921, *Gavriil Nikolayevich Popov. Tvorchestvo. Vremya. Sudba*, Moscow, 2000, 214.

19. Diary, November 21, 1922, *Gavriil Nikolayevich Popov. Tvorchestvo. Vremya. Sudba*, Moscow, 2000, 217.

20. Diary, April 15, 1922, *Gavriil Nikolayevich Popov. Tvorchestvo. Vremya. Sudba*, Moscow, 2000, 216.

21. Diary, September 24, 1922, *Gavriil Nikolayevich Popov. Tvorchestvo. Vremya. Sudba*, Moscow, 2000, 217.

22. Romaschuk interview with the author, February 2018.

23. Romaschuk, *Gavriil Nikolayevich Popov. Tvorchestvo. Vremya. Sudba*, Moscow, 2000, 29.

24. Diary, May 1, 1925, *Gavriil Nikolayevich Popov. Tvorchestvo. Vremya. Sudba*. Moscow, 2000, 223–224.

25. Diary, May 1, 1924, *Gavriil Nikolayevich Popov. Tvorchestvo. Vremya. Sudba*, Moscow, 2000, 223–224.

26. Shcherbachev was a student of Calafati in piano, and in composition of Cherepnin and Shteinberg at the St. Petersburg Conservatoire. Shcherbachev also studied at St. Petersburg University in jurisprudence and philology and played as a concertmaster for Diaghilev's Russian Seasons before the Great War—author.

27. Diary, May 1924, *Gavriil Nikolayevich Popov. Tvorchestvo. Vremya. Sudba*, Moscow, 2000, 222.

28. Protocol of the first meeting of the commission to monitor the pupils of the piano faculty of Leningrad State Conservatoire from May 13 to 31, 1924, where against the name of Popov (No. 15) is written "Academically of average ability, without promise" and further "expel" LGALI, f. 298, op. 1, d. 89) Ed. Apetyan Z.A., *G. N. Popov Iz literaturnovo naslediye. Stranitsi biografii*, Moscow, 1986, 344.

29. Vlasova, E.S., *1948 god v sovetskoy muziki*, Moscow: 21 Classika, 2010, 37.

30. LGAOPCC, f. 2556, op. 1, d. 58, l. 104.

31. Haas, David, *Leningrad's Modernists: studies in composition and musical thought 1917–1932*, New York: Peter Lang, 1998, 24.

32. "Autobiography," *Gavriil Nikolayevich Popov. Tvorchestvo. Vremya. Sudba*, Moscow, 2000, 322.

33. The document affirming Popov's readmission to study was initialed by Chelyapov on June 17, 1925, by the Head Committee of professional-technical education of the Narkompros RSFSR 47038 LGALI, f. 298, op. 2, d. 2597, l. 18.

34. Popov letter to Yavorsky, July 20, 1925, *Gavriil Nikolayevich Popov. Tvorchestvo. Vremya. Sudba*, Moscow, 2000, 38–39.

35. Diary, May 19, 1925, *Gavriil Nikolayevich Popov. Tvorchestvo. Vremya. Sudba*. Moscow, 2000, 224.

36. Romaschuk, *Gavriil Nikolayevich Popov. Tvorchestvo. Vremya. Sudba*, Moscow, 2000, 34.

37. Diary, July 25, 1925, *Gavriil Nikolayevich Popov. Tvorchestvo. Vremya. Sudba*, Moscow, 2000, 225.

38. *Zhizn Iskusstvo* No. 15, 1926.

39. V.M. "Novoye Muzika," *Zhizn Iskussstva*, No. 51, 1926.

40. Milhaud, Darius, *Ma vie heureuse*, Editions Belfond, Paris, 1973, 153.

41. *Rabochy i Teatr*, No. 52, 1926.

42. Asafyev, Boris, "Istorichesky god," *Sovetskaya Muzika*, No. 3, 1933, 102.

43. Apetyan Z.A., ed. *G. N. Popov 1904–1972—Iz literaturnovo naslediye. Stranitsi biografii*, Moscow: Sovetsky Kompositor, 1986, 346.

44. Romaschuk, Inna, "LASM devyanosto let nazad," *Iz Istorii Otechestvennoy muziki XX veka*, MK, No. 1, 2016, 49.

45. Asafyev, Boris, "Portraits of Soviet composers," RGALI, f.2658. op. 1. ed.kh r. 367, l. 107.

46. Raiskin, Iosif, CD booklet for Popov Symphony No. 1, Northern Flowers NF/PMA 9996.

47. Postcard from Popov to Asafyev, dated November 16, 1927. RGALI., f.2658, op. 1., ed. khr. 662.

48. Belyaev, Viktor, "Gavriil Popov," *Sovremennaya Muzika*, No. 1, 1928, 14.
49. Belyaev, Viktor, "Gavril Popov," *Zhizn Iskusstvo*, No. 1, 1928, 14.
50. Hakobian, Leon, *Music of the Soviet Era*, London: Routledge, 2017, 131–132.
51. Romaschuk, Inna, *Gavriil Nikolayevich Popov. Tvorchestvo. Vremya. Sudba*, Moscow, 2000, 98.
52. Romaschuk, Inna, *Gavriil Nikolayevich Popov. Tvorchestvo. Vremya. Sudba*, Moscow, 2000, 37.
53. Romaschuk, Inna, *Gavriil Nikolayevich Popov. Tvorchestvo. Vremya. Sudba*, Moscow, 2000, 37–38.
54. Apetyan, Z.A. (ed.), *G. N. Popov 1904–1972—Iz literaturnovo naslediye. Stranitsi biografii*, Moscow: Sovetsky Kompozitor, 1986, 345.
55. Vainkop, Yuri, *Rabochy i Theater*, No. 49, 1927.
56. Bogdanov-Berezovsky, Venyamin, *Zhizn i Iskusstvo*, No. 11, 1928.
57. Asafyev, Boris, "Portraits of Soviet composers," RGALI, f.2658. op. 1. ed.kh r. 367, l. 100.
58. V'as, (Asafyev, Boris) "G.N. Popov," *Sovremennaya Muzika*, No. 25, 1927, 64–65.
59. The other works heard by him were Stravinsky's Concertino, Casella's Quartet, and Kodaly's Serenade for two violins and viola.
60. Diary, December 6, 1927. *Gavriil Nikolayevich Popov. Tvorchestvo. Vremya. Sudba*, Moscow, 2000, 227.
61. Diary, November 25, 1927, *Gavriil Nikolayevich Popov. Tvorchestvo. Vremya. Sudba*, Moscow, 2000, 227.
62. V. M-yy, *Zhizn i Iskusstvo*, No. 49, 1927.
63. Reed, John (1887–1920) was an American journalist who wrote his *Ten Days that Shook the World* describing the October Revolution of 1917—author.
64. Diary, July 30, 1925. *Gavriil Nikolayevich Popov. Tvorchestvo. Vremya. Sudba*, Moscow, 2000, 225.
65. Sitsky, Larry, *Music of the Repressed Russian Avant-Garde*, Westport, CT: Greenwood Press, 1994, 177–178.
66. Brik, Olesya, *Venskoye Izdatelstvo "Universal Edition" i muzikanti iz sovetskoy Rossi*, St. Petersburg: Novikova, 2011, 133.
67. Brik, Olesya, *Venskoye Izdatelstvo "Universal Edition" i muzikanti iz sovetskoy Rossi*, St. Petersburg: Novikova, 2011, 398–399.
68. Brik, Olesya, *Venskoye Izdatelstvo "Universal Edition" i muzikanti iz sovetskoy Rossi*, St. Petersburg: Novikova, 2011, 183.
69. Gojowy, Detlef, *Neue sowjetische Musik de 20er Jahre*. Laaber-Verlag, 1980, 36.
70. Brik, Olesya, *Venskoye Izdatelstvo "Universal Edition" i muzikanti iz sovetskoy Rossi*, St. Petersburg: Novikova, 2011, 183.
71. Diary, July 4, 1928, *Gavriil Nikolayevich Popov. Tvorchestvo. Vremya. Sudba*, Moscow, 2000, 328.
72. Letter to Kazantseva, December 31, 1928, *Gavriil Nikolayevich Popov. Tvorchestvo. Vremya. Sudba*. Moscow, 2000, 45.

73. Diary, June 5, 1928, *Gavriil Nikolayevich Popov. Tvorchestvo. Vremya. Sudba*, Moscow, 2000, 228.
74. Diary, January 31, 1929, *Gavriil Nikolayevich Popov. Tvorchestvo. Vremya. Sudba*, Moscow, 2000, 228.
75. Diary, September 27. *Gavriil Nikolayevich Popov. Tvorchestvo. Vremya. Sudba*, Moscow, 2000, 1928.
76. Diary, May 20, 1929. *Gavriil Nikolayevich Popov. Tvorchestvo. Vremya. Sudba*, Moscow, 2000, 230.
77. Diary, May 27, 1929, *Gavriil Nikolayevich Popov. Tvorchestvo. Vremya. Sudba*, Moscow, 2000, 230.
78. Asafyev, B., *B.V. Asafyev Sobranie Sochinenii*, Moscow: Academia, 1953, 60.
79. Diary, June 23, 1929, *Gavriil Nikolayevich Popov. Tvorchestvo. Vremya. Sudba*, Moscow, 2000, 329.
80. Diary, June 26, 1929, *Gavriil Nikolayevich Popov. Tvorchestvo. Vremya. Sudba*, Moscow, 2000, 329.
81. Diary, November 5, 1929, *Gavriil Nikolayevich Popov. Tvorchestvo. Vremya. Sudba*, Moscow, 2000, 329.
82. Letter Meyerhold to Popov, October 19, 1929, *Gavriil Nikolayevich Popov. Tvorchestvo. Vremya. Sudba*, Moscow, 2000, 46–47.
83. Diary, October 4, 1929. *Gavriil Nikolayevich Popov. Tvorchestvo. Vremya. Sudba*, Moscow, 2000, 233.
84. Diary, August 18, 1929. *Gavriil Nikolayevich Popov. Tvorchestvo. Vremya. Sudba*, Moscow, 2000, 233.
85. Diary, November 16, 1929, quoted in Iosif Raiskin, CD booklet. NF/PMA 9996.
86. Diary, October 4, 1929. *Gavriil Nikolayevich Popov. Tvorchestvo. Vremya. Sudba*, Moscow, 2000, 234.
87. Diary, August 14, 1929. *Gavriil Nikolayevich Popov. Tvorchestvo. Vremya. Sudba*, Moscow, 2000, 233.
88. Diary, August 25, 1929, *Gavriil Nikolayevich Popov. Tvorchestvo. Vremya. Sudba*, Moscow, 2000, 233.
89. Diary, October 6, 1929, *Gavriil Nikolayevich Popov. Tvorchestvo. Vremya. Sudba*, Moscow, 2000, 234.
90. Diary, November 5, 1929. *Gavriil Nikolayevich Popov. Tvorchestvo. Vremya. Sudba*, Moscow, 2000, 235.
91. A. V., "V poiskakh Sovetskoy Teatr," *Sovremennoy Teatr*, No. 43, 1929.
92. Letter to Kazantseva, October 8, 1930, *Gavriil Nikolayevich Popov. Tvorchestvo. Vremya. Sudba*, Moscow, 2000, 49.
93. Letter to Meyerhold, November 23, 1930, *Gavriil Nikolayevich Popov. Tvorchestvo. Vremya. Sudba*, Moscow, 2000, 49–50.
94. Diary, November 24, 1929, *Gavriil Nikolayevich Popov. Tvorchestvo. Vremya. Sudba*, Moscow, 2000, 235.
95. Diary, January 27, 1931, *Gavriil Nikolayevich Popov. Tvorchestvo. Vremya. Sudba*, Moscow, 2000, 240.

96. Diary, February 2, 1930, *Gavriil Nikolayevich Popov. Tvorchestvo. Vremya. Sudba*, Moscow, 2000, 236.
97. Diary, May 11, 1930, *Gavriil Nikolayevich Popov. Tvorchestvo. Vremya. Sudba*, Moscow, 2000, 236.
98. Gorin, M., *Rabochy i Teater*, No. 29, 1930.
99. Diary, June 18, 1930, *Gavriil Nikolayevich Popov. Tvorchestvo. Vremya. Sudba*, Moscow, 2000, 330.
100. Diary, August 7, 1930, *Gavriil Nikolayevich Popov. Tvorchestvo. Vremya. Sudba*, Moscow, 2000, 237.
101. Diary, August 28, 1930, *Gavriil Nikolayevich Popov. Tvorchestvo. Vremya. Sudba*, Moscow, 2000, 237.
102. Diary, August 29, 1930, *Gavriil Nikolayevich Popov. Tvorchestvo. Vremya. Sudba*, Moscow, 2000, 238.
103. Letter l. Ginzburg to Popov, September 22, 1930, *Gavriil Nikolayevich Popov. Tvorchestvo. Vremya. Sudba*, Moscow, 2000, 48.
104. Diary, October 30, 1930, *Gavriil Nikolayevich Popov. Tvorchestvo. Vremya. Sudba*, Moscow, 2000, 238.
105. Tsymbal, S. *Rabochy i Teater*, No. 66–67, 1930.
106. Diary, December 12, 1930, *Gavriil Nikolayevich Popov. Tvorchestvo. Vremya. Sudba*, Moscow, 2000, 239.
107. Diary, April 23, 1931, *Gavriil Nikolayevich Popov. Tvorchestvo. Vremya. Sudba*, Moscow, 2000, 240–241.
108. Diary, May 17, 1931, *Gavriil Nikolayevich Popov. Tvorchestvo. Vremya. Sudba*, Moscow, 2000, 241.
109. Letter to Kazantseva, April 22, 1931, *Gavriil Nikolayevich Popov. Tvorchestvo. Vremya. Sudba*, Moscow, 2000, 51.
110. Letter to Kazantseva, April 25, 1931, *Gavriil Nikolayevich Popov. Tvorchestvo. Vremya. Sudba*, Moscow, 2000, 51.
111. Diary, August 8, 1931, 2 *Gavriil Nikolayevich Popov. Tvorchestvo. Vremya. Sudba*, Moscow, 2000, 43.
112. Diary, October 1, 1931, *Gavriil Nikolayevich Popov. Tvorchestvo. Vremya. Sudba*, Moscow, 2000, 244.
113. Diary, February 15, 1932, *Gavriil Nikolayevich Popov. Tvorchestvo. Vremya. Sudba*, Moscow, 2000, 244–245.
114. Letter to Malko, August 20, 1931, *Gavriil Nikolayevich Popov. Tvorchestvo. Vremya. Sudba*, Moscow, 2000, 56–59.
115. Bely, V. "O nekotorykh tvorcheskii problemakh proletarskoy muziki," *Proletarian Muzikant*, 1931, supplement to No. 9.
116. "Postanovki V. E. Meyerholda v Leningradskikh teatrakh," *Krasnaya Gazeta*, April 8, 1931.
117. Letter to Meyerhold, September 10, 1931. *Gavriil Nikolayevich Popov. Tvorchestvo. Vremya. Sudba*, Moscow, 2000, 59–62.
118. Letter to Kazantseva, May 18, 1932, *Gavriil Nikolayevich Popov. Tvorchestvo. Vremya. Sudba*, Moscow, 2000, 64.

119. Diary, March 7, 1932, *Gavriil Nikolayevich Popov. Tvorchestvo. Vremya. Sudba*, Moscow, 2000, 246.

120. Kilchevsky, V.I., "K voprosi o shkola Scherbacheva," *Proletarsky Muzikant*, No. 10, 1931, 42–47.

121. Letter to Nikolay D. Popov, May 5, 1932, *Gavriil Nikolayevich Popov. Tvorchestvo. Vremya. Sudba*, Moscow, 2000, 62.

122. Letter to Kazantseva, May 20, 1932, *Gavriil Nikolayevich Popov. Tvorchestvo. Vremya. Sudba*, Moscow, 2000, 65.

123. Diary, August 21, 1932, *Gavriil Nikolayevich Popov. Tvorchestvo. Vremya. Sudba*, Moscow, 2000, 247.

124. Diary, December 26, 1932, *Gavriil Nikolayevich Popov. Tvorchestvo. Vremya. Sudba*, Moscow, 2000, 249.

125. However, it was another composer Yuri Kochurov who was commissioned to write an opera on the same Pushkin work—author.

126. Letter to Samosud, March 29, 1933, *Gavriil Nikolayevich Popov. Tvorchestvo. Vremya. Sudba*, Moscow, 2000, 71.

127. In 1951, he recycled some of his material for the opera in "On the Bank of Barren Waves" for a capella choir. Apetyan, Z.A. (ed.), *G. N. Popov 1904–1972—Iz literaturnovo naslediye. Stranitsi biografii*, Moscow: Sovetsky Kompositor, 1986, 355.

128. Stenographichesky Otchet zasedaniya pravleniya LO SSK po obsuzhdeniyu doklada Arapova o tvorchestve Popova, LGALI, f. 348, op. 1, d. 4,5.

129. Diary, November 20, 1933, *Gavriil Nikolayevich Popov. Tvorchestvo. Vremya. Sudba*, Moscow, 2000, 252.

130. Diary, November 28, 1933, *Gavriil Nikolayevich Popov. Tvorchestvo. Vremya. Sudba*, Moscow, 2000, 253.

131. Letter Prokofiev to Popov, March 5, 1934, *Gavriil Nikolayevich Popov. Tvorchestvo. Vremya. Sudba*, Moscow, 2000, 76–77.

132. Diary, March 14, 1934, *Gavriil Nikolayevich Popov. Tvorchestvo. Vremya. Sudba*, Moscow, 2000, 255.

133. Letter Prokofiev to Popov, March 28, 1934, *Gavriil Nikolayevich Popov. Tvorchestvo. Vremya. Sudba*, Moscow, 2000, 78.

134. The publishing house Triton who first published Popov was a society based in Paris in 1932 for performing new music. Among its members were Honegger, Milhaud, Poulenc, and Prokofiev—author.

135. Diary, April 16, 1934, *Gavriil Nikolayevich Popov. Tvorchestvo. Vremya. Sudba*, Moscow, 2000, 256.

136. Diary, December 5, 1934, *Gavriil Nikolayevich Popov. Tvorchestvo. Vremya. Sudba*, Moscow, 2000, 256.

137. Diary, January 13, 1934, *Gavriil Nikolayevich Popov. Tvorchestvo. Vremya. Sudba*, Moscow, 2000, 254.

138. Diary, December 5, 1934, *Gavriil Nikolayevich Popov. Tvorchestvo. Vremya. Sudba*, Moscow, 2000, 256.

139. Diary, December 20, 1934, *Gavriil Nikolayevich Popov. Tvorchestvo. Vremya. Sudba*, Moscow, 2000, 257.

140. Letter Malko to Popov, August 7, 1934, *Gavriil Nikolayevich Popov. Tvorchestvo. Vremya. Sudba*, Moscow, 2000, 80.
141. Diary, January 5, 1935, *Gavriil Nikolayevich Popov. Tvorchestvo. Vremya. Sudba*, Moscow, 2000, 258.
142. Diary, January 23, 1935, *Gavriil Nikolayevich Popov. Tvorchestvo. Vremya. Sudba*, Moscow, 2000, 259.
143. Apetyan, Z.A. (ed.), *G. N. Popov 1904–1972—Iz literaturnovo naslediye. Stranitsi biografii*, Moscow: Sovetsky Kompozitor, 1986, 242.
144. Diary, February 24, 1930, *Gavriil Nikolayevich Popov. Tvorchestvo. Vremya. Sudba*, Moscow, 2000, 236.
145. Popov, Gavriil, speech at city meeting of Moscow Composers regarding the resolution of the CC of the VKP of February 10, 1948, on opera of Muradeli "The Great Friendship," February 20, 1948. GTSMMK, f. 480, op. 1, ed. khr. 4. l.12.
146. Jokhelson, Vladimir, "Leningradskii Soyuz Sov kompositorov k xvii syesda partii," *Sovetskaya Muzyka*, 1934, 18, Bogdanov-Berezovsky 1934.
147. Popov, Gavriil, *Sovetskaya Muzyka*, No. 3, 1933, 115.
148. Diary, February 22, 1932, *Gavriil Nikolayevich Popov. Tvorchestvo. Vremya. Sudba*, Moscow, 2000, 245.
149. Shostakovich, Dmitry, April 19, 1972, speech at commission on Popov's music quoted in notes, Apetyan, Z.A. (ed.), *G. N. Popov 1904–1972—Iz literaturnovo naslediye. Stranitsi biografii*, Moscow: Sovetsky Kompozitor, 1986, 400.
150. Romaschuk, Inna, *Gavriil Nikolayevich Popov. Tvorchestvo. Vremya. Sudba*, Moscow, 2000, 194.
151. Fanning, David, CD booklet of Popov CD on Telarc CD-80642.
152. Sabinina, Marina, *Shostakovich-symphonist*. Moscow: Kompositor, 100.
153. Dolinskaya, Elena, Ed. Tarakanov, *Istoriya Sovremennoy Otechestvennoy Muzyki*, vypusk 1, 1917–1941, Moscow: Muzyka, 1993, 180.
154. Dolinskaya, Elena, Ed. Tarakanov, *Istoriya Sovremennoy Otechestvennoy Muzyki*, vypusk 1, 1917–1941, Moscow: Muzyka, 1993, 206.
155. Dolinskaya, Elena, Ed. Tarakanov, *Istoriya Sovremennoy Otechestvennoy Muzyki*, vypusk 1, 1917–1941, Moscow: Muzyka, 1993, 206–207.
156. Letter to Malko, August 20, 1931. Apetyan Z.A., ed. *G. N. Popov 1904–1972—Iz literaturnovo naslediye. Stranitsi biografii*, Moscow: Sovetsky Kompozitor, 1986, 56–57.
157. Hakobian, Leon, *Music of the Soviet Age*, Stockholm: Melos, 170.
158. Arapov, Boris, Olympia CD booklet, OCD 576.
159. Diary, March 25, 1935, Apetyan, Z.A. (ed.), *G. N. Popov 1904–1972—Iz literaturnovo naslediye. Stranitsi biografii*, Moscow: Sovetsky Kompozitor, 1986, 260.
160. After the premiere, on March 23, 1935, B. Obnorsky, the head of the Leningrad administration on control of concerts and repertoire, wrote to the artistic director of the Leningrad Philharmonic A Ossovsky stating that the administration "considers impermissible for performances of the symphony by G. N. Popov." Following this ban, there appeared in the *Krasny Gazeta*, an article by Vladimir Jokhelson entitled "With a Foreign Voice." Attacking Popov's symphony, he wrote "this work gives a subjectively limited impression of present day life and distorts it."

Notes iz. Lit, *Gavriil Nikolayevich Popov. Tvorchestvo. Vremya. Sudba*, Moscow, 2000, 363.

161. Diary, March 25, 1935, Apetyan, Z.A. (ed.), *G. N. Popov 1904–1972— Iz literaturnovo naslediye. Stranitsi biografii*, Moscow: Sovetsky Kompositor, 1986, 260.

162. Repertkom which was responsible for programming works for public concerts in the city released a formal interdict on future performances. B. Obnorsky, director of the Leningrad Bureau for the Control of Cultural Events and Repertoire, stated that all performances of the work were forbidden "as reflecting the ideology of classes hostile to us"—author.

163. Diary, March 27, 1935, *Gavriil Nikolayevich Popov. Tvorchestvo. Vremya. Sudba*, Moscow, 2000, 260.

164. Hakobian, Leon, *Music of the Soviet Age—1917–1991*, Stockholm: Melos, 132.

165. Yudin, Mikhail, Stenograficheskiy Otchet zasedaniya pravleniya LO SSK po obsuchendiya doklada B. Arapova o tvorchestvo Popova. Chast 1. LGALI, f. 348, op. 1, ed. kh. 4. L. 18.

166. "Resolutizzi TsK KP(B)," *Leningradskaya Pravda*, February 27, 1935.

167. Notes, *Gavriil Nikolayevich Popov. Tvorchestvo. Vremya. Sudba*, Moscow, 2000, 363.

168. Arapov, Boris, Stenograficheskiy Otchet zasedaniya pravleniya LO SSK po obsuchendiya doklada B. Arapova o tvorchestvo Popova. Chast 1. LGALI, f. 348, op. 1, ed. kh. 4. L. 5 (ob).

169. Bogdanov-Berezovsky, Venyamin, Stenograficheskiy Otchet zasedaniya pravleniya LO SSK po obsuchendiya doklada B. Arapova o tvorchestvo Popova. Chast 1. LGALI, f. 348, op. 1, ed. kh. 4. L. 18.

170. Bogdanov-Berezovsky wrote reviews of the symphony in "Symphonia Popova," *Krasnaya Gazeta* October 11, 1932, On the problem of Soviet symphonism, On the symphonies of G. Popov and Y. Shaporin in *Sovetskaya Muzika*, No. 6, 1934, *Gavriil Nikolayevich Popov. Tvorchestvo. Vremya. Sudba*, Moscow, 2000, 362.

171. Letter Bogdanov-Berezovsky to Popov, May 1, 1935. *Gavriil Nikolayevich Popov. Tvorchestvo. Vremya. Sudba*, Moscow, 2000, 86.

172. Diary, June 11, 1935, *Gavriil Nikolayevich Popov. Tvorchestvo. Vremya. Sudba*, Moscow, 2000, 260.

173. Bratya Tur, "Cherezmernaya Lyubov," *Izvestiya*, June 11, 1935.

174. Letter to Kazantseva, October 28, 1936, *Gavriil Nikolayevich Popov. Tvorchestvo. Vremya. Sudba*, Moscow, 2000, 102.

175. Glikman, Izaak, *Pisma k Drugu*, St. Petersburg: Kompositor, 1993, 287.

176. Interview with Inna Barsova, February 25, 2017.

177. Diary, February 21, 1941, Apetyan, Z.A. (ed.), *G. N. Popov 1904–1972— Iz literaturnovo naslediye. Stranitsi biografii*, Moscow: Sovetsky Kompositor, 1986, 261.

178. Letter to Kazantseva, December 17, 1936, *Gavriil Nikolayevich Popov. Tvorchestvo. Vremya. Sudba*, Moscow, 2000, 105.

179. Vorobyov, Igor, *Social-realism*, St. Peterburg: Kompositor, 261.

180. Diary, August 19, 1935. *Gavriil Nikolayevich Popov. Tvorchestvo. Vremya. Sudba*, Moscow, 2000, 261.
181. Diary, December 19, 1936. *Gavriil Nikolayevich Popov. Tvorchestvo. Vremya. Sudba*, Moscow, 2000.
182. Raiskin, Iosif, CD booklet for Popov Symphony No. 1, Northern Flowers NF/PMA 9996.
183. Apetyan, Z.A. (ed.), *G. N. Popov 1904–1972—Iz literaturnovo naslediye. Stranitsi biografii*, Moscow: Sovetsky Kompositor, 1986, 404.
184. Esfira Shub letter to Popov, June 22, 1937, *Gavriil Nikolayevich Popov. Tvorchestvo. Vremya. Sudba*, Moscow, 2000, 122.
185. Diary, January 8, 1936, *Gavriil Nikolayevich Popov. Tvorchestvo. Vremya. Sudba*, Moscow, 2000, 262.

Chapter 5

Cinema and Theater

A contradiction in Popov's fortunes was that by the time of his symphony's banning in 1935, he was enjoying a phenomenal career in the nascent Soviet film industry. In what was to become his bread and butter, Popov wrote thirty-nine film scores, and the experimentation in the genre helped him develop and perfect ideas in his compositions. His reputation was established in the theater productions of *Oil, Accept Battle,* and *Class,* and for the films, *Song, My Motherland, To Live,* and *Chapayev.* Popov's popular Symphonic Suite No. 1—*Komsomol-Patrons of Electrification* was recycled from the documentary film *KShE* directed by Esfir Shub.

The cinema was quickly becoming one of the most important mediums in the country- in 1917- the Department of Film-Making was established, followed two years later, by the world's first Institute of Cinematography. Apart from the state-run studios, several private film companies operated through the NEP, up to 1931. The first decade of Soviet power witnessed the emergence of directors and cinematographers who have become celebrated in the twentieth century; Eisenstein, Dovzhenko, Pudovkin, Vertov, Barnet, and Shub produced masterpieces of the early silent and sound cinema.[1]

The newsreels by Dziga Vertov (1896–1954) in the *Kino-Pravda* series between 1922 and 1925 established new standards with their experimental and agitational values. Certainly, the success of Eisenstein's *The Battleship Potemkin* (1925), and *October* (1928) characterizing the Russian Revolutions of 1905 and 1917, showed how cinema based on real events could shape new directions in the genre. Vertov's documentary film *Kino-Pravda, Man with a Movie-Camera,* and the film realization of Gorky's *Mother* (1926) by Pudovkin portrayed social-realism on the big screen, while the new concept attracted young women as film directors.

One of the young women directors was Esfir Ilyinichna Shub (1894–1959). Shub, from an early age, was engaged in constructivism, avant-garde theater, and cinema. She collaborated with Meyerhold and Mayakovsky and in the Left Front of the Arts and the Teo Theater. Shub began working in the state film company—Goskino in 1922, by editing Chaplin's *Carmen* (the first Chaplin movie to be shown), and Lang's *Doctor Mabuse* for release in the USSR. Shub's documentary film work was influential on both Eisenstein and Vertov, notably for montage methodology, as the cinema historians Ellis and McLane write, "nothing like Shub's films had existed before them, and her work remains among the finest examples of the compilation technique."[2] In her 1927 newsreels, *The Fall of the Romanovs* and *The Great Path* were transformed into an art form through her directorial interpretation. The Russian film researchers Selunskaya and Zezina write that, "If we compare the original shots with Shub's film, we clearly see the role of the author as historian making sense of and interpreting a historical document."[3] The collaborations in film and music montage between Popov and Shub showcased some of the most outstanding film scores and films of the 1930s.

The most revelatory documentary work was by the futurist cinematographer Dziga Vertov—*I am the Cine-Eye*, who wrote, "I take the strongest and most agile hands from one man, the fastest and best proportioned from another, the most handsome and expressive head from a third, and through montage, I create a new, perfect man."[4] Vertov's film *Simfoniya-Donbass* used industrial sounds in his soundtrack, and again dissonances and tensions in sound were used in the 1933 *Desirtir* film by Pudovkin.

THEATER MUSIC

Before the arrival of sound became available to filmmakers—Popov, like Shostakovich—worked in the theater. In Popov's music for the dramas *Oil*, *Accept Battle*, and *Class* (*The Great Life*), there is a symphonic energy and an undoubted logic in the stylistic switch from the revolutionary motifs to sequences of neo-baroque, all of which are reprised in his orchestral pieces.

Popov's theater debut was for the satire *Oil* based on a lampoon by a quartet of young journalists, Yakov Gorev, Alexander Shtein, and the brothers' Tur (otherwise known as Leonid Tubelsky and Pyotr Ryzhey), about the director of the Red Triangle factory. The drama involves a dispute between the workers and the bosses of a rubber production plant who oppose new research in the industry. The premiere took place on May 9, 1930, at the Leningrad State Drama Theater in a production by the distinguished actor and director Leonid Vivien. Popov wrote thirty-four numbers, including entr'actes and finales in each of the four acts. Several pieces are expressively naturalistic, notably No. 17 "Factory Horn," No. 22a "Race of the Machines," and the grotesquely satirical Nos. 14 and 15. Popov used sharply modernist characteristic sounds with dissonance, passages of ostinato, and rhythmic accents. Popov was sensitive to the industrial theme that embraced the psychosomatics of modern times and the change in consciousness.

In the same year, the Theater of Working Youth (TRAM) in Leningrad staged Nikolay Lvov's play *Accept Battle* including Popov's incidental music.[5] Interestingly, the attraction to symphonism by the composer resulted in his writing a score fusing conflicting emotional feelings, and book-ending the show with citations from the urban song *When There Were Mountains of Gold* and the old revolutionary song *We Are Parting with the Old World*. The press reflected that "the most impressive feature was the unusually powerful music by Popov that was theatrical in the best sense of the word, and not, by any means, tedious. The music permitted a more compelling and sensitive feeling in this production, with the fully expressed music."[6]

This ostensible triumph quickly led to another opportunity for Popov, in 1931 for Alexey Arbuzov's *Class*—which was staged by the Red Theater as *The Great Life*. The theme of the show, directed by Yevgeny Gakkel was about class struggle in a factory.[7] The themes involve the transformation in people's consciousness during the revolution, with the characters' psychology underscored through music. The tuneful subtext swayed the production, and rather than ending with an energetic Komsomol song, the drama ended on a low point with the urban song *There Worked Two Comrades* that heightened the sense of the drama. The vital thread was Popov's abundant use of urban songs, jazz rhythms, and folksong. For example, No. 17 was a romance, No. 18—a street song, No. 34—a foxtrot, No. 35—a balalaika tune, No. 30—a Komsomol song, and No. 32—a folksong. Arbuzov's play is regarded today negatively; however, at the time, the media were positive.[8] "*The Great Life* is really a performance where music is at the heart of the show. All the backups are well constructed, and the accents and parallels are founded on musical principles—the music itself is persuasive, introspective, and offers emotional inflection at different moments."[9]

We have seen how a continuing concern for Popov was dropping work on his symphony so as to fulfill the increasingly frequent commissions for films and the theater. His biographer Romaschuk writes that he was close to committing suicide, so disenchanted was he with life's fortunes.[10] One of the reasons for this trauma was the breakup of his first marriage; however, this was compensated by meeting the composer Irina Kazantseva. They married quickly after his divorce and their two decades of life together was a vitally important factor as Kazantseva gave him succor at this crucial stage in his career, and in the difficult years ahead.

Sound in the Cinema

Meyerhold's invitation to work in his theater to create a "Soviet musical spectacle" in 1930 meant less time on his magnum opus, and there was another offer from the Bolshoi Theater to mark the fifteenth anniversary of the revolution.[11] The scientists Pavel Tager and Alexander Shorin developed a means of sound movies in 1926 (called the Tagerphon) and got backing from the Soviet state. Eisenstein, Pudovkin, Alexandrov, and Vertov issued a joint manifesto on the use of sound in their films, the most progressive advancement arrived in Vertov's *Cinema Eye* in 1925 using radio and film together, and his *Simfoniya Donbas* became the first documentary to use sound. The new era of "talkies" dawned in 1927, with *The Jazz Singer* in the United States (the first sound movies dated from 1931 in the USSR).[12] Popov was commissioned to write the music for one of the first sound films *Song*,[13] directed by Fridrich Ermler at Lenfilm, but as we know, this never left the planning stage.[14] Instead of which Ermler made a sensationally successful film—*The Counterplan*, with a score by Shostakovich.[15]

Another Lenfilm production—*To Live* (1933), from a scenario by Viktor Shklovsky, directed by Semyon Timoshenko was based on the Civil War in the Crimea.[16] Popov's thirty-seven numbers use traditional genres: a gallop, a *tarantella* (recycled in the future film *Spain*, and Third Symphony), a chorale, the Neapolitan song *Santa Lucia*, and a Red Navy song. Popov was suitably enthused by his music that he conceived a *Little Suite* for orchestra, Op. 15b is in eight movements; however, this was never completed.

Popov's next film score was involved in long-term political controversy. *My Homeland* (1932) was directed by Alexander Zarkhi and Iosif Heifetz from a Mikhail Bleiman scenario. The film featured the awakening of class consciousness by a young Chinese man engaged in attacking the East China railway in 1929. The film was successfully released on February 23, 1933, but withdrawn a few weeks later.[17] The censure originated from a complaint to the General Repertoire Department about the unsuitable ideological reliability.[18] The Commissar responsible for cinema—Kliment Voroshilov removed the film from cinemas after complaints from political figures. The Politburo member Sergo Ordzhonikidze wrote to Voroshilov, "Thank you for banning *My Homeland*. It is an insult against the Red Army. The film makers should not be allowed to produce such stuff: they have no conception of the worthiness and honor of the Red Army."[19] As a result, on April 7, the Organizing Bureau resolved to check all scenarios and scripts for forthcoming theater and film productions.[20] The media reaction was different; however, *Leningradskaya Pravda* told its readers that *My Homeland* reflected a "major victory of Soviet art, about real life, is refreshing, and artistically powerful."[21] The film score was also praised. "Popov senses the wealth of means in portraying the musical ideas in film from the audience's level. A Chinese lullaby, the Chinese march, the Campaign, and the Red Army dances—are all tangible musical pieces in themselves, and their strength and integrity—give it genuine dynamic potency."[22]

Collaboration with Esfir Shub

The first overwhelming cinematic success for Popov was *Komsomol: The Patrons of Electrification* (1932)[23] in which music played the dominant spirit.[24] As the composer Bogdanov-Berezovsky commented, "*KShE* is one of the most significant examples in resolving the problem of cinema music."[25] The film was brilliantly orchestrated with fresh ideas and lively harmonies. Shub's film had a subtext and was like a "hidden camera." Intriguingly, the *Overture* shows the film crew at work while the orchestra and conductor begin to record the music. Popov uses the Thereminvox in a passage of mournful lyricism (Lev Theremin is seen conducting electromagnetic waves between two antennae).[26] This segment is followed by a vocalize with soprano and tenor.[27] One of the most striking parts was in the *Waltz*—as the camera slowly swivels—the screen is consumed by electric lightbulbs suddenly lighting up. The frames play their own colorful ballet, with elements of irony expressed by the bass clarinet's fragmented melody. The sound of a rippling stream is conveyed by shimmering notes on the cor anglais, flutes, and bassoons in the *Intermezzo*. The roar of turbines in the hydroelectric dam is conveyed in a vividly shaped pulsating *fugato*. The Armenian mountains are set against the Dzoraget hydroelectric dam, and a passenger train—with its forward-moving rhythm—creates an idiom in which nature is ostensibly controlled by technology. Popov recycled the film score for his Symphonic Suite No. 1, *Overture, Waltz, Intermezzo, Grave*, and *Fugato*. As we know from the previous chapter, the initial response to Popov's Symphonic Suite was positive; however, the musicologist Israel Nestyev in his article "Pseudoscientific cookery" dismissed Popov's music for *KShE* as "a clear-cut example of musical formalism."[28] Subsequently, in 1981 Nestyev confessed that he was mistaken.[29]

The documentary *KShE* with the young film director Esfir Shub initiated a mutually valuable working relationship with Popov.[30] Their rapport was fruitful from the beginning as they bounced ideas off each other, about new ventures, and exchanging telegrams about financial matters, and even to Eisenstein about a film project on Civil Rights in America.[31] Popov's next film with Shub was for another documentary *Moscow Builds the Metro*. Here he describes this as a fresh opportunity for experimenting with his ideas, "my creative plans are clear and unequivocal: two numbers in jazz style, and another pair in classical style (like a) 'Concerto for Strings and Brass.' Jazz—represents enlightenment with accents on a Moscow evening." Shub's shots of the dawn and twilight on Moscow streets are illustrated by syncopating rhythms. Popov contrasted the different scenes with correspondingly lyrical and grotesque episodes. "The 'Concerto Grossi' underground is somber and energetic. These austere pieces of music will be based in two movements of an enormous *Concerto Grosso* for large symphony orchestra of strings and brass (without woodwind and percussion)."[32] This again shows how Popov was using his film scores as steppingstones for future symphonies.

Popov frequently shared his future plans with Shub, and told of his reading a novel by Pyotr Pavlenko about the thirteenth-century knight Alexander Nevsky, and his idea for an opera that would be called *Rus*.[33] Popov asked her to find out if Eisenstein had discussed this plan with Pavlenko. "I would like to get a libretto on this theme, if he hasn't spoken to him, remind Eisenstein. (. . .) I am exploring material for a Soviet opera, and don't want to waste any more time. Certainly, I would really want to write the film score music for *Rus*, but Mosfilm may not invite me, so I won't press them about it."[34] Of course, we know already that instead of Popov writing the music for Eisenstein's film *Alexander Nevsky*, it would be Prokofiev who wrote the soundtrack.

Popov's next collaboration with Shub was for the dramatic war movie—*Spain* (1939) containing twenty-three numbers incorporating 35 minutes of music and contrasts neoclassicism with romantic, pastoral, and planar music. The film is based on twenty-two newsreels—*The Events in Spain* and *Espania* shot during the Spanish Civil War by Boris Makaseyev and Roman Karmen in 1936 and 1937. The scenario was by Vsevolod Vyshnevsky. "We are making neither a chronicle (of events) nor a 'document.' . . . We are making a great tragic film about the people, about Spain and its struggle. We are exploring a fusion of ordinary life, philosophical, military, and history. We see before us Spain at peace, Spain of 1936, 1937, 1938 and Spain in 1939. We see both friends and enemies. We see the fields, coastlines, the cities, the peoples' life, and the Franco putsch."[35] Popov's score was written between March 4 and May 11, 1939, and released in late May 1939. "This is a crucial and thorough work. They have transformed an everyday chronicle into a work of great artistry and passion. The mastery of Shub—allied with the temperament of Vyshnevsky and the talent of Popov is revealed brilliantly."[36] Lev Arnshtam eulogized about Popov's amazing score. "This music flows with the countless folksongs in the film."[37] Popov's music was so richly inventive that he refashioned much of its numbers into the Third Symphony for Strings.

The Civil War Movie—Chapayev

The success of Popov's collaboration with Shub's documentaries was eclipsed by his brilliant score for the Civil War epic feature—*Chapayev*, in which he used a fusion of folksongs through stirring orchestral passages. The film became a legend in Soviet cinema and ticked all the boxes necessary for a major box-office hit. As the scholar Richard Taylor informs, "*Chapayev* is typically considered in terms of the Historical-Revolutionary film and its genre origins are overlooked. However, in terms of its structure-from primeval chaos to order-and in terms of its narrative conception, *Chapayev* is closer to a conventional Western."[38] There is also an association with American films, especially in *The Lost Patrol*.[39] The film was an instant success with both audiences and critics—Popov shared the acclaim with the directors Georgy and Sergey Vasilyev, the cinematographers Alexander Sigayev and Alexander Ksenofontov.[40] "The brilliant melodies from the pen of the Leningrad composer Gavriil Popov make this one of the critically select features of this outstanding Soviet film."[41] The triumph sharply contrasted with the devastating criticism of his First Symphony. According to Richard Taylor, *Chapayev* was among a batch of Soviet films that "portrayed heroic leadership models." Others were *Alexander Nevsky* and *Peter the First*, from the late 1930s.[42] The head of Soviet cinema—Sovkino—Boris Shumyatsky proclaimed *Chapayev* "the best film produced by Soviet cinema in the whole period of its existence . . . a film that represents the genuine summit of Soviet film art."[43]

The film was produced by Lenfilm, and as the film historian Maya Turnovskaya informs us, "The Vasilyev brothers *Chapayev* (. . .) revealed the formula for audience success that survived every succeeding decade right up to the 1980s."[44] A key to the film's success was Popov's arrangement of the Cossack song *The Black Raven*. The film premiered on November 6, 1934, at Leningrad's Titan cinema before going nationwide on November 7 and cueing with the anniversary of the revolution. The film's popularity was reflected by *Pravda* reporting that "the whole country is watching *Chapayev*."[45] Both the Leningrad-based studio and directors were awarded the prestigious Order of Lenin—the highest civilian award at the time. Sergey Eisenstein was suitably impressed and dispatched a congratulatory telegram to the film crew, and the Commissar for Defence Marshal Voroshilov awarded commemorative gold watches to the filmmakers.[46] An avid film buff, it is said Iosif Stalin watched *Chapayev* more than thirty times.[47] Romaschuk comments perhaps unfairly that the movie's success is in the "surprisingly trite effortlessness of the film. The result is a wonderful simplicity through its visual, spoken, and musical sounds creating overall an *opus elementaria*."[48] The film was lauded as an exemplar of socialist realism by rejecting cinematic formalism. "The criterion was the affinity with life in a socialist society and refuting bourgeois, western ideology in cultural life."[49]

When the movie was revived in the 1960s, Popov reflected on making the movie,

We were told it would be better to use more animated orchestral sections in developing a whole series of intense situations, so the directors and I decided to introduce music only when it was organically necessary. It was possible to utilize the chorus in the symphony orchestra and modify the realism of moments like Chapayev's detachment having forty winks before the raid. It was possible to use symphonic means in illustrating the approaching danger unforeseen by Chapayev. . . . It was possible to do this with the orchestra, but we decided this removes somewhat the principle which aspires towards shallow minimalism.[50]

Eisenstein and Bezhin Meadow

Against this ostentatious success, which sharply contrasted with the failure of his symphony, an unfortunate fate befell Popov with Eisenstein's film *Bezhin Meadow*.[51] Eisenstein had previously worked with Popov in 1933 on the eccentric comedy *MMM* in synchronizing music with film scenes. The director emphasized that "it has to be funny!"[52] Since which, Eisenstein had long admired Popov's work, and engaged him for a Mosfilm production for *Bezhin Meadow* during the breaks in filming between 1935 and 1937.[53] The interlude in filming is referred to in a telegram sent by Shub and Popov to Eisenstein asking when the projected film *Baby Chorny* [sic] would be underway (This refers to *Bezhin Meadow*). The director was then staying at the Kyiv Continental hotel.[54]

Eisenstein's *Bezhin Meadow* depicts a tragedy locked in the embrace of death with the principal characters being a mother and her son, religion and the church, the land, and the people. Popov used several songs notably *Along the Valleys, Along the Hills* linking it to the women's chorus in the village church, where it is reprised during the fire. It seemed as if this lament is a sign of the times. Interestingly, Eisenstein wrote to Popov, "The song (in the church) has been edited, as my chauffer expressed ('but the voice of the people is the voice of God')—there can be no better praise. I hope that whatever's left will be in the same spirit."[55] In his film score, Popov seemed to be portraying the collapse of the old peasant life and their traditions. He mixes brass instruments with percussion, contrasting it with voices—with "unpretentious fifths, thirds, and octaves." Eisenstein wanted a wild screeching sound from the women's choir; however, Popov preferred that the singing gradually rises from a *pianissimo* to a familiar descant. Popov wrote to Eisenstein saying that "the (heroic-dramatic) culmination would be for twelve violins and seven cellos (in the style of Bach and Handel), and end on a *fortissimo*," and "close softly and flowingly in a melancholy domain of the unknown."[56]

When he first heard the music, Eisenstein complained that he "was somewhat bewildered because he couldn't imagine the disquiet of the choral singing (on the piano it seems very constrained—screaming, with augmented sixths near to each other). An uproar arose. He said several passages were too complicated (for a women's chorus)." The dispute was resolved when Obolensky, Eisenstein's music assistant, gave his blessing. "Eduard Tisse, and another advisor (Zaitsev) both lent their support."[57] Eisenstein quipped to Popov, "I have the impression that I have a brilliant composer, but has only reached 15% in fulfilling his plans." In responding, rather magnanimously, Popov said that he thought "it's no more than 5%." To which the director countered. "Well, perhaps I am being too liberal."[58] Eisenstein based his film on a true story, and a screenplay by Alexander Rzhevsky, of the young Pioneer Pavlik Morozov, who informed on his father because he supported the kulak's withholding grain. In revenge, Pavlik was murdered by the kulaks. Popov's soundtrack is remarkable in that it is synchronized with the action on film depicting the violence of the revolt. Writing in his diary, Popov wrote, "Today, I am going to Moscow to Eisenstein. I am finishing the first number of the score for *Bezhin Meadow*, a chorus (mixed) plus a brass band with the partisan song *Along the Valleys, Along the Hills*."[59] A week later, Popov writes: "I shall give Eisenstein the *Coda* for the scene of the destruction of the church. The *Coda* is for symphony orchestra of sixty-five musicians, plus organ. The music is only sixty seconds long. On 28 January, we recorded the partisan chorus with brass and percussion."[60] Popov himself conducted the orchestra in another five tracks. "I supplied the temperament and pace (of the music)."[61] Popov was very impressed by the sound recording, but not when the complete film score was recorded in the Large Hall of the Moscow Conservatoire.[62] The film was scheduled for release in the autumn of 1936. This was during a period when the authorities were attacking alleged "formalism" in the arts and the movie was subjected to the similar treatment as Shostakovich's opera *Lady Macbeth*. The theme of *Bezhin Meadow* is overshadowed by collectivization and the battle against the kulaks, and was criticized at a meeting of cinematographers for its "weak ideological content" and "formalism."[63] Alexander Dovzhenko was hostile, while Ivan Pyrev denounced Eisenstein as "anti-Soviet."[64] He was accused of a "combination of ideological poverty that is the mark of Cain."[65] In reply, the chastened Eisenstein asked his fellow directors to help overcome his mistakes, adding that "my talent and glory gave me the right to have a unique vision of the October Revolution. In *The Old and the New*, I sought to give my own special, as it were independent view of the world. I thought I had the right, but it turned out that I did not."[66]

Eisenstein rewrote the scene of the burning church replacing it with an episode where the villagers are trying to put out a fire. In the remake—*Pravda* accused the director of insincerity. "S. Eisenstein disregarded one of the decisive conditions for the development of Soviet art: guidance. He has 'only partially recognized' this."⁶⁷ Thus—after just a few days short of two years on the project—in 1937 it was abandoned.⁶⁸ The film was prohibited, and the score disappeared when the Lenfilm studios were bombed during the siege of Leningrad. Popov recycled his music into the *Symphonic Aria* for Cello and Strings (1945). Despite the film reels being lost, some material remained, and the stills from the original were made into a film by Sergey Yutkevich and Nikolay Kleymanov in 1967.⁶⁹ Inexplicably, the cinematographer Boris Volsky decided to use music from several works (Fourth and Fifth symphonies) by Prokofiev!

The fee scale for the composition of stage works was carefully established by the state. In 1931, ten operas and ballets were scheduled totaling 15,000 roubles; however, following the foundation of the Composers Union, contracts were agreed with promoters. This increased in 1934 when the fees of 106,000 roubles were shared between eighty-five composers. Popov's work became lucrative compared with little or no income from other compositions.⁷⁰ The professionalism and technique to master the necessary skills to capture emotions and action on screen, and timing the action down to a split second was a rare gift. The methodology of working closely with both the director and cinematographer invariably produced highly successful results. Popov utilized a variety of devices from jazz, electronic music, baroque, classical, and folk music to street songs in his film scores.

Opera

As we have noted previously, in 1932, Popov contemplated writing an opera based on Pushkin's *The Bronze Horseman*—after the main character of the controversial poem—*Bedny Yevgeny* (*Poor Yevgeny*). The first choice of a librettist was Boris Pasternak; however, he, in turn, suggested the poet and dramatist Sergey Spassky who turned it down. Several librettists were approached including Semyon Gres, and Osip Brik but nothing emerged. The archives retain sketches for the third scene of the uncompleted opera. Popov's diary tells of "a wonderful variant of the cadenza for Yevgeny's aria. It is quite Italian (in style) and captivating in melodic charm allowing an everlasting development of the same theme. . . . I am so taken with this that I have sketched *The Bronze Horseman* overture in two phrases in the manuscript."⁷¹ Wary that the theme of Pushkin's poem might be contentious, and after discussing the project with friends, he confided to his wife. "No one in Moscow considers the projected opera *Poor Yevgeny* is 'anti-Soviet.' They understand that Pushkin is onstream with Soviet power and that the builders of a new, highly spirited, socialist culture must publicize Pushkin's treasures—this is a responsible and honorable task for the Soviet artist."⁷²

Popov's attempt to interest the Kyiv State Opera in *Poor Yevgeny* after showing them the prepared first scene was unsuccessful.[73] In 1936, Popov's opera was untimely because of the scandal over Shostakovich's opera *Lady Macbeth of Mtsensk District* and the ballet *Limpid Stream*.[74] It was clear that other composers would fall under attack for producing what *Pravda* considered "formalist," and "decadent and bourgeois" music. For Popov, it became evident that writing an opera based on the most controversial work by Russia's greatest poet would be the height of folly. Popov, nevertheless, continued to research Pushkin's writings for an opera that he called "my sacred work."[75]

The Strict Youth

Nevertheless, there would come more misfortune through the proscription of another film. Based on Yuri Olesha's successful play, the score for *The Strict Youth* consumed Popov for two years until 1936. An additional advantage was that the film—produced by Ukrainfilm in Kyiv—employed one of the finest young cinematographers—Abram Room.[76] The plot depicted the characterization of a model young communist in Soviet society. However, its concept was criticized for alleged false idealism and fallaciousness. The film was denigrated as a "lampoon" and censured for "the crudest deviations from the style of socialist realism." Abram Room was forthwith banned from any responsibility for film direction.[77] Popov recycled his score into *Waltz-Canzone*, and the movie was released only in 1974.[78]

With technical innovations sweeping the cinema in the 1920s and 1930s, the film became subject to the party's new regulations on political guidance in the arts—socialist realism, as the British cinematographer Ian Christie here explains.

> The Cultural Revolution had achieved its aim of destroying old structures of legitimacy and creating a new, overriding obligation of loyalty to "the Party" which effectively meant Stalin and those who owed their position to him. The gap between elitist "export" films and those intended for domestic consumption was closed; and home-produced films unambiguously addressed a Soviet audience, albeit an idealized "proletarian" one.[79]

In 1935, Soyuzkino was transformed into the Head Directorate for Cinema and Photographic Industry [GUKF], and, with Boris Shumyatsky in charge, Soviet cinema enjoyed the status of a Government Ministry combining political and artistic responsibilities.[80] For Popov, there would be financial incentives—regardless of whether the film was released, or not—the terms of the contract would be fulfilled. Dziga Vertov affirmed: "They will have better

Violin Concerto

Several years after Albert Coates's suggestion, the Violin Concerto was picked up by Popov again. Interestingly, his wife Irina thought a motif in the Violin Concerto shared an idea from the slow movement of Rachmaninov's Second Piano Concerto. "It appears you are correct: the motif which I wanted to use in the Violin Concerto, is really from the second movement of Rachmaninov's Concerto."[82] However, during the autumn of 1936, Popov shifted his stance following intensive work on the concerto, hoping that the young Boris Fischman could give the premiere.[83] That hope came to nothing when in December 1937, the young violinist canceled owing to a tour of the Far East.[84] There were fears that the young virtuoso was not interested. "He hasn't even looked at my music. I asked to play the concerto to him with Prokofiev and Tseitlin (his teacher) present." This lack of enthusiasm on the part of Fischman may have been due to political uncertainty, as we learn from the same letter. Popov explains further that "In March Gauk is going to perform *KShE* (Symphony Suite No. 1) with his orchestra (First USSR State Orchestra); but before the 'rehabilitation' of myself from 'formalism' he wants to play a couple of my pieces on Russian themes in February (I have in mind writing orchestral arrangements of *Will I Go to the Stream* and *Dance* from my work for Meyerhold). Maybe, I'll add my song of Pavel Korchagin. Together with orchestra, soloists, and chorus, this would seem to be like sitting on the fence."[85]

The Violin Concerto met with a pleasant response from Prokofiev, as Popov wrote to his wife, "He did like the broad melody and the romantically styled 'veneer' (the 'swelling sea' was his expression), but he didn't like the augmented sixths (in the main theme). . . . Well, I do! He approved the first movement and agrees that it can be played on its own because of its integrity in material and scope."[86] Popov wrote that he hoped his orchestration will sound as natural and free as that for Krenek. "I love Krenek's Violin Concerto so much for it's liberal, gutsy, and astringent (generally very skilful) orchestration."[87] Popov's Violin Concerto was formally approved by the Leningrad branch of the Composers Union in 1937; however, the Concerto for Violin and Orchestra Op. 17 is more like a *Poem for Violin and Orchestra* in style. Popov intended the first movement to be free-minded in a positively "idealistic" form. "The culmination of the first movement evokes a magically bright and early summer's morning scented with the fragrance of lilies of the valley."[88] This was the poetic imagery which Popov wanted to express musically and literally.[89] In one of the first drafts, it was subtitled "Spring," the Violin Concerto has "Rossini-like" intonations that energize the opening movement, and there is a Wagnerian citation in the second idea which also appears in the first movement of his Symphony. There is a form of blending the lyrical and romantic or as the composer himself thought there were "elements of sorrow in the song-like exposition."[90]

The Concerto's slow movement *Nocturne* (initially an *Adagio*) has a mockingly written recitative (marked *Largo*, in a cadenza) and a chorale (*Largo*, violin and ensemble). The *Finale* alludes to folksong with refractive folk elements that have a kinship with Tchaikovsky's B-flat minor Piano Concerto. Popov tries to switch from the "new" lyricism of his symphony to lyricism with folksong roots, mentioning that, "I showed Shostakovich the exposition of the Violin Concerto. He approved it, and he thought that the secondary idea was brilliant."[91] Fischman prepared to give the premiere in March 1938 with the Leningrad Philharmonic Orchestra. However, for the second performance in Moscow, it was thought that only the first movement should be performed because of its tremendous development and the affinity with poetic orchestral form.[92] Unfortunately, the premiere was canceled, yet there was still hope that Fischman would play the Violin Concerto, and despite his promises, he never did perform it.[93] In despondency at no performance, Popov wrote complaining that the Composers' Union was failing to fund members' work. His worst fears were confined to his journal, "The (financial) assistance for the second, and third movements of the Violin Concerto has unexpectantly collapsed. Perhaps, I will get a favorable contract for a ballet. But then I will have to lay aside the Violin Concerto. Understandably, all my friends remind me of the obligation to quickly finish the Violin Concerto."[94] Popov showed the score to David Oistrakh, as he wrote to Irina, his wife, "I have rewritten the cadenza. Oistrakh approved it. Oistrakh and I went through the whole violin part of the concerto together (I accompanied him by memory and explained the orchestration to him). He sight reads wonderfully (better than anyone). It seems that he likes the music and considers it playable, (but would play it) only if Polyakin declines to play it. Tomorrow, perhaps, we will meet each other again (he asked me to phone him in the morning)."[95]

Regardless of the concerto's warmth, brightness, and spring-like freshness, the score contained those elements of "formalism" that had been so criticized in the opening movement of the symphony. Popov's concerto was haunted by nostalgia which contrasted with the late romanticism and lyricism of the symphony, and appeared quixotic and illusory. To Popov's enemies, the Violin Concerto contrasted with the brightness of inner life with nostalgia through fragmented harmonies of the real world. Regrettably, the Violin Concerto was not published and only exists in manuscript form.

Concertos for Cello and Piano

The Piano Concerto originates from the late 1920s and shares some of the ideas of the First Symphony. The fragments of the opening seventeen measures are marked *Largo appassionato*, and in the other sketches, there is an expressive dialogue with a lively, vivacious melody and a disquieting feeling as if something is being suddenly destroyed. Popov's first sketches of the Piano Concerto are lost; however, in November 1936 he began recreating the missing sketches, writing in his diary, "I wrote (the entry of the piano solo) and the beginning of the first theme for the orchestra. The beginning of the *Largo* (major-minor resonances on the French horns), the entry of the piano on f and entry of strings."[96] In Moscow, Popov got the idea of writing a Cello Concerto during a discussion with the cellist of the Bolshoi Theater Viktor Kubatsky, who premiered Shostakovich's Cello Sonata, and the premiere of the *Septet*. This idea was only picked up again when he wrote sketches in 1951.[97]

Contemporary concert life was constantly imposing its influence swaying Popov's music; he took in Hindemith's *Mathis de Maler* in both of the Moscow and Leningrad performances under Steidry. "Wonderful, particularly, the second slow movement, and the third—brusque." He heard the premiere of Prokofiev's *Russian Overture* under Unger in Moscow. "A wonderful piece. I heard it twice, and one wants to hear it again and again. I liked the Sixteenth Symphony by Myaskovsky much more than the Fifteenth (under a Tchaikovskian influence). The Sixteenth is more astringent, expressive with even has audacious moments, but is too restrained." Performances of the French modernists Debussy's *Three Nocturnes* and Ravel's *La Bolero* were thought by him very weak.[98]

The Theater of Meyerhold

Vsevolod Meyerhold's concept of "biomechanics" revolutionized Russian theater, and he and Popov collaborated in several notable achievements in the 1930s. Meyerhold believed in a unified musical and dramaturgical power in the theater, and that music must serve the drama of the acting, with the movement on stage emphasizing the importance of expressing the soul of the play. Popov liked to freely use symphonic and jazz elements with quasi-folk and urban songs in the manifold stylistic stage material. As we know, Popov first met the eminent stage director at the All-Union Conference of Dramatists and Composers (Roskomdram) in Moscow in 1929. Popov thought they shared "a belief in the united front struggling for genuine Soviet music."[99]

The hope to create a new Soviet opera by Popov with Meyerhold as director was unfulfilled; however, they found a mutual affinity in their drama theater collaborations. The first fruit from their cooperation was Yuri Olesha's melodrama—*A List of Benefits*. Popov shared his thoughts with Meyerhold: "My aspiration in this show are briefly, 1) the theme must be fashioned judiciously, 2) with insight (in opening up the 'sentiment' of the slogans, as you said at the conference), 3) a form based on symphonic and musical theater, 4) the actors must know how to sing and move (pantomime)."[100] For Popov, the production became a significant achievement, yet because of the issues raised by the dramatist—that is, the role of the intelligentsia in Soviet society—the controversy led to scandal and a tragedy.

The drama portrays the life of the great actor Mikhail Chekhov who left Soviet Russia after the Revolution and enjoyed a successful stage career in the West. The heroine, Lelya Goncharova, lives a life of luxury embracing "a list of benefits" set against "a list of crime." In Paris, she becomes involved in selling artworks on the black market, and tragically loses her life during a demonstration of the unemployed. The play was staged at the Meyerhold Theater (GosTIM) in 1931, and assisted by the artists K. K. Savitsky, and I. Leistikov, with P. Tsetnerovich, A. Nesterov, and S. Kozikov. Popov's music included fragments of waltzes and polonaises by Chopin, Rag-Jazz, Fox-Jazz, and the Chanson of Maurice Chevalier. The finale, however, proved an extraordinary culmination as Popov elucidates. "The music has three themes, a) On the radio (through a loudspeaker), a pianino is accompanied by a solo violin (sentimental and lyrical death of the heroine), from stage right, b) Behind the audience (in the foyer), a jazz band plays (Klavier, 2 sax 'a, Trombe, Trombone, batterie), c) From stage left—a symphonic overture (21 musicians play jazz)."[101] Meyerhold suggested the play ends in this manner: "After the jazz, the tune should emerge from the radio, which plays over the jazz, and (then) blocks it out."[102] Both Popov and Meyerhold were well satisfied. "Your music for *Lists* has become more popular with every performance."[103]

However, the response from the media was disappointing as the critics were unanimous in dubbing the show "reactionary,"[104] other chastisements included "failing to reject the falsehood of petty-bourgeois personal freedom."[105] One review claimed that the play gave a truthful account of contemporary society, where the tragedy of those "groups of the intelligentsia who understood that the old world, the world of capitalism, leads society to depression and war, haven't found their place in the (society of) new, socialist construction."[106] The opinions regarding Popov's score were contradictory: "From the moment that the incidental music (is heard), there appears an odd unfolding of trivial, decadent phantasmagorias of Western-European music."[107] The political aspect of the criticism is raised by Romaschuk, "Here was expressed a virtually class approach to the composer, of clear bourgeois influences, doubt was openly expressed of him as a writer of true revolutionary slogans."[108] Popov was nevertheless ecstatic about working with Meyerhold. "He is an exceptionally sensitive, cultured, and musical person."[109] On his part, the theater director thought that everyone involved "loved it immensely."[110] However, it would be another six years before another production would bring them together, and sadly, it would be their last.

In the autumn of 1937, Meyerhold invited Popov to collaborate on a new show called *One Life*. The play was an adaptation by Yevgeny Gabrilovich of Nikolay Ostrovsky's social realist novel, *How the Steel Was Tempered*.[111] The storyline captures the brief life of the selfless young communist Pavel Korchagin during the Civil War and opens with Popov's grotesquely ironic tune (the hero's motif) played on the accordion. A lively Red Army two-part march is heard—followed by compellingly dramatic episodes and Russian folksong arrangements boosting the emotional power. There was a constant mood of farce and a definitive unhappiness. The subtext was overwhelming in that Popov's parody and irony became the focus of the stage work. "A cautionary show" was how the production was labeled by the media. The preview for critics and government representatives ended in a fiasco—both Popov and Meyerhold were censured, and the play was canceled. Soon afterward, Meyerhold's theater closed on January 7, 1938, ostensibly for reconstruction.[112] At first, Popov considered recycling his score into a *Russian Suite* incorporating a *Song, Merry Song*, and *Dance* for choir and large orchestra. This became a *Divertissement for Orchestra in Nine Miniatures*, Op. 23, and was premiered by the Leningrad Philharmonic Orchestra under Eduard Grikurov on May 5, 1938. The first hearing in the capital came on November 17, 1940, by the Moscow Philharmonic Orchestra under Abram Stasevich.[113]

Meyerhold, Eisenstein, and Alexander Nevsky

On the eve of 1939, Gavriil Popov reflected that he was already thirty-five years old and "yet hardly anything has been done." Resting on his conscience were the two instrumental concertos, a Second Symphony, an opera *Alexander Nevsky*, and much else.[114] Meyerhold, in his new role as the director of the Stanislavsky Music Theater, hoped to team up with Popov on the proposed *Alexander Nevsky* opera, but this collapsed after the arrest of Meyerhold in June 1939. As a consequence, the project was taken up by the Kirov Opera and Ballet Theater. The novel by Pavlenko (which the author had preferred to call *Mister Great Novgorod*). Consenting to making the film, firstly Eisenstein entitled it *The Battle on the Ice*, instead later settled on *Alexander Nevsky* in March 1938.[115] Of course, the appointed composer of the score was Prokofiev and not Popov.[116] This inexplicable turn of fortunes seemed to affect Popov adversely when he saw the completed film at the House of Cinema in Moscow writing to his wife, "Bitter, incomplete, but all the same, a very powerful and talented film. In my speech, I praised Prokofiev, albeit I said the Russian songs lacked any emotion."[117] Regardless of this disappointment, Popov had already started on his epic opera based on the same theme.

Popov approached the Kirov Opera and Ballet Theater with the proposal of *Alexander Nevsky*, and a contract was initialed in May 1938.[118] "I gave a creative promise to pursue epic-heroic music with Russian folk intonations, etc. You can't write it in just two words." Popov invokes here an old Russian proverb, but little did he suspect the problems that would engulf this project.[119] The score was to be completed by the end of the following year, with production to start in the 1939–1940 season.[120] Popov worked on the project with enthusiasm, and by November 1938, he had written sixty-five pages of manuscript—without a libretto. The first libretto was an awkward collaboration shared with Pavlenko and the playwright Alexander Preis; however, the librettist seemingly failed to match Popov's ambition and enthusiasm.[121] In January 1940, after his diversions in cinema, he returned to *Nevsky* and after eight weeks, Popov was able to produce 139 pages of the first act. Glavrepertkom expressed dissatisfaction with the Vatican scene and requested an alternative for the fourth act scenario.[122] Unaware of his collaborator Meyerhold's fate, Popov decided in mid-March 1940 to offer *Nevsky* to the Stanislavsky Opera Theater in Moscow. The reaction was positive as he wrote in his diary, "that is if you can believe the warm comments from Zhukov and Daltseva."[123]

In April 1940, Popov discussed with Mikhail Chulaki at the Leningrad Composers Union the nonperformance of his music at the Philharmonic, as he complained, "A lot of difficult questions were touched upon. The consequence is that you have to work harder to get performed!"[124] His old teacher's warning on his lethargy was coming back to bite. Reflecting on the Soviet representation in the current repertoire, he considered that Prokofiev and Shostakovich were first-rank composers; only Myaskovsky's symphonies could match them. "Shostakovich and Prokofiev are international class, like Hindemith, Schoenberg, Stravinsky, Krenek, (and) R. Strauss."[125] The film work on Shub's documentary *Spain* would take him away from his opera for up two months. As he had done with other film scores, Popov recycled his music into his Third Symphony, "I continue with the *Concerto Grosso*—simple, clear, harsh, emotional, and heroic story about greatness (if I can handle it masterfully) about the greatness of our life, and our human feelings."[126] In October 1939, the first movement was written, but then, nothing more until September 1944—almost five years.

Unable to get a commitment from the Stanislavsky Opera Company on his opera, he was left with only one backer. On June 30, 1940, Popov showed the 155 pages of *Nevsky* to Pasovsky, Baratov, and Shastin, at the Kirov Opera.

"Endorsement was given; however, observations were made regarding the recurring pauses, the accents on chords, however, I pointed out the appeal of flowing (integral) symphonic orchestral harmony in the recitatives, emphasizing the usage of the key musical themes-motifs: funereal (from ancient hymnal chant), and the optimism of song themes by Alexander Nevsky's allies, and the heroic people (my folk mass marching hymnal theme). There was a business-like discussion regarding further work. They are very anxious to move the opera forward. They say that they want to go into pre-production."[127]

However, the writing of the remaining four acts became bogged down with continuous modifications and the burden of the libretto. The second variant did not gain approval from the Kirov Theater, after which little progress was made. The bread and butter of film commissions loomed, and Popov asked the Kirov to double his advance fee, so he did not have to rely on film work. The directorate declined to authorize any advance payments. With this unexpected rebuttal, cinema work remained his sole means of subsistence, and only in December 1940, could he return to the opera. His plight is reflected in a diary entry. "At the time when I am writing the people's chorus of wrath at Tverdilo, and Dmitry's cavatina. A Damocles sword hangs over me with the offer of a two-film contract."[128] Popov was flabbergasted to hear on the radio that his opera was programmed for premieres at both the Kirov and Stanislavsky theaters. By late February 1941, only 40 minutes of music had been composed from the 205 manuscript pages of the great first act.[129] Popov showed *Nevsky* to his colleague Yuri Kochurov who thought "the fishermen's chorus sounded wonderfully Russian."[130] Another supporter was Shostakovich who "praised both the music and its form. He refrains from giving an opinion, instead, he fleetingly praises (or criticizes), in outbursts; repeating the same phrases (as if magnifying their emotional intensity), demanding that I finish the opera as soon as possible this year. He asked me to bring him the score and play it again, to better grasp the spirit of the score."[131]

Four days later, Popov returned Shostakovich's visit. "He was very sympathetic, I sensed something sincere, (that he has) an inner warmth to me after hearing the first scene from *Alexander Nevsky*." In return, Shostakovich presented him with his new Piano Quintet: "To dear Gavriil Nikolayevich Popov, in the hope that his great talent is realized, with love from D. Shostakovich. 20/4/1941. Leningrad."[132] The warmth between the two musicians was evident by Popov's review identifying the connotation of (Shostakovich's) Fifth Symphony for "engaging with the great themes of man, and about the experiences of mankind."[133]

The Nazi invasion on June 22, 1941, enforced a new reality and Popov's plans were almost totally abandoned. Much of the themes for the opera were recycled into the score for the Vasilyev brothers film on which he worked in late July. Noting in his journal,

I am writing the second orchestral episode for *The Voroshilov March* film and *The Defence of Tsaritsyn*. Recently, I have composed two mass marching songs: *March of the Marines* to texts by Vsevolod Rozhdestvensky (a good song!!) and *Arise, Soviet People*. Apart from which, I have written a symphonic poster—*March of the Red Cavalry*, for symphony orchestra and male chorus (at the request of Radio Leningrad)—an adaptation of episodes from *The First Cavalry*. It sounds great. It was performed (and broadcast) on 26 July at 21.10. The head of the radio was satisfied. Recently, I showed (played) Kochurov an extract. This is one of those rare moments of happiness (the ultimate satisfaction from lyrical energy).[134]

Written when the Nazis were closing the ring around Leningrad, this was his last diary entry for almost two years.

The Kirov Opera and Ballet Company was evacuated to the safety of the Urals city of Perm in August 1941. With the tragic death of the librettist Preis in 1942, the third libretto for Popov's opera by Sergey Gorodetsky proved incompatible.[135] After five years of work and now writing the libretto himself, Popov finally completed the enormous first act of *Alexander Nevsky* which amounted to an hour of music in 260 manuscript pages. And it was here everything stopped, regrettably, for little more was added owing to the lack of any real hope for a stage production. Despite having the backing of positively inclined musicians, Popov never did bring this project to fulfillment.[136] Boris Asafyev, a consultant at both the Kirov and Bolshoi companies thought highly of *Alexander Nevsky*. He considered the score effervescent in its classicism and could open up the path for innovative lyrical opera, or opera fresco, as became customary in the second half of the twentieth century. Asafyev considered the unambiguous stylization akin to a fairy tale. "One thinks, such an impression is only because Popov senses perfectly the dramatic potential of the orchestra in appreciation of *melody* and never overcooks it."[137]

Asafyev persuaded the Bolshoi Theater to assume the Kirov Opera's commission of *Alexander Nevsky*. Yet, nothing happened because of the subsequent death of Asafyev in 1949 wrecked any scope for a production. That was not the end of the story however for in the 1970s, the then director of the Bolshoi Theater, Mikhail Chulaki, wanted to stage the completed first act. However, Popov's widow Zara Apetyan refused a performance because the opera was incomplete. To this day, the score of Popov's *Alexander Nevsky* gathers dust in the archives.[138]

In October 1941, the Leningrad branch of the Composers Union heard the first variant of the opera, and despite approval dissatisfaction was expressed with the libretto. Popov's revised version has five acts and seven scenes with the timescale set between 1240 and 1242, during the Teutonic knights incursion into the Russian territory of Pskov. The opening scene depicts a square in Pskov where the populace is preparing for the city's defense. At the city gates, the guards warn: *The Germans are approaching!* Scene two is set in the palace where the boyars are judging the Lithuanian's betrayal. Act two is at Lake Pereslavl, where fishermen are singing, near Alexander's tent. Act three in Novgorod opens with the chorus *Arise, Russian people, arise!* The fifth scene in Act four was set initially in Riga castle, albeit, was switched by Popov to a scene in the Vatican where the Russian knights beseech the Cardinals to release the Papal armies to assist the Russian cause. Act five is at Lake Chudskoye, where Alexander leads his army against the Teutonic knights in the battle on the ice. There is a variant in the sixth scene, where Dmitry and Vasilissa declare their love for each other before the great battle. Scene seven is in the evening, after the victorious battle, and the celebratory Alexander sings, *My brothers! The brotherhood is true, as are all the Russian people!* The chorus sings, *Glory, glory to the Russian people!* The final chorus intones, *Arise, Russian people, know thy strength. The foe has once more been defeated, go forth with pride and courage, joy, joy for the Russian people.*[139]

The manuscript of the first act of *Alexander Nevsky* has an amazingly vivid and intricately written score, in which Popov uses a huge orchestra allowing a unique intonational harmonic structure. The leading characters are the Voyevoda Pavsha, his daughter Vasilisa, the common soldier Dmitry, Pelgusy, and the gardener Tverdilo. Each of the five principal characters has a unique leitmotif associated with the main theme of the Russian people. At an early stage in his writing of the opera, Popov shared his thoughts with the musicologist Pavel Nazarevsky.[140] "Not so much music has been written so far, but the groundwork lies in the heroic elements of harmony for future operas: there is the convention of musical expression, in which the musical language (. . .) based on rich Russian intonation, and the unfamiliar passion of Ancient North-Russian folk melodies offer a dramatic language for opera. The vocal and dramatic energy! Verdi and Tchaikovsky. They are the most perfect embodiment of opera literature."[141] Popov considered an opera based on Lermontov's lyrical-psychological novella *A Hero of Our Time*, but nothing materialized because he failed to find an appropriate libretto. Another notion at the end of 1938 was an opera based on Balzac's novel *Gobsek*. The subject reflects the exposure of the flaws of humanity—but most of all—portrayal of their social origins.

Film Proscription

A typical diversion to Popov's opera writing was producing the film score for *The Guest* (1939), a thriller directed by Adolf Minkin and Herbert Rappaport from a scenario by Lev Kantorovich. The composer was well satisfied by his labor: "In forty days, I have written thirty-seven-thirty-eight minutes of music, I can't be ashamed."[142] The film was proscribed because it featured a Japanese spy in the Soviet Far North—the narrative was considered inappropriate owing to the signing of a Non-Aggression Pact between the USSR and Imperial Japan. Zhdanov at a meeting of the State Committee for Cinematography on May 15, 1941, criticized the "quite low ideological content," adding it "deals with hostile tendencies."[143] Nevertheless, Minkin continued making documentaries, and Rappaport made many more films, three of which were awarded the coveted Stalin Prize.[144] Conveniently, several numbers, *Dreams* (No. 10), and *Morning* (No. 11), were recycled for Popov's Third Symphony.[145]

Motivated by the Civil War—*The First Cavalry* was directed by Yefim Dzigan in March 1940 and released on June 6, 1941, two weeks before the Nazi attack on the USSR. Popov's involvement was entirely owing to the scenarist Vsevolod Vishnevsky. The requirement was for the music of cavalry charges, bugle calls, and mass battles. The scenario depicted the Polish campaign in 1920 and the legendary cavalry led by Budenny and Voroshilov. On seeing the movie, Budenny enthused: "A wonderful piece of work! It is obvious that the scenarist was a former machine gunner in the First Cavalry!"[146] Indeed Vyshnevsky had served as a Red Guards machine gunner on the Neva River and was awarded several medals for valor. Salvaging his film music, Popov produced the symphonic piece *March of the Red Cavalry* for orchestra and male chorus. Millions regularly heard this ephemeral music on Moscow Radio during the war.[147]

Another controversial film was the adventure movie from Yuri Krymov's eponymous novel—*The Tanker Derbent*. The director was Alexander Faintsimmer in an Odesa film production first released on June 9, 1941.[148] The film was criticized because it portrayed sailors as drunkards.[149] The music departs from Popov's other scores by depicting a peaceful atmosphere using jazz syncopations on a saxophone and revealing humorously intimate relationships. Popov was keen to recycle his music. "The music is both emotional, and from the heart." A passage marked *Andante con passione* on strings was considered by Popov as being "nascent for a future string quartet."[150] The movie's popularity led to a revival in 1966.

If jazz syncopations appeared in one film, there were hints of neoclassicism in Abram Room's *Wind from the East* that appeared on February 4, 1941. Based in Western Ukraine, the movie deals with the conflict between religion and socialism. There is a marked contrast by his use of baroque (Bach, Handel) and romanticism (Tchaikovsky and Richard Strauss). Unavoidably, Popov whined, "there has emerged a dreadful film. The music is unbalanced, and many episodes are mutilated by revision and cuts (perfunctorily)." Once more, Popov had visions of recycling his music for future symphonies.

"Actually, the Second is already sketched, so perhaps this will be for the Third."¹⁵¹ Popov was so happy with two of the numbers (No. 3 *Theft of the Land*) that they were recycled for the Third Symphony, and (No. 2 *The Seminary* for organ) for the Sixth Symphony.

Films for the War Effort

The outbreak of war and the rapid advance of the Nazis to the environs of Leningrad in August 1941 led Gavriil and Irina Popov to leave their home at Tsarskoye Selo and to Irina's parents in Leningrad. As the German siege of the city took hold, and unable to be evacuated, they would stay there until February 1942, enduring shelling, and bombing, and the coldest winter in living memory together with a starvation diet.

Popov's successful collaboration with Georgy and Sergey Vasilyev (although credited as "brothers" in their films, they were not brothers in real life) continued with another Civil War series based on the battles in and around the Volga town of Tsaritsyn (Stalingrad).¹⁵² Three movies were planned to cover the conflict. *The March of Voroshilov* and *The Defence of Tsaritsyn* were bestowed the Stalin Prize—two weeks after the premiere on March 29, 1942.¹⁵³ The score's eleven numbers capture the most striking moments—the overture is an arrangement of old Cossack songs, a lyric pastoral *There Flows the Quiet Don*, with a triumphantly vibrant and colorful finale. However, as Popov found himself isolated in Leningrad (the Lenfilm studios evacuated to Alma-Ata in Kazakhstan), the film score was recommissioned to Nikolay Kryukov.

After escaping the Leningrad siege in a convoy across the frozen Lake Ladoga, Popov wrote to Shebalin from his Urals refuge of Molotov (Perm).

> Irina and I left Leningrad on 3 February. On 12 February, we arrived in Lyubim in the Yaroslavl district and for five weeks struggled to recover from pneumonia. We arrived in Molotov on 19 April, and I can walk now. On 20 April, I finished *Heroic Intermedia* for *Alexander Nevsky*. It has been performed seven times for the Mayday concerts by the Kirov Theater. Now I am invited to Alma-Ata (with Irina) by the Central Film Studio, where I intend to finish the *Alexander Nevsky* opera. I would love to see you at Sverdlovsk railway station. Please come if you can manage.¹⁵⁴

Their finances were troubling because Popov requested financial assistance from Muzfond whose director Lev Atovmyan telegraphed 2,000 roubles.¹⁵⁵

When the Popovs got to Alma Ata, they discovered the challenging living conditions in Kazakhstan were worsened by an unforgiving climate and food and energy shortages. Popov wrote to his father in Rostov on Don: "I am working for the Central Film Studio, and writing the film scores for *Partisans* (directed by Ermler) and *Front* (Vasilyev brothers).[156] For eight months, I have been without a piano, but after Leningrad, we are happy to be well and recovered in energy to devote everything to our peoples' struggle with the enemy. The accommodation is difficult. We have been struggling with housing for three months, it is better now."[157] A further burden in their living conditions was sharing a flat with neighbors constantly playing the radio, or records.

The first film scores completed in Alma Ata for Mosfilm were for Grigory Kozintsev's *On One Night*, from the almanac *Our Girls* shared with Prokofiev. The screenplay is a wartime drama about two pilots suddenly seeking sanctuary in a village—one is suspected of being a spy. Inexplicably, the film was never released. The second movie was a joint effort with Velikanov, for a documentary by Dziga Vertov—*The Front—for You*, aka *Kazakhstan-Front* (1942).[158] Popov's music has a symphonic structure: *Allegro Subito, Presto Giocoso, Moderato Presto*, and *Moderato Pesanto* embracing different musical periods and styles from the baroque to constructivism. Vertov's documentary montage is enhanced through Popov's swiftly paced music. Another new collaboration was with the Armenian woman director Arsha Ovanesova—*The Most Precious* at Alma Ata studios.[159] Noteworthy in his score were the writing for strings: *Andante*; *Moderato Cantabile*.

The relationship with the Lenfilm studio was revived with another war movie. The Vasilyev brothers' *The Front* was based on Alexander Korneychuk's play and released on December 27, 1943. The score revives Popovs's earlier work on *Chapayev*, and *The Defence of Tsaritsyn* with an enchanting *Andante* in F which contrasts with the robust *Attack* in D before the *Requiem* in F marking the hero's death. Interestingly, Popov borrows an idea from the finale of Shostakovich's Fifth Symphony The scenarist Korneychuk was awarded the Stalin Prize and the motion picture is credited among the Soviet war classics and got a rerelease in 1975.[160]

One other major film score—leading unswervingly to the Second Symphony—reprised his association with Fridrich Ermler—*She Defended the Motherland*, originally entitled *Partisans* is from a scenario by Alexey Kapler.[161] The movie was released on May 20, 1943 and portrays a young Russian woman—who after seeing the killing of her husband and baby run over by a tank—leads an uprising in her village. The disparate emotions of grief, tragedy, heroism, and courage are invoked compassionately by Popov's stirringly colorful music. The central part of Praskovya was played by Vera Maretzkaya, whose characterization led to a formidable career. The film was successful in portraying the depths of human emotion—rather than through the glorification of war. Popov used folksong and sacred chant, *Ah, You Dark Night, Oh, My Heart Beats*, and the tropar *Christ has Arisen*. Ermler's film was released widely and was known as *No Greater Love* in the United States where it became popular.

Two more film scores engaged Popov during the war, both of which became notable achievements. The documentary *The Victory on the Right Bank of Ukraine* by Alexander Dovzhenko and Yuliya Solntseva was split between the *Symphonic Aria* and *The Great Turning Point*.[162] This was the first of several successful collaborations with the filmmaking husband and wife couple.[163] *The Struggle for Our Soviet Ukraine* (1943), otherwise known as *Ukraine in Flames*, was regarded one of the best documentaries of the Soviet campaigns.

The Second Symphony "Motherland"

The roots of Popov's Second Symphony lay in Ermler's *She Defended the Motherland*, the score of which was promptly recycled into six movements: *Overture*, *Scherzo*, *Cantabile*, *Presto*, *Fugue*, and *Finale*. Writing excitedly in his diary Popov stated, "The symphonic song developed in its innermost fragments and imagery into a *Symphonic Canticle*, becoming the four-movement structure of the Symphony No. 2."[164] Owing to its cinematic origins, the symphony became known as the "Motherland" Symphony. As he wrote in the program notes,

> The terrible images of today's war are etched in my soul and are clearly laid down in the conceptual foundation of the "Motherland" symphony. The first two movements and the last two comprise two sections or halves of the symphony: *Peace and War* intending to recreate the image of our national consciousness in the *Introduction*—through unadorned lyricism, greatness, and contemplation, as if intrinsic in the boundless Russian expanses. The second movement, *Presto giocoso*, is a Russian round dance with images of blazing merriment alternating with lyricism and tenderness. The symphony's second half (*Largo* and *Finale*) plunges the listener into the war. There are exposed images of human grief and suffering amid the terrible losses and trials which befell upon the Motherland, the key imagery of the third movement reaches great tension of protest, rage, and fury to the *Finale*, which is a passage of forceful struggle against the enemy and the people's enlightened strength triumphs. The symphony ends with a gloriously expansive melodious theme reprised from the opening *Introduction* which symbolizes our Motherland's energy and greatness.[165]

The degree to which Popov had retreated from his modernism of the 1920s is clear from the influences from the nationalist school. Romaschuk considers that he was swayed by Taneyev and Shcherbachov, but this was a concession to populism.[166] The Second Symphony was written between

April and October 1943 in Alma Ata. The *Scherzo* has a bright, fun-loving idea on woodwind invoking the carnival scene from Stravinsky's *Petrushka*. Reflecting on his roots, Popov also uses a Don Cossack wedding song, *The Husband Reproaches his Wife*, from the Listopadov collection. The *Largo* opens with a dark theme invoking sadness, and grief, from the folksong *Oh, My Little Heart Groans*, and the church chant *Christ has arisen from the Dead*. The symphony is masterly written, however, is quite unrecognizable from the composer who wrote the extraordinary First Symphony a decade previously.

News about the symphony reached Moscow, and in October Popov was invited to the capital by Khrapchenko at the Committee of Arts. The visit was not a happy occasion, for just days before his arrival, his stepbrother Sergey died from tuberculosis in a Moscow hospital. Initially, Popov stayed at the National Hotel; however, Irina could not join him until May 1944. Following her arrival, they lodged with the Trokhimov family until November 1946, when they were allocated a three-room flat in the city center.[167]

On November 18, Popov played his Second Symphony to Myaskovsky, Shebalin, Shostakovich, Sollertinsky, Shcherbachov, Shaporin, Gauk, and Oborin at the Composers' Union. Myaskovsky endorsed all four movements but criticized some issues. There was a positive response, yet Popov was more forthcoming in writing to Irina. "Everyone gives their approval; however, they noted incongruity between the first two movements and the other two movements. The *Largo* is most favored. Knipper argued that it isn't a symphony. Myaskovsky was perhaps the most positively disposed. Shostakovich doesn't like the *Scherzo* much (for superficiality in content and the thematical material). On the other hand, Shostakovich adored the orchestration—it would sound 'magnificent.' He highly praised, in general, the score, calling me 'one of the best Soviet composers.' Many of the speakers (after all kinds of theoretical conversations, statements, suggestions, and opinions) congratulated me on this new composition."[168] The Committee for Arts commissioned the Second Symphony for a premiere and referred it for a Stalin Prize later in the year. A favorable sidenote was that Vladimir Surin, the deputy chairman of the Committee for Art requested if he could complete *Nevsky* in six months. However, he could not help with his accommodation and only offered assistance in granting travel permits for Irina to come to Moscow.[169]

The premiere of the Second Symphony took place on February 15, 1944, with the USSR State Symphony Orchestra under the baton of Nathan Rakhlin. Popov sent a telegram to his wife writing that the performance enjoyed a "comprehensive success (with) the audience, orchestra, and public opinion."[170] The Ukrainian maestro Nathan Rakhlin was a prizewinner of the All-Union Conducting Competition and a fine interpreter of modern music, who Popov

Figure 5.1 Popov—1944. *Source:* Courtesy of Inna Romaschuk.

thought, "A very talented musician and conductor." Popov was particularly happy that it was well received. "For nine days, the whole of the musical community has been congratulating me for this Symphony. The musicians—in their fashion—have been wonderful." Another source for his upbeat mood was that the secretary of the Composers Union Aram Khachaturyan granted documents for Irina to come to Moscow.[171] With no little irony, Popov noted:

> On 31 May, in *Soviet Art* there appeared a quite informative notice about the symphony in the *Musical Diary* under the monogram of "The Listener." The critique is favorable, but there is one gaffe: it is as if the *Largo* is comparable to (or perhaps suggests) Shostakovich's music. This is not correct as quintessentially; my melodic and thematic material is in the realm of the melodic and passionate diatonic (closer to Tchaikovsky and Mahler). True, the spiritual and recognizable image of the opening idea in the *Largo* approaches the austere, covetous, and acutely reticent imagery of the "tragic" Shostakovich. But the melodic tonality and harmonic scope of the *Largo* is distant from Shostakovich's individuality, and (ever more) my creative style.[172]

A Moscow-based composer and friend of Popov—Nikolay Chemberzhy reflected that "the great significance of this is that the composer has approached, not just this theme, but has handled the modulation of Russian folk song with discrete sensitivity."[173] Asafyev had only praise, writing about

> the energetically audacious music, quite innovatively reveling in alluring folk art from our classical, and particularly poignancy Rimsky Korsakov. Popov has unlocked the dynamic of the ornamental Russian melody. With his audacious lyricism, I would say that he shares with Shaporin—the breath of Russian nationalist vitality, and is mindful of his power and "strength," lovingly enlightening the call to struggle in defense of the motherland.[174]

The transformation between Popov's first two symphonies is discussed here by Levon Hakobian:

> Popov's retreat—largely forced, to be sure—to conservative positions can give rise to a feeling of regret; on the other hand, the symphony "Motherland" obviously surpasses the same composer's First Symphony as regards the unity of thematic material, the coherence of motivic development, and the logistically justified conciseness of form.[175]

Still, his biographer Romaschuk believes the Second Symphony "has several generic levels: firstly, a suite (with features of poetry); song-like (in the style of Glinka and Mahler), and symphonism (with a bi-functional structure)."[176] In Glinka's seminal *Kamarinskaya*, Russian chant secures a fresh classical color that becomes symphonic in nature. If it could never match the originality and brilliance of its predecessor, the Second Symphony won admiration for its orchestration and originality, certainly, the patriotism and its craftsmanship resulted in the award of the Stalin Prize (second class) in 1946. The "Motherland" symphony was frequently performed in the USSR and secured a recording by Hermann Abendroth with the Leipzig Radio Symphony Orchestra.

Following the mauling after the premiere of the First Symphony—certainly, Popov's new symphony registered a personal triumph. However, some musicians were surreptitiously yearning for a fiasco. The nomination by the Committee for Art for a Stalin Prize caused consternation for his erstwhile foes, as Popov recalled, "Tasteless gossips are already congratulating me for having 'the prize in the bag' (but all the same they are eager that my symphony will not get a prize). I am definitely suspending all the hasty 'prize congratulations.'" The Second Symphony was repeated in a revised orchestration on March 10, 1944, again under Rakhlin's baton, and a third hearing at the Central Hall of the Red Army by the same musicians on the following day.[177] Popov was thrilled by Igor Belza's analysis: "this composition is mature and creatively faultless (...) the orchestration of Popov's symphony is really wonderful, powerful, and rich with inexhaustible splendors." Belza added that in its philosophical depth and passionate honesty—"the composer has an affinity with the glorious traditions of Russian music."[178] Muzfond now affirmed funding for Popov's arrangement of the first act of *Nevsky*, and for a "heroic overture cantata" *To Victory* for baritone, chorus, and orchestra. Unwilling to take up a teaching career, Popov turned down a professorship at the Sverdlovsk Conservatoire in the Urals. However, this was a sign that the castigation of his First Symphony seemed to be in the past, yet this ostentatious success was but an interlude before fresh censure would be addressed against Popov.

Plenum of the Composers Union

Regrettably, the criticism of Popov would come from an unexpected source, for between March 28 and April 7, 1944, Dmitry Shostakovich gave the keynote address at a plenary of the Composers Union on Soviet music of the war years.[179] The choice of words used by Shostakovich was surprisingly harsh, and many of those present will have been astonished at his candor,

> One cannot understand the circumstances whereby a composer with such a fine composing technique can take so long to write an opera (that is *The Decembrists*), and how can he work so long on his works and produce them less than that provided by nature? I can make a comparison with one composer from a younger generation of great gifts and outstanding talents. That is G. N. Popov, who, despite his great talent, and great technical development, writes little. Although both composers have a deep-rooted technique, Shaporin and Popov are afflicted by the poison of dilettantism. I am not speaking here of the inability to modulate or of an inability to express their musical ideas. They are both aware of this problem; however, both of these composers are distinguished by inexhaustible dilettantism. In conversation with them, and with others, I have noticed the following. They write a romance, for example. This romance ends so (D. D. Shostakovich during his statement plays examples on the piano not included in the stenogram): it's beautiful, very caressing in F-sharp major, and after this, they finally take another chord of an analogous manner (again he plays an example). And now, the composer begins having terrible fears and doubts. Now, he is thinking about whether it will perhaps be better to end it like this. So, again it is wonderful, no less beautiful, and so on, and so forth. And the composer is hypnotized by such pleasant sounds and cannot make his mind up and is interminably entangled by them. The creative process is exhausted, and there develops a never-ending timescale. It appears that these circumstances are

why neither the brilliant opera *The Decembrists* has been finished, nor has the brilliant opera *Alexander Nevsky* been completed.[180]

The accusations by Shostakovich were scathing of Shaporin and Popov, "dilettantism and for careless creative practice, and what can one say about other less distinguished people whose creative baggage consists of just a few songs!"[181] Shostakovich criticized several prominent musicians, taking care to mention only those whom he genuinely considered gifted composers. Like other contemporary symphonies by Muradeli, Khrennikov, and Balanchivadze—according to Schwartz—the Popov Second Symphony was "laid aside."[182] What caused Shostakovich to criticize his friend Popov so harshly and openly is a mystery. Certainly, there was a significant change in Shostakovich after he moved to the capital, demanding from the authorities a multiroom apartment, a professorial salary of 150,000 roubles, and a chauffeur-driven automobile.[183]

Regardless, there seems to have been an acuity from Shostakovich toward his erstwhile friend and ally. Popov could be deservedly criticized for lethargy, and of prolongingly nurturing his compositions, but could hardly be accused of *dilettantism*. To be slammed for this by his most reliable friend must have been a blow. The criticism is as much a reflection of Shostakovich's inner character as it was of Popov, yet Popov adored Shostakovich all his life. Shebalin also addressed the plenary and made his comments on Popov's Second Symphony. He criticized Prokofiev's cantata *Alexander Nevsky* in the structure of the *Battle on the Ice* "becoming fragile and incomprehensible." Shifting his attention to Popov, Shebalin complained that in his symphony "there is a dissimilar incongruity of purely stylistic nature. One gets the impression that the first two movements belong to one composition, and the *Largo* and *Finale* to another. In such a manner, the conception of the symphony is somewhat of an enigma, and the symphony, in general, is more of a suite, unfree from some stylistic diversity."[184]

It was in the summer of 1944, that Popov took Shostakovich's advice and resumed work on his opera; having received suitable financial support, and now he was trying to concentrate on the *Alexander Nevsky* opera. According to the contract, the piano reduction (by his wife) was worth 5,000 roubles, of which a 25 percent advance was paid out. This allowed him to revise the libretto with Pavlenko, as he mentioned in his diary,

> The writer was sympathetic but hardly accessible (timewise), still engaged with literary fantasy, and the culture of the Russian language, all the same, he doesn't feel the idiom for the human voice. Yes, I acknowledge that my libretto doesn't work out as it ought to. One will have to change course almost everywhere,

reconsider, reconstruct, and partially compose a new text (not mentioning the constant text revisions).[185]

Thoughts about returning to Leningrad (Chulaki at the Kirov Opera was asking him back) were dismissed because his wife's bronchial asthma had improved in Moscow's milder climate. In September 1944, Popov continued work on the second movement of his Third Symphony, which he continued to call a *Concerto Grosso*. Two years later, almost to the day, he finished the symphony with a dedication to Shostakovich. Following the end of the war, in 1945, Popov returned to Leningrad and was distressed at the war-torn state for everything had been lost during the siege. Their flat at Detskoye Selo in the Catherine Palace was ransacked and destroyed by the Germans who had used it as stables.

A unique opportunity opened up after Prokofiev suffered an accident after conducting the premiere of his Fifth Symphony. Prokofiev was engaged to write the film music for *Ivan the Terrible*; however, his wife informed Eisenstein: "I am extraordinarily sad that I have to confirm that Sergey Sergeyevich is unable to write the music for the second part."[186] Prokofiev offered Popov the assignment "it would be good if we could do this together. S.M. Eisenstein will speak with you about this—please don't turn him down!"[187] However, the opportunity was lost because Prokofiev made a speedy recovery and completed the film score for Eisenstein.[188] The disappointment of not working with Eisenstein again must have been hard to take.

In 1945, Lenfilm's *The Great Turning Point* reunited Popov with Fridrich Ermler, in what would be one of Soviet cinema's epic movies. After the disappointment of losing the Eisenstein project, Popov confided to his diary. "I have a difficult and thankless task before me, but I agreed solely because of my working relationship with Fridrich."[189] The production with a Boris Chirskov scenario was known as *General of the Army* on its foreign release, and got the Palme d'Or at Cannes in 1946 (moreover, winning the best screenplay). The film was devoted to the Allies' victory over Germany and correspondingly portrayed feelings of tragedy and joy. As he recorded in his journal, "Yesterday, I wrote *Silence* (in actuality a *Nocturne*) for orchestra. I was still happy because of the lyrical/gloomy/mysterious/fantasy sound of this symphonic piece. The viewer is drawn into amazingly intricate, very musical images."[190] The seven movements include: *Theme of Menace, Breakthrough, Minutka's death, Silence, German Offensive, Klaus is taken Prisoner*, and *Russian Offensive*. The hero of the film is a Soviet general—supposedly Georgy Zhukov—however, in the film he is called Muravyov. The episode *Klaus is taken Prisoner* depicts the surrender of Marshal Klaus Paulus at Stalingrad.

Popov's second project with Dovzhenko and Solntseva was a biopic about the agronomist Ivan Michurin—*An Enlightened Life* (1947). The score was criticized because of its supposed "formalism, and excessively complicated musical language" and "Russian songs are distorted by the composer's harmonic refinements."[191] Popov was wounded by the reaction; nevertheless, he responded through his music. The opening is marked *Andante Energico* and is upbeat in characterizing man's affinity with nature. The scoring is for strings, the *"epigraph"* evokes a picturesque scene, *Moderato Cantabile*, with flutes, and the folksongs *Oh, You, Vanya Lost Your Senses*, and *Ah, the Fields are Boundless* enhance the orchestral color. The finale, *Allegro Moderato*, is energetic, dance-like, and suitably festive—not without elements of nostalgia appropriate to the screenplay.[192]

Popov's film score never made it to the cinemas—the movie was criticized for its lack of ideology—which led to Dovzhenko suffering a heart attack. A revised version was commissioned; however, Popov's film score was scrapped, and instead, Shostakovich wrote the music. About 25 minutes of Popov's score (uncredited) found its way into the remake—*Michurin* which premiered on New Years' Day 1949. The film was well received internationally—receiving an award for the best film at the Marianske Lazne Festival in 1949. Summing up his film work, Romaschuk writes that "*Chapayev*, *KShE*, and *Spain* were not only brilliantly successful but furthermore highly artistic in presenting ideas and imagery in the films. Popov's music entered into the golden treasury of Russian cinema."[193] The film scores presented the significance of writing for the new cinematic genre at a formative time in its development and raised film music to the level of an art form.

NOTES

1. The first science-fiction film *Aelita* was made in 1924, and with shortages of equipment and venues, the earliest films were documentaries to be shown in factories and schools, and for agitational trains during the Civil War—author.

2. Ellis, Jack C. and McLane, Betsy A, *A New History of Documentary Film*. New York, NY: The Continuum International Publishing Group Inc., 2006, 37.

3. Selunskaya and Zezina, "Documentary film-a Soviet source," *Stalinism and Soviet Cinema*, 175.

4. *Lef*, 1923, No. 3, 140; FF, 93.

5. The first night on November 30, 1930, in a stage realization by Mikhail Sokolovsky and Rafail Suslovich—author.

6. Tsymbal, S., "Accept Battle," *Rabochy i Teater*, No. 66–67, 1930, 6.

7. Yevgeny Gustavovich Gakkel (1892–1953) was a distinguished actor and director of drama theatres in Leningrad, notably at the Krasny Theatre and

Komissarzhevskaya Theatres. His son Leonid is one of the most respected music critics in Russia and an authority on piano—author.

8. Alexey Nikolayevich Arbuzov (1908–1986) began his successful theatre career as a mime artist at the Mariinsky Theatre and toured with theatre companies until writing what was his first play "Class" in 1930, afterward he moved to Meyerhold's theatre in Moscow and his first major triumph was with *Tanya* in 1939—author.

9. "Bolshaya Zhisn, Beseda s khudozhestvennym rukovoditelem Krasnovo teatra t. Wolfom," *Rabochy i Teatr*, No. 27, 1931, 15.

10. Romaschuk, Inna, *Gavriil Nikolayevich Popov. Tvorchestvo. Vremya. Sudba*, Moscow, 2000, 42.

11. This never happened despite agreement to write the libretto from Alexey Tolstoy—author.

12. The first feature film with sound "The Road to Life" released on June 1, 1931, won an award at the Venice Film Festival in 1931. The film is based on Makarenko's eponymous novel about orphans in the USSR.

13. Popov wrote the music for this film directed by Ermler; however, the music was not completed.

14. Fridrich Markovich Ermler (1898–1968) was born as Vladimir Markovich Breslav in Resekne in Latvia and became one of the leading film directors making one of the first Soviet sound films with *The Counterplan* featuring music by Shostakovich and became famous also for his screenplays. Starting as an actor, his first film *Scarlatina* was a documentary (1924) and he made some of the finest films of the Soviet era over more than forty years, and was awarded the Order of Lenin and four Stalin prizes—author.

15. The film produced by Lenfilm was made jointly with Leo Arnstein, Sergey Yutkevitch, and Leonid Lobachevsky and was released on November 7, 1932.

16. Semyon Alexeyevich Timoshenko (1899–1958) was an actor, screenwriter, and director who made many films, and his sole film role was in Eisenstein's *Ivan the Terrible* playing the Livonian ambassador. He also wrote two books on acting and the cinema.

17. Heifetz, Iosif, "The Flight and Fall of '*My Rodina*,'" Искусство кино, (Cinema Art), No. 12, 1990.

18. Alexey Stetsky was head of the agitational department of the CC of the VKP(b).

19. RGASPI, f. 74. op. 2. d. 43. l. 60–63.

20. RGASPI, f. 17. Op. 114. d. 435. l. 79–80.

21. Kamegulov, E., "Moya Rodina," *Leningradskaya Pravda*, March 4, 1933.

22. Bogdanov-Berezovsky, Venyamin, "Kompozitor v zvukovom kino," *Krasnaya Gazeta*, April 3, 1933.

23. The film was released in 1932 and was highly praised by Sergey Eisenstein who proposed future projects with Popov.

24. In its acronym for the Young Communist League—often called "*KShE*," represents an important page in Popov's creativity—author.

25. Bogdanov-Berezovsky, Venyamin, "Kompozitor v zvukovom kino," *Krasnaya Gazeta*, April 3, 1933.

26. Lev Sergeyevich Theremin (1896–1993) invented his instrument in 1919 and famously demonstrated the device to Lenin in 1922 who attempted to play Glinka's 'The Lark.' Several designs were made for different purposes, classical, jazz, and rock concerts. Theremin developed his invention widely in the United States before returning to the USSR in 1938—author.

27. The recycled film music for Suite No. 1 was given its premiere by the Leningrad Radio Orchestra under Mikhail Shneiderman on December 23, 1932. Popov's Symphonic Suite No. 1 suffered from the outbreak of criticism following *Pravda*'s piece on Shostakovich's *Lady Macbeth* in which "formalist" composers suddenly found it difficult to get performances of their music. Popov's Suite was not published and only performed again on March 12, 1982, by the USSR BSO under Edward Chivzhel—author.

28. Nestyev, Israel, "Pseudonauchnaya stryapnya," *Sovetskoye Iskusstvo*, January 18, 1939. This was quoted in a review of a book about the Soviet cinema "Music in contemporary cinema" by Jeremiah Ioffe.

29. Romaschuk, Inna, *Gavriil Nikolayevich Popov. Tvorchestvo. Vremya. Sudba*, Moscow, 2000, 71.

30. Esfir Ilyinichna Shub (1894–1959) was a pioneering figure in the early documentary film in the USSR; she was attracted to the genre after she worked in avant-garde theatre in the 1920s collaborating with Meyerhold. She made a series of historical films about the revolution and the fall of the Tsar with an innovative montage methodology.

31. Telegram from Popov, June 2, 1932. RGALI f. 2035, op. 1, ed. khr., 125.

32. RGALI, f. 3035, op. 1, ed. khr., 125. Letter of Popov to Shub, December 9, 1934.

33. February 28, 1938.

34. RGALI, f. 3035, op. 1, ed. khr. 125.

35. Vyshnevsky, Vladimir, "Film—Espania," April 1939 from T. Dmitriev ed. *V.V. Vyshnevsky: Statii, dnevniki, Pisma*, Moscow, 1961, 251–252.

36. Zakharov, A., "Espania," *Kino*, May 15, 1939.

37. Arnshtam, L., "Espania," *Pravda*, June 7, 1939.

38. Taylor, Richard, "Red Stars, Positive Heroes and Personality Cults," *Stalinism and Soviet Cinema*, Oxford: Routledge, 1993, 71.

39. This direct link with the American mass cinema is obvious from the history of 'The Thirteen' by Mikhail Romm which used as a model John Ford's "Lost Patrol."

40. Based on the eponymous novel by Dmitry Furmanov (the screenplay was written by his widow Anna Furmanova, based on his diaries).

41. Tur, Bratya, "Cherezmernaya Lyubov," *Izvestiya*, June 11, 1935.

42. Taylor, Richard, "Red Stars, Positive Heroes and Personality Cults," *Stalinism and Soviet Cinema*, Oxford: Routledge, 1993, 71.

43. Shumyatsky, B.Z., *Kinematografiya millionov*, Moscow, 1935, 148.

44. Turnovskaya, Maya, "The 1930s and 1940s: Cinema in Context," *Stalinism and Soviet Cinema*, Oxford: Routledge, 1993, 47.

45. "Chapayev," *Pravda*, November 21, 1934.

46. The film was rereleased during the war and unsurprisingly, was awarded the Stalin Prize. International recognition was accorded with the award of Best Foreign Film by the US Film Board in 1935, the Grand Prix at Paris in 1937, and the bronze medal at the Venice Film Festival in 1946.

47. In December 1952, the film score was recycled by Popov for a radio dramatization of *"Chapayev"* by the directors Boris Babochkin and Nikolay Litvinov in which it was presented as a symphonic suite with narrator.

48. Romaschuk, Inna, *Gavriil Nikolayevich Popov. Tvorchestvo. Vremya. Sudba*, Moscow, 2000, 217.

49. Christie, Ian, "The Director in Soviet Cinema," *Stalinism and Soviet Cinema*, Oxford: Routledge, 1993, 160.

50. Popov "Chapayev" interview from the 1960s after restoration of the film, Popov archive.

51. Ironically, when the restored film was released in 1958, the film score was replaced by one containing music by Prokofiev.

52. Eisenstein letter to Popov, March 12, 1933, *G. N. Popov Iz literaturnovo naslediye. Stranitsi biografii*, Moscow, 1986, 70.

53. However, this scheme and another proposal from Nikolay Zarkhi for the play 'The Second Moscow' never left the planning stage.

54. Telegram dated October 6, 1936, RGALI, f.1923., op. 1., ed. khr. 3025.

55. Letter Eisenstein to Popov, May 1, 1936, *Gavriil Nikolayevich Popov. Tvorchestvo. Vremya. Sudba*, Moscow, 2000, 98.

56. Letter to Eisenstein, May 14, 1936, *Gavriil Nikolayevich Popov. Tvorchestvo. Vremya. Sudba*. Moscow, 2000, 99.

57. Letter to Kazantseva, January 28, 1936, *Gavriil Nikolayevich Popov. Tvorchestvo. Vremya. Sudba*, Moscow, 2000, 95.

58. Letter to Kazantseva, January 28, 1936. *Gavriil Nikolayevich Popov. Tvorchestvo. Vremya. Sudba*, Moscow, 2000, 96.

59. Diary, *Gavriil Nikolayevich Popov. Tvorchestvo. Vremya. Sudba*, Moscow, 2000, January 22, 1936, 262.

60. Diary, *Gavriil Nikolayevich Popov. Tvorchestvo. Vremya. Sudba*, Moscow, 2000, February 4, 1936, 262.

61. Diary, *Gavriil Nikolayevich Popov. Tvorchestvo. Vremya. Sudba*, Moscow, 2000, February 14, 1936, 262.

62. The film score for *"Bezhin Meadow"* comprises these numbers:
    No. 1 Women's chorus (depicting destruction of the church)
    No. 2 Coda (final destruction of the church)
    No. 3 Lyrical intermezzo (flowering gardens)
    No. 4 Aria (Death of the mother)
    No. 5 Pioneer song (a capella)
    No. 6 Chorus at the fire (symphony orchestra with chorus).

63. Dietsch, Johan, "Herbert Norkus and Pavel Morozov as Totalitarian Child Martyrs: A Study of Political Religion," eds. Klas-Göran Larsson, Johan Stenfeldt, Ulf Zander, *Perspectives on the Entangled History of Communism and Nazism: A Comnaz Analysis*, Lanham: Lexington Books, 2015, 103–118.

64. Esfir Shub and Boris Barnet were reluctant to censure the script; however, Yuri Marian stated that he had despised everything done by Eisenstein since he made *October* in 1927—author.

65. Marian, D., "V otryv ot deistvitelnosti," *Kino*, March 24, 1937.

66. *Kino*, March 24, 1937, 1–2; April 11, 1937, 1.

67. Shumyatsky, B., "Film Bezhin Lug," *Pravda*, March 19, 1937, FF 380.

68. As a result of this failure, Eisenstein was removed of his teaching duties at the Institute of Cinematography in Moscow—author.

69. Kleiman, N., "Eisenstein, Bezhin Lug (First Version), Cultural-Mythological Aspects," *Final Formula Collection*, Moscow: Eisenstein Center, 2004, 126.

70. Vlasova, E.S., *1948 god v sovetskoy muziki*, Moscow: 21 Classika, 2010, 148.

71. Letter to Kazantseva, April 29, 1935, 85.

72. Letter to Kazantseva, March 30, 1936, 97.

73. Letter to Kazantseva, October 13, 1935, Romaschuk, *Gavriil Nikolaevich Popov. Tvorchestvo. Vremya, Sudba*, Moscow, 2000, 93.

74. "Sumbur vmesto muziki," *Pravda*, January 28, 1936.

75. Diary, March 2, 1936, *Gavriil Nikolayevich Popov. Tvorchestvo. Vremya. Sudba*, Moscow, 2000, 263.

76. Abram Mordukovich Room (1894–1976) was among the leading young filmmakers working as a director with Meyerhold in Leningrad as from 1923 and worked in the Eccentric Theatre. He worked also as an actor and as a screenwriter through until the 1970s.

77. Decision of the Ukrainfilm Trust on banning of *The Strict Youth*, June 10, 1936, *Kino*, July 28, 1936.

78. Happily, Room returned to making films, and indeed was awarded the prestigious Stalin Prize in 1945 and 1949—author.

79. Christie, Ian, "The Director in Soviet Cinema," *Stalinism and Soviet Cinema*, 153.

80. Taylor, Richard, "Ideology as Mass Entertainment: Boris Shumyatsky and Soviet Cinema in the 1930s," in Taylor and Christie, *Stalinism and Soviet Cinema*, 193–216.

81. Vertov, Dziga, "My Illness," (1935), FF, 357.

82. Letter to Kazantseva, April 30, 1935, *Gavriil Nikolayevich Popov. Tvorchestvo. Vremya. Sudba*, Moscow, 2000, 85.

83. *Gavriil Nikolayevich Popov. Tvorchestvo. Vremya. Sudba*, Moscow, 2000, 362.

84. Boris Semenovich Fischman (1906–1964), a student of Lev Tseitlin, was winner of the First All-Union musicians' competition in 1933.

85. Letter to Kazantseva, December 4, 1937, *Gavriil Nikolayevich Popov. Tvorchestvo. Vremya. Sudba*, Moscow, 2000, 110.

86. Letter to Kazantseva, December 4, 1937, *Gavriil Nikolayevich Popov. Tvorchestvo. Vremya. Sudba*, Moscow, 2000, 110.

87. Apetyan, Z.A. (ed.) *G. N. Popov 1904–1972—Iz literaturnovo naslediye. Stranitsi biografii*, Moscow: Sovetsky Kompositor, 1986, 263.

88. Popov, Diary, November 7, 1936, *Gavriil Nikolayevich Popov. Tvorchestvo. Vremya. Sudba*, Moscow, 2000, 263.
89. Popov, Diary, April 19, 1934, *Gavriil Nikolayevich Popov. Tvorchestvo. Vremya. Sudba*, Moscow, 2000, 256.
90. Popov, Diary, December 5, 1936, *Gavriil Nikolayevich Popov. Tvorchestvo. Vremya. Sudba*, Moscow, 2000, 257.
91. Popov, Diary, November 7, 1936, *Gavriil Nikolayevich Popov. Tvorchestvo. Vremya. Sudba*, Moscow, 2000, 263.
92. Diary, January 3, 1938. *Gavriil Ni Gavriil Nikolayevich Popov. Tvorchestvo. Vremya. Sudba*, Moscow, 2000, 266.
93. Letter to Kazantseva, December 6, 1937, *Gavriil Nikolayevich Popov. Tvorchestvo. Vremya. Sudba*, Moscow, 2000, 111.
94. Diary, May 7, 1938, *Gavriil Nikolayevich Popov. Tvorchestvo. Vremya. Sudba*, Moscow, 2000, 268.
95. Letter to Kazantseva, December 20, 1939, *Gavriil Nikolayevich Popov. Tvorchestvo. Vremya. Sudba*, Moscow, 2000, 119.
96. Diary, November 11, 1936. *Gavriil Nikolayevich Popov. Tvorchestvo. Vremya. Sudba*, Moscow, 2000, 264.
97. Letter to Kazantseva, November 27, 1935, *Gavriil Nikolayevich Popov. Tvorchestvo. Vremya. Sudba*, Moscow, 2000, 95.
98. Diary, December 19, 1936, *Gavriil Nikolayevich Popov. Tvorchestvo. Vremya. Sudba*, Moscow, 2000, 265.
99. Diary, *Gavriil Nikolayevich Popov. Tvorchestvo. Vremya. Sudba*. Moscow, 2000, 50.
100. Letter Popov to Meyerhold, November 23, 1930, *G. N. Popov Iz literaturnovo naslediye. Stranitsi biografii*, Moscow, 1986, 50.
101. Letter Popov to Kazantseva, April 29–30, 1931.
102. Letter Meyerhold to Popov, May 1931, *G. N. Popov Iz literaturnovo naslediye. Stranitsi biografii*, Moscow, 1986, 52.
103. Meyerhold to Popov, September 6, 1931, *G. N. Popov Iz literaturnovo naslediye. Stranitsi biografii*, Moscow, 1986, 59.
104. Zlessky V, "Spektakl-predostaerezheniye dlya teatra i avtora," *Vechernaya Moskva*, June 12, 1931.
105. Stein A, "O fleite, kotoraya ne zvuchit," *Leningradskaya Pravda*, October 1, 1931.
106. Berezark I, "Problemi intelligentsia na sovetskoy scene," *Nasha Gazeta*, August 31, 1931.
107. Uriel, "Spisok blagodeyanii," *Komsomolskaya Pravda*, June 16, 1931.
108. Romaschuk, Inna, *Gavriil Nikolayevich Popov. Tvorchestvo. Vremya. Sudba*, Moscow, 2000, 42.
109. Letter Popov to Malko, August 20, 1931, *G. N. Popov Iz literaturnovo naslediye. Stranitsi biografii*, Moscow, 1986, 57.
110. Letter Meyerhold to Popov, September 6, 1931, *G. N. Popov Iz literaturnovo naslediye. Stranitsi biografii*, Moscow, 1986, 59.

111. Yevgeny Iosifovich Gabrilovich (1899–1993), a winner of the Stalin Prize and two State prizes, distinguished playwright, and screenwriter.

112. Meyerhold's theatre was rebuilt into the Tchaikovsky Concert Hall in 1940—author.

113. Apetyan, Z.A. (ed.), *G. N. Popov 1904–1972—Iz literaturnovo naslediye. Stranitsi biografii*, Moscow: Sovetsky Kompositor, 1986, 368.

114. He detailed the projects op. 17 Violin Concerto (2–4th parts), op. 22 Lyric cycle of Pushkin poems (orchestration of 3rd and 4th poems), op. 23 Symphony No. 2, op. 24 Piano Concerto, op. 25 "Alexander Nevsky" opera, op. 26 Serenade for winds, then the opera "A Hero of our Time" for the 100th anniversary of Lermontov's death. Popov Diary, December 26, 1938, Iz. Lit. Apetyan, 270.

115. Apetyan, Z.A. (ed.), *G. N. Popov 1904–1972—Iz literaturnovo naslediye. Stranitsi biografii*, Moscow: Sovetsky Kompositor, 1986, 369.

116. Eisenstein's film Alexander Nevsky was filmed between June and November 7, 1938, and following rapid editing the premiere was shown on December 1, 1938, to great acclaim—author.

117. Letter to Kazantseva, December 6, 1938, *Gavriil Nikolayevich Popov. Tvorchestvo. Vremya. Sudba*, Moscow, 2000, 117.

118. Romaschuk, Inna, *Gavriil Nikolayevich Popov. Tvorchestvo. Vremya. Sudba*, Moscow, 2000, 51.

119. Diary, May 7, 1938, *Gavriil Nikolayevich Popov. Tvorchestvo. Vremya. Sudba*, Moscow, 2000, 268.

120. The contract stipulated the libretto was to ready by October 1, 1938, and Popov hoped to complete the score by December 1939; however, this was never completed. Diary iz. Lit.naslediya 369.

121. Alexander Germanovich Preis (1905–1942) wrote the libretti for Shostakovich's *The Nose and Lady Macbeth of Mtsensk*. He also wrote a libretto for Shostakovich based on Gorky's *Mother* in 1935. His work with Popov was heard at the Composers Union in October 1941, after evacuation from the city, he died in Sverdlovsk from dystrophy.

122. Diary, January 10, 1940, *Gavriil Nikolayevich Popov. Tvorchestvo. Vremya. Sudba*, Moscow, 2000, 273.

123. Diary, April 11, 1940. *Gavriil Nikolayevich Popov. Tvorchestvo. Vremya. Sudba*, Moscow, 2000, 274.

124. Diary, April 27, 1940, *Gavriil Nikolayevich Popov. Tvorchestvo. Vremya. Sudba*, Moscow, 2000, 274.

125. Diary, May 10, 1940. *Gavriil Nikolayevich Popov. Tvorchestvo. Vremya. Sudba*, Moscow, 2000.

126. Diary, September 17, 1939, *Gavriil Nikolayevich Popov. Tvorchestvo. Vremya. Sudba*, Moscow, 2000, 273.

127. Diary, July 29, 1940, *Gavriil Nikolayevich Popov. Tvorchestvo. Vremya. Sudba*, Moscow, 2000, 275.

128. Diary, January 4, 1941, *Gavriil Nikolayevich Popov. Tvorchestvo. Vremya. Sudba*, Moscow, 2000, 276.

129. Diary, February 22, 1941, *Gavriil Nikolayevich Popov. Tvorchestvo. Vremya. Sudba*, Moscow, 2000, 278.

130. Diary, April 17, 1941, *Gavriil Nikolayevich Popov. Tvorchestvo. Vremya. Sudba*, Moscow, 2000, 280.

131. Diary, April 17, 1941, *Gavriil Nikolayevich Popov. Tvorchestvo. Vremya. Sudba*, Moscow, 2000, 280.

132. Diary, April 23, 1941, *Gavriil Nikolayevich Popov. Tvorchestvo. Vremya. Sudba*, Moscow, 2000, 281.

133. Popov, "Pobeda sovetskovo symphonism," *Iskusstvo i Zhizn*, (Art and Life) No. 2, 1938.

134. Diary, July 31, 1941, *Gavriil Nikolayevich Popov. Tvorchestvo. Vremya. Sudba*, Moscow, 2000.

135. Sergey Mitrofanovich Gorodetsky (1884–1967) was a poet and translator who was influenced by Blok and later became one of the symbolist poets; however in the Great War, he became a war correspondent and later wrote about the genocide of the Armenians in Turkey. He translated librettos of *Fidelio. Lohengrin, Die Meistersingerin von Nurnberg*, and also for the first Soviet opera about the Civil War. He wrote the libretto for Vladimir Jurowski's opera "Thoughts on Opanas"—author.

136. In Popov's archive, there remains sketches of part of the second act.

137. Asafyev, Boris, B.V. Asafyev, V. 5, Moscow: Academia, 1954, 97–98.

138. Conversation with Inna Romaschuk by the author, February 27, 2017.

139. RGALI, f.648, op. 4, ed.khr. 215.

140. Pavel Pavlovich Nazarevsky (1918–1994) was a musicologist from Popov's hometown who specialized in restoring Cossack musical culture and was active in the Rostov-On-Don Composers Union.

141. Popov, letter of October 19–22, 1939, Apetyan Z.A., ed. *G. N. Popov 1904–1972—Iz literaturnovo naslediye. Stranitsi biografii*, Moscow: Sovetsky Kompositor, 1986, 122.

142. Diary, *Gavriil Nikolayevich Popov. Tvorchestvo. Vremya. Sudba*, Moscow, 2000, 273.

143. Shmyrov, Margolit, "Izyatoye Kino," Moscow, 1995, 64.

144. Herbert Rappaport (1908–1983) was born in Vienna and began his film career at Hollywood for Paramount and as he wanted to make an antifascist film, he agreed to work at Lenfilm in the USSR following his recruitment by Boris Shumyatsky in 1935.

145. Romaschuk, Inna, *Gavriil Nikolayevich Popov. Tvorchestvo. Vremya. Sudba*, Moscow, 2000, 289.

146. Budenny, S.M., "Efim Dzigan," *Zhisn i Film*, Moscow 1981, 116.

147. "I am writing a second orchestral episode for the films *March of Voroshilov* and *Defence of Tsaritsyn* . . . apart from which I have written a symphonic poster—"March of the Red Cavalry," for symphony orchestra and male chorus (on commission from the radio committee)—an adaptation from *The First Cavalry*. It sounds great. They played it (broadcast) on 26 July." The speed at which Popov worked is revealed by the fact that he finished the score on July 2 just ten days after the invasion—author.

148. Alexander Mikhailovich Faintsimmer (1906–1982) enjoyed a long career making his first movie in 1929 and notable for his 1934 film *Lieutenant Kije* with a score by Prokofiev, the suite from which became world famous.

149. 85. RGASPI. *f.* 17. Op. 116. d. 88. *l.* 1.

150. Diary, *Gavriil Nikolayevich Popov. Tvorchestvo. Vremya. Sudba*, Moscow, 2000, 274.

151. Diary, February 14, 1941, *Gavriil Nikolayevich Popov. Tvorchestvo. Vremya. Sudba*, Moscow, 2000, 278.

152. However, the second installment of the series *Tsaritsyn* was not judged suitable as "it departed from the historical and life veracity in depicting the personalities of Stalin and Voroshilov and render a false characterization of the people."

153. "Iz zaklucheniya GFF," Margolit E., Shyrov, *Izyatoye Kino*, Moscow, 1995, 82.

154. Letter to Shebalin, July 8, 1942, *Gavriil Nikolayevich Popov. Tvorchestvo. Vremya. Sudba*, Moscow, 2000, 133–134.

155. Letter to Atovmyan, April 6, 1943, *Gavriil Nikolayevich Popov. Tvorchestvo. Vremya. Sudba*, Moscow, 2000, 135.

156. The film "Partisans" was released as "They fought for the Motherland"—author.

157. Letter to Nikolay Popov, March 27, 1943, *Gavriil Nikolayevich Popov. Tvorchestvo. Vremya. Sudba*, Moscow, 2000, 134.

158. Dziga Vertov (1896–1954) born David Abelovich Kaufman was a legendary documentary filmmaker active in futurism and noted for his Man with a Movie Camera (1929); he produced the first documentary with sound and introduced music enhancing the visual effect in his Simfoniya Donbass (Enthusiasm). His first documentary in 1919 and others were akin to Pathe news reels' films showing the day by day life in the USSR—author.

159. Arsha Ambartsumovna Ovanesova (1906–1990) was born in Nagorno-Karabakh and began making documentary films in 1936; she became a highly talented director specializing in films for children and young people. She was awarded the International Peace Prize and the Stalin Prize for her film *World Youth* (1950). As a teacher she tutored many leading filmmakers in the USSR.

160. Romaschuk, Inna, *Gavriil Nikolayevich Popov. Tvorchestvo. Vremya. Sudba*, Moscow, 2000, 225.

161. Alexey Yakovlevich Kapler (1903–1979) was an outstanding writer and scenarist and began working in the Leningrad Eccentric theatre and with Dovzhenko on the film *Arsenal*, he wrote the screenplay for several revolutionary films of the 1930s and was awarded the Lenin Prize and Stalin Prize. He enjoyed a brief romance with Stalin's daughter Svetlana Alluieva, he was declared an 'enemy of the people' and spent seven years in the Gulag before renewing his film career in 1955, and later became the presenter of a popular TV program about the cinema between 1966 and 1972—author.

162. Alexander Dovzhenko (1894–1956) Dovzhenko was born into poverty in a Ukrainian Cossack family and was one of just three from fourteen children to survive famine. Determined to make a career, he was interested in painting and architecture and became a teacher in a district school. Drawn to politics and participated in the

Civil War in Kiev, he was a diplomat in Warsaw and a cultural commissar in Kiev after which he studied art in Munich prior to working in Soviet cinema. He lived with Yuliya Solntseva an actress who became his codirector on all his films—author.

163. Dovzhenko's trilogy of films *"Zvenigor"* (1928), *"Arsenal"* (1929), and *"The Earth"* (1930) became celebrated worldwide upon release for their graphic realism.

164. Diary, July 3, 1943, *Gavriil Nikolayevich Popov. Tvorchestvo. Vremya. Sudba*, Moscow, 2000, 283.

165. Popov, Gavriil, "Programme notes," February 15, 1944. RGALI, f. 2038.

166. Romaschuk, Inna, *Gavriil Nikolayevich Popov. Tvorchestvo. Vremya. Sudba*, Moscow, 2000, 110.

167. Apetyan, Z.A. (ed.), *G. N. Popov 1904–1972—Iz literaturnovo naslediye. Stranitsi biografii*, Moscow: Sovetsky Kompositor, 1986, 373.

168. Letter to Kazantseva, November 20, 1943, *Gavriil Nikolayevich Popov. Tvorchestvo. Vremya. Sudba*, Moscow, 2000, 137.

169. Letter to Kazantseva, December 14, 1943, *Gavriil Nikolayevich Popov. Tvorchestvo. Vremya. Sudba*, Moscow, 2000, 138.

170. Telegram to Kazantseva, February 18, 1944, *Gavriil Nikolayevich Popov. Tvorchestvo. Vremya. Sudba*, Moscow, 2000, 139.

171. Apetyan Z.A., ed. *G. N. Popov 1904–1972—Iz literaturnovo naslediye. Stranitsi biografii*, Moscow: Sovetsky Kompositor, 1986, 284.

172. Diary, *Gavriil Nikolayevich Popov. Tvorchestvo. Vremya. Sudba*. Moscow, 2000, 292.

173. "Iz stenogrammy obsuzhedeniya Simfoniya 2 v SK," Archive Popova.

174. Asafyev, Boris, "Symphony," vol. V, Asafyev B.V. Selected works, Moscow: Academia, 82–83.

175. Hakobian, Leon, *Music f the Soviet Era*, London: Routledge, 2017, 164.

176. Romaschuk, Inna, *Gavriil Nikolayevich Popov. Tvorchestvo. Vremya. Sudba*, Moscow, 2000, 111.

177. Apetyan Z.A., ed. *G. N. Popov 1904–1972—Iz literaturnovo naslediye. Stranitsi biografii*, Moscow: Sovetsky Kompositor, 1986, 378.

178. Belza, Igor, "Dve simfoniya," *Literatura i iskusstve*, February 19, 1944.

179. Informatsionnii sbornik. Moscow, 1945, Nos. 7–8, 1.

180. "Sovetskaya Muzika v dnei voine," *Sovetskaya Muzika*, No. 11, 1975. *Literatura i iskusstvo*, April 1, 1944. TSGALI, f. 2077, op. 1, ed. khr. 93.

181. RGALI, f. 2077, op. 1, ed. kh. 239, l. 107.

182. Schwartz, Boris, *Music and Musical life in Soviet Russia 1917–1981*, Bloomington: Indiana UP, 1983, 203.

183. Letter Shostakovich to Khrapchenko, May 3, 1945, "Deyatelei Russkovo iskusstva i M. B. Khrapchenko 1939–1948," Perkhin, Moscow: Nauka, 2007, 640.

184. Shebalin, V.Y., *Vospominaniya. Statii. Vystupleniye*, Moscow: Muzyka, 1975, 209.

185. Diary, July 26, 1944, *Gavriil Nikolayevich Popov. Tvorchestvo. Vremya. Sudba*, Moscow, 2000, 284.

186. Nestyev I G. Edelman, *Sergey Prokofiev. Statii. Materiali. 1953–1963*, Moscow: Muzyka, 1962, 287.

187. Letter Prokofiev to Popov, September 12, 1945, *Gavriil Nikolayevich Popov. Tvorchestvo. Vremya. Sudba*, Moscow, 2000, 141.

188. Apetyan Z.A., ed. *G. N. Popov 1904–1972—Iz literaturnovo naslediye. Stranitsi biografii*, Moscow: Sovetsky Kompositor, 1986, 379.

189. Diary, September 10, 1945, *Gavriil Nikolayevich Popov. Tvorchestvo. Vremya. Sudba*, Moscow, 2000.

190. Diary, October 19, 1945, *Gavriil Nikolayevich Popov. Tvorchestvo. Vremya. Sudba*, Moscow, 2000.

191. Schwartz, L. "On Modern Film Music," *Sovetskaya Muzyka*, No. 3, 1948, 6.

192. Romaschuk, Inna, *Gavriil Nikolayevich Popov. Tvorchestvo. Vremya. Sudba*, Moscow, 2000, 251.

193. Romaschuk, Inna, *Gavriil Nikolayevich Popov. Tvorchestvo. Vremya. Sudba*, Moscow, 2000, 210–211.

Chapter 6

1948 and Decline

Written during the last days of the war, the *Symphonic Aria* is imbued by the theme of personal loss. Ostensibly, Popov wrote it in memory of his friend, the writer, Alexey Nikolayevich Tolstoy (1883–1945), as he reflected, "This work is based on two harmoniously musical images: philosophical-heroic and lyrical-romantic."[1] Popov's score uses themes from his film score from the abandoned *Bezhin Meadow*; Popov's piece reflects grief for other friends and colleagues who died during the war: the painter Kirill Petrov-Vodkin, and four composer colleagues—Viktor Tomilin, Pyotr Ryazanov, Vyacheslav Shishkov, and Valery Zhelobinsky. They all shared Popov's values, and the sum of these losses is expressed in this masterly composition. This anguish was overtaken by the death of his father in Rostov on Don on December 15, 1945.[2] Nikolay Popov had been his paradigm throughout his life and given him both inspiration and meaning in life.

The *Symphonic Aria* is written for cello and orchestra and opens with a prologue and closes on a nostalgic coda. At its heart are intermittent recitatives, a transitory *Largo* and *Cantabile* followed by a brief, energetic passage (*Maestoso*) which develops into an *Appassionato*. There is here a parallel with Shostakovich's Second Piano Trio (1944), which was also dedicated to a close friend—Ivan Sollertinsky. However, Popov does not yield to his colleague in freshness and originality. The new piece was approved by the Committee of Arts and a contract agreed. The Deputy-Chairman Vladimir Surin hailed it "simply wonderful!"[3] The premiere of the Symphonic Aria for Cello and Strings was given by Alexander Shtrimer and Popov in a piano reduction at the Chamber Hall of the Moscow Conservatoire on May 1, 1946. The full orchestral variant was premiered by Svyatoslav Knushevitsky with the USSR State Symphony Orchestra under Alexander Gauk on December 19, 1946.

A redeeming feature in Popov's character was that he held no antipathy at Shostakovich's apparent cooling toward him. The newly written Ninth Symphony enthused Popov. "Wonderful tutti, clear ideas (the main idea of the first movement is pure Mozart!). Certainly, it is very individual—Shostakovichian. A great deal of brilliant wit together with sun-filled music. It is mostly accessible. Melodic singing—not perceptibly, but (timbre and quality) is expressive. The tempos of the rapid themes are very dramatic. A wonderful symphony. The finale is wonderful for its gaiety, cheerfulness, polish, and tempo!! Well done Mitya!"[4]

The Kyiv Philharmonic concert season opened with Popov's Second Symphony in October 1946. The conductor Nathan Rakhlin wrote to Popov: "I was sad beyond words that you weren't (present) because it is quite impossible to describe the performance. You know that I don't exaggerate, but this was something close to perfection."[5] The conductor who had premiered the Second Symphony inquired when the Third would be ready. Popov was now an honored composer, a measure of which was that the 1946 Stalin Prize second class brought him a financial reward of 80,000 roubles.

The ostensible success of the *"Motherland"* symphony allowed him the assurance to complete his Third Symphony in 1946. Popov's work was briefly interrupted by composing the incidental music to *Key to Berlin* at Moscow's Theater of the Revolution. Concerns were arising from the delay in the Third Symphony led to the Committee for Arts asking for repayment of the 11,000 roubles advance.

The Third Symphony is known as "The Heroic" and unsurprisingly deals with the problems of war and peace. There are allusions to neoclassicism and the idiom is compellingly dramatic with two *Scherzo* movements, but the *Largo* lies at the heart of the symphony, as his biographer writes, "The idea emerged from the profundity of life—and life's eternal contradictions."[6] There come together notions about an eternally freethinking, remarkable, and cheerful people, and the other Spain which can be seen through the paintings of Goya. Romaschuk continues that "it's not only the native color and its crowded atmosphere mixed with the sparkle of life but the eternal question, which is shouting out 'Why?' This unrequited question is important to understand the philosophical and human themes in *The Heroic* Symphony."[7]

There is in Russian music an empathy with Spanish culture, reflected most significantly by the nationalist school, above all by Glinka's *Summer Nights in Spain*, and Rimsky Korsakov's *Capriccio Espagnole*. One other model for the symphony was the Second Viennese School. The idea for Popov came from Schoenberg's *Verklärte Nacht*. "I listened to his expressive melodies and recognized a great ability to create an emotionally smoldering musical structure. I sensed elements of Wagnerian symphonism, through to Richard Strauss."[8]

Popov's latest work has a kinship too with Honegger's Second Symphony and shares a laconism in the orchestral color. A unique feature is the citations of Catalan and Basque folk music, and there is a theme which is also used by Shostakovich in his Fourteenth Symphony (in his Lorca poem setting). Cast in five movements, the Third Symphony is remarkable for its imagery, energetic drama, and motoric dance rhythms. The relationship with Spanish dance motifs emphasizes elements of the grotesque. Popov was well satisfied on completing the Third Symphony on September 21, 1946: "Shcherbachov believes Symphony No. 3 is my best achievement."[9] The premiere was given in Moscow on January 31, 1947, by Abram Stasevich conducting the USSR State Symphony Orchestra, leading Popov to enthuse in his diary, "Applause broke out after the third movement; then, after the fourth, and fifth. Of course, they only performed it at 70% in the expression and depth of perspective. Stasevich hasn't quite grasped it, the committee (of the Stalin Prize awards) will seemingly not back the Symphony No. 3."[10] The Leningrad Philharmonic Orchestra, under Stasevich, performed the Third on March 9, 1947. Popov made use of this opportunity to spend a month in the city supervising the rehearsals and taking in the occasion of his symphony played by the country's premier orchestra, and pleased the composer as he noted that, "It was a great success. All and sundry, with a few exceptions, congratulated me."[11] The performance led to many positive reactions and one colleague mentioned that Popov was continuing Beethoven's symphonism.[12] Popov managed to secure a future concert of his *Symphonic Aria* at the Philharmonic.

During the weeks spent in his former home, Popov rediscovered Leningrad and its almost mystical cultural ethos. Popov wrote home to Irina. "The open window looks onto Lavrov Street (parallel with Kirochnaya). The fresh air in Leningrad is wonderful. The city is unusually beautiful: stern and severe in outline against the silhouettes of buildings and the streets, squares, and embankments. The mighty Neva is magical in its expanse, profuse blue, sea ozone, and the wonderful Ladoga."[13] Since his student years, he adored jazz, smoked cigars, and carried himself like a dandy in Leningrad society. Popov's good looks and *bonhomie* found favor with women and he habitually signed himself off as "Gabriel Popov."

Popov's Third Symphony was proposed for the Stalin Prize; however, as Popov wrote, "for unknown reasons, the discussion of my Third Symphony by a plenary meeting of the Committee (for Stalin Prizes) postponed the discussion to the following session in 1947."[14] Regardless of the early positivity, no award was given. Part of the reason may be explained by Myaskovsky's disapproval—the most influential musician on the Stalin Prize Awards Committee, who dismissed it as "preposterous: excellent music, but quite muddled up both in the composition and orchestration."[15] The Third Symphony was neither mentioned nor discussed at further sessions of the committee.¹⁶ The possibility of an accolade was put on ice because of the developing campaign against formalism in January 1948.

The ostentatious success of Popov's immediate postwar work allowed him to conceive the idea of an unfulfilled ballet *Amur and Psyche*. However, Moscow life brought with it new tasks and other responsibilities. Popov was co-opted onto the expanded Composers Union Organizing Committee (which also included Prokofiev, Shebalin, Khrennikov, Polovinkin, and Knipper) in 1946.¹⁷ He joined a commission to work out improved leadership responsibilities of the Composers' Union and align it with the Writers' Union.¹⁸ There came with these obligations business tours around the country, firstly to the Caucasus to audition works for the Stalin Prize. For the first time, he could visit parts of the country long unfamiliar to him. Popov was impressed by the museums, ancient architecture, art galleries, and the hospitality of people in Georgia, Armenia, and Azerbaijan. What would prove to be a providential visit was the trip to Riga in 1946. There he addressed the plenary of the Latvian Composers Union and attended concerts of the Baltic Republic's contemporary music. Khachaturyan told him after his invigorating speech. "Well, here we have a new potential chairman!"¹⁹ Popov fell in love with Riga, sharing his passion in his journal, "Cleanliness, comfort, greenery, parks, flowers, lovely lilacs, narcissus, roses, and lilies of the valley. The surrounding area and the sea are wonderful. I bathed (in the Gulf of Riga) on 30 May. I am bewitched with the spiritual joy, and stirring feeling from the sea!!!"²⁰ Among those he met was a fellow delegate to the Latvian capital—the Armenian musicologist Zara Apetyan, who would in time become, Popov's third wife.

Back in Moscow, Konstantin Ivanov conducted the Second Symphony with the USSR State Symphony Orchestra to great success and repeated the symphony in Kharkiv in April 1946. At last, following years of homelessness, the Popovs were granted a three-room flat on Mozhaisk Avenue where they moved in on November 16, 1946. There was more praise for his Third Symphony; however, Shostakovich found the occasion to find faults. Shostakovich criticized it for deficient musical development, absence of humor, and overcrowded tension, and a lack of psychological pauses.²¹ Now, in late 1946, Popov returned to his *Nevsky* opera working on the libretto with Gorodetsky; however, in January 1947, the Bolshoi Theater called him in for what he presumed to be a discussion on his long-anticipated opera, what emerged instead was a commission for an opera on a modern theme. A contract was duly initialled on July 23, 1947, for the stage work entitled *The Contemporaries*, and his collaborators were to be Mark Tseitlin and Gorodetsky.²² The latter showed little interest, and the project quickly lost track—if it ever had any. By the summer of 1947, Popov began to have misgivings. "It is with terrible fear, anxiety, and concern that I reflect upon this new opera. (about a 'hero of our time'—a Leningrad inventor). I want to call the opera *Dreams*. Or the hero is an engineer-inventor—a poet of great hopes—but he cannot fulfil them!"[23] In November 1947, Popov was awarded the illustrious title of Merited Artist of the RSFSR—an award he felt was profoundly undeserved owing to his many unfinished projects.[24]

In the first days of February 1948, Popov heard the first three movements and cadenza of Shostakovich's unfinished Violin Concerto, and enthused, "Excellent! It reminds me somewhat (in the spirit of the writing and orchestration) of his Sixth Symphony. The third movement—*Passacaglia*—is fine in its choral-harmonic structure particularly in the woodwind. I wait (to hear) its swift finale."[25] This hearing was one of the few positive notes in what would be a miserable year for Soviet music. Popov was a member of the Composers Union Secretariat that was attacked for "formalism," added to which was his alleged aiding and abetting "Western musical values." Supplementary to the formalist sobriquet was "renunciation of the basic principles of classical music," the propagation of "atonality, dissonance, and disharmony," and "muddled, nerve-racking sounds turning music into cacophony."[26] On January 13, Andrey Zhdanov named Popov in a list with Kabalevsky and other "offending" composers, but on February 3, in a statement from Khrapchenko of the Committee of Arts, Popov's name was absent—yet a week later—he was returned to the proscribed company with Kabalevsky, now exempt.[27]

The Central Committee resolution published in *Pravda* on February 10, 1948, rebuked Khachaturyan, Myaskovsky, Muradeli, Popov, Prokofiev, Shebalin, and Shostakovich. Among the suggested reasons for Popov's substitution for Kabalevsky is that the latter's wife, Larisa Pavlovna Chegodayeva was influential on the CC and had asked for her husband to be excused. Whether this is true cannot be verified for Chegodayeva did not hold any important position, albeit, Kabalevsky's first spouse Edvarda Iosifovna Bluman worked at the Ministry of Foreign Trade. Now, the "turncoat" Kabalevsky strongly criticized his "formalist" colleagues at meetings of the Composers Union, and who, like Khachaturyan, was a member of the VKP(b).

On February 20, 1948, at a meeting of the Composers Union Moscow branch, Popov expressed regret for the "harmful tendencies" in his past music. "While melody is the foundation of my musical creativity and has always been the main factor, it is difficult for me to resist a strong attraction for the whole range of contemporary new-fangled and musically expressive resources."[28] He promised to purge negativity and to "realize the most valuable decrees of the Party and honorably fulfill my creative tasks in the name of our great servitude to our people and the glorious Motherland."[29] Popov acknowledged that his polyphony, and "hypertrophy of polyphonic practice," and orchestral dramaturgy "wanted for orchestral beauty." He stated also that the negativity in his scores was through the frequent use of the percussion—although he had always tried to limit their use except for the cinema and theater. Not unlike his symphonies, it is impossible not to read a measure of sarcasm and irony in several of the phrases expressed by Popov, notably "valuable decrees," "servitude," and "honorably fulfill."

Regardless, Popov came under attack during heated discussions at the Leningrad Union of Composers on March 1–3. Mikhail Chulaki gave the main address in which Popov's *Grosse Klaviersuite* was cited as "formalist," as was Deshevov's opera *Rails*, and early piano pieces by Shostakovich.[30] Nevertheless, unlike the Moscow meetings, there was a relatively open debate. Mravinsky expressed his strong support for Shostakovich and his music, dismissing the accusations of formalism.[31] The Leningrad meetings were more intense and supportive of the "formalists," yet a subdued atmosphere prevailed at the Moscow Conservatoire meeting attended by some five hundred students and staff. The Eighth and Ninth symphonies by Shostakovich, Popov's Third Symphony, and Prokofiev's Seventh and Eighth Piano Sonatas were all in the firing line.[32] The First Composers Union Congress was held on April 19–25, 1948. Following the opening day, Popov did not attend any further sessions. It is said that the former ASM members gathered at Myaskovsky's home on his name day to confer on the events and that Popov himself was among the "conspirators."[33]

Of the alleged "formalist composers," only Myaskovsky refrained from any form of apology—everyone else acknowledged their guilt and pledged to restructure themselves.[34] Romaschuk writes that Popov's compositional style did not change significantly over forty years, but it looks as if his language became pretentious and more accessible.[35] Popov was swayed to making his peace with the new leadership of the Composers Union and adopted socialist realist texts. He arranged several admirably written choruses: *Cossack Humoresques* based on texts by the symbolist Ilya Selvinsky, where he found ample scope for a capella choir through the richly ambient, sharply contrasting colors of the Don Cossack folksongs.[36] Popov attempted to reassert his artistic status with his cycle of romances and his redemption was acknowledged ostensibly by the Committee for Arts.[37]

A sign of the compromise by Popov was *The Field Is Being Harvested* for boys' choir based on socialist realist poetry by Alexey Mashistov. This was incorporated into the Suite—*Our Dear Lands*, including the songs *Our Garden* (words by Mashistov), and *The Languid Cuckoo* (Alexander Prokofyev) embellishing the turn to a more plausible genre.[38] *We Are the Free Youth of the World* (texts by Mstislav Levashov), for mixed choir and piano, and *Everything That Is Desired and Beautiful* (1948), for mixed a capella choir continued the trend.[39] Popov's turn to populism was unacknowledged in a vitriolically hostile essay by the young musicologist Israel Nestyev entitled "The allure of bourgeois modernism in the works of G. Popov."[40] Popov was mischievous enough to find a means of writing music of irony contrary to the meaning of his texts. A discerning reflection shows Popov never relented in his harmonic and stylistic individualism.[41] His colleagues noted that the harmonies of his choruses were "refined" and embraced challenging choral passages, within the socialist realist lexicon.

THE FOURTH CHORAL SYMPHONY

In May 1948, Popov began working on a new symphony. "I have written a movement for a Concerto for a Capella chorus with the theme of *The Soviet Army—Glory!* (based on texts by Mikhail Golodny).[42] The Concerto is to be in four parts. The Committee for Arts has endorsed the music."[43] There was moral encouragement from Shcherbachov and Bogdanov-Berezovsky in Leningrad for his changed course.[44] There remained other concerns for Popov, as he noted, "I have to write the Choral Concerto, and repeat the whole score (260 pages) of the piano arrangement of the *Alexander Nevsky* opera (for a dreadful presentation to the Committee for Arts: What will they say? What if they don't support my completion of the opera?" According to the contract, the Choral Concerto was to be finished by October 1, 1948.[45] This deadline—like most others—was not met, and he struggled to gather together the draft and libretto for *Nevsky*. "True, they have recognized my 'talent' in the first act, but are scared to death by the 'wild harmonies' and other problems."[46] In February 1949, matters got much worse for Popov when Nikolay Goryaninov, the head of Theater at the Committee for Arts, demanded the return of the advance for the opera. Popov's sketches for the second act had been approved by Igor Ilyin, but Goryaninov—who had not heard any of the new music—overruled Ilyin and threatened to tear up the contract.[47]

The *Choral Concerto* made slow progress; however, Popov entitled what he called his new Fourth Symphony subtitled *Glory to the Homeland!* for a capella chorus was completed on September 18, 1949.[48] Disregarding the recently voiced fealty to his detractors, Romaschuk believes that after the 1948 Zhdanov condemnations, few musicians would have conceived this music, and that Popov's music was ahead of its time. "The program and its texts were aimed at some kind of consciously public festivity, similar both in style and language to the mass song."[49] The Fourth Symphony embodied Popov's conception of choral writing characterized through the human voice in a poly-melodic (polyphonic stylization) score.

There was a mixed response when Popov unveiled his symphony to the Composers Union Secretariat on September 23, 1949, noting in his journal,

"They all praised the music, but criticized its length and the symphony's technical difficulties."[50] Myaskovsky said it was one of the few pieces (performed) that was worthy of any praise.[51] Koval and Zakharov suggested cutting it down to twenty-five to thirty minutes; however, Popov refused to make any cuts. Other complaints were that "it was too difficult to sing," according to Schwartz—the "contribution was minimal."[52] On November 30, 1949, the second movement *Spring* was performed by the Gnessin Institute Chorus, supplemented by twenty-six singers from the Bolshoi Theater Chorus directed by Alexander Khazanov at the Chamber Hall of the Moscow Conservatoire. The soloists were the mezzo-soprano Valentina Gagarina and the lyric tenor Solomon Khromchenko. The performance was "disappointing. The soloists were worse than the chorus. Considering that the chorus's role is greater, they couldn't spoil the general impression. The audience responded wonderfully to *Spring*, and I was twice called on stage and the chorus (130 singers) joined in the ovation. All week everyone has been congratulating me for this artistic triumph."[53] A subsequent recording for radio was made with the same performers, and a replacement tenor—Anatoly Orfenov. What became known as the *Choral* Symphony was published by Muzfond of the Composers' Union.[54] Popov's work was unanimously approved for a Stalin Prize, but the awards committee decided to pass it over to another year because only one movement was performed.[55] There was admiration from Alexander Anisimov, the vice-chairman of the Committee for Arts. "Your *Choral* Symphony is the ultimate in realist art."[56] Regardless of this, and despite the positive response in Moscow and Leningrad (where Popov performed it at the Capella), the Fourth *Choral* Symphony was not heard again. Marian Koval wrote positively: "The symphony captivates its audience for its beautiful melodies and rich choral sound."[57] The new leader of the Composers' Union Tikhon Khrennikov said that the symphony creates "a great impression on the audience with its innermost spirit and good purposefulness."[58]

The *Choral* Symphony is based upon the traditions of Russian choral music, from Bortnyansky and Berezovsky, but also Bach, Beethoven, and Verdi.[59] Regardless of having few performances, Popov's *Choral* Symphony may well have inspired Alfred Schnittke's Fourth Symphony, and the *Ten Revolutionary Poems* (1951), and Thirteenth Symphony *Babi Yar* (1962) by Shostakovich. The poems by Selvinsky were considered fresh and contemporary, although today they are passé, there is an emotional charge, and is forcefully dramatic. Romaschuk considers the subtext has more fundamental themes that are portrayed unequivocally through the musical imagery, "Ancient Russia, Russia, its voices (invoking distant echoing bells, 'gusli' folk instruments, expansive hymnal chants, and potent 'spring-like' torrents) in the first movement, there are recollections of the war, with operatic elicitations in the second movement, a lament (in the form of a requiem) in the third movement, finally, the culminating movement is an apotheosis, reminding one of the stirring Glinka's chorus from *Life for the Tsar* -*Glory!*"[60]

TALES ABOUT LENIN

The disappointment of no complete performance and little recognition of his Choral Symphony was a setback. Attracted to the choral genre he began writing a new-fangled choral score *Tales about Lenin*, based on an ancient Slavonic chant, transcribed by Fyodor Konashkov.[61] The work was written in April 1950 for a bass soloist and male voice choir to piano accompaniment with an alternative orchestral version. The work was approved by the Union of Composers and scheduled for a premiere in December 1950 with Myaskovsky's Twenty-Seventh Symphony and Prokofiev's oratorio *On Guard of Peace*, but the premiere was canceled because the choir could not learn it in time. This unfortunate sequence of events reveals the lack of respect given to Popov.[62] Another source of disappointment was that Alexander Gauk's scheduled broadcast was prohibited by Moscow Radio.[63]

The premiere of the *Tales* was given on April 6, 1951, by the soloist Alexey Ivanov, with Gauk conducting the Moscow Radio Symphony Orchestra and Chorus. There was approval from Kukharsky who commented, "This work is astonishingly talented. I cannot recall anything similar to this recently or at the Composers' Union."[64] The second performance of Popov's *Tales about Lenin*, however, came only eighteen years later in 1969 given by the bass-baritone Evgeny Vladimirov, the male choir of the Yurlov State Choir, and the Moscow Philharmonic Orchestra under Israel Guzman. The occasion was to celebrate the birth centenary of the founder of the Soviet state. Melodiya issued a recording, and the score was published in 1962 (first version) and reissued in 1972. It was only then that *Tales* received any attention and became widely performed. Romaschuk writes that the "reappearance" of this work by an "avant-garde" composer proved somewhat disappointing to those who remembered his best work. Colleagues considered Popov had left his notions behind in the 1920s and 1930s, and everyone had lost interest.[65]

Popov continued to garner work from the cinema allowing him experimentation in different styles with some degree of self-confidence that his work could attain recognition distant from the center of musical life. The next decade witnessed twelve film scores helping revive his prewar realizations, though none equaled their brilliant success. Another blow was the death of Popov's librettist for *Nevsky*—Pyotr Pavlenko in June 1951—as Popov noted in his diary, "I have lost my main collaborator in the preliminary creative work to complete my opera *Alexander Nevsky*." It appeared that he had still not lost hope in what he called his magnum opus.[66]

QUARTET SYMPHONY

Throughout his career, Popov loved to share his musical ideas with his friends and his first wife, Olga Palui was a constant muse, writing to her, "I want so much to play this music to you. It is overflowing (in the first three movements) with passionate melody, determination, struggle, intensity, and tenderness. It is like a chamber symphony for (string) quartet."[67] Popov composed what he would call his Quartet Symphony between June and September 1951. In a radio interview, Popov said his notion was for "the sound of four magnificent instruments like a whole orchestra in an intuitively emotional transcendence."[68]

Popov's first and only string quartet is dedicated to Pyotr Pavlenko.[69] The Moscow premiere by the Union of Composers Quartet (later renamed the Borodin Quartet) on December 4, 1951, met with mixed opinions. Popov wrote to Khachaturyan, "I am sorry that you didn't hear the inspiring and artistic performance. This challenging piece surges with virtuosic and musically dynamic imagery, with the players 'in discourse with the audience' in a magnificently epic lyricism, and energetic images of thoughts and feelings."[70]

The Quartet Symphony shares a kinship with the First Symphony in its inner struggle of juxtaposing elements all of which are sensitively and sentimentally ornamented (quasi-citation in the finale of the folksong "In the garden the chrysanthemums have flowered"). However, there is an unrelenting movement, and the *Adagio* invokes ancient Russian chant in the spirit of 'Glory.' Popov thought that the piece would not be welcomed because of the intense musical and psychological ideas, fearing that the critics would "knock my head off."[71] Shebalin praised the "poetry, and inspiring, moving, unmistakable innovative talent." On the other hand, Shostakovich complained that the music was excessively neurotic. Regrettably, the Quartet Symphony has not become established in the Russian quartet repertoire.

THE FIFTH SYMPHONY

There came more sadness through the death of several colleagues and close friends. Following the death of Pavlenko in 1951, in the following year, Vladimir Shcherbacov and Yuri Kochurov died. Popov eulogized Shcherbachov as "the creator of an entire school of composing representing an entire epoch in Soviet composition, and I am orphaned. My friend and leader has died—my musical father."[72] Popov lamented greatly the passing of Kochurov - an extraordinarily gifted composer who was steadfast to modernist music. Popov wrote that, "In two and a half months, I have lost two of my closest musical friends."[73] Myaskovsky's death from cancer in 1950 was another grievous loss as the symphonist had often mentored Popov. The greatest loss for Popov came in October 1953 when following a prolonged illness, his wife died, Popov wrote, "The blackest day in my life of 49 years: today at 3.10 in the morning, my beloved, irreplaceable and unthanked Irinochka died."[74]

The first thoughts of the Fifth Symphony appear in a diary entry from November 1951. The symphony reflects upon Popov's creativity torn between storms and tragedies and the quixotic frustrated picturesque dreams of "pastoral" life. Popov elicits his thoughts "the first movement is multifaceted with a psychological subtext, but there is one theme which appears almost unnoticed and assumes great significance in a profoundly lyrical dreamworld."[75]

The expansive opening of the Fifth Symphony in its narrative about the threat to life (the second movement *Menace*, while the third movement *Struggle*) has a kinship with the Quartet Symphony in the fourth movement *Elegy*, and the fifth movement *Pastoral*. The vibrant lyrical and sentimental outlines of the two works are distinguished by the dramaturgical tone and high-pitched *Scherzo* (grotesque) motifs. Nathan Rakhlin (who gave the premiere) enthused. "There is so much passion, feelings, suffering, and potency in your Fifth—it is as if you are giving everything to it. So much sweat, blood and energy have to be given by both orchestra and conductor. It is splendidly powerful and Russian in spirit."[76] These thoughts were shared by Shostakovich. If his Third Symphony was inspired by Schoenberg, the Fifth is the closest that Popov came to the symphonies of Gustav Mahler.

The Fifth Symphony took another four years to emerge fully and started off in a modest fashion, as Popov disclosed, "In April, I started writing a symphonic poem. It is about nature, the labor of man in nature, and the joys of life. I have written the opening (a morning in nature), as a lyrical-epic theme (singing broadly, on subtly rich harmonies)."[77] The origin is in that Mikhail Chulaki at the Ministry of Culture offered a commission for an orchestral work to be called *Russian Pastorals* to mark the Exhibition of Economic Achievements in Moscow opening in 1953.[78] What became Popov's Fifth reflects upon the "thaw" and "liberalization" in Soviet life, a period witnessed by both Shostakovich's Tenth Symphony and the premiere of the Violin Concerto. There is also a parallel between Popov's Fifth and Myaskovsky's valedictory Twenty-Seventh Symphony (1950), as Romaschuk justifies, "The inspiring mood recreates with surprising warmth the sound of nature's beauty."[79]

Popov heard Shostakovich's Tenth before its Leningrad premiere,[80] and noted the particularly melancholic character at the performances on December 17 and 18, 1953, and four times in rehearsal and studying the score. Curiously, Popov discovered a "borrowing" from one of his own works,

The theme of the opening to the first movement (in the jargon by Vainkop in the program notes), in my opinion (and Arapov's) is that the main theme of the first movement—is borrowed from the main theme of my *Grosse Klaviersuite*, Op. 6, composed in 1927, and fortunately published in 1929 and 1936. The only difference is the absence by Shostakovich of octaves in the second quarter of the second bar. It's possible that Mitya simply forgot about the existence of this theme. He knew it well enough before as he heard it in concerts and at home and even told me that he would disseminate it—that is playing it in public—because he liked it very much.[81]

The Fifth Symphony made slow progress because of his continuing film work. By April 1956, Popov had written 135 pages, as he tells in his diary, "It is in my head and fingers (on the piano) through to the finale. But the score is challenging (because of the many tonal nuances)."[82] The Fifth Symphony was completed on August 18, 1956, and orchestrated almost a year later on June 28. Konstantin Sakva, the deputy chairman at the Ministry of Culture, praised its great beauty, and "the abundant depth and ideas" but thought it would be difficult to perform. This was endorsed by the composer Nikolay Timofeev. "The whole symphony is written with a profound sense of song—everything is melodic—which is very alluring. Boris Chaykovsky mentioned that "there are challenges for the conductor." The work's origins as a symphonic poem were noticed by Arapov, "it's a symphonic poem. There is so much romanticism." However, Bogdanov-Berezovsky thought "it refashioned an association with Scriabin," while the conductor Rozhdestvensky concurred it would be challenging, "its beautiful music but there is a congestion of tutti."[83]

Interestingly, during the World Festival of Youth in 1956, Popov introduced the Fifth to the visiting Scottish composer Erik Chisholm and the Swedish composer Sven-Erik Johansson.[84] Chisholm said that the symphony is romantic, emotional, sounds well, but would be magnificent because it is wonderfully orchestrated. The Scot offered to Popov, "I will write about the symphony in the western press and send the article to you. And you will send me a bottle of vodka."[85] After taking in Shakespeare's *King Lear* at the Russian Drama Theater in Minsk, Popov began working on a new opera, writing to Apetyan, "Shakespeare is brilliant. *Lear* is one of his most striking tragedies." The incidental music used in the Minsk production was by Beethoven and poorly performed. "The clear imagery and polished form of the Shakespearean tragedies demand insightful music specially composed for it."[86] Popov suggested the project to Vladimir Fedorov—chief director of the Minsk Opera Theater who prepared a libretto in 1955. The exasperated Fedorov wrote. "How much time do we need to write music and texts? This opera has to be written in one breath!"[87] The news of Popov's *King Lear* reached the directors of the Kirov Opera who asked him to quickly finish the opera for a future production. Agonizingly, Popov confided to his diary that he had writers' block, "But I cannot start it." After eight years, it appears the project completion was beyond him.[88] There are forty-four pages of the manuscript for Popov's *King Lear* which was fated to be another doomed opera project.[89] Both the libretto and music came to nothing and the music was recycled for the Sixth Symphony. Yuri Grigorovich and Margarita Dovlatova at the Kirov Ballet asked him to write a ballet based on his *Divertimento*, but again this was a fiasco owing to Popov's lack of organization and lethargy.[90]

In 1958, marking a decade following the infamous resolution, the CPSU CC reviewed the measures against the leading Soviet composers and abridged them without absolute redemption. The news of this half-baked rehabilitation was nevertheless welcome, as he writes, "Today many congratulated me on this resolution."[91] In his personal life, he married his musicologist friend of many years Zara Apetyan, and with cultural affairs transformed by the "Thaw," the doors opened to foreign travel. Popov joined a delegation of film workers to visit Czechoslovakia in July 1958.[92] On his fifty-fifth birthday in September 1959 he reflected that so much had gone into the cinema, radio, and theater and that he often struggled for existence. "So little has been achieved in such a long life." There came other distractions in a tourist visit to the United Kingdom taking in Edinburgh, Glasgow, Oxford, Stratford-on-Avon, Birmingham, Sheffield, and London between August 14 and 31, 1959, flying there via Copenhagen, and returning by boat via Stockholm and Helsinki. Much pleasure was experienced visiting Shakespeare's birthplace and seeing *King Lear*, writing home, "The poetry of the nature (in Stratford) makes one want to create a symphonic picture—'Trees and swans at Stratford upon Avon.'"[93] Other highlights were visiting the 1959 Edinburgh International Festival, Loch Lomond and the Promenade concerts directed by Sargent and Barbirolli (he particularly enjoyed the latter conductor) at the Royal Albert Hall.[94]

At the beginning of 1958, the Second Symphony was inexplicably dropped from the program of a concert at the Moscow Conservatoire. The composer Yuri Shaporin sent off an angry epistle to *Pravda*.

> The program for the symphony concert at the Conservatoire on 14 January scheduled Popov's Second Symphony. This work by a Soviet composer has not been performed for a long time, and in my opinion, is interesting both for its notion and talent. Hence, the enterprise by the conductor, USSR Peoples Artist Nathan Rakhlin in reviving a half-forgotten symphony deserves praise. Imagine the surprise of the audience, and that of the composer who attended the concert, when the symphony suddenly, and without explanation was replaced by another work. It seems that such a disrespectful attitude towards the work of a Soviet composer should be severely condemned.[95]

Popov's cinema work in Soviet cinema in this period includes *Unfinished Novel* (1955) and *Poem of the Sea* (1958) which share a common melancholia. Significantly, *Unfinished Novel* by Lenfilm reunited Popov with Fridrich Ermler. In writing to Olga Palui, "This is a film about love. There is considerable lyricism in the music. The movie's content and the music is intimate and modern. I have worked with satisfaction on each episode."[96] Based on a Konstantin Isayev melodrama, the narrative tells of a crippled ship engineer (Sergei Bondarchuk) who is helped to recover his career by a doctor (Elina Bystrytskaya) with whom he falls in love.[97] Popov cites Tchaikovsky in recreating a world of broken human feelings in attempting the impossible. The film score influenced the writing of Popov's Fifth Symphony.

The *Poem of the Sea* was a project by Alexander Dovzhenko; however, the director died on the eve of filming leaving his wife to make the movie. The plot follows a soldier who returns home to oversee the building of a hydroelectric dam. Popov's score was the epicenter of the film.[98] There were positive reviews, but the party considered the media analysis "practically anti-Soviet, slandering those involved in man-made projects, and the Soviet people."[99] In the ensuing debate, Nekrasov claimed the film was out of date in its portrayal of "pomposity" and the "grand style" of Soviet cinema.[100] Andrey Konchalovsky, however, called Dovzhenko's scenario "brilliant," claiming that it predated Fellini's *8 ½*.[101] The film was a labor of love for Dovzhenko's widow Yuliya Solntseva who was awarded a prize at the London Film Festival in 1962. A posthumous lifetime award of the Lenin Prize was awarded to Dovzhenko with credits going to the actor Boris Andreyev and Solntseva at the 1959 Moscow Film Festival. An interesting side note was that the Bolshoi Theater tenor Ivan Kozlovsky appeared in the movie. As was the case in all Dovzhenko's work, Ukrainian culture played an intrinsic part with the score citing Ukrainian folksongs.

One other film which courted controversy—Ermler's *Broken Dreams* (1953) was released only nine years later as *The Summoned Supper*. This was a short color movie based on Ermler's satire *The Devil in a Mask*. The topical theme was considered too near the bone, though Ermler's notion was celebrated by the satirist actor Arkady Raikin's 1974 Lenfilm film *People and Mannequins*. Popov's music has never seen the light of day. In 1952, Popov worked on a score based on a scenario by Boris Chirskov for Ermler—*The Conquerors* where he attempted to introduce an epic lyricism; however, owing to numerous changes in the script, the whole project was abandoned in 1953. Popov uses a grotesque scherzo recycling the fugue from his *Grosse Klaviersuite*.

Of lesser impact was *Children of the Partisans* (1953–1954) in which Popov collaborated with the Byelorussian composer Dimitri Lukas. The patriotic movie was directed by Lev Golub and Nikolay Figurovsky from a script by Grigory Lentulov.[102] Popov's score for a children's movie at the Gorky film studio was realized in Vitaly Voitetzky's *With One's Own Hands* (1956).[103] The film depicted a dispute of agricultural methods from Dmitri Zorin's play *Our Days*. The Albanian/Mosfilm war epic directed by Yuri Ozerov *Fortune*, aka *The Storm* (1959) portraying the Albanian resistance struggle was shot in Durres, Albania, and Romania.[104] Popov wrote the music between September 18 and October 21, 1959. The score for Jan Frid's film *Glory of the Baltic* was a one-off film for Lenfilm in which a lighthearted portrayal was but a money-making exercise for Popov.[105] Another avenue for Popov during this period was for radio theater in Gogol's *The Tale of How Ivan Ivanovich Quarreled with Ivan Nikiforovich* (1952), and a Dickens adaptation (1952) of *Nicholas Nickleby*, and another Zorin play—*The Eternal Source* (1957).

Visiting Leningrad in November 1959, Popov showed the Fifth Symphony to Mravinsky who gave his approval.[106] Popov thought that the only question would "be which conductor would be in charge. In Moscow, they are proposing that Svetlanov conducts the Fifth. It is said that he is good and has recently improved greatly as an outstanding musician."[107] Rather than the young Svetlanov, it was Stasevich who conducted the premiere of the Fifth with the USSR State Symphony Orchestra on March 17, 1960. For once, Popov could find something to enthuse about from a symphonic premiere, "The orchestra played magnificently." However, he considered the conductor hadn't grasped the score and failed to give the maximum emotional and sound potential.[108] The Composers Rest Home in Repino near Leningrad was where Popov started writing his next and valedictory Sixth Symphony, along with several choral pieces including *The Bronze Horseman*, in November 1959.[109] At the Prague Spring Festival, two months later, he introduced the Fifth Symphony to Karel Shein, the second conductor of the Czech Philharmonic who gave his agreement and asked for the *Septet*. There is no record of either work being performed in Czechoslovakia. Following a two-month holiday at Sukhumi in Abkhazia, Popov and Zara Apetyan returned home in November 1961 for the recording of the Second Symphony by the All-Union Radio Symphony Orchestra under Gennady Provatorov on November 21 and 22.[110]

In April 1962, a rare performance of Scriabin's *Prometheus* Symphony was given by Ivanov and the USSR State Symphony Orchestra which greatly impressed Popov and Apetyan.[111] This rare performance excited Popov as he recorded in his journal, "Brilliant music! With the chorus, and even (in the finale—five minutes) the play of colors (against a white velvet curtain—on an elliptical spot). It was wonderful! But Scriabin's instructions in the score should be observed."[112] On January 21, 1963, Gurgen Karapetyan directed the Fifth Symphony with the USSR State Symphony Orchestra—according to Popov—the radio broadcast lasted longer (forty-five minutes) than under

Stasevich (thirty-nine minutes). Nevertheless, Popov appreciated both the conducting and performance.[113] In 1963, following a gap of three decades, the *Septet* was revived at the Gnessin Institute Concert Hall in Moscow. The event was remarkable in the revival of his forgotten graduation piece Popov noting that, "Many asked when this modernist work (*Septet*) was written and exclaimed in surprise that thirty-six years had passed since the premiere. Everyone asked why has the *Septet* not been played for over three decades???"[114]

A PERIOD OF REFLECTION

Popov frequently reflected himself returning to his roots—attempting to rediscover the source of his remarkable creative urge. Life in the USSR of the 1950s and 1960s made him feel lonely and out of favor. Popov - for the young composers who were forging new paths - was a name from the past: Gubaidulina, Denisov, Karetnikov, Ledenev, Silvestrov, Slonimsky, Tischenko, and Schnittke. There were now different trends in music; the "folklore wave" adherents to nationalist music; Sviridov, Yeshpai, Shchedrin, Slonimsky, Tormis, Kancheli, and Terteryan belonged to the "new contemporary line." Some continued the tradition of Myaskovsky and Shostakovich; Boris Chaykovsky, Weinberg, Peiko, Bunin, Levitin, Leman, Ustvolskaya, Volkhonsky, and Karen Khachaturyan embraced modernism and startling new tendencies.

The Third Symphony was revived in a subscription concert of the Moscow Philharmonic Orchestra on October 25, 1963. However, performing and interpretative issues continued to concern Popov as he shared in his diary.

> The public received it well, afterward, Shostakovich phoned and congratulated me for the wonderful music and on the success, saying that he liked the symphony. Mosolov and Karen Khachaturyan also approved the symphony, although (they) criticized the performance. . . . I was especially upset by the lifeless, wretched playing in the fourth movement (*Largo*). . . . That is why I have to conduct my symphonies.[115]

The gift of producing a performance nevertheless seemed now to be beyond him, but he had dreams "of conducting my music with the USSR State Symphony Orchestra."[116] Regrettably, the country's leading ensemble was beyond his powers, but in November 1963, Popov fulfilled a craving by conducting his incidental music for *Yegor Bulychev and the Others* at the Moscow Arts Theater. The Composers Union and the Ministry of Culture presented a reception to Popov on his sixtieth birthday, as he admitted, "I can't speak at funerals (tears) and such (sentimental) congratulatory rituals

. . . there come tears."[117] In his honor, the *Septet*, the Quartet Symphony, the *Waltz Canzone* from *The Strict Youth*, *Pages from an Album*, and *In the Album* were all performed. Inexplicably, the concert took place after his actual birthday. Aram Khachaturyan wrote to Popov ironically. "If you have (celebrated) some kind of jubilee just now, then I congratulate you warmly and wish you happiness."[118]

Memories of his cinematic successes surfaced when Popov worked on a biopic about the film directors *The Vasilyev Brothers*, directed by Darya Shpirkan (1964).[119] The film reunited several of the surviving actors, notably Boris Babochkin, the hero of *Chapayev*. The sixteen numbers frame a montage of lyrical episodes epitomizing their work together: *Sergey's Youth, Sergey Departs for the Front-line, The Death of Lenin, Feat on the Ice, Work on Chapayev, Sergey's Funeral*. Popov's eventful film career culminated with the Pushkin fairy tale *The Tales of Tsar Sultan*, directed by Alexander Ptushko (1965–1966).[120] As much a career award as it was for this latest film, Popov's film score was given a special award at the Leningrad Third All-Union Film Festival in 1968. As was his habit, the score was recycled for *Symphonic Pictures* and Five a Capella Choruses. The Five Choruses were published in 1970 by Sovetsky Kompositor.

THE VALEDICTORY SIXTH SYMPHONY

Popov's last contribution to the symphony started life as the *Russian Festive Overtures* (1963) although he had started a new symphony some years before. Like a ball gathering moss, his musical ideas were rich enough to engender conceiving a symphonic poem—*Poem of Joy* (1966). This theme developed when Popov considered a more approachable *Ode of Joy*, or *Russian Capriccio* (1967). The Sixth Symphony bears an unusual subheading, reflecting on its inner nature as a rondo-sonata for symphony orchestra. One can reflect upon his former mentor Asafyev's old familiar question of the 1930s, "looking at expressive qualities and forms—in whatever degree, they answer the needs of our time—obviously there emerge arguments and questions: what should the Soviet symphony be?"[121] Certainly, Popov was a composer who enlightened music with energy reflecting the time in which he was living, and sought an innovative language, as Asafyev stated, "of an intellectually thoughtful dialogue."[122]

As we have seen, it was another question getting Popov's music performed in the concert hall. In Nathan Rakhlin—he had now a committed conductor—and in 1967, Rakhlin was given charge of the Kazan State Symphony Orchestra, and hoped that Popov would try his hand at conducting. "I think the idea of playing the Second Symphony under the 'direction of the composer' a very good proposal, and we will do this. Then I will take care of the Third, and dream of the Fifth, and make our listeners happy with a worthy performance of your new Poem."[123] Unfortunately, none of these projects were fulfilled.

In 1967, Popov and Apetyan traveled to Romania where the Second Symphony was performed by the Bucharest Radio Symphony Orchestra under Emanuel Elenescu, noting in his diary that, "It sounded arid and there was a poor rubato in the Russian chant (particularly in the first and third movements) nevertheless they played the symphony with gusto."[124] During the two-week visit, he was impressed by performances of *Don Carlos*, *Lohengrin*, *Rigoletto*, *Carmen*, *La Boheme*, and *The Sleeping Beauty* at the Bucharest Opera and Ballet Theater. Toward the end of the year, the Quartet Symphony was revived by the Union of Composers Quartet (later to be known as the Shostakovich Quartet).[125] Regrettably, Popov's music was now rarely seen on concert bills in the country; however, a mark of respect was accorded him when Popov got the second-highest number of votes in the Moscow branch (after Shostakovich) in 1968 in the elections to the RSFSR Composers Congress.[126] At the close of the year, Popov heard a recital of Wagner's "Wesendonck" lieder which enraptured him as he noted in his diary, "How many times have I been again convinced of the profoundly modern romanticism of Wagner's genius. Wagner was not only the greatest genius in music, but the father of all new music over 500 years." It seemed that Popov forgot about his past reverence of Mahler's symphonies for he charged him of using "trivial material, and of plagiarising Tchaikovsky and Wagner."[127] In October 1967, the *Septet* was recorded in Moscow under Popov's guidance. The LP came out in 1969 and the composer spent many hours searching the record shops in Leningrad and reporting to his wife in Moscow that, "It became clear after a few hours that they had them in stock, but had sold out."[128]

In 1969, the Sixth Symphony "*Festivo*" was finally completed. As Romaschuk writes, the symphony portrays "festive games, farce, drama, and, even tragedy."[129] Popov here briefly relates, "On 4 November, I finished the score of the Sixth Symphony (*Festivo*) for large orchestra and organ. The symphony is in three unbroken movements without break—approximately twenty-eight minutes. I am very cautious about the fate of the Sixth Symphony because it is both psychologically and technically very complex (for conductor and orchestra). There are fast tempos, stormy-scherzo gusts, and storms."[130] The Ministry of Culture of the RSFSR gave its approval, commending it "very rich, Russian, innovative, sincere, bright, and joyous." Well aware of past concerns over scheduling his latest music Popov was relieved to be told by an official Nina Lebedeva: "Everything is in order. The symphony is approved." Owing to past experiences, Popov was worried if this was only her opinion.

The Sixth was premiered by Alexander Dmitriev and the USSR State Symphony Orchestra on April 17, 1970, in the Large Hall of the Moscow Conservatoire. The final entry in Popov's diary relates to the symphony's premiere. "The conductor (Alexander Dmitriev) is talented, lyrical, technical, and has great taste. He lacks some temperament (but probably needs more rehearsals, because it was played with more reserve than necessary). There were places where the symphony sounded excellent, but there were lapses. The audience took to the symphony very well. At present, there is no expectation of any more performances."[131] An old former friend and opponent of his First Symphony—Valerian Bogdanov-Berezovsky—wrote to him that "your Sixth Symphony created a strong impression on me for its original ideas, the innovative form (compositional structure), freshness, and rich language. I congratulate you with all my heart."[132]

On the same day as the Sixth was accepted for performance, the second edition of Popov's *Septet* was agreed for publication for the first time since 1928 by Universal Edition in Vienna. Popov decided that it would be called the Chamber Symphony.[133] Popov looked out the unfinished Violin Concerto. "One has to concentrate on completing the great Concerto (in a spring-symphonic four-part cycle)."[134] It was only his death at the early age of sixty-seven years that halted its completion and that of a Seventh Symphony. Gavriil Nikolayevich Popov died at the Union of Composer's rest home at Repino near Leningrad on February 17, 1972. The First Symphony remains his magnum opus—perhaps the most neglected Russian symphony of the twentieth century. What might have developed for Popov if this symphony was accepted into the concert repertoire—we will never know. Perplexingly, Shostakovich wrote: "To dear Gavriil Popov with the hope that his enormous talent will be discovered." Hakobian wrote that Popov "potentially could (have) become one of a half-dozen greatest composers of this country."[135] Reflecting on what we have learned about the life and sufferings of Popov, and the unfinished three concertos, the operas, and the massive first act of what he called his magnum opus—the opera *Alexander Nevsky*—more needs to be researched, and most importantly his symphonies need to be revived in the concert hall.

NOTES

1. Popov, G. N., manuscript, RGALI, Archive.
2. Diary, Apetyan, Z.A. (ed.), *G. N. Popov 1904–1972—Iz literaturnovo naslediye. Stranitsi biografii*, Moscow: Sovetsky Kompositor, 1986.
3. Diary, July 18, 1945. Apetyan, Z.A. (ed.), *G. N. Popov 1904–1972—Iz literaturnovo naslediye. Stranitsi biografii*, Moscow: Sovetsky Kompositor, 1986, 288.

4. Diary, September 21, 1945, Apetyan, Z.A. (ed.), *G. N. Popov 1904–1972—Iz literaturnovo naslediye. Stranitsi biografii*, Moscow: Sovetsky Kompositor, 1986, 288–289.

5. Letter Rakhlin to Popov, October 25, 1946, Apetyan, Z.A. (ed.), *G. N. Popov 1904–1972—Iz literaturnovo naslediye. Stranitsi biografii*, Moscow: Sovetsky Kompositor, 1986, 143.

6. Romaschuk, Inna, *Gavriil Nikolayevich Popov. Tvorchestvo. Vremya. Sudba*, Moscow, 2000, 89.

7. Romaschuk, Inna, *Gavriil Nikolayevich Popov. Tvorchestvo. Vremya. Sudba*, Moscow, 2000, 89.

8. Popov, Gavriil, "Po povodu Leningradskikh konzertov," Manuscript Archive Popov.

9. Raiskin, Iosif, CD booklet, NF/NMA 9972.12-13.

10. Diary, February 7, 1947. Apetyan, Z.A. (ed.) *G. N. Popov 1904–1972—Iz literaturnovo naslediye. Stranitsi biografii*, Moscow: Sovetsky Kompositor, 1986, 294.

11. Raiskin, Iosif, CD booklet, NF/NMA 9972.13.

12. Diary, March 11, 1947, Apetyan, Z.A. (ed.), *G. N. Popov 1904–1972—Iz literaturnovo naslediye. Stranitsi biografii*, Moscow: Sovetsky Kompositor, 1986, 294–295.

13. Letter to Kazantseva, July 19, 1949. Apetyan, Z.A. (ed.), *G. N. Popov 1904–1972—Iz literaturnovo naslediye. Stranitsi biografii*, Moscow: Sovetsky Kompositor, 1986, 150.

14. Raiskin, Iosif, CD booklet, NF/NMA 9972.13.

15. Letopis, diary of Myaskovsky, February 3, 1947, f. 2040.

16. Notes, Apetyan, Z.A. (ed.), *G. N. Popov 1904–1972—Iz literaturnovo naslediye. Stranitsi biografii*, Moscow: Sovetsky Kompositor, 1986, 408.

17. RGALI, f.2077, op. 1, d.139, l.14 (Protocol 6, April 5, 1946), pt.1.

18. RGALI, f.2077, op. 1, d.139, l.60-60ob. (Protocol 19, October 8, 1946) pts.1–3.

19. Diary iz. Lit, June 6, 1946. Apetyan, Z.A. (ed.), *G. N. Popov 1904–1972—Iz literaturnovo naslediye. Stranitsi biografii*, Moscow: Sovetsky Kompositor, 1986, 291.

20. Diary, June 6, 1946. Apetyan, Z.A. (ed.), *G. N. Popov 1904–1972—Iz literaturnovo naslediye. Stranitsi biografii*, Moscow: Sovetsky Kompositor, 1986, 291.

21. Diary, November 16, 1946. Apetyan, Z.A. (ed.), *G. N. Popov 1904–1972—Iz literaturnovo naslediye. Stranitsi biografii*, Moscow: Sovetsky Kompositor, 1986, 293.

22. Notes, Apetyan, Z.A. (ed.), *G. N. Popov 1904–1972—Iz literaturnovo naslediye. Stranitsi biografii*, Moscow: Sovetsky Kompositor, 1986, 409.

23. Diary, June 24, 1947, Apetyan, Z.A. (ed.), *G. N. Popov 1904–1972—Iz literaturnovo naslediye. Stranitsi biografii*, Moscow: Sovetsky Kompositor, 1986.

24. Diary, November 6, 1947, Apetyan, Z.A. (ed.), *G. N. Popov 1904–1972—Iz literaturnovo naslediye. Stranitsi biografii*, Moscow: Sovetsky Kompositor, 1986.

25. Diary, February 5, 1948. Apetyan, Z.A. (ed.), *G. N. Popov 1904–1972—Iz literaturnovo naslediye. Stranitsi biografii*, Moscow: Sovetsky Kompositor, 1986, 296.

26. RGASPI, f.17, op. 3, d.1069, ll.42-49 (February 10, 1948).
27. Vlasova, E.S., *1948 god v sovetskoy muziki*, Moscow: 21 Classika, 2010, 272.
28. Popov, Gavriil, "Rech na obschegorodskom sobranii kompositorov g. Moskvy po povodu postanovleniya TsK VKP(b) ot 10 fevralya 1948 ob opera V. Muradeli 'Velikaya druzhba'. February 20, 1948. G.Ts.M.M. K im. M. I. Glinki, f. 480, op. 1, ed. kh. L. 4.
29. Popov, Gavriil, "Rech na obschegorodskom sobranii kompositorov g. Moskvy po povodu postanovleniya TsK VKP(b) ot 10 fevralya 1948 ob opera V. Muradeli 'Velikaya druzhba'. February 20, 1948. G.Ts.M.M. K im. M. I. Glinki, f. 480, op. 1, ed. kh. L. 11.
30. RGALI, f. 2077, op. 1, ed. kh. 241, l. 95, 97.
31. Tassie, Gregor, *Nikolay Myaskovsky: The Conscience of Russian Music*, Lanham: Rowman & Littlefield, 2014, 280.
32. TsAOPIM, f. 44, d. 177, l. 6.
33. Tomoff, Kirill, *Creative Union: The Professional Organization of Soviet Composers, 1939–1953*, Ithaca, NY: Cornell University Press, 2006, 148.
34. Tassie, Gregor, *Nikolay Myaskovsky: The Conscience of Russian Music*, Lanham: Rowman & Littlefield, 2014, 282.
35. Romaschuk, Inna, *Gavriil Nikolayevich Popov. Tvorchestvo. Vremya. Sudba*, Moscow, 2000, 176.
36. Ilya Lvovovich Selvinsky (1899–1968) began writing poetry in 1915, he took part in the civil war for the Red Army, and later became a constructivist writer, and in the 1930s, avant-garde poet, he was criticized for his anti-artistic, harmful poetry in 1937, and later in 1943. However, he was forgiven and continued a successful career—author.
37. RGALI, f. 962, op. 3, ed. kh. 1956 l. 27, 28.
38. Alexey Ivanovich Mashistov (1904–1987) a poet and most noted for his songs set by contemporary socialist realist composers. Alexander Andreyevich Prokofyev (1900–1971) was a poet who was attracted to nature and to socialist realism, he was active in journalism and founded the Leningrad literary journal *Neva*—author.
39. Mstislav Alexandrovich Levashov (1912–1973) was a poet and writer, also active in journalism.
40. Nestyev, Israel, "V plenu u burzhuasnovo modernism/ o tvorchestva g. Popova," *Sovetskaya Muzyka*, 10, 1948.
41. Romaschuk, Inna, *Gavriil Nikolayevich Popov. Tvorchestvo. Vremya. Sudba*, Moscow, 2000, 60.
42. Golodny, Mikhail, "Sovetskoy Armii-slava!" *Znamya*, No. 2, 1948.
43. Diary, May 19, 1948, Apetyan, Z.A. (ed.), *G. N. Popov 1904–1972—Iz literaturnovo naslediye. Stranitsi biografii*, Moscow: Sovetsky Kompositor, 1986, 296.
44. Diary, July 27, 1948, Apetyan, Z.A. (ed.), *G. N. Popov 1904–1972—Iz literaturnovo naslediye. Stranitsi biografii*, Moscow: Sovetsky Kompositor, 1986, 296–297.
45. Diary, July 27, 1948, Apetyan, Z.A. (ed.), *G. N. Popov 1904–1972—Iz literaturnovo naslediye. Stranitsi biografii*, Moscow: Sovetsky Kompositor, 1986, 297–298.

46. Diary, October 21, 1948, Apetyan, Z.A. (ed.), *G. N. Popov 1904–1972— Iz literaturnovo naslediye. Stranitsi biografii*, Moscow: Sovetsky Kompositor, 1986, 298.

47. Diary, February 20, 1949, Apetyan, Z.A. (ed.), *G. N. Popov 1904–1972—Iz literaturnovo naslediye. Stranitsi biografii*, Moscow: Sovetsky Kompositor, 1986, 298–299.

48. Diary, November 16, 1949, Apetyan, Z.A. (ed.), *G. N. Popov 1904–1972— Iz literaturnovo naslediye. Stranitsi biografii*, Moscow: Sovetsky Kompositor, 1986, 299.

49. Romaschuk, Inna, *Gavriil Nikolayevich Popov. Tvorchestvo. Vremya. Sudba*, Moscow, 2000, 61.

50. Diary, Apetyan, Z.A. (ed.), *G. N. Popov 1904–1972—Iz literaturnovo naslediye. Stranitsi biografii*, Moscow: Sovetsky Kompositor, 1986, 299.

51. Tassie, Gregor, *Nikolay Myaskovsky: The Conscience of Russian Music*, Lanham: Rowman & Littlefield, 2014, 304.

52. Schwartz, Boris, *Music and Musical Life in Soviet Russia 1917–1982*, 1983, Indiana UP, 229.

53. Diary, December 8, 1949, Apetyan, Z.A. (ed.), *G. N. Popov 1904–1972— Iz literaturnovo naslediye. Stranitsi biografii*, Moscow: Sovetsky Kompositor, 1986, 300.

54. Apetyan, Z.A. (ed.), *G. N. Popov 1904–1972—Iz literaturnovo naslediye. Stranitsi biografii*, Moscow: Sovetsky Kompositor, 1986, 82.

55. Diary, December 22, 1949, Apetyan, Z.A. (ed.), *G. N. Popov 1904–1972— Iz literaturnovo naslediye. Stranitsi biografii*, Moscow: Sovetsky Kompositor, 1986, 300.

56. Anisimov vice-chairman of Committee for Arts, Diary, January 5, 1950, Apetyan, Z.A. (ed.), *G. N. Popov 1904–1972—Iz literaturnovo naslediye. Stranitsi biografii*, Moscow: Sovetsky Kompositor, 1986, 300.

57. Koval, Marian, "Slava Otchizne," *Literaturnaya Gazeta*, December 14, 1949.

58. Khrennikov, Tikhon, "Zavoevat vsenarodnoye priznaniye," *Sovetskom iskusstsve*, December 10, 1949.

59. Diary, Apetyan, Z.A. (ed.), *G. N. Popov 1904–1972—Iz literaturnovo naslediye. Stranitsi biografii*, Moscow: Sovetsky Kompositor, 1986, 229.

60. Romaschuk, Inna, *Gavriil Nikolayevich Popov. Tvorchestvo. Vremya. Sudba*, Moscow, 2000, 90.

61. Fyodor Andreyevich Konashkov (1860–1941) was a storyteller who collected folk legends and tales in his expeditions around Russia—author.

62. Diary, January 3, 1951, Apetyan, Z.A. (ed.), *G. N. Popov 1904–1972—Iz literaturnovo naslediye. Stranitsi biografii*, Moscow: Sovetsky Kompositor, 1986, 302.

63. Diary, April 27, 1951, Apetyan, Z.A. (ed.), *G. N. Popov 1904–1972—Iz literaturnovo naslediye. Stranitsi biografii*, Moscow: Sovetsky Kompositor, 1986, 303.

64. Kukharsky, V., TSGALI, f. 2077, op. 1, ed. khr. 431, l. 160–161.

65. Romaschuk, Inna, *Gavriil Nikolayevich Popov. Tvorchestvo. Vremya. Sudba*, Moscow, 2000, 61.

66. Diary, June 19, 1951, Apetyan, Z.A. (ed.), *G. N. Popov 1904–1972—Iz literaturnovo naslediye. Stranitsi biografii*, Moscow: Sovetsky Kompositor, 1986, 306.

67. Popov letter to O. Palui, August 27, 1951, Apetyan, Z.A. (ed.), *G. N. Popov 1904–1972—Iz literaturnovo naslediye. Stranitsi biografii*, Moscow: Sovetsky Kompositor, 1986, 160.

68. "Interview with Popov," Typewritten text, Archive Popov, RGALI.

69. Romaschuk, *Gavriil Nikolayevich Popov. Tvorchestvo. Vremya. Sudba*, Moscow, 2000, 65.

70. Popov letter to Khachaturyan, June 4, 1967, Apetyan, Z.A. (ed.), *G. N. Popov 1904–1972—Iz literaturnovo naslediye. Stranitsi biografii*, Moscow: Sovetsky Kompositor, 1986, 182.

71. Diary, November 14, 1951, Apetyan, Z.A. (ed.), *G. N. Popov 1904–1972—Iz literaturnovo naslediye. Stranitsi biografii*, Moscow: Sovetsky Kompositor, 1986, 308.

72. Diary, March 2, 1952, Apetyan, Z.A. (ed.), *G. N. Popov 1904–1972—Iz literaturnovo naslediye. Stranitsi biografii*, Moscow: Sovetsky Kompositor, 1986, 312.

73. Diary, June 4, 1952, Apetyan, Z.A. (ed.), *G. N. Popov 1904–1972—Iz literaturnovo naslediye. Stranitsi biografii*, Moscow: Sovetsky Kompositor, 1986.

74. Diary, October 1, 1953, Apetyan, Z.A. (ed.), *G. N. Popov 1904–1972—Iz literaturnovo naslediye. Stranitsi biografii*, Moscow: Sovetsky Kompositor, 1986, 318.

75. Diary, November 8, 1951, Apetyan, Z.A. (ed.), *G. N. Popov 1904–1972—Iz literaturnovo naslediye. Stranitsi biografii*, Moscow: Sovetsky Kompositor, 1986.

76. Rakhlin letter to Popov, December 2, 1967, Apetyan, Z.A. (ed.), *G. N. Popov 1904–1972—Iz literaturnovo naslediye. Stranitsi biografii*, Moscow: Sovetsky Kompositor, 1986, 184.

77. Letter to O. Palui, May 23, 1953, *Gavriil Nikolayevich Popov. Tvorchestvo. Vremya. Sudba*, Moscow, 2000, 163.

78. Apetyan, Z.A. (ed.), *G. N. Popov 1904–1972—Iz literaturnovo naslediye. Stranitsi biografii*, Moscow: Sovetsky Kompositor, 1986, 385.

79. Romaschuk, Inna, *Gavriil Nikolayevich Popov. Tvorchestvo. Vremya. Sudba*, Moscow, 2000, 68.

80. Shostakovich's Tenth Symphony was premiered on December 17, 1953, by the Leningrad Philharmonic under the baton of Mravinsky.

81. Diary, December 25, 1953, Apetyan, Z.A. (ed.), *G. N. Popov 1904–1972—Iz literaturnovo naslediye. Stranitsi biografii*, Moscow: Sovetsky Kompositor, 1986, 322.

82. Diary, April 24, 1956, Apetyan, Z.A. (ed.), *G. N. Popov 1904–1972—Iz literaturnovo naslediye. Stranitsi biografii*, Moscow: Sovetsky Kompositor, 1986, 326.

83. Diary, June 27, 1957, Apetyan, Z.A. (ed.), *G. N. Popov 1904–1972—Iz literaturnovo naslediye. Stranitsi biografii*, Moscow: Sovetsky Kompositor, 1986, 326.

84. Erik Chisholm was then a lecturer in Cape Town South Africa and went to Moscow for the 1956 World Youth Festival—author.

85. Diary, August 3, 1957, Apetyan, Z.A. (ed.), *G. N. Popov 1904–1972—Iz literaturnovo naslediye. Stranitsi biografii*, Moscow: Sovetsky Kompositor, 1986. 327.

86. Letter to Apetyan, February 14, 1953, Apetyan, Z.A. (ed.), *G. N. Popov 1904–1972—Iz literaturnovo naslediye. Stranitsi biografii*, Moscow: Sovetsky Kompositor, 1986, 162.

87. Letter Fedorov to Popov, March 18, 1955, Apetyan, Z.A. (ed.), *G. N. Popov 1904–1972—Iz literaturnovo naslediye. Stranitsi biografii*, Moscow: Sovetsky Kompositor, 1986, 167.

88. Letter to O. Palui, May 28, 1961, *Gavriil Nikolayevich Popov. Tvorchestvo. Vremya. Sudba*, Moscow, 2000, 173–174.

89. Apetyan, Z.A. (ed.), *G. N. Popov 1904–1972—Iz literaturnovo naslediye. Stranitsi biografii*, Moscow: Sovetsky Kompositor, 1986, 386.

90. Letter to Apetyan, June 14, 1961, Apetyan, Z.A. (ed.), *G. N. Popov 1904–1972—Iz literaturnovo naslediye. Stranitsi biografii*, Moscow: Sovetsky Kompositor, 1986, 174–175.

91. Diary, June 8, 1958, Apetyan, Z.A. (ed.), *G. N. Popov 1904–1972—Iz literaturnovo naslediye. Stranitsi biografii*, Moscow: Sovetsky Kompositor, 1986, *G. Popov, ed. Z. Apetyan, Muzyka, Moscow, 1986*, 328.

92. Diary, August 6, 1958, 3, *G. Popov, ed. Z. Apetyan, Muzyka, Moscow, 1986*, 28.

93. Letter to Apetyan, August 26, 1959, *G. Popov, ed. Z. Apetyan, Muzyka, Moscow, 1986*, 171.

94. Diary, September 12, 1959, Apetyan, Z.A. (ed.), *G. N. Popov 1904–1972—Iz literaturnovo naslediye. Stranitsi biografii*, Moscow: Sovetsky Kompositor, 1986, 329.

95. *Pravda*, January 16, 1958.

96. Popov letter to O. Palui, July 8, 1955, Apetyan, Z.A. (ed.), *G. N. Popov 1904–1972—Iz literaturnovo naslediye. Stranitsi biografii*, Moscow: Sovetsky Kompositor, 1986, 167.

97. Sergey Bondarchuk became a famous film actor and director and is celebrated for his 'Story of a Life' and for 'War and Peace,' whereas Bystrytskaya became a leading actress, singer, and teacher—author.

98. Romaschuk, Inna, *Gavriil Nikolayevich Popov. Tvorchestvo. Vremya. Sudba*, Moscow, 2000, 69.

99. Sulgin, Mikhail, "O Varshavskom," *Iskusstsvo Kino*, 2000, No. 7.

100. Nekrasov, Viktor, 'Слова «великие» и простые,' *Искусство кино*, 1959, No. 5.

101. Konchalovsky, "A Great Deception," *Sovershenno sekretno*, 2000.

102. Lev Vladimirovich Golub (1904–1994) was a Byelorussian film director who specialized in films for children about the revolution or the war. Nikolay Nikolayevich Figurovsky (1923–2003) was a writer, actor, and director. He appeared as an actor in the famous war film '*The Young Guard*' (1948).

103. Vitaly Pantelelimovich Voiteztky (1909–1977) directed only three films and he also worked as an assistant on other films—author.

104. Yuri Nikolayevich Ozerov (1921–2001) was a distinguished director who fought in the Second World War and specialized in war movies, notably making a

trilogy of epic films about the war. His brother Nikolay was a famous sportsman and commentator—author.

105. Jan Borisovich Frid (1908–2003) made a long series of romantic and comedy films for the Lenfilm studios.

106. Unfortunately, the Fifth was not performed by the Leningrad Philharmonic Orchestra—author.

107. Diary, November 21, 1959, Apetyan, Z.A. (ed.), *G. N. Popov 1904–1972—Iz literaturnovo naslediye. Stranitsi biografii*, Moscow: Sovetsky Kompositor, 1986, 329.

108. Diary, March 25, 1960, Apetyan, Z.A. (ed.), *G. N. Popov 1904–1972—Iz literaturnovo naslediye. Stranitsi biografii*, Moscow: Sovetsky Kompositor, 1986, 330.

109. Diary, November 21, 1959, Apetyan, Z.A. (ed.), *G. N. Popov 1904–1972—Iz literaturnovo naslediye. Stranitsi biografii*, Moscow: Sovetsky Kompositor, 1986, 329–330.

110. Diary, November 25, 1961, Apetyan, Z.A. (ed.), *G. N. Popov 1904–1972—Iz literaturnovo naslediye. Stranitsi biografii*, Moscow: Sovetsky Kompositor, 1986, 333.

111. Ivanov used a specially built color projector for the first time in a performance—author.

112. Diary, April 20, 1962, Apetyan, Z.A. (ed.), *G. N. Popov 1904–1972—Iz literaturnovo naslediye. Stranitsi biografii*, Moscow: Sovetsky Kompositor, 1986, 333.

113. Diary, March 16, 1963. Apetyan, Z.A. (ed.), *G. N. Popov 1904–1972—Iz literaturnovo naslediye. Stranitsi biografii*, Moscow: Sovetsky Kompositor, 1986, 333.

114. Diary, November 14, 1963, Apetyan, Z.A. (ed.), *G. N. Popov 1904–1972—Iz literaturnovo naslediye. Stranitsi biografii*, Moscow: Sovetsky Kompositor, 1986, 333–334.

115. Diary, October 30, 1964, Apetyan, Z.A. (ed.), *G. N. Popov 1904–1972—Iz literaturnovo naslediye. Stranitsi biografii*, Moscow: Sovetsky Kompositor, 1986, 335.

116. Diary, December 6, 1963, Apetyan, Z.A. (ed.), *G. N. Popov 1904–1972—Iz literaturnovo naslediye. Stranitsi biografii*, Moscow: Sovetsky Kompositor, 1986, 334.

117. Diary, September 17, 1964, Apetyan, Z.A. (ed.), *G. N. Popov 1904–1972—Iz literaturnovo naslediye. Stranitsi biografii*, Moscow: Sovetsky Kompositor, 1986, 335.

118. Khachaturyan. Aram, Apetyan, Z.A. (ed.), *G. N. Popov 1904–1972—Iz literaturnovo naslediye. Stranitsi biografii*, Moscow: Sovetsky Kompositor, 1986.

119. Darya Vyacheslavna Shpirkan (1904–1970) worked as scenarist and director on "Two Friends" (1941) and "The Brothers Karamazov" (1968).

120. Alexander Lukic Ptushko (1900–1973) worked on mostly children's films some of which were awarded prizes at major international film festivals including Cannes, Edinburgh, and Venice.

121. Asafyev, Boris, "Istorichesky god," *Sovetskaya Muzika*, No. 3, 1933, 113.

122. Asafyev, Boris, "Istorichesky god," *Sovetskaya Muzika*, No. 3, 1933, 14.

123. Letter Rakhlin to Popov, September 28, 1967, Apetyan, Z.A. (ed.), *G. N. Popov 1904–1972—Iz literaturnovo naslediye. Stranitsi biografii*, Moscow: Sovetsky Kompositor, 1986, 183.

124. Diary, March 12, 1967, Apetyan, Z.A. (ed.), *G. N. Popov 1904–1972—Iz literaturnovo naslediye. Stranitsi biografii*, Moscow: Sovetsky Kompositor, 1986, 336.

125. Diary, October 5, 1967, Apetyan, Z.A. (ed.), *G. N. Popov 1904–1972—Iz literaturnovo naslediye. Stranitsi biografii*, Moscow: Sovetsky Kompositor, 1986, 337.

126. Diary, May 20, 1968, Apetyan, Z.A. (ed.), *G. N. Popov 1904–1972—Iz literaturnovo naslediye. Stranitsi biografii*, Moscow: Sovetsky Kompositor, 1986, 337.

127. Diary, December 16, 1968, Apetyan, Z.A. (ed.), *G. N. Popov 1904–1972—Iz literaturnovo naslediye. Stranitsi biografii*, Moscow: Sovetsky Kompositor, 1986, 338.

128. Letter to Apetyan, August 3, 1969. Apetyan, Z.A. (ed.), *G. N. Popov 1904–1972—Iz literaturnovo naslediye. Stranitsi biografii*, Moscow: Sovetsky Kompositor, 1986, 186.

129. Romaschuk, Inna, *Gavriil Nikolayevich Popov. Tvorchestvo. Vremya. Sudba*, Moscow, 2000, 75.

130. Diary, November 6, 1969, Apetyan, Z.A. (ed.), *G. N. Popov 1904–1972—Iz literaturnovo naslediye. Stranitsi biografii*, Moscow: Sovetsky Kompositor, 1986, 338.

131. Diary, April 22, 1970. Apetyan, Z.A. (ed.), *G. N. Popov 1904–1972—Iz literaturnovo naslediye. Stranitsi biografii*, Moscow: Sovetsky Kompositor, 1986, 339.

132. Letter Bogdanov-Berezovsky to Popov, July 18, 1970, Apetyan, Z.A. (ed.), *G. N. Popov 1904–1972—Iz literaturnovo naslediye. Stranitsi biografii*, Moscow: Sovetsky Kompositor, 1986, 188.

133. Diary, December 30, 1969. Apetyan, Z.A. (ed.), *G. N. Popov 1904–1972—Iz literaturnovo naslediye. Stranitsi biografii*, Moscow: Sovetsky Kompositor, 1986, 338–339.

134. Letter to Nazarevsky, September 8, 1971, Apetyan, Z.A. (ed.), *G. N. Popov 1904–1972—Iz literaturnovo naslediye. Stranitsi biografii*, Moscow: Sovetsky Kompositor, 1986, 189.

135. Hakobian, Leon, *Music of the Soviet Age*, Stockholm: Melos, 1998, 133.

Chapter 7

Man and Machines!

Few twentieth-century composers represented the new industrial age more than the Russian modernist musician—Alexander Mosolov. He was born in Kyiv on July 29, 1900 (August 11 New Style) to Vasily Alexandrovich Mosolov and Nina Alexandrovna (nee Romanova). Alexander's father was a lawyer; however, the musical genes came from his mother (1882–1953), who studied piano at the Kyiv Music Institute and possessed a fine lyric-coloratura voice.

When Alexander was three years old, the family moved to Moscow, where his mother joined the Bolshoi Theater Chorus and appeared as a soloist in Meyerbeer's *Les Huguenots*—under the pseudonym of Antonina Miller. In later years, she appeared at regional theater companies as Natalya A. Koltsova. Vasily Mosolov died suddenly in 1905, and without a breadwinner—Nina Mosolova's salary at the Bolshoi Theater was inadequate—the way out of the family's difficulties came through remarrying a close friend of the family. This new union was to lead to significant consequences.

Nina's new husband was the Ukrainian composer, conductor, and music critic Boris Vladimirovich Podgoretsky (1873–1919). He composed several romances for Nina which she performed at her song recitals.[1] Through Podgoretsky's concert career and his network of associates, the family traveled extensively in Europe before the Great War. However, according to Leonid Rimsky, the relationship with Podgoretsky did not last for she divorced and married the artist Mikhail Varfolomeyevich Leblanc (1875–1940). At this time, Leblanc was teaching at the Moscow Institute of Painting—according to one of his students Yevgeny Spassky, Leblanc was an outstanding character of openness, a truly noble man bearing a cheerful and pleasant outlook.[2] Leblanc embraced an interest in cubism, futurism, supremacism, realism, and naturalism.

Demanding professionalism—opposing academicism in art—Leblanc remained true to impressionism, and his works reflect both tranquility and innovation. Leblanc studied with Vasnetsov, Leonid Pasternak, Serov, Korovin, and Repin. In Paris, between 1910 and 1912, he studied at the Académie de la Grande Chaumière, and with Matisse. In the 1910s, Leblanc participated in the World of Art, the Jack of Diamonds, and the Fire-Color exhibitions in Russia. In the first years of Soviet power, Leblanc worked at the Commissariat of Enlightenment and helping form the Union of Artists.[3] Leblanc's paintings were exhibited in St. Louis (1903), Berlin (1922), Venice (1924), and New York (1929). Alexander Mosolov imbued Leblanc's directness, openness, and uncompromising attitude to art, which was seen subsequently as open bravado by his friends and contemporaries.[4]

From his early childhood, Alexander grew up in an artistic environment and became well versed in different cultural trends; through his aunt Emilia Ivanovna Bisneck, he learned German. Alexander spent three years in Europe with his parents, at first, in 1908 and 1909, and later between 1911 and 1914, all of which considerably widened his education and outlook—Alexander also became fluent in French and English, and studied music in London, Paris, and Berlin.[5] Nina's third husband, Michel Leblanc, had a considerable sway on Alexander, particularly in his mien. In Moscow, the family lived at No. 3 Bolshaya Bronnaya Street in central Moscow.

Against the pleasing domestic life, there were contrasting aspects in Alexander's character, as Barsova relates. "The morality of his actions showed an intolerance bordering on the impermissible, but this was born from impatience and a desire for independence. At sixteen, he ran away to the front but was sent home, and at the Flerovsky No. 10 Boys' Gymnasium of the Teacher's Society, he was expelled several times for dangerous behavior."[6] This institution was one of the finest educational establishments, where the fees were twice that of its competitors. Alexander's fellow pupils included Chaliapin's son Boris, the future philosopher Igor Ilyinsky, and Chekhov's nephew Lev Knipper—an upcoming modernist composer. Alexander completed his studies at the Gymnasium in 1916. Before the revolution, Nina transformed their home into a place for artists' meetings and chamber recitals; these musical soirees were often given by the distinguished singer Maria A. Olenin-D'Alheim and her husband Pierre, founders of the House of Song in the capital. Among the visitors was the composer and teacher—Reinhold Glière (1875–1956). Alexander studied piano with the young avant-garde composer Alexander Shenshin (1890–1944), a descendent of the Russian romantic poet Afanasy Fet.[7]

REVOLUTION AND CIVIL WAR

Following October 1917, the uprising was greeted enthusiastically by Alexander Mosolov as he recalled later, "I was attracted to the ideals of the world revolution, and signed up into the revolutionary people's ranks."[8] Mosolov worked at the Secretariat of the Peoples Control under K. I. Lander—the administration of the new Soviet regime. Mosolov's duties included the delivery of documents to the Bolshevik Commissars—including on three occasions—to the head of the government—Vladimir Lenin. Alexander Mosolov's enthusiasm for Soviet power would come to be tested, for, in the unfolding Civil War, Tsarist generals mounted a revolt, and on May 10, 1918, he enlisted in the First Moscow Red Guard Cavalry.[9]

The first action that Mosolov took part in was in the fighting against General Denikin's White Guards to the West of the capital. Following the successful campaign ending with the defeat of rebels at the gates of Moscow, Mosolov took part in further battles in Poland and Ukraine, his Cavalry Regiment was led by Georgy Kotovsky—one of the most celebrated military leaders in the Red Army.[10] The young man who had assimilated a cultured European lifestyle was profoundly disturbed by the brutality of the conflict and was injured during heavy battles in 1920, as he reflected later, "The war taught me a great deal: we killed people in the artillery, and we were killed, I saw a lot of filth, pain, deaths."[11] Suffering from post-traumatic stress disorder, Mosolov was treated at the First Psychiatric Hospital in Moscow from which he was discharged on August 20, 1920, and assigned to the reserve.[12] For valor shown in the defense of Moscow, and his two years of battle service, Mosolov was awarded two Orders of the Red Banner.

Moscow Conservatoire—Glière and Myaskovsky

The recuperation from the agonies of the Civil War, the influence of his parents, and the attraction of music allowed Mosolov a fresh start in life with music his passion. Prior to entering the Conservatoire, he studied privately with Glière, and in September 1922, Mosolov entered Glière's composition class, sharing his studies in Grigory Prokofyev's piano class. Mosolov's keyboard skills were so promising that in the following year, 1923, he moved to the class of Konstantin Igumnov (1873–1948), who was one of Russia's most distinguished pianists. The state of the arts in the first years of Soviet Russia was in constant turmoil. Inna Barsova offers an intriguing explanation of the plight of the intelligentsia,

> The "twenties" were judged not only in the terms of the period but for it's profoundly rich content. In the "twenties," people shared ideas with each other, and

needed each other, and often shared a common fate. For those artists who had put their futures with the revolution—particularly young people—the ideology of the revolution was socially irredeemable with the ideology of the reconstruction of life, which meant the arts had to find a new position for itself. Everyone understood that this was impossible without the renewal of art. However, the generally accepted position was that the art of the revolutionary epoch must be revolutionary—not only in content—but in form. This conviction was shared by most of the creative intelligentsia from recognized innovators such as Mayakovsky, and Meyerhold, to the young members of the "Blue blues" or the students of Vkhutemas.[13]

Barsova observes that during this period, artists in Western Europe like Brecht, Éluard, and Aragon were attracted to revolutionary ideas. Ahead of the 1926 performance of Myaskovsky's Sixth Symphony in Prague, the musicologist Zdeněk Nejedlý wrote that "the parallel between revolutionary music in political thoughts and revolutionary music in the practical notion has its own characteristic in themes of revolutionary events."[14]

It is clear that Mosolov's character—particularly in his youth—possessed a burning desire to achieve great things in life. Barsova writes that Mosolov was a child of his times—born in the year of a new century, it was difficult to foresee what his fate or future was to be, but his character was already formed from an early age. Mosolov's youthful maturity corresponded with the young Prokofiev or Shostakovich. Barsova writes that there are strong indications to his precipitous advance, "One is surprised by the acceleration of his musical development. It appears that he began composing only in 1921. But, after three years, Mosolov was the author of many works and—in another year—was a recognized representative of the Moscow music school."[15] A notable observation by Barsova is his affinity with the era in which he was living. "Every cell of his being, each design of Mosolov was passionate in belonging to 'his own time.' Mozhei Nappelbaum's portrait of 1928 epitomizes the young Mosolov perfectly as a young man of fashion."[16]

Reinhold Glière was first to recognize the potential of Mosolov yet expressed apprehension about his cherished student's welfare, writing to him, "If you have a depressed mood and things seem difficult, write to me. I want you to be successful in your studies. Neither doubt your own efforts, nor your talents, but don't force yourself in studying, and don't rush to grasp compositional technique."[17] This was before Glière's departure to Baku (for his commissioned opera *Shakh-Senem*), for, in February 1924, Mosolov joined the class of Nikolay Myaskovsky. Rather than disrupt his studies, this was a mark of good fortune for Mosolov, because Myaskovsky was the leading composer in Moscow and an advocate of modernism. Mosolov's professors represented two traditions in the Russian composing

Figure 7.1 Mosolov—1928. *Source*: Photography by Mozhei Nappelbaum Courtesy of Universal Edition A.G., Wien.

school: Myaskovsky was a student of Rimsky Korsakov and Lyadov, while Glière had studied with the dean of the Moscow school, Sergey Taneyev—a disciple of Tchaikovsky. Glière preferred to write in the late romantic style; however, Myaskovsky embraced both late romanticism and modernism. The Second and Third Piano Sonatas by Myaskovsky were exciting, unconventional pieces, while the Fourth and Sixth postrevolutionary symphonies were modern esoteric works with original, troubling themes. The Sixth was considered to reflect the plight of the intelligentsia in the face of the revolution and is spoken of as a requiem to his father who had been shot by Red Army soldiers in 1918.

Nikolay Yakovlevich Myaskovsky (1881–1950) was the leading symphonist and disciple of new music in Russia. The American scholar Amy Nelson writes: "He was the mentor of Polovinkin, Mosolov, Shebalin, and other young composers affiliated with the ASM."[18] If Myaskovsky entertained doubts about young Mosolov, he had no misgiving as to his outstanding musical talent, something disclosed to him by his colleague Glière. "Alexander Mosolov is fantastically talented, brilliant, intelligent, but audacious." Foreseeing problems to come, Myaskovsky revealed to Prokofiev in a letter, "Mosolov—though our censorship cannot bear him—is very talented."[19]

Active in music publishing, Myaskovsky was a leading member of the ASM, and closely involved in orchestral life in Moscow. Expanding on this, the musicologist Anna Ferenc writes, "the positions occupied by many of these individuals in conservatoires, state agencies, and all divisions of Narkompros, in particular, allowed them to achieve their objectives and to influence and encourage a younger generation of composers that included Alexander Mosolov, Leonid Polovinkin, Vissarion Shebalin, Vladimir Deshevov, and Dmitry Shostakovich."[20] Under his peers' sway, Mosolov enthusiastically joined the ASM, through which he met with leading European composers visiting Moscow—Hindemith, Bartók, Berg, Honegger, Reger, and Milhaud.

The Piano Sonatas and Legenda

Myaskovsky frequently offered Mosolov suggestions for his projects—and reflecting years later, "didn't try to force matters—his credo was in aspiring for the 'last word' in musical technique because invention doesn't have any personal purpose."[21] Unfortunately, we cannot judge his early work for the earliest pieces by Mosolov in 1921 and 1922 are almost entirely lost. According to Barsova, "His first experiences were thrown on the page in whole notes without indications." Certainly, from the piano sonatas, Mosolov turned to "left" radicalism in music, far away from academicism. According to the musicologist Yuri Kholopov, "The path along which he moved is distinguished by the piano compositions—the Second (a little earlier written) and the First Sonata. The composer decisively departs from the traditions of the later Russian school to a blazing dissonance in the cascades of chords and 'machine-like' aggressive rhythms."[22] It is possible to make comparisons against the leading modernists of the period. Kholopov expands that "the foundations of Mosolov's musical thought is a new tonality (atonality), similar to the type of tonality of Prokofiev (in his *The Gambler* opera), and Shostakovich (in his First Piano Sonata), but is distant from the tonality of Scriabin—Roslavets—and the Yavorsky school. The razor-sharp dissonant texture is repeatedly controlled by brutally straight melodic lines in which, Mosolov, regardless of its affinity with 12 tone chromatics, all the same, Mosolov's 'atonal' language is distinguished from Schoenberg."[23]

Between 1924 and 1928, Mosolov composed thirty different pieces, only one or two of which were suitable to establish him as the leading avant-garde composer of the day. The music poured so profusely from his pen that writers said of "Mosolov gaining the notoriety of being a single-minded avant-gardist."[24] His exceptional modernism was no more obvious than in the Piano Sonata No. 1 (1924). Mosolov gives the indication of a tonality of C; however, this is only a generalized indication. There is just one movement, yet, there are swift changes in tempo and character: *Lento lugubre*, *Allegro feroce*,

Allegretto poco innocente, Subito strepiso, Lento, Mesto, poco ironico, Allegro grave, Lento sostenuto. Kholopov considers that "the sonata is surprizing for its breadth of scope, freshness of thought, musical language and effective sound." There was acclamation from another avant-gardist Nikolay Roslavets who called it "a true encyclopaedia of modernism where one can find gathered all the (. . .) tricks of the most audaciously high-pitched 'sensations' in the spirit of Prokofiev, Stravinsky, (and) the Western masters of polytonality."[25] There were significant Mosolovian influences on his contemporaries; Shostakovich's First Piano Sonata, as Hakobian explains, "shares with Mosolov a disposition to use such devices as percussion effects in the lower registers, in tone-clusters, chords with false eighths, etc., as well as a peculiar version of piano 'impressionism.' The latter is evident especially in the *Lento* episode just before the sonata's fast and loud coda. Here the dense pedal and the texture based on the superposition of three planes separated in space are reminiscent of Mosolov's piano *Nocturnes* (composed in the same year), being at the same time highly atypical of the rest of Shostakovich's piano music."[26]

The Second Piano Sonata in B minor (1923) bears the inscription "From Old Notebooks" and predates the First Sonata and is a nod to his compatriot Prokofiev. There are three movements, *Sonata: Andante non troppo, Espressivo*; *Adagio: Sostenuto severo*; and *Finale: Allegro tumultoso, Infernale*. The mood is reflective, and at times the listener feels as if entering a dream-like world, but there are repeated interruptions with flashing dissonant chords before the idiom switches again to a restful world of other imagery. Several ideas appear to be miniature citations from Prokofiev's piano sonatas, but Mosolov contrasts these themes with his own chords of harsh dissonance and rhythms. The innovation of the early sonatas is similar to the early Prokofiev, abiding by the Liszt-Scriabin mode where the opening tone row is played in equally quiet and fiery moods, followed by tritons and minor seconds giving color to the music. Critics however quickly condemned the Third Sonata for being "formalist satire and jokes."[27] Regrettably, we can't share in the anecdotal side of Mosolov for the Third Sonata is lost.

The Fourth Sonata was dismissed for being "defiant and insolent. (. . .) Only a pact with the devil could incite the composer to such ferocious jumps and the infernal crashes which permeate his Sonata—an extreme manifestation of the anti-melodic style, the principles of which were laid down by Prokofiev. (. . .) Though somewhat monotonous, it is, nevertheless, fairly impressive."[28] Regardless of this reluctant praise, the consequences of the link with Prokofiev (who was then an émigré in France) were damaging. Certainly, as Roslavets above informs us, there are musical associations in Mosolov's music with his celebrated compatriot. In the slow movement of

Mosolov's Piano Sonata No. 1, there is a barely suppressed violence, and a notable feature in the inner voices is a citation of the Latin *Dies Irae* motif.

Another parallel between Prokofiev and Mosolov is that the early sonatas are phenomenally difficult to perform with elaborate rapid leaps and obligatory crossovers throughout. The complete cycle of the five piano sonatas was first performed in an evening of Mosolov's music on September 29, 1925, by the composer (Mosolov was a virtuoso), and he accompanied songs performed by his mother, Nina. The Moscow musicologist Leon Hakobian reflects that

> The version of modernism professed by Mosolov, in contrast to that of Roslavets, is of a rather non-systematic elemental type. Mosolov is fond of tone-clusters, instants of quasi-serial or quasi-"synthetic chord" technique, sharp percussion effects in the extreme low register of the instrument; at the same time, he did not avoid triads and other familiar harmonic structures, paying a special homage, however, to structures containing the interval of diminished eighths (e.g., 3-3-5, 3-4-4, 3-5-3, etc.). Mosolov's early language is marked by abrupt, unexpected changes of mood, and by an extravagant rudeness, reminding (the listener) of "barbarian" ostinatos and the emphatically "square," "chopped" rhythms of early Prokofiev.[29]

The Fifth Sonata, Op. 12 (1925) is traditional only in that it has four movements and is influenced by Liszt and Scriabin, and Myaskovsky. Furthermore Hakobian delineates Mosolovian musical techniques,

> Its first movement follows a sufficiently clear sonata scheme, the second is a slow "Elegy," while the third is a march-like scherzo (*Scherzo marziale*)—in other words, the proportions between the movements look quite traditional. The contrast between these three movements is, however, largely neutralized by numerous shifts of tempo and mood within them, as well as by a certain uniformity of harmonic and thematic structures. The slow Finale, (. . .) imparts to the whole a radically new—one might say philosophical—dimension. As if in tribute to his teacher Myaskovsky as the author of the Sixth Symphony, the piece contains a strange conglomerate of heterogeneous quotations. The descending *lamento* figure in the bass appears as the movement's principal background leitmotif; in due course, it alternates with a "softened" version of the "Dies irae" motif, stated in the high register, just as it appears in the second movement of Myaskovsky's Sixth, then with the tune of a Russian playful ditty transferred to the extreme bass and a traditional Turkmen tune—all these thematic elements being abundantly interspersed with tone clusters and other sharply dissonant vertical combinations.[30]

The former Polivanovsky Gymnasium was the venue for many of Mosolov's musical premieres. The first piano sonatas, the *Legend* for cello and piano, three lyrical pieces for viola and piano, and around twenty vocal miniatures were performed on September 29, 1924, at the State Academy of Arts on Kropotkin Street. The performers included Mosolov, his first wife Elena Fyodorovna Kolobova (1892–1948),[31] his mother Nina Mosolova, the cellist A. N. Yegorov, the violist A. G. Blum, the Bolshoi Theater soloist A. N. Sadomov, and the singer Y. A. Dikushina-Karysheva.[32] The ASM hired the concert hall as its platform for both new Soviet and European music for the next few years. There would come a time when the ASM would lose this fine venue for contemporary music, as we shall discover.

The mid-1920s was a time of enormous restructuring in musical education, mostly by the effort by Proletkult which relied on support from the Bolshevik Government. The RAPM and ORKiMD created the Rabfaks that opened up entry to the conservatoires by students from the poor. The faction which grouped themselves around the self-anointed "Red Professors" in Moscow attempted to "cleanse" the Conservatoire of "alien" elements. Mosolov and the radical musician Alexander Davidenko were expelled from the Conservatoire in May 1924, allegedly for "unsatisfactory fulfillment of productivity."[33] Mosolov wrote: "In the last six years, I have only twice lost my temper: the first time was with (Nadezhda) Bryusova and they nearly expelled me from the Conservatoire for that."[34] Mosolov was accused of skipping lectures and failing to complete tasks from his professors. The scholar Martynov tells us that "with the support of patronage networks, both, within, and beyond the Conservatoire, Mosolov and Davidenko were allowed to continue their studies. For Davidenko—who had been thrown out for missing class—the lobbying by Kastalsky, Myaskovsky, Konius, and Glière proved sufficient to gain reinstatement."[35] The support by Kastalsky was significant as he was with the leftist RAPM, while Glière's affidavit supplemented Mosolov's petition for reinstatement—underscoring his merits (Mosolov's illness and Glière's absence forestalled him from completing his studies in the preceding academic year). There were also Mosolov's loyalty to Soviet power, his voluntary army service, and disability suffered serving in the Red Army, in addition to his combat awards.[36] This appeal was sympathetically received by Boris Krassin—the chairman of Muzsektor, who efficaciously allowed Mosolov to continue his studies.[37]

The avant-garde composer of the late Soviet period—Edison Denisov wrote that Mosolov's "early compositions by their standard and talent, and clarity exceed everything that Prokofiev was writing."[38] Mosolov was attracted to constructivism—the new style which rejected art for art's sake, inspired by the industrial themes reflecting the new societal and political realities in the Soviet republic. People believed that society would form a new type of person. Man would be part of a cogwheel, and the country would be like a huge factory building a new bright future. Art followed in the stream of this rapid industrialization of society and music would play its part. Myaskovsky asked his student, "Are you not afraid, my friend, to turn everything upside down, are you not terrified at killing music?"[39] To which Mosolov responded "One has to do away with fear, to enter a new level. But what is there—do we need to know? Should we be afraid of the abyss?"[40]

In 1925, Mosolov graduated with an impressive folio: a Trio for clarinet, cello, and piano (later entitled *Ballade*); the Fourth and Fifth Piano Sonatas; and the symphonic poem *Twilight*. For his final examination, he composed *The Sphinx*—a cantata for large orchestra, choir, and tenor based on Oscar Wilde. A recital on June 6, 1925, at the Chamber Hall of the Conservatoire, presented his settings to Pushkin's *Three Keys* Op. 9 (1924) and *Two Poems* Op. 20 (1925), a vocalize performed by Viviana Telezhinskaya to accompaniment by Mosolov. Unfortunately, these pieces are lost. The concert featured fellow students Gaigerova, Davidenko, Fere, Shekhter, Bely, and Sokolov—all composition students of Myaskovsky, Catoire, and Glière.[41]

Political and religious content prevailed in several large-scale Mosolov pieces, the *Anti-Religious Symphony* for narrators, choir and orchestra, and the operetta *The Christening of Russia*, which are both lost.[42] In his more intimate piano pieces, Mosolov was influenced by Myaskovsky's Third Sonata, the Sixth of Feinberg, and Scriabin's late sonatas. Barsova writes: "The psychological and philosophical exalted outbursts mixed with ... irony, all share a stylistic concept with late romanticism (retrospectively: Feinberg, Myaskovsky, Scriabin, still further back, Liszt, with his Faustian and Mephistophelean antinomies) was already a trademark and not a pose by Mosolov in his life and conflicting inner world. There is a startling leaning by the young man to portray images of the night and the twilight by choosing subjects and texts in a coloristic shadowy dark quality."[43] This is evident in the settings; the romance *Night* Op. 1 (from Pushkin), *The Grey Twilight* (from Blok, a romance from a series of vocal miniatures *In the Darkness*), *In the Silent Night*, and *The Terrible Chill of Evening* (both from the cycle—*Ten Poems by Blok* (1925), Op. 10, or 10bis, the symphonic poem *Twilight* (1925), Op. 9 dedicated to Blok, and the piano miniatures *Two Nocturnes* (1926), Op. 15.

Change in Style

The year 1926 marked a change in compositional style both in Mosolov's mood and tone. We can separate the student period from 1923 to 1925 from the mature 1926 to 1929, and by the genre in which he was working. Now, instead of sonatas, he would write symphonic miniatures, concertos, and for ballet and opera.

The period from 1917 to 1932 appeared like a chain of continual events in Russian cultural life set against tremendous societal transformations—the time was one of swiftly moving happenings in which the old society was squashed by the quickly moving mass of revolutionary changes. The emigration of the former aristocracy and landowners together with the remnants of the Romanov dynasty was countered by a Soviet working class hungry for power and setting to rights the old injustices before the revolution. The brutality of the Civil War helped fashion the dynamics of the new society, after the destruction, hunger and the deaths of several million men and women there came dozens of fledgling organizations. The NEP introduced an environment which benefited the avant-garde artists particularly after 1921 when private publishers, studios, and trading companies were set up. In this environment, the avant-garde composers flourished with new theaters and cinemas, and concert promoters using all available stages for performances. It was during this timescale that Mosolov began writing his five piano sonatas, *Legenda* for cello and piano, and song settings from Goethe, Pushkin, Lermontov, Tyutchev, and Blok. The second phase in Mosolov's creativity is after leaving the Conservatoire and the formation of the Union of Composers in 1932. As we shall see, this period was the richest vein of composition in Mosolov's career, following which his music reached a maturity in style embracing folk song and traditional forms. The third chapter in his career came in the years 1937–1938. Following this *annus horribilis*, Mosolov wrote in a late romantic style, yet, not without a rich thread of musicality in his symphonies, concertos, songs, and choruses through to his final years—but after 1932—the avant-garde Mosolov was gone.

The British scholar Neil Edmunds writes: "Individuality was the opposite of what the proletarian music movement expected from its ideal citizen-composers as illustrated by numerous articles written by the proletarian music movement's composers that emphasized how being a composer was just a job like any other."[44] It was in the piano sonatas that the modernism of Mosolov revealed itself sharply. Marina Frolova-Walker comments that "Mosolov's abrasive ultra-modernist Fourth Piano Sonata stood out, promising a refreshing change in ASM's direction."[45] Concerning Mosolov's early creativity, the Petersburg musicologist Igor Vorobyov writes: "It is not enough to point out the similarity of 'machine' themes by Mosolov (the Fifth Sonata, *The Foundry*, etc.) or the themes symbolizing revolutionary struggle and labor by Shostakovich (the 2nd and 3rd symphonies) with the thematics of Scriabin. (. . .) Noticeable, in the context of urbanism, is the intonational affinity shared by the symphonic poem *Komsomoliya* by N. Roslavets, and the symphonic rhapsody *October* by I. Schillinger."[46] This affinity with contemporary art forms was an illusion, as Vorobyov continues for Mosolov, "The symphonic utopia of the 1920s seemed to be pragmatic and functional when transformed into musical forms of the *Monument to the Third International* by Vladimir Tatlin—the height of which pointed to 'forward and upwards'—yet failed to define the transcendental and spiritual-moral concept of the ascent."[47]

The ASM *Contemporary Music* carried reviews, articles, and analysis of both contemporary Soviet and Western music, and, from 1926, the ASM concerts benefited from newly written works by Bartók, Schoenberg, Eisler, Casella, and Hindemith. In the spring of 1926, Darius Milhaud arrived in Moscow and played music by Satie, Poulenc, and Auric at the State Academy of Art. Shortly afterward, Alfredo Casella visited for concerts. In 1927, Honegger, Berg, and Hindemith all toured the Soviet Union, and Berg's *Wozzeck* was performed in Leningrad, in only its second staging outside of Berlin. Mosolov was appointed the Russian secretary of International Society of Contemporary Music (ISCM) in 1927 and 1928. While international success continued, in Moscow, as we know from previous chapters, the control of publishing fell into the hands of the RAPM and their acolytes.

The RAPM specified four musicians groups for being ideologically impure, among whom were the people of "Golovanovschina" which were characterized as "grey epigones, dead" and "belonging to the past."[48] The second was the ASM which was considered "foreign to the working classes, and revealing in their music—the ideology and interests of the culture (. . .) of the leading Russian bourgeoisie, and intelligentsia (. . .) and frequently associated to the West."[49] Unfortunately, for Mosolov, the verdict was already out—the ultra-left considered that his music posed a threat to Soviet music, regardless of his Civil War gallantry.

To the wrath of the proletarian musicians, Mosolov played the part of a solitary genius creating controversy wherever and whenever he appeared. Indeed, of all those composers associated with the ASM, Mosolov was the most unlikely to conform to stereotype, which ultimately led to his expulsion (albeit short lived) from the Composers Union in 1936 on trumped-up charges. For all his brilliance, Mosolov was unstable, as Barsova describes: "Shostakovich said that Mosolov didn't know how to behave; he was incapacitated during the war, and this led to consequences. In 1927, there came the first attacks against Mosolov, and *The Foundry* was banned. He could fight someone in a restaurant, insult people, and laugh at them—he enjoyed a normal relationship with Shostakovich. There was a long friendship with (the harpist) Vera Dulova. There are many anecdotes that one can't repeat in public—it's not surprising that he insulted someone who then took action against him."[50]

The influence of new European music—mixed with his fresh ideas—was instilled by Mosolov during this intense period of the 1920s; he wrote that "the epoch has made us drunk. . . . We sense new rhythms, forms, thoughts. . . . We need to learn how to master them . . . speed, movement, rhythms. Faster, faster. . . . It is impossible to stop."[51] His mentor

Myaskovsky said: "The epoch is offering temptation, and you give in to them. Are you not destroying your soul? And in the name of what?"[52] Myaskovsky was concerned about his favorite student in a letter to him, "Sonatas, concertos, symphonies, romances, eccentricities. . . . Perhaps it is time to stop?" However, Mosolov argued, "There isn't enough time. I am afraid that I am not strong enough. After (the war) one can't return to the world as it was before. I feel the rhythm of time. . . . I want to prove this. I want to understand, where is God?" Myaskovsky reproached him, "Really, now what would your papa say?"[53]

The Constructivist

As Roslavets informs us, it was clear that Mosolov was "a representative of extreme left modernism. His (first) sonata is a true bible of modernism in which all the harmonic tricks are concentrated in the spirit of Prokofiev and Stravinsky."[54] The five sonatas bear a common trait of immense power, under-bearing dark and gloomy ideas, reflecting the times, and embracing novelty.

In 1928, Myaskovsky wrote to Prokofiev about the latest sensation by his former pupil—*The Foundry* "Mosolov is becoming more and more witty and sharp."[55] In his response, Prokofiev noted that "the score sounds very well." However, "there is terribly little material, apart from which it is continually repetitive and depresses me, albeit I did the same with my *Scythian Suite*."[56] Prokofiev explains the problems for Parisian audiences after hearing Mosolov's brilliant symphonic miniature. "In Paris, there is a requirement for Soviet music somewhat different from that required in Moscow: in Moscow, they demand boldness most of all, in Paris, they have already embraced Soviet audaciousness, but they are often expressing anxiety that there is a dearth of content. One needs to excuse the French because their acquaintance with Soviet music started with Mosolov's *The Foundry*."[57]

Paradoxically, it was Mosolov's liberty in thought that ultimately blighted his development as a composer. The leading music critic and composer Boris Asafyev was a strong supporter of Mosolov—under the pseudonym of Igor Glebov—and attacked the critics of new music in a witty and rather caustic article called *Pismakh glukhikh lyudey* (*Letters of deaf people*). Viktor Belyaev wrote an article of searching wisdom about Mosolov's gifts. The young composer Alexander Cherepnin (in exile in France) wrote to Mosolov. "I love *Legenda* very much and strongly believe in the forceful value of your gifts. I will be delighted if you can acquaint me with your latest compositions—particularly of chamber music, or music for the radio. I may perform or help to sway concerts. And if you have the time, tell me about your affairs and life, just, if the chance arises, I can enlighten the public."[58]

Figure 7.2 Mosolov—*The Foundry* (First Page). *Source*: © Copyright Le Chant Du Monde. Reprinted by permission of Hal Leonard Europe Ltd.

Making a living from music alone was precarious, particularly when private enterprise was allowed through the NEP. Hence, on January 1, 1926, Mosolov started teaching at the Malakhovsky Musical Courses in Moscow. Another chore that gave him space for writing was as the head of the Chamber Music Section at the Moscow Academy of Arts. Mosolov added to his bow by reviewing Hindemith's music, and to his earnings, by giving solo recitals almost entirely of Western music. On December 6, 1926, in the ASM concert welcoming Alfredo Casella to Moscow, music by Feinberg, Polovinkin, Alexandrov, Melkikh, Mosolov, and Gamburg was performed for their Italian visitor.[59] The young pianist—soon to become Mosolov's first wife—Elena Kolobova performed in the recital.[60]

Here we have a sketch of the young, seemingly notorious Mosolov of the 1920s, Vera Dulova remembered that "he was an intellectual and a brilliantly educated gentleman and some of us familiar with his 'explosive' character feared his cane."[61] These reminiscences by the young harpist Vera Dulova tell of Mosolov cutting quite a striking figure with his sharp dress style and walking stick leading girls to call him "Dorian Grey." Following the scandalous performances of Mosolov's music there reigned a pandemonium of shouts and yelling which was contrasted by the hurrahs and loud applause from his acolytes.

Piano Concerto No. 1

If the piano sonatas caused a hullabaloo, Mosolov's First Piano Concerto (1926–1927) reprised even more discontent and praise among audiences. After the premiere in Leningrad on February 12, 1928, Shebalin wrote that the concerto "was performed by its composer, as it should be, and apparently all of its deliberate 'tricks' succeeded. Some of the audience attempted to hiss after the performance—but without avail—responding to the applause—the composer returned on stage three times."[62] The concerto was heard in Moscow on October 14 at the Large Hall of the Conservatoire with Mosolov taking the solo part, again under Malko. The concerto was heard in Vienna and London during the 1931 and 1932 seasons.[63] The conductor Malko who introduced the piano concerto to European audiences informed Myaskovsky, "It seems Mosolov's concerto, following the unexpected success of *The Foundry* . . . is now fashionable."[64]

Barsova rationalizes the impact that the Mosolov Piano Concerto had upon contemporary musicians. "Mosolov liberated the concerto from subjective emotions, with his post-Scriabinism. He brought a freshness in 'tonality,' which, by the 1930s, was already significantly diminished (and which) was becoming dominant, the joy of motoric, celebratory toccatas, and humor. It was the first anti-romantic concerto in Soviet music (appearing six years before Shostakovich's concerto)."[65] A contemporary reviewer proclaimed that "the nature of his music is severe and harsh. There are no sweet sounds, no meditations—it is anti-psychological, earthy in its materialism, and sporadically simultaneously with machine rhythms. Mosolov is a musical constructivist."[66]

The Piano Concerto No. 1 is in the style of a *Concerto Grosso*, akin to Ernst Krenek's *Concerto Grosso* No. 2 for violin, viola, and cello; Hindemith's *Concerto*, Op. 38; and Casella's *Partita* (all three of which were heard in Leningrad in the 1920s).[67] They all share the influence of neoclassicism—here, interestingly, is what Mosolov wrote about Hindemith, "The distinguishing features of his music . . . appear to be . . . qualitatively—perhaps exclusively—the cult of paradoxes, which is expressed spontaneously in relationship with each other—thematically excellent—and in the concept of expression—exceeds all other German composers in this form, with improvised music, often unpleasant, in separate, untidy themes, and, a harmonically, somewhat weak moderation."[68] The Piano Concerto No. 1 is scored for strings (8,6,4,3,2) with flute, piccolo, oboe, clarinet, bassoon, two horns, trumpet, trombone, timpani, Piatti, military Tamburo, Gran Casa, and tam-tam. Intriguingly, Mosolov includes nine variations with portraits of contemporary composers—musical humoresques—"as if several were parodies on the style of eminent composers."[69]

Mosolov's orchestral score is relentlessly unforgiving, the first movement *Andante lugubre* opens on a *Phrygian* E minor with the bassoon playing at its highest register. There materializes a rather mysterious march that breaks into brass clusters and a motoric ferocity with the piano adopting a toccata style. The second movement, *Tema con Concertini*, is a set of variations—nine in all—including a waltz, and a nocturne, in which music by Hindemith, Casella, and Stravinsky are caricatured. In the third movement, *Allegro. Molto marcato*, the Moscow-based scholar Hakobian exemplifies: "the quality of 'structural scarcity and syntactical paucity'—more or less in its place in a short piece on an industrial theme—is emphasized to an even more noticeable degree. Only the work's middle movement, *Tema con concertini*, which contains moments' of finer instrumental texture—though the humor of the piece, intended to represent a series of musical caricatures hinting of the most eminent composers of the epoch (. . .) is at present hardly intelligible."[70] Such criticism may appear dismissive in the reflection of almost a century, yet there is no question—at the time—Mosolov's First Piano Concerto was an outstanding standard-bearer for the Soviet avant-garde. Elena Dolinskaya of the Moscow Conservatoire writes,

> Although a small orchestra is used, the composer doesn't treat it as a chamber ensemble, there is a considerable string section, with a large percussion group and wind. The initial sound image of the concerto is created by a toccata

Figure 7.3 Mosolov—Piano Concerto No. 1 (First Page). *Source*: © Copyright 1972 by Universal Edition A.G., Wien.

expression, with totally dissonant harmonies, and constructivist rhythms. (. . .) In the constructivist concept of the concerto, the composer unifies both innovation and tradition. In the latter, there is a shared three-part structure, where the entire first movement (a sonata with antithetical reprise) corresponds with the closing toccata. The great originality of the concerto is in the central movement which is the heart of the work. It is like a cycle of variations for orchestra (Tema con concertini) initially there appear variations, ending on the solo trombone in a reprise of the opening idea. The tonal form of the theme is original—eleven unrepeated sounds, as if in a "false" twelve tonal series.[71] There dominates a spirit of *buffonado*, the color of which gives especially an improvisational beginning. The variations appear in turn categorically—march, nocturne, waltz (No. 4, 5, and 6).[72]

The Foundry: The Music of Machines

The background to Mosolov's most celebrated piece is a ballet commissioned by the Bolshoi Theater in 1926. The ballet scenario by Inna Chernetskaya comprises of four episodes: (1) *Entrance—The Foundry*, (2) *In Jail*, (3) *At the Ball*, (4) *On the Square* (*March*).[73] Regrettably, the manuscript for the music of the last three movements has not been discovered. *The Foundry: The Music of Machines* was first published in 1928. The 3-minute piece was premiered by the Orchestra of the Revolution under Konstantin Saradzhev on December 4, 1927, in the Moscow Hall of Columns, at a matinee concert marking the tenth anniversary of Soviet power.[74] Making up the rest of the bill were Shostakovich's Symphony No. 2 *To October*, *Prologue* by Polovinkin, and Roslavets's cantata *October*. Amy Nelson writes that "Mosolov's orchestration invokes the din of the factory by dragging a stick across a sheet of corrugated metal. If his colleagues had an affinity with 'industrial' orchestral devices. (. . .) Perhaps identifying acceptable 'content' (would) ensure that the content would be unmistakeably clear."[75]

There was immediate approval from audiences for this adventurous piece and the use by Mosolov of a terse use of sonata, toccata, and fugue format. However, it was the treatment of the orchestra and his espoused harmonic language that aroused more interest than Polovinkin's music. Anton Uglov commented that

> Mosolov has written very wittingly and refreshingly before in the chamber genre, yet, here he reveals himself as an interesting master in the symphonic scheme. In the suite from *Steel*, he doesn't pose any elaborate questions, as in the Quartet or in his vocal pieces. The timbre of his writing is lavish, concentrated, and sometimes unusually inventive. In this context, one needs to see that in the shattering roar of *The Foundry* scene, Mosolov has unearthed a stunning "industrial" force—refraining from simply reproducing crude sound. This extract screams about how much one should be "grateful" to industrial themes—if only it were from a leading musician.[76]

The theme of musical "constructivism" is exemplified spectacularly well in *The Foundry* and is often compared to Honegger's *Pacific 231*. However, in close comparison of the two works, Mosolov provides a percussive tour de force evoking the sound of factory machinery in the most brutalist musical language through his use of harshly severe ostinato rhythms with momentary timbre and melodic blocks to imitate the movement and sounds of a modern factory. Honegger was not the only parallel, as the American writers Leslie-Anne Sayers and Simon Morrison graphically suggest,

> The last measure of *The Foundry* bears some resemblance to the last measure of *L'pac d'acier* (the former comprises a thirty-second note run to a unison C, the latter a sixteenth note run to a unison A), but the preceding measures do not. Mosolov's factory breaks down, unable to meet its production quota despite repeated rhythmic retooling, and the final *sforzando* caps a meltdown of the orchestral metal works. Prokofiev's factory, in contrast, promises to operate forever, irrespective of human and material wear and tear or overtime costs. The unison A marks the descent of the theater curtain, not the closure of the plant.[77]

Arthur Honegger elucidates himself on his *Pacific 231*. "What happened was something similar to wide-ranging choral variations with throughout a contrapuntal line in the spirit of the Bach style."[78] Certainly, in the rapidly changing world of new technology, Poulenc and Milhaud composed works evoking the terrifying world of machines, but no one captivated his audiences as did Mosolov's symphonic miniature. The RAPM music critic Semyon Korev wrote excitedly,

> The first section is most successful as an illustration. The principal rhythmic-melodic figure, which is very expressive, runs through the entire section—from beginning to end—creating a vivid musical picture of a factory running at full tilt. But the composer did not limit himself to the creation of a mere "naturalistic" scene. He goes beyond and is richer. Without changing his main musical theme but concentrating intensely on the logic of the gradual build-up, the composer transcends the illustration as he approaches the climax. His solid melodic-rhythmic figures begin to sound so victorious and uplifting (especially when the brass add their sustained chords over the rhythmic-melodic background) this vivid overture—while losing none of its illustrative character—is transformed into a mighty hymn to mechanized labor. The overture is constructed solidly and expressively, and has every reason to become very popular, and is justly warranted. Programmatic works will undoubtedly find their place in Soviet music, and the path opened by *The Foundry* will lead to further achievements.[79]

A present-day appraisal by Vorobyov offers us further insight into Mosolov's *The Foundry*. "Actually, the variants, of total ostinato, of qualitative plastics in this famous work represent, all the same, the method of movement in circles. Only, not in the horizontal plane, but, in the vertical, which naturally makes the form more dynamic and approaches the culminatory reprise."[80] A unanimous success among Soviet audiences, Mosolov's symphonic cameo *The Foundry* became an international sensation following the European premiere in Liege at the ISCM Festival on September 6, 1930, and later famously in Hollywood in 1932.[81] The American scholar Anna Ferenc considers that "the composition's portrayal of machines in motion through a layering of motoric, dissonant, and percussive ostinatos actually has much in common with the earlier Cubo-Futurist aesthetic."[82]

It is unfortunate that Mosolov shares the fate of a small number of composers whose fame is almost entirely owing to a single brief and brilliant orchestral work. Perhaps the secret is in capturing the moment in time of a harshly modern world embracing new technology. The cluster of Soviet conductors, Gauk, Ginzburg, Khaikhin, Polovinkin, and Stolyarov, programmed *The Foundry* to enthusiastic audiences all over the Soviet Union. The score was published three times between 1928 and 1934 by Muzsektor

Figure 7.4 Mosolov—1928. *Source*: Photography by Mozhei Nappelbaum – Courtesy of Universal Edition AG.,Wien.

and by Universal Verlag in Vienna.[83] The most distinguished conductors of the period, Leon Baton, Victor de Sabata, Hermann Scherchen, Leopold Stokowski, and Arturo Toscanini, performed *The Foundry* in concerts of twentieth-century music. The fame of the piece lasted until the Cold War, when it disappeared together with many Soviet works; however in recent years, it has reappeared both in performances and recordings by orchestras in Europe and America.

The Song Cycles

If *The Foundry* appeased both modernists and conservatives, it seemed as if a brief interregnum before a fresh wave of controversy raged around Mosolov. The source of another uproar was the song settings—the *Three Children's Scenes*, Op. 18, and the *Four Newspaper Advertisements*, Op. 21. As Barsova explains, "It would have been untrue to state that the composer met with a complete lack of understanding."[84] This appraisal is confirmed by Mosolov's friend and former teacher, Alexander Shenshin, who noticed "a genuine sharpness and facility for clarity in expression. In the *Three Children's Scenes*, this expression is purely by external means (meowing, shuddering, and dragging, etc.), then in the *Four Newspaper Advertisements*, it follows a path of probing visible characteristics. The performer needs not only great musicality but considerable acting preparation."[85] It appears that the commentators considered the pieces more of a provocation. The *Three Children's Scenes* portrays a child tormenting a cat and the natural groaning of a bare toddler. In Mosolov's Op. 21 collection, a somber yet intricately created score satirized banal newspaper announcements about a lost dog, a rat catcher, and another about the sale of leeches. The ASM paper *Contemporary Music* had nothing but praise for Mosolov's talent, mastery, and innovation.[86] However, as to be expected, the RAPM detractors condemned Mosolov's work for being morally demeaning and worthless mischief whose naturalistic excesses fell far short of genuine art, and which ought to direct attention to more significant, worthwhile ideas.[87]

The *Three Children's Scenes* was described by the critics as "ultra-realist" through using children's language, animal, and street noises transposed into musical scores—and worse, according to pundits—the youngsters in Mosolov's piece seemed to be very unhappy and living a cheerless life. Mosolov's use of adverts from *Izvestiya* created sharply ironic and witty musical images from humorless words. Mosolov was trying to characterize with bitter social musical satire the NEP corruption during a time of declining morality in Soviet Russia. The RAPM press didn't see it that way, and one critic who attended the first performance of the *Three Children's Scenes* accused the songs of being "utterly alien to our Soviet reality."[88] Marian

Koval went further denouncing Mosolov as a "class enemy"; moreover, Viktor Bely now considered *The Foundry* a representation of "slave labor" insinuating that Mosolov thought this way about Soviet workers.[89]

The US scholar Olga Forsch discussed the attraction by young writers of the period to the ordinary life of people in the big cities—one of the most prominent authors was the respected satirist Mikhail Zoschenko. However, for Mosolov, it was a wicked parody on merchant life, and, in his *Three Children's Scenes*—a charming yet ironic expression of the world of children. Barsova considers that this fascination for "ordinary life and the world of the fairy tale was most relevant in Mosolov's song cycles."[90] A quite different opinion dominated media opinion of the day. "It's impossible to consider this seriously as a song arranged for music from newspaper advertisements: 'A dog is lost' or 'A sea of cockroaches' etc." However, in purely musical terms, there were favorable comparisons made between the emotional world of Mosolov's *Three Children's Scenes* and Musorgsky's song cycles. Remarkably, the *Three Children's Scenes* and the *Four Newspaper Advertisements* continue the tradition of Musorgsky's *Rayok* and *The Seminarist*. One specific parallel is in the declamatory repetition of children's speech patterns. There is here, as Barsova points out, "an intonational-stylistic theater. In this 'theater,' there participate several, so to speak, 'masked languages.'" Furthermore, Barsova argues:

> In the *Four Newspaper Advertisements*, the idea of the composition was more polemical. Although the music for prosaic text has a long-standing tradition in Russia and was regarded in the nineteenth century as a struggle for truth in art just like the challenge "to new shores" (*The Marriage* by Musorgsky), however, the usage of non-literary texts in the twentieth century has an element of aesthetic epitaph. Individually, there was the idea of "musical chronicles" as if hanging in mid-air. In Berlin, there were performances of *Zeitungsausschnitte* by Hanns Eisler that created a scandal—and in Leningrad—the performance of the vocal feuilleton by Valerian Bogdanov-Berezovsky *On the Base of a Duck* (from the text by the then-popular satirist A. Zorich). That was a challenge to the "sacred heaven" of the chamber music world, to academic dryness, which stalled at a glimpse at their place of the "world picture" of the twenties. And, only now, when we place the *Four Newspaper Advertisements* in the wide-ranging context of Soviet art of that time, there comes to the fore another aspect: the pitiless satire of raising one's head during the period of the NEP marketplace, of exposure of the "social type," about which so much was discussed and written during that period. The emotional world of the *Four Newspaper Advertisements* is distinguished by the composer's vocal lyrics. He is anti-lyrical, anti-psychological, and, at the same time, is quite characteristically spiky. The hero of Mosolov's vocal miniature is the social mask, as much is born of the

contemporary mercantile Meyerhold scenes, in the characters from *The Bedbug*, and *The Mandate*.[91]

At the beginning of 1927, the RAPM media published an editorial entitled *The Left Wing of Contemporary Music*, in which the principal culprit was Alexander Mosolov. Other modernist composers were attacked, but Mosolov was the main target, dismissing him for the apparent portrayal of loneliness, and tragic fantasies in his recent works—all of which contrasted with real life. "What does all this mean? (...) well, the composer is irrelevant to Soviet reality, he doesn't fit in and finds himself isolated." The anonymous writer continued: "In 1924, he brought cynicism, mockery, and 'funereal moods,' to our music, and in 1926—the 'ultra-realism' of a naked man, of mediocre music at the level of a prosaic subject like Mosolov's 'newspaper advertisements,'—a subject which may be as necessary as a floor rag, but only in as much as an irrelevant person is as desirable as a dirty floor." In his closing remarks, "Mosolov and his supporters don't have anything in common with progress, for they are reactionary, intimidating and no longer welcome."[92] The article was headed by a quote from Nikolay Bukharin—a member of the Bolshevik leadership, noted for his leftist opinions (which led to his trial and execution in 1936). "The author who cannot fit in and has become too foreign in our Soviet life will feel themselves cast out."[93]

This brutally dismissive judgment did not lead to a downturn in the performances of Mosolov's music at home and abroad. What was most extraordinary in the editorial was the importance given to Mosolov's position in the modernist group of composers, placing him above Roslavets, Shostakovich, and others. However, it was just the beginning of a prolonged campaign against Mosolov and the avant-garde.

In the following month, in February 1927, Mikhail Druskin, as the secretary of the Leningrad branch of ASM, invited Mosolov to bring his latest music for performances in the spring.[94] The composer arrived in Leningrad for a recital in May at the Glazounov Hall of the Conservatoire to perform his *Three Pictures*, Op. 23a; *Two Dances*, Op. 23b; *Two Nocturnes* for piano, Op. 15; and the Fourth Sonata, Op. 11. The songs—*To a Friend, Four Pieces*, Op. 7; *Four Newspaper Advertisements*; and the *Three Children's Scenes*—were performed by Irina Polyanovskaya (accompanied by Mosolov). The second part of the concert featured modernist works by Kushnarev, Aseyev, Schillinger, and Deshevov.[95] Mosolov's vocal works were very significant in the music of Soviet Russia, as Hakobian points out, "Mosolov caused a considerable disquiet with two short song cycles for soprano voice with piano accompaniment: the *Three Children's Scenes*, Op. 18 and the *Four Newspaper Advertisements*, Op. 21. The texts for the first cycle were written by Mosolov himself in the spirit of Musorgsky's *Nursery*, though with some risqué details, such as the representation of the child's physiological impatience in the 'third scene.' As to the cycle of *Four Newspaper Advertisements*—in the history of Russian music—this was, probably, the very first example of setting to music such unpoetical texts (borrowed from the Moscow paper *Izvestiya*) as, for instance: 'A dog has run away, a bitch, English setter, white, with coffee spots. Caution against buying and sale. The deliverer will be rewarded,' or 'Personally exterminate rats and mice, have references, twenty-five years of experience.' The music of both cycles shows few signs of the usual Mosolovian straightforward 'brashness' instead is distinguished by a remarkable inner concentration, with intense and meticulous declamation, and plenty of masterly elaborated details giving birth to a rich game of discrepancies between words and music. The extremely fine and witty orchestration of both cycles was realized by the Soviet composer Edison Denisov in 1981."[96]

Some Soviet writers explained the nature of Mosolov's musical absurdity in everyday terms, considering the *Four Newspaper Advertisements* as musical satire directed against the philistines and the nouveaux riches in the age of NEP.[97] Hakobian disagrees saying that "this does not seem convincing since it is really very difficult to see in Mosolov's settings any invective. It would be perhaps more adequate to assess the humor of Mosolov as a remarkable example of the typically Russian kind of the comic based essentially on the effects of the absurd; if his songs have any point, it is directed not so much against the defects of real-life—as against the established views concerning the relation between art and reality—and hence refers to some important philosophical and aesthetical issues."[98]

It might be more insightful to judge the songs as Inna Barsova suggests, representing a reflection on the decline of morality in the decade after the revolution. One other interpretation alludes to the symbolism portrayed in the music: "The composer disrobed the ugly philistine masks, symbols of the past and present life—the very masks against which Zoshenko was fighting with such an outstanding talent."[99] Lyudmila Nikitina points to the influence on Shostakovich's music. The heroes of Zoshenko are present in the personalities of Mosolov's *Four Newspaper Advertisements*. In honing his portrayals, Mosolov used a high-pitched harmonic language, underlined by dissonance, with grotesque melodic changes and even a dissimilarity in styles. "Shostakovich himself turned to similar satirical irony in his later song settings of *The Satires* based on Sasha Cherny."[100]

Further influence of Mosolov's song cycles can be observed in Shostakovich's *The Nose* (1927) chamber opera as Hakobian suggests, "the distorted quotation from Tchaikovsky's *Lullaby*, and from a popular street tune in the children's scenes, the funeral march rhythms on the words about 'rat extermination,' and the nostalgically melancholy insertion in the purest

D minor in the advertisements are 'tricks' of the kind highly characteristic of *The Nose*."[101] To the mainstream commentators, the vocal cycles were fascinating for their wit and invention, in Yuri Vainkop's opinion, they were "a little distant, but not dissimilar to what is heard in Musorgsky."[102]

Reflecting on the death of Lenin (1870–1924), Mosolov composed the chorus *The Year 1924*. However, the RAPM composer Marian Koval dismissed Mosolov's piece. "At last, we find in the musical literature a work dedicated to Lenin, and a composition clearly hostile and offensive to the proletariat. This chorus with orchestra (. . .), is clearly music by the class enemy."[103] The Moscow academic writer Stepanova regrets that so little of Mosolov's vocal legacy is appreciated today. "The composition by Mosolov of cantatas and other choral pieces still await restoration to the concert platform, only after which may we judge their artistic importance."[104] However, for Mosolov, as Leonid Rimsky suggests, the song cycles would prove the preparation for his next major step—writing for opera.[105] So impressed was Prokofiev by his young compatriot that he wrote enthusiastically to Diaghilev. In a letter of September 21, 1928. "I recommend Mosolov reservedly because those things known to me are not without yesterday's modernism and are somewhat static. But since then, I have come across his *Four Newspaper Advertisements* for voice and piano, which are delightfully razor-sharp and eye-catching, yet (they) can't compare with *Machines agricoles* by Milhaud, which he says he isn't familiar with. Apart from which, he has written a string quartet and a piano concerto which I haven't seen."[106] Alas, nothing ever came from this suggestion as the impresario died shortly after receiving this letter.

NOTES

1. Podgoretsky composed a huge number of works including the opera *Bednaya Liza*. The score of which was presented to the library of the Kyiv State Conservatoire by Mosolov in 1968—author.

2. Leblanc September 13, 1875, was born in Gorodische in Mtsensk district into a peasant family. He studied with the great Russian painters Levitan and Vasnetsov. In 1910, he lived in Paris and as from 1912 he taught at the Moscow Art Studio and from 1918 at the Moscow dept. of people's education, later in the 1930s at the Institute of Higher Architecture, at the Stanislavsky Studio, and at Mosfilm. He died on December 22, 1940. His work was exhibited at the Tretyakov gallery at the Russian museum and at the Scriabin house museum—author.

3. Rimsky, Perepiska A.V. Mosolova, materialy i dokumenty iz evo arkhiva, *Iz proshlovo muzikalnovo kultury, vyp. 3*, Moscow: Kompozitor, 1982, 9–10.

4. Rimsky, Perepiska A.V. Mosolova, materialy i dokumenty iz evo arkhiva, *Iz proshlovo muzikalnovo kultury, vyp. 3*, Moscow: Kompozitor, 1982, 10.

5. Archives of SSK USSR, lichnoye dela, No. 374, l. 4 i 6, No. 84, l.44.

6. Barsova, Inna, "Rannee tvorchestva A. Mosolova," *A.V. Mosolov, Statii i Vospominanii*, Moscow: Kompositor, 1986, 46.
7. His full name was Fet-Shenshin—author.
8. Rimsky, Leonid, Perepiska A.V. Mosolova, materialy i dokumenty iz evo arkhiva, *Iz proshlovo muzikalnovo kultury, vyp. 3*, Moscow: Kompositor, 1982, 10.
9. Rimsky, Perepiska A.V. Mosolova, materialy i dokumenty iz evo arkhiva, *Iz proshlovo muzikalnovo kultury, vyp. 3*, Moscow: Kompositor, 1982, 10.
10. Barsova, Inna, "Rannee tvorchestva A. Mosolova," *A.V. Mosolov, Statii i Vospominanii*, Moscow: Kompositor, 1986, 81–82.
11. Mosolov-Myaskovsky correspondence—Archive Nina Meshko translated by the author.
12. Archives of N. Meshko, also of Moscow State Control op. 15, No. 1946, l. 8. Svideltelstvo No. 12430, Barsova, 82.
13. Barsova, Inna, "Rannee tvorchestvo Aleksandra Mosolova," *Mosolov, A.V. Mosolov, Statii i Vospominanii*, Moscow: Kompositor, 1986, Meshko, 44.
14. "Soobsheniye," *Sovremennaya Muzika*, Nos. 13–14, 1926, 108.
15. Barsova, Inna, "Rannee tvorchestva a. Mosolova," *A.V. Mosolov, Statii i Vospominanii*, Moscow: Kompositor, 1986, 46.
16. Barsova, Inna, "Rannee tvorchestva a. Mosolova," *A.V. Mosolov, Statii i Vospominanii*, Moscow: Kompositor, 1986, 46.
17. Letter Glière to Mosolov, February 19, 1924, "Perepiska A.V. Mosolova," Rimsky, *Iz proshlovo sovetskoy muzikalnovo kultura*, Ed., Livanova, Moscow: Kompositor, 1982, 55.
18. Nelson, Amy, *Music for the Revolution: Musicians and Power in Early Soviet Russia*, Pennsylvania UP, 2004, 159.
19. Prokofiev—Myaskovsky "Perepiska A.V. Mosolova," Rimsky, *Iz proshlovo sovetskoy muzikalnovo kultura*, Ed., Livanova, Moscow: Kompositor, 1982, 263. In regard to vocal cycles by Mosolov.
20. Ferenc, Anna, "Music in the Socialist State," *Soviet Music and Society under Lenin and Stalin*, London: Routledge, 2009, 11.
21. *N. Ya. Myaskovsky*, t. 1., 101.
22. Kholopov, Yuri, "Alexander Mosolov i evo fortepiannaya muzyka," *A. Mosolov. Izbranniye Sochineniya dlya fortepiano*, Moscow: Muzyka, 1991, 3.
23. Kholopov, Yuri, "Alexander Mosolov i evo fortepiannaya muzyka," *A. Mosolov. Izbranniye Sochineniya dlya fortepiano*, Moscow: Muzyka, 1991, 3.
24. Belyaev, Viktor, "Aleksandra Vasilyevich Mosolov," *Sovremennaya Muzyka*, 1926, 13–14.
25. "Rabis," *Rabochy Iskusstvo*, 1927, 4, 15
    Uglov, Anton, *Izvestiya*, February 24, 1927.
26. Hakobian, Leon, *Music in the Soviet Era*, London: Routledge, 2017, 57.
27. Anon, "Levy flange," *Muzyka i Revolutssi*, No. 1, 1927, 4.
28. Uglov, Anton, *Izvestiya*, February 24, 1927.
29. Hakobian, Leon, *Music of the Soviet Age*, Stockholm: Melos, 1998, 50.
30. Hakobian, Leon, *Music of the Soviet Era*, Stockholm: Melos, 1998, 43–44.

31. Elena F. Kolobova studied with Goldenweiser at the Moscow Conservatoire graduating in 1916, and performed widely all over Russia, and began teaching in 1921, and became head of piano studies at the Conservatoire, and also taught at the Gnessin Music Institute, among her pupils was the conductor Yevgeny Svetlanov—author.

32. RGALI, f.2040, op. 3, ed.khr.102, l. 17.

33. Rimsky, L. A., "A.V. Mosolov. Biograficheski ocherk," *A.V. Mosolov. Statii i Vospominaniya*, Ed. N.K. Meshko, Moscow, 1986, 13.

34. Mosolov to Asafyev, October 22, 1927, RGALI, f. 2658, op. 1, e.kh. 633.

35. Martynov, N., *A. Davidenko. Tvorchesky put, cherty stilya*, Leningrad: Kompozitor, 1977, 13.

36. Archive Moscow State Control, op. 15, No. 1946, l. 11.

37. Glière's telegram to Mosolov, Mosolov's affidavit, Krassin's petition, and supplementary documents are in Rimsky's "Perepiska A. V Mosolova, materials, I documents is archive," *Iz proshlovo Sovetsky culture*, vol. 3, Livanova, 1982, 55–56.

38. Denisov, Edison, *Tempo*.

39. Tassie, Gregor, *Nikolay Myaskovsky: The Conscience of Russian Music*, Lanham: Rowman & Littlefield, 2014.

40. Mosolov, Myaskovsky perepiska, Rimsky, Perepiska A.V. Mosolova, materialy i dokumenty iz evo arkhiva, *Iz proshlovo muzikalnovo kultury, vyp. 3*, Moscow: Kompozitor, 1982, 10.

41. "24 pokazatelny konzert," Moskovskaya Gosurdarstvenny Konservatoire, June 6, 1925, Barsova, 82–83.

42. Based on a scenario by N. Aduev—author.

43. Barsova, Inna, "Rannee tvorchestva A. Mosolova," *A.V. Mosolov, Statii i Vospominanii*, Moscow, 1986, 48–49.

44. Edmunds, Neil, *The Soviet Proletarian Music Movement*, Oxford: Peter Lang, 2000, 29.

45. Frolova-Walker, Marina, *Music and Soviet Power 1917–1932*, London: Boydell, 2017, 160.

46. Vorobyov, Igor, *Social Realism*, St. Petersburg: Kompozitor, 2013, 261.

47. Vorobyov, Igor, *Social Realism*, St. Petersburg: Kompozitor, 2013, 262.

48. Golovanschina was named after the eminent conductor of the Bolshoi Theater who was accused of being anti-Soviet and anti-Semitic, although much of the "evidence" for this was false and was simply based on his being a "representative" of the old Tsarist Russian regime. Golovanov was dismissed although he returned some years later—author.

49. Lebedinsky, L., "Obschestvenniye gruppirovki muzykantov v CCCP," *Muzykalnoye obrazovaniye*, No. 4–5, 1928, 89.

50. Interview with Inna Barsova, February 25, 2017.

51. Mosolov-Myaskovsky correspondence—Archive Nina Meshko—translated by the author.

52. Mosolov-Myaskovsky correspondence—Archive Nina Meshko—translated by the author.

53. Mosolov-Myaskovsky correspondence—Archive Nina Meshko—translated by the author.

54. Roslavets, Nikolay, "Notnaya polka," *Rabis*, 1927, No. 4(46), 15.
55. Kabalevsky, D.B. (ed.), *Perepiska Prokofieva i Myaskovsky*, Moscow: Sovetsky Kompositor, 1977, 266.
56. Kabalevsky, D.B. (ed.), *Perepiska Prokofieva i Myaskovsky*, Moscow: Sovetsky Kompositor, 1977, 355.
57. Kabalevsky, D.B. (ed.), *Perepiska Prokofieva i Myaskovsky*, Moscow: Sovetsky Kompositor, 1977, 415.
58. Letter A. Cherepnin to A. Mosolov of April 12, 1929 (Archive N. Meshko).
59. *Vechernaya Moskva*, December 6, 1926.
60. A banquet was hosted by the association in honor of Casella and a photograph appeared in the media which made a big occasion of the Italian's visit with another concert featuring modern Italian music at the Conservatoire, and another in which Casella conducted a concert of Vivaldi, Rieti, Balakirev's *Islamey* (in his orchestration), and his rhapsody '*Italia*' at the Hall of Columns on December 5.
61. Dulova, Elena, V., from Kapustin, M., 'Vera Dulova,' Moscow, 1981, 32.
62. Shebalin, Vissarion, *Literaturnaya naslediye*, Moscow: Sovetsky Kompositor, 1975, 107.
63. Archive Nina Meshko—translated by the author.
64. Malko, Nikolay, *Vospominaniya, Statii, Pisma*, Moscow: Muzyka, 1972, 224.
65. Barsova, Inna, "Rannee tvorchestva A. Mosolova," *A.V. Mosolov, Statii i Vospominanii*, Moscow: Kompositor, 1986, 67.
66. Uglov, Anton, "Pervye Konzert Sovfila," *Izvestiya*, October 17, 1927.
67. The Krenek piece was performed on October 13, 1926, conducted by Vladimir Dranishnikov. Hindemith's was conducted by Fritz Steidry at the Leningrad philharmonic on October 20, 1926, while the Casella piece was performed November 27, 1926, under Hans Knappertsbusch.
68. Mosolov, A., "Noviye Kamerny konzert i P. Hindemitha," *Sovremennaya muzika*, No. 11, 1927, 18.
69. Belyaev, Viktor, "A.V. Mosolov," *Sovremennaya Muzika*, No. 13–14, 1926, 88.
70. Hakobian, Leon, *Music of the Soviet Era*, London: Routledge, 2017, 46.
71. There is a similar nature in Rodion Shchedrin's Piano Concerto No. 3—author.
72. Dolinskaya, Elena, Ed. Tarakanov, *Istoriya Sovremennoy Otechestvennoy Muzyki*, vypusk 1, 1917–1941, Moscow: Kompositor, 1993, 173–175.
73. *Sovremennaya Muzika*, No. 24, 1927, 21.
74. The conducting was shared with Boris Khaikhin—author.
75. Nelson, Amy, *Music for the Revolution*: *Musicians and Power in Early Soviet Russia*, Pennsylvania UP, 2004, 201.
76. Uglov, Anton, "Simfonicheskoye novinki," *Izvestiya*, February 12, 1928.
77. Sayers, Lesley-Anne and Morrison, Simon, "Prokofiev's *Le pac d'acier*," *Soviet Music and Society under Lenin and Stalin*, London: Routledge, 2009, 89.
78. Honegger, Artur, *O musikalnom iskusstve*, Leningrad: Muzyka, 1979, 164.
79. Korev, Semyon, "Sovetskaya simfonicheskaya Muzika: yubileynii Oktyabriskiye kontserti," *Sovetskoye Iskusstvo*, No. 7, 1927, 51–52.

80. Vorobyov, Igor, *Social Realism*, St. Petersburg: Kompositor, 2013, 261.
81. Barsova, Inna, "Rannee tvorchestva A. Mosolova," *A.V. Mosolov, Statii i Vospominanii*, Moscow: Kompositor, 1986, 84.
82. Ferenc, Anna, "Music in the Socialist State," *Soviet Music and Society under Lenin and Stalin*, London: Routledge, 2009, 12.
83. In the archive of N. Meshko there are reviews of concerts in Prague, Warsaw, Philadelphia, and Lisbon. In the USSR, the most enthusiastic conductor was Stolyarov.
84. Barsova, Inna, "Rannee tvorchestva A. Mosolova," *A.V. Mosolov, Statii i Vospominanii*, Moscow: Kompositor, 1986, 78.
85. Shenshin, Alexander, "Notografiya," *Sovremennaya Muzika*, No. 25, 1927, 72.
86. Belyaev, Viktor, "Aleksandra Vasilyevich Mosolov," *Sovremennaya Muzyka*, 1926, 81–88.
87. Tsekhnovitser, Orest, "Novaya Muzyka i proletariat," *Novaya Muzyka*, No. 2, 1927–28, 15.
88. Anonym, "'Levy' flang sovremennoy muzyki," *Muzyka i Revolutssi*, No. 1, 1927, 5.
89. Bely, Viktor, "O nekotorykh tvorceskikii problemakh proletarskoy muziki," *Proletarian Muzikant*, 1931, 57.
90. Barsova, Inna, "Rannee tvorchestva A. Mosolova," *A.V. Mosolov, Statii i Vospominanii*, Moscow: Kompositor, 1986, 79.
91. Barsova, Inna, "Rannee tvorchestva A. Mosolova," *A.V. Mosolov, Statii i Vospominanii*, Moscow: Kompositor, 1986, 83–84.
92. *Muzika i Revolutsii*, No. 1, January 1927, 3–7.
93. Bukharin, Nikolay, "Formalny method v iskusstv," *Pechat i Revolutssi*, 1925, kn. 3, 257.
94. Meshko, Nina, Archive, *Sovetskaya Muzyka*, No. 7, 1989, 85.
95. Meshko, Nina, Archive, *Sovetskaya Muzyka*, No. 7, 1989, 85.
96. Hakobian, Leon, *Music of the Soviet Era*, London: Routledge, 2017, 44.
97. Barsova, Inna, "Rannee tvorchestva a. Mosolova," *A.V. Mosolov, Statii i Vospominanii*, Moscow: Kompositor, 1986, 84.
98. Hakobian, Leon, *Music of the Soviet Era*, London: Routledge, 2017, 44.
99. Sarnov, "Prishestvie kapitana lebyadkina," Moscow, pik. 1993.
100. Nikitina, L., *Istoriya Sovremennoy Otechestvennoy Muzyki*, vypusk 1, 1917–1941, Moscow: Muzyka, 1993, 260–261.
101. Hakobian, Leon, *Music of the Soviet Era*, London: Routledge, 2017, 44.
102. Vainkop, Y.Y., "Konzert LASM," *Rabochy i Teatr*, 1927, No. 23, 13.
103. Koval, Marian, "Lenin v musike," *Proletarsky Muzikant*, No. 1, 1930, 9–13.
104. Stepanova, I., *Istoriya Sovremennoy Otechestvennoy Muzyki*, vypusk 1, 1917–1941, Moscow: Muzyka, 1993, 273.
105. Rimsky, L., "Perepiska A.V. Mosolova, materialy i dokumenty iz evo arkhiva," *Iz proshlovo muzikalnovo kultury, vyp. 3*, Moscow: Kompositor, 1982, 18.
106. *Sergey Diaghilev i russkoye iskusstvo*, Tom 2, Moscow, 1982, 142–143.

Chapter 8

The Stage Works

If Mosolov's song cycles remained unknown to a wider audience—the orchestral works were winning more of a reputation—and despite the venomous attacks from his proletarian critics, according to Frolova-Walker, Mosolov managed to sustain "a high profile thanks to the ultra-modern Piano Concerto, deepening the synthesis of expressionist atonality and machine music that won him acclaim in *The Foundry*."[1] Barsova writes that "for Mosolov, the stylistic change of 1926 was not something that came from European style—allowing an appraisal of the character of his creative musical language. Much of Mosolov's style from this period disappeared forever, still, its essence remained unbroken. This unassuming trait of the twenties relates to his harmonic material."[2]

STRING QUARTET NO. 1

By the late 1920s, the cult of futurism, machines, and futurological utopias was quickly losing its appeal. The "naïve-romantic way of life" that was discussed by Asafyev in 1927 was shocked by the urbanist musical movement in the fear that the "spirit," "nature," "love and other human emotions" had become inaccessible in this world.[3] One of the musical pieces that would dispel Asafyev's fears was Mosolov's String Quartet No. 1 when it was premiered by the Stradivarius Quartet on February 20, 1927, at the Mozart Concert Hall on Bolshaya Dmitrovka 17 in Moscow. The piece immediately secured considerable enthusiasm among both critics and audiences for its intriguing and quite astonishing notions, and as much as for its jazz-like rhythms and ostensibly "boisterous music."[4] This review in the state broadsheet *Izvestiya* attempts to draw on the diversity of the new piece,

The composer is on the extreme left of our music. Among the many groups of friends who share his proclivity, he has managed to occupy an exclusive individuality, which is equally stimulating, and entertaining. His compositions are interesting and extraordinary. He is least interested in melody and harmony, but in all kinds of possible rhythmic sounds which are both impressive and attractive. His music is inventive, picante, absolutely alluring, and exciting. The quartet is unusually original in that there are very intermittent solo melodies (in the *Andante*) that are enveloped by *flageolets*, pizzicatos, and chords. There are unadorned cries of bacchanalia in the most unusually unrelated sounds heard through a rhythmic harmony among the jam-packed deviations in the quartet. Generally, in it's' style, this is one of the "leading examples" of violent music.[5]

Mosolov used motifs of Turkmen folk music—not for the first time, and "it seems that not only Turkmen folk provenance 'floats' in intensely dissonant contexts" in his String Quartet.[6] Hakobian suggests that Mosolov makes use of Bartók's techniques by altering the timbre of the instruments. The Quartet No. 1 was given its European premiere by the Kolisch Quartet of Vienna (Kolisch, Kuner, Lenner, Heifetz) at the Frankfurt on Main ISCM Festival in 1927. The ASM journal wrote, "this young composer (who was) educated by Glière and Myaskovsky has proven his talent. This four-part composition is like a variety of themes similar to the mosaic from a recitative in which there are the typical makings of a Russian nationalist."[7] Dzimitrowski of the publishers Universal Edition in Vienna wrote to Mosolov that the piece enjoyed great success.[8] Paul Stefan noted an "unusually talented composition which makes its composer one of several hopes among the younger generation of our composers."[9]

There were concerns, however, in Mosolov getting paid, as Derzhanovsky describes. "Mosolov phoned and reported that. . . . Dzimitrowski wrote he hadn't received the 200 marks for the performance of the Mosolov Quartet in Frankfurt. . . . Mosolov is luckless, regardless of his Frankfurt success (very good reviews) and a five-year contract with Universal Edition, he is sitting penniless, and running to his mummy every day to eat, and smoking the thousands of papirosi that he acquired in May."[10] The Mosolov couple then lived at Durnovsky Street, while his parents stayed at the family home on Bolshaya Bronnaya Street.

There were other musical successes—Mosolov's *Two Nocturnes* for Piano (1926) in which Hakobian tells us "the characteristic rudeness of Mosolov's writing yields to a delicate and subtly differentiated three-staff 'impressionistic' texture. Two years later, there appeared another tribute to Turkmenian folklore, the three-movement virtuoso piano suite *Turkmenian Nights* (1928) in which the borrowed tunes are once more treated in an audaciously 'modernistic' manner."[11] The constructivism in Mosolov's orchestral scores may well have influenced contemporaries in Leningrad, notably the Second Symphony by Shostakovich and Vladimir Deshevov's opera *Ice and Steel*.

THE HERO

The first of Mosolov's four completed operas—*The Hero* was a one-act comic opera. Barsova writes that as an antipode to the ill-fated ballet—*Steel*, the chamber opera—*The Hero* has "the conceptual scheme of a false hero. No little secret surrounds this opera from the moment of its writing to this day."[12] Mosolov's stage work was scheduled for a world premiere in Frankfurt on Main in 1928, and later on July 15, in Baden-Baden.[13] For technical reasons, the first performance was moved to Baden-Baden; however despite the active promotion of *The Hero* on the edge of the Black Forest, the production never happened.[14] Barsova writes that "they canceled at the last minute because the score didn't arrive in time."[15] In December 1928, Asafyev queried Mosolov about his latest stage work. "I am overjoyed both by the quantity and abundance of your composing. What is *The Hero* about, and how long will it be?" The half-hour-long stage work—with a libretto by the composer—tells the story of a ham-fisted coward who is erroneously mistaken for a celebrity fencing master by the inhabitants of a small city, and which suitably inspires an irresistible fear on the part of his dueling challenger. The scoring is for chamber orchestra, and—as was Mosolov's practice—a large percussion section is employed. Vorobyov considers that "Mosolov's *The Hero* is the missing link in the history of Soviet music, which, together with *The Nose* of Shostakovich points to the existence of an independent path, between the 20s and 30s, in Soviet musical theater of an alternative to the dominance of historical or revolutionary operas."[16] On the other hand, in Hakobian's consideration, Mosolov's opera yields to Shostakovich's *The Nose* (written in the same year) "in the sharpness of its musical characterizations, and reveals the young composer's weakness in coping with large forms with an orchestra."[17]

The whereabouts of the score and parts were a mystery despite it being mentioned in correspondence during the 1920s; Mosolov's *The Hero* appeared in both his discussions, and letters to Asafyev, and with the Russian department of Universal Edition in Vienna. Abram I. Dzimitrowski—the head at the Russian section in Universal Edition wrote to Mosolov on March 29, 1929. "I have already put in writing that *The Hero* (all the materials) are with me." More than two months later, Dzimitrowski again wrote to Moscow. "Dear Mr. Mosolov, as all the theaters are presently preparing for next season, we are actively searching for the best stage for the premiere of your chamber opera *The Hero*. We have seen that we do not have a contract for this composition, so we are sending this to you at once and request that, in reply, you will receive a copy signed by us."[18] Mosolov responded,

> Abram Isaakovich! I am immediately sending you the signed agreement for publication of *The Hero* and notify that the supplement with Universal Edition needs a piano score. Hence, someone has to produce an appropriate piano score, albeit at my expense. I will be very, very glad to hear that *The Hero* has at last found its sanctuary and will be very pleased to get the corrections. With great impatience, I await your letter in response to my urgent inquiries.[19]

The next episode in the saga emerged on February 5, 1931, when Dzimitrowski informed Mosolov that "*The Hero* is with the Darmstadt opera, and we shall inform you as soon as we know that it is in production."[20] There the story ended for almost half a century.

Forty-eight years later, in 1979, the narrative of *The Hero* was picked up when the musicologist Inna Barsova attended a symposium on Mahler in Vienna. Quite by accident, "I discovered the score of *The Hero* together with the previously unknown letters at the Vienna Stadt-und-Landesbibliothek."[21] In the advance publicity at Baden-Baden for *The Hero*, it had been billed as "a one-act musical work, with brief character content." Barsova continues: "Undoubtedly, such a commission was provocative in presenting a curious and witty piece. The Festival, in the previous year, had staged operas of short time spans, the sketch by Hindemith *Hin und zurück* (lasts 12 minutes), the 'opera-minute' of Darius Milhaud *L' enlèvement d'Europe* (lasts but nine minutes)."[22] The source of the opera is mysterious for Erich Doflein suggested that "the scene could have been from a short novel by Dostoyevsky."[23] Elena Georgievna Dulova, Mosolov's friend, suggested the idea is from Alexey Tolstoy.[24] However, Barsova is certain that neither Dostoyevsky nor Tolstoy provided Mosolov with his literary inspiration.[25] Barsova writes that it was the writer Kozma Prutkov who presented Mosolov with an absurd dramaturgy more typical of the twentieth century. "Notably, his dramatic works, his *Fantasy*—a one-act comedy along with the operetta in three acts *Cernoslov, sirech Frenolog* and a drama in three acts *Lyubov i Silin*. Christened the 'impartial child of Russian leading democratic satire,' Prutkov trailed behind a rich national culture: the satirical *Fantasy* 'introduces a characteristic quality from the absurd to vaudeville.'[26] "Russian vaudeville assumed diverse aspects of tragedy, comedy, and operetta in the vaudeville conceived by Kozma Prutkov."[27] There exists, moreover, a kinship between Mosolov's work and Hindemith's *Hin und zurück*. Hindemith's piece includes a Professor, Nurse, and Servant Girl, while *The Hero* has a Fencing Professor, a Doctor, and a Servant Girl. There is another association by the occasional use of German words and phrases. One can also see the

Figure 8.1 Mosolov—The Hero (First Page). *Source*: © Copyright 1989 by Universal Edition A.G., Wien.

influence of the farce that became prevalent in the 1920s with Meyerhold's staging of Fernand Crommelynck's *Le Cocu magnifique* portraying—with huge success—a tragic farce in the genre of a utopia.[28]

Mosolov categorized *The Hero* (dedicated to Viktor Belyaev) as a one-act opera for singers and chamber orchestra (one act with three scenes), Op. 28. The final page of the score indicates that it was completed in Moscow on June 18, 1928. The orchestra is for minimum strings, flute, oboe, clarinet in A, horn in f, Trumpet in A, Bass Trombone, Timpani, triangle, Piatti, and Tamburo militare. The orchestration follows much the same size as that for Shostakovich's *The Nose*, written at the same time.

The plot starts with a quarrel followed by the challenge to a duel, which leads to the death of the fencing professor and ending in exaltation by the townsfolk. Barsova writes: "The *Antihero* created by Mosolov—as a tragic farce is like a logical extension to his scenic constructivism." There are two diametrically opposing aspects in the chamber opera. On one side, there is "great intensity, a dramatic symphonic development that is countered by the vaudeville, and banal speech on stage."[29] Unlike Shostakovich, who matured from his constructivism in the 1920s, from *The Nose* to *Lady Macbeth* (*of Mtsensk District*), neither Deshevov's ballet *Ice and Steel* nor Mosolov's *The Hero* progressed because there were no performances. Mosolov's *The Hero* had to wait until 1989 for its first performance in the Soviet Union.[30]

Asafyev expressed sympathy with Mosolov's problems at the Triton music publishers and Muzsektor (which had stopped his music from being published). "Your fate is not to be envied. One wants to help, but I am at a loss. I don't really know because we have also been provoked in our musical affairs. I still don't know how to cope." However, with obstacles mounting at home, Asafyev advised Mosolov to contact the Swiss conductor Hermann Scherchen. "Send your music there and mention my name. Scherchen will definitely be willing to propagandize your work. It is important that he performs something at a radio concert."[31] Hermann Scherchen was the General Music Director at Konigsberg between 1928 and 1931 and one of the most enthusiastic conductors of contemporary music and Soviet compositions. Mosolov's hopes were rewarded for Dzimitrowski writing from Vienna informed him, 'I have just received a letter from Scherchen asking me to grant him the premiere of the (First Piano) Concerto in Germany.'[32]

In commemoration of the tenth anniversary of the October Revolution, in 1927, the Bolshoi Theater offered a commission to Anatoly Alexandrov, Mosolov, Leonid Polovinkin, and Shostakovich to write one-act ballets—*The Four Ages of Moscow*. The notion was to present the city at different historical times; Polovinkin was to portray a scenario set during the reign of Ivan the Terrible in 1567, while Alexandrov was assigned a ballet for the year—1818, while the Civil War in 1919 was to be depicted by Shostakovich, and Mosolov's contribution by Mosolov was to be set in the far-off future. As one could guess from the haphazard nature of the project, neither Mosolov's *Moscow 2117* nor any of the other ballets were ever presented by the Bolshoi Ballet. The failure of this fiasco was unveiled by the RAPM broadsheet. "The artistic council of GATOB (the Bolshoi Theater) has dropped the idea of *The Four Ages of Moscow* ballet because of the libretto's anti-artistic motives dealing with the period of serfdom through to the twentieth century, up to and after the October Revolution."[33] The flawed libretto was not the only shortcoming in the abandoned project, as Marian Koval here wants us to believe,

> It's difficult to discuss Mosolov's music because his composing is almost like a primitive invention of tonality. Mosolov concocts some sort of sound and rhythmic structure, generally quite crude, which both surprises and deafens his audience and is repetitive. Using such means, he proceeds to the next episode using a harsh tonal construction little different from before. That is what is being created by the "left music" of Mosolov. In the fourth act of *The Four Ages of Moscow*, there emerges a remarkably powerful and profusely psychological anguish. The dances of the maidens and young boys show how the composer completely misreads childrens' psyche. One cannot grasp at all why the maidens' first dance, and the dance of the boys in the second scene convey such misery. This performance could be called better the dances of the buffalos. Those present at the audition expressed shock at not finding any modern rhythm, or indeed any pathos in Mosolov's music. But, even if one approaches Mosolov's music properly—where is the composition's lucid intensity? There is nothing. The music is abstract, without any content, and stressful, nor does it stimulate any artistic feelings.[34]

This relates to the audition of the second and fourth acts of the ballet performed on September 28, 1929, at the Beethoven Hall of the Bolshoi Theater from a libretto by Mikhail Boitler and Ivan Aksenov arranged by the conductor Yuri Fayer. Unfortunately, we have no means of evaluating Mosolov's score as both the manuscript and parts are long lost.

THE DAM

After the cancellation at the Bolshoi Theater of his ballet, Mosolov reached a crisis with an embargo on his works. In addition to the ballet, and the rejection of his other music, now another stage work by Mosolov came under fire. The commissioning of which was on the recommendation of the influential Boris Asafyev. The staging was part of a project for new Soviet operas by the Leningrad State Opera Theater. In explaining the suitability of the scenario,

Asafyev wrote on May 30, 1929. "Zadykhin's subject is appropriate because Mosolov is the only composer who can sustain the related issues in juxtaposing a catastrophe with forceful willpower and reason (. . .). Similar to Deshevov, Mosolov is fully prepared enthusiastically—and there is an appropriately strong positivity in the music. I consider—without condition—that we have to award him the third of these commissioned operas.[35] Mosolov will surely work particularly intensively and quickly."[36] Mosolov wrote the five acts between 1929 and 1930.

Mosolov dedicated the opera to Myaskovsky, with a libretto by Yakov L. Zadykhin (initially shared with Lydia Seifullina).[37] However, Mosolov had second thoughts about the opera's title. "The very name *The Dam* doesn't suit its purpose. *Steps of the Third* is much better and evocative."[38] Mosolov had in mind the momentous third year of the first Five-Year Plan—fulfilled two years early. The opera's five acts have ten scenes with the narrative set in the 1920s and 1930s. The scenario portrays the construction of a hydroelectric dam and the relocation of the villagers following the flooding of their village. Despite a breakdown, the workers manage to repair the functioning of the turbines of the new dam.

The libretto caused sharp differences at the plenary of the artistic and political council of the theater—all of which was comprehensively documented in the RAPM press—who accused *The Dam* of "further developing urbanism," and *Proletarian Musician* advocated struggle "against the tendencies of a bourgeois path in the development of Soviet opera." The writer went on to warn of "the danger of a scandalous musical theater taking the side of the reactionary forces."[39] Regardless of the attacks by the RAPM media, in December 1930, the opera went into rehearsal, however it was withdrawn in the spring of 1931. Mosolov himself explains,

> I composed a grandiose scenic presentation—*The Dam* in five acts. The theme is about the construction of an electric power station far-flung in the USSR. The political arts council approved it, and everything was scheduled for performance (in 1930). However, following the appointment of a new director (Comrade Buchstein), the opera was halted, and a first act preview was arranged at which Comrade Kilchevsky (Leningrad RAPM) and Buchstein criticized the opera's music with disparaging demagoguery. What is most thought-provoking is that the opera was halted six weeks before the public preview, and neither the artists, orchestra, nor the conductor were given 50% of the essential musical material. The criticism (of the opera) related only to the first act, and the remaining music was of little interest. It would appear that the Putilov plant comrades were correct when they stated that "no one understands anything, and there is little consideration given for the performance. One has to complete the entire work and only then discuss it." As for myself, I can only say that I do not understand what is going on.[40]

The problems of Mosolov's stage work were neither in the libretto, nor in the plot because the narrative revealed a conflict between the old and new world; the old—represented by the kulak Puschin, and the monk Gavriil, the old woman Sekleteya, her son Ivan, and the village people. The new world wins with the death of Sekleteya, and the arrest of Puschin, Ivan, and Gavriil, allowing the dam to be completed. Mosolov's music clashes frequently with the text and action on stage by creating a subtext in his portrayal of the psychological battle within the opera. Following his practice in *The Hero*, Mosolov uses grotesquely satirical imagery. Vorobyov considers this presentation is a parody of society, having parallels with Musorgsky's *Khovanschina*, and *The Legend of Kitezh* by Rimsky Korsakov.

Yakov Zadykhin's libretto itself is not controversial for it subscribes to the popular themes of the period during industrialization and the building of a new hydroelectric dam in the depths of Siberia. The cast includes builders and workers, and villagers, village women, "brothers and sisters," pioneers, masons, carpenters, and construction workers. The construction engineer Gard and the Bolshevik Party official are taken by actors. The engineer Sharov is a dramatic tenor, while the kulak Puschin is a bass, Sekleteya is a mezzo-soprano, and her son Ivan is a baritone.

Mosolov uses a phonetic and stylistic language that reflects on the abstruse, and crude language used by the constructivists and the futurists of the 1910s and 1920s. There is also an unusual semantics in the names of the opera's leading characters. Each name represents its phonetic symbol of the quintessential function of the person, invoking a kinship with the theater of the absurd developed by Khlebnikov in 1913. Several characters have social masks of a grotesque nature; Puschin is an old Russian name symbolizing a strong character, Gavriil the monk, Sekleteya is a rare name symbolizing the departing world; Sekleteya—skeleton-death; it's not incidental that the pioneer children harass her, "You, old woman, die, and we shall live longer!" The gossips Fefela and Nenela have almost Dada sound-like sounds "fe-fe, ne-ne" like "ba-ba," "be-be," and so on. The "positive" characters have social masks in their names reflecting on abstruse futurology. The name of the chief constructor named Gard signifies importance from the abbreviations such as RAPP, RAPM, and RSFSR at the time. It is associated with decisiveness and an uncompromising nature (Gard-grad-gorod-city) as an image of building or construction. The futurist Khlebnikov devised a phonetic scheme of word meanings, depicting what each letter in a name or word should imply.[41] The meaning of each of the letters G—great vibration A—going against a movement R—the division of property D—movement from one world to another. Vorobyov suggests that the choice of this name conveys the essence of the opera's narrative showing "the tragic division of the old Russia into Soviet Russia and dying Russia?"[42] In the opera, Gard is surrounded by engineers, managers, and party leaders, all of whom play dramatic roles as representatives of the new world, and there is both cynicism and aggression in their voices, and an abstract, intonational musically impersonal nature to their singing.

In his appraisal of Mosolov's opera, Vorobyov explains that "the opera portrays worker's heroism opposed by counter-revolutionary forces, whereby the worker is opposed by a monster. This loose collision of 'good' and 'evil' was wholly egalitarian, accessible without conflict, and hence optimistic (really, all difficulties seemed to be peripheral in the opera). It's not accidental that the industrial art of the 1920s, and at the beginning of the 1930s (theater, cinema, literature), was distinguished by poster art, documentary, and was exaggerated by agitational-propaganda extravagance. Therefore, the dramatic canvass of the work lacked any subtext."[43] The simple plot of the libretto was not matched by a similar musical text for throughout, the music counters the action on stage, there are other characters depicted wholly separate from the singing in the opera, presenting a deeply psychological drama, and a more complex conflict than that between old and new. The Petersburg scholar Vorobyov considers Mosolov did not realize the full consequences of his stage work, and more than likely, could not foresee the result.[44] "The image of the dam acquired terrifying features of some kind of Moloch, the hero of socialist construction seemed to be the destroyer, and the representatives of the old world—not champions, but supplicants. And this is where the composer himself, as was the librettist, on the side of those forces created by them and they were destroying. The contradiction was evident."[45] From an examination of the correspondence between the Deputy Director of the Leningrad Opera Theater K. I. Reingerts and Mosolov, it is apparent—at the beginning of April 1931—that the opera was received positively in the rehearsals. As the final production was drawing closer, the staff of the Leningrad Opera and Ballet Theater wrote a collective letter to Mosolov.[46]

> There is ongoing intensive work on your opera. The colleagues of the theater, everyone is as one and both the artistic and technical personnel decided—whatever happens—to complete the production by the middle of December. To fulfill the set task—we must work at a shock tempo, and all our forces and the whole theater are involved in this work. The least slackening of the tempo, and the least holdup, hinders the schedule of the premiere and contravenes our plan. At present, there appears only the problem of the orchestration of the score. The four acts are presently in production, but we haven't received the final act from you. It would be upsetting, if our common work, in which you—as the author of the opera are taking part—wasn't completed in the agreed timescale because you held back the final orchestrated act. Therefore we appeal to you: if the orchestration isn't ready, then hurry and complete it. Every lost day is important for us. We, shock workers of GATOB call you to our ranks so we can pull our forces

together to fulfill the earliest appearance on the Soviet stage of a Soviet opera. We hope that you respond to our call and join with us in our slogan: Not one hour lost, Not one hour of lethargy, With comradely greetings.[47]

Among those who defended the opera at the artistic council was Shostakovich, "the opera must be staged as soon as possible," an opinion shared by the composers Arseny Gladkovsky, Anatoly Kankarovich, the musicologist Ivan Sollertinsky, and the director Sergey Radlov. Regrettably, the groundswell of criticism from the influential Golovanov and the RAPM members proved overwhelming.[48] The Nemirovich-Danchenko Theater in Moscow offered further possibilities for production, however, because of opposition from the proletarian musicians, the whole project was dropped.[49]

Nevertheless, the failure to stage *The Dam* (and other projects) was because the RAPM was now in control of the artistic councils of the theaters. Alekseyenko writes that this opera reflected the stylistic evolution of Mosolov when he was tortuously mixing different trends in his music. His early style sharply contrasted with attempts to create more positive imagery by responding to social themes of the time. A noticeable aspect in *The Dam* is Mosolov's observance of the Russian opera tradition. This is characterized by the fullness of the characters, in the mass scenes with singing ensembles, choruses, and dramaturgy. Similar to the parallel universe explored in *Khovanschina*, Mosolov presents two different worlds: the building of a new society, and the dying world of Russia.[50] Mosolov uses the style of the grotesque by characterizing figures from the past, and contrasting them with modern voices. This is a methodology used by Stravinsky in *Mavra* (1922), Berg in *Wozzeck* (1927), and Shostakovich in *The Nose* (1928).[51] In *The Dam*, Mosolov uses familiar songs throughout, notably *The Internationale*, the old revolutionary song *Brave, Arise Comrades to Your Feet*, and urban songs. The magnitude of Mosolov's opera was not lost on one musicologist in the city. "Among all the Soviet operas which appeared in the period of 'contemporary' music, certainly, there was not one, that would have compensated most for all the most negative aspects of the movement, as *The Dam* by A. Mosolov."[52]

SYNOPSIS OF *THE DAM*

Act One opens in the evening forest with a mill on stage, and construction work can be heard in the distance. Polya enters and sings of her difficult life with husband and father-in-law, dreaming of a brighter life. Sharov, an engineer enters from hunting in the forest, and both he and Polya look at the peasants bearing candles praying for destruction of the dam. Sharov takes Polya's hands, and sings that people don't understand that the dam will benefit everyone. Ivan, Polya's husband, appears and seeing her with Sharov questions her what she is up to. Fefela prophesizes the taking of their land and the victory of the AntiChrist communists. Darkness falls as the prayer transcends into a poignant dance. Scene two is set at night. The riverbank, forest, and overhanging cliffs. The dam workers are at work. Floodlights. Bura complains that Serega's father is a kulak opposed to the construction of the dam. Serega sings, "Father and I are on different paths." A great locomotive steams away in the foreground. Sharov reads a declaration by the chief constructor Gard. "Construction transfers to the main task—work on the main structure—to install the sluices." Everyone is happy and sings an upbeat song accompanied by a balalaika, followed by dancing. Sharov sees a gloomy Ivan and tells him that Sekleteya, and he have to leave the mill because it's going to be flooded. Ivan replies, "We will see who is who." Serega and Podduzhny sing boldly about a young engineer girl, and everyone is cheerful at work.

Act Two. The scene opens in the collective farm office. Above hangs a banner "Electrification plus Soviet power—this is communism." Village girls sing about love. A meeting is prepared to resolve the villagers' evacuation. Serega appears with an accordion and plays a quadrille. Podduzhny enters and a pioneer group is heard beating drums, singing "Hey! Aye, We are Pioneers, New life, new beginnings!" The scene becomes full of people. Polya is upset, she doesn't know what to do, to leave home or stay with Ivan. The majority of villagers are against evacuation. Sekleteya tries to oppose the evacuation, but the pioneers cry out "We ask the old granny not to interfere." Serega throws water over the drunken Yepishka, everyone laughs, and Serega sings about leaving to begin a new life. The voting begins and there is a majority for evacuation. Sekleteya leads the old women and men away to pray. Polya and Ivan join them. Second scene. Gard's office. A great window. Engineers are crowded around the small table. The party leader enters with Bura. They discuss possible sabotage on the dam construction. Sharov enters with Sekleteya and others. She pleads for the fields not to be flooded. Gard answers saying that factories will depend on the dam in the bright future. Evacuation is necessary and compensation will be given. Sekleteya warns the dam will be destroyed. "We don't want to see your dam!" Gard sends a telegram requesting extra security. Sharov and Gard go to the window watching the lights of the construction singing: "A poor silly old woman."

Act Three. Late night. Floodlights shine on the construction site. Sharov is worried because of problems with the dam. The workers gossip about mistakes by the head engineer. Water is leaking and Ivan doesn't respond with help of his rescue brigade, and he is sacked. A fault causes a catastrophe, the workers flee. Sharov tries to stem the flow of the leak. Ivan pulls levers and Sharov falls into the water. Gard arrives and stops the panic. Second scene. Early morning. Riverbank. Yepishka is fishing. He regrets the loss of his river to the dam. Suddenly, he sees the unconscious Sharov in the water. Polya appears and seeing Sharov realizes that she loves him. Yepishka decides to hide Sharov in the forest because of his guilt for the accident.

Act Four. At Puschin's home. The granary. The men are singing. "Today is the day of Saint Vlasya and the dam is breached. Let everyone get merry and sing." Sekleteya enters. She is happy and today she says it's not sinful to drink. Yepishka runs in, "The dam is repaired. The water is breached again." Fefela and Nenela enter and tell of seeing Sharov and Polya in the forest. Ivan runs off into the forest. The merrymaking continues amid wild dancing. Second scene. The forest. A clearing. A hut. Polya looks at her beloved Sharov. Sharov comes to and wonders what happened and why Polya is beside him. Ivan runs in and tries to shoot Sharov. Polya stops him and the bullet hits Ivan instead. Polya weeps over her dying husband, but Ivan tells her "I took care of him," saying that he pushed Sharov into the water. Sekleteya, Yepishka, and the others enter and Sharov is taken away while Sekleteya weeps over her dead son.

Act Five. The workers are working at the dam. Its break time. It's very hot. Bura tells the party leader and the engineer that in a month or two, the dam will be finished. Sekleteya enters. She falls to her feet and mourns that despite losing her son, she will fight the anti-christ to her death. She plunges into the river and drowns. Interlude. The dam. The water flows through the sluices. Fefela and Nenela stand on the clifftop. They are burning. Sekleteya is no more. Gavriil and Puschin have been arrested by the GPU. "Where do they get strength from? There is only one way—to pray in the sacred house." Scene two. The hydroelectric dam. A square. An amateur band is playing. Banners hang: "Electrification plus Soviet power—this is communism!" Everyone is pale and sad. Schur and the party leader enter in a radiant mood. The peasants have to come out. Although there is a proletarian dictatorship there is a place for the peasants. The workers sing "The International," followed by the peasants. The meeting begins. Gard congratulates everyone on the successful completion of the dam. He switches on the power. The lights illuminate the scene, and everyone is triumphant. Polya and Sharov are in the crowd. Gard sings. "We are little pieces of dust in the big wide world. And we've made energy benefit us. All by your sweat, will, and labor! Shall we stop moving forward?" General festivities and dancing close the opera.

The significance of the opera is raised by Vorobyov writing that *The Dam* "was the last major work wholly associated with the aesthetics of the Russian avant-garde. This relationship was not only in a distinctive musical language but in the daring and inflexibility with which Mosolov synthesized different genre images."[53] The opera uses sound effects familiar from works by Avraamov, Satie, Russolo, Varèse, Shostakovich, and Deshevov in both technical innovations, and unconventional instruments to show everyday sound effects. "There was also a trend to introduce neo-musical speech in operas by Prokofiev, Schoenberg, Shostakovich, Stravinsky, and Berg by terminating the anti-romantic rethinking of opera as a musical genre."[54]

Expanding on the avant-garde stage works of the period, Vorobyov writes, "Opera based on an industrial subject is a means of curbing the romantic emphasis: the musical dynamics should not contrast with the dynamics of the action. Hence, realism, even natural effects, especially factory whistles, clarion calls, telephone ringing, explosions, and including dramatic actors as performers, and in the finale, the sound of an amateur band playing on their untuned instruments, and ultimately the cinema."[55] Meyerhold believed that the theater should "mobilize all accessible means to achieve the greatest agitational feeling on the audience."[56] As we now know, *The Dam* was canceled, and the score and parts lay in the archive of the Mariinsky Theater, until the opera was performed at the Music Theater of St. Petersburg Conservatoire in March 2012 during the "From the Avant-Garde to Our Times" festival.[57]

Regardless of the debacle of Mosolov's ballets and operas, there remained strong support for Mosolov as more commissions arrived at his door. Shortly after the disappointment over *The Dam*, Mosolov composed the incidental music for the Young Pioneers Rally at the Moscow Dynamo stadium on August 25, 1929. This event took the form of the futurist inspired demonstrations from the post-1917 years. Mosolov collaborated with the artist Valentina Mikhailovna Khodasevich and the Leningrad-based theater director Sergey Ernestovich Radlov. Khodasevich explains that "Radlov hurriedly wrote the scenario when we started work on it. At the Meyerhold Theater (when the company was touring), they prepared a creative management center. Together with Radlov, Meyerhold's young assistants helped in directing everyone."[58] Mosolov's incidental music was heard in the "construction" movement when three thousand Pioneers formed a five-pointed star. According to Khodasevich, "the star shuddered: at first they held up their hands, from which there emerged the celebratory musical symphony, and slowly, and triumphantly (the star) rose still higher and higher to grow, with factory horns, amid multi-staged factory groups in windows (. . .) the terrible cacophony sounds of strange roaring and shrieks' under which there flew into the air the colossal images of the enemy: Chiang Kai-shek, Mussolini, the Archbishop of Canterbury, and Lord Baden-Powell."[59] Mosolov's musical contribution is long lost, and only reminiscences allow us an impression of this event. Of course, this style has its origins in the futurist movement blending poster art, music, and movement. After this ostentatious success, on June 15, 1930, Mosolov was invited to work at the Moscow Radio Centre. Mosolov spent only a few weeks in post.

RAILS RINGING

It is remarkable that in parallel with *The Dam*, Mosolov worked on another stage work based on a play by Semyon Kirshon, *Rails Ringing* commissioned by the Second Belorussian Drama Theater in Gomel. Sergey G. Rozanov, the artistic director of the Drama Theater himself produced the opera libretto.[60] The proposal was for music to be shared among Alexandrov, Polovinkin, Starokadomsky, Oransky, Mosolov, and Milyutin. The suggestion was for separate episodes portraying a satirical parody with Gypsy, English foxtrot, and related sound effects.[61] Mosolov's music uses unconventional glissandos on trombones, plucking on strings, and typically rude blasts on the brass. This show was part of the pervasive popular crusade mocking the "beautiful world" of NEP in Russia. For example, in the episode *Mine No. 3*, the song "the worker John was simple" was modified for the Soviet public.[62] Mosolov responded, "Forgive me for delaying my music for *Rails*. I have tried to do as you wish; I have used all sorts of modern songs—and it has come out brilliantly! I beg you not to think about how it sounds on the piano—just wait to hear the orchestral rehearsal. It's a pity that I won't hear or see either music, or the play itself, and visually experience my composition of theater music."[63] After the premiere on December 31, 1928, Rozanov in rather a mixed fashion wrote to Mosolov regarding his music. "It is not entirely coherent but is quite good in parts, particularly the finale, the bells, and Vasily's dream. But where is the continuation of 'the dream' (or dreams?) Vasily is not complete. The Cheteka (Georgian dance) is also not bad. However, the foxtrot as a parody is distasteful. The song is excellent. The public happened to like it. On any account, your work is acceptable."[64] This rather unequivocal appraisal cannot be judged as the music suffered the fate of so many of Mosolov's works of the period and is missing.

The Russian scholar Nikolay Alekseyenko makes the point that "at the beginning of the 1930s, there entered a period of storm and stress in Mosolov's work, he made a sharp break from his earlier writing and began a new, self-contradictory style from the past. (. . .) The stylistic accent taken by Mosolov in the 1930s affected all his future creativity."[65]

What caused this sharp creative transformation? One specific reason was the role played by the partisan criticism from RAPM. However, there were subjective reasons for this development. This metamorphosis was also a response to the arts and the push toward clarity and simplicity in the 1930s. It appears that Mosolov felt an organic necessity to find another form of musical expression. In any account, Mosolov sustained a high degree of professionalism and masterly technique. The feeling to the actuality in time which molded Mosolov's music in the 1920s did not desert him because much of the music he was writing in the 1930s fitted in with contemporary Soviet music.

If there was a mixed success in performances in the Soviet Union, it was quite different in the West where Mosolov was becoming more popular following performance of *The Foundry* at the ISCM festival in Liege in 1930.[66] According to *Anbruch* of Vienna, Mosolov's *The Foundry* was "performed with sensational success all over the world."[67] Constructivism had found its incarnation in the freshly written compositions of Deshevov and Mosolov, who used "instruments" such as corrugated sheet metal, whistles, and saucepans as well as "prepared" pianos to evoke the aural environment of the machine age in their music.[68]

The "new Soviet music" was becoming more experimental by employing avant-garde orchestration and Shostakovich, Knipper, and Deshevov were matching the diversity of instrumentation for different ensembles. The artistic radicalism in Mosolov's constructivism and Georgy Rimsky-Korsakov's work with microtones was more than matched by the creative conservatism of such prominent figures as Myaskovsky and Gëdike.[69] Mosolov was the outstanding figure of new Russian music whose latest compositions epitomized the revolution and fresh innovative ideas in twentieth-century art. An indication of this was that Mosolov was praised by his colleagues for gaining international recognition at the ISCM concerts.[70] This was quite opposite to the position of the RAPM who dismissed Mosolov as being "utterly alien to our Soviet reality."[71]

In the 1930s, the stylistic change in Mosolov's writing was as much a consequence of maturity and a reflection of the changing status quo. Nevertheless, numerous traits of the young Mosolov would continue to appear, including some of the devices he employed in his earliest pieces. As we know, several important pieces were lost for different reasons, and as Rimsky writes the 1930s were worrying for only three major pieces remain from this decade and much of the blame may be placed at the door of the composer himself, for he made little attempt to preserve his work. "It is surprising how a creatively industrious Mosolov could not be concerned about his personal archives. Several have been preserved—it appears—without any thanks to the composer."[72]

Among the new pieces which suffered from Mosolov's lack of attention was the Piano Concerto No. 2. The work was well received and enjoyed some success when it was premiered on April 21, 1932, with the composer at the keyboard, under Leonid Polovinkin at the Large Hall of the Moscow Conservatoire. However, only the first movement and part of the finale remain from the three movements—*Difiramb*, *Serenada*, and *March*.[73] We know from contemporary reviews however that the concerto is dominated by one theme throughout, which is sustained by a typically mechanical rhythm emphasizing the piano's potential and versatility as a percussion instrument;

Mosolov makes use of Kirghiz folk music, tone clusters, ostinato, and polytonality. As one might expect from an increasingly hostile media, Mosolov's latest piece was judged negatively,

> The main feature in the concerto appears to be the extraordinary staticity and restraint in its musical construction. (...) It is characteristic that one theme proceeds not from its inner development, but is repeated, and becomes quite simply tiresome ... the use of the piano ... mainly ... proceeds to a unison duplicated orchestral part which is "buoyed" by embellished passages ... the use of which is repeatedly like a "percussion" instrument, and in Mosolov's searching for any possible trickery (like for example, the never-ending *glissando* of the trombone in the first movement), which is accentuated by some offensive and unacceptable bourgeois creativity thrust upon our ears.[74]

If his music was misunderstood or poorly received at home, in the West Mosolov was still good box office for the Piano Concerto No. 2—with Mosolov at the keyboard—was scheduled for a European premiere on October 27, 1933, by the Vienna Concert Orchestra under I. Bortnikov. However, this never took place owing to the failure by the composer to get a visa.[75] As we will discover later, there may have been a specific cause for this denial. Certainly, matters were changing in regard to a pause in cooperation with foreign agencies by the Soviet authorities. We do not know of the specific trigger for this cancellation; however, a letter to Mosolov by Abram Dzimitrowski of Universal Edition in Vienna enlightens us on the difficulties which had now developed in Mosolov's career.

Deeply respected Alexander Vasilyevich!

> I still haven't received answers from my letters to Arkadyev, Chernyavsky, Raysky, Goldenweiser and others. Approaches to the local embassy and personal contacts haven't led to any response. As you may be assured, in the advance publicity you are programmed as the soloist. I have requests for you from Paris and Milan. My letter to you of 25 August hasn't been answered either. You see, from one angle, I want to work intensively, and I am sure this exchange of artists will lead to good results, from another angle, it's not a particularly pleasant posture from those people who received me so well there (in Moscow). I don't understand what is going on. In any case, I do not intend to continue in these circumstances, when there is such an attitude to affairs from people who should be interested in this upcoming work. Now concerning you: I must print the posters and publish the media propaganda by the 24th of this month. If I don't have an answer by then—sad as it is for me—I shall have to cancel the program, and am

afraid that it will not be so easy to find the opportunity abroad for your performances. I am sorry and unhappy about this—after such good beginnings—this much expected cultural work is now being destroyed through some unknown factor, and is being shattered through the unbusinesslike irresponsibility of the people on whom it all depends.[76]

Nevertheless, despite this failure, Dzimitrowski continued to arrange performances of Mosolov's music, the last correspondence to the composer is dated in 1935 and relates to a successful performance of Mosolov's "Turkmenian Nights" in Brussels, and moreover, he asks Mosolov to write a new Piano Trio.[77] A sign of the times was a statement by Platon Kerzhentsev at a meeting of the Composers Union. 'When Comrade Prokofiev said that they like, (in the West the music of) Mosolov, Popov or Shostakovich, this doesn't serve as proof of the outstanding qualities of these composers and even more so doesn't demonstrate the revolutionary aspects of their works.'[78]

LES CLOCHES DE CORNEVILLE

Mosolov's orchestration for the revival of a French 'opera-comique' earned him an unexpected endorsement. The new production of Robert Planquette's *Les Cloches de Corneville* premiered on November 19, 1932, at the Nemirovich-Danchenko Theater in Moscow. Mosolov introduced jazz rhythms and other "innovations" into the instrumentation of this nineteenth-century operetta. The new scoring was so successful that the revived stage work enjoyed 250 performances in the theater's touring all over the country. The old libretto was rewritten by V. G. Zak and V. M. Inber transforming the Marquise Henry de Cornville into a director, author, principal actor, and director of the wandering troupe. Jean-Baptist Villiers sought a theater of tragedy and satire; the wealthy farmer Gaspar became an abbot and castle owner, his daughter Serpoletta—the prima donna of the troupe, and his niece Germaine—an orphan and the student of the abbot is a sadist and there is a womanizing town mayor. The updated version allowed for a new scenario giving a social aspect and a morally incorruptible character appropriate to modern Soviet life, as is mentioned here in a documentary about the theater's productions of the 1930s by the theater historian Pyotr Markov.

> The theater not only created its own version but gave the music a fresh orchestral sound. Mosolov reorchestrated *Les Cloches* by excising incomplete developments in musical fragments. Through his extraordinary ingenuity, Mosolov (as

a composer) is wholly different from (the composer) Planquette, but in general, is fitting for nineteenth-century opera-comique. The steadfast urbanist was drawn to the technique of orchestral perfection, and Mosolov has transformed the modest Planquette into a composer of irony in our times and with instruments unknown to Planquette. More than which—he used them to color his ironic relationship to Planquette, and the subject of the comedy. The glissando of trombones, unexpected syncopations, and rhythmic dissonances is mixed with the prosaic and light accompaniment of Planquette. This fresh stylization in orchestration destroyed the clarity of musical construction, and it depended heavily on the vocal sketches. The experience of the music of *Les Cloches,* was accurate in one part, but seemed quite false in others.[79]

The reviews were dissimilar in their praise:

I consider that Mosolov has taken the correct path by painting fresh, contemporary hues to Planquette's music. The glissandos of muted trombones and muted trumpets resembled characters on stage. The voices remained in one's memory as one listened to their tête-à-têtes. There was so much positivity from the composer in his prominent saxophone melodies. The sharply vibrant tenor-saxophone was magnificent. Numerous contributions from the rarely used xylophone, and penny whistle, and instruments in jazz, modest by any means, and long since gone from modernist orchestration.[80]

The popular *Komsomolskaya Pravda* was not so upbeat:

With the tastelessly naïve musical "delights" of *Les Cloches de Corneville,* Mosolov has supplied a blend of jazz orchestration, using all the innovative methods of musical "greasepaint." This has given him a triumph right across the board. But what has resulted is diametrically opposite to what the producers of the show wanted and has taken the show to themes—which make it more distant in its societal context.[81]

As one could expect, there was criticism of the jazz rhythms, "the roaring and boisterous noises are beyond comprehension. (. . .) This is unnecessary nonsense and does not enhance our music."[82] The production involved the country's finest artists—Ostroumov, Kemarskaya, Orlova, Kuznetsova, and Kandelaki toured Leningrad, Odesa, Kharkiv, and Donetsk. The conductors were Grigory Stolyarov and the young Kirill Kondrashin. Nadezhda Kemarskaya wrote that the production enjoyed an affinity with both audiences and singers.

The format was based on discussions between Vladimir Nemirovich-Danchenko and the dramatist and translator Mikhail Petrovich Galperin. The veteran theater director Vladimir Nemirovich-Danchenko was excited by the staging in one of the last great theatrical productions of the decade. Mosolov dedicated a waltz to Kemarskaya in the third act for her characterization of Serpoletta.[83] The scenarist Vera Inber wrote to Mosolov. "Dear Alexander Vasilyevich, I am sending you the texts, almost all of them. There is no Germaine No. 10 (it is already written, but needs to be corrected). There is also the Quintet and part of the Villiers Waltz. But you don't really need all this. Phone me tomorrow in the morning—or today after three. I will give you all the material. I don't have any copies, so don't lose them. Greetings, Vera Inber."[84] It would appear from Inber's last phrase that Mosolov's habit of losing his music was well known to many in the Moscow music world.

TRAVELS TO CENTRAL ASIA

One of the changes in Mosolov was his attraction to folklore from the Central Asian republics in a search for fresh themes for his music and perhaps for different means of expression. Mosolov had already used a Turkmen folk theme in his Fifth Piano Sonata in 1925, the Turkmen Suite for Piano, and in his First String Quartet. The mounting allure to the colors and modulations of ethnic music encouraged Mosolov to follow the example of Bartók and he traveled to Central Asia to study local folk music.

In 1931, he spent part of the summer in Kirghizia, and he repeated the experience in 1932 by an extended voyage including again Kirghizia.[85] While he was there, owing to additional assignments, we know from his contract that the expedition was extended, from August 31, he went "to Dagestan, Odesa, Tbilisi, and Yerevan filming a picture *Advance* about socialist reconstruction in the Dagestan mountains."[86] Unfortunately, the film project ended in a fiasco, leaving him in dispute with the authorities. This was not the last in a series of conflicts that ultimately blighted his career. Mosolov worked side by side with the former RAPM activist Boris Shekhter (and Myaskovsky pupil) on the orchestral piece *Turkmenian Suite* (1932),[87] which was for some time considered the almost perfect model of the "East-Western" synthesis in music.[88]

According to documents, Mosolov later participated in making a film in Turkmeniya.[89] Mosolov wrote: "I went on a working trip to Turkmenia (1935), but having lived there half a year, I argued with the management and returned to Moscow."[90] There were pieces which were lost, among which was an orchestral piece *Uzbek Dances* (1935) mentioned in a letter from Myaskovsky to Prokofiev.[91] On leaving Baku by train to Moscow Mosolov left behind on the platform a yellow suitcase containing many of his scores, and despite efforts, the suitcase has never been found.

In 1936, Mosolov again went to work in Central Asia, the occasion on this visit was—as he wrote to Myaskovsky—he had signed a contract for a Turkmen musical drama, and in a bizarre glimpse of his witty humor was anecdotally involved in "discussions on Turkmen musical motives in the Spanish language."[92] There was also a proposal for a new stage work—*The Stone Guest* at the Ashkhabad Drama Russian Theater. On his travels, Mosolov was issued with a Browning revolver, then standard practice in regions where safety was not always guaranteed. "I traveled to Kirghizia," and made arrangements of some 100 Kirghiz songs (several have been published).[93] Following the brilliant success of his youth—both at home and abroad—in the 1930s, much was expected of Alexander Mosolov who had managed to embrace new means of expression in diverse genres—a cloud, however, soon fell upon him which caused the great cataclysm of his career.

NOTES

1. Frolova-Walker, Marina, *Music and Soviet Power 1917–1932*, Oxford: Boydell, 2017, 199.
2. Barsova, Inna, "Rannee tvorchestva a. Mosolova," *A.V. Mosolov, Statii i Vospominanii*, Moscow: Kompositor, 1986, 88.
3. Glebov, Igor, 'Russkaya simfonicheskaya muzika za 10 let' *Muzika i Revolutsiya*, No. 11, 1927, 23.
4. The Stradivari ensemble was regarded as the leading quartet of the period composed of B. M. Simsky, B. Y. Vitkin, G.S. Gamburg, and V. L. Kubatsky.
5. Uglov, A., "Tsikl Stradivariuses," *Izvestiya*, March 20, 1927.
6. Hakobian, Leon, *Music of the Soviet Era*, London: Routledge, 2017, 46.
7. *Sovremennaya Muzika*, 1927, No. 24, 47.
8. Letter to Dzimitrowski to Mosolov July 11, 1927, Nina Meshko archive, *Sovetskaya Muzyka*, July 1989, 86.
9. "Kvartet A. Mosolova na festivale internationalovo obshestva sovremmennaya muziki vo Frankfurte," *Sovremennaya Muzika*, No. 24, 1927, 47.
10. Diary of Derzhanovsky of July 29, 1927 (GTSMMK, f.3, inv. No. 1640, ed. khr. 23, l. 2).
11. Hakobian, Leon, *Music of the Soviet Era*, London: Routledge, 2017, 46.
12. Barsova, Inna, "Rannee tvorchestva a. Mosolova," *A.V. Mosolov, Statii i Vospominanii*, Moscow: Kompositor, 1986, 97.
13. Letter Mosolov to Asafyev October 1, 1928. Nina Meshko archive, *Sovetskaya Muzyka*, July 1989, 86.
14. In the publication by G. B. Bernandt *Opera dictionary* the date of July 15, 1928, in Baden-Baden is erroneous, 1962, 364.
15. Preisner, E., "Festival Kamerny muziki v Baden-Baden," *Muzikalnovo obrazovaniye*, No. 45, 1928, 46.
16. Vorobyov, Sinaiskaya, *Kompositori Russkovo Avangarda*, St. Petersburg: Kompositor, 2007, 142.

17. Hakobian, Leon, *Music of the Soviet Era*, London: Routledge, 2017, 46.
18. Dzimitrowski to Mosolov, June 1, 1929.
19. Nina Meshko archive, *Sovetskaya Muzyka*, July 1989, 86.
20. Nina Meshko archive, *Sovetskaya Muzyka*, July 1989, 86.
21. Barsova, Inna, "Rannee tvorchestva a. Mosolova," *A.V. Mosolov, Statii i Vospominanii*, Moscow: Kompositor, 1986, 99.
22. Barsova, "Rannee tvorchestva a. Mosolova," *A.V. Mosolov, Statii i Vospominanii*, Moscow: Kompositor, 1986, 99.
23. Doflein E., (Freiburg i[n] Br[eislau]), "Kammeroper," *Melos*, 1928, H.7, s. 338.
24. Dulova E., manuscript Mosolov, 99.
25. Barsova, Inna, "Rannee tvorchestva a. Mosolova," *A.V. Mosolov, Statii i Vospominanii*, Moscow: Kompositor, 1986, 99.
26. Zaslavsky, D.I., "Kozma Prutkov i 'Sovremennik," *Sochineniya Kozmy Prutkova*, Moscow, 1955, 5.
27. Barsova, Inna, "Rannee tvorchestva a. Mosolova," *A.V. Mosolov, Statii i Vospominanii*, Moscow: Kompositor, 1986, 99.
28. Turovskaya, M., *Sochineniya Kozmy Prutkova*, Moscow, 1955.
29. Vorobyov, Sinaiskaya, *Kompositori Russkovo Avangarda*, St. Petersburg: Kompositor, 2007, 144.
30. Barsova, Inna, "Rannee tvorchestva a. Mosolova," *A.V. Mosolov, Statii i Vospominanii*, Moscow: Kompositor, 1986, 97–99.
31. Asafyev letter to Mosolov, December 15, 1928, *Sovetskaya Muzyka*, July 1989, 86.
32. A letter of June 10, 1929, Nina Meshko archive, *Sovetskaya Muzyka*, July 1989, 86.
33. *Proletarsky Muzikant*, No. 4, 1929, 40.
34. *Proletarsky Muzikant*, No. 5, 1929, 30–31.
35. Here reference is to the operas *Ice and Steel* by Deshevov and that by Mikhail Yudin which was never completed—author.
36. Otsyv B.V. Asafyeva ob eskizakh oper M Yudina i A. Mosolova khranitsya v LGALI (f. 4463, op. 1, ed. khr. 1210, l. 96-96 ob.).
37. Documents on libretto and staging of '*The Dam*' from February 18 to 27, 1930, LGALI, f.4463, op. 1, ed. khr. 1204.
38. Mosolov letter to Nikolayev May 19, 1930. Central Music Library of Mariinsky Theatre.
39. Kilchevsky, V., "Na Leningradsky front," *Proletarsky muzikant*, No. 2, 1931, 34.
40. Mosolov letter to Stalin, *Sovetskaya Muzika*, No. 7, 1989, 89.
41. Khlebnikov, Velimir, "Khudozhniki Mira!" *Tvoreniya*, Moscow: Sovetsky pisatel, 1987.
42. Vorobyov, Igor, *Russkiye avangarda i tvorchestvo Alexandra Mosolova 1920–1930 godov*, 2006, St. Petersburg: Kompositor, 129.
43. Vorobyov, Sinaiskaya, *Kompositori Russkovo Avangarda*, St. Petersburg: Kompositor, 2007, 146.

44. Vorobyov, Sinaiskaya, *Kompositori Russkovo Avangarda*, St. Petersburg: Kompositor, 2007, 146.
45. Vorobyov, Sinaiskaya, *Kompositori Russkovo Avangarda*, St. Petersburg: Kompositor, 2007, 147.
46. Letter from the direction of the GATOB brigade to Mosolov of November 8, 1930—Archive of Nina Meshko.
47. November 8, 1930, Brigade of GATOB, Vorobyov, Sinaiskaya, *Kompositori Russkovo Avangarda*, St. Petersburg: Kompositor, 2007, 147–148.
48. Kilchevsky, V., *Proletarsky Muzikant*, No. 2, 1930, 34.
49. Alekseyenko, N., "O tvorchestve A. V. Mosolova, tridtsatii-semidesyatikh godakh," *A.V. Mosolov, Statii i Vospominanii*, Moscow: Kompozitor, 1986, 125–129.
50. Alekseyenko, N., "O tvorchestve A. V. Mosolova, tridtsatii-semidesyatikh godakh," *A.V. Mosolov, Statii i Vospominanii*, Moscow: Kompozitor, 1986, 129.
51. Alekseyenko, N., "O tvorchestve A. V. Mosolova, tridtsatii-semidesyatikh godakh," *A.V. Mosolov, Statii i Vospominanii*, Moscow: Kompozitor, 1986, 131.
52. Bogdanov-Berezovsky, V., *Sovetsky Opera*, Leningrad, 1940.
53. Vorobyov, Igor, *Russkiye avangarda i tvorchestvo Alexandra Mosolova 1920–1930 godov*, St. Petersburg: Kompozitor, 2006, 187.
54. Vorobyov, Igor, *Russkiye avangarda i tvorchestvo Alexandra Mosolova 1920–1930 godov*, St. Petersburg: Kompozitor, 2006, 188–189.
55. Vorobyov, Igor, *Russkiye avangarda i tvorchestvo Alexandra Mosolova 1920–1930 godov*, St. Petersburg: Kompozitor, 2006, 189.
56. Meyerhold from Volovik I. O., "O Massovykh muzykalnyy deystvakh 20 x godax," *Sovetskaya Muzyka*, No. 1, 1976, 90.
57. This production, albeit with cuts and music by Yevgeny Petrov is available on YouTube: https://www.youtube.com/watch?v=6jI_n7f-1oQ.
58. Khodasevich, T., "Massoviyiy deistvi, zrelischa i prazdniki," *Teatr*, No. 4, 1967, 12–19.
59. Khodasevich, T., "Massoviyiy deistvi, zrelischa i prazdniki," *Teatr*, No. 4, 1967, 12–19.
60. The theater is now called the Belarus State Drama Theater named after Yan Kolas—author.
61. Letter from Rozanov to Mosolov November 7, 1928. RGALI f.1408, op. 1. Ed .khr. 248, l. 1–2.
62. 'Mine No. 3' is a song by V. Y. Kruchenin from texts by P. D. German 'He was a miner, a simple worker.'
63. Letter Mosolov to Rozanov December 5, 1928, RGALI f.1408, op. 1, ed. khr. 339, l. 1.
64. Rozanov to Mosolov January 22, 1929, RGALI f.1408, op. 1, ed. khr. 248, l. 4.
65. Alekseyenko, N., "O tvorchestve A. V. Mosolova, tridtsatii-semidesyatikh godakh," *A.V. Mosolov, Statii i Vospominanii*, Moscow, 1986, 123–125.
66. Schwartz, Boris, *Music and Musical life in Soviet Russia 1917–1981*, Bloomington: Indiana UP, 1983, 50.
67. *Anbruch*, 1931, XIII, 23.

68. Nelson, Amy, *Music for the Revolution: Musicians and Power in Early Soviet Russia*, Pennsylvania UP, 2004, 41–42.
69. Nelson, Amy, *Music for the Revolution: Musicians and Power in Early Soviet Russia*, Pennsylvania UP, 2004, 50.
70. Nelson, Amy, *Music for the Revolution: Musicians and Power in Early Soviet Russia*, Pennsylvania UP, 2004, 167.
71. Bugoslavsky, Sergey, "Bloknot muzykanta," *Zhizn iskusstsv*, No. 6, 1925, 11.
72. Rimsky, L., "A.V. Mosolov: biographicheskii ocherk," *A.V. Mosolov, Statii i Vospominanii*, Moscow: Kompositor, 1986, 22.
73. GTSMMK, f.3 inv. 2366. Poster in the archive of Derzhanovsky.
74. Kryukov, N., "Kompositori na pereputi," *Sovetskoye Iskusstvo*, May 9, 1932, No. 21.
75. Rimsky, L., "A.V. Mosolov: biographicheskii ocherk," *A.V. Mosolov, Statii i Vospominanii*, Moscow: Kompositor, 1986, 23.
76. Letter from Abram Dzimitrowski to Mosolov, September 15, 1933. Rimsky, *Perepiska Mosolova*, Moscow: Sovetsky Kompositor, 1982, 73.
77. Vorobyov, Igor, *Russkiye avangarda i tvorchestvo Alexandra Mosolova 1920–1930 godov*, St. Petersburg: Kompositor, 2006, 213.
78. *Prokofiev o Prokofiev: Statii, interviews*, Moscow: Sovetsky kompositor, 1991, 156.
79. Markov, P., *Vl. I. Nemirovich-Danchenko i muzikalnovo teatra evo imeni*, Moscow, 1937, 128.
80. Gabrilovich, E., "Udacha spectacle," *Sovetskoye Iskusstvo*, December 3, 1932.
81. Tirs, K., "Corneville kolokola," Teatr imeni Nemirovich-Danchenko, *Komsomolskaya Pravda*, November 30, 1932.
82. Mchelin, V., "Kultura operetta," *Sovetskoye Iskusstvo*, December 3, 1932.
83. Rimsky, L., Mosolov, 27. From an interview with Kemarskaya. The concert was April 4, 1933, and also included *The Foundry* conducted by Polovinkin.
84. Nina Meshko archive, *Sovetskaya Muzyka*, July 1989, 86.
85. Archive of Nina Meshko a letter from Atovmyan asking for use of a browning revolver for his projected tour to the southern republics.
86. Document of contract from Vostok film Nersessov.
87. Hakobian, Leon, *Music of the Soviet Era*, London: Routledge, 2017, 94.
88. Zukkerman, 1936, quoted in Rimsky, Perepiska A.V. Mosolova, materialy i dokumenty iz evo arkhiva, *Iz proshlovo muzikalnovo kultury*, vyp. 3, Moscow: Kompositor, 1982, 12.
89. Archive of SK USSR, lichnoye dela No. 374, l. 8. No other documents exist.
90. Archive SSK USSR, lichnoye dela No. 84, l. 46.
91. December 6, 1935, Perepiska, 444.
92. Rimsky, L., "A.V. Mosolov: biographicheskii ocherk," *A.V. Mosolov, Statii i Vospominanii*, Moscow, 1986, 28.
93. Handwritten notes by Mosolov from March 1938—Nina Meshko archive, *Sovetskaya Muzyka*, July 1989, 87.

Chapter 9

Trial and Renewal

In the 1930s, according to his widow, Mosolov said that he could no longer write as in the past because he had changed his form of musical thinking.[1] This could be through maturity in style as much as a change in his circumstances, as discussed in the previous chapter, and we know that there were similar transformations in the styles of both Shostakovich and Prokofiev during this decade.

The infamous 1936 critique in *Pravda* on Shostakovich's stage works occurred when, according to Schwartz, both Roslavets and Mosolov "were silenced, Myaskovsky and Shcherbachov had become middle-of-the-road composers, Knipper and Deshevov had turned to realist music."[2] Certainly, in discussions at the Composers Union branches in Moscow and Leningrad, it was Mosolov, Popov, and Heinrich Litinsky who were mentioned most often regarding their controversial musical styles.[3] Mosolov had already suffered through both non-publication and few performances of his music, and now he felt obliged to appeal over the heads of his determined opponents. In the first weeks of 1932, following another series of media attacks from the RAPM, the mood of depression so afflicted Mosolov that he thought the only outlet for his music was in the West. It seemed there were no prospects for his music to be heard; there was no alternative for him but to leave and seek assistance from the highest authority in the land. This was upon the advice of several colleagues, notably the musicologist Viktor Belyaev and the composer Vissarion Shebalin.

MOSOLOV'S APPEAL TO STALIN

There already existed a precedent for aggrieved members of the arts appealing to Stalin. On March 28, 1930, the distinguished writer and playwright Mikhail Bulgakov asked to get his plays staged again in Moscow, and a year later, in June 1931, Yevgeny Zamyatin, the Leningrad satirist, wrote to Stalin regarding the non-publishing of his literary works.[4] It would appear no one else in the country shared the degree of responsibility and audacious influence over events as did the Communist Party General Secretary Iosif Stalin.

At a loose end in his personal and professional dilemma, Mosolov wrote a protracted entreaty to Stalin for support.[5] "I am neither published nor performed. I feel myself to be persecuted and an entirely disenfranchised musician. I don't know what to do, but I can't work in such conditions."[6] Mosolov expounded on the circumstances of his abandoned opera *The Dam* at the Leningrad Opera and Ballet Theater and went further by itemizing the gradual decline in his career. "For three years (since 1929), they have not published me at all, since 1928, performances of my works have been gradually suspended, and in 1930–1931, not a single opus has been brought to performance, whether it be mass songs, large symphonic, or stage works. Slowly, but surely, all the music institutions in Moscow have become afraid of my 'odious' name, and are cutting any ties with me under the pretext of the lack of work, or because of the 'harmfulness' of my music."[7] Mosolov described the great success of *The Foundry*, which had now been banned by the State Music Publishers, and despite requests from Universal Edition in Vienna for the score and parts, the Moscow publishers had threatened to destroy the engraved plates. Finally, he asked Stalin to use his authority so that the RAPM relented from their persecution of him, and if failing this, that he be allowed to leave the Soviet Union to continue his career in Western Europe. "I don't want to be a musical failure! I compose because I want to!" Together with this letter, Mosolov sent Stalin an envelope with copies of reviews and articles from performances of his music in Europe and the Americas. He mentioned the concert in Vienna where 2,000 people gave his *The Foundry* a standing ovation. "They appreciate me abroad, they are playing my music, even if they call me a Bolshevik." There is no indication that Stalin responded to this letter; however, Mosolov was called into the party headquarters where he deliberated over his affairs with Rabichev, and notably, with Pyotr Petrovich Postyshev, who was the secretary responsible for agitation and propaganda at the Central Committee. A consequence was that a meeting of the Politburo discussed Molotov's situation and that of Soviet music.

The consequences of this letter led to exceptional events, as Vladimir Derzhanovsky relates,

> Mosolov couldn't bear the shameless and idiotic persecution from the RAPM anymore (which you know very well), so he wrote a letter to Stalin, the final

paragraph of which—I confess that I had a hand in—describes, in general, the outrageous state in musical life, and the disruption by the RAPM. Mosolov's letter, which demonstrates his faith in the Party, was acknowledged with extraordinarily benign consideration. Now, the RAPM has been crushed, their poisonous *Proletarian Musician* has been taken away from them, and most likely their members will be removed from responsible positions in concert, education, and publishing affairs.[8]

Of course, it may have been wholly coincidental that these major changes occurred soon after Mosolov's letter to Stalin, yet the affair of the steadfast Soviet composer unable to work amid attacks by the ultra-leftists could have been an element in the catalyst for banning the RAPM and establishing the Union of Composers in April 1932. There were other grounds for this makeover because it concurred with the demise of the proletarian writers' organization, RAPP, and the foundation of the Writers Union. For Mosolov, personally and professionally, there were no dramatic consequences, certainly, his Second Piano Concerto was premiered in 1932, the orchestration of *Les Cloches de Corneville*, and the State Publishers Muzyka published the cycle of *Three Songs* for Voice and Orchestra Op. 33, in 1934, released from its banning, *The Foundry* was reprinted (for the third time), and the early *Three Lyric Songs* Op. 7 appeared in 1935. That summer, as we know, Mosolov traveled to the southern republics to research folklore, following Bartók's example. There was no substantial upturn in public performances, however.[9]

Film Music

As we know, the cinema attracted many composers, not only as a supplementary source of income but also as a means for experimentation in their expression. Mosolov had not considered the medium as an important avenue for his work; however, his first encounter proved an astonishing vision of what would become Mosolov's short-term future. In 1934, Mosolov was engaged by the Vostokfilm studios to write a film score based on Nikolay Pogodin's play *The Aristocrats* about a labor camp, directed by Yevgeny Chervyakov.[10] In order to familiarize himself with the milieu, Mosolov traveled to the Medvezhgorsk penal colony that was involved in the construction of the White Sea-Baltic canal on the banks of Lake Onega.[11] When the film was released in 1936, Mosfilm retitled the movie as *The Prisoners*—notably the first and only Soviet film to show political and criminal prisoners.[12] According to the film historians Selunskaya and Zezina, "The shots of the camp and the White Sea Canal construction remain the only film evidence of their kind."[13] In the press the movie was severely criticized for the "crude" portrayal of the "naturalism" of camp life, corruption, criminal jargon, and the frivolous heroine Sonya's fighting with other prisoners. Following the first showing, the studio was told to "concentrate attention to the intuitive and forthright imagery of the distinguished Chekist officers."[14] The studio director Samsonov recommended: "The picture, in my opinion, shouldn't be how the playwright wants. The name *The Prisoners* doesn't mean anything and doesn't motivate the moviegoer. It would be better to rename the film *Awakening* or *Those Without Purpose, There is No Way Back* or *Vanquished Chaos*, etc, etc."[15] Mosolov spent some two weeks on-site, and although his film score was abandoned, at least he was reimbursed for his contribution. The movie remake was shot in Karelia with the music inexplicably composed by Yuri Shaporin. A more entertaining diversion for Mosolov at the time was attending a reception at the Metropol Hotel hosted by the Composers Union for the guest conductors Jerzy Sěnkar and Albert Coates on December 30, 1934. Apart from the engaging evening with champagne and caviar, an advantageous outcome was that both conductors went on to perform his music in Europe in the coming seasons.

Scandal and Imprisonment

Following the publication in *Pravda* of the critique "Muddle instead of Music" in January 1936, the Moscow and Leningrad branches of the Union of Composers debated the campaign against "formalism" and "decadent music." Mosolov was in the frame of those accused together with Popov, Sollertinsky, Shcherbachev, and Shostakovich by the former activists of the RAPM and ORKiMD. The lead in the accusations was Beskin, the consultant for the Commissar for Enlightenment, who complained that "young formalists can't reform themselves. You are not doing what is required. You can write poorer music, but you write what we want, and we want social realism."[16] Mosolov was identified as a "Westerner," and his music was adjudged as lifeless. The former RAPM member, Viktor Bely opined that *"The Foundry* was not written by a great talent."[17] In a separate event, Mosolov was accused of insulting a waiter in a restaurant, and despite being initially cleared of any misbehavior, the affair was used by his detractors to make an example of him along with the accusations of "formalism" and "Western decadence." This was based on a scandalous evening with his friends, the actor and director Alexei Diky, the poet Pyotr Oreshin, the dramatist Konstantin Listov, and the Kyiv-based actor Alexei Vatulya. The former members of the RAPM and ORKiMD wanted blood and Mosolov proved a worthy victim. Klara Vaks, the wife of the composer Tikhon Khrennikov, complained that "several comrades have portrayed the lifestyle and morality of Mosolov—and taking into consideration his behavior at the Press House restaurant on 31 January—and this is not the only example—for there have been numerous incidents in his life (. . .) the general meeting of the Union of Soviet Composers has decided to expel Mosolov from the Union of Composers."[18] The Art Workers Union RABIS was more lenient and only suspended Mosolov's membership. Just as bizarre was that owing to appeals by his peers, Mosolov was restored as a full member just a few months later.[19] All of these events would, however, lead to the most serious consequences just one year later.

In the same year, 1936, Mosolov was engaged to write works based on Turkmen folklore in an expedition arranged by the Turkmenian SSR in Ashkhabad. Mosolov visited Turkmenia in June that year, agreeing to compose several works based on Turkmen national song, including a projected opera and an oratorio called *Turkmenian Song about Stalin*, as he described to Myaskovsky on August 8.[20] However, on Mosolov's arrival in Ashkhabad, he was met with generous hospitality which went far beyond normal limits, as a result, after some weeks, he was described as being dissolute, drunken, and behaving like a hooligan, spending most of his time at the bar in the Intourist hotel and at inns in the locality. It seemed as if little time was spent by Mosolov on researching Turkmen folk culture, for he returned home with little or nothing to show for his efforts.[21] It was this alleged behavior which was used by the satirists in a nationwide broadsheet which threw his career into even greater notoriety than before.

If contemporary life remained challenging, still new contracts arrived among which was writing the music for a Red Square parade by the Moscow Institute of Physical Culture. On July 12, 1937, we know from Barsova that Mosolov "revealed himself as a highly qualified specialist (. . .) providing a high-quality musical contribution on Red Square."[22] This engagement was a prestigious event for Mosolov; however, the time seemed ominous because the first weeks of autumn were full of media reports about trials of citizens accused of carrying out sabotage and anti-Soviet activity.

Unfortunately, after the previous year's accusations, Mosolov's detractors were not silent for long; on September 18, 1937, he was maliciously characterized in unflattering cartoon images in the Government newspaper *Izvestiya*. The brothers' Tur were well-known satirists whose speciality was in scandalizing various public figures—both foreign and Soviet.[23] As we know from a previous chapter, Gavriil Popov had been supported by the same pair of satirists who enjoyed considerable sway in media and public opinion. In this feuilleton *"The Deviation of a Genius,"* Mosolov is portrayed as a drunkard and debauchee, behaving "with the air of an enemy of the people." At the time, this was the most damaging accusation possible. However, the lampoon went further "these (literary mamas) depict the 'personal life' of a literary person, with remarkable genius, show the political face of the enemy."[24] Mosolov's efforts at composing a Turkmen opera were mockingly illustrated, "With the raising of the curtain, the trumpets will blast on a prolonged note in A."[25] Also, it was alleged that not all of Mosolov's contractual obligations were fulfilled with Vostokfilm studio in Armenia and that Mosolov had walked away from the project with thousands of state funds in his pocket.[26] Mosolov protested to the Moscow branch of the Composers' Union and September 28, the secretary wrote to the paper contradicting the allegations and asking for a withdrawal. "It is necessary to make a correction in relation to the false information about this matter in the feuilleton." The newspaper failed to print a withdrawal or indeed any correction, nevertheless, matters soon became deadly serious. Under Article 58.10 of the criminal code, Mosolov was arrested on November 4, 1937.[27] Mosolov was convicted on December 23, 1937, by a court of three judges, for "counter-revolutionary propaganda." The sentence given down was for eight years, but the sentencing took place without any judgment or assessment of the "alleged offenses" by the tarnished "troika" court. Based on this "technicality," the case could proceed to the appeal court.

Before this plea could be heard, Mosolov was dispatched into the prison system. He served more than eight months in a labor camp situated several hundred kilometers to the north of Moscow. The location must have seemed brutally ironic after Mosolov's futile film score about a prison camp, and the calamitous opera *The Dam*.[28] The Volzhskiy camp was on the banks of the Sheksna River, 3 kilometers from the mouth of the river where a hydroelectric dam was being built. The location was a forest logging camp under control of the NKVD. During his detention, a sign of Mosolov's extraordinary talent was unearthing themes for his future Concerto for Harp, and a Cello Concerto. Fortunately, the petition launched in March 1938 by Myaskovsky and Glière to the Soviet president Mikhail Kalinin was successful and on July 15, 1938, Mosolov was granted release, but without the right to reside in Moscow, Leningrad, or Kyiv for five years.[29] Mosolov was released on August 26 and allowed to travel to the Maloyaroslavets railway station on the Moscow district line.[30] A mark of providence in Mosolov's release was that at the time of the appeal, several hundred political prisoners were released in 1938 and 1939 owing to the amnesty upon Lavrenty Beria's appointment as chairman of the NKVD.[31] An extra "improvement" to Mosolov's situation was that he was only restricted from living in Moscow for twelve months.[32] On reflection, it would appear that Mosolov's punishment was lenient considering that his friend, the writer—Pyotr Oreshin who was involved in the infamous restaurant brouhaha was arrested and executed in 1938.[33] Mosolov's restoration to membership of the Composers Union came in August 1941 through Myaskovsky's recommendation and which exempted Mosolov from serving at the front line.[34]

The Concerto for Harp

The lingering genius of Mosolov was reflected in the Concerto for Harp performed by Vera Georgievna Dulova at the opening concert of the Decade of Soviet Music on November 18, 1939, at the Moscow Conservatoire. There was huge interest in Mosolov's reappearance on the concert stage with many of the audience sitting in the passageways; afterward, students approached Myaskovsky, who, "in his quiet voice—and a rare smile—said that he highly cherished his former student."[35] It may well have been Myaskovsky that guaranteed the scheduling of Mosolov's Concerto for Harp. Myaskovsky observed that in his "turning from modernism, Mosolov had treaded towards misbehavior" (bearing in mind his vocal cycles), now he had made a "sharp turn around to socialist realism with impressionist colors, brilliantly orchestrated with clear brilliance, including a celeste."[36] The Harp Concerto was so successful that one movement (the *Toccata*) was repeated at the closing Festival concert on December 11. Sharing the bill with the Mosolov piece were Prokofiev's cantata *Alexander Nevsky*, Khachaturyan's Piano Concerto, and Muradeli's First Symphony.[37]

Barsova suggests that including Mosolov's new work at such a prestigious festival in the capital was not only a mark of respect for Mosolov but also a sign of forgiveness by the music authorities.[38] Another sign of rehabilitation was his inclusion in a group of musicians touring to Kharkiv in Ukraine, from November 26 to November 30, 1939. We know from the program of the concert on November 29 that it featured Mosolov's *Turkmen* overture, a *Rhapsody Kirghizia* for large symphony orchestra for soloist and choir, and the Concerto for Cello and Orchestra (1937), and Pushkin and Lermontov romances.[39] All of these are lost, including the *Rhapsody Kirghizia* which dates from before 1937.[40] This concert tour—under the auspices of the Committee for Arts—restored Mosolov to public life, and it seemed that Mosolov's constructivism and modernism were now a distant memory.

Further evidence of this recognition (not without irony) was the publication of Mosolov's setting to Zharov's *Table Song for Stalin* in the newspaper *Izvestiya* on December 21, 1939, in honor of the leader's sixtieth birthday. The Harp Concerto comprises of four movements; however, Mosolov removed one movement (later recycled as the Dance Suite for Harp in 1945). The opening movement *Sostenuto-Lento-Adagio* includes a brilliant cadenza in which the soloist's virtuosity is tested in a fiendishly difficult passage, while the second movement *Nocturne* is lyrical and beautiful in its effusive orchestration. The *Gavotte* is brief and charming in its musicality, while the *Toccata* is challenging with harsh rhythms demanding intensity from the soloist's playing fingers like tiny hammers. As we know, the new piece was successful—the two central movements were encored at the premiere. The transformation in his style of writing was already apparent in 1938 and succinctly identified acquiescently by Myaskovsky—Mosolov's work had become lyrical and emotionally charged—gone was much of the dissonance and jerky rhythms, with perhaps a refined modernity in its place. The writer Nikolay Alekseyenko reflects that "contemporary listeners noticed the attention paid not only to the orchestral colors in which Mosolov showed himself an established master. There was something different in the simplicity of the harmonic language with attention given to the melodic aspect of his musical expression."[41]

Mosolov's Concerto for Harp became one of his most frequently performed pieces in the Soviet Union and a standard repertoire piece for classical harp players. The first Soviet composer to write for the instrument—Reinhold Glière—considered that the work was "masterly written" and the critics were unanimous in their praise.[42] Commenting further, the composer Vano Muradeli wrote "this composition is a lyrical narrative, at times, tender and warm (the nocturne!), at times, brilliant bearing witness of the great transformation in the creativity of the composer, and a fresh emotional feeling in his environment."[43] Another commentator added his voice. "Mosolov's pioneering piece appears to be a major step forward in the creative development of the composer. The delicate, transparent orchestration, and diversity in the high quality musical fabric (particularly in the second and fourth movements) unquestionably places Mosolov's Concerto for Harp among the finest compositions written for the instrument. The concerto was brilliantly performed by Vera Dulova."[44] Rimsky writes that it represented: "A victory for Mosolov—the justified outcome of the composer's thoughts 'about the times and about himself,' and, in this triumph there was nothing unforeseen in the stature of the talent which was Mosolov."[45] The Mosolov Harp Concerto remains today among the obligatory works for international harp competitions.

Folksongs

We have seen that some time before the Concerto for Harp, there had already emerged a change in Mosolov's style which was apparent after visiting Kirghizia, Dagestan, Armenia, Georgia, and Turkmenia during the 1930s. Through his arrangements of folksongs for orchestral suites, rhapsodies, and dances, Mosolov found a new unpretentiousness in his style, and it seemed that the exciting trendsetter and visionary of a decade before had disappeared for good. Mosolov made arrangements of three songs for voice and orchestra based on Turkmen, Kirghiz, and Afghani folksongs, and a Turkmen lullaby for a capella choir. The vocal works that appear to have vanished include his Pushkin settings. *There Burns a Spark of Desire in My Blood*, *The Last Flower*, *I Love You—Otherwise*, *I will Go*, *In Your Light*, and two Lermontov settings, *The Mountain Heights*, and *From Under the Secret, Cold Mask*.

These songs reflect a quite different composer from the one who wrote the auspicious *Three Children's Songs*. Regrettably, *In Your Light* was the only song to be published. A concert of Mosolov's songs was given in the Beethoven Hall at the Bolshoi Theater and broadcast on nationwide radio in 1936. Rimsky writes that in the Mosolov settings, there appeared previously unknown new-fangled qualities of melodic language. There was now an emotionalism, depth, and fragility in poetic truth to the original poems allowing a classicism in their form and which significantly simplified their harmonic language.[46]

Turkmenian folksongs inspired several pieces for a cycle of orchestral suites, yet the Uzbek Suite of 1936 is lost and probably unperformed. Nothing survives from a plan to write a symphony for the birth centenary of the poet Lermontov. If the composer had changed his musical style, his penchant to forget and discard his compositions was unmoved. Regardless of Mosolov's return to normality, the Concerto for Harp was only published in 1972, and the new opera *The Signal* of June 1941 was published in 1942.[47] Owing to the term of his sentence and subsequent release, it is thought that Mosolov stayed with friends outside the Moscow city limits. On February 7, 1940, Andrey Vyshinsky, the deputy chairman of the Council of Peoples Commissars signed a request for the term of residence to be reduced, and probed the NKVD to amend the court's original judgment, removing any criminality from his name. During the first months of the war, Mosolov served in civil defense and helped organize anti-gas attacks at the offices of the Composers' Union on Arbat Square. Like Shostakovich, he stood guard on the roofs of buildings and disposing of incendiaries from German bombers. He also joined a group preparing for weapon practice on the Western approaches of Moscow in the event of a Nazi breakthrough.[48]

The Wartime Operas

As a veteran of the Civil War, it is curious that in the first months of the conflict, Mosolov worked on a one-act opera *The Signal* from a libretto by Osaf Litovsky. Here, motivated by the outbreak of the war on Soviet soil, *The Signal* "continues the traditions of Russian heroic-patriotic opera. The dramaturgy is founded on a conventional plan in which the contrasting sides are expressed by music of conflicting intonational thematic complexes and generic characteristics."[49] Mosolov's arias are bright and harmonically appealing, reflecting a fresh emotionalism. In the second scene, the telegraphist Shirokov's arioso sings the motherland leitmotif which is at the heart of the opera. The poster art concept of Mosolov's stage work is shared by Surkov's patriotic *Songs of the Courageous*, and the films by Pyrev *Secretary of the Raikom*, and Ermler's *They Defend the Motherland*. Another unfulfilled, yet interesting project was a musical comedy based on the antifascist satire by A. Argo and S. Serpinsky. The score was completed on October 14, 1941, yet the opera was rejected by theaters in Sverdlovsk and Stalingrad.[50]

The first of Mosolov's patriotic pieces is the symphonic poem *Ukraine* for soloists, chorus, and orchestra. This was followed by a cycle of choruses portraying Tsarist military leaders—Alexander Nevsky, Alexander Suvorov, and Mikhail Kutuzov. The oratorio *Hero-City* was published with the hymns *Moscow*, the ballad *Leningrad*, the nocturne *Stalingrad*, and the marches *Sevastopol* and *Odesa*.

The first year of war proved industrious because Mosolov—in parallel with *The Signal*—created yet another stage work. Based on Lermontov's *Masquerade*, Mosolov's fourth opera is again in one act, with six scenes, and unlike his previous attempt, is romantic in tone and content. Mosolov's style is fashioned on the nineteenth-century Russian romance; there are several leitmotifs, one being the theme from the second scene of the heroine Nina's lost bracelet, during which a series of variations are heard. The second leitmotif from the third scene arioso is the hero Arbenin's contemplations on love. The centerpiece of the opera—in Alekseyenko's opinion—is Nina's romance "At the Countess's Ball." The opera ends tragically in the tableau of Nina's bedroom scene. The opera was commissioned by the Nemirovich-Danchenko Company in Moscow; however, it was never staged, and the contracts nullified. Fourteen excerpts from *Masquerade* were published in two hundred copies in 1944. A hint as to the tragic lack of success comes from Mosolov's own words: "I may compose music, but I am quite unprepared to make any 'accommodation,' or attempt to get it performed."[51]

Mosolov composed works in diverse genres during the war among the brightest of which are the Quartet No. 2 (1943) and the cantata *October* (1942) used texts by Rudnev which were well written and warmly received. Mosolov's patriotic settings from Demian Bedny's *Motherland* were arranged for choir and piano (1943). Other pieces from the war years are his *Three Elegies* on words by Denis Davydov for voice and piano (1944) and the *Five Waltzes* for voice and piano (1945). Mosolov's *Five Poems of A. Blok*, including *In the Divan Corner*, and *I Lived There* are elegiac, however anguish and anger dominate in *The Guitar Strings Were Tight*, and *The Evening Quiet Shadows*, while the Blok cycle closes brightly in *I Rise in the Misty Morning*. Common to all is a Mosolovian laconic psychological mood.

Symphony in E Major

An important work of the war years is the four-movement Symphony in E major (1944).[52] Mosolov employs a three-part orchestra with eight horns, six trumpets, five trombones, percussion, two harps, piano, and celeste.

The ensemble is on a par with the orchestral forces used by Prokofiev and Shostakovich in their war symphonies and in his own *The Foundry*. The orchestration reflects the wartime period by invoking excitingly dramatic tension and an electrifying intensity set against a gorgeous panoply of color. Throughout, Mosolov develops the main themes masterfully while adroitly making use of several folksongs. The symphony encapsulates the new Mosolovian style; the only consistency between the old modernist Mosolov and the new is the remarkable high degree of musical excellence and brilliant orchestration.

The opening *Largo* typifies Mosolov's "new" style, evoking Borodin's Second Symphony with the octave unisons and polyphony of the inner voices. The protracted main idea on the low strings is united by the brass and woodwind in a meditative mood, the secondary stronger theme introduced on the violins is like an awakening, and the tubular bells maintain an upbeat tone assisted by the flutes and clarinets. There is a rise in tension and a feeling of great anticipation to an exciting culmination that is annulled by a beautiful melody and a mood of peace and joy. The oboe invokes a childlike simplicity in Mosolov's theme *Oh Rasseya, My Rasseya*. When the main idea enters on the strings, it is picked up by the percussion, on the bells, harp, and flutes, and builds to a colossal volume, reminiscent of Shostakovich's *Leningrad* Symphony, but without the latter's march-like intonation. A third songful theme is introduced by the flute and carried by the woodwind and strings with the movement closing on an optimistic note. The second movement, *Largo sostenuto*, opens with octave unisons, and soon distinctive Russian folk melodic rhythms enter on the clarinet and develop to a climax of celebration, but holding back, as if in restraint. Lyadov's *Eight Russian Folk Songs* are cited in a nod to the nationalist school, followed by a marvelously intertwined subtle polyphony from which emerge joyful harmonies, and closing on a rather pitiful note on the oboe. In the third movement, *Largo maestoso* Mosolov brings out all his invention and brilliance in orchestral colors—reflecting the human soul with tender intonation on harps against the pizzicato strings. In the finale, the composer uses folksongs from the Napoleonic wars *Oh Rasseya, My Rasseya* from his wartime cycle of *Five Russian National Songs of the 1812 War* (this idea was reprised in Mosolov's Second Quartet). Following the trumpets and horns chorale, an intense and dramatic section dominates from which there develop a great march using every section of the orchestra—almost like a great locomotive in momentum—evoking memories of his most famous piece. The rhythmic tension generated is thrillingly exciting, and the main theme arrives to bring this symphony to a celebratory close with the snare and bass drums used with full force, and slowly, but at last, the first theme reenters as a hymn in the concluding bars. Alekseyenko notes that there is a common feature here with Myaskovsky's late symphonies, "The E major symphony is the most expansive both in its size and in overall sound. It was only here that the composer employs his own orchestral hybrid with a large orchestra. The symphony could not but reflect this wartime spirit."[53]

By the time the Red Army had cleared the last remaining Nazi troops from Soviet territory in 1944, the Soviet Government rewarded composers and musicians who had helped on the "music front." Mosolov received 12,000 roubles for his contribution, but of all Soviet composers, the highest financial award was to Shostakovich of 32,000 roubles.[54]

Cello Concerto No. 2

The *Elegy* for cello and piano most certainly rekindles themes of the lost Mosolov Cello Concerto of 1937, and when he showed this piece to Myaskovsky, it was suggested that he incorporate the *Elegy* for a Cello Concerto.[55] The main idea is melodious, lyrical, and inspired by Myaskovsky's most verdant style, and adorned by the warm late romanticism and lyricism in his cello works. As Alekseyenko points out, "It's possible that Myaskovsky's love of the violoncello influenced Mosolov. Whatever way, Mosolov's violoncello line (from the 1940s to 1960s) was analogous to the late romanticism of Myaskovsky, in grasping the cantilena of the instrument."[56] Certainly, the Cello Concerto No. 2 picks up the same stylistic harmonies of his Concerto for Harp from which original sparks of modernism emerge like bursts of sunshine on a cloudy day.

In the opening *Elegy*, there is a solemn dancing rhythm in the pizzicato of the violins against the harmony of the cello, yet, the theme dies away, and light and hope emerge only when the celesta introduces an illuminating vividness. There appears a new grace note, and fanciful invocations in the *Intermezzo*, with fascinating harmonies, heard on flutes, xylophone, celesta, bells, and harp glissandos, create an extraordinarily stimulating musical realm. The finale, *Ballade*, opens with an enchanting theme, followed by a dashingly exciting, march-like idea. The cello's cantilena explores several modulations, and as the drama and tension are whipped up, there arrives a cadenza invoking the polyphony of J. S. Bach, and soon after, the coda brings a vigorous and daring culmination.

The new Cello Concerto was completed in 1944; however, it was not premiered until January 23, 1947, by Alexander Stogorsky (brother of Gregor Pyatigorsky) with the Georgian conductor Odyssey Dimitriadi directing the Moscow Philharmonic Orchestra at the Central House of Arts Workers. The work was welcomed by critics and audiences, notably by the former proletarian writer Semyon Korev, "the composition has many achievements," noting "the somewhat artificial and deliberately difficult musical language of the former Mosolov has now become meaningfully simple and more expressive."

There was a welcome for "the wonderful lyricism of the first movement's theme" and the "temperamental intermezzo." However, the finale was criticized because "the listener is disturbed by the sweeping mood as he leaves behind the musical imagery of the earlier movements."[57] This rebuke led to Mosolov rewriting the finale to make it more accessible. Stogorsky to whom the work is dedicated championed the concerto in Baku, Voronezh, Gorki, and in Novosibirsk, and extensively in coming seasons. The score was only published in 1983 but has never found a permanent place in the cello repertoire.

Postwar Compositions

Mosolov returned to writing for the voice—most notably with two cycles based on Blok, the first from 1946, *A Spring Day Passed Without Anything*, and *On Achievement, On Feats, On Glory*, and his second cycle of the same year, *In the Corner of the Divan, That Life Has Passed, There Played Guitar Strings, The Quiet Evening Clouds*, and *I Arose on a Misty Morn*.

Attracted to the symphonic genre, Mosolov wrote his Symphony No. 2 in D Major (1946); however, there is little record of either publication or indeed of any performances and this piece currently lies gathering dust in the archives. This work was followed four years later, by the *Song* Symphony in B Major with the four movements carrying the helpfully explanatory titles: *A Spring Morning, A Song about the Feat, An Evening in the Fields*, and *A Song about Labor*. The *Song* Symphony represents his accommodation with the 1948 Composers Union Congress and the trend for song symphonies based on Russian folksong. Mosolov's collection of *Ten Melodies of the Kuban Cossacks* were recycled in another Mosolovian song-symphony *Symphonic Pictures from the Life of the Kuban Cossack Collective Farmers* (1950).[58] However, this major work by Mosolov remains unpublished. The *Song* Symphony—with its rich folklore—characterizes much of his writing from the period.[59] The opening movement contains an alluring Kuban song *The Night Is Present*. Here is an unusual evocation of his shadowy nocturnal vocal works from the 1920s, but this is dispersed with a song-like charm in the second movement, and the upbeat colorful harmonies prevail with dance melodies in the third and fourth movements. The folk dance imagery is underlined by colorful harmonies, and two accordions (bayans) introduce folk themes in the central section of the third movement with the pizzicato strings evoking domras and balalaikas. This use of folk instruments was highlighted in Mosolov's orchestral suites: *Kubanskaya* and the *Suite from the Kuban Cossacks*.

In January 1947, composers were offered commissions for operas and ballets of up to 60,000 roubles for an opera and 40,000 for a ballet.[60] Mosolov acquiesced to write a ballet entitled *On Friendship between the Bashkir and Russian Peoples*.[61] This became another unrealized project owing to the limited stipulations exposing fundamental weaknesses and few anticipated stage works were produced in this project. Only Yuri Shaporin's *The Decembrists* and Tikhon Khrennikov's *Frol Skobeyev* enjoyed successful stage productions. The most controversial stage work was by the Georgian composer and Myaskovsky student—Vano Muradeli. The opera was successfully staged as *The Extraordinary Commissar* in several opera houses through 1947; however, it was rechristened for the Bolshoi Opera production as *The Great Friendship*. The Moscow premiere became the target of the party's anger in the now scandalous affair of 1948.

The 1948 Composers' Congress

We already know of the meetings in January and February 1948 which announced the Resolution on Formalism and the attacks of leading composers: Khachaturyan, Muradeli, Mosolov, Popov, Prokofiev, Myaskovsky, Shebalin, and Shostakovich. At the Composers Union Congress in April 1948, the new General Secretary Tikhon Nikolayevich Khrennikov criticized Mosolov and the Leningrad modernist Vladimir Deshevov for their "long-forgotten eccentricities," formalistic experimentation, and abstract musical idiom that had caused a "breach between the listener and musical art." Indictments followed for producing "images and emotions alien to Soviet realistic art-expressionistic anxiety, of neuroticism, and escaping into abnormal, repulsive, and pathological phenomena."[62] The ferocity of the language was reminiscent of the attacks by the members of the RAPM and ORKiMD in the 1920s, but now it was former members of the RAPM who enjoyed the reins of power.

Composers were to write works that were simple, melodic, and easy to listen to, free of "formalist" ideas or technique. Following this advice, Mosolov contributed a *Choral Suite* which was approved by the newly appointed Secretariat of the Composers Union in December 1948.[63] One other choral piece was the cantata *Glory to the Soviet Army*.[64] This work was started in 1947, and Mosolov wrote several patriotic vocal pieces, also from the same year is the oratorio celebrating the anniversary of the city's foundation *Moscow* for soloists, choir, and orchestra with texts by Klenov, Oshanin, and Solovyov. Other works in a similar genre were a capella choruses—*On Lenin* from a poem by Mashistov, and *Motherland* from Alexander Prokofyev's poems (1948). Mosolov's song cycles based on Pushkin (1948 and 1949) included *Cossack*, and three songs *Remembrance, Desire,* and *To the Sea*. Several chamber compositions date from this period, notably the Sonatina for Cello and Piano (1946), Four Pieces for Bassoon and Piano, a *Dance Suite* for Harp, and Four Pieces for Oboe and Piano (1947). Of particular interest is the *Serenade* for Mandolin and Piano (1950), and another piece composed for Stogorsky were Three Pieces for Cello and Piano based on folksongs (1950–1951). Again, with Stogorsky in mind is *Elegia* and *Dance* (1947). All of these chamber works represent a very high standard, and throughout show the innovative composing of Mosolov regardless of the criticism of the Composers' Congress. The disappointment of his Cello Concerto to win the public's hearts did not sway the composer from writing for the instrument again and the *Elegiac Poem* (1960) did not change matters. Following an audition by the Composers Union secretariat, and despite a recommendation from Shostakovich, the piece was proscribed.

Kuban Cossack Music

Reprising his explorative journeys to the Caucasus and Central Asia in the 1930s, Mosolov now researched the folk traditions in the Kuban Cossack country of South Russia. Mosolov fell in love with the beauty of the region and started using themes of Kuban Cossack folklore. In August 1953, the composer traveled to the Maryansky, Anapa, and Novorossiysk districts in the Krasnodar region. This initiated the first part of Mosolov's Kuban period in which he methodically studied Kuban Cossack culture. Mosolov studied contemporary and ancient Cossack songs visiting many villages and hamlets and collecting some 160 songs. He also explored the recordings made by G. M. Plotnichenko, a professional composer from the Krasnodar area, and collaborated with G. A. Koval, the director of an amateur Cossack choir. In 1959, Mosolov prepared his collection for publication and wrote several papers on the folklore of the Kuban region.[65]

There was a surprising variety in the compositions that Mosolov wrote during the early 1950s: *Songs of the Terek Cossacks* (which is lost), a Suite *Kuban Stanitsa* for chorus and folk orchestra (1952), another piece which is abandoned is for a capella chorus—*Mother Kuban*. In 1953, he composed *Young Cossacks* for chorus and folk orchestra and another suite for similar forces—*Kuban Collective Farm* (1954). Mosolov set poems by Pyatko—*Steppe Songs of the Kuban* for chorus and folk orchestra (1954). During this period, the composer gathered four volumes of folksongs: sixteen Kuban Songs (1951–1952), twenty-four Terek Cossack Songs (1953), Abkhazian Folk Songs, together with eleven Stavropol Songs and various folksongs (1952 and 1953). The remarkable professionalism and standing are reflected by Mosolov's three essays about musical life which were published in *Sovetskaya Muzika*, and which, apart from his early critical papers about contemporary music in the 1920s, are the summation of his musicological works.[66]

Symphony on Kuban Folksong

In 1950, Mosolov composed a programmatic symphony on themes of the Kuban Cossacks. After six months' work, he couldn't avoid being tied to "the archaically beautiful Kuban melodies" from the 1898 Bigdaem song collection.[67] Mosolov traveled to South Russia to embrace the idiom.[68] Among the fruits of this period are two orchestral suites written for Russian folk orchestra based on Kuban folksongs. In Nalchik, the regional capital of the Kabardinian autonomous republic, he arranged a quantity of gorgeous folksongs, the most successful of which was the *Song of the Nart*. Mosolov met local musicians there, including the conductor A. G. Shachgaldyanom, the composer T.K. Sheiblero, the musicologist K. K. Khavpachev, and the poets A. P. Kheshokov, A. K. Shomakhach, A. O. Shogentsukov, and the dramatist and writer A. T. Shortanov. The richly colorful folksongs of the region had been garnered efficaciously by Myaskovsky, Prokofiev, and Alexandrov during their imposed exile in the town following the Nazi invasion in the autumn and winter of 1941.[69] Mosolov's *Song of the Nart* was performed in Nalchik, while the chorus *Unbroken Friendship* was heard in the regional capital of Ordzhonikidze, and extracts from the Cello Concerto No. 2 were broadcast on local radio under the baton of his colleague Shachgaldyanom, who became a faithful interpreter.

Of considerable interest are the *Four Songs for Small Orchestra* from diverse cultural backgrounds: *Indian Song, Irish Song, Chinese Song,* and *Polynesian Song*. The fact that Mosolov was regularly offered contracts for work reveals that the Committee for Arts still valued his talent. On his return from the Kuban region, Mosolov wrote extensively in numerous genres. The most significant of these are for the voice: the cycle of Ten Russian Songs: *Lyrics of the Old Village* (1958). Of outstanding quality is his setting *The Russian Woman* (1952), from the nineteenth-century writer Nekrasov, and from Blok—*He took a Guitar* (1956). Several compositions were on socialist realist themes—a cantata for chorus and orchestra based on texts by Pyatko—*Ode to the Party* (1963) and the oratorio *Glory to Moscow* from Zharov (1967). There were chamber instrumental pieces all using folk themes—one of which recycled Kabardinian folk motifs for his Piano Quintet (1956) and the Third Quartet—subtitled *Suite on Themes from Patriotic Soldiers and Partisan Songs of 1812*. Mosolov's Third Concerto for Cello and Orchestra was from Kabardinian-Balkar songs (1956); sadly, these two pieces are now lost.

Mosolov's Symphony in C major (1958–1959) was written a year before the *Elegiac Poem* for Cello and Orchestra. Regrettably, like its predecessor, the symphony awaits a premiere as the manuscript languishes in the archives gathering dust. In his return to choral music, Mosolov's *Song about Soviet*

Russia (1958) for a capella choir uses poems by Litvinov, and again, he turned to socialist realist texts for his four-part chorus *About Lenin* based on Mayakovsky's poem (1959–1961). In a similar vein, and in the same timeline, are the two choruses on Lenin—*Hey Russia*, and *The Year 1924* by Mashistov. This concept was followed up in 1962, when he wrote six orchestral poems about the former Soviet leader, in a capella chorus—*Thoughts* using texts by Alymov, Bedny, and Mashistov, and again Mayakovsky for his chorus *The Red Banner*, and *Put the Hammer and the Poem* (1963). Mosolov's popular *Children's Choruses* for voice and piano entitled *Natasha's Day* (1967) are set to poems by Nikolay Ushakov and Alexander Prokofyev.

Nina Meshko

A huge influence on the latter part of his career was the musicologist who would become his second wife. Nina Konstantinovna Meshko (1917–2008) was the director of the Northern Russian Peoples Chorus, a professional ensemble that performed traditional and classical music in the northern city of Archangelsk. This development in his private and professional life enriched the twilight years of his late career, distancing himself from his former memories and disappointments, allowing him both personal happiness and a degree of freedom and comfort. There were too autonomous concert promoters, radio stations, and publishers providing a fresh outlet for Mosolov. In appraising the last decade, Barsova reflects on the benign "influence of Meshko, for after his heart attack he wrote his Fifth Symphony from which (Mosolov was) happy that he could find a relationship with another musician, distant from the past, and discover a new life—he was entertaining, and for instance, unbroken in spirit."[70]

Symphony No. 5

Another late work in which Mosolov tries to find closure is the valedictory Fifth Symphony (1965) that follows upon the Symphony No. 4 (1963), subtitled *Four Poems about the Virgin Lands*, and the *Russian Overture* (1963). The Fifth was composed after recovery from a life-threatening heart attack, and appears to have influenced Mosolov to reflect on his past, and conspicuously reprocess motifs and styles from his most rewarding music of the "golden twenties" when he was the trailblazer of the Soviet avant-garde. The symphony is masterly written with a brilliantly scored orchestration, often throughout there emerge memories from past works notably in dissonances unconventional in symphonies of the 1960s. Characteristic is the first movement, *Largo-Allegro-Maestoso* which cites a seafarer's song *You Don't Know Dear; You Don't Go*.[71] The citations appear sometimes as fearless octaves;

however, they are like fresh extensions from similar material, in a series of sophisticated variations. In the second movement, *Adagio-Sostenuto Andante-Allegretto-Andante-Maestoso-Largo* the composer cites the *Adagio* from his Second Piano Sonata (1924). An example of the theme is a folksong expressed on the bassoon in the entry to the finale, *Andante recitativo-Allegro-Maestoso-trionfale* (where the bass-clarinet is heard, but an octave higher). The melancholy which dominates the second movement is transformed by the energy of the finale and its life-affirming coda. Alekseyenko wonders if this is "nostalgia, or is it a rebirth of a dissonant sound world from the past—linked with folklore—and the modernism of the sixties? What is significant here is the mastery of including themes from the 1920s, regardless of being stylistically unfamiliar."[72] Mosolov's Fifth Symphony was originally in four movements (the slow movement as a polyphonic *Andante* was incorporated into the second movement, *Andante-Maestoso-Largo*). The problem for Mosolov was that very few of his works were performed, and if at all, were neither repeated, nor recorded. There were few musicians willing to champion this one-time leader of the Russian avant-garde. The symphony was not published until 1991, and was heard for the first time only in 2019, and is dedicated to Nina Meshko.[73]

Peoples' Oratorio

Following renewed recognition on local radio and TV, Mosolov's folk choruses were broadcast nationally on Moscow Radio. However, the work to which Mosolov devoted much of his time was the *Peoples Oratorio for G. I. Kotovsky* (1970). This was his last completed work. The subject was based on the friendship and experiences shared with a longtime friend and comrade from the Civil War. The legendary figure of Grigory Ivanovich Kotovsky was a distinguished soldier and officer who fought in both the Great War and the Civil War and was a celebrated figure until his rather peculiar murder in 1925.

The dedication by Mosolov commemorated the forty-fifth anniversary of Kotovsky's death. "To the most valiant of the brave, the strongest of the strong, and the most humble of the modest—dedicated to the unforgettable memory of my commander Grigory Ivanovich Kotovsky."[74] The text of the oratorio is from Eduard Bagritsky's 1926 poem *Thoughts about Opanas*. The poem became the basis for the libretto commissioned by the Nemirovich-Danchenko State Theater in 1933. Bagritsky elicited that, "I wanted to portray the Civil War and everything that I witnessed. I wanted to write in the style of the old Ukrainian folk songs using the rhythmic style of Taras Shevchenko, which is relevant today."[75] The poem was controversial in its day for the content and manner in which Bagritsky wrote, and this work on which Mosolov was closure from the two years of terrible conflict that he endured in the bitterly fought Civil War. Interestingly, there appear in the oratorio text which is missing from Bagritsky's original. Mosolov underlined the theme of nationalism which is a motif throughout all the six movements of the oratorio. The musical language is almost entirely based on ancient lyrical and drawn-out (protyazhny) songs and marching songs from both the Civil War and the Second World War. The two tonal centers are equally heroic and lyrical and characterize the compass of the oratorio—the fighting and suffering of the Ukrainian people. The hostile force is the Makhno rebellion against the young Soviet republic. Several of the choruses point to the structure of the oratorio and its center—*Song of the Old Women from the Village Robbed by Makhno, The Day Is Hot! The Earth Is on Fire!*, and *Kotovsky's Trumpets Ring the Alarm*. The first choruses, second, third, and fifth parts are couplets, with a greater or lesser degree of tonal variation for soloists and choral reprieves. The orchestra is for a three-part ensemble with a large percussion section. Typically, Mosolov writes in a colorful, richly illustrative musical imagery with brilliant orchestration, in which he introduces an outlandish "instrument"—"horse hoofs" invoked by a snare drum giving the illusion of galloping cavalry. Both these "devices" create an ostinato sound. This work marks the high point in Mosolov's works for chorus and orchestra. Regrettably, Mosolov's work remains unpublished and like much of his late works lies in the archives awaiting discovery.

On August 11, 1970, Mosolov's seventieth birthday was observed, albeit the celebrant was congratulated not for his early work but for his traditional compositions. The Ministry of Culture noted that this "talented composer made a valuable contribution to the development of Soviet music, enriching the repertoire of Russian folk choirs."[76] The great popularity worldwide of Mosolov's music in the first decades of Soviet power (and the income from sales of his music in the West) was overlooked in the birthday celebrations. The speeches by Tikhon Khrennikov and Viktor Bely (both former members of the RAPM) ignored Mosolov's music from the 1920s and 1930s. Of the eight Mosolov symphonies, to date, only the E major symphony of 1944 and the Fifth have been published and recorded, while not one of his operas have been recorded.[77]

Mosolov possessed a sharp wit and sense of humor—and the explosive temperament—reappeared whenever he witnessed injustice or malpractice. He was pained when he reflected, "how can I write music if I haven't heard my compositions for the last sixteen years?" He found an affinity and long-standing friendship with another "victim" in the neglected Gavriil Popov, and regretted that the music of Myaskovsky, Shebalin, and Polovinkin was ignored and unperformed. That imitable sense of black humor was evident when Mosolov phoned someone whom he hadn't met or seen for ages, by introducing himself: "this is the late Mosolov speaking!"[78]

Piano Concerto No. 3

From his early years, it was the very process of exploration and composition that stimulated Mosolov, and as soon as the writing process was finished, he seemed to have little motivation in pursuing performances. Mosolov rarely responded to pleas for revision because he found it impossible to rekindle the original inspiration. Inevitably, this led to many works being both unpublished and unperformed. Regardless, throughout his career, Mosolov unleashed an unending conveyor belt of music in different genres. In the last nine years of his life, he composed a symphony, two oratorios, 150 choral pieces, a cycle of children's songs, and folk pieces. One of the last works was his Piano Concerto No. 3 (1971); however, rather than write a new work, Mosolov merely recycled old material, utilizing the themes, albeit altering them slightly. He made notes in the sketches of the Third Concerto to "look at the score" of his Second Piano Concerto of 1932.[79] The Piano Concerto No. 3 can be considered at best the modern-day reincarnation of the Second Piano Concerto.

Alexander Mosolov died on July 12, 1973, in Moscow, and his ashes were interred at the Vvedensky Crematorium four days later. He left unfinished a Sixth Symphony and an opera based on Chernyshevsky's *What Is to Be Done?* It is clear that despite his loss of vision, the fires of creativity were still burning within Mosolov. Nina Meshko loyally copied his music. "He dictated, sang, and played with his right hand, but the writing was taken down by me."[80] The lust for life continued to the end, with his sense of humor matched by a sharp wit that managed to overcome every obstacle. It was only after his death that his legacy was recognized, and leading Russian musicians began to perform and record his music. A sign of how much his music had changed so dramatically from his avant-garde youth was that in an epitaph, Dmitry Kabalevsky described him as "the singer of his motherland."[81]

The Mosolov Revival

There came a renaissance of Mosolov's music in the Soviet Union when *The Foundry* was performed and recorded by the distinguished conductor Yevgeny Svetlanov and the USSR State Symphony Orchestra in 1973. Rimsky commented that this recording "exonerated the traditional impression (. . .) started by the motoric 'avant-garde' opus that brought a fresh breath of air during the 1920s."[82] In Warsaw, *The Foundry* was used in the ballet $E=MC^2$. "This music represents a dynamic Perpetuum mobile with a clear build to culmination (like Ravel's *Bolero*). Together with the effective scenic acting, it led to creating an artistically convincing performance."[83] Another opinion of the same production, "This music is effusively modern and distinguished in many ways from our contemporary opuses because, excepting the enhanced naturalistic factory noises, there is here a powerful melody that is embodying the creative labor of man."[84]

The Polish production in 1974 was not the first to present Mosolov's masterpiece in the theater. In 1932, the Russian-born choreographer Adolph P. Bolm staged his ballet *Mechanical ballet* in the United States.[85] The *Three Childrens' Songs* and *Four Newspaper Advertisements* were revived by Larissa Davydova and Vasily Lobanov at the House of Composers on December 16, 1978, in Moscow. Remarkably, fifty years after the premieres of his works on German soil, at the Festival of Soviet Music in Cologne in 1979, Mosolov's *The Foundry* and the String Quartet No. 1 were performed with music by other avant-garde composers—Lourié, Schillinger, Alexandrov, Deshevov, and Roslavets's *Song Cycles* (1913–1914), and the *Nocturne* for harp, oboe, two violas, and cello.[86] The 1980 Moscow Autumn Festival revived the First Piano Concerto half a century after the premiere. For the first time, several of the important early works were recorded by the Soviet state record company Melodiya.

The Moscow poetess, Larisa Vasilyevna invoked Alexander Mosolov by relating him to Pierre Besukhov and Steve Obolensky as a character from Tolstoy's novels. This similarity with two of the most likable, humane, and reasoned men from Russian literature unveils what this man and musician was in real life, and not the vulgar, spoilt youth as he is often portrayed—he could have lost his way—yet he was able to maintain a sense of dignity to the end. Mosolov was a modernist who could have been even more significant if he lacked the caprice of refusing to revise compositions, yet his greatest hindrance was the attacks from the proletarian musicians of the 1920s and 1930s, and perhaps if he performed his music in the West, he could have developed quite differently, but then we know that the European modernists all changed stylistically in the 1930s and 1940s.

The composer Edison Denisov appraised both Mosolov and Roslavets in more laudatory terms than Prokofiev and Shostakovich—at least regarding their works of the 1920s.[87] Hakobian suggested that if Mosolov had enjoyed greater artistic freedom in his development, "he could have grown into a really remarkable and independent figure, perhaps a Russian counterpart to Edgard Varèse."[88] It took three years after his passing before *Sovetskaya Muzyka* could publish an article about his early career by Inna Barsova and rather ironically edited by one of his former nemeses Viktor Bely.[89] Alexander Mosolov embraced constructivism, and modernism - revealing one of the great trendsetters in twentieth-century music.

NOTES

1. Alekseyenko, Nikolay, "O tvorchestve A. V. Mosolova, tridtsatii-semidesyatikh godakh," *A.V. Mosolov, Statii i Vospominanii*, Moscow: Kompositor, 1986, 168.
2. Schwartz, Boris, *Music and Musical Life in Soviet Russia 1917–1981*, Bloomington: Indiana University Press, 1983, 124.
3. Schwartz, Boris, *Music and Musical Life in Soviet Russia 1917–1981*, Bloomington: Indiana University Press, 1983, 128.
4. Barsova, Inna, "Iz neopubilikovannykh arkhivov Mosolova," *Sovetskaya Muzyka*, No. 7, 1989, 91.
5. Barsova, "Iz neopubilikovannykh arkhivov Mosolova," *Sovetskaya Muzyka*, No. 7, 1989, 89–91.
6. Mosolov to Stalin, "Iz neopublivonnovo arkhiva A. V. Mosolova," Ed. by Barsova, *Sovetskaya Muzyka*, No. 7, 1989, 80–92.
7. Mosolov to Stalin, "Iz neopublivonnovo arkhiva A. V. Mosolova," Ed. by Barsova, *Sovetskaya Muzyka*, No. 7, 1989, 80–92.
8. Derzhanovsky to Prokofiev, April 16, 1932, LPA, f.29, f.290.
9. Barsova, Inna, "Iz neopubilikovannykh arkhivov Mosolova," *Sovetskaya Muzyka*, No. 7, 1989, 92.
10. The canal was built in twenty months and commissioned on June 20, 1933—author.
11. *Bolshaya Sovetskaya Encyclopaedia*, second edition, 1950, vol. 4, 461.
12. Barsova, Inna, "Dvadzatii gody," *Sovetskaya Muzyka*, No. 8, 1989, 70.
13. Selunskaya and Zezina, "Documentary Film—A Soviet Source," *Stalinism and Soviet Cinema*, Oxford: Routledge, 1993, 182.
14. TSGALI, "Zaklyuchenii," material k kartine. 1934–1936, f. 2450, op. 2, ed.kh r. 628, 254.
15. TSGALI, "Zaklyuchenii," material k kartine. 1934–1936, f. 2450, op. 2, ed.kh r. 628, 270.
16. Goryacheva, T.V., "Sotzrealism kak osoznannaya neobkhodimost: Mastera avangarda v kontsa 1920-x-nachala 1930-x," *Festival iskusstve imeni Nikolaya Roslavetsa i Nauma Gabo: Materialy mezhdunarodnoy nauchno-teoreticheskoy konferentsii*, Bryansk: Bryanskoye Muzykalnoye uchilische, 1994, 46.
17. Bely, Viktor, "Protiv formalisma i falshi. Tvorcheskii Diskussiya v moskovskom soyuze kompositorov," *Sovetskaya Muzyka*, No. 3, 1936, 20.
18. Vaks, Klara, "Kompositor Mosolov isklyuchen iz SSK," *Sovetskaya Muzyka*, No. 3, 1936, 104.
19. Vaks, Klara, "A.K. Mosolov," *Sovetskaya Muzyka*, No. 7, 1936, 104.
20. A. Mosolov letter to Myaskovsky, Rimsky, "Iz proshlovo sovetskoy muzykanovo kultury," vyp. 3, 1982, 74–75.
21. Barsova, Inna, "Dvadzatii gody," *Sovetskaya Muzyka*, No. 8, 1989, 71.
22. Barsova, Inna, "Dvadzatii gody," *Sovetskaya Muzyka*, No. 8, 1989, 70.
23. Tur, Brothers, "Deviations of a Genius," *Izvestiya*, September 18, 1937.
24. Tur, Brothers, "Deviations of a Genius," Izvestiya, September 18, 1937.
25. Tur, Brothers, "Deviations of a Genius," Izvestiya, September 18, 1937.

26. Tur, Brothers, "Deviations of a Genius," *Izvestiya*, September 18, 1937.
27. Barsova, Inna, "Iz neopubilikovannykh arkhivov Mosolova," *Sovetskaya Muzyka*, No. 8, 1989, 70–71.
28. Barsova, Inna, *Sovetskaya Muzyka*, No. 8, 1989, 72.
29. Vypiska iz protokola, archive of Nina Meshko, *Sovetskaya Muzyka*, No. 8, 1989, 72.
30. Barsova, Inna, "Iz neopubilikovannykh arkhivov Mosolova," *Sovetskaya Muzyka*, No. 8, 1989, 72.
31. Barsova, Inna, "Iz neopubilikovannykh arkhivov Mosolova," *Sovetskaya Muzyka*, No. 8, 1989, 73.
32. Barsova, Inna, "Iz neopubilikovannykh arkhivov Mosolova," *Sovetskaya Muzyka*, No. 8, 1989, 70–72.
33. Beltov, E., "Rasstrelyannaya literatora," *Vechernaya Moskva*, July 19, 1988.
34. Vlasova, E.S., *1948 god v sovetskoy muziki*, Moscow: 21 Classika, 2010, 285.
35. Dulova, E. G. "*Dnevniki yunosti*," Fragment of manuscript to Rimsky, "A.V. Mosolov: biographicheskii ocherk," *A.V. Mosolov, Statii i Vospominanii*, Moscow: Kompositor, 1986, 24.
36. Dulova, E. G. "*Dnevniki yunost*," Fragment of manuscript to Rimsky, "A.V. Mosolov: biographicheskii ocherk," *A.V. Mosolov, Statii i Vospominanii*, Moscow: Kompositor, 1986, 24.
37. Concert Programme archive of Nina Meshko, *Sovetskaya Muzyka*, No. 8, 1989, 74.
38. Barsova, Inna, "Iz neopubilikovannykh arkhivov Mosolova," *Sovetskaya Muzyka*, No. 8, 1989, 74.
39. Archive of Nina Meshko, *Sovetskaya Muzyka*, No. 8, 1989, 74.
40. Alekseyenko, "O tvorchestve A. V. Mosolova, tridtsatii-semidesyatikh godakh," *A.V. Mosolov, Statii i Vospominanii*, Moscow: Kompositor, 1986, 143.
41. Alekseyenko, "O tvorchestve A. V. Mosolova, tridtsatii-semidesyatikh godakh," *A.V. Mosolov, Statii i Vospominanii*, Moscow: Kompositor, 1986, 147.
42. RGALI, f. 2085, op. 1, ed. khr. 351, L.37.
43. Muradeli, Vano, "Novoye v sovetskoy muziki," *Sovetskoye iskusstvo*, January 9, 1940.
44. Kreitner, G., "Decada sovetskoy muziki," *Moskovskoy Bolshevik*, November 23, 1939.
45. Rimsky, L., "A.V. Mosolov: biographicheskii ocherk," *A.V. Mosolov, Statii i Vospominanii*, Moscow: Kompositor, 1986, 24.
46. Rimsky, L., "A.V. Mosolov: biographicheskii ocherk," *A.V. Mosolov, Statii i Vospominanii*, Moscow: Kompositor, 1986, 28.
47. Barsova, Inna, "Iz neopubilikovannykh arkhivov Mosolova," *Sovetskaya Muzyka*, No. 8, 1989, 74.
48. Barsova, Inna, "Iz neopubilikovannykh arkhivov Mosolova," *Sovetskaya Muzyka*, No. 8, 1989, 75.
49. Alekseyenko, "O tvorchestve A. V. Mosolova, tridtsatii-semidesyatikh godakh," *A.V. Mosolov, Statii i Vospominanii*, Moscow: Kompositor, 1986, 149.

50. A mysterious consequence is that several arias from the opera "Aria of Valya" and "Aria of Nikolay Kotlyarevsky" and "Aria of the parachutists" written to texts by Rudnev are in Nina Mesko's archive—author.

51. Rimsky, L., "A.V. Mosolov: biographicheskii ocherk," *A.V. Mosolov, Statii i Vospominanii*, Moscow: Kompositor, 1986, 30.

52. "Simfoniya ob Otechestvennoy voine—proizvedeniye A, Mosolova," *Vechernaya Moskva*, July 17, 1942.

53. Alekseyenko, "O tvorchestve A. V. Mosolova, tridtsatii-semidesyatikh godakh," *A.V. Mosolov, Statii i Vospominanii*, Moscow: Kompositor, 1986, 157.

54. Vlasova, E.S., *1948 god v sovetskoy muziki*, Moscow: 21 Classika, 2010, 190.

55. This is unclear because of Mosolov's own recollections of the work, making allusions to it in letters and conversations—author.

56. Alekseyenko, "O tvorchestve A. V. Mosolova, tridtsatii-semidesyatikh godakh," *A.V. Mosolov, Statii i Vospominanii*, Moscow: Kompositor, 1986, 148.

57. Korev, S., "Simfonicheskoye sobraniye. V centralny dom rabotnikov iskusstve," *Vechernaya Moskva*, February 10, 1947.

58. Mosolov, A., "Poezdka v kubanskie kolhozy," *Sovetskaya Muzika*, No. 5, 1950, 46.

59. Alekseyenko, N., "O tvorchestve A. V. Mosolova, tridtsatii-semidesyatikh godakh," *A.V. Mosolov, Statii i Vospominanii*, Moscow: Kompositor, 1986, 157.

60. RGALI, f.648, op. 5, ed.kh. 148, l.24-27.

61. Vlasova, E.S., *1948 god v sovetskoy muziki*, Moscow: 21 Classika, 2010, 219.

62. *Sovetskaya Muzyka*, No. 1, 1948, 54–62.

63. RGALI, f.962, op. 3, ed.kh.1956 (1), l.27, 28.

64. Vlasova, E.S., *1948 god v sovetskoy muziki*, Moscow: 21 Classika, 2010, 344.

65. Mosolov, A., "V Stanitskakh Kubani," *Sovetskaya Muzyka*, No. 1, 1953, 61–65.

66. Mosolov, A., "Poezdka v kubanskie kolhozy," *Sovetskaya Muzika*, No. 5, 1950, 44, "V Stanitskakh Kubani" No. 1, 1953, 61–65, "V Stepyakh Stavropolya," *Sovetskaya Muzika*, No. 3, 1956, 99.

67. "Pesni Kubanskikh kosakov. Materiali k izucheniya Kubanskovo kosachevo voiska," Vypusk 1-8. *Sobranii deistvitelnom chelnom Kubanskovo staticheskovo komiteta k 200-letnemy jubilee Voiska.*

68. Mosolov, A., "Poezdka v kubanskie kolhozy," *Sovetskaya Muzika*, No. 5, 1950, 44.

69. Myaskovsky wrote his Twenty-Third Symphony based on Kabardinian themes, Prokofiev also used local folklore for his Quartet No. 2, and Alexandrov used material for his opera—author.

70. Author interview with Inna Barsova February 25, 2017.

71. Kondratyeva, Svetlana, *Russkiye Narodny Pesni Pomorye*, Moscow, 1966.

72. Alekseyenko, "O tvorchestve A. V. Mosolova, tridtsatii-semidesyatikh godakh," *A.V. Mosolov, Statii i Vospominanii*, Moscow: Kompositor, 1986, 161–162.

73. Alekseyenko, "O tvorchestve A. V. Mosolova, tridtsatii-semidesyatikh godakh," *A.V. Mosolov, Statii i Vospominanii*, Moscow: Kompositor, 1986, 158.

74. Nina Meshko archive, *Sovetskaya Muzyka*, July 1989, 88.

75. Bagritsky, Eduard, *Pesnya pro Opanas*, Moscow: Gosudarstvenniye Izdatelstvo Khudozhestvennoye Literatura, 1935, 5.

76. Telegram from deputy minister of culture G. P. Alexandrov of August 10, 1970—Archive of Nina Meshko.

77. For instance, the key theme of the third movement from the E major symphony reappears in the first movement of the Second Symphony written two years later. The first idea from the first movement of the E major symphony is reprised for the leading melody in the finale of his Third Symphony. Furthermore, the central theme of the Second Symphony's first movement becomes the leading idea in the C Major Symphony of 1959. The leading theme from the finale from Symphony No. 2 becomes the second idea in the first section of the second movement of the Third Symphony. The secondary theme of the third movement in the Second Symphony becomes the core idea in the opening to the third movement of the Song-Symphony and the lead theme in the first movement of his Fifth Symphony. Similarly, the main idea in the finale of the Song-Symphony is recycled as the second theme in the third movement of the Third Symphony. The second movement (*Largo*) of the E Major Symphony is the second movement (*Largo sostenuto*) of the Second Symphony with orchestral variations—author.

78. Rimsky, L., "A.V. Mosolov: biographicheskii ocherk," *A.V. Mosolov, Statii i Vospominanii*, Moscow: Kompositor, 1986, 36.

79. Alekseyenko, N., "O tvorchestve A. V. Mosolova, tridtsatii-semidesyatikh godakh," *A.V. Mosolov, Statii i Vospominanii*, Moscow, 1986, 167.

80. Rimsky, L., "A.V. Mosolov: biographicheskii ocherk," *A.V. Mosolov, Statii i Vospominanii*, Moscow: Kompositor, 1986, 36.

81. Kabalevsky, D.B., "Pevets rodnoy strany," *Sovetskaya Kultura*, July 27, 1973.

82. Rimsky, L., "A.V. Mosolov: biographicheskii ocherk," *A.V. Mosolov, Statii i Vospominanii*, Moscow: Kompositor, 1986, 37.

83. Kurysheva, Tatyana, "Varshavskaya osen-73," "Dva mneniya o konzertakh festivalya," *Sovetskaya Muzika*, No. 2, 1974, 126.

84. Solodukho, A., "Varshavskaya osen-73," "Dva mneniya o konzertakh festivalya," *Sovetskaya Muzika*, No. 2, 1974, 123.

85. Rimsky, L., "A.V. Mosolov: biographicheskii ocherk," *A.V. Mosolov, Statii i Vospominanii*, Moscow: Kompositor, 1986, 43.

86. Schwartz, Boris, *Music and Musical Life in Soviet Russia*, Bloomington: Indiana University Press, 1983, 625.

87. Kholopov and Tzernova, "Edison Denisov," *Moscow Kompositor*, 1993, 154.

88. Hakobian, Leon, *Music of the Soviet Age: 1917–1987*, Stockholm: Melos, 1998, 54.

89. *Sovetskaya Muzyka*, 1976, 12, 77–87.

Conclusion

As we have seen, the first decades of the twentieth century witnessed outstanding examples in modernism; among the brave explorers of new worlds in sound and harmony were musicians from across the developed world; Bartók, Hindemith, Krenek, Ives, Prokofiev, Satie, Schoenberg, Shostakovich, Strauss, and Stravinsky. Through their brutal rhythms and dissonance their music both shocked and fascinated audiences more familiar with the romanticism of Brahms, Tchaikovsky, Verdi, and Wagner. Among the most sensational were Richard Strauss's *Salome* and its "Dance of the Seven Veils," Schoenberg's String Quartet No. 2, and *Pierrot lunaire*, Stravinsky's *Le Sacre du Printemps*, Edgar Varèse's *Arcana*, and Erik Satie's *Rag-Time Parade* among much else. In Russia, the avant-garde was first influenced by European trends, yet their modernism embraced all the disciplines; from Malevich to Kandinsky, to the poets Severyanin and Blok, the architects Tatlin and Gabo to the composers Prokofiev and Stravinsky. The utopian idealism of the Russian avant-garde seemed to possess a wild and chaotic momentum lending it a dynamic and powerfully explosive effect that was expended in three revolutions.

It is clear that the changing political and economic structures in Europe enforced stylistic changes on the arts; ideology has always enforced its strictures in society, but this was not the only reason for the decline of the avant-garde. The great financial collapse in 1929 caused enormous societal damage across the world's markets, transforming great wealth into penury, many millions lost their livelihoods overnight, and children were thrown into poverty. That could not have but a catastrophic effect in society, nowhere more so than in the arts and music. Much of the audiences disappeared, and the days of the avant-garde were, for the time being, over. The Great Depression of the 1930s changed the arts, yet there were other reasons for the avant-garde disappearing. One of the factors in composers changing their style was through gaining maturity, the search for expression continues, but with greater knowledge and mastery in composition and technique.

In the Russian context, many argue that *Pravda*'s criticism of Shostakovich's *Lady Macbeth of Mtsensk* forced the change by the composer from "formalism" and modernism toward traditional classical forms; however, we know that there were already signs of a stylistic change. As in the case of the purported "reply to just criticism" in Shostakovich's symphony, the British musicologist Malcolm MacDonald shows, "The Fifth's apparently sudden stylistic shift to a more immediately comprehensible and classicizing tonal language, often seen as a response to the *Pravda* denunciations of early 1936, is in fact fully anticipated in the Cello Sonata, which may therefore be taken as evidence that Shostakovich was already developing in this direction."[1] Shostakovich's Cello Sonata, Opus 40 was written in 1934, two years before the infamous critique "Muddle instead of Music."

In Europe, following the Nazis' ascent to power, Schoenberg departed for the United States, where he quickly abandoned his twelve-note theory in some of his works. This was observed in the work of one of the most distinguished modernists in Germany. The musicologist Jonathan Petropoulos notes that "with the shift away from his most aggressively modernist music behind him, and with a sense that Nazi music policy was inchoate and inconsistent, Paul Hindemith set out to find a place in the Reich. He understood that his best hopes rested on developing personal relationships with those in positions of influence and took steps to cultivate allies."[2] It seems that this development for the composer was not only for political or societal reasons but simply to benefit his audience, as the scholar David Stanley Smith explains, "At one time, (Hindemith) was an extreme modernist but lately has softened his style so that it is accessible to the average listener."[3] Unfortunately for Hindemith, the Nazi regime had no place for him and he found that work was fast disappearing. Petropoulos informs us that "yet despite the deteriorating situation, Hindemith remained in Nazi Germany in the mid-1930s and continued to hope for official acceptance."[4] However, the Nazis were determined to rid themselves of any insubordinate musicians, on the ship taking him into exile, Hindemith wrote to his sister. "If I could return with good grace and with the prospect of a somewhat secure existence, I would have the ship turned around right away."[5] In America, Hindemith found fame as a respected teacher and never wrote compositions in the startling and exciting modernism of before, and despite returning to Europe after the war, his newly written music seemed to lack the spark and fire of his youth.

Indeed, for modernist composers seeking sanctuary from the Nazis, American society appeared as unreceptive to new music as Hitlerite Germany, albeit for the most bizarre reasons. The British scholar Frances

Stonor Saunders states that "America's cultural mandarins detected a contrary virtue: for them, (modernism) spoke to a specifically anti-Communist ideology, the ideology of freedom, of free enterprise."[6] The House Committee Un-American Activities, set up in 1938, did not favor some musicians who had sought refuge from fascism. Petropoulos points out that "Congressman George Dondero, a Republican from Missouri, proclaimed 'modernism to be, quite simply part of a worldwide conspiracy to weaken American resolve,' and rumors even circulated that certain abstract works were encoded maps to US missile fields and military installations. Most observers, however, took a very different view of modernism."[7]

Staying with the fate of Paul Hindemith, we find that he became a quite different musician from that of just a few years before. According to the scholar Michael H. Kater,

> already the German premiere of his opera *Mathis der Maler* in Stuttgart in December 1946 was an anachronism for a once avant-garde composer. His neo-classicism was deemed incrementally out of date at Darmstadt until he had to make room for Schoenberg around 1949. Thus Hindemith himself became embittered, to the point where the systematic refutation of the serialism of the Second Viennese School became a major theme of his last ten years. So although he had the ear of the follower of modernism for some time, he was perceived as sufficiently conservative, especially in memory of the *Mathis der Maler* symphony of 1934, to please the members of the Old Guard—to the same degree that he was criticized by such Young Turks as Henze.[8]

With the arrival in the United States of exiles from European tyranny, the modernist composers found a quite different cultural idiom. As Metzer writes, "Conservative Americans indebted to such Victorian perspectives as virtuousness and a belief in unshakeable universal truths often struggled against the modernist fascination with uncertainty, irrationality, raw emotion, immorality, mechanization, complexity, and new art forms."[9] The most radical was Schoenberg, who was greeted by such epithets, such as from Henry Finck, "The Musical Messiah—or Satan?"[10] Schoenberg's atonalism was attacked as if an atrocity by critics in the US media as "monstrous crimes against beauty."[11] Arnold Schoenberg was, of course, the most exceptional of the avant-garde composers who found a career in the United States in the 1930s. His departure from the groundbreaking music of the early 1900s became conclusive when he discovered music was but a commodity in America. As Boris Schwartz informs us, "After his move to the United States, so it has been averred by some, Schoenberg made concessions to a more conventionally adjusted music audience by at times retracting the serial style of composition in favor of traditionally tonal constructions."[12]

Of course, like Hindemith, the Austrian serialist became an acclaimed teacher in California, albeit becoming a hermitic composer unwilling to reprise the outstanding fame of his fin de siècle life in Vienna. The West Coast of the United States was a world away from the horrors of the Second World War; hence the advantages of a secure professorship, together with regular conducting opportunities, offered a means that he could not have imagined in Nazi-run Austria. Already he was aware of what music the Americans wanted from him, and it wasn't serial music. The scholar Michael Kater writes that "it is true that many, if not most, Americans found twelve-tone music difficult to comprehend."[13] Schoenberg quickly unveiled for his new audiences a piece more akin to their conservative tastes. The late English music writer Peter Heyworth comments that "when Schoenberg's new Suite for String Orchestra in G major was performed in New York by the Philharmonic Symphonic Orchestra under Klemperer in the summer of 1935, apparently marking a return to tonality, the sophisticated *New York Times* critic Olin Downes was dismayed, finding it 'thickly and muddily written,' in an 'affectation of the old sturdy manner, and thereafter mordant counterpoint.' For him, it was 'Ersatz music, music on and of paper.'"[14] There were more hostile appreciations of Schoenberg's turn to tonality from other critics. The left-wing musician Charles Seeger described the Suite as "old spoiled wine in old spoiled bottles" "safe for bourgeocracy."[15] In the *New York Times*, Downes exclaimed that audiences could "now expect atonal fugues by Shirley Temple."[16] While the critic Winthrop Sargeant wrote, "Has the much-advertised Californian sunshine thawed out the gloomy apostle of the twelve-tone Grundgestalt and left him singing roundelays among the poppies?"[17]

Yet all the Suite was doing was marking the beginning of a phase in which Schoenberg took the liberty of switching between serialism and tonality (by which he may have intended to show that he still was master of the universal art of composition; he said later that he has given in to a long-standing desire "to return to the old styles").[18] Altogether, there was, as Stuckenschmidt has rightly pointed out, no question of "turning back."[19] In her study of Schoenberg's life in the United States, Sabine Feisst wrote, "He has been pitied and America blamed for its 'commercially' orientated institutions that hindered his productivity and the reception of his music. But Schoenberg himself has also been criticized for being elitist and unwilling to adapt to American life; and conversely, he has been rebuked for his attempts to accommodate to America by sometimes compromising his progressive compositional approach."[20]

In the American period, Schoenberg alternated between the old and new styles. Before arriving in Boston in 1933, Schoenberg had been working on a Concerto for String Quartet and Orchestra after a Concerto Grosso by

Handel, not an atonal work.²¹ Next came the Suite for String Orchestra of 1934, again in a tonal mold, perhaps to please himself but also to be playable by US youth orchestras.²² For Schoenberg's following compositions, the serial compositions proved difficult to play, pushing instrumentalists to the limits of their capacity. That was exemplified by the Violin Concerto, Op. 36 (1934–1936). Dedicated to Webern, it was first performed by violinist Louis Krasner, with the Philadelphia Orchestra under Leopold Stokowski on December 6, 1940.²³

The Dutch musicologist Francis Maes writes about the different aspirations of the avant-garde,

> The so-called New Music that emerged after 1910 was in many ways a deliberate attempt to discard existing institutions. The avant-garde aimed not only at technical and stylistic innovation, but also at a transformation of the entire musical apparatus. While the Western avant-garde aspired to dismantle the traditional institutions, however, Soviet culture clung to them. The difference between the two music cultures was greatest during the postwar period. The Cold War was reflected in the musical sphere by a radical split between an institution-supporting form of music with an emphasis on ideological importance, on the Soviet side, and an institution-transcending aesthetic stressing the transformation of the musical material, on the Western side.²⁴

In the West, Soviet music was at a peak in popularity during the Second World War, but this all quickly changed after the wartime alliance crumbled, and most of all, the change in alliances was reflected in modernist music by the changing political climate between the former allies. There were however positive advantages for Schoenberg as Jennifer DeLapp describes,

> The reputation of Schoenberg's music benefited from Cold War politics as well. (. . .) Schoenberg's dodecaphony became not only a politically correct compositional approach, but also a symbol of creative freedom in both America and Europe. (. . .) The demand for music conveying socialist and patriotic messages declined with the end of the war, and McCarthyism arguably propelled left-wing artists (including Copland) to abandon their politically engaged art in favor of the "safe" territory of abstract expression.²⁵

Amid this, there emerged questions of who the true modernists were, and here unveiled by these two examples. The avant-garde composer Charles Wuorinen wrote that, "Squabbles about which group continued Schoenberg's heritage and was the 'real' avant-garde emerged as well. Viewing themselves as Schoenberg's true heirs, 'uptown' composers dismissed downtown music as 'theatrico-musical expressions' and 'Cagean amateurism' and questioned

Cage's studies with Schoenberg."[26] Conversely, downtown composers "poked fun at the 'university' avant-garde and its 'anti-experimental Einstein(s).'"[27]

The case of Igor Stravinsky is of course quite similar; however, he managed to change his musical style as quickly as he switched from producer to promoter, and astonishingly managed to attain his brilliance in whatever genre and style he composed in from modernism to neoclassicism, and serialism. Naturally, he was well aware that music is but an article of trade, and fashion comes and goes as quickly as the weather changes. There were also discernable transformations in his adaptability to political systems as is noted here by the scholar James R. Currie, "Traces of Stravinsky's tendency towards conflating artistic order with an implied social order make their pressure felt strongly at such moments, bringing us close to the man who was attracted to Mussolini and fascism."[28] It would appear that the life of a perpetual émigré had its influences on his creativity, the Czech novelist Milan Kundera suggested that there was a link between Stravinsky's exile status and his "neoclassical" stylistic play. "Without doubt, Stravinsky, like all others, bore within him the wound of his emigration; without a doubt, his artistic evolution would have taken a different path if he had been able to stay where he was born."[29] Other exiles maintained their style of expression, for instance, as the academic Stephen Graham writes, "Running throughout Weill's varied career was what Hinton calls a desire for 'reform,' as can be seen in everything from the socialist epic theater of *Die Dreigroschenoper* (1928) to the formally daring albeit highly tuneful psychoanalytical Broadway musical *Lady in the Dark* (1941), and from the hybrid opera-musical *Street Scene* (1946) to the anti-apartheid show *Lost in the Stars* (1949)."[30]

Stephen Graham again informs us of the diverse forms of expression of the French avant-garde school,

> Eric Satie's music could explore humor, farce and popular music styles, as, for example, in the ragtime of a short piece like *Le Piccadilly* (c1904, pre-echoing the Debussy of *Le Petit nègre*, 1909) or the gunshots, typewriters and tottering oom-pah of his ballet *Parade* (1924), or, on the other hand, entertain with the conceptual hi-jinks of something like *Vexations* (1893), without ever getting beyond the feel of a cross-cultural encounter. The same could be said of the composer-members of *Les Six* in the 1920s and 1930s, where cabaret and jazz aesthetics come together (creatively, but perhaps uneasily) with modernist sounds and ambitions in pieces like Darius Milhaud's *La Creation du monde* (1922–1923) and Francis Poulenc's Concerto for Two Pianos (1932).[31]

The change of style from the "old" avant-garde in Germany is interesting, for, if one compares the output by Richard Strauss, for example, during the Weimar period, and then during the Third Reich. The British scholar James

Currie once again tells us that "the content of Strauss's operatic works from *Der Rosenkavalier* onwards, which so frequently turn to comedy, seems studiously to avoid the potential for political controversy and biting cultural critique that Offenbach's works, with such virtuosity, simultaneously encourage and circumvent."[32]

Reflecting on the three "apostles" of Russian music, it is useful to examine their careers from the angle of their relevance to music in the prerevolutionary and postrevolutionary periods, and what their importance is today. In the case of Roslavets, Popov, and Mosolov, it is clear that each composer was unique, while sharing a modernity, there remained a pioneering strain in their composing through to the end of their lives. There also existed specific problems in their careers; in the case of Popov, many were self-inflicted because of the lethargy and indolence of the writing process from the initial conception through to the final orchestration; the masterly First Symphony took at least two revisions through seven years and reorchestrating the score after the one and only performance. This compares with his Second Symphony which took six months after composing the original film music. Despite fifteen years work, Popov's *Alexander Nevsky* opera is complete in only one of the planned five acts. Of course, we know that writing for theater and film was his "bread and butter," yet we also know that other composers like Prokofiev and Shostakovich were earning a living from theater and film, yet seemingly their concert works were not hindered through a prolonged time. If Popov could have written his symphony and released his completed score to one of the several interested European and American conductors, then perhaps his career could have developed in quite a different plan. Popov remained an open and warm human being despite the enormous hindrances set before him during the 1930s by the proletarian musicians, if his First Symphony was recognized as a great Russian symphonic work, then perhaps Soviet music would have advanced quite differently. We shall never know.

Roslavets was born into poverty and seeing the imprisonment of his brother by the Japanese in 1904 and his witnessing the brutal handling of student protests in 1905 helped to radicalize him. This intolerance became more embedded by rebelling against the teaching in the Conservatoire and emboldened him on a search for new methodology—reinforced after hearing the mystical chord of Alexander Scriabin. The period was revolutionary in more than a political or societal sense because of the transformative effects of the painters, writers, composers, and philosophers who were then taking Russia to unknown frontiers, often along utopian lines, and often engendered by revolutionary politics. Roslavets became part of the idealist Proletkult project to bring the arts to the masses and joined the Social-Revolutionary Party which was in coalition initially with the Bolsheviks. In all this he appeared to remain a loyal supporter of the political system through until his death in

1944. Mosolov was as loyal to the Soviet system as Roslavets, and he fully engaged in the cause by signing up for the Red Army during the Civil War. The injuries sustained in the fighting had an effect on his physical and mental health, yet, before the conflict there were signs of unusually eccentric behavior by his running away from school to join the fighting in the Great War. His background was a privileged one with him accruing a wide spectrum of knowledge and artistic interests. Both Mosolov and Popov deserve their place as leading avant-garde composers in the Soviet Union, yet their legacy rests on a small number of pieces from the 1920s, while the remainder of their careers was spent on music which was middle stream, exceptionally well written—with a thread of genius—but no longer displaying the extraordinary brilliance of their youth. Roslavets, on the other hand, left a large number of outstanding music in almost all genres, and it is intriguing that at least 50% of his works are lost or destroyed.

Dmitry Shostakovich was one of the most astonishing avant-garde composers in the 1920s, yet much of his career has been misrepresented by different groups in the world of music. The Dutch musicologist Francis Maes identifies the suitability of Volkhov's *Testimony* for the musical world, "the public was given precisely what it seemed to have been waiting for. The book filled a need. (. . .) At the end of the 1970s, the music market set out to make Shostakovich's oeuvre part of the general repertoire. The reason is simple: Shostakovich wrote music for two of the most important institutions of modern concert life, the symphony and the string quartet."[33] Maes suggests that Volkhov's book conjured up the image of the repressed musician who instead of being an "official Soviet composer" was "a lifelong dissident, who behind the façade of his music had been making ironic comments about the Soviet regime the whole time."[34] Tchaikovsky, of course, was on good terms with the Imperial Court and always played a fine line between what was permissible or not with both his stage works and other pieces with his patrons, whether it be Nadezhda von Meck or the Court. Leon Hakobian here enlightens us on the societal transformations in the early Soviet period,

> As is commonly believed, in the mid-1920s, when Shostakovich was making his first steps as a professional musician, the musical scene represented a field of battle between two major forces. One of them consisted of more or less apolitical professionals formed during the so-called Silver Age of Russian culture, and their most enlightened pupils. The representatives of this group, according to the cataloging in 1923 by the party's "number two," Leon Trotsky, were considered fellow travelers (*poputchiki*): though being sympathetic to the aims of the revolution, they still had to be re-educated (or, using the peculiar terminology of the 1920s, "reforged") in the spirit of Bolshevism. The second force was represented by adherents of the so-called proletarian culture—dogmatists

and careerists, whose mental outlook was narrow and professional qualifications were low, but whose proletarian, Bolshevik views were firm and unbending. The first group promoted the traditional approach to artistic creation as a highly individual affair, while the second group recognized only class interest, refusing to the individual right of self-expression.[35]

Of course, in the last years of the Silver Age, there were other composers who laid a path for the avant-garde in Russia, among the most significant are Mikhail Matyushin, Arthur Lourié, and Joseph Schillinger.

MIKHAIL MATYUSHIN

One of the most significant figures in the Russian avant-garde—born into poverty—Mikhail Vasilyevich Matyushin (1861–1934) was the sixteenth child of a peasant family living in the Volga river port of Nizhny-Novgorod. The bastard son of Nikolay Saburov—from a famous acting family—Mikhail was brought up single-handedly by his mother Irina Matyushina—a former serf. We know that his attraction to music came from singing in a church choir and learning to play the violin. Mikhail attended the Free Music School in his hometown and continued studying at the Moscow Conservatoire (1876–1881) in violin with Professor A. A. Gilf and in harmony with Professor Sergey Taneyev. Attracted to foreign languages, through self-study Mikhail learned French, German, and English.

It was evident that Matyushin showed outstanding talent, for between 1882 and 1913, he was appointed a member of the first violins in the Imperial Court Orchestra. Eager to broaden his knowledge, he studied painting between 1894 and 1898 with the Polish impressionist painter Jan Ciągliński (1858–1912) in whose studio he met his second wife, the poet Elena Guro (1877–1913). He also studied with Léon Bakst (1866–1924) and later with Guro joined the avant-garde group around the painter, composer, and businessman Nikolay Kulbin (1868–1917). This association led to his paintings being shown at the "Exhibitions of Modern Art" in 1908, where he met Malevich. In 1909, Matyushin and Guro broke away from Kulbin, disagreeing with his group's eclecticism, decadence, and the allure to Vrubel's mystical works.

Now, in 1910, Matyushin and Guro became the de facto leaders of the Cubo-Futurist school in Russia (at the same time as the Italian futurists) when they issued their manifesto "Trap the Judges." Matyushin was influenced by the theosophy of Pyotr Ouspensky, notably his "Tertium Organum: A Guide to the Mysteries of the World." He also developed a friendship with the libertarian and idealist philosopher Nikolay Lossky, whose book *The World as an Organic Whole* shaped his philosophy in years to come. At this time, he started teaching the violin (pro bono) at the Peoples' Conservatoire in Moscow. Matyushin's first musical compositions were settings of Elena Guro, writing a symphonic suite *Harlequin* for her book *"Sharmanka"* in 1909. There followed the incomplete *Dances of Venera* (1910–1914). Regrettably, only the violin part remains of this music. In 1912, he wrote *Autumn Dream* for violin and piano, which appeared in Guro's eponymous publication in 1912, and *The Crane* collection of poems in 1915.

In St. Petersburg, Matyushin helped organize the "Union of Youth" embracing Alexey Kruchenykh, Mayakovsky, Khlebnikov, Goncharova, the Burlyuk brothers, Larionov, Tatlin, Filonov, and others. We have a sketch of Matyushin from this time by the journalist Yevgeny Adamov, "The meeting was opened by a long disheveled futurist with a long bare neck and wooden voice. 'We declare war against individual sentimentality!' he began, reading a lengthy, like himself, list of his enemies. 'We declare war against the following tendencies in art: science, psychology, responsible society, homogeneity and civil thought.'"[36] Matyushin's home became the de facto center of the futurist movement through into the 1930s, and as a forum about modern art and hosting rehearsals for his opera *Victory over the Sun*.

In 1913, at the First All-Russian Congress of Futurist poets, Matyushin read a paper on "New Music." This was his theory of quarter-tone music and quarter-tone notation—called "budetlyan notation" to be unveiled in his new opera. The score for the opera's introduction was published in memory of his wife (Elena Guro died from leukemia at the age of thirty-five) in *"The Three"* collection of poetry in 1913, and by the publishing cooperative "Svet" later that year. The opera was to be the first in a trilogy, the second—*Victory over the War* and lastly, *Victory over Imperialism*. It coincided with the launch by Matyushin, Kruchenykh, and Malevich of their futurist manifesto "A Slap in the Face of Public Opinion."

The budding theatrical offshoots of the futurist movement—the play *A Tragedy: Vladimir Mayakovsky* and Matyushin's *Victory over the Sun* opera both date from 1913. The libretto was by Velimir Khlebnikov and Alexey Kruchenykh, with costumes and sets by Malevich. The characters include Nero and Caligula, Sportsmen, Funeral directors, Telephone operator, Narrator, Aviator, and much else. Vorobyov writes that "this futurist opera was the first blow against the classical canons of the genre, and its unique manifesto of the aesthetics of negativity." The writers essentially produced an anti-opera, "more precisely, an imitation of all the features of the 'queens' of classical music theater, but turned inside out."[37] The creators used images of the Commedia dell Arte, mysteria, and even the circus. They attempted to shock, and politicize, to provoke, and promote an aesthetic aggression, with a living manifesto of art played out on stage. Rather than stir debate, the "Union of Youth" aimed to scandalize and force their identity in the history of art. Matyushin's music was aleatoric, extremely free, and the chorus simply created a cacophony of noise akin to the "zaum" poetry of Kruchenykh with its unique neology of syllables and phonetic entity. The score provides for cannon fire, machine noises, and other sound effects.

Matyushin blended the use of polychords in harmonics and quarter tones with unique "Budetlyan" notation. His collaborators believed the sun represented the everyday falseness of the infallibility of modern society, and that one day humans can "capture" the sun to suit their purposes. It was in this show that Malevich's Black Square first made its appearance.[38]

Vorobyov writes that Malevich first unveiled his philosophy of symbolism through Suprematist characters and partly by the Black Square.[39] The show's success was greater than anyone could have imagined for the opera became one of the models of the new artistic world of the 1910s. The local press reported that "on stage, there strode some kind of scarecrows dressed as executioners from the Middle Ages, and (...) spoke various gibberish, evidently designed at causing a scandal."[40] Another witness recorded on "the coming and going of the most disparate masks. The backdrops changed, and the mood changed. Sirens were heard, and shots fired. The challenge was thrown down, and the struggle began. Who and with whom? No one knows."[41] Matyushin explained that his "opera has a profound inner content through making fun of the old romanticism and emptiness of words. The entire *Victory over the Sun* triumphs over old-fashioned traditional feelings about the sun and about beauty."[42] The anarchic style is illustrated here in Kruchenykh's script.

Actor on stage—I don't have everything at home!
Loud voice off stage—Correct!
Student—This isn't so witty.
Voice from above—Don't stop us listening.
(Whistling and applause)
The lady (at the top of her voice)—Quiet!
Several voices in unison—This is a futurist!
Several ladies' voices—You yourselves are futurist!
Several men's voices—This isn't for you, why are arguing?[43]

Malevich, one of the creators of this groundbreaking stage work, said that with this opera, "the curtain was immediately torn away from the hollering conscience of the old way of thinking, opening before their eyes the many wild paths stretching to the earth and the sky. We opened up a new road for theater."[44] The writer Tomashevsky reflected that "all the futurists were enraptured by Matyushin's music, especially Kruchenykh. 'Wonderful!' He shouted, pitifully waving his arms. Amazing! This isn't Tchaikovsky!"[45]

Kruchenykh shouting to all that would hear him that "literature, lubok and the madhouse are all hitched up together!"[46]

Little remains of Matyushin's score for *Victory over the Sun*; however, the stage work has been staged on several occasions on different continents. Malevich reprised the show without any music in Vitebsk in 1920 using the sets and costumes by his student Vera Ermolayeva. The opera of the ridiculous unsurprzingly gained adherents in Europe. In Hannover, in 1923, another Russian futurist El Lissitzky staged *Sieg Über die Sonne* in an electric showing of color lithography *Figurinen. Die plastische Gestaltung der electromechanischen Schau*. In 1993, the opera was revived in St. Petersburg at the Lensoviet Theater, without Matyushin's music, yet continuing the original stage concept. Since which, in Russia, the Stas Namin ensemble revived the stage work, and this *Theater of the Absurd* has been staged in Berlin and America continuing this avant-garde show a century after its premiere and seemingly as ever relevant or irrelevant to new generations.

Creating new groundbreaking stage works was not his only innovatory design for in 1916, Matyushin built a new form of violin using different woods, which he favored over his Italian violin. The idea was that this violin "would be more accessible for mass production and make it closer to the broad masses."[47] The instrument had something in common with the "gusli" folk instrument and other adaptations progressed over several years and were demonstrated at the Museum of Culture and Art in 1924. The *Don Quixote* piano suite (1914) concludes Matyushin's cycle devoted to Guro's poetry in "The Crane" in 1915, and along with his *Autumn Dream* demonstrates his new compositional technique. In 1919, after four years, again from Kruchenykh's libretto, Matyushin completed his second opera—*Victory over the War*.

All these avant-gardists Matyushin, Malevich, and Filonov shared a belief in the theory of perceptual millenarianism that stipulates that the possibilities of human perception remain unknown—and that a person can perceive 360 degrees, visualizing a rear plane. The avant-garde group formed a group called "See and Know."[48] Following the October Revolution, Matyushin and his colleagues took over the former Imperial Academy of Arts, opening up Free Workshops with himself starting a studio on Color. In 1921, the authorities decreed that the workshops be taken over by neoclassical painters, although both Matyushin and Malevich continued to teach at the Petrograd Institute of Art and Culture.

In 1923, Matyushin wrote a composition based on quarter tones for violin and piano that was performed incomplete on February 18 by the composer and Maria V. Ender at the home of Georgy M. Rimsky Korsakov (which was attended by Shostakovich). Rimsky Korsakov—nephew of the famous nationalist composer, together with E. D. Sholpo—explored a system of "graphic tonality." Matyushin continued working on his quarter-tone system and published an article in 1925—"De Music" which he followed up by forming a performing ensemble for quarter-tone music and conducted its concerts between 1925 and 1932. Among his final pieces are sketches for a stage work *On Spatial Dimensions* (1920) and *The Origin of Color and Size* (1923). Matyushin continued to explore the possibilities of color and dimension in his *Handbook on Color* published in 1932 and started researching his memoirs *The Creative Path of an Artist*, which was completed by his student Maria Ender—the second part of his *Handbook on Color* remains unpublished. Matyushin died in Leningrad on October 14, 1934.

ARTHUR LOURIÉ

Arthur Lourié (1892–1966) is most celebrated as the "Minister for Music" in the first Bolshevik government and was hugely influential in the administration of the arts during the early years of Soviet culture. A dedicated futurist, Lourié may have been an unlikely candidate for such an auspicious role; however, Vorobyov is succinctly accurate when he describes Lourié as "an actor, instantly reacting to all the enhancing changes taking place on stage in his artistic life, and so by transformation, occupied that niche of creativity, which at any moment, was most provident. There is in Lourié's creative path something similar to the stylistic evolution of I. Stravinsky."[49] Vorobyov considers Lourié's life path "embraced romanticism, the futurist revolution, then socialist revolution, and finally, travel and wandering."[50]

Naum (Arthur) Izraelevich Lourié was born a merchant's son on May 14, 1892, in the Gubernia of Mogilev, which lies between Minsk and Moscow, and presently is in Belarus. At six years, the family moved to Odesa, where he studied music, literature, and the Roman and Greek classics. Together with his mother, in 1905, he visited Vienna, where a performance of Wagner's *Tannhäuser* made a huge impression. Four years later, he began studies at the St. Petersburg Conservatoire with a disciple of Yesipova and Leschetizky—Vladimir Drozdov (1882–1960), and later with Marina Barinova, and composition with Glazunov. Barinova described Lourié as "original, both very clever and gifted, but a creature of fashion, wholly decadent. Lourié was in great need because his financial resources didn't allow him the space he dreamed of. Lourié was perpetually involved in all kinds of societies about contemporary art and acquainted me with the pioneering artist Kulbin."[51]

In 1910, concurrently with his music studies, he read philosophy at St. Petersburg University, and began rebelling against the Rimsky Korsakov system, and left the Conservatoire without graduating. Lourié's newly made acquaintance Nikolay Kulbin was an artist, musician, and theoretician of the Russian avant-garde. Often called the father of the avant-gardists, Kulbin's ideas of the synthesis of art, on "free music" the use of untraditional means of expression (quarter-tone, complex modal harmony), hugely influenced Lourié.[52] "Nikolay Ivanovich Kulbin introduced me somehow to a volume of the orthodox liturgy customs saying, 'Here, Artem, listen to this perhaps it will be useful to you.' Nikolay Ivanovich wasn't mistaken; contact with the traditions opened up before me a new, unknown world of melodic treasures, in the practices of church-monastery ancient chant."[53] Influenced by Christianity, Lourié was baptized into the Orthodox church in 1912 and took the pseudonym of Arthur Vincent, in honor of Schopenhauer and Van Gogh; in the following year, he married Jadwiga Wilhelmovna Tsybulskaya. As of 1912, Lourié became the leading figure of the café-cabaret "Brodyachaya Sobaka" (The Wandering Dog) in St. Petersburg society—at this time, another focal point of the decadent/futurist movement.

We have a sketch by the writer Kuprin of the young futurist Lourié loving to dress "in a bright green costume of fantastic material adorned by huge, great buttons in a tea blouse, with green buttons in the front, behind, and on the cuffs (...) wearing large open slippers with French ladies heels."[54] Barinova gives us another picture of Lourié. "His age was difficult to judge (from 20 to 35). He was talented, undoubtedly, both as a pianist and composer. Besides his masterly writing, he could commit the crudest, appalling errors. Lourié aspired to everything new that was perfect and sophisticated. He dressed in a blouse with large buttons, spoke very stylishly, and was friendly with all the young writers, and was well connected with Lunacharsky."[55]

Lourié was now writing his finest music; predominately for the piano; the cycle *Synthèses* (1914) where he experiments with twelve-tone music, and the composition dedicated to Picasso—*Forms en l'air* (1915) with visually expressionist segments throughout the score. Several of his piano pieces fail to reach the unusual explorative nature of the *Greek Songs*, and the *Suite japonaise* which show influences of Debussy and Scriabin. The vocal cycles *Chetki* are extraordinary for their modal effects—from Anna Akhmatova—then a young poetess with whom he enjoyed a tempestuous love affair. There were other vocal pieces from Verlaine, Sologub, Mallarme, Blok, Sappho, and others. Among his highlights at the "Brodyachaya Sobaka" cabaret club was an evening in January 1914 wholly devoted to Lourié's compositions.

The two poems from Verlaine and three piano pieces from "The Book of Masks" were performed on either side of Lourié's oration—"About Music (Interpretation. Overcoming impressionism. Synthesis-primitivism)." This was followed in February by the manifesto "The West and Us" unveiled with the painter Georgy Yakulov and the poet Benedict Livschitz. This treatise developed his notions of "free music" based on the formative principles and new sound systems (including quarter tones). In 1915, his paper "To Music of the Highest Chromatic Scales" appeared in the *"Streletz"* (*The Archer*) futurist collection. According to Vorobyov, "the composer preached about the absolute independence and 'foundation' of the branches of the Russian avant-garde. As a result, according to N. Kulbin, the Italian futurist 'Marinetti was astonished beyond belief by Arthur Lourié.'"[56] Despite pointing to the significance of micro chromatics in the development of twentieth-century music, he hardly ever used micro chromatic technique in his music. Lourié in the first issue of "Lad" (*Modal*) proclaimed the creation of music free of any links with the past. This essentially futurist announcement was expressed in the spirit of the revolutionary symbolism of Alexander Blok—the dominant figure of Russian symbolist poetry.

It was during a chance meeting between Vasily Kandinsky, Lourié, and the Commissar of Enlightenment Lunacharsky in 1917, whereby Lourié was offered the position of being in charge of music in the new Bolshevik administration. It was clear from his first major statement that the concept of futurism dominated the cultural policy of the new Soviet Government, "In the present heroic days, the spirit of music reveals the burning rhythms of the world uprising. (. . .) Without finding the spirit of music and musical thought in the formal educational academic music, (. . .) the Music Department declares that in all its forms music is now free from all presently existing false canons and laws of musical scholastics."[57] The same publication informed the world of the creation of the ASM.

Lourié developed into a political activist, a major state leader—all shared with being a composer, pianist, and public orator. This combination of roles led to a departure from Scriabinism and experimentation. Vorobyov writes that he became closer to Prokofiev and Stravinsky, *Les Six* and neoclassicism by embracing a new simplicity. A typical example is the settings to Mayakovsky's "Our March"—one of his first revolutionary compositions. One other piece which remains experimental is "UPMANN. A smoking anecdote" for plastic movement accompanied by the piano combining jazz rhythms and Chinese pentatonics. This stylistic pluralism led to the avant-garde hermetical novelty of his later period such as the "Dialectical Symphony" following which he began returning to sources and a nostalgic mood in his compositions.[58]

In 1919, Lourié composed "In the Temple of the Golden Dream" cantata from Blok's poetry, and in 1920–1921, wrote a ballet from Akhmatova's scenario *The Snow Mask* with settings from the symbolist poet's texts. Lourié wrote that "Blok was the most perfect person I ever met with." The artistic relationship was portrayed by Asafyev. "They are united by the elusive, yet universally sacred Dream of feminity."[59]

Lourié was moved from head of Music at Muzo to a position at the Institute of Art History in 1921. Following criticism by the proletarian musicians, during a visit to France, Lourié decided not to return to the Soviet Union in 1922. Settling in Berlin, he reprised his relations with Busoni, and moved to Paris, where he collaborated with Stravinsky, and significantly influenced several compositions by his older compatriot. This was evident with Lourié's A Little Chamber Music (1924), on Stravinsky's *Apollon musagète* (1927), similarly so for Concerto spirituale (1929) shaping Stravinsky's Symphony of Psalms (1930). Furthermore, Stravinsky picked up Lourié's method of using blank spaces instead of empty bars in his later notation. Lourié championed Stravinsky in his early Paris years, sharing the family household, although, in the late 1920's, Stravinsky turned against Lourié and barely mentioned him in the future. Following the Nazi invasion of 1940, Lourié moved to the United States with his emigration assisted by Koussevitzky, and he eventually settled into a teaching appointment at Princeton. Several of his works were conducted by Koussevitzky, Ansermet, Munch, Stokowski, and Furtwangler, and other leading conductors. His major work—an opera based on Pushkin—*The Blackamoor of Peter the Great*—took him ten years but has not been staged. He wrote a huge number of mostly unperformed works that today languish in the archives. His final opus Funeral Games in Honor of Chronos (1964), for three flutes, piano, and crotales dates from two years before his death.

JOSEPH SCHILLINGER

One of the forgotten avant-garde composers, Joseph (Iosif) Schillinger (1895–1943), is perhaps among the most fascinating for his exploration of new musical structures and electronic technology. As the Russian musicologist Inna Barsova writes, "Iosif Schillinger lived two lives, one in Russia, from which he left in 1928, and to which he never returned, the other in the United States of America. His life in Russia also falls into two periods, wholly dissimilar from each other."[60]

Iosif Moiseyevich Schillinger was born on August 31, 1895 in Kharkiv. His father was a promising violinist, but he went into business, while his mother Anna Gilgour ran a milliners that served the Imperial Court. It was hoped that Iosif would carry on the family enterprise; however, music and mathematics became his passions in life. There would be other interests that developed prodigiously in later years and had a decisive influence on his career. We may grasp a sense of his character from the early age of eighteen months as he tells us, "I was extremely interested in the mechanics of biological and aesthetic things. I broke open the head of a doll to find out how she opened and closed her eyes."[61] At the age of five years, his parents took him to hear Glinka's *A Life for the Tsar* at the Kharkiv Opera Theater which "didn't leave a strong musical impression on me, although, music has since fascinated me." According to Schillinger—underlined by him—"at home, there was absolutely no musical milieu. From the age of five, I started to improvise rhythmic sentences, and from seven—poetry; the need to compose music came at ten years, but a bit earlier, (at nine) there appeared very clear musical impressions by listening to symphonic music." Hearing Gounod's *Faust* led to him composing a waltz in F, and at fifteen, after being given a piano, he studied Saccetti's "Musical Education" for three months, and composed almost thirty pieces for piano, for voice and piano and the violin. "In this period, I sensed a unique (no earlier, or later) attraction to creativity."[62] Interestingly, Kharkiv was an important center for the arts, as several futurist poets including Nikolay Aseyev, Grigory Petnikov, and Velimir Khlebnikov were active there. Later, in 1918–1920, Schillinger set their poems for his early song cycles.[63] The Kharkiv futurist journal *The Path to Creativity* was the first to publish Schillinger's essays on musical theory.

Iosif began studying music systematically, using Bussler's book on harmony, and counterpoint with a student of the Imperial Capella. In 1912, he studied with Alexander Horowitz—a professor of piano at the Kharkiv Conservatoire, and music critic and uncle of Vladimir Horowitz. This was excellent preparation for Schillinger's entrance to the St. Petersburg Conservatoire in September 1914, as he recollects, "At once, I leaped into the musical life of St Petersburg, never missing one important event in the flow of musical life."[64] Schillinger studied conducting with Nicolas Cherepnin (1873–1945), composition with Vasily Calafati (1869–1942), and counterpoint and form with Jāzeps Vītols (1863–1948) graduating in 1918. According to a survey, the greatest influences in St. Petersburg for him were "Scriabin (extensively and forcefully from 1915 to 1922), in parallel with Ravel and Medtner (regardless of their dissimilarities); from 1922, mainly Stravinsky and perhaps insignificantly—Prokofiev."[65] One other mentor was Schoenberg, owing to his "colossal constructivist energy; (however) the question of the emotional effect by Schoenberg on my recent works, I consider is unclear."[66] He viewed the Austro-German schools and the Russian romantic school of the nineteenth century, with antipathy, as well as the Russian circle around Myaskovsky of the 1920s.

Schillinger shared with Lourié and Roslavets's disappointment and rebellion against his schooling, accusing the teachers of dilettantism, and thought his time there was lost. It was this experience that inspired Schillinger to develop his own teaching methodology.[67] Following graduation, Schillinger returned home to become a highly respected instructor and conductor of the Kharkiv State Symphony Orchestra. He was appointed a professor and deacon of composition at the Kharkiv Music Academy, and the head of Music at the Narkompros, and through several years, was a consultant for the State

Opera, and conductor, choirmaster, lecturer, and organizer of the Variety Symphony Orchestra of Ukraine. For someone so young, this was an exceptional burden on his shoulders. The first compositions by Schillinger to be performed were the Cello Sonata and his settings from Rilke and Verlaine on December 8, 1918. An important piece was his Ocean Sonata for piano Op. 5 (1918–1923) and the Little Suite for Double-Bass and piano Op. 7 (1921). Schillinger's Violin Sonata Op. 9 (1921–1922) was performed by Nathan Milstein and Abram Makarov on February 8, 1922, in Kharkiv and repeated a year later in Petrograd.

Schillinger's teaching methodology led to an invitation by the Commissariat of Enlightenment to teach music theory in Moscow, and subsequently in Petrograd where he developed his musical technique teaching at the State Institute of Art History, and at the Central Musical Technicum. Active in the ASM, he shared the chairmanship with Boris Asafyev. From his early years, Schillinger was drawn to the synthesis of art and religion. Again we learn from his examination that "this attraction (ending around 1921) has had no favorable influence on my creativity, changing from 1921 to a form of 'rationalism' (and my interest jumped first) to the philosophy of mathematics, the symbolism of numerals, the interrelations of time and space, and also the theory of relativity by Einstein, enshrined in his form of 'rationalized mathematical emotionalism.'"[68] In an article about his career, Schillinger divided his creativity into two periods of writing, "The ten years of composing (1917–1927) is really in two stages. The first (1917–1922) period is of technical maturity and searching for one's own path. This period ended with my Violin Sonata (Op. 9) and Eastern Vocalises (Orientalia Op. 10)."[69] During the 1920s, Schillinger wrote exclusively in two genres: vocal miniatures calling them poems, and instrumental pieces. Schillinger wrote that, "Generally, one can define two types of preparation: 1) so to speak 'improvisational,' when there (usually) a rhythmic scheme, comes at first 'acquiring' quite unfree sound material straight through to its completion." The second type of preparation was "structurally abstract" with a prior plan "for major works ('as in the concrete carcass of constructing American skyscrapers'). In such there 'proceeds the building of the thematic material' and in the given 'constructive plan,' there occur moments when 'against the considered productive plan' there advances some different character, arising from the 'pressure of the sound material.' Schillinger thought that 'improvisation' assists the melodic line."[70]

Between 1922 and 1928, Schillinger wrote comparatively little; amounting to several song cycles, a Sonata-Rhapsody for piano, vocalzes, and four orchestral works. This period was devoted to preparing his major theoretical work along this path, one of his essays verifies his exploring of technique—"Threshold to the New Bach" (1922), foresees a different approach to the modal organization of music.[71] Schillinger surveyed the musical line from Orlando Lasso and Palestrina to Chopin, Wagner, Liszt, and Scriabin writing that "in creating new modern polyphonic styles, (. . .) we have the basis to expect a new Bach, not 'neo-Bach,' but a real genius able to create an original style of contemporary polyphony."[72] In this perspective, he pointed to Roslavets and Schoenberg who had "succeeded in creating enormous achievements in this direction."[73] Schillinger thought the arrival of the new Bach was close and that he expected a vast ocean of new polyphony to be opened up not by a squeaky organ or a feeble orchestra, but by the perfection of the radio-apparatus of Lev Theremin.

In his essay, he offered the Schillinger Complex for analysis of new structures in modern music. One of the means that he examined was cinematography, among which are his experimentation in the Op. 12 and Op. 14 Piano Miniatures, and the Symphonic Rhapsody "October" Op. 19. Notably, one of the miniatures "L' Excentriade" was performed in public by Shostakovich in February 1925.[74] Once again we learn from his survey that "the works followed upon 1) the principle of cinema montage and 2) chordal 'complexes.'"[75] In responding to a questionnaire, Schillinger answered, "Cinema for me—is the main axis in several art forms, and regardless of its relative infancy as an independent branch of art. I consider that cinema has been a favorable influence on my music."[76]

Of Schillinger's orchestral works, the "March of the Orient" Op. 11 (1924) was premiered together with Shostakovich's First Symphony and Julia Weisberg's cantata "The Twelve" on May 12, 1926. Shostakovich reflected that Weisberg's piece was "nasty music, yet Schillinger's 'March of the Orient' was much better. In general, we thought my symphony was the very best piece."[77] Given the celebrity of Shostakovich's symphony, it was unfortunate that Schillinger's piece was billed in the same concert because it is clearly masterful, and rather than engaged by the orientalism of the vocalizes, is more toward the barbaric dancing (or march) of *Prince Igor*.[78] Lasting just more than 3 minutes (similar to Mosolov's *The Foundry*), Schillinger uses a huge orchestra of triple wind, six horns, three trumpets, and trombones, and tuba, plus extended percussion, and two harps. Schillinger's Complex is evident in the rhythmic ostinatos. The piece is sustained by a continuing repeated complex of different basses.

The Petrograd engineer Lev Theremin invented a revolutionary musical gadget in 1920, and Schillinger became his most enthusiastic collaborator after meeting with him in the early 1920s. Sabaneyev writes,

> The sound of this contraption (Thereminvox) is quite pleasant, reminding one of a distant voice with closed lips. The main resources of this device are the ability to give different timbres (tonal colors), a powerful means to tonal

expression, regardless of tuning (sound stability), the capacity to reach a high frequency with comparative little loudness, and a very great beneficial accuracy in the quality of the complete electro-technical device (. . .) and finally, a valuable superiority in the movement of sound over distance and even in "several examples," it is possible, at the same time, to be played by one performer at several different locations.[79]

Schillinger's Symphonic Rhapsody "October" (1927) for piano and large orchestra was premiered by the Persimfans ensemble on November 21, 1927, with Alexander Kamensky as the soloist. Schillinger's Sonata-Rhapsody and Beethoven's Fifth Symphony made up the rest of the program, which opened with *The Internationale*. According to the composer, "October" was to achieve several tasks, "1) to clearly present in wide-ranging sound the musical imagery of our epoch, 2) to build the form of this work in such a manner that it responds to the present consciousness (and contemporary tonal recognition), and on the other hand corresponds to the standard of composing technique; 3) to grasp the possibility of a fuller understanding, notably the characterization in different moments of themes (ten years of the October Revolution) and in musical language."[80] Barsova writes that by ostensibly celebrating the revolution, Schillinger was taking his expression to the limit, whereby "the listener—including the powers that be—tire of understanding and question what is this—skepticism, or a rush of loyalty?"[81] Schillinger justifies himself, "I adopted both revolutionary folksongs, and ordinary folksongs from the period of the October Revolution." Among the quotes are "L' Marsellaise," the "Internationale," "Bravely, to your feet, comrades," along with urban street songs such as "Alesha-sha." Musically, Schillinger introduces elements of cinematic montage by switching swiftly changing thematic rhythms, in what he called "cine-dynamic symphonism" treating this as a "new form of music."[82] This formula was most truthfully realized decades later, in Barsova's opinion, in Shostakovich's Eleventh Symphony and the First Symphony by Schnittke.[83] The composer introduces diverse styles in his piece: "symphonic and chamber style, military, jazz, salon (piano), and finally, cacophony (in the finale)."[84] In the fragment devoted to jazz, Schillinger introduced three saxophones—something unique in Soviet music. The rapid switch from the funeral lament of the old revolutionary song "You fell as victims" to the "salon" section of a beautiful piano cadenza created a wholly disconcerting change in mood for listeners.

Attracted to the syncopation of jazz music, Schillinger formed the first Jazz Orchestra in Soviet Russia which became soon immensely popular in Moscow and Leningrad. On April 28, 1927, the ensemble gave their debut at the Leningrad State Capella under the direction of the pianist Leopold Teplitzky. In his preconcert talk, in explaining the origins of jazz and the social significance of the genre, Schillinger expressed the hope that this would widen audiences to jazz through the slogan "Music for the People." There were different responses to the big-band concert—many were enthusiastic—"Jazz-band will be the music of the future," and "Let Jazz-Band be the soul of Russia's working life!"[85] The repertoire included jazz arrangements from Rimsky Korsakov, Verdi, Gounod, and Rubinstein, and pieces by Irving Berlin, George Gershwin, and Frank Jeremiah Blake. This enthusiasm for electronic music and jazz led however to attacks from the RAPM. Our old friend from the RAPM, Marian Koval attacked it as "an invasion of reactionary music finding an affinity with the NEP."[86]

At this period of sharp criticism from the proletarian musicians, a mark of providence arrived for Schillinger with a letter of invitation to visit New York. This may have been facilitated by his aunt who had emigrated to America. Formally, he was invited by the American-Soviet Cultural Society to lecture about Soviet music. The Society committee included Joseph Achron, Kurt Schindler, Leopold Stokowski, Sergey Radamsky, and Edgar Varèse. The invitation was also intended to develop relations with the Leningrad Association for Contemporary Music. In July 1928, Schillinger traveled to America via Berlin, staying in the German capital until November, before making his way to Cherbourg, and across the Atlantic to New York. In Germany, he attempted to arrange concerts of Soviet music, notably mentioning a Berlin Philharmonic concert of Shostakovich, Deshevov, Schillinger, and Alexander Krein under the baton of Klemperer. In Königsberg, the Prussian State Orchestra under Hermann Scherchen gave a radio broadcast of Soviet music.[87] He reached out to Sergei Eisenstein, en route to Hollywood proposing cooperation on film scores.[88] Interestingly, he wrote about the German film industry and took part in an experimental studio on Film kunst, in which Schoenberg, Hindemith, Toch, and Meisel were also participating. It was in Berlin that Schillinger composed his *First Airphonic Suite* for the Thereminvox and Orchestra.[89] Before leaving Germany, he arranged a chamber concert by German musicians of works by Roslavets, Polovinkin, Alexander and Grigory Krein, Alexandrov, Gnessin, Veprik, Schillinger (two poems by Aseyev and Pesenka), and Popov.[90]

Schillinger arrived in New York on November 13, 1928, on the ocean liner Majestic. The society welcomed him with a concert of his music on February 2, 1929, including the premiere of his Dance Suite for Cello, Op. 20, which became popular for its Blues, Waltz-Boston, and Ragtime. Schillinger described himself as an emotional constructivist unlike the Austro-German form of constructivism. There he developed his collaboration with Lev Theremin, who was also in America to introduce his invention by opening a patent and a company there. Schillinger's newly written *First Airphonic Suite* for Thereminvox and orchestra was premiered by the Cleveland Orchestra under Nikolay Sokoloff in 1929 with Theremin as the soloist winning an ovation from the audience.

This concert led to considerable fame for both Schillinger and Theremin with the inventor becoming a major celebrity in the United States. Toscanini, Stokowski, Ravel, Menuhin, and many luminaries visited his newly opened studio to hear the potential of the gadget. Schillinger's final written composition—influenced by his friend Asafyev—was the "North-Russian Symphony"—commissioned by RCA in 1930; however, it remains unperformed despite interest from Nikolay Malko. It may have been the problem of getting his music performed was the reason for Schillinger giving up composition in his last decade of activity. However, Schillinger said that the process had grown out of him and that he wanted to devote himself to what he called his most important duty in teaching his new methodology in composition.

Schillinger collaborated with Theremin on developing an apparatus that would compose music to a degree of perfection for contemporary musicians by mathematical calculation. This was called the Rhythmicon, the invention, and the experimentation of which also involved the young composer Henry Cowell. In the wake of the Thereminvox's popularity, Charles Ives wrote enthusiastically about the potential to Nicolai Slonimsky,

> The great relief for me is that this new instrument will actually be closer to an instrument than a machine. There will be "levers" and pedals, with which one can easily change the "tempo," and also the "sound" and so forth. The question is not to construct a new instrument—but I suggest it must be done—of how to improve it, study it, move it on,—but in that is there enough time left to present it in Paris, and if so, how to do this in the best way possible.[91] Henry thinks as I do—that after the instrument is demonstrated at the New School of Social Studies next Thursday, we shall understand better how to do this. Yesterday, I sent a cheque to Mr. Theremin—and he has commenced work on it.[92]

However, despite its many positive elements, the Rhythmicon was unsuccessful. Work stopped on the gadget after Theremin returned to the Soviet Union in 1938. It was only in 1971 that it was improved in a performance by Stanford Symphony Orchestra using a computer. "It sounded sterile, antiseptic, lifeless—like a robot with a synthetic voice."[93]

If the Rhythmicon proved disappointing, the Thereminvox was applied by several leading composers including Edgar Varèse, Bohuslav Martinů, and Percy Grainger, apart from which, the instrument acquired great popularity in the cinema—especially for science fiction movies. In this manner, it enjoyed so much success that its use in the cinema after 1945 became more than fashionable.[94] Interestingly, such popular songs as "Good Vibrations" by the Beach Boys used this instrument, and many other pop groups of the 1960s, and subsequently by Pink Floyd and Deep Purple up to the present day, and the best-known variant is Peter Moog's electronic synthesizer.

The most revelatory aspect of Schillinger's theoretical work was opening up composition through mathematical formulae. No longer was the creation of music the preserve of geniuses, Schillinger thought that everyone could compose music without discovering melodies or harmonies. Schillinger was unique in that he was one of the few avant-garde composers who developed a unique teaching methodology and school of composition. He taught a large number of American musicians, including George Gershwin, Tommy Dorsey, Benny Goodman, Glenn Miller, Earle Brown, Oscar Levant, and Henry Cowell. Perhaps the most significant influence was on Gershwin's *Porgy and Bess*, as Nicolai Slonimsky suggests, "taking Schillinger's technique of harmonic layers in the orchestral parts. (. . .) He also used Schillinger's ideas on the sound and time extended consequences, including the expanded range of intervals in the theme."[95]

In May 1935, four months before the Broadway premiere, Gershwin wrote to Schillinger. "I have finished the composition of the opera—in the piano version, and also the orchestration of the first act and am working on the second act score, but this is moving slowly. I would like to see you one of these days, and perhaps, continue taking lessons, as I am planning to stay in New York all the summer."[96] In all the American composer studied with Schillinger for four and a half years as Schillinger wrote to David Evan, "in rhythm, melody, counterpoint, etc. apart from orchestration."[97] According to Earl Ferris, Gershwin composed only one melody "Summertime" in his stage work, while all the remaining melodies were composed using Schillinger's methodology. It is also thought that Clara's lullaby is from an old Ukrainian folksong "Oi khodit son kolo vikon" popularized by the Ukrainian Choir of Alexander Koschitz.[98] Gershwin was similarly influenced by his teacher in the "I Got Rhythm" orchestral piece with piano. Vernon Duke wrote that Schillinger's technique brought unforeseen freedom to Gershwin's musical expression.[99] Glenn Miller's "Moonlight Serenade" started life as an exercise from Schillinger's System.

Upon the suggestion of Henry Cowell, the young composer John Cage wrote to Schillinger about his interest in experimental electronic music. This was following his studies with Schoenberg in 1940, and several letters were exchanged, yet unfortunately, Schillinger couldn't assist Cage with advice on electronic music because Lev Theremin had returned to the Soviet Union.[100] According to Schillinger's widow, Cage visited him and played together on the piano using Schillinger's theories. The young American was so impressed that he didn't notice the torrential rain on returning home.[101]

In his final years, before his death from cancer, Schillinger widened his interests to industrial and stage design, graphics, and photography. The

American composer Charles Previn was attracted to Schillinger's system after Gershwin introduced him to his theory. Following a correspondence course, Previn spent three hours studying harmony with Schillinger when he visited California, recalling that, "I wouldn't give the impression that it's possible to study harmony in three hours, it's clear that it's not like that. But the mathematical analysis allows Schillinger to classify the different types of harmony, the sequences and voice-leading in limited condensed forms, the development of which demands months of practical work." Previn commented that everything is laid out in fine detail in the two-volume study of the Schillinger System of Musical Composition. "During my study of the 'System,' I discovered through correspondence, that it was being studied by several other Hollywood composers. Among whom were Herbert Spencer and Edward Powell from 20th Century Fox, Lenny Hayton from MGM, and Frank Skinner, the present musical director of Universal Pictures." Previn found that Schillinger's theories were indispensable both for conducting and "for writing specialized music material for our stagings."[102] He also collaborated with Walt Disney on the montage of cartoons and music in the early 1930s. His major treatise in two volumes "The Schillinger System of Musical Composition" was published only after his death. In 1945, Schillinger's theory began to be taught at the Juilliard School in New York. Schillinger himself stated, "My system, in a short time, has conquered the American market for applied music (radio, theater, cinematograph, television etc.) to such a level that today, it is difficult to find any music director, conductor, composer, or orchestrator of name, who hasn't used my methodology, or has not been one of my students. In purely statistical figures, the influence of my system is felt in 70% of the mass American musical product."[103] Schillinger had a studio in New York equipped with the latest technology for sound recording. Today, several schools teach his original theory of composition, and a website offers online teaching in Schillinger's groundbreaking methodology. Schillinger's death from cancer at the age of only forty-seven—at the height of his creativity and work—has its parallels with the early passing of other major composers, sadly today Joseph Schillinger is a forgotten figure in world music.

Of course, in twentieth-century music, Igor Stravinsky was the trailblazer of modernism in music with his breathtaking ballets, especially the 1913 *Le Sacre du Printemps* in Paris producing one of the biggest shocks in music. The argument that the changes in Russia brought a new simplicity appears contrived when we consider the transformation in Stravinsky's music in the 1920s and 1930s, as Maes explains, "The retrospective element in Stravinsky's neoclassicism—the evocation of historical styles—was not the main reason for the prestige he enjoyed among young French composers. Together with Cocteau, the members of Les Six applauded his 'new simplicity,' his 'purified style,' and his classical clarity and directness."[104] Francis Maes goes further to explain the cause for the "new" Stravinsky writing that the émigré Russian's "neoclassicism was closely connected with a new type of social elitism. It was part of the reaction of the social upper crust to the chaos of the war. The underlying objective of neoclassicism was to safeguard culture from the masses and from the nouveaux riches. It was art for the educated, which in the rhetoric of the time meant people of good breeding."[105] The émigré composer Nikolay Medtner complained of French societal attitudes, as he wrote to Rachmaninov, "The public, who had filled the Grand Opéra to overflowing, this public who takes it as an insult if someone should appear in its midst in anything but tails or a smoking jacket (for which reason I had to hide myself and my little grey jacket in the highest loges)—this public steadfastly withstood every slap in the face and every humiliation, and what is more, rewarded the author with deafening applause."[106] Of course, Stravinsky was not impartial to this new world of bourgeois snobbery, as again Maes tells us, "Stravinsky came down openly on the side of the social elite. He sought out the company of the emigrant titled nobility, became a staunch follower of the Romanovs, and cultivated his aristocratic status. His political sympathies became totalitarian and fascist. He called Mussolini the hope of the world."[107] Maes considers that by turning to neoclassicism, "Stravinsky turned his back on Russian music."[108]

At this time, in the mid-1920s, his compatriot Prokofiev exiled in France had already written in neoclassical forms, reprised modernism with the Second Symphony. He had planned a symphony of "iron and steel"; however, he met only with negativity in the critics' reviews, dismissing it as "vulgar and brash." The symphony was based on music from Prokofiev's constructivist ballet *Le pas d'acier* (1925)—about modern-day life in the USSR—which was commissioned by Diaghilev for the Ballets Russes. The composer said it was "a decisive step leading me towards chromaticism and diatonics. (. . .) A whole series of keys are written for the white keys."[109] In 1930, and trying to show he had relented on his former *enfant terrible* of the past, Prokofiev wrote, "We want a simpler and more melodic style for music, a simple, less complicated emotional state, and dissonance again relegated to its proper place as one element of music. . . . I think we have gone as far as we are likely to go in the direction of size, or dissonance, or complexity in music. Music, in other words, has definitely reached and passed the greatest degree of discord and complexity that can be attained in practice. I want nothing better, more flexible, or more complete than the sonata form, which contains everything necessary for my structural purposes."[110] Francis Maes writes that "Prokofiev had shown himself to be a traditionalist even before he contemplated a permanent return to the Soviet Union. Hence it is more likely that his decision to go back to Russia was in part the result of his musical development."[111]

The formation of mass cultural groups and demonstrations using music, and poster art were one of the most vivid expressions of this new Soviet culture. The utopianism of the futurists in the Silver Age transposed into a quite different quality and significance in the USSR. Arts exhibitions, films, radio, literature, and architecture were designed to project the strength of the country's power that would be ready to defend itself against any external threat. The Russian philosopher Sergey Tretyakov constituted the association between symbolism and futurism, on the one hand, and socialist realism, on the other. Writing that the Soviet artist had to grasp "Not life in its inertia and dependence on an established pattern of things, but a dialectically perceived reality that is in a state of perpetual formation—reality understood as progress toward the commune, which is not to be forgotten for a single minute."[112] Tretyakov defined the artist in Soviet society as a "psycho-engineer," or a "psycho-constructor," and an expression wrongly attributed to Stalin as "engineers of the human mind."[113] Herein perhaps are some of the concepts of the original futurists albeit transformed in the new modern age.

The latest wave of "new" avant-garde music in the USSR arrived in the Festivals of New Music in Leningrad in the 1970s and 1980s. There appeared new names such as Edison Denisov, Arvo Pärt, and Arnold Schnittke who offered a freshness of ideas in the generations following Prokofiev and Shostakovich. Today, these names have been added to by Gubaydullina, Shchedrin, Silvestrov, Slonimsky, Tischenko, Ustvolskaya, and Weinberg and others to the annals of the Russian avant-garde. This groundswell of new music would not have been possible if not for the experimentalism by Lourié, Mosolov, Popov, Roslavets, Schillinger, and Matyushin in the first decades of the last century. In recent years both Lourié's and Roslavets's music have become widely available in recordings and their music is slowly gaining a place in mostly chamber recitals, while Mosolov and Popov have a small but growing representation on Compact Disc and the internet, regrettably, Matyushin and Schillinger are almost absent from recorded music media—much more is needed for them to find their place in the music world.

In the twenty-first century, modernist composers no longer scare away audiences with their dissonance, shrieking chords, or disturbing augmented sixths. Modern music shares the effects of serialism, atonality, minimalism, micro tonalism, and a host of other "isms" in the creativity of Adams, Boulez, Cage, Glass, Gorecki, Ligeti, Messaien, Milton Babbitt, Morton Feldman, Penderecki, Reich, Thorvaldsdottir, Xenakis, and many others. Now in the third millennium, audiences are better educated and sophisticated, and as a result, it is no longer a rarity that music of the once lampooned avant-gardists share concert programs with Haydn, and Mozart, Ravel, and Shostakovich.

Festival administrators, concert program creators, and record company producers seem anxious to discover new voices to freshen the catalogs and repertoire, and internet streaming and other new technologies help dust off the forgotten and neglected masterpieces of yesterday. Our world has become smaller, and the sharing of ideas enrich our culture—hopefully, this narrative of the Russian avant-garde will stir readers to further their interest and seek out this startling music whether online or most hopefully in the concert hall.

NOTES

1. MacDonald, Malcolm, "Shostakovich's string concertos and sonatas," *The Cambridge Companion to Shostakovich*, CUP, 2008, 117.
2. Petropoulos, Jonathan, *Artists under Hitler: Collaboration and Survival in Nazi Germany*, Yale University Press, 2015, 92.
3. Smith, David Stanley, quoted in Kater, *Composers of the Nazi Era: Eight Portraits*, New York: Oxford University Press, 2000, 33.
4. Petropoulos, Jonathan, *Artists under Hitler: Collaboration and Survival in Nazi Germany*, Yale University Press, 2015, 102.
5. Paul to Gertrude Hindemith (February 14, 1940), quoted in Kater, *Composers of the Nazi Era*, 46.
6. Stonor Saunders, Frances, *The Cultural Cold War: The CIA and the World of Arts and Letters*, New York: The New Press, 1999, 253–254.
7. Petropoulos, Jonathan, *Artists under Hitler: collaboration and survival in Nazi Germany*, Yale University Press, 2015, 328.
8. Kater, Michael H., *Composers of the Nazi Era: Eight Portraits*, New York: OUP, 2000, 280.
9. Metzer, D.J., "The Ascendancy of Musical Modernism," 14–34, Sabine Feisst, *Schoenberg's New World*, Oxford UP, 2011, 31.
10. Finck, Henry, "The Musical Messiah-or Satan?" *Nation*, November 15, 1915.
11. Foote, Arthur, "Will the Music of Ultra-Modernists Survive?" Etude 34, No. 5 (May 1916), 331 and Henry Holden Huss, "The Anarchic Element in Some Ultramodern Futurist Music," *Art world* 2, No. 2 (May 1917), 139–141.
12. Schwartz, Boris, "The Music World in Migration," in Jarell C. Jackman and Carla M. Borden, eds. "The Muses Flee Hitler: Cultural Transfer and Adaption," 1930–1945 (Washington, D.C, 1983), 141; Ernst Krenek, "Americas einfluss auf eingewanderte komponisten," in Traber and Weingarten, *Verdrangte Musik*, 104.
13. Kater, Michael H., *Composers of the Nazi Era: Eight Portraits*, New York: OUP, 2000, 192.
14. Heyworth, Peter, *Klemperer*, 2:53; Olin Downes's critique in *The New York Times* of October 18, 1935, quoted in Ennulat, "Schoenberg Correspondence," 226.
15. Seeger, Charles (Carl Sands), "Schoenberg's Latest Composition," *New York City Daily Worker*, October 23, 1935.
16. Downes, Olin, "New Suite by Arnold Schoenberg," *New York Times*, October 13, 1935.

17. Sargeant, Winthrop, "Arnold Schoenberg and the Atonal Style," *Brooklyn Daily Eagle*, October 6, 1935.

18. Schoenberg quoted in Hilmar, *Schoenberg: Gedenkausstellung 1974*, Vienna: Universal Edition, 1974, 334.

19. Stuckenschmidt, Hans Heinz, *Schoenberg: His Life, World and Work*, New York: Schirmer, 1977, 113.

20. Feisst, Sabine, *Schoenberg's New World*, Oxford UP, 2011, 3.

21. Schoenberg to Berg, [august. 1933] and September 17, 1933, in brand et al., "Berg-Schoenberg Correspondence," 444–445; *Schonberg to Webern*, September 16, 1933, in Hilmar, "Schoenberg and Webern," 54; ng 16:720.

22. Schoenberg quoted in Hilmar, *Schoenberg: Gedenkausstellung 1974*, Vienna: Universal Edition, 1974, 334.

23. Ibid, 340; Rusamen, "Schoenberg in America," 473.

24. Maes, Francis, *A History of Russian Music*, London: University of California Press, 2006, 346.

25. DeLapp, Jennifer, "Copland in the Fifties: Music and Ideology in the McCarthy Era," (PhD, University of Michigan, 1997), 104–105.

26. Wuorinen, Charles, "The Outlook," 54; and Gunther Schuller, "Schoenberg's Influence," in TASC, 260; Andrea Olmstead, *Conversations with Roger Sessions*, Boston: North-Eastern Press, 1987, 237.

27. Brown quoted in Amy Beal, *New Music, New Allies: American Experimental Music in West Germany from the Zero Hour to Reunification*, Berkeley: University of California Press, 2006, 140.

28. Currie, James R., "Modernism – Out of the Spirit of Comedy," *The Routledge Companion to Modernism in Music*, London: Routledge, 2019, 46.

29. Kundera, Milan, "Improvisation in Homage to Stravinsky," in *Testaments Betrayed*, translated by Linda Asher, London and Boston: Faber and Faber, 1995, 97–98.

30. Graham, Stephen, "Modernism for and of the Masses?" *The Routledge Companion to Modernism in Music*, London: Routledge, 2019, 243.

31. Graham, Stephen, "Modernism for and of the Masses?" *The Routledge Companion to Modernism in Music*, London: Routledge, 2019, 244.

32. Currie, James R., "Modernism – Out of the Spirit of Comedy," *The Routledge Companion to Modernism in Music*, London: Routledge, 2019, 37.

33. Maes, Francis, *A History of Russian Music*, London: University of California Press, 2006, 345–346.

34. Maes, Francis, *A History of Russian Music*, London: University of California Press, 2006, 347.

35. Hakobian, Leon, "Shostakovich, Proletkult and RAPM," *Shostakovich Studies 2*, CUP, 2016, 263.

36. Adamov, Yevgeny, "Pobeda and solntsem," *Den*, 1913.

37. Vorobyov, Igor, Sinaiskaya, Anastasia, *Kompositori Russkovo avangarda*. St. Petersburg: Kompozitor, 2007, 33.

38. Malevich to Matyushin, February 15, 1914. *Nashe Naslediye*, 1989, 8. 134–135.

39. Vorobyov, Igor, Sinaiskaya, Anastasia, *Kompositori Russkovo avangarda*. St. Petersburg: Kompositor, 2007, 37.

40. "Opera futuristov," *Peterburgskaya Gazeta*, 1913.

41. Mgrebrov, A. as quoted in Vorobyov, Sinaiskaya, *Kompositori Russkovo avangarda*, St. Petersburg: Kompositor, 2007, 38.

42. Matyushin, Mikhail, Vorobyov, Sinaiskaya, *Kompositori Russkovo avangarda*, St. Petersburg: Kompositor, 2007, 39.

43. Adamov, Yevgeny, "Pobeda and solntsem," Den, 1913.

44. Malevich, Kazimir, "Teater," 1917. Vorobyov, Sinaiskaya, *Kompositori Russkovo avangarda*, St. Petersburg: Kompositor, 2007, 39.

45. Tomashevsky, K., "Vladimir Mayakovsky," *Teater*, No. 4, 1938.

46. Kruchenykh, A., "Pobeda na solntsem. Podgotovka texta, predisloviye i oformleniye R. V. Duganova," Moscow, Vienna, 1993. Vorobyov, Sinaiskaya, *Kompositori Russkovo avangarda*, St. Petersburg: Kompositor, 2007, 40.

47. Matyushina, Olga, *Negasimiye iskry*, Leningrad, 1960.

48. Clark, Katerina, Petersburg, *Crucible of Cultural Revolution*, Harvard UP, 1998, 44.

49. Vorobyov, Sinaiskaya, *Kompositori Russkovo avangarda*. St. Petersburg: Kompositor, 2007, 49.

50. Vorobyov, Sinaiskaya, *Kompositori Russkovo avangarda*, St. Petersburg: Kompositor, 2007, 49.

51. Barinova, Marina, *Muzyka i ee predstavitely v moyei zhisnei*, St. Petersburg: Kompositor, 2002.

52. Vorobyov, Sinaiskaya, *Kompositori Russkovo avangarda*, St. Petersburg: Kompositor, 2007, 51.

53. Lourie, Arthur, "Nash marsh," *Novy Zhurnal*, No. 94, New York, 1968.

54. Ali-Khan (A. Kuprin), Pokhozhdeniya "Zelenoi loshadki," *Novaya Russkaya Zhizn*, April 21, 1921, Helsinki.

55. Barinova, Marina, *Muzyka i ee predstavitely v moyei zhisnei*, St. Petersburg: Kompositor, 2002.

56. Vorobyov, Sinaiskaya, *Kompositori Russkovo avangarda*, St. Petersburg: Kompositor, 2007, 66.

57. Lourie, Arthur, *Lad*, 1919, Vorobyov, Sinaiskaya, *Kompositori Russkovo avangarda*, St. Petersburg: Kompositor, 2007, 68.

58. Vorobyov, Sinaiskaya, *Kompositori Russkovo avangarda*, St. Petersburg: Kompositor 2007, 62.

59. Asafyev, Boris., *Russkaya Poeziya v russkoi muzyke*, 2 editions, Petrograd, 1924.

60. Barsova, Inna, "Put Kompositora," *Dve Zhizni Iosifa Shillingera*, Moscow State Conservatoire/Smithsonian American Art Museum, 2015, 11.

61. JSP. Series 1. Box 20. Folder 11. From "Pereros muzyky kak takovyu," Elena Gubinetz, *Dve Zhizni Iosifa Schillingera*, Moscow State Conservatoire/Smithsonian American Art Museum, 2015, 250.

62. Anketa, po psychology muzikalnovo tvorchestvo. Iosif Schillinger otvechaet na voprosy R.O. Grubera// VMOMK. F. 285. Ed. Khr. 21/10.

63. Barsova, Inna, "Put Kompositora," *Dve Zhizni Iosifa Schillingera*, Moscow State Conservatoire/Smithsonian American Art Museum, 2015, 13–14.
64. Anketa. l. 1–1.
65. Anketa, l. 3.
66. Anketa, l. 2.
67. Anketa, l.1.ob.
68. Anketa, l. 3.ob.
69. Schillinger, I.M., "O sebye i o svoyei Rapsodii," *Persimfans*, No. 3–4, 1927–1928, 12.
70. Anketa, l. 4.
71. *Dve Zhizni Iosifa Shillingera*, Moscow State Conservatoire/Smithsonian American Art Museum, 2015, 207–208.
72. Schillinger, I., "V preddveri novovo Bacha," *Ezhegodnik Petrogradskikh gosudarstvennykh akademicheskikh teatrov*, No. 5, 1922, 22.
73. Schillinger, I.M., "V preddveri novovo Bacha," *Ezhegodnik Petrogradskikh gosudarstvennykh akademicheskikh teatrov*, No. 5, 1922, 23.
74. Khentova, S., *D. Shostakovich. Zhizn i Tvorchestvo*: v 2 tomakh, tom 1. Leningrad: Kompozitor, 1985, 529.
75. Anketa, l. 1 ob.
76. Anketa, l. 1 ob.
77. "Mne ispolnilos vosemnadtsat let . . ." (Pisma D.D. Shostakovicha k L. N. Oborinu)/ publ. M. G. Koslovoi/ *Vstrechi s proshlom*: Cb. Materialov TSGALI SSSR. Vyp. 5, Moscow, 1984, 259.
78. Barsova, Inna, "Put Kompositora," *Dve Zhizni Iosifa Shillingera*, Moscow State Conservatoire/Smithsonian American Art Museum, 2015, 48–49.
79. Sabaneyev, Leonid, *Teatralny Izvestiya*, No. 3, February 17–20, 1922, 3,5.
80. Schillinger, I.M., "O sebye i o svoyei Rapsodii," *Persimfans*, Nos. 3–4, 1927–1928, 12.
81. *Dve Zhizni Iosifa Shillingera*, Moscow State Conservatoire/Smithsonian American Art Museum, 2015, 54.
82. Schillinger, I.M., "O kompositsii symphonicheskoi rhapsodii," *Oktyabr*, 12.
83. *Dve Zhizni Iosifa Shillingera*, Moscow state conservatoire/Smithsonian American Art Museum, 2015, 68.
84. Schillinger, I.M., "O kompositsii symphonicheskoi rhapsodii," *Oktyabr*, 12.
85. JSP. Ser. 1. Box 15. Folder 15,16.
86. Koval, Marian, "Propaganda Jazz-banda," *Muzyka i Revolutsiya*. Nos. 5–6, 1927, 49.
87. Schillinger to Yuri Shaporin, October 4, 1928, RGALI. f. 2642. op. 1. ed. Khr. 459. l. 1–2.
88. Schillinger to Eisenstein, October 11, 1928, RGALI. f. 1923. op. 1. ed. khr. 2244. L. 1–1 ob.
89. Schillinger to Gruber October 14, 1928, VMOMK. F. 285. No. 1069.
90. Schillinger to Yuri Shaporin, November 1, 1928, RGALI. f. 2642. Op. 1. Ed .khr. 459. l. 3.
91. The Paris concert was on February 21, 1932.

92. Charles E. Ives to Henry Cowell, Slonimsky, N., *Music since 1900*, fourth edition, New York, 1971, 1331.

93. Slonimsky, N., *Music since 1900*, fourth edition, New York, 1971, 219.

94. Rhea, T., "The Evolution of Electronic Musical Instruments in the United States," Ph. D. Diss./George Peabody College for Teachers, 1972, 58–59.

95. Slonimsky, N., "Review of the Shillinger System of Musical Composition," *The Musical Quarterly*, No. 32, 1947, 455–470.

96. Gershwin to Schillinger, Schwartz Ch., *Gershwin, His Life and Music*, Indianapolis: New York, 1973, 124.

97. Schillinger to David Evan, FJSC. Box 1A.

98. Ferris, E., "Inside Stuff," *Variety*, April 4, 1956, 49.

99. Duke, Vernon, "Gershwin, Shillinger and Dukelsky," *The Musical Quarterly*, No. 32 1947, 110.

100. Gubinetz, Elena, "Pereros muzyky kak takovyu," *Dve Zhizni Iosifa Schillingera*, Moscow State Conservatoire/Smithsonian American Art Museum, 2015, 259–261.

101. Schillinger, F., *Joseph Schillinger*, 198.

102. Previn, Charles, "Schillinger's Influence on Film Music," *Music News*. 1947. March. Vol. 39. No. 3, 39–40. *Dve Zhizni Iosifa Schillingera*, Moscow State Conservatoire/Smithsonian American Art Museum, 2015, 408–410.

103. I.M. Schillinger to Nikolay Malko, September 27, 1942. "Pereros muzyky kak takovyu," Elena Gubinetz, *Dve Zhizni Iosifa Schillingera*, Moscow State Conservatoire/Smithsonian American Art Museum, 2015, 262.

104. Maes, Francis, *A History of Russian Music*, London: University of California Press, 2006, 288.

105. Maes, Francis, *A History of Russian Music*, London: University of California Press, 2006, 288.

106. Nikolay Medtner to Sergey Rachmaninov, May 28, 1924, quoted in Taruskin, *Stravinsky and the Russian Tradition*, 1516.

107. Maes, Francis, *A History of Russian Music*, London: University of California Press, 2006, 289.

108. Maes, Francis, *A History of Russian Music*, London: University of California Press, 2006, 291.

109. Samuel, Claude, *Prokofiev*, London: Calder and Boyars, 1970, 98–99.

110. *The New York Times*, 1930, quoted in Harlow Robinson, *Sergey Prokofiev*, 243.

111. Maes, Francis, *A History of Russian Music*, London: University of California Press, 2006, 321.

112. Tretyakov, Sergey, quoted I Gutkin, *Legacy of the Symbolist Aesthetic Utopia*, 191.

113. Tretyakov, Sergey, quoted I Gutkin, *Legacy of the Symbolist Aesthetic Utopia*, 190.

Bibliography

PRIMARY SOURCES

Apetyan, Z.A., ed. *G. N. Popov 1904–1972 - Iz literaturnovo naslediye. Stranitsi biografii*, Moscow: Sovetsky Kompositor, 1986.

Alekseyenko, Nikolay, "O tvorchestvo A.V. Mosolova tridtzatykh-semidecyatykh godov," ed. N. K. Meshko, *Mosolov A., Statii i Vospominanii*, Moscow: Sovetsky Kompositor, 1986.

Barsova, Inna, "Rannee tvorchestvo Aleksandra Mosolova," ed. N. K. Meshko, *Mosolov A., Statii i Vospominanii*, Moscow: Sovetsky Kompositor, 1986.

Barsova, Inna, *Sovetskaya Muzyka*, No. 7, 1989.

Barsova, Inna, *Kontury stoletiya: Iz Istorii russkoy muzyki XX veka*, Sankt Petersburg: Kompositor, 2007.

Barsova, Inna, "Put Kompositora," *Dve Zhizni Iosifa Shillingera*, Moscow State Conservatoire/Smithsonian American Art Museum, 2015.

Hakobian, Leon, *Music of the Soviet Age, 1917–1987*, Stockholm: Melos, 1998.

Hakobian, Leon, *Music of the Soviet Era, 1917–1991*, London: Routledge, 2017.

Lobanova, Marina, *Nikolay Andreyevich Roslavets: i kultura evo vremeni*, Moscow: Petroglif, 2011.

Lobanova, Marina, "Naidenniye rukopisi N.A. Roslavetsa," *Sovetskaya Muzyka*, No. 10, 1989.

Lobanova, Marina, "Strasti po Nikolaye Roslavetsu," *Rossiskaya Muzikalnaya Gazeta*, No. 10, 2002.

Mosolov, A., "Noviye Kamerny konzert i P. Hindemitha," *Sovremennaya muzika*, no. 11, 1927.

Mosolov, A., "Poezdka v kubanskie kolhozy," *Sovetskaya Muzika*, No. 5, 1950.

Mosolov, A., "V Stanitskakh Kubani," No. 1, 1953.

Mosolov, A., "V Stepyakh Stavropolya," *Sovetskaya Muzika*, No. 3, 1956.

Popov, Gavriil, "Pobeda sovetskovo symphonism," *Iskusstvo i Zhizn*, No. 2, 1938.

Popov, Gavriil, "Po povodu Leningradskikh konzertov." Manuscript Archive Popov.

Popov, Gavriil, *Sovetskaya Muzyka*, No. 3, 1933.
Romaschuk, Inna, *Gavriil Nikolayevich Popov. Tvorchestvo. Vremya. Sudba.* Moscow: Izdatelstvo Instituta Ippolotit-Ivanova, 2000.
Rimsky, L. A., "A.V. Mosolov. Biograficheski ocherk," ed. N.K. Meshko, *A.V. Mosolov. Statii i Vospominaniya*, Moscow, 1986.
Roslavets, E.F., *Sovetskaya Muzyka*, No. 5, 1989.
Roslavets, Nikolay, "Druzhestvenny otvet Ars. Avraamovu," *Muzika*, No. 215, 1915.
Roslavets, N.A., *Abaza A.M.*, "Muzyka," No. 208, 1915.
Roslavets, Nikolay, "Sem let Oktyabrya v muzyke," *Muzykalnaya Kultura*, No. 3, 1924.
Roslavets, Nikolay, "Dialektikus, O Reaktionnom i Progressivnom v Muzyka," *Muzykalnaya Kultura*, No. 1, 1924.
Roslavets, Nikolay, "Nashi zadachi," *Muzykalnaya Kultura*, No. 1, 1924.
Roslavets, Nikolay, "Beglym ognem," *Muzykalnaya Kultura*, No. 8, 1924.
Roslavets, Nikolay, "Nikolay Roslavets," *Sovremennaya Muzyka*, No. 2, 1924.
Roslavets, Nikolay, (manuscript), Frankfurt-am-Main, 1997, *Roslawetz und Kultur und seiner zeit.*
Roslavets, Nikolay, "Otchet o rabote Lekstionno-repertuarno-izdatelskoy sektsii I konzertnovo podotdela muzykanovo otdela Moskovskoy proletkulta," ed. S.R. Stepanova, *Muzykalnaya zhizni Moskvy v pervye gody posle Oktyabya 1917–1920. Khronika, dokumenty, materialy*, Moscow, 1972.
Roslavets, Nikolay, "Muzyka," *Sovetskoye Iskusstsv*, No. 5, 1927.
Roslavets, Nikolay, "Lunaire Pierrot—Arnold Schoenberg," *K Novym beregam*, No. 3, 1923.
Roslavets, Nikolay, "O sebye i svoim tvorchestva," *Sovremennaya Muzyka*, V. 1924.
Roslavets, Nikolay, "Sovetskaya Muzika," *Rabis*, No. 43(85), 8/11/1927.
Roslavets, Nikolay, "Notnaya polka," Rabis, 1927, no. 4(46).
Roslavets, Nikolay, *Working Book on the Technique of Musical Composition. Parts of Theory and Practice. Research.* (1931). Roslavets, Nikolay, "*Research on Musical Sound and Tonality*" probably was written in Tashkent (1933).
Roslavets, Nikolay, "Pedagogical Principles of the New System of Musical-Creative Education" (1930).
Roslavets, Nikolay, "The New System of Composer's Education. Course of the Norms for Theoretical and Practical Attainment of Methods and Means of Musical Composition" (1935).
Schwartz, Boris, *Music and Musical Life in Soviet Russia 1917–1981*, Bloomington: Indiana UP, 1983.
Schillinger, I.M., "O kompositsii symphonicheskoi rhapsodii," *Oktyabr*, 12.
Schillinger, I.M., "O sebye i o svoyei Rapsodii," *Persimfans*. 1927–1928. No. 3–4.
Schillinger, I.M., "V preddveri novovo Bacha," *Ezhegodnik Petrogradskikh gosudarstvennykh akademicheskikh teatrov*. 1922. No. 5.
Vorobyov, Igor and Sinaiskaya, Anastasia, *Kompositori Russkovo Avangarda*, Sankt Peterburg: Kompositor, 2007.
Vorobyov, Igor, *Russky Avangard: Manifesti, deklaratsii, programmniye statii (1908–1917)*, Sankt Peterburg: Kompositor, 2008.

Vorobyov, Igor, *Russkiye Avangard i Tvorchestvo Aleksandra Mosolova 1920–1930 x godov*, Sankt Peterburg: Kompositor, Sankt Peterburga, 2006.
Vorobyov, Igor, *Social Realism*, St Peterburg: Kompositor, 2013.

SECONDARY SOURCES

"Kvartet A. Mosolova na festivale internationalovo obshestva sovremmennaya muziki vo Frankfurte," *Sovremennaya Muzika*, No. 24, 1927.
"Russkiye Narodny Pesni Pomorye," Moscow, 1966.
"Simfoniya ob Otechestvennoy voine," proizvedeniye A, Mosolova, *Vechernaya Moskva*, 17 July 1942.
"Sovetskaya Muzika v dnei voine," *Sovetskaya Muzika*, No. 11, 1975. *Literatura i iskusstvo*, 1 April 1944.
A.B., "Cantata N. Roslavetsa Oktyabr," *Sovetskaya Muzyka*, No. 24, 1927.
Adamov, Yevgeny, "Pobeda and solntsem," *Den*, 1913.
Ali-Khan (A. Kuprin), Pokhozhdeniya "Zelenoi loshadki," *Novaya Russkaya Zhizn*, 21/4/1921, Helsinki.
Anon, "24 pokazatelny konzert," Moskovskaya Gosurdarstvenny Konservatoire, 6 June 1925.
Anon, "Bolshaya Zhisn, Beseda s khudozhestvennym rukovoditelem Krasnovo teatra t. Wolfom," *Rabochy i Teatr*, No. 27, 1931.
Anon, "Chapayev," *Pravda*, 21 November 1934.
Anon, "Khorovaya rabota v Soyuz tekstilshikov," *Muzyka i Revolution*, No. 1, 1926.
Anon, "Novy ustav associatsiya sovremennoy muziki," *Sovremennaya Muzika*, No. 32.
Anon, "Personalia," *Sovremmennaya Muzika*, vypusk 7, Moscow, 1925.
Anon, "Prigovor suda po delu SOPHILa," *Vechernaya Moskva*, 24 March 1931.
Anon, "Puti razvitiya muziki," *Stenograficheskyy Otchet Soveschaniye po voprosam muziki*, 1930.
Anon, "Velikii Octobrya," *Muzyka i Revolutsii*, No. 11, 1927.
Anonym, "'Levy' flang sovremennoy muzyki," *Muzyka i Revolutssi*, 1927, 1.5.
Arnshtam, Lev, "Espania," *Pravda*, 7 June 1939.
Asafyev, Boris, "Istorichesky god," *Sovetskaya Muzika*, No. 3, 1933.
Asafyev, Boris, *Russkaya Poeziya v russkoi muzyke*, 2 editions, Petrograd, 1924.
Barinova, Marina, *Muzyka i ee predstavitely v moyei zhisnei*, St Petersburg: Kompositor, 2002.
Barsova, Inna, *Sovetskaya Muzika*, No. 8, 1989.
Belodubrovsky, Mark, "Nash zemlyak," *Sovetskaya Muzika*, No. 5, 1989.
Beltov, E., "Rasstrelyannaya literatora," *Vechernaya Moskva*, 19 July 1988.
Bely, Viktor, "Fakty i tsifri protiv ocherednoi kleveti na RAPM," *Proletarsky muzykant*, No. 9, 1931.
Bely, Viktor, "Levaya fraza muzykalnaya reaktsii," *Muzykalnaya Obrazovaniya*, No. 1, 1928.
Belyaev, Viktor, "Aleksandra Vasilyevich Mosolov," *Sovremennaya Muzika*, 1926.

Belyaev, Viktor, "Gavriil Popov," *Sovremennaya Muzika*, No. 1, 1928.
Belyaev, Viktor, "Muzykalnoye vystavki," *Muzykalnaya kultura*, No. 1, 1924.
Benois, Alexander, "Khudozhestvennoye heresy," *Zolotoye Runo*, No. 2, 1906.
Berezark I, "Problemi intelligentsia na sovetskoy scene," *Nasha Gazeta*, 31 August 1931.
Blok, Alexander, *Zapisniye knizhki*. 1901–1920. Moscow, 1915.
Bogdanov-Berezovsky, Venyamin, "Kompositor v zvukovom kino," *Krasnaya Gazeta*, 3 April 1933.
Bolshaya Sovetskaya Encyclopaedia, second edition, 1950, vol. 4.
Braudo, Yevgeny, "Na konzertakh (O Roslavets i Gr. Krein)," *Novy zritel*, No. 13, 1924.
Braudo, Yevgeny, "Organizator zvuk," *Vestnik rabotnikov iskusstsv*, No. 2, 1925.
Braudo, Yevgeny, *Die Musik*, XX: (April 1928).
Bugoslavsky, Sergey, "Bloknot muzykanta," *Zhizn iskusstsv*, No. 6, 1925.
Bukharin, Nikolay, "Formalny method v iskusstsv," *Pechat i Revolutssi*, 1925, kn. 3.
Clark, Katerina, *Moscow: The Fourth Rome. Stalinism, Cosmopolitanism, and the Evolution of Soviet Culture, 1931–1941*, Cambridge, MA: Harvard UP, 2011.
Clark, Katerina, *Petersburg: Crucible of Cultural Revolution*, Harvard UP, 1998.
Currie, James R., "Modernism – Out of the Spirit of Comedy," *The Routledge Companion to Modernism in Music*, London: Routledge, 2019.
DeLapp, Jennifer, "Copland in the Fifties: Music and Ideology in the McCarthy Era" (PhD, University of Michigan, 1997).
Denisov, Edison, "Ne lyublyu formalnoye iskusstsvo," *Sovetskaya Muzika*, No. 12, 1989.
Detsvo i yunost Kasimir Malevich, Harsevitch, Stockholm, 1976.
Dietsch, Johan, "Herbert Norkus and Pavel Morozov as Totalitarian Child Martyrs: A Study of Political Religion," *Perspectives on the Entangled History of Communism and Nazism. A Comnaz Analysis*, New York and London.
Doflein, E., (Freiburg i[n] Br[eislau]), Kammeroper, - *Melos*, 1928, H. 7.
Dolinskaya, Elena, "Posdny period tvorchestva Shostakovicha," *Shostakovich posvyashaetsa: 1906–1996*, 1997.
Dolinskaya, Elena, Ed. Tarakanov, *Istoriya Sovremennoy Otechestvennoy Muzyki*, vypusk 1, 1917–1941, Moscow, 1993.
Downes, Olin, "New Suite by Arnold Schoenberg," *New York Times*, 13/10/1935.
Drozdov, A., "Simfonicheskoye konzert GAKhN," *Muzika i Revolutsiya*, No. 12, 1927.
Duke, Vernon, "Gershwin, Shillinger and Dukelsky," *The Musical Quarterly*, No. 32, 1947.
E.M., "Poslednee slovo otzhivayuschey kultura," *Muzika i Revolutsiya*, No. 9, 1927.
Edmunds, Neil, *The Soviet Proletarian Music Movement*, Oxford: Peter Lang, 2000.
Ellis, Jack C. and McLane, Betsy A., *A New History of Documentary Film*. New York, NY: The Continuum International Publishing Group Inc., 2006.
Fairclough, Pauline, "From Enlightened to Sublime: Musical Life under Stalin, 1930–1948," *Russian Music since 1917*, London: British Academy, 2017.

Bibliography

Fanning, David, "Shostakovich and Structural Hearing," ed. Fairclough, *Shostakovich Studies 2*, Cambridge University Press, 2016.
Fanning, David, CD booklet of Popov CD on Telarc CD-80642.
Feisst, Sabine, *Schoenberg's New World*, Oxford UP, 2011.
Ferenc, Anna, "Music in the Socialist State," ed. Neil Edmunds, *Soviet Music and Society under Lenin and Stalin*, London: Routledge, 2009.
Ferenc, Anna, "Reclaiming Roslavets: The Troubled Life of a Russian Pioneer," *Tempo*, No. 182, 1992.
Finck, Henry, "The Musical Messiah-or Satan?" *Nation*, 15/11/1915.
Foote, Arthur, "Will the Music of Ultra-Modernists Survive?" *Etude* 34, no. 5 (May 1916), 331 and Henry Holden Huss, "The Anarchic Element in Some Ultra-modern Futurist Music," *Art World* 2, no. 2 (May 1917).
Frolova-Walker, Marina and Walker, Jonathan, *Music and Soviet Power 1917–1932*, London: Boydell, 2017.
Gabrilovich, E., "Udacha spectacle," *Sovetskoye Iskusstvo*, 3 December 1932.
Gershwin to Shillinger, Schwartz, Charles, *Gershwin, His Life and Music*, Indianapolis; New York: Bobbs-Merrill Company, 1973.
Glebov, Igor, "Russkaya simfonicheskaya muzika za 10 let," *Muzyka i revolutsiya*, No. 11, 1927.
Grabar, *Valentin Serov v vospominaniyakh, perepiska i dnevnikakh*, tom. 2.
Graham, Stephen, "Modernism for and of the Masses?" *The Routledge Companion to Modernism in Music*, London: Routledge, 2019.
Grigoryeva, Galina, *Stilevy problemi russkoy sovetskoy muziki vtoroi poloviny XX veka*, 1989.
Gubinetz, Elena, "Pereros muzyky kak takovyu," *Dve Zhizni Iosifa Shillingera*, Moscow State Conservatoire/Smithsonian American Art Museum, 2015.
Gutkin, Irina, "Legacy of the Symbolist Aesthetic Utopia: From Futurism to Socialist Realism," 183–84. eds. Irina Paperno and Joan Delaney Grossman, *Creating Life: The Aesthetic Utopia of Russian Modernism*, 1677-06. Stanford, 1994.
Haas, David, *Leningrad's Modernists: Studies in Composition and Musical thought 1917–1932*, New York: Peter Lang, 1998.
Hakobian, Leon, "Shostakovich, Proletkult and RAPM," *Shostakovich Studies 2*, Cambridge UP, 2016.
Heifetz, Iosif, "Взлёт и падение «Моей Родины»," *Искусство кино*, No. 12, 1990.
Heyworth, Peter, *Klemperer*, 2:53; Olin Downes's Critique in *The New York Times* of 18 October 1935, quoted in Ennulat, "Schoenberg Correspondence."
Honegger, Arthur, *O musikalnom iskusstve*, Leningrad, 1979.
Jokhelson, Vladimir, "Leningradskii Soyuz Sov kompositorov k xvii syesda partii," *Sovetskaya Muzyka*, 1934.
Jokhelson, Vladimir, "The Creative Discussion in Leningrad," *Sovetskaya Muzyka*, No. 4, 1936.
Kabalevsky, D.B., "Pevets rodnoy strany," *Sovetskaya Kultura*, 27 July 1973.
Kaltat, Lev, "O podlinno-burzhasnoi ideologii gr. Roslavetsa," *Muzykalnaya Obrazovaniye*, 1927.
Kamegulov E., "Moya Rodina," *Leningradskaya Pravda*, 4 March 1933.

Karatygin, V., "Noveishiye techeniya v russkoy muziki."
Katanyan, V. *Mayakovsky – Khronika zhizni i deyatelnosti*, Moscow, 1985.
Kater, Michael H., *Composers of the Nazi Era: Eight Portraits*, New York: OUP, 2000.
Keldysh, Yuri, "Stalnoy skok Prokofieva," *Muzykalnoy obrazovaniye*, No. 3, 1928.
Kerzhentsev, P.M., "Puti razvitiya muziki," *Stenograficheskiy Otchet Soveschaniye po voprosam muziki pri APPO TsK VKP(B)*, Moscow, 1936.
Khentova, S., D. *Shostakovich. Zhizn i Tvorchestvo*: v 2 tomakh, tom 1, Leningrad: Sovetsky Kompozitor, 1985.
Khodasevich, T., "Massoviyiy deistvi, zrelischa i prazdniki," *Teatr*, No. 4, 1967.
Kholopov and Tzernova, "Edison Denisov," *Moscow Kompositor*, 1993.
Khrennikov, Tikhon, "Zavoevat vsenarodnoye priznaniye," *Sovetskom iskusstve*, 10 December 1949.
Kilchevsky, V., "Na Leningradsky front," *Proletarsky muzikant*, No. 2, 1931.
Kilchevsky, V., *Proletarsky Muzikant*, No. 2, 1930.
Kleiman, Levina, "Bronenosets Potemkin," Moscow, 1969.
Kleiman, N., "Эйзенштейн, 'Бежин луг' (первый вариант), культурно-мифологические аспекты," /*Формула финала: сборник*, Moscow: Эйзенштейн-центр, 2004.
Konchalovsky, A. S., "Возвышающий обман," Moscow, *Совершенно секретно*, 1999.
Korev, Semyon, "Glaviskustsvo," *Proletarskaya Muzyka*, No. 3, 1930.
Korev, Semyon, "Simfonicheskoye sobraniye. V centralny dom rabotnikov iskusstve," *Vechernaya Moskva*, 10 February 1947.
Korev, Semyon, "Sovetskaya simfonicheskaya muzyka: jubilniye Oktyabrsiye kontserti," *Sovetskoye Iskusstvo*, No. 7, 1927.
Koval, Marian, "Lenin in Music," *Proletarsky Muzikant*, No. 1, 1930.
Koval, Marian, "Propaganda Jazz-banda," *Muzyka i Revolutsiya*. 1927. May–June, No. 5–6.
Koval, Marian, "Slava Otchizne," *Literaturnaya Gazeta*, 14 December 1949.
Kreitner, G., "Decada sovetskoy muziki," *Moskovskoy Bolshevik*, 23 November 1939.
Kruchenykh, A., "Pobeda na solntsem. Podgotovka texta, predisloviye I oformleniye R. V. Duganova," Moscow, Vienna, 1993. Vorobyov, Sinaiskaya, *Kompositori Russkovo avangarda*. kompositora, St Petersburg, 2007.
Kryukov, Nikolay, "Kompositori na pereputi," *Sovetskoye Iskusstvo*, 9 May No. 21, 1932.
Kundera, Milan, "Improvisation in Homage to Stravinsky," in *Testaments Betrayed*, translated by Linda Asher, London and Boston: Faber and Faber, 1995.
Kurysheva, Tatyana, "Varshavskaya osen-73—Dva mneniya o konzertakh festivalya," *Sovetskaya Muzika*, No. 2, 1974.
Langunova, Olga, "Nikolaj Andreevic Roslawetz."
Larsson, Klas-Goran, Johan Stenfeldt, and Ulf Zander, *Perspectives on the Entangled History of Communism and Nazism: A Comnaz Analysis*, Lanham: Lexington Books, 2015.

Lebedinsky, Lev, "O muzykalnoy praktike, obshestvennikh gruppirovkakh muzykantov k nashey politike po otnosheniyu k nim," *Proletarsky muzikant*, No. 2, 1930.

Lebedinsky, Lev, "Obschestvenniye gruppirovki muzykantov v CCCP," *Muzykalnoye obrazovaniye*, No. 4–5, 1928.

Lebedinsky, Lev, "Otchet o deyatelnosti soveta Associatsii proletarskikh muzykantov, borbe za proletarskoy muzyki i dalneishikh zadacha RAPMa," pt. 1, *Proletarsky Muzykant*, No. 3–4.

Lebedinsky, Lev, *8 let Borby za proletarskoy musiku*, Moscow, 1931.

Lourie, Arthur, "Nash Marsh," *Novy Zhurnal*, No. 94, New York, 1968.

Lunacharsky, Anatoly, "Nash muzykalnyy front," Moscow.

Lunacharsky, Anatoly, "Teatr sevodnya," Moscow.

MacDonald, Malcolm, "Shostakovich's String Concertos and Sonatas," *The Cambridge Companion to Shostakovich*, CUP, 2008.

Maes, Francis, *A History of Russian Music*, London: University of California Press, 2006.

Malevich, Kazimir, "Detsvo i yunost Casimira Malevicha," *Glavi iz Avtobiografii khudozhnika*, Stockholm, 1976.

Malevich, Kazimir, "O sebye, sovremmeniki o Malevichi," *Pisma, dokumenty, kritiki*, tom 1., Vakar, Mikenko, Moscow, 2006.

Malevich, Kazimir, "Teater," 1917.

Malko, Nikolay, *Vospominaniya, Statii, Pisma*, Muzyka, Moscow, 1972.

Margolit, Shmyrov, "*Izyatoye Kino*," Moscow, 1995.

Marian, D., "V otryv ot deistvitelnosti," *Kino*, 24 March 1937.

Markov, P., *Vl. I. Nemirovich-Danchenko i muzikalnovo teatra evo imeni*, Moscow, 1937.

Martynov, N., *A. Davidenko. Tvorchesky put, cherty stilya*, Leningrad: Sovetsky Kompositor, 1977.

Martynova, Svetlana, "Pavel Lamm v tyurmakh i sslykhakh: Po stranitsam Vospominanii O. P. Lamm."

Mchelin, V., "Kultura operetta," *Sovetskoye Iskusstvo*, 3 December 1932.

Mende, Wolfgang, "Music Censorship in the Era of NEP and Cultural Revolution: The Case of Nikolay Roslavets," *1948 and All That: Soviet Music, Ideology and Power*, Cambridge, 2009.

Metzer, D.J., "The Ascendancy of Musical Modernism," 14–34, Sabine Feisst, *Schoenberg's New World*, Oxford UP, 2011.

Milhaud, Darius, *Ma vie heureuse*, Paris: Editions Belfond, 1973.

Morrison, Simon and Lesley-Anne Sawyers, "Prokofiev's *Le Pac d'Acier*," *Soviet Music and Society under Lenin and Stalin*, London: Routledge, 2009.

Muradeli, Vano, "Novoye v sovetskoy muziki," *Sovetskoye iskusstvo*, 9 January 1940.

Muzika i Revolutsii, No. 1, January 1927, 3–7.

Myaskovsky, N. Ya., *N. Ya. Myaskovsky*, tom 2, Moscow: Gosizdat, 1964.

Myaskovsky, Nikolay, *Muzika*, No. 197, 1914.

Nekrasov, Viktor, "Слова «великие» и простые," Искусство кино, 1959, № 5.

Nelson, Amy, *Music for the Revolution: Musicians and Power in Early Soviet Russia*, Pennsylvania UP, 2004.
Nestyev, Israel, "Pseudonauchnaya stryapnya," *Sovetskoye Iskusstvo*, 18 January 1939.
Nestyev, Israel, "V plenu u burzhuasnovo modernism i o tvorchestva G. Popova," *Sovetskaya Muzyka*, No. 10, 1948.
Nikitina, L., *Istoriya Sovremennoy Otechestvennoy Muzyki*, vypusk 1, 1917–1941, Moscow: Muzyka, 1993.
Ovrutsky L., Razgon, "Terror ugnettennikh i terror pobeditelei," *Rodina*, No. 5, 1990.
Petropoulos, Jonathan, *Artists under Hitler: Collaboration and Survival in Nazi Germany*, Yale University Press, 2015.
Podmarkova, L. A., *N. A. Roslavets—kompositor, pedagog, obshestvenniy deyatel*, Elets, 2003.
Preisner, E., "Festival Kamerny muziki v Baden-Baden," *Muzikalnovo obrazovaniye*, No. 45, 1928.
Previn, Charles, "Shillinger's Influence on Film Music," *Music News*. 1947. March. Vol. 39. No. 3, 39–40. *Dve Zhizni Iosifa Shillingera*, Moscow State Conservatoire/ Smithsonian American Art Museum, 2015.
Proletarsky Muzikant, No. 4, 1929, 40.
Proletarsky Muzikant, No. 5, 1929, 30–31.
Raaben, L., *Istoriya Russkovo i Sovetskovo skripachnovo iskusstvo*, Leningrad, 1978.
Raiskin, Iosif, CD booklet for Popov Symphony No 1, Northern Flowers NF/PMA 9996.
Rhea, T., "The Evolution of Electronic Musical Instruments in the United States," PhD Diss./George Peabody College for Teachers, 1972.
Roslavetsa, Natalya N.R., "Music in Post-war France," *Muzykalnaya Kultura*, No. 3, 1924.
Sabaneyev, Leonid, *Muzyka v Klube*, Moscow, 1926.
Sabaneyev, Leonid, *Teatralny Izvestiya*, No. 3, 17–20 February 1922.
Sabinina, Marina, *Shostakovich-symphonist*, Moscow: Muzyka, 1976.
Samuel, Claude, *Prokofiev*, London: Calder and Boyars, 1971.
Sargeant, Winthrop, "Arnold Schoenberg and the Atonal Style," *Brooklyn Daily Eagle*, 6/10/1935.
Schoenberg, Arnold. *Gedenkausstellung 1974*, Vienna: Universal Edition, 1974.
Schwartz, Boris, "The Music World in Migration," eds. Jarell C. Jackman and Carla M. Borden, "The Muses Flee Hitler: Cultural Transfer and Adaption," 1930–1945 (Washington, DC, 1983), 141; Ernst Krenek, "Americas einfluss auf eingewanderte komponisten," in Traber and Weingarten, *Verdrangte Musik*.
Schwartz, L., "On Modern Film Music," *Sovetskaya Muzyka*, No. 3, 1948.
Seeger, Charles (Carl Sands), "Schoenberg's Latest Composition," *New York City Daily Worker*, 23/10/1935.
Selunskaya and Zezina, "Documentary Film—A Soviet Source," *Stalinism and Soviet Cinema*, Oxford: Routledge, 1993.
Sergey Diaghilev i russkoye iskusstvo, Moscow, 1982, t. 2.
Shaw, George Bernard, *Papers*, British Library Add 85031, n.p.

Shebalin, Vissarion Yakovlevich, *Vospominaniya. Statii. Materialii*, Moscow: Sovetsky Kompositor, 1975.
Shebalin, Vissarion, "Diskussiya o sovetskom simfonisme," *Sovetskaya Muzika*, No. 5, 1935.
Shenshin, Alexander, "Notografiya," *Sovremennaya Muzika*, No. 25, 1927.
Shostakovich, Dmitry, "Soviet Music is Lagging Behind," *Sovetskaya Muzika*, No. 3, 1933.
Shumyatsky, Boris, "Film Bezhin Meadow," *Pravda*, 19 March 1937.
Shumyatsky, Boris, "Kinematografiya millionov," Moscow, 1935.
Sitsky, Larry, *Music of the Repressed Russian Avant-Garde*, Westport, CT: Greenwood Press, 1994.
Slonimsky, N., "Review of the Shillinger System of Musical Composition," *The Musical Quarterly*, 1947. No. 32.
Slonimsky, N., *Music since 1900*, fourth edition, New York: Scribner, 1971.
Sollertinsky, Ivan, "Diskussiya o sovetskom simfonisme," *Sovetskaya Muzika*, No. 5, 1935.
Solodukho, A., "Varshavskaya osen-73—Dva mneniya o konzertakh festivalya," *Sovetskaya Muzika*, No. 2, 1974.
Sovetskaya Muzika, 1948, 1, 54–62.
Sovetskaya Muzika, 1976, 12, 77–87.
Sovremennaya Muzika, 1927, no. 24, 47.
Spring, Derek, Taylor, Richard, and Christie, Ian, "The Director in Soviet Cinema," *Stalinism and Soviet Cinema*, Oxford: Routledge, 1993.
Stein A, "O fleite, kotoraya ne zvuchit," *Leningradskaya Pravda*, 1 October 1931.
Stepanova, I., *Istoriya Sovremennoy Otechestvennoy Muzyki*, vypusk 1, 1917–1941, Moscow, 1993.
Stites, Richard, "Russian Popular Music to 1953," *Soviet Music and Society under Lenin and Stalin*, edited by Neil Edmunds, London: Routledge, 2009.
Stonor Saunders, Frances, *The Cultural Cold War: The CIA and the World of Arts and Letters*, New York: The New Press, 1999.
Stuckenschmidt, Hans Heinz, *Schoenberg: His Life, World and Work*, New York: Schirmer, 1977.
Sulgin, Mikhail, "O Varshavskom," *Iskusstvo Kino*, No. 7, 2000.
Tassie, Gregor, *Nikolay Myaskovsky: The Conscience of Russian Music*, Lanham: Rowman & Littlefield, 2014.
Taylor, Richard, "Ideology as Mass Entertainment: Boris Shumyatsky and Soviet Cinema in the 1930s," in Taylor and Spring, *Stalinism and the Soviet Cinema*, London: Routledge, 2013.
Taylor, Richard, "Red Stars, Positive Heroes and Personality Cults," *Stalinism and Soviet Cinema*, London: Routledge, 2013.
Tirs, K., "Corneville kolokola, Teatr imeni Nemirovich-Danchenko," *Komsomolskaya Pravda*, 30 November 1932.
Tomoff, Kirill, *Creative Union: The Professional Organization of Soviet Composers, 1939–1953*, Ithaca, NY: Cornell University Press, 2006.

Tretyakov, Sergey, quoted Irina Gutkin, *Legacy of the Symbolist Aesthetic Utopia*, Stanford: Stanford UP, 1993.
Tsekhnovitser, Orest, "Novaya Muzyka i Proletariat," *Novaya Muzyka*, No. 2, 1927–28.
Tsymbal, S., "Accept Battle," *Rabochy i theatre*, No. 66–67, 1930.
Tur, Bratya, "Cherezmernaya Lyubov," *Izvestiya*, 11 June 1935.
Tur, Bratya, "Deviations of a Genius," *Izvestiya*, 18/9/1937.
Tur, Bratya, *Izvestiya*, 18 July 1937.
Turnovskaya, Maya, "The 1930s and 1940s: Cinema in Context," *Stalinism and Soviet Cinema*, London: Routledge, 2013.
Turovskaya, M., *Sochineniya Kozmy Prutkova*, Moscow, 1955.
Uglov, Anton, (pseudonym for D. Kashintseva) "Simfonicheskoye novinki," *Izvestiya*, 12 February 1928.
Uglov, Anton, (pseudonym for D. Kashintseva) "Tsikl Stradivariuses," *Izvestiya*, 20 March 1927.
Uglov, Anton, (pseudonym for D. Kashintseva), "Drugaya Kamerny muziki," *Izvestiya*, 24 February 1927.
Uglov, Anton, (pseudonym for D. Kashintseva), "Pervye konzert sovfila," *Izvestiya*, 17 October 1927.
Uglov, Anton, (pseudonym for D. Kashintseva), *Izvestiya*, 24 Feb 1927.
Uriel, "Spisok blagodeyanii," *Komsomolskaya Pravda*, 16 June 1931.
Vaidman, P. E., *Neizvestny Tchaikovsky- chelovek i khudozhnik*, Moscow: P. Jurgenson, 2009.
Vainkop, Yuri, "Konzert LASM," *Rabochy i Teatr*, No. 23 1927.
Vaks, Klara, "A.K. Mosolov," *Sovetskaya Muzyka*, No. 7, 1936.
Vasilenko, S.A., *Vospominaniya*, Moscow: Kompositor, 1979,
Vaxberg, A., *Tsaritsa dokazeltelstv: Vyshinsky in evo zhertv*, Moscow, 1992.
Vlasova, E.S., "Venera milosskaya i printsipi 1789 goda," statii pervaya, *Muzykalnaya Academia*, 1993.
Vlasova, E.S., *1948 god v sovetskoy muzyki*, Moscow: 21 Classika, 2010.
Volkogonov, Dmitry, *Trotsky: The Eternal Revolutionary*, London: HarperCollins, 1997.
Vygodsky, "1905 god v muziki," *Muzykalnaya obrazovaniye*, No. 1–2, 1926.
Wuorinen, "The Outlook," 54; and Gunther Schuller, "Schoenberg's Influence," in TASC, 260; Andrea Olmstead, *Conversations with Roger Sessions*, Boston: North-Eastern Press, 1987.
Yampolsky, M., *Les ecrans de la liberte: URSS, 50 ans de cinema retrouve*, Paris, 1989.
Yavorsky, B. L., *Statii, Vospominanyii, Pisma*, Moscow, 1972, vol. 1.
Zakharov, "Espania," *Kino*, 15 May 1939.
Zaslavsky, D.I., "Kozma Prutkov i 'Sovremennik," *Sochineniya Kozmy Prutkova*, Moscow, 1955.
Zlessky, V., "Spektakl-predostaerezheniye dlya teatra i avtora," *Vechernaya Moskva*, 12 June 1931.

Catalog of Works

NIKOLAY ROSLAVETS

Stage works

Pakhta (Cotton)—1931–1932—pantomime ballet in three acts—manuscript
Chorus and orchestra
The Heaven and Earth—1912—mystery based on Byron—manuscript
On the death of the Earth—symphonic poem for baritone, choir, and orchestra—lost
October—cantata for mezzo-soprano and baritone, mixed choir, and orchestra—manuscript
Komsomoliya—symphonic poem for mixed choir and orchestra, 1928—Schott ED 8256
The Black City—symphonic poem for bass, choir, and orchestra, 1929—lost
On the death of Mayakovsky—funeral fragment for bass and orchestra to words by Panchenko, 1930—manuscript
A capella choir
Ave Maria to words by Ellis, 1910—manuscript
Symphonic Orchestra
Symphony in C minor, 1910—Kompositor International Mainz 51585
In the hours of the New Moon, 1912—Schott ED 8107
Man and the Sea, 1921—symphonic poem—lost
Symphony in four movements, 1922—manuscript drafts
Symphony No. 2, 1923—manuscript drafts
Work for symphony orchestra (Lento), 1920—manuscript drafts
Work for symphony orchestra, 1920–1930—manuscript drafts
Soviet Uzbekistan—symphonic poem, 1932—manuscript drafts

Girya—Uzbek folksong for symphony orchestra, 1932–1933—manuscript drafts
Work for symphony orchestra, 1930s—manuscript drafts
Violin and Orchestra
Reverie, 1907—manuscript drafts
Violin Concerto No. 1, 1925—SCHOTT ED 7823
Violin Concerto No. 2, 1936—Kompositor International Mainz 52700
Chamber Ensemble
Chamber Symphony for eighteen performers, 1934–1935—Kompositor International Mainz 51581
Nocturne, 1913—SCHOTT ED 8129
Quartet for domra on Chechen folksongs, 1934–1935—manuscript drafts
String Quartet
Minuet, 1907—manuscript
Quartet in F major—first movement, 1910—manuscript
Quartet No. 1, 1913—SCHOTT ED 8126
Quartet, 1916—sketches of 2 and 3 movements
Quartet, 1919—manuscript drafts
Quartet No. 3, 1920—SCHOTT ED 8127
Quartet, 1920–1924—lost
Turkestan Quartet, 1930s—lost
Quartet No. 4, 1939—manuscript drafts
Quartet No. 5 in E major, 1941—SCHOTT ED 8128
For Violin, Cello, and Piano
Trio No. 1—lost
Trio No. 2, 1920—SCHOTT ED 8059
Trio No. 3, 1921—SCHOTT ED 8035
Trio No. 4, 1927—SCHOTT ED 8036
Trio No. 5—lost
Four Uzbeki folksongs, 1930s—lost
For Two Violins
Serenade, 1909—manuscript
For Violin and Piano
Morgenstimmung, 1907—manuscript
Romance, 1907—manuscript
Elégie, 1908—manuscript
Reverie, 1908—manuscript
Romance, 1908—manuscript
Arabesques, 1909–1910—manuscript
Trois poèmes, 1909/1910—SCHOTT ED 17036-9
Rondeau-polonaise, 1910—manuscript
Sonata No. 1, 1913—Sikorski 1428

Composition, 1914–
Poème, 1915—SCHOTT ED 8261
Sonata No. 2, 1917—SCHOTT ED 8059
Three Dances, 1923—SCHOTT ED 8261
Sonata No. 3—lost
Sonata No. 4, 1920—SCHOTT ED 8044
Sonata No. 5, 1922–1923—lost
Invention, 1935—SCHOTT ED 17036-9
Nocturne, 1935—SCHOTT ED 17036-9
Waltz, 1935—manuscript
Lullaby, 1935—manuscript
Scherzo, 1935—manuscript
Dance, 1935—manuscript
Gavotte, 1935—manuscript
Seven pieces in the first position, 1930s—SCHOTT ED VLB 131
Sonata No. 6, 1930s—SCHOTT ED 8431
Legenda, 1941—SCHOTT ED 8261
24 Preludes, 1941–1942—SCHOTT ED 7940
For Viola and Piano
Sonata No. 1, 1926—SCHOTT ED 8177
Sonata No. 2, 1930s—SCHOTT ED 8178
For Cello and Piano
Dances of the White Maidens, 1912—SCHOTT ED 8045
Sonata No. 1, 1921—SCHOTT ED 8038
Thoughts/Meditation, 1921—UE 9203
Sonata No. 2, 1922—SCHOTT ED 8039
For Piano
Trois compositions, 1914—SCHOTT ED 7907
Trois etudes, 1914—SCHOTT ED 7907
Sonata No. 1, 1914—SCHOTT ED 7941
Deux compositions, 1915—SCHOTT ED 7907
Sonata No. 2, 1916—SCHOTT ED 8391
Berceuse, 1919—SCHOTT ED 17041-3
Danse, 1919—SCHOTT ED 17041-3
Valse, 1919—SCHOTT ED 17041-3
Quatre compositions, 1919–1921—SCHOTT ED 17041-3
Cinq preludes, 1919–1922—SCHOTT ED 7907
Deux poèmes, 1920—SCHOTT ED 7907
Sonata No. 3—lost
Sonata No. 4, 1923—lost
Sonata No. 5, 1923—SCHOTT ED 8392
Sonata No. 6, 1928—manuscript sketches

Poème berceuse, 1939—lost
For Voice and Piano
Two romances from Balmont, 1909—SCHOTT ED 8435
Morana (Evening field), 1909–1911—SCHOTT ED 8435
Swans from Ivanov, 1910–1911—SCHOTT ED 8435
Beatrice from Gumilyov, 1910–1911—SCHOTT ED 8435
I don't remember about yesterday from Blok, 1910–1911—SCHOTT ED 8435
Four romances, 1911—SCHOTT ED 8435
Sad landscapes from Verlaine, 1913—SCHOTT ED 8436
Three compositions for voice and piano, 1913—SCHOTT ED 8436
Four compositions for voice and piano, 1913–1914—CHOTT ED 8436
Flight from Kamensky, 1915—SCHOTT ED 8436
Songs of Harlequin from Guro, 1915—SCHOTT ED 8436
Through the Velvet Curtain from Voloshin, 1918—SCHOTT ED
My past is lost from Blok, 1919—SCHOTT ED 8437
Four poems by Zinaida Gippius, 1919—SCHOTT ED 8437
On the Saime from Bryusov, 1920
In the far-off light from Bryusov, 1920—SCHOTT ED 8437
Four poems by Sologub, 1919—SCHOTT ED 8437
Four poems by Pavlovich, 1922—SCHOTT ED 8437
Agitational music
Songs of the Revolution, 1921–1926—SCHOTT C 54051
October for a capella, 1926—Gosizdat 1926
Iron flowers, unfinished—manuscript
Communist international for a capella, 1923—manuscript
Communist funeral march for a capella, 1923—manuscript
Poems of the Working Profession, 1924–1926—Gosizdat 1925
Songs about 1905 for voice and piano, 1925–1926—Gosizdat 1925, 1926
Lullaby for voice and piano, 1920s—manuscript
Metalworker for mixed choir, 1925—Muzsektor 1925
Song about the red banner for women's choir, 1926—Muzsektor 1926
Workers' palace for mixed choir, 1926, Muzsektor, 1926
Hymn of the Soviet workers militia, Publishing house of the All-Russian union of peasant writers 1926
Working woman, 1928—manuscript
Women's share for voice and piano, 1929, authors' publication
You Give! For voice and piano, 1929—Dahesh publishers 1929
Knock the door! Komsomol march, Muzgis 1930
Baraban (Drum), for two-part choir and balalaikas, Tea-Kino-Pechat 1930
Militant callsign, 1930, Tea-Kino-Pechat 1930
Give us the five-year plan in four years, 1930—Dayesh publishers 1930

Avia march—Red army songs—1931
Aurora for voice and piano, 1939, Songs of the Red Fleet 1939
Four Songs for Radio, 1930s—All-Union Radio Archive
Tabachok for voice and piano, 1942, Muzgis 1942
Songs of the 1920s–1940s,—manuscript

GAVRIIL POPOV

Piano Pieces
Images—
Le Fond
Retentissement
Expressia and *Melody*, Op. 1
Septet, Op. 2
Two Vocalises, Op. 3
Concertino for violin and piano, Op. 4
Dance Suite for piano, Op. 5
Grosse Klavier Suite, Op. 6
Orchestral works
Symphony No. 1, Op. 7
Theatre suite—Oil
Theatre Suite—Accept Battle
Film score—Motherland
Film score—Komsomol—patrons of electrification,
Symphonic Suite No. 1, Op. 12
Little Suite, Op. 15b
Film score—Chapayev
Concert poem for violin and orchestra, Op. 17
Film score—Strict Youth
Film score—Bezhin Meadow
Film score—Spain, Symphonic fragments
Lyric suite after Pushkin, Op. 22
Divertissement, Op. 23
Piano Concerto, Op. 24
Serenade for Wind, Op. 26
Film score—They Defend the Motherland
Symphony No. 2 "Motherland," Op. 39
Symphony No. 3 "Heroic," Op. 45
Symphonic Aria, Op. 43
Quartet Symphony
Symphony No. 5 "Pastorale," Op. 77

Symphony No. 6 "Festive," Op. 99
Stage works
Alexander Nevsky, Op. 25
Choral works
Overture-cantata—"To Victory"
Poem cantata—"Glory, glory to our dear Party"
Symphony No. 4 "Glory to the Motherland"
Suite for Choir—"Our Dear Land"
Vocal symphonic poem—"Tale on Lenin"
Lyrical concertino for mixed choir, "Family of Eagles"
Five choruses—"Tale of Tsar Sultan"

ALEXANDER MOSOLOV

Piano pieces

Two etudes (Op. 3) lost
Piano Sonata No. 1, Op. 3
Piano Sonata No. 2, Op. 4 (lost)
Piano Sonata No. 3, Op. 11 (Op. 8) lost
Piano Sonata No. 4, Op. 11
Piano Sonata No. 5, Op. 12
Deux Nocturnes, Op. 15
Two Poems, Op. 20—lost
Three Pictures, Small Pieces for piano, Op. 23a
Two Dances, Op. 23b
Turkmen Nights, Fantasy for Piano (1929)
Two pieces on Uzbeki themes, Op. 31
Nine Children's Pieces (1956)

Vocal pieces

Romance *Night* based on Pushkin, Op. 1
In the Darkness, song cycle from Blok, etc.—lost
Two songs on Pushkin
To a Friend, Three lyric songs, Op. 7
Three Keys based on Pushkin, Op. 9
Ten poems from Blok, Op. 10
Ten poems to words by Blok—lost
Four Newspaper Advertisements, Op. 18
Three Children's Scenes, Op. 21

Songs from words by Mayakovsky,
Khodasevich, and Khlebnikov—lost
Three Songs for voice and orchestra, Op. 33
Four romances to words by Pushkin (1936)—lost
Three romances to Lermontov (1936)—lost
Table Song for Stalin words by Zharov (1939)
Five Poems on words by Pushkin
Three Elegies for voice and piano from Davydov (1944)
Three Waltzes for voice and piano (1945)
Five poems to A. Blok (1944)
Five Poems to Blok (1946)

Chamber pieces

Ballade, Trio for clarinet, cello and piano, Op.
Legend for Cello and Piano, Op. 5
String Quartet No. 1, Op. 24
String Quartet No. 2 (1943)
Dance Suite for Harp Solo (1945)
Sonatina for cello and piano (1946)
Four Pieces for Oboe and Piano (1947)
Four Pieces for Bassoon and Piano (1947)
Two pieces for cello Elegia and Dance (1947)
Serenade for mandolin and piano (1950)
Three pieces for cello and piano from folksongs (1951)
Piano Quintet on Kabardinian songs (1956)

Orchestral pieces

Twilight, symphonic poem—lost
Piano Concerto No. 1, Op. 14
The Foundry: Music for Machines (Zavod)—Op. 19
Piano Concerto No. 2
Uzbek Suite (1936)—lost
Gavotte and Minuet for orchestra
Turkmen overture (1937)—lost
Cello Concerto No. 1 (1937)—lost
Harp Concerto, Op. 39
Symphony in E major (1944)
Cello Concerto No. 2
Symphony in C major, Op. "Kuban Collective Farm"
Four Songs for Small Orchestra (1954)

Song of the Nart—Suite for Orchestra (1954)
Unbroken Friendship—Suite for Orchestra (1954)
Cello Concerto on Kabardian songs (1956)—lost
Symphony in C major (1958)
Elegiac Poem for Cello and Orchestra (1961)
Violin Concerto
Russian Overture for orchestra (1963)
Symphony No. 5 (1965)
Piano Concerto No. 3 (1971)

Choral pieces

The Sphinx, cantata on words by Oscar Wilde—lost
The Year 1924 choral and orchestral cantata—lost
The Christening of Russia operetta—lost
Offering—Music for First All-Union Pioneers Meeting
Anti-religious Symphonic Poem, for narrators, orchestra, and choir, Op. (1929)—lost
Rhapsody on Kirghiz themes for soloist, chorus, and orchestra (1937)—lost
Ukraine—symphonic poem for soloists, chorus, and orchestra (1941)
Cycle of choruses portraying Tsarist military leaders—Alexander Nevsky, Alexander Suvorov, and Mikhail Kutuzov (1941–1942)
Oratorio *Hero-City* was published with the hymns *Moscow* (1941)
Ballad *Leningrad*
Nocturne *Stalingrad*
Marches *Sevastopol*, and *Odesa*
October, cantata from Rudnev (1942)
Motherland chorus and piano from Bedny (1943)
Five Russian National Songs of the 1812 War (1942)
Cantata *Glory to the Soviet Army* (1947)
Moscow cantata (1947)
Choral Suite (1948)
On Lenin for a capella chorus (1948)
Motherland for a capella chorus (1948)
Cycle to Pushkin (1949)
Song Symphony in B major (1949)
Kuban Stanitsa Suite for chorus and folk instrument orchestra (1952)
Songs of the Terek Cossacks (1953)—lost
Mother Kuban for chorus (1953)
Young Cossacks Suite for chorus and folk instrument orchestra (1954)
Kuban Collective Farm Suite for chorus and folk instrument orchestra (1954)

Steppe Songs of the Kuban Suite for chorus and folk instrument orchestra (1954)
Lyrics of the Old Village—Ten folksongs (1958)
Natasha's Day—Children's Songs (1958)
Song about Soviet Russia for a capella chorus based on Litvinov (1958)
About Lenin for chorus from Mayakovsky (1961)
Hey Russia a capella based on Mashistov (1961)
The Year 1924 a capella chorus based on Mashistov (1961)
Thoughts a capella chorus from Mayakovsky (1962)
The Red Banner a capella chorus from Mayakovsky (1963)
Put the Hammer and the Poem from Mayakovsky (1963).
Symphony No. 3, Op "Virgin Lands"
Tractor's Arrival at the Kolkhoz
Suite—*Soldiers' Songs*
Nine Choruses—*Front Roads*
Eight Choruses—*Collective Farm Meadows*
Ode to the Party for chorus and orchestra (1963)
Glory to Moscow based on Zharov oratorio (1967)
Peoples Oratorio for G. I. Kotovsky for soloists, chorus, and orchestra (1970)
Stage works
The Hero, Op. 28
2117 for *The Four Ages of Moscow* ballet—lost
The Dam, opera in five acts, Op. 35—manuscript
Incidental music for Planquette's *Les Cloches de Corneville* (1932)
Signal (1941)
Masquerade (1942)

MIKHAIL MATYUSHIN

Canzone—*Music for Harlequin* (1909)
Suite for Violin and Piano—Autumn Dream (1912)
Victory over the Sun—opera (1913)
Don Quixote (1914)
The War—sketches for one act opera (1915–1919)
On Space Dimensions—sketches (1920s)
Composition in 4 tones foe Violin and piano (1923)
Birth of Color and Size composition (1923)
For further details on Arthur Lourié, his compositions and available recordings www.arthurelourié.ch
For further details on Joseph Schillinger, his compositions, and theoretical works www.schillingersociety.com

Discography

NIKOLAY ROSLAVETS

Violin Sonata No. 1—Solomia Soroka and Arthur Greene—Naxos 8.557903, Mark Lubotsky and Julia Bochkovskaya—Olympia OCD 558 (1995)

Violin Sonata No. 2—Mark Lubotsky and Julia Bochkovskaya—Olympia OCD 558 (1995)

Violin Sonata No. 4—Solomia Soroka and Arthur Greene—Naxos 8.557903, Mark Lubotsky and Julia Bochkovskaya—Olympia OCD 558 (1995), Rasma Lielmane, Peter-Jurgen Hofer—Genesee Records GRN-4252 LP (1980)

Violin Sonata No. 6—Solomia Soroka and Arthur Greene—Naxos 8.557903, Mark Lubotsky and Julia Bochkovskaya—Olympia OCD 558 (1995), Kamilla Schatz, Oliver Triendl—Telos Music TLS 226 (2016)

Viola Sonata No. 1—Andrei Gridtchuk, Alexander Blok—Brilliant Classics 9174, Le Chant du Monde LDC 288 047, Yuri Bashmet, Mikhail Muntian—RCA Red Seal Victor 09026612732 (1991)

Viola Sonata No. 1—(transcribed for Cello) Lachezar Kostov and Viktor Valkov—Naxos 8.570996, Victoria Chiang, Randall Hodgkinson—Centaur CRC 2450, Lawrence Power, Simon-Crawford Phillips—ECS 911756

Viola Sonata No. 2—Andrei Gridtchuk, Alexander Blok—Brilliant Classics 9174, Le Chant du Monde LDC 288 047, Victoria Chiang, Randall Hodgkinson—Centaur CRC 2450

24 Preludes for Violin and Piano—Mark Lubotsky and Julia Bochkovskaya—Olympia OCD 559 (1995), Kamilla Schatz, Oliver Triendl—Telos Music TLS 226 (2016), Carolyn Stuart, Svetozar Ivanov—Gega GD 340 (Preludes 4, 9, 11, 12, 17, 20, and 24)

Nocturne—Mark Lubotsky and Julia Bochkovskaya—Olympia OCD 559 (1995), USSR Bolshoi Theatre Soloists Ensemble, Alexander Lazarev—Melodiya SUCD 10-00077, Moscow Contemporary Music Ensemble—Triton MECC-26010 (1992) (orch. By Edison Denisov), Carolyn Stuart, Svetozar Ivanov—Gega GD 340

Three Dances—Mark Lubotsky and Julia Bochkovskaya—Olympia OCD 559 (1995), Solomia Soroka and Arthur Greene—Naxos 8.557903, Carolyn Stuart, Svetozar Ivanov—Gega GD 340

Poem lyrique—Mark Lubotsky and Julia Bochkovskaya—Olympia OCD 559 (1995)

Poem romantique—Carolyn Stuart, Svetozar Ivanov—Gega GD 340

Three Poems—Carolyn Stuart, Svetozar Ivanov—Gega GD 340

Morgenstimmung—Carolyn Stuart, Svetozar Ivanov—Gega GD 340

Reverie—Carolyn Stuart, Svetozar Ivanov—Gega GD 340

Elégie—Carolyn Stuart, Svetozar Ivanov—Gega GD 340

Cello Sonata No. 1—Lachezar Kostov and Viktor Valkov—Naxos 8.570996, Sergei Soudzilovski and Andrei Diev—Brilliant Classics 9174, Le Chant du Monde LDC 288 047, Alexander Ivashkin, Tatyana Lazareva—Chandos CHAN 9881 (2000), Moscow Contemporary Music Ensemble—Triton MECC-26010 (1992), Boris Pergamanischikov, Pavel Gililov—Orfeo C249921 (1991)

Cello Sonata No. 2—Lachezar Kostov and Viktor Valkov—Naxos 8.570996, Alexander Ivashkin, Tatyana Lazareva—Chandos CHAN 9881 (2000)

Cello Sonata No. 3—Seraphin Trio—Signum SIG 013-00 LP (1986)

Five Preludes—Alexander Ivashkin, Tatyana Lazareva—Chandos CHAN 9881 (2000)

Meditation—Lachezar Kostov and Viktor Valkov—Naxos 8.570996, Alexander Ivashkin, Tatyana Lazareva—Chandos CHAN 9881 (2000), Moscow Contemporary Music Ensemble—Triton MECC-26010 (1992)

Dances of the White Maidens—Lachezar Kostov and Viktor Valkov—Naxos 8.570996, Alexander Ivashkin, Tatyana Lazareva—Chandos CHAN 9881 (2000), Alexander Ivashkin, Ingrid Wahlberg—Manu 1426 (1993)

Piano Trio No. 1—Trio Fontenay—Teldec/Warner Classics 256469324-4 (2000)

Piano Trio No. 2—Trio Fontenay—Teldec/Warner Classics 256469324-4 (2000)

Piano Trio No. 3—Moscow Trio—Brilliant Classics 9174, Le Chant du Monde LDC 288 047, Trio Fontenay—Teldec/Warner Classics 256469324-4 (2000), Clementi Trio Koln—Largo 5112 (1987)

Quartet No. 1—Novosibirsk "Filarmonika" Quartet—Arte Novo ANO 487222, Haba Quartet, New Class—NEOS (1998)

Quartet No. 2—Haba Quartet, New Class—NEOS (1998)

Quartet No. 3—Novosibirsk "Filarmonika" Quartet—Arte Novo ANO 487222, Chilingirian Quartet—Conifer Classics 75605 51252 (1994), Leipziger String Quartet—MDG Gold MDG 3071192-2 (2003), Studio for New Music String Quartet—Moscow Conservatory SMCD 0159 (2014), Haba Quartet, New Class—NEOS (1998)

Two Pieces for String Quartet—Moscow Contemporary Music Ensemble—Triton MECC-26010 (1992)

Piano Sonata No. 1—Marc-Andre Hamelin—Hyperion CDA66926 (1996), Irina Emeliantseva—NEOS 10902 (2008)

Piano Sonata No. 2—Marc-Andre Hamelin—Hyperion CDA66926 (1996), Irina Emeliantseva—NEOS 10902 (2008), Anya Alexeyev—Marquis 81415 (2010)

Piano Sonata No. 5—Marc-Andre Hamelin—Hyperion CDA66926 (1996), Natalia Pankova, Brilliant Classics 9174, Sarah Rothenberg—GM Recordings GM2040CD, Le Chant du Monde LDC 288 047, Irina Emeliantseva—NEOS 10902 (2008)

Three Compositions—Marc-Andre Hamelin—Hyperion CDA66926 (1996), Sarah Rothenberg—GM Recordings GM2040CD, Roger Woodward—Celestial Harmonies 13255-2 (2011), Irina Emeliantseva—NEOS 10902 (2008), Mats Persson—Caprice CAP 1071 (1975), Anton Batagov—MCA Classics AED 10354 (1991)

Three Etudes—Marc-Andre Hamelin—Hyperion CDA66926 (1996), Irina Emeliantseva—NEOS 10902 (2008), Anya Alexeyev—Marquis 81415 (2010)

Two Compositions—Marc-Andre Hamelin—Hyperion CDA66926 (1996), Irina Emeliantseva—NEOS 10902 (2008)

Two Poems—Marc-Andre Hamelin—Hyperion CDA66926 (1996), Yuri Favorin—Melodiya MEL CD 1001965 (2012), Irina Emeliantseva—NEOS 10902 (2008), Christophe Sirodeau—Arkadia AK 152.1 (1994), Anya Alexeyev—Marquis 81415 (2010)

Five Preludes—Marc-Andre Hamelin—Hyperion CDA66926 (1996), Yuri Favorin—Melodiya MEL CD 1001965 (2012), Sarah Rothenberg—GM Recordings GM2040CD, Vladimir Feltsman—Nimbus Alliance NI 6377 (2018), Steffan Schleiermacher—hat ART CD6157 (1994), Irina Emeliantseva—NEOS 10902 (2008), Lynelle James—Blue Griffin BGR 435 (2017), Anton Batagov—MCA Classics AED 10354 (1991), Christophe Sirodeau—Arkadia AK 152.1 (1994), Anya Alexeyev—Marquis 81415 (2010)

Prelude—Marc-Andre Hamelin—Hyperion CDA66926 (1996), Sarah Rothenberg—GM Recordings GM2040CD, Irina Emeliantseva—NEOS 10902 (2008), Massimiliano Damerini—Arts Music 47216-2 (1998), Christophe Sirodeau—Arkadia AK 152.1 (1994)

In the hours of the New Moon—BBC Scottish Symphony Orchestra. Ilan Volkhov—Hyperion CDA67484, Rundfunk Symphonie Orkester Saarbrucken, Heinz Holliger—WERGO 6207-2 (1990)
Chamber Symphony No. 2—BBC Scottish Symphony Orchestra. Ilan Volkhov—Hyperion CDA67484
Violin Concerto No. 1—Alina Ibragimova—BBC Scottish Symphony Orchestra. Ilan Volkhov—Hyperion CDA67637 (2008), Tatyana Grindenko, Rundfunk Symphonie Orkester Saarbrucken, Heinz Holliger—WERGO 6207-2 (1990)
Violin Concerto No. 2—Alina Ibragimova—BBC Scottish Symphony Orchestra. Ilan Volkhov—Hyperion CDA67637 (2008)
"For 25 October"—V.M. Politkovsky—MuzTrest 16201 78 (1920s)

GAVRIIL POPOV

Chamber Symphony Op. 2—St. Petersburg Academic Symphony Orchestra, Alexander Titov—Northern Flowers NF/PMA 9996, Moscow Chamber Ensemble, Alexander Korneyev, Olympia OCD 588, USSR Bolshoi Theatre Soloists Ensemble, Alexander Lazarev—Melodiya SUCD 10-00077
Grosse Klaviersuite, Op. 6—Yuri Favorin, Melodiya MEL CD 1002459
Symphony No. 1, Op. 7—St. Petersburg Academic Symphony Orchestra, Alexander Titov—Northern Flowers NF/PMA 9996, Moscow State Symphony Orchestra, Gennady Provatorov—Olympia OCD 576, London Symphony Orchestra, Leon Botstein—Telarc CD-80642
Symphonic Suite No. 1, Op.—Rimma Glushkova, Alexander Polyakov, Moscow Radio TV Symphony Orchestra, Edvard Chivzel—Olympia OCD 598 (1982)
Symphony No. 2, "Motherland," Op. 39—USSR Radio and TV Symphony Orchestra, Gennady Provatorov—Olympia OCD 576, Leipzig Radio Symphony Orchestra, Hermann Abendroth—Eterna
Symphonic Aria for Cello and String Orchestra, Op. 43—St. Petersburg Academic Symphony Orchestra, Alexander Titov—Northern Flowers NF/PMA 9972
Symphony No. 3 "Heroic," Op. 45—St. Petersburg Academic Symphony Orchestra, Alexander Titov—Northern Flowers NF/PMA 9972
Symphony No. 5 in A major, "Pastorale" Op. 77—USSR State Symphony Orchestra, Gurgen Karapetian—Olympia OCD 598 (1963)
Symphony No. 6, "Festive," Op. 99—USSR Radio Symphony Orchestra, Edvard Chivzhel—Olympia OCD 588 (1984)

ALEXANDER MOSOLOV

Piano Sonata No. 1, Op. 3—Daniel Lombardi—Arte Nova ANO 277930, Sarah Rothenberg—GM Recordings GM2040CD, Olga Andryuschenko Grand Piano GP703-04 (2015), Stefan Schleiermacher—Capriccio C5241 (20), Thomas Gunther—Cybele 161403 (2012), Larry Sitsky—Move MD 3328 (2010) Geoffrey Douglas MadgeDante PSG 9118 (1991)

Piano Sonata No. 2 in B minor, Op. 4—Herbert Henck,—ECM Records ECM 1569, Olga Andryuschenko Grand Piano GP703-04 (2015), Thomas Gunther—Cybele 161403 (2012) Geoffrey Douglas Madge—BV Haaste Records BV HAASTE 025 LP (1979) Dante PSG 9118, Yuri Lisichenko—Etcetera KTC 1161 (1995), Anton Batagov—MCA Classics AED 10354 (1991)

Legend for Cello and Piano, Op. 5—Ringela Riemke, Stefan Schleiermacher—Capriccio C5241, Alexander Ivashkin, Ingrid Wahlberg—Manu 1426 (1993)

Piano Sonata No. 4, Op. 11—Thomas Gunther—Cybele 161403 (2012), Daniel Lombardi—LINE CACD 9.00613P (1999), Daniel Lombardi—Arte Nova ANO 277930, Rusudan Khuntsaria—BMG Classics 74321 562632 (1985) Geoffrey Douglas Madge—Dante PSG 9118 (1991)

Piano Sonata No. 5, Op. 12—Daniel Lombardi—Arte Nova ANO 277930, Sarah Rothenberg—GM Recordings GM2040CD, Herbert Henck,—ECM Records ECM 1569, Olga Andryuschenko Grand Piano GP703-04 (2016), Thomas Gunther—Cybele 161403 (2012), Rusudan Khuntsaria—BMG Classics 74321 562632 (1985) Geoffrey Douglas Madge—Dante PSG 9118 (1991), Yuri Lisichenko—Etcetera KTC 1161 (1995)

Turkmen Nights (Fantasy for Piano)—Daniel Lombardi—Arte Nova ANO 277930, Olga Andryuschenko Grand Piano GP703-04 (2015)

Piano Concerto No. 1, Op. 14—Rusudan Khuntsaria, USSR State Symphony Orchestra, Vladimir Kozhukar—Olympia OCD 176/BMG Classics 74321-562632 (1985), Rundfunk Symphonie Orkester Berlin, Stefan Schleiermacher, Johannes Kalitzke, Capriccio C5241

Deux Nocturnes, Op. 15—Herbert Henck,—ECM Records ECM 1569, Olga Andryuschenko Grand Piano GP703-04 (2016), Thomas Gunther—Cybele 161403 (2012), Vladimir Feltsman—Nimbus Alliance NI 6377 (2018), Roger Woodward—Celestial Harmonies 13255-2 (2011), Rusudan Khuntsaria—Melodiya LP C10 3115307 (1991) BMG Classics 74321 562632 (1985), Yuri Lisichenko—Etcetera KTC 1161 (1995), Steffan Schleiermacher—hat ART CD6157 (1994), Anton Batagov—MCA Classics AED 10354 (1991), Mihkel Poll—Ondine (2020)

Four Newspaper Advertisements, Op. 18—Nelli Lee, USSR Ministry of Culture Orchestra, Gennady Rozhdestvensky—Melodiya SUCD 10-00077/

BMG Classics 74321-562632 (1985), Natalia Zagorinskaya, Triton 17-004 (1995), Natalia Pschenischikova, Rundfunk Symphonie Orkester Berlin, Johannes Kalitzke, Capriccio C5241, Natalia Gerassimova, Vladimir Skanavi—Le Chant Du Monde LDC 288025 (1990)

Zavod—Op. 19—USSR State Symphony Orchestra, Yevgeny Svetlanov—Olympia OCD 176/BMG Classics 74321-562632 (1985) (1973), Royal Concertgebouw Orchestra, Riccardo Chailly—DECCA 4834345 (1993), Los Angeles Philharmonic Orchestra, Esa-Pekka Salonen—DG 4777348 (2007), Orchestre Symphonie de Paris, Julius Ehrlich—Columbia Masterworks M 347(1938) 78 Shellac, London Philharmonic Symphony Orchestra of London, Argeo Quadri—Westminster MLAB-7004, Nixa MLB 20000, Mono LPs Sonotape SW1005 Mono tape (1955), Turin Orchestra of the Italian Broadcasting Authority, Victor de Sabata—Parlephone 56548 (matrix 2-84588-2), Rococo Records 2075 LP/NAXOS 8.110859 (December 30, 1933), Rundfunk Symphonie Orkester Berlin, Johannes Kalitzke—Capriccio C5241, Orchestre de la Société de Concerts la Conservatoire, Pierre Dervaux—Le Voix De Son Maitre—FALP 474 , Vladimir Stoupel—piano arrangement

Children's Scenes, Op. 21—Nelli Lee, USSR Ministry of Culture Orchestra, Gennady Rozhdestvensky—Melodiya SUCD 10-00077/BMG Classics 74321-562632 (1985), Natalia Zagorinskaya, Triton 17-004 (1995), Natalia Gerassimova, Vladimir Skanavi—Le Chant Du Monde LDC 288025 (1990)

Three Small Pieces, Op. 23a—Olga Andryuschenko Grand Piano GP703-04 (2015), Larry Sitsky—Move MD 3328 (2010), Steffan Schleiermacher—hat ART CD6157 (1994)

Two Dances, Op. 23b—Olga Andryuschenko Grand Piano GP703-04 (2015), Vladimir Feltsman—Nimbus Alliance NI 6377 (2018), Larry Sitsky—Move MD 3328 (2010), Steffan Schleiermacher—hat ART CD6157 (1994)

String Quartet No. 1, Op. 24—Novosibirsk "Filarmonika" Quartet—Arte Novo ANO 487222, Utrecht String Quartet—MuseikGroep Nederland NM EXTRA 98020 (2000)

Harp Concerto, Op.—Taylor Anne Fleshman, Moscow Symphony Orchestra, Arthur Arnold—NAXOS 8. 574102 (2019)

String Quartet No. 2—Elena Pak, Orestes Shurgot, Sergei Tischenko, Natalia Savinova—Triton 17-004 (1995)

Symphony in E major, Op.—St. Petersburg Academic Symphony Orchestra, Alexander Titov—Northern Flowers NF/PMA 9978

Symphony No. 5 (1965)—Moscow Symphony Orchestra, Arthur Arnold—NAXOS 8.574102

Harp Concerto (1939)—Taylor Ann Fleshman, Moscow Symphony Orchestra, Arthur Arnold—NAXOS 8.574102

Dance Suite for Harp Solo, Op.—Vera Dulova—Talents of Russia RCD 16205

Cello Concerto No. 2, Op.—Sergei Sudzhilovsky, Russian Cinematographic Symphony Orchestra, Sergei Skripka—Olympia OCD 592, Dmitry Yeremin, St. Petersburg Academic Symphony Orchestra, Alexander Titov—Northern Flowers NF/PMA 9978

Four Pieces for Oboe and Piano—Pyotr Fedkov and Viktor Yampolsky—Triton 17-004 (1995)

Four Pieces for Bassoon and Piano—Alexander Popov and Victor Yampolsky—Triton 17-004 (1995)

Tractor's Arrival at the Kolkhoz, Rundfunk Symphonie Orkester Berlin, Johannes Kalitzke—Capriccio C5241

Suite—*Soldiers' Songs*—Osipov Russian Folk Orchestra—Vital Gnutov—Olympia OCD 176

Nine Choruses—*Front Roads*—Soloists, USSR TV and Radio Chorus, Nikolay Kutuzov—Olympia OCD 176

Eight Choruses—*Collective Farm Meadows*—Soloists, USSR TV and Radio Chorus, Nikolay Kutuzov—Olympia OCD 176

Fantasia on the Russian folksong "Evening Bells"—Osipov Russian Folk Orchestra, Nikolay Kalinin—Melodiya SUCD 20-00292

"Farewell by the Birch Tree"—Northern Russian Folk Choir, Nina Meshko—Melodiya CO-01672 (1969) LP

Violin Concerto—Leonora Dmitreko (violin), Moscow Contemporary Music Ensemble, Alexei Vinogradov Triton 17-004 (transcription by Yuri Kasparov for violin from the Cello Concerto) (1995)

Elegiac Poem for Cello and Orchestra—Sergei Sudzhilovsky, Russian Cinematographic Symphony Orchestra, Sergei Skripka—Olympia OCD 592

The Dam—Premiere of 21 March 2012 in St. Petersburg: https://www.youtube.com/watch?v=WBkznuHlna8

Plotina: https://yandex.ru/video/preview/?text=mosolov%20plotina&path=wizard&parent-reqid=1620031577321974-12337328597301593061 00141-production-app-host-vla-web-yp-223&wiz_type=vital&filmId=7632089817370948463

MIKHAIL MAYUSHIN

Matyushin—*Victory over the Sun*—Stas Namin performance at Basle: https://yandex.ru/video/preview/?text=matyuyshin%20victory%20over%20the%20sun%20stas%20namin&path=wizard&parent-reqid=1620032071995382-3941900526211213871001 03-production-app-host-vla-web-yp-251&wiz_type=vital&filmId=876730269304347125

Mikhail Matyushin : Excerpts from *Victory over the Sun*: https://yandex
.ru/video/preview/?text=matyuyshin%20victory%20over%20the%20sun
&path=wizard&parent-reqid=1620031878160859-980576192845802
139300103-production-app-host-vla-web-yp-164&wiz_type=v4thumbs
&filmId=8116065292465340613

https://yandex.ru/video/preview/?text=matyuyshin+victory+over+the+sun
&path=wizard&parent-reqid=1620031878160859-980576192845802
139300103-production-app-host-vla-web-yp-164&wiz_type=v4thumbs
&filmId=3534750253577280795&url=http%3A%2F%2Fwww.youtube
.com%2Fwatch%3Fv%3DykbSeIQ2vgI

For further details on Arthur Lourié, his compositions and available recordings www.arthurlourié.ch

For further details on Joseph Schillinger, his compositions, and theoretical works www.schillingersociety.com

Index

Abasa, Arkady, 18; teaching of Roslavets, 18
Abendroth, Hermann, 185
Achron, Joseph, 327
Adamov, Yevgeny, 316
Adams, John, 332
Akhmatova, Anna, 23, 113, 320–21; association with Lourie, 320–21
Aksenov, Ivan, 263
Alexandrov, Anatoly, 71, 73, 141, 241, 262, 271, 301, 327
Alexandrov, Georgy, 162
Alexandrovsky, Vasily, 84
Alymov, Sergey, 297
Anisimov, Alexander, 208
Ansermet, Ernest, 132, 144, 322
Antheil, George, 6, 327
Apetyan, Zara, 147, 177, 204, 212–13, 215, 217
Aragon, Luis, 230
Arapov, Boris, 123, 136, 139, 146, 213
Arbuzov, Alexey, 161, 190
Argo, Abram, 290
Asafyev, Boris, 8, 69, 72, 101, 103, 123, 125–26, 129, 132, 135–36, 144–45, 147, 177, 185, 239, 257, 259, 262–63, 321, 324, 328; association with Lourie, 321; association with Mosolov, 239, 253, 257, 259, 262–64, 277–78; association with Popov, 125–26, 129, 132, 135–36, 144–45, 147, 177, 185, 217; association with Roslavets, 101–2; association with Schillinger, 324, 328
Aseyev, Nikolay, 5, 36, 249, 323
Atovmyan, Lev, 180
Auer, Leopold, 19
Auric, Georges, 238
avant-garde, 2–10, 12–14, 19, 69, 73, 76, 102, 113, 126, 148, 160, 191, 221, 228, 232, 235, 237, 242, 249, 269–70, 272, 297–98, 300–301, 307–9, 311–12, 314–15, 318–22, 329, 332–33; meaning of, 6–7, 69, 148, 320–21; origins of, 4, 7, 19, 307, 311, 318–20; revival of, 4, 8, 113, 209, 235, 300–301, 318, 332. See also futurism; modernism; socialist realism; symbolism
Avraamov, Arseny, 10, 27, 40, 43, 73, 95

Babbitt, Milton, 6, 332
Babochkin, Boris, 192, 217
Bach, J.S., 129, 131, 146, 166, 179, 208, 245, 292, 324–25; influence on Popov, 129, 131, 166; influence on Schillinger, 325

367

Bach-Busoni, 124
Bagritsky, Eduard, 298–99
Bakaleinikov, Vladimir, 19
Bakst, Léon, 315
Balanchivadze, Andria, 187
Balmont, Konstantin, 23, 26
Balzac, Honoré de, 178
Barbirolli, Sir John, 213
Barinova, Marina, 122, 319
Barnes, Julian, 1
Barnet, Boris, 159
Barsova, Inna, 147, 230, 232, 236, 247–48, 259, 262, 326
Bartók, Bela, 13, 71, 73, 78, 232, 238, 258, 276, 283, 307; influence on Mosolov, 232, 258, 276, 283
Baton, Leon, 247
Baudelaire, Charles, 63
Bedny, Demyan, 290, 297
Beethoven, Ludwig van, 13, 95, 131, 146, 208, 212, 326; influence on Popov, 122, 131, 146, 203, 208; influence on Roslavets, 77, 96
Belodubrovsky, Viktor, 17, 21, 57, 112–13
Bely, Andrey, 9, 23–24, 26, 82, 98, 101, 236, 248, 284, 299, 301
Belyaev, Viktor, 69, 73, 262, 281
Belza, Igor, 186
Benois, Alexander, 33
Berezovsky, Dmitry, 208
Berg, Alban, 6, 81, 126, 136, 141, 232, 238, 267, 270; influence on Mosolov, 267, 270; influence on Popov, 136, 142
Beria, Lavrenty, 286
Berio, Luciano, 6
Berlin, Irving, 326
Berlioz, Hector, 148
Bisneck, Emilia, 228
Blake, Frank Jeremiah, 326
Bleiman, Mikhail, 162
Blok, Alexander, 2, 21, 23–24, 33, 35, 44, 56, 62, 236–37, 290, 293, 296, 307, 320; influence on Lourie, 320–21; influence on Mosolov, 236–37, 290, 293, 296, 307; influence on Roslavets, 21, 23–24, 26, 33, 44, 56, 62. *See also* symbolism
Blum, A.G., 235
Bluman, Edvarda, 205
Bobrov, Sergey, 5
Bogdanov, Alexander, 56
Bogdanov-Berezovsky, Valerian, 128, 136, 146, 206, 213, 219, 248
Boitler, Mikhail, 263
Bolm, Adolph, 301
Bolshakov, Konstantin, 43
Bondarchuk, Sergei, 214
Borisovsky, Vadim, 81
Borodin, Alexander, 291
Bortnikov, I., 273
Bortnyansky, Dmitry, 208
Boulez, Pierre, 332
Brahms, Johannes, 307
Braudo, Yevgeny, 27, 45–46, 96
Brecht, Bertolt, 230
Brik, Olesya, 131
Brik, Osip, 168
Brown, Earle, 329
Bryusov, Valery, 21, 26–27, 33, 38, 56, 61, 95; influence on Roslavets, 21, 27, 33, 38, 61, 95. *See also* futurism
Bryusova, Nadezhda, 68, 71, 74, 235
Bubnov, Nikolay, 134, 137
Budenny, Semyon, 179
Bukharin, Nikolay, 8, 249, 255; influence on the RAPM, 8, 249
Bulgakov, Mikhail, 66, 282; appeal to Stalin, 282
Bunin, Revol, 216
Bürger, Peter, 7
Burlyuk, David, 4, 19, 21, 26, 32–34, 36, 38, 41–43, 52, 56, 316; association with Roslavets, 19, 21, 26, 32, 36, 38–39, 41–43, 56; background, 4, 15, 34; leadership of the Russian futurists, 15, 34, 36. *See* avant-garde; futurism
Burlyuk, Nikolay, 34, 36, 41, 316

Busoni, Ferruccio, 122
Bystrytskaya, Elina, 214

Cage, John, 6–7, 311–12, 329, 332; association with Schillinger, 329
Calafati, Vasily, 323
Carter, Elliott, 6
Casella, Alfredo, 71, 238, 241–42
Catherine II, 66, 119, 136, 188
Catoire, Georgy, 62, 236
Chagall, Mark, 82
Chaliapin, Boris, 228
Chaliapin, Fyodor, 2, 8, 69, 228
Chaplin, Charles, 160
Chaykovsky, Boris, 213, 216
Chegodayeva, Larisa, 205
Chekhov, Anton, 12, 120
Chekhov, Mikhail, 173
Chelyapov, Nikolay, 97
Chemberzhy, Nikolay, 185
Cherepnin, Alexander, 239
Cherepnin, Nikolay, 2, 8, 69, 323
Chernomordikov, David, 8, 72, 74
Chernyavsky, Mykola, 273
Chernyshevsky, Nikolay, 300
Chervyakov, Yevgeny, 283
Chevalier, Maurice, 173
Chirskov, Boris, 188, 214
Chisholm, Erik, 213
Chopin, Frederic, 129, 173, 325; influence on Popov, 129, 173; influence on Schillinger, 325
Christie, Ian, 169
Chulaki, Mikhail, 175, 177, 188, 206, 211
Chulkov, Georgy, 23
Chuzhak, Nikolay, 9,
Ciągliński, Jan, 315
Clark, Edward, 141
Coates, Albert, 141, 170, 284
Cocteau, Jean, 330
Copland, Aaron, 311
Cowell, Henry, 6, 328–29, 337; association with Schillinger, 328–29
Crommelynck, Fernand, 262

Cubo-Futurism, 5, 15, 246, 315. See also futurism
Curry, James, 312–13

Davidenko, Alexander, 9, 98, 101, 106, 235–36; collection of Chechen folk songs, 106
Davydov, Denis, 290
Davydova, Larissa, 301
Debussy, Claude, 29, 45, 77, 83, 96, 172, 312, 320; influence on Lourie, 320; influence on Popov, 172; influence on Roslavets, 29, 96
DeLapp, Jennifer, 311
Denikin, Anton, 229
Denisov, Edison, 1, 81, 90, 113, 118, 216, 235, 250, 253, 301, 305, 332; appreciation of Mosolov, 235, 250, 301; appreciation of Roslavets, 81, 113, 301
Derzhanovskaya, Yekaterina, 45
Derzhanovsky, Vladimir, 26, 45, 69, 71–72, 91, 101, 108, 258, 282
Deshevov, Vladimir, 3–4, 6, 8, 130, 232, 249, 259, 262, 264, 272, 281, 301, 327
Desormiere, Roger, 141
Diaghilev, Sergey, 251
Dickens, Charles, 215
Dikushina-Karysheva, Y.A., 235
Diky, Alexey, 284
Dillon, V. I., 64
Dimitriadi, Odyssey, 292
Disney, Walt, 330; collaboration with Schillinger, 330
Dmitriev, Alexander, 219
Doflein, Erich, 260
Dolinskaya, Elena, 143–44
Dondero, George, 309
Dorsey, Tommy, 329; study with Schillinger, 329
Dostoyevsky, Fyodor, 2, 34–35
Dovlatova, Margarita, 213
Dovzhenko, Alexander, 159, 167, 182, 189, 214

Downes, Olin, 310
Dranishnikov, Vladimir, 141
Drozdov, Vladimir, 319
Druskin, Mikhail, 134, 249
Druzhinin, P., 95
Dulova, Elena, 260
Dulova, Vera, 238, 241, 287–88
Dzegelyonok, Vladimir, 71
Dzigan, Yefim, 179
Dzimitrowski, Abraam, 258–59, 262, 273–74

Edmunds, Neil, 236–37
ego-futurism, 4, 40. *See also* futurism
Einstein, Albert, 35, 324
Eisenstein, Sergey, 5–6, 149, 159, 162–63, 165–67, 174, 188, 190, 192–93, 195, 327; association with futurism, 5–6, 159; collaboration with Popov, 149, 163–64, 166–67, 174, 188, 192; collaboration with Prokofiev, 149, 164, 174, 188, 195. *See also* futurism
Eisler, Hanns, 95, 110, 238, 248; association with modernist songs, 95, 110, 248
Elenescu, Emanuel, 218
Éluard, Paul, 230
Ender, Maria, 318–19
Erdenko, Mikhail, 19
Ermler, Fridrich, 162, 181–82, 188, 214, 289
Ermolayeva, Vera, 318

Faintsimmer, Alexander, 179
Fanning, David, 10
Favorsky, Pavel, 95
Fedorov, Vladimir, 213
Feinberg, Samuil, 12, 71, 73, 79, 136, 236, 241
Feisst, Sabine, 310
Feldman, Morton, 6, 332
Fellini, Federico, 214
Fere, Vladimir, 3, 131, 236
Ferenc, Anna, 232

Ferris, Earl, 329
Fet, Afanasy, 228
Figurovsky, Nikolay, 214
Fillipova, Maria, 103–4
Filonov, Pavel, 38, 93, 145, 316; association to modernist music, 93, 145
Finck, Henry, 309
Fischman, Boris, 170–71
folk music, 2, 48, 59, 69, 103–6, 110, 119, 125, 161, 164–65, 168, 171–72, 174–76, 178, 181, 183, 185, 189, 203, 206, 208, 210, 214, 216, 222, 237, 258, 273, 276, 283, 285, 288–89, 291, 293, 295–96, 298–300, 304, 318, 326, 329; association with Matyushin, 318; association with Mosolov, 103, 237, 258, 273, 276, 283, 285, 288–89, 291, 293, 295–96, 298–300; association with Popov, 119, 123, 125, 161, 164–65, 168, 171–72, 174–76, 178, 181, 183, 185, 189, 203, 206, 208, 210, 214, 298; association with Roslavets, 22, 59, 104–5, 110; association with Schillinger, 326, 329
Frid, Jan, 215
Furtwangler, Wilhelm, 322
futurism, 4–5, 9–10, 33–34, 36–38, 40, 56, 64, 98–99, 197, 228, 257, 321, 332; decline in Russia, 10, 99, 257; influence on Russian music, 27, 33, 36–38, 56, 64, 98, 321; influence on Soviet art, 5, 56, 98–99, 197, 321, 332; origins in Russia, 4, 34, 40, 228. *See also* Cubo-Futurism; ego-futurism

Gabo, Naum, 307
Gabrilovich, Yevgeny, 174
Gagarina, Valentina, 208
Gakkel, Yevgeny, 161, 189
Galin, G., 94
Galperin, Mikhail, 275
Gamburg, Grigory, 241

Gauk, Alexander, 170, 183, 201, 209, 246; performance of music by Mosolov, 246; performance of music by Popov, 170, 201, 209
Gëdike, Alexander, 68, 272
George, Stefan, 33
Gershwin, George, 13, 326, 330, 337; association of *Porgy and Bess* with Schillinger, 329; study with Schillinger, 13, 329, 337
Gilels, Elizaveta, 111
Gilf, A., 315
Gilgour, Anna, 322
Ginzburg, Lev, 134, 246
Gippius, Zinaida, 2, 26, 44, 52, 61; influence on Roslavets, 26, 44, 52, 61. *See also* symbolism
Gladkovsky, Arseny, 140, 267
Glass, Philip, 6
Glazounov, Alexander, 124, 319
Glière, Reinhold, 3, 8, 22, 48, 101, 228–30, 235–36, 252–53, 285, 287–88; appeal to Kalinin for release of Mosolov, 286; teaching of Mosolov, 8, 228–30, 235–36, 252–53
Glikman, Izaak, 147
Glinka, Mikhail, 13, 123, 185, 202, 209, 322
Glukh, Mikhail, 140
Glushenko, Fyodor, 79
Gnedov, Vasilisk, 15, 32, 35–36, 40–43, 52, 56; association with Roslavets, 32, 35–36, 40–43; career of, 40–41, 56. *See also* futurism
Gnessin, Mikhail, 62, 74, 121, 137–38, 327; association with Popov, 121; association with Roslavets, 74
Goethe, Johann Wolfgang, 237
Gogh, Van, Vincent, 320
Gogol, Nikolay, 2, 215
Goldenweiser, Alexander, 22, 138, 273
Goldstein, Boris, 111
Goldstein, U.M., 64
Golodny, Mikhail, 206

Golovanov, Nikolay, 22, 99, 138, 238, 253, 267; criticism of by RAPM, 238; criticism of Mosolov, 267; dismissal from Bolshoi Theater, 99
Golub, Lev, 214
Golyshev, Yefim, 3, 13, 27
Goncharov, Ivan, 120
Goncharova, Nataliya, 316
Gongini, Barbara í, 7
Goodman, Benny, 329; teaching by Schillinger, 329
Górecki, Henryk, 323
Gorev, Yakov, 160
Gorky, Maxim, 9, 35, 49, 57, 159, 195, 215; declaring of socialist realism, 9
Gorodetsky, Sergey, 177, 204
Goryaninov, Nikolay, 206
Gounod, Charles, 323, 326
Goya, Francisco, 202
Grabar, Igor, 44
Graham, Stephen, 312
Grainger, Percy, 328
Grechaninov, Alexander, 2, 69
Gres, Semyon, 168
Grigorovich, Yuri, 213
Grikurov, Eduard, 174
Grindenko, Tatyana, 79
Gubaydullina, Sophia, 1, 216, 332
Guro, Elena, 4, 15, 26, 32, 37, 44–45, 82, 315–16. 318; involvement in futurism, 4, 15, 26, 37, 82, 315; marriage to Matyushin, 37, 315; settings by Matyushin, 315–16, 318; settings by Roslavets, 33, 44–45. *See also* Cubo Futurism; futurism
Guzikov, Igor, 19
Guzman, Boris, 133
Guzman, Izrael, 209
Gyumilov, Nikolay, 23–24, 26

Hakobian, Leon, 11, 40, 101, 127, 144, 185, 219, 234, 250, 258, 301, 314
Handel, George Frederick, 166, 179, 311; influence on Popov, 166, 179
Haydn, Joseph, 332

Hayton, Lenny, 330
Heifetz, Iosif, 162
Heifetz, Jascha, 2, 258
Henze, Hans Werner, 309
Hershkowitz, Philip, 3
Hindemith, Paul, 10, 13, 73, 78, 95, 123, 127, 130, 136, 138, 172, 175, 232, 238, 241–42, 260, 307–10; influence on Mosolov, 12, 232, 238, 241–42, 260; influence on Popov, 123, 127, 129–31, 136, 138, 172, 175
Hoffmann, Joseph, 122
Honegger, Arthur, 13, 71, 78, 95, 203, 232, 238, 245; influence on Mosolov, 12, 232, 245; influence on Popov, 203; influence on Roslavets, 78, 95
Horowitz, Alexander, 323
Horowitz, Vladimir, 323
Hřimalý, Jan, 18–19, 47; appreciation by Roslavets, 21; career as violinist in Europe, 18–19, 47; teaching of Roslavets, 21
Hřimalý, Vojtech, 19
Hřimalý, Vojtech jr, 19

Igumnov, Konstantin, 22, 101, 229
Ilyin, Igor, 207
Ilyinsky, Alexander, 19–20, 22
Ilyinsky, Ilya, 228
Inber, Vera, 275–76
Ippolitov-Ivanov, Mikhail, 3, 19–22, 48, 123; career as composer, 21–22, 48; career as conductor, 21–22; career as Conservatoire director, 22–23; teaching of Roslavets, 19–22
Ivanov, Georgy, 209
Ivanov, Konstantin, 204, 215; conducting of music by Popov, 204
Ivanov, Vyacheslav, 23–24, 26, 56
Ives, Charles, 6, 307, 328; association with Schillinger, 307

Jazz music, 9, 77, 110, 135, 144, 161–63, 168, 172–73, 179, 191, 203, 274–75, 312, 321, 326–27, 336; influence on Lourie, 321; influence on Mosolov, 257, 274–75; influence on Popov, 135, 139, 144, 161, 163, 168, 172–73, 179, 203; influence on Roslavets, 110; influence on Schillinger, 326–27
Johansson, Sven-Erik, 213
Jokhelson, Vladimir, 137, 145–47, 156, 160; criticism of Popov, 137, 146, 156, 160; praise for Popov, 146

Kabalevsky, Dmitry, 4, 8, 12, 141, 205, 300
Kalinin, Mikhail, 286
Kalinnikov, Vasily, 22
Kalinnikov, Viktor, 22
Kamensky, Alexander, 326
Kamensky, Vasily, 4, 15, 19, 26, 34, 36, 39, 41, 43, 52, 56, 61, 82, 95; association with Roslavets, 19, 26, 36, 39, 43, 56, 61, 82, 95; career and life of, 34, 41, 43, 56, 82. See also futurism
Kancheli, Gia, 1, 216
Kandelaki, Vladimir, 275
Kandinsky, Vasily, 12, 33–34, 307, 321
Kankarovich, Anatoly, 267
Kantorovich, Lev, 178
Kapler, Alexey, 181
Karapetyan, Gurgen, 215
Karatygin, Vladimir, 45
Karetnikov, Nikolay, 216
Karmen, Roman, 164
Kastalsky, Alexander, 8, 235
Kater, Michael, 309–10
Kazantseva, Irina, 161, 170, 180, 184, 211
Keldysh, Yuri, 67–68, 98, 100
Kemarskaya, Nadezhda, 275–76
Kerzhentsev, Platon, 96, 274
Khachaturyan, Aram, 8, 12, 184, 204–5, 210, 217, 287
Khachaturyan, Karen, 216
Khaikhin, Boris, 246
Kharms, Daniil, 99

Khavpachev, K.K., 296
Khazanov, Alexander, 208
Kheshokov, A.P., 296
Khlebnikov, Velimir, 4–5, 34, 36, 38, 41, 56, 82, 265, 316, 323. *See also* futurism
Khodasevich, Valentina, 271
Khrennikov, Tikhon, 187, 204–5, 208, 284, 294, 299
Khromchenko, Solomon, 208
Kilchevsky, Vladimir, 264
Kirillov, Vladimir, 84
Kirov, Sergei, 145
Kirshon, Semyon, 270
Kleiber, Erich, 134, 147; interest in music of Popov, 134
Klemperer, Otto, 131, 134, 147, 310, 327, 333; interest in music of Popov, 134, 147
Klenov, Andrey, 294
Kleymanov, Nikolay, 168
Klimov, Mikhail, 130
Knipper, Lev, 8, 12, 16, 142, 204, 228, 281; career and life of, 8, 16, 204, 228; music by, 12, 272, 281
Knushevitsky, Svyatoslav, 201
Kochurov, Yuri, 136, 155, 176–77, 210; association with Popov, 136, 155, 176–77
Kodaly, Zoltan, 71
Kogan, Leonid, 111
Kolisch, Rudolf, 258
Kolobova, Elena; marriage to Mosolov, 235; sharing piano recitals with Mosolov, 235, 241
Konashkov, Fyodor, 209
Konchalovsky, Andrey, 56, 214
Kondrashin, Kirill, 275
Konius, Georgy, 19, 69, 73, 82, 235
Korchagin, Pavel, 174
Korev, Semyon, 68, 85, 96, 99–100, 245, 292; criticism of Roslavets, 97, 100; praise of Mosolov, 245, 292; praise of Roslavets, 85–86
Korneychuk, Alexander, 181

Korovin, Konstantin, 228
Kotek, Iosif, 19
Kotovsky, Georgy, 229, 298
Koussevitzky, Serge, 2, 69, 322
Koval, G.M., 295
Koval, Marian, 9, 43, 98, 101, 208, 248, 251, 263, 326
Kozikov, S., 173
Kozintsev, Grigory, 181
Kozlovsky, Ivan, 214
Krasev, Mikhail, 102
Krasner, Louis, 311
Krassin, Boris, 235
Krein, Alexander, 327
Krein, Anatoly, 327
Krein, Grigory, 327
Krenek, Ernst, 71, 98, 134, 136, 146, 170, 175, 242, 254, 307, 333; influence on Mosolov, 242; influence on Popov, 134, 136, 146, 170–71, 175
Krimmer, Eduard, 139
Kruchenykh, Alexey, 34, 37, 82, 316–18. *See also* futurism
Krymov, Yuri, 179
Kryukov, Nikolay, 136, 149, 180
Ksenofontov, Alexander, 165
Kubatsky, Viktor, 126, 172
Kukharsky, Vasily, 209
Kulbin, Nikolay, 315, 319, 321
Kundera, Milan, 312
Kuprin, Alexander, 35, 320
Kushnarev, Christopher, 249
Kustodiev, Boris, 2
Kuznetsova, Maria, 275

Labriola, Antonio, 70
Laforgue, Jules, 28–29; influence of poems on Roslavets, 28–29
Lamm, Pavel, 111
Lander, Karl Ivanovich, 229
Langovaya, Nataliya: association with Roslavets, 23, 39; dedicatee of songs by Roslavets, 24, 39; letter to Roslavets, 103; marriage to Roslavets, 23

Langovoi, Alexey, 44
Larionov, Mikhail, 316
Lasso, Orlando, 325
Lebedinsky, Lev, 8, 68, 72, 74, 78, 81–82, 96, 98, 100
Leblanc, Michel, 227–28, 251; exhibiting of paintings of, 228; guidance to Mosolov, 227–28; study in Paris, 228
Ledenev, Roman, 216
Lehner, Eugene, 258
Leistikov, Ivan, 173
Leman, Anatoly, 216
Lenin, Vladimir, 13, 56, 229, 251, 297
Lentulov, Aristarch, 19, 36, 38–39, 56, 215, 316. *See also* futurism
Lermontov, Mikhail, 104, 178, 237, 287, 290; setting of music by Mosolov, 237, 287–90
Levant, Oscar, 329; teaching by Schillinger, 329
Levashov, Mstislav, 206
Levitin, Yuri, 216
Ligeti, György, 6, 332
Lisitzky, El, 318
Listopadov, Alexander, 183
Listov, Konstantin, 284
Liszt, Franz, 83, 124, 233–34, 236, 325; influence on Mosolov, 233–34, 236; influence on Schillinger, 325
Litinsky, Heinrich, 281
Litovsky, Osaf, 146, 289
Livschitz, Benedict, 320
Lobanov, Vasily, 301
Lobanova, Marina, 28–29
Lossky, Nikolay, 315
Lourie, Arthur, 3, 6, 12, 14, 27, 58–59, 67, 69, 74, 113, 301, 315, 319, 321, 323, 332; appointment to Bolshevik government, 58, 321; association with Akhmatova, 320–21; association with futurism, 321; association with symbolism, 321; birth and christening, 319; composing styles, 322; emigration to Europe and America, 322; influence of Debussy, 320; influence of Prokofiev, 321; influence of Scriabin, 323, 325; influence of Stravinsky, 319, 321–22; influence on Stravinsky, 321–22; settings to Blok, 320–21. *See also* futurism
Lukas, Dmitri, 214
Lunacharsky, Anatoly, 56, 78, 82, 89, 97–98, 115, 320–21; appointment of Lourie as head of music, 58, 320–21; attack upon modernist composers, 78, 82, 97–98
Lutosławski, Witold, 6
Lvov, Nikolay, 161
Lyadov, Anatoly, 231, 291
Lyubera, Lina, 1

Maes, Francis, 2, 6, 8–9, 311, 314, 330–31
Mahler, Gustav, 131, 184–85, 211, 218, 260; influence on Popov, 131, 184, 185, 211, 218
Makaseyev, Boris, 164
Malevich, Kazimir, 3–4, 12, 17, 33, 35, 56, 99, 102, 307, 316–18; childhood and youth with Roslavets, 18, 19; collaborations with Roslavets, 41, 56; descriptions of Roslavets, 35–37; drawing of Roslavets, 19. *See also* futurism
Malinovskaya, Elena, 138
Malko, Nikolay, 101, 132, 134, 136, 142, 241; association with Mosolov, 241, 254; association with Popov, 132, 134, 136, 142, 144, 154, 156–57, 194; association with Schillinger, 328, 337; conducting of modernist music, 101
Mallarmé, Stéphane, 320
Maretzkaya, Vera, 181
Marinetti, Filippo, 4, 321; founding of futurist movement, 4; rejection by Russian futurists, 4
Markov, Pyotr, 324

Marshad, David, 120; teaching of Popov, 120
Martinu, Bohuslav, 328; association with Thereminvox, 328
Marx, Karl, 56, 69
Mashistov, Alexey, 206, 294, 297
Maslakovetz, Alla, 130
Matisse, Eduard, 228
Matyushin, Mikhail, 3–5, 14, 36–37, 99, 315–16, 332; association with futurists, 36, 37, 315–17; attraction to symbolism, 316; career as a violinist, 316; childhood and education, 315; death in Leningrad, 319; marriage to Elena Guro, 316; opera *Victory over the Sun*, 37, 317–18; study of painting, 316; teaching in Petrograd, 318–19; writing of textbooks on Color, 319. See also avant-garde; futurism
Mayakovsky, Vladimir, 3–6, 34, 36, 41, 56, 58, 82, 98, 135, 137, 142, 160, 230, 297, 316, 321; acting and directing career, 82, 86, 95, 98, 135, 230, 335; association with futurism, 4, 6, 15, 34–35, 38, 41, 51, 56, 82, 86, 316; association with Lourie, 321; association with Matyushin, 316; association with Mosolov, 297; association with Popov, 135, 137, 139, 142; association with Roslavets, 3–4, 56, 58, 95; revolutionary activity, 3–4, 6, 56, 58, 139, 316; suicide of, 98, 137
Medtner, Nikolay, 2, 8, 62, 69, 323, 331
Meisel, Edmund, 327
Melkikh, Dmitry, 241
Menuhin, Yehudi, 328; interest in the Thereminvox, 328
Meshko, Nina, 297–99; association with Mosolov, 297–98
Messiaen, Oliver, 332
Meyerbeer, Giacomo, 227
Meyerhold, Vsevolod, 3–4, 35, 43, 82, 98, 133–36, 144, 160, 170, 172–74, 230, 270; association with futurism, 3–4, 35, 43, 51, 56, 83, 98, 230; association with Mosolov, 249, 262, 270; association with Popov, 133–37, 139–40, 144, 153, 162, 170, 173–75, 194; theater methodology, 172–74, 190, 249, 270, 279. See also futurism
Milhaud, Darius, 79, 125, 151, 155, 232, 238, 245, 251, 260, 312; association with Mosolov, 232, 245, 251, 260; association with Popov, 125, 151, 155; association with Roslavets, 79
Miller, Glenn, 329; study with Schillinger, 329
Milstein, Nathan, 48, 324; premiere of Schillinger's sonata, 324
Minkin, Adolf, 178–79
Mirzoyeva, Maria, 64
modernism, 2, 6–9, 12, 25, 32–33, 44–45, 61–65, 76, 82, 95, 122–23, 126, 143, 182, 207, 216, 230–35, 237, 239, 251, 287, 292, 298, 301, 307–9, 312, 330–31. *See also* symbolism; synthetic chord
Mogilevsky, Alexander, 19
Moog, Peter, 329; development of Schillinger's device, 329
Morozova, K.M., 135
Morrison, Simon, 1
Mosolov, Alexander, 3–4, 6, 8, 12, 95, 97, 113, 137, 205–6, 216, 250, 325; arrest and sentencing, 286; association with Cubo-futurism, 246; association with Meshko, 297; association with symbolism, 250; attacks by RAPM, 82, 249, 263, 267, 281–82; attitude to the revolution, 229, 282; behaviour and scandal in media, 276–77, 283–85; birth, family and education, 227; chamber works, 233, 236; change to style of industrial themes, 237; *The Dam*, 263–69; early compositions, 232–33; First Piano Concerto, 241–43; *The Foundry*, 85, 238, 240, 244; *The Hero*, 259–62;

influence of Bartók, 232, 258, 276, 283; influence of Berg, 267, 270; influence of Hindemith, 12, 232, 238, 241–42, 260; influence of Honegger, 12, 232, 245; influence of Musorgsky, 248–49, 251, 265; influence of Prokofiev, 230, 232–35, 239, 245, 270, 291, 296; influence of Scriabin, 232–34, 236–37, 241; influence of Stravinsky, 2, 233, 239, 242, 267, 270; joining the Army and wounding in the Civil War, 228–29; joining the Conservatoire and study with Gliere and Myaskovsky, 229; letter to Stalin and consequences, 282–83; maturity in style, 257, 271, 281; Mosolov, parody of Rimsky Korsakov, 265; Mosolov, stage works, 257; piano sonatas, 232–34; revival of career, war and post-war music, attraction to choral music, 295–97; revival of music, 299–300, 332; settings to Blok, 236–37, 290, 293, 296, 307; use of the synthetic chord, 234
Mosolov, Vasily, 227
Mosolova, Nina, 227, 234–35
Mozart, Wolfgang Amadeus, 130, 202, 332
Mravinsky, Yevgeny, 206, 215
Munch, Charles, 322
Muradeli, Vano, 187, 205, 287, 294
Musorgsky, Modest, 22, 248–49, 251, 265; influence on Mosolov, 248–49, 251, 265
Mussolini, Benito, 312, 331
Myaskovsky, Nikolay, 8, 12–13, 22, 103, 108, 111, 114, 136, 138, 141, 172, 175, 183, 203, 205–6, 208–9–211, 216, 230, 232–32, 235–36, 238–39, 241, 272, 276–77, 281, 285–88, 291–92, 294, 299, 323; appeal for Mosolov, 235; review of Roslavets, 31, 36, 45, 46, 60, 64, 69, 72, 73, 79, 91, 93, 109–10; tutoring of Mosolov, 229–34. See also modernism

Nappelbaum, Mozhei, 230
Nazarevsky, Pavel, 178
Nejedlý, Zdeněk, 230
Nekrasov, Nikolay, 296
Nekrasov, Viktor, 214
Nelson, Amy, 231, 244
Nemirovich-Danchenko, Vladimir, 275–76
Nesterov, A., 173
Nestyev, Israel, 11, 163, 206
Neuhaus, Heinrich, 101
Nevsky, Alexander, 290
Nietzsche, Friedrich, 93
Nikolaev, Leonid, 123–24
Nikolay I, 94
Nikolay II, 119

Obnorsky, Boris, 145–46
Oborin, Lev, 183
Obradovich, Sergey, 84
Obukhov, Nikolay, 13, 27
Odoyevsky, Alexander, 94
Oistrakh, David, 111, 171; work on the Popov Violin Concerto, 171
Olenin-D'Alheim, Maria, 228
Olenin-D'Alheim, Pierre, 228
Olesha, Yuri, 169
Oliveros, Pauline, 7
Oransky, Viktor, 271
Ordzhonikidze, Sergo, 162
Oreshin, Pyotr, 95, 284, 286
Orfenov, Anatoly, 208
Orff, Carl, 10
Ormandy, Eugene, 12
Oshanin, Lev, 294
Ostroumov, Lev, 275
Ostrovsky, Nikolay, 174
Ovanesova, Arsha, 181, 197
Ozerov, Yuri, 215

Palestrina, Giovanni, 325
Palui, Olga, 125, 210, 214; letters from Popov, 210, 214, 223–24; marriage to Popov, 125
Pärt, Arvo, 1, 332

Partch, Harry, 6
Pasovsky, Ariy, 175
Pasternak, Boris, 5, 36, 168
Pasternak, Leonid, 228
Pavlenko, Pyotr, 164, 174–75, 187, 209–10; writing of libretto for Popov's *Alexander Nevsky*, 164, 175, 187, 209
Pavlovich, Nadezhda, 61–63
Pechnikov, Alexander, 19
Peiko, Nikolay, 216
Penderecki, Krzysztof, 332
Picasso, Palo, 320
Pilnyak, Boris, 140
Planquette, Robert, 274–76
Plotnichenko, G.M., 295
Podgoretsky, Boris, 227
Poe, Edgar Allan, 28
Poggioli, Renato, 6–7
Pogodin, Nikolay, 283
Polovinkin, Leonid, 8, 85, 96, 126, 136, 204, 231–32, 241, 244, 246, 262, 271–72, 299, 327
Polyakin, Miron, 171
Pomorsky, Alexander, 94
Popov, Gavriil, 3, 8; article in *Izvestiya*, 147, 285; association with Eisenstein, 161–64; association with Prokofiev, 132, 140–41; association with Shostakovich, 123, 142, 313; association with Shub, 149, 159–60, 163; attempt to stage *Alexander Nevsky*, 218–19, 299; attraction to engineering and architecture, 120–21; banning and appeal for lifting of ban, 145–47, 284; birth and origins, 119; Composers Congress, 294; Composers Union, 204–6; death of, 219, 332; death of second wife, 211; early compositions, 121; early education, 120; entry to Leningrad Conservatoire, 122–23; expulsion from conservatoire, 124; Fifth Symphony, 210; film scores, 133, 159–60, 163; First Symphony, 111, 131–34, 137–45; Fourth Symphony, 206–7; influence of Bach, 129, 131, 166; influence of Beethoven, 122, 131, 146, 203, 208; influence of Berg, 136, 142; influence of Chopin, 129, 173; influence of Handel, 166, 179; influence of Hindemith, 123, 127, 129–31, 136, 138, 172, 175; influence of Honegger, 203; influence of Mahler, 131, 184, 185, 211, 218; influence of Prokofiev, 123, 127, 133, 136, 140–41, 170, 172, 175; influence of Rachmaninov, 121, 170; influence of Rimsky Korsakov, 121, 185, 202; influence of Schoenberg, 123, 125, 136, 146, 175, 202, 211; influence of Scriabin, 122, 125, 133, 148, 212, 215; influence of Strauss, 83, 175, 179, 202; influence of Stravinsky, 2, 123, 127, 130, 132, 134, 136, 142, 146, 175, 183; influence of Tchaikovsky, 131, 141, 171, 178–79, 184, 214, 218; post-war compositions, 201–4, 209; recordings of First and Second symphonies and Septet, 215, 218; rehabilitation after 1948, 213; Second Symphony, 148, 180–83; Septet, 126–28, 132, 134, 216; Sixth Symphony, 180, 215, 217–19; stage works, 160, 168–69; Third Symphony, 162–63, 175, 179–80, 188, 202–4; visit to Great Britain, and Czechoslovakia, 213; writing of, *Alexander Nevsky*, 174–77, 186–87
Popov, Nikolay, 180; arrest and release, 121; death of, 201; teaching of son, 120
Popova, Lyubov, 120–21
Postyshev, Pyotr, 282
Poulenc, Francis, 13, 238, 245, 312
Powell, Edward, 330
Preis, Alexander, 175
Presman, Matvei, 120
Press, Mikhail, 19
Previn, Charles, 330

Prokofiev, Sergey, 1–4, 8, 10, 12–13, 22, 27, 28, 62, 69, 73, 95, 96, 98, 144, 149, 164, 170, 172, 175, 187, 204–5, 209, 232–34, 287, 294, 301, 307, 321, 323, 331–32; association with Mosolov, 270, 274, 276, 291; association with Popov, 127, 132–33, 136, 141, 175, 181; attempt to arrange concerts for Popov, 141; influence on Lourie, 321; influence on Mosolov, 230, 232–35, 239, 245, 270, 291, 296; influence on Popov, 123, 127, 133, 136, 140–41, 170, 172, 175; influence on Schillinger, 323; offer of Eisenstein film to Popov, 188; proselytization of Mosolov, 239, 251. See also avant-garde; modernism

Prokofyev, Alexander, 206, 294, 297
Prokofyev, Grigory, 229
Provatorov, Gennady, 215
Prutkov, Kozma, 260
Ptushko, Alexander, 217
Pudovkin, Vsevolod, 159–60
Pugachev, Emelyan, 119
Pushkin, Alexander, 22, 34, 35, 94, 139, 168–69, 217, 236–37, 288, 294, 322; settings by Lourie, 322; settings by Mosolov, 236–37, 287–88, 294; settings by Popov, 139, 168–69, 195, 217; settings by Roslavets, 94
Pushkov, Benedict, 140, 145
Pyatigorsky, Grigory, 292
Pyrev, Ivan, 167, 289

Raaben, Leonid, 19
Rabichev, 282
Rabinovich, David, 97
Rachmaninov, Sergey, 1, 8, 69, 121, 170, 331; influence on Popov, 121, 170
Radamsky, Sergey, 327
Radlov, Sergey, 267, 270
Radzhabov, Yunas, 106
Raikh, Zinaida, 135, 139

Raikin, Arkady, 214
Raiskin, Iosif, 148
Rakhlin, Nathan: conducting of Popov's symphonies, 183, 185, 202, 211, 213, 217
Rappoport, Herbert, 178–79
Raskatov, Alexander, 109
Ravel, Maurice, 78, 172, 301, 323, 328, 332
Raysky, Nazary, 273
Razin, Stepan, 119
Rebikov, Nikolay, 78
Reed, John, 130
Reger, Max, 83, 232
Reich, Steve, 332
Reingerts, K.I., 266
Renzin, Issay, 130
Repin, Ilya, 228
Respighi, Ottorino, 98
Rilke, Rainer Maria, 324
Rimsky Korsakov, Georgy, 272, 318
Rimsky Korsakov, Nikolay, 22, 66, 92, 122, 132–33, 185, 202, 231, 265, 319, 326; influence on Popov, 121, 185, 202; rejection of methodology by Roslavets and Schillinger, 20, 22, 26, 319
Rockefeller, John David, 13, 328
Rodchenko, Alexander, 3, 12
Rodzinski, Artur, 141
Romaschuk, Inna, 122–23, 143, 161, 165, 173, 182, 185, 189, 208, 218
Room, Abram, 133, 169, 179
Roslavets, Andrey, 17, 18
Roslavets, Nikolay, 3, 6, 8, 12, 21, 23–26, 35, 43, 64, 85, 232–33, 239, 244, 281, 313, 323, 325, 327; activities in Kharkiv, 62, 63; agitprop music, 58, 75, 84, 85, 148; antipathy to Stravinsky, 95; appointment as Editor of Music Press, 67; articles on music education, 67, 69, 75, 83; articles on synthetic chord, 75, 76, 83; association in Bolshevik music administration, 59, 60, 107;

association with futurism, 35–39, 56, 64; association with symbolism, 21, 23–26, 35, 43, 64, 85; attacks from RAPM, 73, 74, 83, 99–100; attraction to radicalism, 20, 26, 55; award of Silver medal, 21, 25; behaviour and disposition, 20, 36, 37, 70, 71; birth and family background, 17; call up to the army, 28; chamber music, 23–25, 60; compositions in Kharkiv, 63–65; compositions on Uzbeki folk music, 104–6, 110; conducting his ballet, 105; death of, 114; decline in health, 112; diploma award work, 20, 21, 23, 25; discovery of the synthetic chord, 28, 29, 39; dismissal from Music Press, 99–100; enlisting at Moscow Conservatoire, 18; exploration of synthetic chord in songs and chamber works, 39, 60, 64; family circle, 20, 23, 24; final chamber works, 112–13; first attraction to violin and music, 17; first compositions, 20, 21, 23, 24; first teacher, 18; first Violin Sonata, 31; forming a musical band, 18; influence of Beethoven, 77, 96; influence of Debussy, 29, 96; influence of Hindemith, 71, 78, 95; influence of Honegger, 78, 95; influence of Prokofiev, 95; influence of Schoenberg, 12, 21, 27–29, 31, 36, 39, 45–46, 78, 82–83, 92, 95–96, 108, 110; influence of Scriabin, 22, 24–25, 29, 31–32, 35–36, 39, 65, 75, 78, 83, 92, 109; influence of Stravinsky, 2, 82; involvement in debates on music in USSR, 66–67, 69, 73–75, 83, 92; involvement in revolution, 55, 56, 107; marriage to Natalia, 24; meeting with Malevich, 18; move to Kharkiv, 59, 62; political activity in Elets, 57, 107; problem in payments for theatre work, 112; reception to his music in the west, 79; release from the army, 28; remarriage and move to Tashkent, 102–3; resignation from the Party, 59, 60, 99; retirement and heart attack, 112; return from Kharkiv, 66, 70, 71; return from Tashkent and appointment to teaching and editorial positions, 107; revival of his music and recordings of major pieces, 113, 301, 332; settings to Blok, 21, 23–24, 26, 33, 44, 56, 62; song cycles, 23–25; study with Hřimalý, 18, 20, 21; study with Ilyinsky, 19, 20; study with Ippolitot-Ivanov, 19, 20; study with Vasilenko, 21; teaching at the Conservatoire, rejection of, 20, 22, 26; and Violin Concerto No 2, 111; work in ballet and radio, 104; work on railways, 18; writing of Chamber Symphony No 2, 108–10; writing of the Violin Concerto No 1 and Chamber Symphony, 79–81

Rossini, Giacomo, 171
Rozanov, Sergey, 271
Rozhdestvenskaya, Nataliya, 125
Rozhdestvensky, Gennady, 213
Rubinstein, Anton, 326
Rudnev, Daniil, 290
Russolo, Luigi, 13
Ryazanov, 125, 130
Ryazanov, Pyotr, 140, 201
Ryzhey, Pyotr, 160

Sabaneyev, Leonid, 39, 52, 59, 63–67, 69, 71, 73–74, 79, 87, 89, 91, 102, 114, 325–26, 336; appraisal of Roslavets, 39–40, 63–66, 79, 91; appraisal of the Thereminvox, 325–26
Sabata, de Victor, 247
Saburov, Nikolay, 315
Sadomov, A.N., 235
Safonov, Vasily, 19, 120
Saint-Simon, Henri de, 7

Sakva, Konstantin, 213
Samosud, Samuil, 135, 139
Sappho, 320
Saradzhev, Konstantin, 244
Sargeant, Winthrop, 310
Sargent, Sir Malcolm, 213
Sati, Erik, 7, 238, 307, 312
Savitsky, K.K., 173
Scherchen, Hermann, 134, 147, 247, 262, 327
Schillinger, Joseph, 4, 13–14, 62, 63, 98, 102, 148, 237, 249, 301, 315, 332; activity as teacher of conducting, 323–24; adoption by the Juilliard School and other music schools of his theory, 330; appraisal of his influence on US music, 329–30; association with symbolism, 324; attraction from Schoenberg, 323, 325, 327; attraction from Scriabin, 323, 325; attraction to composition, 324–25; attraction to electronic music, 325; attraction to Jazz and establishment of jazz orchestra, 324–26; attraction to music, mechanics and mathematics, 322–23; birth and family background, 322; composition of works on revolutionary themes using Therminvox, 325, 326; compositions in the USA, 328; death of, 330; development of his teaching methodology, 324, 328–29; influence from Prokofiev, 323; influence of Chopin, 325; invitation to the USA for talks, 327; proselytization of Soviet music in Berlin, 327; public speaker and organiser in Kharkiv, 324; study and rejection of teaching at the St Petersburg Conservatoire, 323; teaching of Gershwin, and other musicians in the US, 329–30. *See also* futurism; modernism
Schindler, Kurt, 327
Schnittke, Alfred, 1, 208, 326, 332
Schoenberg, Arnold, 6, 13, 21, 27, 28, 34, 36, 45, 50, 71, 82, 83, 92, 95, 96, 108, 110, 115, 123, 125, 136, 142, 145–46, 175, 202, 232, 237, 270, 307–11, 323, 325, 327; antipathy by Popov, 142; influence on Mosolov, 232; influence on Popov, 123, 125, 136, 146, 175, 202, 211; influence on Roslavets, 12, 21, 27, 31, 36, 45–46, 78, 92, 95–96, 108, 110. *See also* avant-garde; modernism
Schopenhauer, Arthur, 320
Scott, Cyrill, 71
Scriabin, Alexander, 2–3, 12, 21, 24, 25, 29, 32, 35, 36, 39, 65, 75, 78, 84, 92, 120–23, 148, 213, 215, 232, 234, 236, 241, 313, 320, 323, 325; influence on Lourie, 320–21; influence on Mosolov, 232–34, 236–37, 241; influence on Popov, 122, 125, 133, 148, 212, 215; influence on Roslavets, 22, 24–25, 29, 31–32, 35–36, 39, 65, 78, 83, 92, 109; influence on Schillinger, 323, 325
Seeger, Charles, 310
Seifullina, Lydia, 264
Selvinsky, Ilya, 4, 6, 208
Sëngar, Eugene, 284
Sergeyev, Konstantin, 8, 68, 72, 99–100
Serov, Valentin, 44, 228
Serpinsky, S., 290
Severyanin, Igor, 4, 21, 26, 32, 34, 35, 40, 43, 307. *See also* ego-futurism; futurism
Shachgaldyanom, A.G., 296
Shakespeare, William, 212–13
Shaporin, Yuri, 136, 138, 145, 183, 185–87, 213, 284, 294
Shatalov, A., 94
Shaub, Vasily, 121–22, 132
Shchedrin, Rodion, 1, 216, 332
Shcherbachov, Vladimir, 8, 13, 123–24, 126–27, 130, 132, 134, 136–37, 147, 151, 182, 203, 207, 210, 281, 284;

influence on Popov, 123–24, 126–27, 132, 134, 136, 182, 203, 207, 210
Shebalin, Vissarion, 8, 72, 103, 135–38, 141, 145, 147, 180, 183, 187, 204–5, 210, 231–32, 241, 281, 294, 299, 327
Sheiblero, T.K., 296
Shein, Karel, 215
Shekhter, Boris, 9, 98, 101, 236, 276
Shenshin, Alexander, 136, 228, 247
Shirinsky, Sergey, 64
Shishkov, Vyacheslav, 201
Shklovsky, Viktor, 162
Shogentsukov, A.O., 296
Sholokhov, Mikhail, 119
Sholpo, E.D., 319
Shorin, Alexander, 162
Shortanov, A.T., 296
Shostakovich, Dmitry, 1–4, 8, 10, 12–13, 73, 85, 96, 99, 101, 110–11, 123, 126–27, 129–35, 137–38, 141, 144, 148, 169, 172, 175–76, 181–84, 201–2, 204–5, 210–11, 218, 232–33, 237–38, 242, 244, 250, 259, 262, 267, 270, 272, 274, 281, 284, 291–92, 294, 301, 307–8, 313–14, 318, 325–27, 332; association with Mosolov, 232–33, 237–38, 242, 244, 249–50, 259, 262–63, 267, 269–70, 274, 291, 295, 301; association with Popov, 123, 130, 134, 147, 247; criticism of Popov, 186–87; influence by Popov on the Fourth Symphony, 133, 142; influence by Popov on the Tenth Symphony, 211–12. See also avant-garde; modernism
Shpilman, Semyon, 64
Shpirkan, Darya, 217
Shreker, Franz, 98
Shtein, Alexander, 160
Shteinberg, Lev, 149
Shteinberg, Maximilian, 122–23, 137
Shtrimer, Alexander, 201
Shub, Esfir, 149, 158–60, 163, 166
Shulgin, Lev, 8, 68, 78, 83
Shumyatsky, Boris, 165, 169

Sigayev, Alexander, 165
Silvestrov, Valentin, 1, 216, 332
Sitsky, Larry, 6
Skinner, Frank, 330
Slonimsky, Nicolas, 1, 328–29
Slonimsky, Sergey, 216
socialist realism, 9, 22, 77, 146, 165, 169, 221, 287, 332; attraction to, 22, 165, 287, 332; influence on music, 9, 22, 77, 165, 169, 287, 332; meaning of, 9, 146; origins of, 9. See also avant-garde; futurism
Sofronitsky, Vladimir, 123
Sokoloff, Nikolay, 328
Sollertinsky, Vladimir, 8, 133, 183, 201, 284
Solntseva, Yulia, 182, 189, 214
Sologub, Fyodor, 26, 35, 56, 61, 63, 320
Solovyov, 236, 294
Spassky, Sergey, 139, 168
Spassky, Yevgeny, 227
Spencer, Herbert, 330
Stalin, Iosif, 10, 43, 147, 165, 169, 179–80, 186, 202–3, 282–83, 285, 287, 332
Stanchinsky, Alexey, 27
Stanislavsky, Konstantin, 174
Starokadomsky, Mikhail, 271
Stasevich, Abram, 203, 215
Stefan, Paul, 258
Stiedry, Fritz, 130, 142, 144–45, 172, 254; conducting of Popov's symphony, 144–45
Stockhausen, Karl Heinz, 6
Stogorsky, Alexander, 292–93, 295
Stokowski, Leopold, 12, 247, 311, 322, 327
Stolyarov, Grigory, 246, 275
Stonor Saunders, Francis, 308–9
Strauss, Richard, 6, 10, 83, 136, 175, 179, 202, 307, 312–13; influence on Popov, 83, 175, 179, 202; influence on Roslavets, 83. See also avant-garde; modernism

Stravinsky, Igor, 2, 6, 12–13, 62, 73, 82, 95, 98, 123, 127, 130, 132, 134, 136, 141, 146, 152, 175, 239, 242, 267, 270, 307, 312, 319, 321, 323, 330–31; antipathy by Roslavets, 95; association with Lourie, 2; influence on Lourie, 319, 321–22; influence on Mosolov, 2, 233, 239, 242, 267, 270; influence on Popov, 2, 123, 127, 130, 132, 134, 136, 142, 146, 175, 183; influence on Roslavets, 2, 82; influence on Schillinger, 2, 323; influence on Stravinsky from Lourie, 322. See also avant-garde; modernism

Surin, Vladimir, 183, 201

Surkov, Alexey, 289

Svetlanov, Yevgeny, 215, 300

Sviridov, Georgy, 1, 216

symbolism, 5, 21, 23–26, 35, 43, 64, 85, 317, 321, 324, 332; influence on music, 21, 23–26, 35, 43, 64, 85; influence on Soviet art, 5, 85, 321, 332

synthetic chord, 12, 24, 27, 29, 32–33, 35, 38–41, 58, 60–61, 63–64, 75, 77, 79, 81, 83, 91, 93, 95, 107–8, 112–13, 234; meaning of, 24, 27, 40, 58, 75, 83, 108, 112–13, 234; origin of, 12, 24, 27, 35, 234; use of, 24, 27, 29, 32–33, 38–41, 58, 60–61, 63–64, 75, 77, 79, 81, 83, 91, 93, 95, 107, 113, 234. See also Roslavets

Tager, Pavel, 162

Tairov, Alexander, 56

Taneyev, Sergey, 48, 65, 113, 123, 182, 231, 315; influence on Popov, 123, 182; influence on Roslavets, 65, 113; teaching of Matyushin, 315

Tatlin, Vladimir, 3–4, 56, 237, 307, 316

Tchaikovsky, Pyotr, 1, 47–49, 66, 113, 131–32, 141, 171–72, 178–79, 184, 195, 214, 218, 231, 250, 307, 314, 317; influence on Mosolov, 250; influence on Popov, 131, 141, 171, 178–79, 184, 214, 218; influence on Roslavets, 66, 113

Telezhinskaya, Viviya, 236

Teplitzky, Leopold, 326

Teplov, Pyotr, 70, 71

Terteryan, Avet, 1, 216

Theremin, Lev, 12–13, 328–29; compositions by Popov, 12, 163; compositions by Schillinger, 325, 327–28; development of other electronic gadgets with Schillinger, 328–29; invention of the Thereminvox and other devices, 163; return to the USSR, 329

Thorvaldottir, Anna, 332

Timofeyev, Nikolay, 213

Timoshenko, Semyon, 162

Tischenko, Boris, 1, 216, 332

Tisse, Eduard, 167

Tolstoy, Alexey, 136, 138–39, 144, 201

Tolstoy, Leo, 35, 120, 160

Tomilin, Viktor, 201

Tormis, Veljo, 216

Toscanini, Arturo, 12, 247, 328

Trotsky, Lev, 8, 69–70, 314

Tseitlin, Lev, 13, 170, 204

Tsetnerovich, Pavel, 173

Tsybulskaya, Jadwiga, 320

Tubelsky, Leonid, 147

Tur, The Brothers, 147, 160, 285

Turchaninov, Dmitry, 119

Turgenev, Mikhail, 120

Tyulin, Yuri, 125, 130, 147

Tyutchev, Fyodor, 237

Ushakov, Nikolay, 297

Uspensky, Pyotr, 315

Ustvolskaya, Galina, 1, 216, 332

Vaks, Klara, 284

Van Gogh, Arthur Vincent, 320

Varèse, Edgarde, 6, 13, 144, 269, 301, 307, 327–28; association with Popov, 144; comparisons with Mosolov,

13, 269, 301. *See also* avant-garde; modernism
Vasilenko, Sergey, 3, 19, 21, 25, 71, 109; musical works and career, 21, 71; opinion of Roslavets' music, 21, 25; teaching of Roslavets, 19, 21, 25, 109. *See also* symbolism
Vasilyev, Georgy, 165, 176, 180–81, 217
Vasilyev, Sergey, 165, 176, 180–81, 217
Vasilyeva, Larissa, 301
Vasnetsov, Viktor, 228
Vatulya, Alexey, 284
Velikanov, Vasily, 181
Veprik, Alexander, 71, 327
Verdi, Guiseppe, 178, 208, 307, 326; influence on Popov, 178, 208
Verhaeren, Emil, 95
Verlaine, Paul, 21, 32, 33, 320, 324; influence on Roslavets' vocal works, 21, 32–33, 39; settings by Lourie, 320; settings by Schillinger, 324
Vertov, Dziga, 6, 159–62, 169, 181
Vītols, Jāzeps, 323
Vivien, Leonid, 160
Vladimirov, Evgeny, 209
Vlasov, Vladimir, 3
Vlasova, Ekaterina, 58, 60, 93, 123
Voitetzky, Vitaly, 215
Volkhov, Solomon, 1, 314
Volkogonov, Dmitry, 70
Volkonsky, Andrey, 216
Voloshin, Maximilian, 23, 24, 44
Volsky, Boris, 168
Vorobyov, Igor, 3–5, 148, 237, 246, 259, 266, 269, 317, 319
Voroshilov, Kliment, 95, 162, 165, 176, 179
Voschene, L., 104
Vrubel, Mikhail, 315
Vvedensky, Alexander, 99
Vyshinsky, Andrey, 289
Vyshnegradsky, Ivan, 13, 27
Vyshnevsky, Vsevolod, 164, 179

Wagner, Richard, 38, 49, 83, 122, 133, 171, 202, 218, 307, 325; antipathy by Roslavets, 38, 83; influence on Popov, 122, 133, 171, 202, 218; influence on Schillinger, 25
Webern, Anton, 6, 71
Weill, Kurt, 110
Weinberg, Moshe, 1, 216, 332
Weisberg, Julia, 122, 325
Wellesz, Egon, 6
Wuorinen, Charles, 311

Xenakis, Iannis, 6, 332

Yavorsky, Boleslav, 8, 43, 52, 69, 82, 124, 151, 232; antipathy to Roslavets, 43, 82; association with Popov, 124
Yesenin, Sergey, 66
Yeshpai, Andrey, 216
Youmans, Vincent, 101
Yudin, Mikhail, 145
Yudina, Maria, 123, 127, 130
Yurovsky, Alexander, 72, 79
Yutkevich, Sergey, 168

Zadykhin, Yakov, 264–65
Zak, Avenir, 275
Zakharov, Vladimir, 208
Zamyatin, Yevgeny, 66, 140, 282
Zarkhi, Alexander, 162
Zharov, Alexander, 95, 287, 296
Zhdanov, Andrey, 93, 179, 205, 207
Zhelobinsky, Valery, 201
Zhilyaev, Nikolay, 8, 13
Zhitomirsky, Daniil, 101
Zhivotov, Alexey, 126
Zhukov, Georgy, 188
Ziloti, Alexander, 28
Zoric Alexander, 248
Zorin, Dmitri, 215
Zoschenko, Mikhail, 250
Zverev, Nikolay, 120

About the Author

Gregor Tassie was born in Bristol, England, and studied with the distinguished Scottish avant-garde composer John Maxwell Geddes. He also studied engineering, Russian, and music at Glasgow University and taught in Glasgow until 2013. He was artistic director of the Prokofiev Centenary Festival in 1991 and arranged concerts by professional musicians from Eastern Europe during the 1990s. He writes regularly for *Musical Opinion*, *Classical Record Collector*, *Gramophone*, and has worked as a consultant for BBC Radio and in documentary film. He has authored essays on leading Russian composers: Myaskovsky, Roslavets, Popov, Mosolov, Sviridov, Tischenko, Shebalin, and many artists and musicians such as Richter, Kogan, Yudina, Shafran, Golovanov, Gauk, Ivanov, and others. He writes about concerts and musical performances throughout Europe, including major arts festivals in Austria, Germany, Switzerland, and Russia. He is the author of *Yevgeny Mravinsky: The Noble Conductor* (Scarecrow, 2005), *Kirill Kondrashin His Life in Music* (Scarecrow, 2010), and *Nikolay Myaskovsky: The Conscience of Russian Music* (Rowman & Littlefield, 2014). Currently, he is writing a biography about a celebrated Russian musician and researching a monograph about the Russian composer and musical theoretician Sergey Taneyev.

www.ingramcontent.com/pod-product-compliance
Lightning Source LLC
Chambersburg PA
CBHW071357300426
44114CB00016B/2091